What is a question-mark?
A flowering stone
It is, and is its own
Answer. Dark
And hard is a stone, its skin
Is manifold,
And rolled tight to hold
What within?
A stone has no insides
And its perfection
Is to be sheer protection.
What it hides
Is what it is. We,
Seeing it back
Brazen in daylight, ask
What can it be?
Then does the graceful flower
By wonder grown
Over the world-shaped stone
Bend for an hour.

Dictionary of Literary Biography

American Poets Since World War II

Part 2: L–Z

Dictionary of Literary Biography • Volume Five

American Poets Since World War II

Part 2: L–Z

Edited by Donald J. Greiner
University of South Carolina

Cumulative Index Volumes 1-5

A Bruccoli Clark Book
Gale Research Company • Book Tower • Detroit, Michigan 48226
1980

Planning Board for
DICTIONARY OF LITERARY BIOGRAPHY

John Baker
Richard L. Darling
William Emerson
A. Walton Litz
Orville Prescott
William Targ
Alden Whitman

Matthew J. Bruccoli, *Editorial Director*
C. E. Frazer Clark, Jr., *Managing Editor*
Richard Layman, *Project Editor*

Copyright © 1980
GALE RESEARCH COMPANY

Library of Congress Cataloging in Publication Data

Main entry under title:

American poets since World War II.

   (Dictionary of literary biography ; v. 5)
   "A Bruccoli Clark book."
   Includes bibliographies.
   1. American poetry--20th century--Bio-
bibliography.   2.   Poets, American--20th century--
Biography.   3. American poetry--20th century--
History and criticism. I. Greiner, Donald J.
II. Series: Dictionary of literary biography :
American series ; v. 5.
PS323.5.A5   821'.54'09   80-16058
ISBN 0-8103-0924-6

Contents

*Indicates master entries

Contents

Acknowledgments

This book was produced by BC Research.

Karen L. Rood was the in-house editor.

The production staff included Mary Bruccoli, Joyce Fowler, Timna Gainey, Sharon K. Kirkland, Nadia Rasheed, Cynthia H. Rogers, Jean W. Ross, Shirell Simmons, Robin Sumner, Theodora J. Thompson, and Lynne C. Zeigler.

George Geckle, chairman of the Department of English at the University of South Carolina, provided the editor the necessary release time. The editor's secretary, Etseghenet Assefa, typed most of the correspondence. Harriet Oglesbee and her interlibrary loan staff at the Thomas Cooper Library of the University of South Carolina tracked down fugitive books with courtesy and efficiency. Walter W. Ross III did the necessary library research with the valuable assistance of the following librarians at the Thomas Cooper Library: Michael Havener, Donna Nance, Jean Rhyne, Ellen Tillett, Joyce Werner, and Beth Woodard. Photographic copy work for this volume was done by Pat Crawford; and assistance in locating photographs was provided by the University of Connecticut Library and Washington University Libraries, St. Louis.

The following photographers generously allowed us the use of their photos: Amanda Blanco, Boris Bohun-Chudyniv, Nicholas Clifford, Linda L. Fry, Bernard Gotfryd, John Gruen, Maxwell Mackenzie, Charles Morales, Pat Padgett, Everett Peirce, Paul Pitts, Layle Silbert, Joey Tranchina, Thomas Victor, and Herb Weitman.

Finally, grateful acknowledgment is due the subjects of entries in this book who were kind enough to read their entries for accuracy. Without the assistance of all these people, this book would not have been possible.

Dictionary of Literary Biography

American Poets Since World War II

Part 2: L–Z

Dictionary of Literary Biography

DENISE LEVERTOV
(24 October 1923-)

SELECTED BOOKS: *The Double Image* (London: Cresset, 1946);

Here and Now (San Francisco: City Lights Books, 1956);

Overland to the Islands (Highlands, N.C.: Jonathan Williams, 1958);

With Eyes at the Back of Our Heads (New York: New Directions, 1960);

The Jacob's Ladder (New York: New Directions, 1961; London: Cape, 1965);

O Taste and See (New York: New Directions, 1964);

The Sorrow Dance (New York: New Directions, 1967; London: Cape, 1968);

Relearning the Alphabet (New York: New Directions, 1970; London: Cape, 1970);

To Stay Alive (New York: New Directions, 1971);

Footprints (New York: New Directions, 1972);

The Poet in the World (New York: New Directions, 1974);

The Freeing of the Dust (New York: New Directions, 1975);

Life in the Forest (New York: New Directions, 1978);

Collected Earlier Poems: 1940-1960 (New York: New Directions, 1979).

Denise Levertov is an important and established poet of the 1960s and 1970s whose poems are widely admired and anthologized, whose poetic theories are quoted by fellow practitioners, and whose teachings have influenced many beginners. She is an extremely fine craftsman, and her greatest talent is surely her profound understanding of her medium, of language as a sign system that is not only private and public but also aural and visual. Levertov's sense of the word is rich and comprehensive; words are not simply referents or evocations, but rather, in her favorite paraphrase of Wordsworth, "Language is not the dress but the incarnation of thought." Poems are verbal constructions, and every possible effect upon the reader's intellect and senses must be wrung from the words of the poem, but poems are never merely manipulations of words. The poem must be the result of perception so intense that it becomes meditation and can only arise from a profound attention to the immediate business of living. A careful tension between commitment to the craft and immersion in experience, or between the poet making and the poet seeing, therefore sustains Levertov's best lyrics. She, however, considers this tension as simply the way poets are: "the poet does not see and then begin to search for words to say what he sees: he begins to see and at once begins to say or to sing, and *only in the action of verbalization does he see further.* His language is not more dependent on his vision than his vision is upon his language."

Perhaps the underlying impetus of her poetry is stated in the line she often quotes from Ranier Maria Rilke, "unlived life, of which one can die." Levertov seems never to have been guilty of living the unlived life and never hesitates to make her life the occasion, if not the subject, of her poems. For this reason, a knowledge of her life enriches responses to her poetry.

Levertov was born in Ilford, Essex, England. Her father was a Russian Jew who converted to Christianity, became an Anglican minister, and dedicated his life to the unification of Christianity and Judaism. Paul Philip Levertoff was a descendant of Schneour Zalman, the founder of Habad Hasadism, a religious movement that Levertov describes as containing "a very great strain of asceticism, yet along with it there was a recognition and joy in the physical world." Her mother, Beatrice Spooner-Jones, was Welsh and a descendant of Angel Jones of Mold, a tailor and a preacher. This background, rich in the Judeo-Christian tradition, seems to shine forth from Levertov's poetry, for although she is not avowedly religious, she always displays reverence for the natural world and the humanity that inhabits it, as

Denise Levertov

well as high seriousness about the responsibility of living and of writing poems. In her poem to her two spiritual forebears, "Illustrious Ancestors," she turns her heritage into a credo: "Well, I would like to make / thinking some line taut between me and them, poems direct as what the birds said, / hard as a floor, sound as a bench, / mysterious as the silence when the tailor / would pause with his needle in the air."

Levertov never attended grammar school as a child and never went to university as a young woman, but for an aspiring poet, the education she did receive seems, like Robert Browning's, made to order. Her mother read aloud to the family the great works of nineteenth-century fiction, and she read poetry, especially the lyrics of Tennyson: "one can learn a lot from Tennyson. And so I had him practically stuck under my armpit for several years of my childhood." Her father, a prolific writer in Hebrew, Russian, German, and English, used to buy secondhand books by the lot to obtain particular volumes. Levertov grew up surrounded by books and people talking about them in many languages in "the strange assemblage of dancers, evacuees, refugees, Russian exiles, and misfits that formed our household." She studied traditional ballet for several years, which she believes strengthened her sense of rhythm, and she painted. Although she says she was not a good painter, her poems reveal an eye for the nuances of color: "I discovered / the colors in the wall that woke / when spray from the hose / played on its pocks and warts— / a hazy red, a / grain gold, a mauve / of small shadows, sprung / from the quiet dry brown."

She began writing poetry as a child, and at twelve sent some of her poems to T. S. Eliot, who responded with a long letter of advice. At sixteen she met poet and critic Herbert Read and began a correspondence with him. Her first volume of poetry, *The Double Image*, was published just after the war in 1946. The poems in it were written during the war years, three of which Levertov spent as a civilian nurse in St. Luke's Hospital, Fitzroy Square, London. As a nurse she encountered poverty and disease and death, but the immediacy of these experiences—recalled later in prose—is not to be found in *The Double Image*. The poems are rather in the neoromantic mode of British poetry of the 1940s. They deal with feelings of isolation and separation, a sense of lost childhood, a belief in the saving powers of love, and realizations of time and death. The shadow of war is ever-present and is dealt with directly in "Christmas 1944": "Bright cards above the fire bring no friends near, / fire cannot keep the

Denise Levertov

cold from seeping in." The poems in this volume, written in traditional metrical and stanzaic patterns, tend to start from abstractions, from titles such as "Childhood's End," "Five Aspects of Fear," "To Death," or "Extravagant Time," which are then fleshed out with generalized natural images of perhaps waves or leaves or stones. Such vague seeing has never since been characteristic of her poetry, nor does she usually proceed from abstractions. But *The Double Image* is a brave and tender volume that reveals a poet of promise ready to discover her own voice and her own form.

Poems from *The Double Image* were included in Kenneth Rexroth's anthology *New British Poetry* (1949), but another volume of her poetry did not appear until *Here and Now* in 1956. During the ten years between her first two volumes, Levertov underwent some major changes. In 1947 she married an American soldier, the novelist Mitchell Goodman; in 1948 she moved to New York City; in 1949 her son Nikolai was born. But more extraordinarily, she learned a new life, a new language, and a new poetry. She was henceforth to be an American poet, writing in the American idiom.

The strains in the transformation can hardly be sorted out, but certainly an important one was that Levertov discovered her true mentor, William Carlos Williams, and learned to depend upon the red wheelbarrow, to search for no ideas but in things. As early as 1948, however, probably before she was comfortable enough in the American dialect to appreciate Williams fully, she was moving toward the "here and now" on her own. Her 1979 volume, *Collected Earlier Poems: 1940-1960*, contains a poem written before she settled in America: "Too Easy: to Write of Miracles." In it, she seems to reject her previous voice, finding that it is "Easy like the willow to lament," but "difficult to write / of the real image, real hand, the heart / of day or autumn beating steadily: / to speak of human gestures, clarify / all the context of a simple phrase / —the hour, the shadow, the fire, the leaf on a bare table." This admiration for the actual was intensified as she learned New York City, its streets, its people, and its voices; many of her poems written in the early 1950s are evocations of New York scenes, discoveries of the poetry inherent in the street. She also became friends with Robert Creeley, who published her poems in *Origin* and *Black Mountain Review*, and with Robert Duncan. Both Creeley and Duncan taught with Charles Olson at Black Mountain College, and thus Levertov has been considered a member of the Black Mountain school or of the Olson group. She does consider Creeley and Duncan the foremost poets among her contemporaries, but she has remarked that a "school" is any group of poets who talk and write letters to each other. Her own development as a poet has certainly proceeded more according to her own themes, her own sense of place, and her own sensitivities to the music of poetry than to poetic manifestos. Her artistic kinship is with Gerard Manley Hopkins, Rilke, Williams, H.D. (Hilda Doolittle), Wallace Stevens, and perhaps Thoreau.

The poems in *Here and Now* and *Overland to the Islands* (1958), two volumes that Levertov believes should have been published as one, reveal a poet who has found her own voice. She has learned to discover poetry in the intense perception of the immediate—Ralph Mills describes her verse as "poetry of the immediate"—and she has rejected traditional poetic forms in favor of "free verse," of a line scored to reveal the process of the poet thinking and perceiving. The occasions of these finely realized songs are various: scenes of city life, events in human lives, perceptions of natural images, scenes of life in Mexico, and thoughts on love and marriage. The reader is always inspired and sometimes directly told to live life more fully, more deeply, more finely attuned to the quick. In the title poem, "Overland to the Islands," she urges, "Let's go—much as that dog goes, / intently haphazard." And she announces her own direction: "Under his feet / rocks and mud, his imagination, sniffing, / engaged in its perceptions— dancing / edgeways, there's nothing / the dog disdains on his way, / nevertheless he / keeps moving, changing / pace and approach but / not direction—'every step an arrival.' "

In 1959 James Laughlin of New Directions decided that Levertov indeed had a voice of her own, and she became a New Directions author. *With Eyes at the Back of Our Heads* was published in 1960, and its title indicates her belief in indirection, as does the fine poem "Pleasures": "I like to find / what's not found / at once, but lies / within something of another nature, / in repose, distinct." Many of the poems in this volume begin with natural images and become reflections on the transforming and redemptive powers of the imagination. She observes a lagoon, and the perception of it "draws the mind / down to its depths / where the imagination swims, / shining dark-scaled fish, / swims and waits, flashes, waits and / wavers, shining of its own light." The imagination can perceive and create accord between the mind and the natural world; it can also create poetry. Levertov finds great joy in her vocation, a joy revealed in her well-known poem, "To the Snake": "Green Snake—I swore to my companions that certainly / you were harmless! But truly / I had no certainty, and no hope, only desiring / to hold you, for that joy, / which left a long wake of pleasure. . . ."

In *The Jacob's Ladder* (1961) Levertov continues defining the task of the poet, "to labor / planting the vegetable words / diversely in their order / that they come to virtue!," and the language of poetry, "Not 'common speech' / a dead level / but the uncommon speech of paradise." In "Six Variations" she offers a virtuoso performance— almost in the manner of Alexander Pope—in manipulating the sonorities and rhythms of the line: "when your answers / come / slowly, dragging / their feet" . . . "time / for a lagging leaden pace, a short sullen line, / measure / of heavy heart and / cold eye." She plays with sound, "Shlup, shlup, the dog / as it laps up / water / makes intelligent / music," and luxuriates in assonance, "Lap up the vowels / of sorrow," "Hone the blade / of a scythe to cut swathes / of light sound in the mind." The poet is a verbal fabricator, but he must also attempt to ascend "The Jacob's Ladder"; he "must scrape his knees, and bring / the grip of his hands into play.

The cut stone / considers his groping feet. Wings brush past him. / The poem ascends."

Perceptions of the natural world frequently become poems for Levertov; in *O Taste and See* (1964) she also uses—or generates—material from dreams and visions. She believes firmly in the romantic view of the imagination; it is a gift granted to artists who must be ready for visitations of the creative impulse. The muse cannot be ordered or cajoled, only prepared for, as her beautiful poem "To the Muse" concludes: "Perhaps / a becoming aware a door is swinging, as if / someone had passed through the room a moment ago—." The creative process, she writes in her essay "Working and Dreaming," does involve labor, but it consists largely in the "focussing of attention *upon what is given*, and not in the 'struggle for expression.' That is where the basic misunderstanding lies."

Although she insists upon visions and visitations, Levertov is a conscious artist, clear and explicit in her prose about the genesis, transformations, and intentions of her poems. In her essay "Some Notes on Organic Form" (first printed in *Poetry* magazine, 1965), she offers perhaps one of the clearest sets of directions for writing a poem to be found anywhere:

> I think it's like this: first there must be an experience, a sequence or constellation of perceptions of sufficient interest, felt by the poet intensely enough to demand of him their equivalence in words: he is *brought to speech*. Suppose there's the sight of the sky through a dusty window, birds and clouds and bits of paper flying through the sky, the sound of music from his radio, feelings of anger and love and amusement roused by a letter just received, the memory of some long-past thought or event associated with what's seen or heard or felt, and an idea, a concept, he has been pondering, each qualifying the other; together with what he knows about history; and what he has been dreaming—whether or not he remembers it—working in him. This is only a rough outline of a possible moment in life. But the condition of being a poet is that periodically such a cross section, or constellation, of experiences (in which one or another element may predominate) demands, or wakes in him this demand: the poem.

This essay has been reprinted several times, most notably in Stephen Berg and Robert Mezey's anthology *Naked Poetry* (1969). It has become something of a credo for practitioners of free verse, who do not like to be thought of as libertine. For Levertov, organic poetry is not formless at all, merely freed from imposed forms: "In organic poetry the metric movement, the measure, is the direct expression of the movement of perception." She makes a careful distinction—which many academic poets and critics refuse to recognize—between free verse and organic poetry: "where true 'free verse' is concerned with the maintenance of its freedom from all bonds, 'organic' poetry, having freed itself from imposed forms, voluntarily places itself under other laws: the variable, unpredictable, but nonetheless strict laws of *inscape*, discovered by *instress*." Levertov uses Hopkins's term *inscape* to mean the intrinsic form of an experience, intellectual, emotional, or sensory; *instress* is the apperception of *inscape*. Thus, form is discovered in the experience, and "content and form are in a dynamic state of interaction." In a conversation with Walter Sutton published in the *Minnesota Review* in 1965, she explains the discovering and composing process that resulted in the poem "The Tulips." This essay and one entitled "Work and Inspiration: Inviting the Muse" are perhaps the best paths into her poetry.

Her early mentor, Herbert Read, wrote of art, "What history demands in its long run, is the object itself—the work of art which is itself a created reality, an addition to the sum of real objects in the world." Levertov copied these words into her notebook when she was eighteen and took them seriously; they gave her "a measure to try and fill." They underscore Levertov's sense of the poet as maker, and she continued to refine and clarify her theory of prosody in interviews and in such essays as "Line-Breaks, Stanza-Spaces, and the Inner Voice" and "On the Function of the Line."

Into considerations of the making of poems burst a new sense of the proper subject matter of poetry. The years of Vietnam turned Levertov into a political activist. She participated in antiwar rallies and demonstrations, she joined the counterculture and eventually went to Hanoi, and her husband Mitchell Goodman was a codefendant in the draft-resistance conspiracy trial of Dr. Benjamin Spock. She began to write political poetry, believing that "we need poems of the spirit, to inform us of the essential, to help us *live* the revolution." *The Sorrow Dance* (1967) is composed of eight sections that reveal her progressive political involvement. The volume begins with poems about the experiencing of love and joy, poems filled with delight at the restorative powers of the natural world. But the death of her sister Olga in 1964 inspired a reexamination and refocusing of her emotional life.

"Grief, I have denied thee" she writes in "A Lamentation," and the Olga poems follow. Some of Levertov's finest poetry is written about her sister and their early lives together. Her evocations of their intensely lived childhood are stunning. Olga was a political activist, and as Levertov recollects Olga's life and admits her sense of kinship with her sister ("your life winds in me"), she seems drawn toward a similar social commitment. The last portion of *The Sorrow Dance* is "Life at War," and in it are the first poems of protest, "You who go out on schedule / to kill, do you know / there are eyes that watch you, / eyes whose lids you burned off," and poems of rage at "the scheduled breaking open of breasts whose milk / runs out over the entrails of still-alive babies."

Levertov's critics have generally responded unfavorably to her political poetry, believing that the rhetoric of protest violates the language of poetry and that poetry and politics are best kept apart. Levertov detests such a separation: "Poetry is necessary to a whole man, and that poetry be not divided from the rest of life is necessary to *it*. Both life and poetry fade, wilt, shrink, when they are divorced." She has been known to disturb the gentility of poetry readings by demanding that attention be paid to a political refugee, and her fellow poets are sometimes bemused by her persistent seriousness. But she has never relented or retreated, and sometimes her defeats become poems: "The Day the Audience Walked Out on Me and Why." She has sharp words for the comforts of noncommitment in academe: "the people who write banal poetry . . . usually seem to be the same academics who talk a liberal line concerning education and politics . . . but who, when it comes to some crucial issue, such as a student protest, will not commit themselves far enough to endanger their own security." It is easy enough now to say that student protests were not in fact crucial issues. But Levertov thought they were. Her sense of the moral necessity of opposing a war she believed unjust is surely related to her personal history. She did not grow up in a middle-class American household, but in a family that had experienced the displacement of two world wars. Her parents, as prisoners of war, were under house arrest in Leipzig during World War I. During World War II, their house was a center for the reception and relocation of Jewish refugees from Hitler. It is hardly likely that of all poets Denise Levertov would have chosen to ignore the political and social issues of the 1960s.

In 1970 *Relearning the Alphabet* was published. It is a large volume containing many poems on social themes: the war, the Detroit riots, Biafra, and war resisters. Levertov cannot fathom the ability of others to live normally when "We are at war, / bitterly, bitterly at war" and when she herself is so filled with doubt, misgivings, and feelings of dislocation and diminution, "Reduced to an eye / I forget what / I / was." Her plight is certainly understandable, but her poetry suffers here from weariness and from a tendency toward sentimentality. "A Tree Telling of Orpheus" reaffirms her belief in the poet's vocation and in the value of his singing. But in the long poem "From a Notebook," Levertov's own song seems loose and toneless. This work is a poetic collage of musings, quotations, letters, thoughts about friends, and her experience in the People's Park resistance in Berkeley. It does not cohere—except externally as the reader brings to it his own recollections of those troubled times. The title poem, "Relearning the Alphabet," is a series of short poems each written around what she would call the "horizon note," the central sound, of a letter of the alphabet. In this poem she attempts to reaffirm a self transformed by social anguish. "Heart breaks but mends / like good bone."

Levertov's war poetry was collected in *To Stay Alive* (1971). This volume contains the Olga poems and other poems from *The Sorrow Dance*, the protest poems from *Relearning the Alphabet*, and more protest poems written in the mode of "From a Notebook." Her intention was to assemble all the parts of her response to the war in a volume that would have "some value not as mere 'confessional' autobiography, but as a document of some historical value, a record of one person's inner/outer experience in America during the '60's and the beginning of the '70's." *To Stay Alive* is a historical document and does record and preserve the persons, conversations, and events of those years. Perhaps, as the events recede in time, these poems will seem true and just, rather than inchoate, bombastic, and superficial. History, after all, does prefer those who take stands. (Without them there would be no history.) As W. H. Auden said in his poem to William Butler Yeats, time always pardons writers' politics; it pardons them for writing well.

Readers of Levertov's 1972 volume, *Footprints*, were pleased to discover that she had not forsaken writing well. Most of the poems in *Footprints* were written concurrently with the Notebook poem of *To Stay Alive*; thus, Levertov in that venture was trying out another voice, one she evidently felt appropriate to her public role, not rejecting the themes or the craft of her earlier poems. In the brief title poem she writes: "day reveals / a perspective of lavender caves / across the snow. Someone / entered the dark woods."

She has not abandoned her own dark woods of dreams and visions, of perceiving and making. She hears "the crickets practice their religion of ecstasy." She appreciates "Brass tacks that glint / illuminations of darkness / and hold down feet to earth," and she feels "The pulse of life-pain / strong again, count it, fast but not fluttering." Social themes are still present, but they are more finely realized, more thoroughly transmuted into poetry.

One of the most interesting poems in the volume is "A New Year's Garland for My Students/MIT: 1969-70." Thirteen vignettes of the members of a poetry seminar reveal Levertov's sensitivity as a teacher and her ability to turn psychological acuity into precise word portraits. In one student she sees herself, "trudging home from the library lugging / too many books," and in another she observes, "The people in you: some are silent." Levertov has taught at the YMHA Poetry Center, Drew University, City College of New York, Vassar College, the University of California at Berkeley, Massachusetts Institute of Technology, the University of Cincinnati, and most recently at Tufts University. In an essay, "The Untaught Teacher," written for the anthology *Writers as Teachers, Teachers as Writers* (1970), she describes her experiences as a teacher, her approaches, and her intentions. As one might expect, she brings to the classroom the seriousness and intensity that she brings to every activity in her life.

For a conference on myth in 1967, Levertov wrote an essay, "The Sense of Pilgrimage," in which she discusses the pilgrimage theme as the central myth of her own poetry. In each of her volumes she has displayed a careful sense of the composing of not just poems but volumes of poetry. Thus, *The Freeing of the Dust* (1975) is divided into nine sections, nine stages, which map a spiritual journey of their maker. The volume begins with poems of journeying, poems of a renewed sense of earth's fertility, and poems recollecting the intensity of love. In part 4 are more poems of the war and poems inspired by her trip to Hanoi. One of her best antiwar poems is here, "The Pilots," in which she tries to sort out her feelings about a meeting with actual agents of the war. The poems in part 6 are in the confessional mode of Robert Lowell and deal with her divorce in 1972 after twenty-five years of marriage, and her gradual adjustment to aloneness. A long poem in part 7, "The Growth of a Poet," reveals Levertov again defining her vocation: "To make poems is to find / an old chair in the gutter / and bring it home / into the upstairs cave." And in "Conversation in Moscow" she speaks with a

Russian poet. Her voice is that of an activist, but now an activist poet: "we mustn't, any of us, lose touch with the source, pretend it's not there, cover over / the mineshaft of passion" from whence come "the scales of its laughing, improbable music, / grief and delight entwined in the dark down there." The volume constitutes a journey toward integration and cohesion, an attempt to hold in balance, with equal poetic intensity, both despair and the wildest joy.

Life in the Forest (1978), Levertov's most recent volume, is again carefully composed poem by poem to constitute a further chapter in her pilgrimage. It is also another attempt to maintain a balance, here between two different poetic styles. She says in her introduction that she was "impelled by two different forces." One was to write in a more discursive and expansive mode, using a longer line, to render other persons and scenes in the manner of Cesare Pavese. The other was "to try to avoid overuse of the autobiographical, the dominant first person singular of so much of the American poetry—good and bad—of recent years." This statement seems a strange claim for a volume in which half of the poems are written in the first person and in which there are so many extremely personal poems—about her mother's death in Mexico, her regrets as a daughter, her ill-fated love affair, her son, her house, even her used wedding ring. It is difficult not to see as autobiographical such lines as: "I in America, / white, an / indistinguishable mixture / of Kelt and Semite, grown under glass / in a British greenhouse, a happy / old-fashioned artist, sassy and free." She is, however, trying to write in two styles, to continue to write the tight, carefully honed sonorous lyric that she has mastered, as well as to extend her poetic range to a more social and conversational voice, revealing the self in dialogue with others, in dialogue with herself. In this sense the poems are less personal because they are less interior. In the best of them she is able to take joy in presenting herself, whole and complete and ready: "a kind of sober euphoria makes her believe / in her future as an old woman, a wanderer, / seamed and brown," "an old winedrinking woman, who knows / the old roads, grass-grown, and laughs to herself. . . ."

The volume does contain some poems that are observations of other persons and other scenes. It also contains poems on social themes, some of which seem strangely naive. *Life in the Forest* thus reveals a poet expressing herself in a variety of voices: a self perceiving others, a self discursive and personal, a self formalized and controlled, a self committed and didactic. Although some of these poems seem less than successful, some are very fine indeed and remind the reader of the strength and resilience of Levertov's talent:

> The woman whose hut was mumbled by termites
> —it would have to go,
>> be gone,
>> not soon, but some day:
>> she knew it and shrugged—
> had friends among the feathers,
> quick hearts.

Denise Levertov is an extremely active woman of letters. Her poems and essays have been published in countless literary journals from the most ephemeral to the most staid. She has translated poetry from several languages and has published a volume of her translations of Eugène Guillevic. For three years she was poetry editor of the *Nation*. She has given scores of readings, held numerous teaching positions, and been awarded grants and prizes. Her prose has been collected in two volumes, *The Poet in the World* (1974) and *Denise Levertov: In Her Own Province* (1979). The latter volume, which contains interviews, essays by Levertov, and essays on Levertov, was withdrawn from publication because of numerous errors. (Levertov is serious as a scholar too.)

The most comprehensive criticism of Levertov's poetry is Linda Wagner's *Denise Levertov* (1967) and Ralph Mills's chapter on Levertov in his *Contemporary American Poetry* (1965). Explication of her poetry, however, is seldom necessary; it is almost always accessible. She asks only that her readers listen to her poems and experience them as "sonic entities," rather than as problems to be solved. This is a reasonable request, for Levertov is a singer. Her song is clear and beautiful and true. Listening to it is a rich reward. —*Carolyn Matalene*

Other:

Out of the War Shadow: An Anthology of Current Poetry, edited by Levertov (New York: War Resisters League, 1967);
In Praise of Krishna: Songs from the Bengali, translated by Levertov and Edward C. Dimcock, Jr. (Garden City: Doubleday, 1967; London: Cape, 1968);
Eugène Guillevic, *Selected Poems*, translated by Levertov (New York: New Directions, 1969);
Linda W. Wagner, ed., *Denise Levertov: In Her Own Province*, includes essays by Levertov (New York: New Directions, 1979).

Bibliography:

Robert A. Wilson, *A Bibliography of Denise Levertov* (New York: Phoenix Book Shop, 1972).

References:

Ralph Mills, Jr., *Contemporary American Poetry* (New York: Random House, 1965), pp. 176-196;
Linda W. Wagner, *Denise Levertov* (New York: Twayne, 1967);
Wagner, ed., *Denise Levertov: In Her Own Province*.

PHILIP LEVINE
(10 January 1928-)

SELECTED BOOKS: *On the Edge* (Iowa City: Stone Wall Press, 1961);
Silent in America: Vivas for Those Who Failed (Iowa City: Shaw Avenue Press, 1965);
Not This Pig (Middletown, Conn.: Wesleyan University Press, 1968);
5 Detroits (Santa Barbara: Unicorn Press, 1970);
Thistles (London: Turret Books, 1970);
Pili's Wall (Santa Barbara: Unicorn Press, 1971);
Red Dust (Santa Cruz: Kayak Books, 1971);
They Feed They Lion (New York: Atheneum, 1972);
1933 (New York: Atheneum, 1974);
On the Edge & Over (Oakland, Cal.: Cloud Marauder Press, 1976);
The Names of the Lost (New York: Atheneum, 1976);
Ashes: Poems New and Old (New York: Atheneum, 1979);
7 Years from Somewhere (New York: Atheneum, 1979).

Philip Levine was born in Detroit to Russian-Jewish immigrant parents. After graduation from Wayne State University in 1950, he worked at a series of menial jobs and then left Detroit "for good." He married Frances Artley in 1954, and they lived in North Carolina, Florida, and Iowa (where he received an M.F.A. from the University of Iowa in 1957), until Levine was awarded the Stanford University Fellowship in Poetry and moved to California, becoming a faculty member at Fresno State College in 1958. He has received, among other awards, the Frank O'Hara Prize in 1972, a National Institute of Arts and Letters Award in 1973, and a Guggenheim Fellowship in 1973.

Philip Levine

Like other city children who came to individual consciousness before World War II, Levine met his enemy in the gray arenas of industrialism, where the grownups worked obsessively because *their* enemy was the Depression's spectre of idle poverty. Even beyond World War II, the Cold War, the tumultuous 1960s, and the numb 1970s, this generation lives with memories of factory hum and stink, vacant lots, junkyards, and railroad tracks; their residual child knowledge of the wasteland of land wasted by greed still rises every day with the sun. For the poets among them, there is the need to embrace this world in words, but the world resists. Levine, however, more than most poets, brings it to life in such poems as "Coming Home, Detroit, 1968," from *They Feed They Lion* (1972):

> A winter Tuesday, the city pouring fire,
> Ford Rouge sulfurs the sun, Cadillac, Lincoln,
> Chevy gray. The fat stacks
> of breweries hold their tongues. Rags,
> papers, hands, the stems of birches
> dirtied with words. . . .
>
> . . . .
>
> until the lights change and you go
> forward to work. The charred faces, the eyes
> boarded up, the rubble of innards, the cry
> of wet smoke hanging in your throat,
> the twisted river stopped at the color of iron.
> We burn this city every day.

Levine's hero is the lonely individual who tries and often fails in his struggle within this big industrial machine, the state. In a 1978 interview with Calvin Bedient, Levine observes that for years he has written political poetry with a tendency toward anarchism, a sort of apolitical anarchism in that he does not expect systems of government to fall away. He sees anarchy as useful for opening up sympathies, as the annihilation of power, and as a "way" in which one's loyalty is to people, not to a code or a bureaucracy. "The state," he says, "*is the* enemy." Much of this distrust of the state comes from his Jewish heritage, but as Levine says in a 1975 interview for the *Ohio Review*, "I think a lot of it comes from the time of someone precisely my age in America discovering, when they're quite young— fourteen or fifteen or something—an immense lie. . . . Your country wasn't what you had been told it was, the others weren't what you'd been told they were. . . . The Constitution was not the beautiful document; nobody ever listened to it anyway, and the guys who wrote it had slaves. This sudden, just fantastic shock—and then it went on and on—it went on through the forties and into the fifties. Our great

allies in the movies, the Russians, overnight became some fiendish devils."

Even as a child Levine began to develop strong political awareness. By the time he was thirteen, he was listening to the older men in his neighborhood debate about anarchism and communism. Coming from a Jewish household, he was subject to the persecution of "minor-league fascists" in Detroit. He became fascinated with the Spanish Civil War when very young as "one more advance of fascism"; men such as Ferrer Guardia and José del Castillo became his political heroes, but relatives, friends, and fellow factory and farm workers also assumed heroic proportions:

> I try to pay homage to the people who taught me my life was a holy thing, who convinced me that my formal education was a lie; these were the men and women I met as an industrial worker and bum in America; they were mainly Southerners—so many of whom had come to Detroit in my boyhood to find work—and they were closer, I believe, to some great truths about people, to the truth that we are the children of God, and that we were meant to come into this world and live as best we could with the beasts and the trees and plants and to leave the place with our love and respect for it intact, and to leave it our selfs. These people, both Black and white, were mainly rural people, and the horror of the modern world was clearer to them than to me, and the beauty and value of the world was something they knew in a way I did not, first hand. So, I learned from them and I owe them my hope and maybe more.

This "maybe more" is love. Many of Levine's poems serve the demand of love—which is to embrace, to incorporate, not merely the bodies of others, but their feelings and experience, their memories. While this impulse is implicit in Levine's first two volumes, it is more directly stated in *They Feed They Lion* (1972), *1933* (1974), and *The Names of the Lost* (1976). In "Hold Me," one who has died demands, "Was I dust that I should fail?" The poet recalls his "tiny Russian Grandpa" with *his* memories of "sweat, black shag, horse turds on the wind, / the last wooden cart rattling down / the alleys," and cries in the last stanza:

> I am the eye filled with salt,
> his child climbing the rain, we are
> all the moon, the one planet, the hand
> of five stars flung on the night river.

It is as though Levine wills all that he loves onto one planet to keep it against loss. In the beginning of the long poem "Letters for the Dead," he says,

Joey Tranchina

[I] thought of you one by one
and tried to hold your faces
in my eyes

tried to say
something to each of you
of what it is
without you.

Although there is "always a new dark," what
happens each day is

       not snow but
       seeds fallen
       through the roof
       of my life
       on the stained table
       the glass
       the silent phone

          the unanswerable letter,

as Levine struggles to incorporate all that he loves
into the boy's dream

       of a single self
   formed of all the warring selves split
      off at my birth
      and set spinning.

Levine lives on the sharp edge of irony. His love,
the urge to incorporate, will fail with the deaths of
those he loves, with his own death, with time. He is
not God but he tries to love as if he were:

      Someone
    must remember it over
    and over, must bring
    it all home and rinse

each crushed cell
in the waters of our lives
the way a God would.

His first book of poems, *On the Edge*, published in 1961, demonstrates Levine's early and abiding preoccupation with narratives and portrait poems that celebrate the heroism of the ordinary individual living out his stubborn joys and hopes in the face of the fear, pain, and loneliness of the human condition. The German officer losing his sense of identity in "The Distant Winter," the deserters from the French-Algerian army in "The Negatives," the poet himself in the doctor's waiting room in "Passing Out" are all such characters. His portraits, as in "The Drunkard" and "On the Edge," frequently show the subject losing in the struggle, although the portrait is painted with respect. In this and succeeding books, Levine is especially, although not exclusively, concerned with the plight of urban and suburban humans whose pain derives from or is exacerbated by the exploitations of a complex of corporate, industrial, military, and political interests.

Because Levine's poems "remember . . . over and over" not only political heroes but also members of his own family, living and dead, they are essentially narrative in nature, and his primary concern is with what is *out there*, in contrast to that of many of his contemporaries who share the postmodernist concern with words as the process by which one perceives what is out there. In the 1975 *Ohio Review* interview, Levine comments that he enjoys writing narratives and agrees that he is "a storyteller" who once wanted to write fiction. Many critics have responded approvingly to this narrative, realistic aspect of his work. Ira Sadoff in a 1977 review of *Names of the Lost* praises Levine's commitment "to write poetry that explores the relationships between self and other, between the personal and social worlds," at a time "when much American poetry has become self-conscious, exploring the psyche almost to the point of narcissism," and Richard Schramm, reviewing *They Feed They Lion* in 1972, praises the "vibrant realness" of Levine's work as opposed to "the anaemia of self-ness prevalent elsewhere."

Over the years the concerns of the poems have largely remained the same. The history of Levine's poetry is mainly the history of his poetic line, from the traditional meters of his early poems through the syllabic work of his middle period to the more open lines of his recent work. The narrative nature of his poems presents a problem here, for while the lyric can move with the rhythm of its successive images and the words that comprise them, the narrative

moves with the rhythm of events in the story line, apart from the poem's surface. If a poem's primary interest is with characters and events outside its surface—not just with the pattern created by words themselves—the poet risks producing prose. Indeed, critics have noted this tendency in Levine's work. Charles Molesworth, for example, has observed that some of the poems in *Not This Pig* (1968) tend to proceed "through rhetorical rather than metaphorical devices," and Hayden Carruth warns that "more than most, he should beware the contagion of the casual." Levine himself in a 1978 interview with Calvin Bedient commented, "I don't know if I'm trying to create a language. I've never really thought about that. In a curious way, I'm not much interested in language. In my ideal poem, no words are noticed. You look through them into a vision of . . . just see the people, the place." And in the *Ohio Review* interview he speaks critically of poets who "never wrote about anything. They wrote about the surface of their poems. My poems wouldn't be worth a damn if they were just the surfaces of the poems. . . ." Here then is the challenge Levine has set for himself: to develop a line that will serve his narrative vision without wholly succumbing to the essentially lyrical postmodern preoccupation with the surface of the poem.

As may be expected, Levine does not always meet this challenge. In "Lights I have Seen Before," a poem committed to nine six-line stanzas whose lines have respectively seven, five, four, five, four, and seven syllables, one may observe the dangers posed to Levine's voice by a prior commitment to a syllabic rather than an accentual metrical system:

> Between the cry of matter
> and the cry of those
> whose lives are here
> what is there to choose
> but failure? What
> can one say to oneself that
>
> will make it believable?
> and I am on my
> block, slowing for
> clusters of children
> who hear nothing.

The arbitrary line length and the absence of accentual rhythms in combination with the abstract diction lead perilously close to the flatness of prose. In "An Abandoned Factory, Detroit," the iambic pentameter becomes merely self-perpetuating, and the last three lines seem motivated by no urgency, only the necessity to fill out the final lines of the three-stanza, *abcabc* pattern:

> Men lived within these foundries, hour by hour;
> Nothing they forged outlived the rusted gears
> Which might have served to grind their eulogy.

Usually, however, metrical forms serve Levine well. While his later syllabics often provide merely a mechanical means of ending each line, thus blunting his energies, a commitment to accentual meters apparently provides him with just enough limits to channel his voice and make it stronger. Levine is extremely skilled in his ability to handle spondaic accents, enjambment, and delicate rhymes, as these lines to his wife in "To Fran" indicate:

> She packs the flower beds with leaves,
> Rags, dampened papers, ties with twine
> The lemon tree, but winter carves
> Its features on the uprooted stem.
>
> I see the true vein in her neck
> And where the smaller ones have broken
> Blueing the skin, and where the dark
> Cold lines of weariness have eaten
>
> Out through the winding of the bone.
> . . . .
> I turn to her whose future bears
> The promise of the appalling air,
>
> My living wife, Frances Levine,
> Mother of Theodore, John, and Mark,
> Out of whatever we have been
> We will make something for the dark.

This poem illustrates not only Levine's technical competence but also, in the irony of the last line, his ability to ride the thin edge of hope and despair.

One of the most interesting poems is "Sierra Kid," a long narrative poem of twenty-two stanzas, launching itself appropriately in balladlike rhythms and subtly modulating through its major sections until in the fifth, final section the control is appropriately and primarily syllabic: the Sierra Kid, having achieved mythic stature through hardship and suffering in the wilderness, returns to civilization and finds the A & P parking lot:

> I came to touch
>
> The great heart of a dying state.
> Here is the wound!
> It makes no sound.
> All that we learn we learn too late,
> And it's not much.

With the publication of *Not This Pig*, Levine's poetic voice emerged more insistently. The lyric poems are fewer, the narratives and portraits accounting for most of the poems in the book. The proletarian hero is still here: "the old champion in a sweat suit" in "A New Day" whose "fat slides under his shirt" finds

> No fresh start and no bird song
> And no sea and no shore
> That someone hasn't seen before.

In the all-night restaurant before dawn Levine wants

> to sweeten the sandwich of the child,
> to waken the cook, to stop the Negro from
> bearing witness to the world,

but he is "not Prince Valiant," and they hear "the 8 o'clock whistles blasting from heaven, / and with no morning the day is sold." Outside "The House of the Hanged Child," "three men in their stiff vests are listening" with "no songs, no radios in the electric morning":

> their hair has coarsened; their lips,
> their brows and hands have darkened
> in the frame of white America.
> They are becoming
> speechless, they are becoming
> Portuguese.
> . . . .
> Near the cypresses shading the white
> Impala no one can drive
> a small dark brother leans
> toward the freeway and the music,
> burning like a hive of tears.

This poem also illustrates Levine's growing mastery of the line as he elaborates upon his original seven-syllable pattern. The lines in the poem's three stanzas of successively seven, eight, and nine lines each vary from five to eleven syllables. Each line has three stresses, although this is occasionally modulated to two, four, or five; more important, the lines move into iambics and anapests as the rhetorical and emotional rhythms demand. The result is a line that is moving and momentous.

Not all of the poems are formally this successful. "Above it All," "Commanding Elephants," "Obscure," and "Barbie & Ken, Ken & Barbie" move along in what Robley Wilson, Jr., in a 1968 review, calls "relentless syllabics-in-sevens." To these relentless sevens Levine sacrifices line after line, losing meaning as well as energy. These lines from "Commanding Elephants," for example, seem arbitrary:

Let me Begin again

~~Beginnings~~

Let me begin again as a speck
of ~~dust~~ dust caught in the night winds
sweeping out to sea. Let me begin
~~for the second time knowing~~
this time knowing the world is
salt water & dark clouds, the world
is grinding & sighing all night, & dawn
comes slowly & changes nothing. Let
one ~~return to the world~~
me go back to land after a lifetime
of going nowhere. ~~let me become~~
            This time loafed
white in the feathers of some scavenging gull
  above the black ship that docks
  & dredges upon the oily waters of
your harbor. This leaking freighter
has ~~carried~~ brought a hold full of crayfish
from Spain, great jeroboams of dark
Algerian wine, & quill pens that won't
write. English the sailors have stumbled
off toward the bars or the bright houses
the captain closes his log & falls asleep.
1/10/28. Tonight I shall enter my life
after being at sea, for ages, anxiety ~~~~
~~in Detroit~~
in a hospital named for an automobile.
the one child of millions of children

who has flown alone by the stars
~~his eyes bright against~~
above the black wastes of moonless waters
that stretched forever, who has turned
golden in the full sun of a new day.
~~The single child cried alone~~
A tiny wise child who this time will love
his life because it is like no other.

"Let me Begin again," manuscript

And in the bathroom farther
Than he could go the high-top
lace-up boots, the kind the scouts
wore and he'd worn since

he was twelve.

Such line divisions serve neither meaning nor rhythm. In their mechanical obedience to the rule of seven they stifle the energies of the poem. One more example, from "Obscure," also indicates the dangers of overindulgence in sustained syllabics:

for first she must
sit still in a workingman's
bar in Calwa, just under
the raised television set
where her shot glass has lain down
in a puddle. She has seen
so much, and knows so little.

One wonders why the poet chooses such arduous and prosaic lines over possibly clearer, more colloquial possibilities. Perhaps a case could be made for their withdrawn quality, but there are too many other line divisions that seem to do disservice to Levine's energies to overlook this problem.

The most exciting development in this volume is Levine's new power with open forms. "The Everlasting Sunday" and "Rats," both organically constructed, foreshadow the passion and sensitivity of *They Feed They Lion*. These lines from "Rats" move like stealthy, persistent animals and suggest a menace and vitality that go beyond the meaning of the words. It is clear that Levine is, as he says,

listening to myself,
to my breathing and to
the noise my breathing makes.

they are moving, the shadows,
out of time, out
of sight, somewhere out
there in the darkness, and
when the lights
come back they are no longer
where they were.

The small-press publication of *Pili's Wall* and *Red Dust* in 1971 marked important changes in Levine's imagery as well as a franker use of open forms. *Pili's Wall* is really one long poem composed of ten short meditations based on a child's stick figures etched into a stone and plaster wall. Photographs of these figures accompany the poems, which are more elliptical and discontinuous than

Levine's previous work, gaining in intensity and presence:

I press my hand over
my mouth, I see nothing.

A blood bean
leaps at the foot of the wall

And I am with my face
turned in.

Out of lime
Out of thatch, straw, stones

Out of the years
of peeling and crying

Out of saying No
No to the barn swallow, No

to the hurled stone
No to the air

Out of *You can't*
to the crying grain, *you won't*

to the lost river
of blackening ivy

out of blind
out of deaf, closed, still

I stand and stand and stand into
this wall.

The poems in *Red Dust*, many of which appear later in *Ashes: Poems New and Old* (1979), reflect much the same concerns as *Not this Pig* but move with more organic, authoritative rhythms, like these lines from "In the New Sun":

Awake
in Tetuan, the room filling
with the first colors, and water running
in a tub.

The imagery in *Red Dust* has also grown more powerful. Images start in the real world, then slide into the psyche to resonate metaphorically, as in "For Luis Omar Salinas":

Sinks whispering in the cold, pinball
machines that sweat,
sacks of memorial letters
crying for help. . . .
. . . .
the drive-ins are
shrouded in mist, the stars
coming apart, and nothing waits inside
the halos of sleep.

Philip Levine

They Feed They Lion, published in 1972, established Levine as an important American poet descended from Walt Whitman and William Carlos Williams in his celebration of the American common man in the city. Although some poems, because of mechanical line divisions, still teeter on the borders of prose, most of the poems demonstrate that Levine has incorporated the growth evident in *Pili's Wall* and *Red Dust* in this volume. Besides a sensitive and brilliant sequence entitled "Thistles" and dedicated to George Oppen, the most noteworthy is the title poem, which epitomizes the best of this volume's qualities. Its lines are incantations, their power derived from anaphora, alliteration, and strong sprung rhythm. Its images are sharply concrete and discontinuous, referring to the most brutal sensory experiences in the marginal existence of the blacks who leave the rural South for factory work in the North.

The essence of the poem is its ambiguity, especially the syntactic ambiguity of the refrain "They Lion grow" and the concluding line "They feed they Lion and he comes." "They" may be read as manufacturers or workers, "grow" as produce or become, and "Lion" as direct object or predicate adjective. In the closing line, "feed" may be read as transitive or intransitive; "they" may be a dialect possessive or a new subject in a series of short clauses; and "comes" may or may not have a sexual connotation. The cumulative result of rhythm, imagery, and syntax is the creation out of suffering and exploitation of a creature (or a people) at once angry and forgiving, menacing and loving, oppressed and dignified.

The years following the publication of *They Feed They Lion* seem mainly to have been a period of consolidation for Levine. *1933*, published in 1974 and taking its title from Levine's poem commemorating the death of his father in that year, contains many portraits of relatives and friends recalled from his early childhood. In this volume it is clear that Levine has continued to perfect his imagery, his use of colloquial language, and the organic poetic line. These lines from "1933" capture the relentless movement of domestic life:

> my mother waits for the horsecart to pass
> my mother prays to become fat and wise
>   she becomes fat and wise
> the cat dies and it rains
> the dog groans by the side door
> the old hen flies up in a spasm of gold. . . .

"At the Fillmore" shows colloquial language moving rhythmically from line to line in hypnotic cadence with the sensuous imagery:

> She dozed in the Ladies
> wondering should she
> return. This warmth
>
> like the flush of juice
> up the pale stem
> of the flower, she'd known
>
> before, and its aftermath—
> seeing the Sisters
> and the promises again.

Most of the poems in *On the Edge & Over* (1976) were reprinted from earlier volumes, and most of the new poems it contains appear in *The Names of the Lost*, also published in 1976. This book is essentially elegiac in tone, and in it Levine seems to be working toward a new type of line, neither organic nor metrical-accentual, but rather a somewhat abstractly constructed, usually five-or-six-syllable, two-or-three-stress line that threatens to flatten the effect even of such moving pieces as "A Late Answer," which concludes:

> Somewhere
> we'll leave the world weighing
> no more than when we came,
> and the answer will be
> the same, your hand in mine,
> mine in yours, in that clearing
> where the angels come toward us
> without laughter, without tears.

Ashes: Poems New and Old (about half the poems are reprinted from *Red Dust*) and *7 Years from Somewhere*, both published in 1979, signal a major change in Levine's poetry. There are fewer portraits, fewer narratives, and many lyrical poems. The elegiac tone remains, but the elegy is for the past selves of Philip Levine. Many of the poems are retrospective, the poet reviewing his youth as he sees the years "turning toward home" in "Here and Now," "The Life Ahead," and "Andorra." "Each year," he says, "I tire a little more," and "each hour of this life I see the darkness more clearly." Levine has been undertaking a coming-to-terms with time and the self in "Peace" and "Lost and Found," in which there is a marked transition from past into present time:

>   the sun
> has cleared the trees, the wind
> risen, and we, father and child,
> hand in hand, the living and
> the dead, are entering the world.

16

From the past Levine has reentered this world, one he twice refers to as "what no one promised, here and now." Accompanying this reentry into the present is an intensification of the surrealistic imagery seen in earlier poems like "The Midget" and "The Rats" from *Not This Pig*. In "Here and Now," he thinks he can "hold the darkness the way a man / holds a cup of coffee before / he wakens," and in "Planting," a soldier

                    writes a letter
        to the year and explains
        how he was meant to make
        something else, a ball
        of earth out of his ears
        . . . .
        was meant to grow small
        and still, a window
        on the world, a map
        that can show him home.
        He goes out to the fields
        and plants it word by word,
        hurling it into the wind
        and feels it come back, soft,
        burning, heavy with rain.

This return to the present also is probably closely connected with recent changes in the poet's line. In some poems, as in "The Gift," there is further movement toward an abstract, regularized, five-to-seven-syllable line with two or three stresses that seems to reduce the energy of the poem; in others there is a greater authority and rhythmic variation, as in these lines from "The Helmet":

        They did not lie down
        face to face
        because of the waste
        of being so close
        and they were too tired
        of being each other
        to try to be lovers
        and because they had
        to sit up straight
        so they could eat.

This split in the development of the poet's line recalls the formal problem that was created by the primarily narrative nature of the poems. Levine may now be approaching the solution more closely than ever in his growing concern with his language and his lines as they reflect his poetic vision. This is an exciting development; Levine's reader has come to know the poet's public self, his sympathy for the oppressed, and his reverence for human dignity. But

the reader expects and desires in the poem an exploration of Levine's idiosyncratic shaping imagination, his passion for the word as it enables him, in the present, to perceive people and place. This revelation will inform Levine's line with even greater lyric power and precision. As he says in "Any Night":

                I will have to learn
        to sing in the voices of pure joy
        and pure pain. I will have to forget
        my name, my childhood, the years
        under the cold dominion of the clock
        so that this voice, torn and cracked,
        can reach the low hills that shielded
        the orange trees once. I will stand
        on the back porch as the cold
        drifts in, and sing, not for joy,
        not for love, not even to be heard.
        I will sing so that the darkness
        can take hold and whatever
        is left, the fallen fruit, the last
        leaf, the puzzled squirrel, the child
        far from home, lost, will believe
        this could be any night.

                                —*Joan Taylor*

Interviews:

"Touch Them Because They Gave Me My Life: An Interview with Philip Levine," *American Poetry Review*, 1 (November-December 1972): 35-37;
"And See if the Voice Will Enter You: An Interview with Philip Levine," *Ohio Review*, 26 (Winter 1975): 45-63;
Calvin Bedient, "An Interview with Philip Levine," *Parnassus*, 6 (1978): 40-51.

References:

Calvin Bedient, "Four American Poets," *Sewanee Review*, 84 (Spring 1976): 351-359;
Bedient, "Horace and Modernism," *Sewanee Review*, 85 (Spring 1977): 361-370;
Thom Gunn, "Modes of Control," *Yale Review*, 53 (March 1964): 447-453;
Richard Howard, "Centers of Attention," *Poetry*, 125 (March 1975): 354-359;
Richard Hugo, "Philip Levine: Naming the Lost," *American Poetry Review*, 6 (May-June 1977): 27-28;
David Kalstone, "The Entranced Procession of the

Philip Levine

Philip Levine

Dead," *Parnassus*, 3 (Fall-Winter 1974): 41-50;
William Marling, "Like Dynamite Evaporating," *Southwest Review*, 62 (Summer 1977): 325-326;
Robert Mazzocco, "Matters of Life and Death," *New York Review of Books*, 22 (3 April 1975): 20-23;
Ralph J. Mills, " 'The True and Earthly Prayer': Philip Levine's Poetry," *American Poetry Review*, 3 (March-April 1974): 44-47;
Charles Molesworth, "The Burned Essential Oil: The Poetry of Philip Levine," *Hollins Critic*, 12 (December 1975): 1-15;
Joyce Carol Oates, "Books of Change: Recent Collections of Poems," *Southern Review*, 9 (Autumn 1973): 1015-1016;
Jay Parini, "The Small Valleys of Our Living," *Poetry*, 130 (August 1977): 293-303;
Robert Pinsky, Review of *The Names of the Lost*, *New York Times Book Review*, 20 February 1977, pp. 6, 14;
Stanley Poss, Review of *1933*, *Northwest Review*, 14, no. 2 (1974): 113-118;
Richard Schramm, "A Gathering of Poets," *Western Humanities Review*, 26 (Autumn 1972): 389-392;
Robert Spector, Review of *They Feed They Lion*, *Saturday Review of Literature*, 55 (11 March 1972): 80-81;
Robley Wilson, Jr., "Five Poets at Hand," *Carleton Miscellany*, 9 (Fall 1968): 117-120;
Stephen Yenser, "Bringing it Home," *Parnassus*, 6 (1977): 101-117.

JOHN LOGAN
(23 January 1923-)

SELECTED BOOKS: *A Cycle for Mother Cabrini* (New York: Grove, 1955);
Ghosts of the Heart (Chicago: University of Chicago Press, 1960);
Spring of the Thief (New York: Knopf, 1963);
The Zigzag Walk (New York: Dutton, 1969);
The Anonymous Lover (New York: Liveright, 1973);
The House that Jack Built (Omaha: Abattoir Editions, 1974);
Poem in Progress (San Francisco: Dryad Press, 1975);
Aaron Siskind: Photographs / John Logan: Poems (Rochester, N.Y.: Visual Studies Workshop, 1976);
The Bridge of Change (Brockport: BOA Editions, 1979);
The Ballet of the Ear, ed. Donald Hall (Ann Arbor: University of Michigan Press, forthcoming, 1981).

John Logan, born in Red Oak, Iowa, received his undergraduate degree in biology (*magna cum laude*) from Coe College in 1943, and his M.A. in English from the State University of Iowa in 1949; he has done graduate work in philosophy at Georgetown University and Notre Dame University. He was married in 1945, and later divorced; Logan has nine children. He has taught at St. John's College in Annapolis, Maryland, Notre Dame, the University of Washington, San Francisco State University, and, since 1966, the State University of New York at Buffalo. His work has earned extensive critical acclaim; he has been awarded Wayne State University's Miles Modern Poetry Prize in 1968, a Rockefeller Foundation grant in 1969, the National Institute of Arts and Letters Morton Dauwen Zabel Award in 1974, a State University of New York Research Foundation Fellowship in Poetry in 1979, and a Guggenheim Fellowship in 1980. He is a former poetry editor of both the *Nation* and the *Critic*, as well as a former poetry columnist for the latter. He is also founder and coeditor of *Choice*, a magazine of poetry and graphics.

Although Logan's poetry has received the admiration of distinguished poets and critics and has been compared by James Dickey to that of Thomas Merton and Robert Lowell, it is only in recent studies that his work has been viewed as distinctively humanist both in its central concerns with man and his capabilities and in its continuing emphasis on classical allusions, both ancient and modern.

The philosophical foundation of Logan's work has been closely related to the existential humanism of Martin Heidegger, whose aim is an authenticity and wholeness of human 'being'. Logan too wants to rescue man from the meaningless void of nihilism. His honesty and directness are a way of facing his own being and acquiring self-knowledge, of seeing his life in its entirety (including his death). This perspective necessitates a sense of loss and dread, but it also allows a human being to achieve authenticity. Logan's voice of conscience and responsibility consistently urges the reader to transcend and transform the inauthentic life, to find freedom in the resolution to become oneself, to be whole. The duty to understand one's self is an obligation to realize one's inner capabilities by choosing to do so, despite what one is given as the conditions of existence. Logan's poetry is, on the surface, disarmingly casual and immediate, but at its center engagingly metaphysical and meditative.

The poems are intense and personal, and have been praised by Dickey for conveying "to a remarkable degree that degreeless and immeasurable and unanalyzable quality . . . called . . . reverence for

18

life." Robert Bly has identified Logan as "one of the five or six finest poets to emerge in the United States in the last decades," and notes that his language is always "being used to build something, rather than to reflect something." Bly's observation serves to recall both Heidegger's conception of language as the house of Being and Logan's use of each book of poems as a unit in the creation of a coherent structure.

A Cycle for Mother Cabrini (1955), his first book, is a celebration of the immigrant nun who helped shape the city of Chicago by building schools, hospitals, and orphanages. In retrospect, Logan's recurrent themes are here like the skeleton of an incipient skyscraper or a diagram of a looming metaphorical structure. The title poem touches on several of his general concerns: the sources of one's identity, dread transformed to hope, poetry as transformation, the willingness and courage to take risks, and the search for authentic being. "A Dialogue with La Mettrie" affirms the human spirit, repudiates the reductive mechanistic view of man, and reflects the poet's interest in fundamental questions of philosophy. The lives of literary characters, from Robert Southwell to Augustine, are integral to subsequent poems in the volume; the frequency of allusion to classical figures establishes, more than allegiance, the deeper presence of Logan as poet, as a being who carries on their presences, in the continuum of poetic language.

Ghosts of the Heart, published in 1960, continues the themes mentioned above. The opening poem, "The Lives of the Poet," is a short biography of Arthur Rimbaud that expresses the notion that all poets, after discovering the inner life and being moved by the faith of their fathers, become voyagers or subjects of change. "On the Death of the Poet's Mother Thirty-Three Years Later" begins with an image of the poet as a child overwhelmed by a bronze-colored dog that further on becomes the Roman she-wolf that nurtured Romulus and Remus, the legendary founders of the city of Rome. The poem also alludes to Virgil's *Aeneid*. Here the search for authentic self is for origins, for the identity to be found in both personal memory and public record. Each poem in part 1 of this volume is preceded by an epigraph and/or followed by an after note as a constant reminder of the poem's location in the context of an omnipresent history. "Protest after a Dream" introduces part 2, which describes a search heightened by a questioning of the past and a movement into the present: "If they cannot make us well, as it looks, / What the hell good are our books?" The subsequent poems of this section depict the vulnerability of openness while dramatizing the

responsibility to know and share vital truths with family, friends, or fellow wanderers. Part 2 closes with a resolution to his son: "as I can I will help you with my love." Part 3 moves into the realm of the more personal past and the polarities of ecstasy and grief, of exotic paradise and anguished failure; it is a summons to remember, to be mindful of the potential human being that exists in anticipation of its own possibilities. In the last poem, "A Trip to Four or Five Towns," the poet loves his friends, unlike Romulus, who killed his brother; but like Romulus, who disappeared in a thunderstorm, the poet disappears in an airliner, taking the ghosts of his heart with him. This second book also contains a number of poems celebrating other poets, including Homer, Byron, Heinrich Heine, Hart Crane, and William Carlos Williams. These poems, mediated by his knowledge, say as much about Logan's intentional location of the self-as-poet as they do about the figures they celebrate.

Spring of the Thief (1963), Logan's third volume, has a cryptic dedication with an unattributed quotation from the philosopher-theologian Karl Rahner (who studied under Heidegger). The quotation says in part: "The art is to help men become what they really are." If men are to understand each other and themselves, it will be through the magic of language, Logan says, which alone allows men to stand in openness to what is.

In "The Experiment that Failed," a poem about a fatal transfusion that took place in the fifteenth century, the underlying paradox is that the hope for a transmuted life led to death. In the poems about portraits of the foot by the photographer Aaron Siskind, a deep desire for change begins to find some satisfaction in the powers of imagination; the foot that might be a hand almost becomes a bird.

The widely praised title poem of *Spring of the Thief* questions the nature of Being and suggests that it is essentially an eternal transformation that one witnesses in the "freshness" of things. Other poems increase the attention to nakedness and to the consequent inverted, juxtaposed, or rearranged identities. The volume tapers to a close with a metaphorical fishing trip wherein the poet is both fisherman and fish, a still ambiguous being.

A change takes place in *The Zigzag Walk*, published in 1969. The voice is less erudite and more natural, and the poetic structures are more varied; there is also a focus on landscape that is not present in the earlier volumes. In the first section, the pursuit of self-knowledge and freedom becomes symbolic in the exploration of various geographies, and the struggle for survival isolates and imprisons the poet.

The second and third sections include transla-

steam-4-

hostile teacher, watchman.
But a little later they came too, and their women
and others in that gentle lunatic
                                    light
come to bathe and sing with us.
But ~~Because~~ in this
                        hot spring
water everything
                    eventually heals:
for, by
        the sea
it flows from these ancient, California hills,
which are the trans-
                    formed,
giant bodyof a once
powerful, turquoise-adorned
Indian Prince,
            and the sulphur is the changed,
sharp incense
            he burned daily as he chanted
year and year over for the sick young princess--
~~until~~ he died of grief,
                    still unable to help,
                                        he thought.
can ~~But~~ Everybody here who comes together
                                in ~~belief~~

is somehow bound, bathed and made whole
e-
    ven as was she
by the gradual, glinting water
of his warm, continual tears for *our* sister.

John Logan
Buffalo. Dec. 11'72

"*Poem: tears, spray and steam,*" revised typescript

20

tions of German and Hungarian poetry, and homages to Rainer Maria Rilke and Herman Melville that deal with alienation and grief again but also with a movement beyond the limits of conventional love. In "Homage to Herman Melville," David, the protagonist of the poem, puts "an end to his paternity and to his past. / The future is an untravelled gulf." Memory, a defense against self-forgetfulness and an instrument of establishing origins and personal history in the earlier volumes, is seen here as an instrument of decay. The fourth section consists of five elegies in a repeated confrontation with the mystery of death, and it ends with the exhausted poet in flight, spiritually communing with his dead grandmother on Easter.

The last section asserts the power of friendship; male and female companions give strength and "make us want to stay alive." "Lines for Michael in the Picture" articulates a relentless courage to love in the face of a changing situation, and Michael becomes an artistic blend of brother, friend, son, and father. There is a palpable yearning for personal, but not physical, contact throughout these poems. A bipolar level of existence is achieved in the realization that intimate human interaction is essential to fulfillment of the self as well as fulfillment of the other. "The Search," which concludes the volume, dismisses various explorations of the other, repeating five times the question, "For whom do I look / seek?" and concludes, "Perhaps it is you whom I seek."

One critic, Karl Malkoff, emphasizes that in this volume Logan is "pointing out that it is necessary to love in order to live, and that the problems inherent in the human condition make love as complicated and difficult as it is necessary." A. Poulin, Jr., notes that "final transcendence can be achieved only when and if the self has fully responded to human and earthly experience." *The Zigzag Walk*, erratic, full, and searching, responds to such experience. Elinor Cubbage notes that "Love is Logan's reason for writing, living. A worshipping of life, his poetry revolves around the ability of his art to reach out successfully to a reader. . . . I can only wish that all poets, when at their best, had this poet's commitment to life."

The title of the fifth volume, *The Anonymous Lover* (1973), echoes the term *Anonymous Christian*, which is Karl Rahner's description of genuinely religious people who might seem to have no faith whatsoever but will be redeemed by a loving, incomprehensible God. The opening poem, "Cape Elizabeth: A Photograph," urges the reader to watch with the poet for a light ship on the horizon. The

responsibility inherent in "Only the Dreamer Can Change the Dream" is one of building a home of one's own, of creating a house that "rise- / s silent as a ship does." "Poem for My Son," rich in humor and integrity and a criticism of insufficient loving, also employs the image of the house. It is evoked as an image of philosophy, as a fulfillment of the human spirit. In *The Poetics of Space*, Gaston Bachelard discusses self-prophecy as a function of art, and he remarks that the house image "is a principle of psychological integration . . . [and] would appear to have become the topography of our intimate being." The house image recurs, in one form or another, throughout the book, creating a suite of rooms, some erotic and sensual, as in "New Poem," some aesthetic, as in "Three Poems on Aaron Siskind's Photographs," and others tenderly human, as in "Return to the Island." ("Three Poems on Aaron Siskind's Photographs" was republished with others, in 1976, in a volume of poems and graphics, *Aaron Siskind: Photographs / John Logan: Poems*.) *The Anonymous Lover* differs from the previous work by the presence of humor, most noticeably in the expansive poem "Heart to Heart Talk with My Liver." The change in the poet's symmetry

Thomas Victor

John Logan

represents a development of the self-deprecatory into the comic, culminating in a spirit of health and aliveness by which the poet becomes his "own deliverer."

One critical response, by William H. Chaplin, observes that: "No poet, since Freud's discoveries have become the common property of the mind, has written with fuller mastery of the circumstances in which this longing [for the 'spirit of health'] finds itself baffled and fulfilled than John Logan. He has gone far to answer Freud's misbegotten charge that poetry is another form of fantasy; for he has . . . dramatized the way the need for transcendence goes beyond fantasy to become actual." Chaplin further observes that Logan's poetry is free of "the reductive truths of psychoanalysis." Richard Howard says, "The poems of *The Anonymous Lover* are perhaps the first in the history of the art which are set down, by an authentic artist, to take care of themselves." John R. Carpenter notes how the poems build up "into large, deliberate structures," and how this volume might be seen as the house of human love.

The House That Jack Built, primarily a volume of rich, intense, autobiographical prose, was published in 1974. Although limited to the poet's childhood, it is important for the revelations of poetic roots to be found in the indelible images and experiences from Logan's earliest years: the boy being overpowered by his family's red dog, being punished for telling the truth, traveling and singing with his father, writing on the sidewalk with a fountain pen, searching for his mother's grave, and experiencing the joy inherent in lyrical language.

Poem in Progress (1975), an eight-part poem in which "the house image" becomes a boat, continues the voyage in which the poet, through the essential union of friendship, becomes father, son, and brother. Here the allusions are more contemporary and help to remind the reader that a denial of his own ambiguous and androgynous soul is a trap of his dualistic logic (i.e., male or female, good or evil, father or friend?), which often blocks the quest for the true self. The simultaneous interest in American geography and the body, evident since *The Anonymous Lover*, is integrated here in an affirmation of the social bond.

Subsequent poems, still uncollected, move clearly into the social and public realm. Both "Dublin Suite: Homage to James Joyce" and "The Bridge of Change" expand to epic proportions the parameter of Logan's carefully structured body of work. In retrospect, the overall affirmation and glorification in his poetry celebrates the poet-as-speaker, or the artist-as-hero, as creator of monuments of language.

Referring to the misreadings of Logan's poetry by some critics, Robert Boyers says in *Contemporary Poets*, "Too often the rather prosaic voice and straightforward presentation of sequential observations have been mistaken for ideological certitude and dully competent versification. Only in a recent study by Jerome Mazzaro has the relation between Logan's poetic artifacts and his thematic concerns been successfully explained." The emergence of Logan as an existential humanist in the ranks of major American poets has been augmented by an unfolding view of the world similar to Alfred North Whitehead's concept of the universe as a harmonious process of developing organisms. Logan continues to please and delight his readers with a love born of desire and courage and a fullness of living.

—*Dan Murray*

Other:

"The Organ Grinder and the Cockatoo," in *Modern American Poetry*, ed. J. Mazzaro (New York: McKay, 1970);

Hart Crane, *White Buildings*, foreword by Logan (New York: Liveright, 1972);

"The Success," in *The Poet's Story*, ed. Howard Moss (New York: Simon & Schuster, 1973), pp. 107-115;

"On My Early Poetry," in *American Poets in 1976*, ed. William Heyen (Indianapolis: Bobbs-Merrill, 1976), pp. 146-164;

"Poets and Poetry Today," in *New Naked Poetry*, ed. Stephen Berg and Robert Mezey (Indianapolis: Bobbs-Merrill, 1976);

Shreela Ray, *Night Conversations with None Other*, foreword by Logan (San Francisco: Dustbooks, 1977);

Daniela Gioseffi, *Eggs in the Lake*, foreword by Logan (Brockport, N.Y.: BOA Editions, 1979).

Periodical Publications:

POETRY:

"Poem for my Brother," *Ironwood*, no. 4 (1974): 5-6;

"Prose Poem: On Returning Home," *Boundary 2*, 4, no. 1 (1975): 174-175;

"Five Preludes for Buffalo's own Forest Lawn," *Ohio Review*, 16 (Winter 1975);

"At Drumcliffe Churchyard, County Sligo," *Kayak*, no. 42 (1976);

"The Bridge of Change," *Paris Review*, no. 69 (Spring 1977): 50-55;

"Elegy for Dylan Thomas," *Ironwood*, no. 11 (Spring 1978): 72-74;

"Ten Poems on Mark Logan's Photographs," *Choice*, 10 (Summer 1979): 221-230;

"The Library," *Poetry*, 134 (June 1979): 144-145;

"The Unknown Lover," *West Hills Review*, 1 (Fall 1979): 53;

"From Dublin Suite," *Modern Poetry Studies*, 9 (1979): 188-190.

FICTION:

"The Picture for the Publisher," *New World Writing*, no. 11 (1957);

"The Bishop's Suite," *New Yorker*, 33 (1 June 1957): 81-84;

"The Last Class," *Kenyon Review*, 20 (1958): 373-392;

"The House that Jack Builds," *Chicago Review*, 12 (Autumn 1958): 19-26;

"Fire," *Big Table*, 1 (Summer 1959): 24-27;

"The Panic Round," *Epoch*, 11 (Winter 1961): 34-43;

"The Loss," *Critic*, 20 (December 1961-January 1962): 26-30;

"The Cigars," *Minnesota Review*, 5 (January-April 1965): 35-38.

NONFICTION:

"John Gruen's Settings for Wallace Stevens," *Hudson Review*, 9 (Summer 1956): 273-276;

"Sorrow in the Poet in the Man in the Animal," *Chicago Review*, 12 (Autumn 1958): 29-32;

"Dylan Thomas and the Ark of Art," *Renascence*, 12 (Winter 1960): 59-66;

"New Catholic Poets," *Critic*, 19 (October-November 1960): 77-87;

"Broadside Attack on the Patriarchs of Modern Poetry," *Commonweal*, 73 (20 January 1961): 438-440;

"The Poetry of Isabella Gardner," *Sewanee Review*, 70 (Spring 1962): 257-260;

"Interior and Exterior Worlds," *Nation*, 204 (24 April 1967): 541-542;

"Psychological Motifs in Melville's *Pierre*," *Minnesota Review*, 7 (Spring 1967): 325-330;

"The Bear in the Poet in the Bear," *Nation*, 207 (16 September 1968): 244-245;

"A Note on the Inarticulate Hero," *New Mexico Quarterly*, 38, no. 4 / 39, no. 1 (Winter-Spring 1969): 148-153.

References:

Charles Altieri, "Poetry as Resurrection: John Logan's Structure of Metaphysical Solace," *Modern Poetry Studies*, 3 (1973): 193-224;

Alfred Barson, "The Walking Poems: Logan's Mature Voice," *Modern Poetry Studies*, 9 (1979): 191-196;

Marvin Bell, "Homage to the Runner," *American Poetry Review*, 4, no. 5 (1975);

Bell, "Logan's Teaching," *Voyages*, 4 (Spring 1972): 38-39;

Bell, "What Poetry Means to John Logan: An Interview," *Trace*, no. 43 (May 1961): 230-234;

Robert Bly, "John Logan's Field of Force," *Voyages*, 4 (Spring 1972): 29-36;

Bly, "The Work of John Logan," *Sixties*, no. 5 (Fall 1961): 77-87;

Glauco Cambon, *Recent American Poetry* (Minneapolis: University of Minnesota Press, 1962), pp. 36-42;

John R. Carpenter, "The Anonymous Lover," *Poetry*, 125 (December 1974): 171-172;

Paul Carroll, "Was Frau Heine a Monster," in his *The Poem In Its Skin* (New York: Follett Publishing, 1968), pp. 110-136;

William Chaplin, "Identity and Spirit in The Recent Poetry of John Logan," *American Poetry Review* (May-June 1973): 19-24;

Chaplin, "The Third Presence," *Ohio Review*, 15 (Spring 1974): 115-119;

Elinor Cubbage, "John Logan's 'The Zigzag Walk,'" *Modern Poetry Studies*, 9 (1979): 168-178;

James Dickey, *Babel to Byzantium: Poets and Poetry Now* (New York: Farrar, Straus & Giroux, 1968), pp. 164-167;

Gene Frumkin, "The Spiraling Notebook of John Logan," *Ironwood*, no. 11 (Spring 1978): 75-86;

Richard Howard, *Alone with America Essays on the Art of Poetry in the United States Since 1950* (New York: Atheneum, 1969), pp. 306-317;

Howard, "Cutting at the Joint," *American Poetry Review*, 2 (September-October 1973): 7-8;

Harold Isbell, "Growth and Change," *Modern Poetry Studies*, 2 (1971);

Karl Malkoff, *Crowell's Handbook of Contemporary American Poetry* (New York: Crowell, 1973);

Jerome Mazzaro, "The Poetry of John Logan," *Salmagundi*, 2 (Fall 1968): 78-95;

Mazzaro, "Integrities," *Kenyon Review*, 32 (1970): 163-168;

Robert Phillips, "John Logan's 'The Anonymous Lover,'" *Modern Poetry Studies*, 9 (1979): 178-180;

A. Poulin, Jr., "Unpredictable as Grace," *Nation*, 209 (29 December 1969): 734-735;

Michael Rust, "Singing for the Shadow," *Voyages*, 4, no. 3-4 (Spring 1972): 40-47;

Phyllis Thompson, "Journey to the New Waters of Brother, Sister," *Modern Poetry Studies*, 9 (1979): 197-210.

Robert Lowell

Ashley Brown
University of South Carolina

BIRTH: Boston, Massachusetts, 1 March 1917, to Robert Traill Spence and Charlotte Winslow Lowell.

EDUCATION: Harvard University, 1935-1937; A.B., Kenyon College, 1940; Louisiana State University, 1940-1941.

MARRIAGE: 2 April 1940 to Jean Stafford, divorced. 28 July 1949 to Elizabeth Hardwick, divorced; children: Harriet Winslow. 1972 to Caroline Blackwood; children: Robert Sheridan.

AWARDS: National Institute of Arts and Letters Award, 1947; Guggenheim Fellowship, 1947; Pulitzer Prize for *Lord Weary's Castle*, 1947; Consultant in Poetry, Library of Congress, 1947-1948; Harriet Monroe Poetry Award (University of Chicago), 1952; Guinness Poetry Award (Ireland), 1959; National Book Award for *Life Studies*, 1960; Bollingen Poetry Translation Prize, 1962; Levinson Prize (*Poetry* magazine), 1963; Golden Rose Trophy (New England Poetry Club), 1964; Sarah Josepha Hale Award, 1966; Pulitzer Prize for *The Dolphin*, 1974; Copernicus Award (Academy of American Poets), 1974.

DEATH: New York City, 12 September 1977.

BOOKS: *Land of Unlikeness* (Cummington, Mass.: Cummington Press, 1944);
Lord Weary's Castle (New York: Harcourt, Brace, 1946);
Poems 1938-1949 (London: Faber & Faber, 1950);
The Mills of the Kavanaughs (New York: Harcourt, Brace, 1951);
Life Studies (New York: Farrar, Straus & Cudahy, 1959);
For the Union Dead (New York: Farrar, Straus & Giroux, 1964; London: Faber & Faber, 1965);
The Old Glory (New York: Farrar, Straus & Giroux, 1965; London: Faber & Faber, 1966; revised edition, New York: Farrar, Straus & Giroux, 1968);
Near the Ocean (New York: Farrar, Straus & Giroux, 1967; London: Faber & Faber, 1967);
The Voyage & Other Versions of poems by Baudelaire (London: Faber & Faber, 1968; New York: Farrar, Straus & Giroux, 1969);
Prometheus Bound (New York: Farrar, Straus & Giroux, 1969; London: Faber & Faber, 1970);
Notebook, 1967-68 (New York: Farrar, Straus & Giroux, 1969); revised and republished as *Notebook* (New York: Farrar, Straus & Giroux, 1970; London: Faber & Faber, 1970);
The Dolphin (New York: Farrar, Straus & Giroux, 1973; London: Faber & Faber, 1973);
For Lizzie and Harriet (New York: Farrar, Straus & Giroux, 1973; London: Faber & Faber, 1973);
History (New York: Farrar, Straus & Giroux, 1973; London: Faber & Faber, 1973);
Selected Poems (New York: Farrar, Straus & Giroux, 1976);
Day by Day (New York: Farrar, Straus & Giroux, 1977).

For some readers and critics the late Robert Lowell stood at the center of his literary generation, and by the mid-1960s one admirer, Irvin Ehrenpreis, was referring to "The Age of Lowell." One can see why. Lowell was associated with nearly all the important American poets of the first half of this century, and long before the end of his life he seemed to be their heir. His appeal was not only literary. He involved himself to an unusual degree with the public events of his time, just as he brought his private life into public view by way of his poems. He was at once the poet of the American empire (sometimes resembling Virgil, sometimes Juvenal, sometimes Horace) and the alleged father of "confessional poetry." In some respects it is still too early to assess his career. He wrote a very great deal during his last decade, from 1967 to 1977, but so far few readers have assimilated the late work. His great poems, or at least the familiar ones, all come before 1967. In the near future there will doubtless be much scholarly work done with Lowell's poetry; few poets have revised so rapidly and extensively. A Variorum Lowell may or may not make these things easier for readers.

Robert Traill Spence Lowell was born in Boston. His family, long distinguished in that city, included a number of literary persons: his Lowell grandfather (for whom he was named), James Russell Lowell, and Amy Lowell. For two years he attended St. Mark's School in Massachusetts (of which his grandfather had once been headmaster).

On the faculty was Richard Eberhart, a young American poet, about whom Lowell said many years later, "there was someone there whom I admired who was engaged in writing poetry."

He went to Harvard, like all Lowells before him, but he left after two years. Although he was already acquainted with Robert Frost, he sought his instruction in poetry elsewhere. About this time, in 1937, he met the English novelist Ford Madox Ford, who was about to go to Tennessee to visit Allen Tate and his wife, the novelist Caroline Gordon; Ford evidently invited the young man to accompany him. Thus Lowell was brought into the presence of a distinguished Southern poet who was to have a considerable influence on his work. He pitched a tent in the Tates' front yard and spent the summer there, writing poetry in an almost obsessive way. In the fall of that year he went to Kenyon College in Ohio to study with John Crowe Ransom (Tate's first master); he remained there till 1940, when he graduated with a *summa cum laude* degree in classics. Among the close friends he made were Randall Jarrell, the poet, and Peter Taylor, the short-story writer. At the same time, in 1940, he became a Roman Catholic and married a young novelist, Jean Stafford. (Jean Stafford, who died in 1979, was the author of three novels and several collections of stories; she occasionally figures in Lowell's poetry.) To round out his education with the Southern literati, Lowell studied for a year at Louisiana State University with Cleanth Brooks and Robert Penn Warren.

He worked for a time in New York City with the Catholic publishing house of Sheed and Ward, but he and Jean Stafford spent 1942-1943 in the mountains of Tennessee, where they shared a house with the Tates. It was here that many of the poems in his first book were written. Then, in the middle of World War II, he was jailed as a conscientious objector to the Allied bombing of German civilians. (This interlude in his life is the basis of a poem called "Memories of West Street and Lepke" in *Life Studies*.) In 1944 his first book, *Land of Unlikeness*, was published in a small edition by the Cummington Press in Massachusetts; it was introduced by Allen Tate.

Tate's introduction is a brilliant account of Lowell's poetry at that time, and in two sentences he foretold what the course of Lowell's career would be: "On the one hand, the Christian symbolism is intellectualized and frequently given a savage satirical direction; it points to the disappearance of the Christian experience from the modern world, and stands, perhaps, for the poet's own effort to recover it. On the other hand, certain shorter poems, like 'A Suicidal Nightmare' and 'Death from Cancer,' are richer in immediate experience than the explicitly religious poems; they are more dramatic, the references being personal and historical and the symbolism less willed and explicit."

An example of the former kind of poetry that Tate mentions is the opening stanza of "On the Eve of the Feast of the Immaculate Conception":

> Mother of God, whose burly love
> Turns swords to plowshares, come, improve
>   On the big wars
> And make this holiday with Mars
> Your Feast Day, while Bellona's bluff
> Courage or call it what you please
>   Plays blindman's buff
>   Through virtue's knees.

Here the ironic contrast between the Mother of God and the Roman goddess of war is boldly stated as a metaphysical conceit; the sarcasm is only too evident. This passage comes close to being the norm for *Land of Unlikeness*. The strength of feeling never relents. Both private and public aspects of Lowell's life at this time account for the tone of the poetry: his defiance of his parents in different ways, one of them being his conversion to Catholicism; and the wartime events that he saw as more complicated than most people would. (Early in the war, however, he attempted to enlist in the navy.) The terms of this kind of poetry are large, almost cosmic, and they sometimes lead to the excesses of metaphor that one associates with the decline of the metaphysical style in the seventeenth century. Most of these poems have never been reprinted, at least not in their original form.

The other kind of poetry that Tate describes is just beginning to emerge in this first book; it can be seen at its best in the sequence on Lowell's grandfather Arthur Winslow. The "personal and historical" references are very specific; and one can easily say in retrospect that Lowell's particularity is one of his strong points as a poet. This sequence was reprinted in his famous second book, *Lord Weary's Castle* (1946), where the particularity is even more evident. In the early version, for instance, he speaks of "The craft that netted a million dollars, late / Mining in California's golden bays / Then lost it all in Boston real estate." In the revised version in *Lord Weary* the poeticism of "California's golden bays" becomes "Hosing out gold in Colorado's waste," which is probably more accurate as family history, and certainly more precise in physical details. The precision is there even when Lowell is imagining a situation. In "Exile's Return," the first poem in *Lord Weary's Castle*, he describes a scene that is evidently wartime Germany; it looks authentic. What the poet has in fact done is to lift details from Thomas Mann's story, "Tonio Kröger" (1903) and rearrange them, heighten them, for maximum effect. Lowell very early became a master at making poetry out of prose; his eye for the precise detail is unusually keen.

At this stage in his career he resembled at least one classic American writer, Nathaniel Hawthorne, in that he seemed to do his best work when he turned his attention to the history of his own people. And for a young writer in the mid-twentieth century, there was an accumulated literary history such as did not exist when Hawthorne started. Hawthorne himself is part of this history; so is Jonathan Edwards, and two of the finest poems in *Lord Weary's Castle* ("Mr. Edwards and the Spider" and "After the Surprising Conversions") are transmuted from well-known passages in Edwards's highly charged prose. One intensely satirical poem, the sonnet called "Concord," was carried over from *Land of Unlikeness* to *Lord Weary's Castle*, but with the most drastic changes. In the earlier version Ralph Waldo Emerson is the special focus of criticism: "Concord, where the Emersons / Washed out the blood-clots on my Master's robe." Two years later this passage becomes, less severely,

> Concord where Thoreau
> Named all the birds without a gun to probe
> Through darkness to the painted man and bow:
> The death-dance of King Philip and his scream
> Whose echo girdled this imperfect globe.

Here Emerson is not directly named; nor does his disciple Thoreau come in for the same criticism. But the last line, which is carried over almost intact, is itself an "echo" of Emerson's most famous line in "The Concord Hymn."

It was Herman Melville, however, who most deeply engaged Lowell's imagination in those days. "The Quaker Graveyard in Nantucket," a magnificent baroque elegy in seven parts, would have been impossible without *Moby-Dick* (1851). (Lowell's poem was originally called "To Herman Melville.") It no doubt owes much to the John Milton of "Lycidas" (1637), and indeed this is appropriate, because Lowell's poem is about the death of his cousin Warren Winslow, a naval officer who drowned in the North Atlantic during the war. But the rhetoric is closer to Melville, as in this passage:

> The winds' wings beat upon the stones,
> Cousin, and scream for you and the claws rush
> At the sea's throat and wring it in the slush
> Of this old Quaker graveyard where the bones
> Cry out in the long night for the hurt beast
> Bobbing by Ahab's whaleboats in the East.

Melville remained an important point of reference in Lowell's mind if not in his poetry, which became less baroque. Near the end of his life he put *Moby-Dick* beside the great epics of earlier literary periods. In an unfinished essay called "New England and Further," part of which was published in 1979, he wrote:

> Often magnificent rhythms and a larger vocabulary make it equal to the great metrical poems. . . . It is our best book. It tells us not to break our necks on a brick-wall. Yet what sticks in the mind is the Homeric prowess of the extinct whaleman, gone before his prey.

The kinesthetic quality of the passage quoted from "The Quaker Graveyard" is fairly typical of early Lowell. Here and there, as in the sixth section of the poem ("Our Lady of Walsingham"), a quiet moment occurs; but generally the rhetoric surges in response to a deeply felt subject.

Lord Weary's Castle received the Pulitzer Prize in 1947. By that time it had been reviewed at length; one review in particular, Randall Jarrell's in the *Nation* (18 January 1947), became famous in its own right as an example of a poet-critic's generously recognizing the arrival of a young master. Indeed his description of Lowell's central theme—the "wintry, Calvinist, capitalist world" against which the poet set himself—was the basis for much subsequent commentary.

Lowell's poetry continued to move in the direction that Allen Tate had predicted it would: the poems became more dramatic as they depended less on the "willed" Christian symbolism. The characteristic poems of the next few years were in fact dramatic monologues. Seven of them made up *The Mills of the Kavanaughs* (1951). The title poem, which is Lowell's longest single work (608 lines, arranged in 38 rhymed stanzas), has never gone down well with even his most sympathetic critics. Its narrative does not move; its large symbolism is forced. The heroine, a widow lamenting her husband, identifies herself with Persephone, whose statue stands in the grounds of her husband's house in Maine. But there is no real action. On the other hand, two of the shorter poems, running to three or four pages, are highly successful: "Mother Marie

Therese" and "Falling Asleep over the Aeneid." They are written in heroic couplets and may owe something to Robert Browning and Yvor Winters, but they sound like Lowell, with their vigorous run-over lines and emphatic rhythms. "Mother Marie Therese" is also a poem of lament, in this case for a nun who drowned in 1912 (Lowell may have been thinking of Gerard Manley Hopkins's 1875 poem "The Wreck of the Deutschland" here); the speaker is herself a Canadian nun "stationed in New Brunswick." The poem is wonderfully conversational at times, but it gathers up to a pitch of feeling at the end, when the poet somewhat boldly rounds it out with three couplets using the same rhyme.

"Falling Asleep over the Aeneid" is a masterpiece; Robert Fitzgerald recently called it "that marvel of dreamwork as historical imagination." The speaker, an old man in Concord, reading Virgil on Sunday morning, is immediately brought before us:

> The sun is blue and scarlet on my page,
> And *yuck-a, yuck-a, yuck-a, yuck-a*, rage
> The yellowhammers mating. Yellow fire
> Blankets the captives dancing on their pyre,
> And the scorched lictor screams and drops his rod.

Lowell has perhaps learned something about composition from Wallace Stevens's "Sunday Morning," where bird and fruit and sun, introduced in the opening lines, are carried through the poem in a series of transfigurations. Here the flame colors of the bright morning sun are intensified by the yellow wings of the birds that the old man only *hears*, but then the colors are absorbed by the fire that leaps from the page, as it were, with the lictor's scream. (The funeral of the heroic young Pallas in the *Aeneid* is the episode that takes over the old man's dream.) Fire and bird move through the poem in many ingenious ways, and they prepare for the end, where the dreamer recalls his uncle, a young Union officer in the Civil War, "Blue-capped and bird-like," at *his* funeral. Thus two eras of history are brought into relationship as we return to the present.

When *The Mills of the Kavanaughs* was published in 1951, Lowell was living in Italy. His marriage with Jean Stafford had ended in 1948; in the following year he married Elizabeth Hardwick, a novelist from Kentucky. The Lowells lived at different places in Europe, but Italy seemed to have the greatest attraction for him, as it did for so many other American poets during the 1950s. (Eventually, after his death, some of his Italian friends, including

his translator, brought out an impressive volume of tributes.) He was also becoming known in London, and as early as 1950 Faber and Faber, the publishing house of which T. S. Eliot was a director, began to publish his work. In time his reputation in London was possibly even larger than it was in the United States. But after the death of his mother in 1954 in Italy, he returned with his wife to live in a house on Marlborough Street in Boston. He had left the Catholic church. Perhaps for the moment there was nothing urgent to write about, and the few poems that he composed during this period were usually elegies for literary friends such as Ford Madox Ford and the philosopher George Santayana, whom he had visited in Rome.

The great change that came over his poetry in the late 1950s is now well known. In 1957 he was writing his autobiography in prose, and this became the actual source for a group of highly personal poems that, to some early readers, were only chopped-up prose fragments. The first of the new poems, and probably the most famous, is "Skunk Hour," which was started in August 1957. It is modeled on Elizabeth Bishop's "The Armadillo," according to Lowell's own account. (Miss Bishop's poem, which is set in Brazil, is dedicated to Lowell.) Her versification and open texture suggested an "easier" mode of poetry. In each case a single animal emerges at the end of the poem in a kind of affirmation. According to Lowell (whose account of the poem's composition is found in *The Contemporary Poet as Artist and Critic*, edited by Anthony Ostroff, 1964), he worked backward. The poem became intensely personal in a way that Miss Bishop's is not. Finally he wrote the four opening stanzas (half the poem) as a social setting: a declining Maine seaside town. The characteristic pronoun here is *our*, but the sense of community is precarious. The heart of the poem is the pair of stanzas that comes between the social setting and the image of the skunk and her kittens who take over the deserted town at the end:

> One dark night
> my Tudor Ford climbed the hill's skull;
> I watched for love-cars. Lights turned down,
> they lay together hull to hull,
> where the graveyard shelves on the town. . . .
> My mind's not right.
>
> A car radio bleats,
> "Love, O careless Love. . . ." I hear
> my ill-spirit sob in each blood cell,
> as if my hand were at its throat. . . .

Robert Lowell

I myself am hell;
nobody's here—

This is quintessential Lowell. Intensely private though it is (to a certain kind of reader it comes close to being a psychiatric case history), it has its public dimension. As some readers have noted, it is a version of the "dark night of the soul" of San Juan de la Cruz, although without the sense of a spiritual progression that the great Spanish mystic followed. "I myself am hell" is borrowed from *Paradise Lost*: Satan, spying on Adam and Eve. Between these two noble literary sources Lowell drops a phrase from a rather banal song that is being half-heard by millions, but it attains a certain pathos in this context. The speaker verges, perhaps, on a self-pity that could be disastrous for the poem ("the hill's skull" suggests Golgotha), but there is also a laconic detachment that comes out in "I myself am hell," which stands in a line by itself, like "My mind's not right" in the preceding stanza. Most readers cannot avoid knowing what Lowell brings into so many of these poems: his recurrent mental illness. Robert Fitzgerald, who knew him well, has stated this firmly but sympathetically: "behind those poems and henceforth all his work is his breakdown of 1949 and the necessity he now felt of governing his greatness with his illness in mind. Manic attacks now and again would put him in the hospital, overborne by the fever that one had felt to be just beyond some of his poems from the beginning."

"Skunk Hour," although first in order of composition, comes last in the group of fifteen poems that Lowell calls "Life Studies." It is led up to gradually by poems about an uncle, Great-Aunt Sarah, his Winslow grandparents, his father, his mother; the family relationships intensify painfully. There are beautiful idyllic moments; thinking of his grandparents, he says:

Then the dry road dust rises to whiten
the fatigued elm leaves—
the nineteenth century, tired of children, is gone.
They've all gone into a world of light; the farm's my
own.

But as the reader moves closer to the present, the tone is clipped and sardonic:

Father's death was abrupt and unprotesting.
His vision was still twenty-twenty.
After a morning of anxious, repetitive smiling,
his last words to Mother were:
"I feel awful."

Robert Lowell

The poet's father is the central figure in a prose memoir, "91 Revere Street," which forms the centerpiece of *Life Studies* (1959). Rather curiously, it does not immediately precede the group of family poems. Intervening are four poems on literary figures (Ford, Santayana, the poets Delmore Schwartz and Hart Crane) whom Lowell admired. Ninety-one Revere Street was the address of the house where the Lowells lived for a few years in the 1920s; here the psychological battle between husband and wife was fought out. Lowell's mother, neurotic but obviously strong in her own way, won; she forced her husband to retire from the navy. He moved into the business world with a marked lack of success, and the poem called "Commander Lowell" presents his declining years without comment; he is almost a figure of comedy. He died in 1950. But while he was alive, Lowell wrote and published in *Lord Weary's Castle* a poem called "Rebellion," which suggests a more painful relationship between father and son. Once, during his Harvard days, he knocked his father down in a quarrel over a girl. Lowell returns to this incident in a short sequence of poems, "Charles River," in *Notebook, 1967-68* (1969).

His mother is never really described, although her presence is strongly felt in various places. She is, finally, an object; one can only speculate on the feelings that lie back of this passage:

When I embarked from Italy with my Mother's body,
the whole shoreline of the *Golfo di Genova*
was breaking into fiery flower.
The crazy yellow and azure sea-sleds
blasting like jack-hammers across
the *spumante*-bubbling wake of our liner,
recalled the clashing colors of my Ford.
Mother travelled first-class in the hold;
her *Risorgimento* black and gold casket
was like Napoleon's at the *Invalides.* . . .

The "Life Studies" sequence composes a kind of fragmentary novel in verse, not unlike James Joyce's *A Portrait of the Artist as a Young Man* (1916). Since Lowell was an influential teacher by now (he held temporary posts at several American universities), a number of younger writers who were at one time his students—such as W. D. Snodgrass and Anne Sexton—were associated with him as "confessional" poets. Yet this association appears to have been somewhat exaggerated. Snodgrass's *Heart's Needle* (1959) was written before *Life Studies*, and the anguished revelations of Anne Sexton and Sylvia Plath are poetry of a rather different kind from Lowell's. Their work, for the most part, lacks his wit and detachment and public dimension.

Life Studies has been considered a landmark in contemporary poetry by many critics; its importance was almost immediately recognized, and in 1960 Lowell received the National Book Award. About this time he moved to New York City with his wife Elizabeth Hardwick and daughter Harriet. Thus began a decade during which he was involved in public affairs, or at least public artistic projects, including the theatre. Early in the decade he read a new poem, "For the Union Dead," at an arts festival on the Boston Common. It is a more accessible piece than most of *Life Studies* or certainly *Lord Weary's Castle*, even for those readers (or auditors) uninstructed in Boston history and the aftermath of the Civil War. The open texture of *Life Studies* has now been extended to the modern scene and the history that has led up to it. Although "For the Union Dead" starts out as a private meditation, it soon moves to Boston Common itself:

Parking spaces luxuriate like civic
sandpiles in the heart of Boston.
A girdle of orange, Puritan-pumpkin colored girders
braces the tingling Statehouse,

shaking over the excavations, as it faces Colonel Shaw
and his bell-cheeked Negro infantry
On St. Gaudens' shaking Civil War relief,
propped by a plank splint against the garage's
                       earthquake.

This passage takes the reader to the central historical situation. Colonel Robert Shaw of Boston, who commanded a regiment of black troops, was killed in July 1863, in an assault on Fort Wagner, South Carolina. Although Lowell presents him as an example of idealism and youthful beauty, he was scorned by his father; he was buried in a ditch, where his "body was thrown / and lost with his 'niggers.' " Lowell juxtaposes the events of three generations: Shaw's actual death and anonymous burial; the dedication of the memorial to him and the Union dead in the 1890s; and the present moment, when ideals, it is suggested, have eroded along with much else:

The ditch is nearer.
There are no statues for the last war here;
on Boylston Street, a commercial photograph
shows Hiroshima boiling

over a Mosler Safe, the "Rock of Ages"
that survived the blast. Space is nearer.
When I crouch to my television set,
the drained faces of Negro school-children rise like
                       balloons.

Future readers may require footnotes to identify a few of the details from the 1960s—the civil-rights struggle, the advertising slogans of the period, even the design of American automobiles. Lowell's sense of particularity is brilliant; the details could hardly be better chosen. But here the reader is close to the pop art of the 1960s, with its jaunty arrangements of familiar objects, its air of being both inside and detached from popular culture. The poem, however, is beautifully composed. The motif of the fish, introduced in the opening stanzas with the old South Boston Aquarium, is sarcastically alluded to midway ("Their monument sticks like a fishbone / in the city's throat"), and then it rounds out the poem:

> The Aquarium is gone. Everywhere,
> giant finned cars nose forward like fish;
> a savage servility
> slides by on grease.

"For the Union Dead" gave the title to Lowell's next book, which came out in 1964. This collection is very miscellaneous in character. It includes personal vignettes, poems derived from the prose of friends such as Elizabeth Bishop and Mary McCarthy, recastings of older poems by Lowell himself, even commissioned poems. "Hawthorne" was written to commemorate the Centenary Edition of that author's works published by the Ohio State University Press. This and its companion piece, "Jonathan Edwards in Western Massachusetts," as Lowell says, are based on prose passages by their subjects. These poems are highly interesting to Lowell's public, of course, because they return to New England writers who have always meant a great deal to him. His attitude toward them is now more relaxed along with the mode of the verse.

One sequence in this collection is almost entirely concerned with the public world: "July in Washington," "Buenos Aires," and "Dropping South: Brazil." They suggest a quasi-political attitude that would soon become very explicit in Lowell's work. He chose the first one, in fact, when he was asked to submit a favorite poem from his own work, along with a work he admired from the past, to an anthology, *Preferences* (1974), edited by Richard Howard. Lowell paired "July in Washington" with Melville's "The House-Top," a poem about the draft riots in New York City in July 1863. Howard in a brief commentary mentions the "seditious tropical summers of America's cities" that are often a background to political stresses if not disasters. Lowell's poem this time is built up on the motif of the circle. The actual plan of Washington makes this credible, but the opening couplet involves more:

"The stiff spokes of this wheel / touch the sore spots of the earth." Then the poem on Buenos Aires has its focus in a graveyard of Republican martyrs during a chilly Argentine winter. In the poem on Brazil, although it is done mainly from the point of view of a tourist on Copacabana beach, Lowell reflects that "inland, people starved, and struck, and died— / unhappy Americas, ah *tristes tropiques!*"

In 1969, Lowell remarked in an interview with the Caribbean novelist V. S. Naipaul, "America with a capital A I find a very hard thing to realise. It's beyond any country, it's an empire. I feel very bitter about it, but pious, and baffled by it." This summary of his feelings has a certain ambiguity about it. He had long been concerned about the outcome of American history, like an earlier Bostonian, Henry Adams, and his feeling that it was being betrayed ran very strong. In 1965 he was invited by President Johnson, as one of a small group of distinguished American artists, to attend the White House Festival of the Arts. He turned down the invitation in a public statement of protest against the American involvement in the Vietnam War: "We are in danger of imperceptibly becoming an explosive and suddenly chauvinistic nation, and we may even be drifting on our way to the last nuclear ruin." Then in October 1967, he participated with several other literary figures in the famous "march" on the Pentagon, which ended with mixed results but was highly publicized. Lowell himself wrote two poems about it for *Notebook*, but a more famous and extensive account of this incident, in which he has a prominent part, is found in Norman Mailer's *The Armies of the Night* (1968).

Lowell was becoming known in other ways. Like many other modern poets, he was attracted by the theatre. In 1961 he was asked to translate Jean Baptiste Racine's *Phèdre*; he did this in heroic couplets as being the nearest English equivalent to the French alexandrines. Critical opinion has been mixed about the result, and perhaps it should be regarded as an "imitation" of Racine. (In 1961, the same year as his *Phaedra*, Lowell brought out his controversial book called *Imitations*, which consists of versions of poetry from several languages.) This was the first of the theatre projects that Lowell started, and *Phaedra* was seriously considered by two Broadway producers in 1962. Another venture was his collaboration with Leonard Bernstein on a symphony, *Kaddish*; before it broke off, Lowell wrote three poems, remarkably formal, even stately, for a musical setting. (They were published for the first time in *Ploughshares* in 1979.) In 1965 Lincoln Center commissioned an acting version of Aeschylus's *Oresteia*; this was mostly finished but never produced; eventually it was published in 1979. Lowell's prose version of Aeschylus's *Prometheus Bound* was actually produced at the Yale Drama School with an international cast two years before it was published in 1969.

By far his most successful work for the theatre was the group of short plays called *The Old Glory* (1965). There was at least one good reason for this success. Originally intending to write an opera libretto based on Melville's "Benito Cereno" (1856), Lowell instead quickly wrote a play. Then he added two plays from stories by Hawthorne, "Endicott and the Red Cross" and "My Kinsman, Major Molineux." Taken together (with "Benito Cereno" presented last), they compose a trilogy on the emergence of the United States out of its colonial past. According to Lowell in a late interview in London, the title, *The Old Glory*, has two meanings: "it refers both to the flag and also to the glory with which the Republic of America started." Thus his lifelong engagement with Hawthorne and Melville—his major American sources, one might say—paid off handsomely again. The original production of the play in New York, a considerable critical success, received a number of prizes.

In 1967 Lowell brought out *Near the Ocean*, a handsome book (illustrated by the famous Australian painter, Sidney Nolan) that contained his most formal poetry since *The Mills of the Kavanaughs*. The earlier book was mostly written in heroic couplets; part of this one is written in tetrameter couplets, the poetic form of which the seventeenth-century poet Andrew Marvell was the master in English verse. Lowell's versification is not as strict as Marvell's, but almost playfully he runs his couplets through sentences of eight lines, the length of a stanza. The tone is playful, too, as the reader moves in and out of a charming domestic scene (a house Lowell inherited in Maine) in the manner of Marvell's "Upon Appleton House," which may well be the general model; he uses the same eight-line stanza. But Lowell, like his great predecessor, touches on some serious issues. The opening lines of the first poem in the sequence, "Waking Early Sunday Morning" (now rather famous among Lowell's readers), make that clear:

> O to break loose, like the chinook
> salmon, jumping and falling back,
> nosing up to the impossible
> stone and bone-crushing waterfall—
> raw-jawed, weak-fleshed there, stopped by ten
> steps of the roaring ladder, and then

> to clear the top on the last try,
> alive enough to spawn and die.

It is part of the attractiveness of these poems that they can advance so quickly to matters of Church and State and Society and absorb them into their easy rhythms:

> O to break loose. All life's grandeur
> is something with a girl in summer . . .
> elated as the President
> girdled by his establishment
> this Sunday morning, free to chaff
> his own thoughts with his bear-cuffed staff,
> swimming nude, unbuttoned, sick
> of his ghost-written rhetoric!

The President is Lyndon Johnson; the occasion is the summer of 1965. Lowell has recently turned down the invitation to the White House Festival of the Arts, and this witty passage does indeed stand in contrast to the now-forgotten speeches by the official hack writers. But Lowell can be forceful about some things; in Central Park, almost at the door of his apartment house, he finds fear and poverty lurking amid the flowering shrubs; public sexual activity in the park is perhaps a correlative to these grimmer aspects of the contemporary scene. Lowell had a divided mind about the five poems in this group. While he retained the poems in this "Near the Ocean" group in his *Selected Poems* (1976), he cut four of them down, so drastically in some cases that they hardly resemble the originals. Such was his restless way with his own work.

The second half of *Near the Ocean* consists of translations or "imitations"—the precise term is not easy to establish here. The poets whom he uses are mainly Horace, Juvenal, and Dante (*Inferno*, 15). Of these distinguished works, much the longest is Juvenal's Satire 10, "The Vanity of Human Wishes," occupying forty of Lowell's pages. Since we already have Samuel Johnson's famous "imitation" of this poem, we might remark that Lowell's version is closer to Juvenal than Johnson's. Lowell's is done in blank verse. (Juvenal of course used no rhymes.) And the effect of the Lowell version is to suggest, somehow, a comparison between Juvenal's Rome and the American empire of the 1960s. Although the tone of this great work is truly Juvenalian in Lowell's hands, it has a thematic connection with the "Horatian" poems in the first part of the book. (Marvell, the general model there, is perhaps the most Horatian of English poets.)

No sooner had *Near the Ocean* been published and *Prometheus Bound* been produced at Yale in

Robert Lowell

1967 (the latter work, the most extravagant thing that Lowell ever wrote, is also an indirect commentary on the 1960s), than Lowell started on a large venture of another sort. This is *Notebook 1967-68*. Lowell's friend John Berryman had already begun his ambitious and much-praised *Dream Songs* (the first part, published in 1964, won the Pulitzer Prize), and now the small audience for contemporary poetry watched two important writers quickly building up large sequences of short poems. (They were both published by Farrar, Straus and Giroux.) In each case the overall form was the diary. Berryman used an original six-line rhymed stanza throughout; Lowell committed himself to the unrhymed sonnet. The resemblances and differences between the two are fascinating to study. Berryman, who killed himself early in 1972, probably had no intention of rearranging the plan of his work, but Lowell's took some unexpected turns very shortly.

Notebook 1967-68 is a kind of diary, but the form is cyclical: Lowell prints a list of dates for 1967-1968 at the back of the book to remind the reader of the year's disasters, beginning and ending with the Vietnam War and including the assassinations and major political upheavals. Even though public events seem to get out of control and affect everyone's destiny, there are moments of reminiscence and private satisfaction (Randall Jarrell and Peter Taylor at college in the 1930s, or Elizabeth Schwartzkopf singing in New York). There are also many characters out of history, European and American. Although the poems are arranged in groups, some of them are not closely connected: for instance "Names," which merely brings together the figures of Sir Thomas More, Napoleon, and others. As Lowell himself says, the pattern is "jagged" and created largely by association. At the end a small group dedicated to his wife Elizabeth Hardwick is somewhat inconclusive. In the following year Lowell issued a revised and expanded edition. Some of the material here is more private than ever; it is even drawn from people's letters and conversations.

In 1973 Lowell brought out three books simultaneously: *For Lizzie and Harriet*, *The Dolphin*, and *History*, all written in unrhymed sonnets. In these volumes he has broken up the expanding *Notebook* project (undated in the revised, 1970 edition) into public and private sectors. *For Lizzie and Harriet* deals with Elizabeth Hardwick and their daughter; many of the poems were scattered through the two editions of *Notebook*. The poems in *The Dolphin*, however, are mostly new; they are concerned with his third wife, the Englishwoman Caroline Blackwood, whom he married in 1972,

their son Sheridan, and his life in England. There are obvious personal reasons, then, for separating the phases of a complicated existence.

As for *History*, the largest of the three books, it contains most of the "public" poems from *Notebook*, sometimes reworked, with about eighty new poems. Many of these are about prominent literary figures, from Juvenal to John Berryman, but there are a fair number about men of power as different as Robespierre, Ché Guevara, and Martin Luther King. The arrangement is now linear or chronological, and almost every period of Western history is touched on. Lowell was always deeply interested in history; he knew the great historians better than most people. And so here is his personal vision of history, fragmentary though it appears. History is, in its way, a kind of epic; and Lowell would probably have agreed with Ezra Pound that an epic is simply a poem about history. It is Pound, finally, whom Lowell most resembles among the modern poets. Lowell met him as early as 1948, when he was the Consultant in Poetry at the Library of Congress. (Pound was kept in St. Elizabeths Hospital in Washington from 1945 to 1958.) He admired Pound, often saw him in Washington and sometimes later in Italy, and kept his portrait above the desk in his study. By the time of *History* the scale and variety of Lowell's work began to resemble Pound's: the extensive translations and "imitations," the restless quest for new models, the ventures into personal epic. There is also an unevenness that is undeniable, in *History* as in the *Cantos*; and in Lowell's case the commitment to the unrhymed sonnet may have been a limitation of a kind. Everything has to be put in the same mold. The *Cantos*, at least the early ones, often have a sustained yet varied rhythmic interest that Lowell hardly approaches. Had he lived, Lowell would probably have done something more with *History*, which contains much of a lifetime's experience.

There are further rearrangements in the *Selected Poems* of 1976, a kind of interim volume. In a sense Lowell agreed with the general estimate of his work by including almost everything from *Life Studies* except the prose centerpiece. Like Pound's *Hugh Selwyn Mauberley* (1920), it seems to be something that all readers endorse. At this point Lowell was writing the poems that would make up his last book—the last book published in his lifetime, *Day by Day*, which appeared shortly before his death in September 1977. These late poems continue what he called his "verse autobiography," but often in a somewhat muted way. He no longer uses the elaborate narrative structure of some of the earlier poetry, or even the unrhymed sonnets of the *Notebook* period. His new marriage brings some happiness, especially with his infant son, but there are tensions and breakdowns, usually brought into his poems in this hesitant and oblique manner:

> To each the rotting natural to his age.
> Dividing the minute we cannot prolong,
> I stand swaying at the end of the party
> a half-filled glass in each hand—
> I too swayed
> by the hard infatuate wind of love
> they cannot hear.

This book, unexpectedly, was the end of Lowell's career. Since his death the *Oresteia* translation of the 1960s has been published, and probably a collection of his prose will appear, but most of his work has been before the public a long time. Well before his death he had assumed a great authority in the literary world; he was profoundly respected by his elders such as Eliot. If this was not the Age of Lowell, it was certainly a literary epoch in which he had an extraordinary part.

Other:

Jean Baptiste Racine, *Phaedra*, in *Phaedra and Figaro*, translated by Lowell (New York: Farrar, Straus & Giroux, 1961; London: Faber & Faber, 1963);

Imitations, edited and translated by Lowell (New York: Farrar, Straus & Giroux, 1961; London: Faber & Faber, 1962);

Aeschylus, *The Oresteia*, translated by Lowell (New York: Farrar, Straus & Giroux, 1979).

Interviews:

"The Art of Poetry III: Robert Lowell," *Paris Review*, no. 25 (Winter-Spring 1961): 56-95;

"Et in America ego—the American poet Robert Lowell talks to the novelist V. S. Naipaul about art, power, and the dramatisation of the self," *Listener*, 4 September 1969, pp. 302-304.

References:

Rolando Anzilotti, ed., *Robert Lowell: A Tribute* (Pisa: Nistri-Lischi Editori, 1979);

Steven Gould Axelrod, *Robert Lowell: Life and Art* (Princeton: Princeton University Press, 1978);

Philip Cooper, *The Autobiographical Myth of Robert Lowell* (Chapel Hill: University of North Carolina Press, 1970);

John Crick, *Robert Lowell* (Edinburgh: Oliver & Boyd, 1974);

Richard J. Fein, *Robert Lowell* (New York: Twayne, 1970);

Robert Fitzgerald, "The Things of the Eye," *Poetry*, 132 (May 1978): 107-111;

Michael Lond and Robert Boyers, ed., *Robert Lowell: A Portrait of the Artist in His Time* (New York: David Lewis, 1970);

Norman Mailer, *The Armies of the Night* (New York: New American Library, 1968);

Jerome Mazzaro, *The Poetic Themes of Robert Lowell* (Ann Arbor: University of Michigan Press, 1965);

Thomas Parkinson, ed., *Robert Lowell: A Collection of Critical Essays* (Englewood Cliffs, N.J.: Prentice-Hall, 1968);

Marjorie Perloff, *The Poetic Art of Robert Lowell* (Ithaca: Cornell University Press, 1973);

Salmagundi, special Lowell issue, 1 (1966-1967): contains seven essays on Lowell;

Peter Taylor, "Robert Trail [*sic*] Spence Lowell," *Ploughshares*, 5 (1979): 74-81;

Alan Williamson, *Pity the Monsters: The Political Vision of Robert Lowell* (New Haven: Yale University Press, 1974);

Stephen Yenser, *Circle to Circle: The Poetry of Robert Lowell* (Berkeley: University of California Press, 1975).

HAKI R. MADHUBUTI
(DON L. LEE)
(23 February 1942-)

BOOKS: *Think Black* (Detroit: Broadside Press, 1967);

Black Pride (Detroit: Broadside Press, 1968);

Don't Cry, Scream (Detroit: Broadside Press, 1969);

We Walk the Way of the New World (Detroit: Broadside Press, 1970);

Directionscore: Selected and New Poems (Detroit: Broadside Press, 1971);

Dynamite Voices: Black Poets of the 1960's (Detroit: Broadside Press, 1971);

From Plan to Planet. Life Studies. The Need for Afrikan Minds and Institutions (Detroit: Broadside Press / Chicago: Institute of Positive Education, 1973);

Book of Life (Detroit: Broadside Press, 1973).

Don L. Lee was born in Little Rock, Arkansas,

the son of Jimmy and Maxine Graves Lee. He attended Dunbar Vocational High School in Chicago, Chicago City College (A.A., 1966), Roosevelt University in Chicago (1966-1967), and the University of Illinois, Chicago Circle. From 1960 to 1963 he served in the U.S. Army. Lee has had a varied background. He was an apprentice museum curator at the DuSable Museum of African American History in Chicago from 1963 to 1967. While in Chicago, he worked as a stock department clerk for Montgomery Ward in 1963-1964, as a post office clerk in 1964-1965, and he was a junior executive for Spiegel Incorporated in 1965-1966. In the late 1960s, however, he abandoned the business world for the academic one, becoming a writer-in-residence at Cornell University in Ithaca, New York (1968-1969), at Northeastern Illinois State College in Chicago (1969-1971), at Morgan State College in Baltimore (1972-1973), and at Howard University in Washington, D.C. (1970-1975). He is an editor for *Black Books Bulletin* and Third World Press, both in Chicago, as well as director of the Institute of Positive Education, an independent black institution in Chicago. In 1969, he received a National Endowment for the Arts Grant and in 1973, a Kuumba Workshop Black Liberation Award. He has been a member and vice-chairman of the African Liberation Day Support Committee, and he is a former member of the executive council of the Congress of African People. He began writing under the name of Haki R. Madhubuti in 1973.

In her introduction to Lee's book *Don't Cry, Scream* (1969), Gwendolyn Brooks describes his poetry as unconcerned with "correctness" and "elegance." Rather, he deliberately chooses to use nonstandard English, esoteric hip street slang, jazzlike varied repetition of words and phrases, abbreviations that mimic the sounds of black vernacular, letters that are drawn out to become words, and words that are drawn out to imitate musical notes, moans, and screams. This, he believes, makes his ideas more accessible to his intended reader, who is not the average black reader of poetry and who is certainly not the average white reader of poetry, but who is, rather, the average black person who reads, speaks, and understands black vernacular. Lee quotes Allama Muhammad Iqbal: "There should be no opiumeating in Art. The dogma of Art for the sake of Art is a clever invention of decadence to cheat us of life and power." Lee agrees. His poetry is written for the black masses who buy his books in the tens of thousands. According to Helen Vendler, his poems "have sold over 100,000 copies without any large-scale advertising or mass distribution."

As a poet and critic, Lee is far less concerned with poetry than with politics. In his preface to *Don't Cry, Scream*, he insists that "most, if not all, blackpoetry will be *political*. I've often come across black artists (poets, painters, actors, writers, &c.) who feel that they and their work should be apolitical; not realizing that to be apolitical is *to be* political in a negative way for blackfolks. There is *no* neutral blackart; either it *is* or it *isn't*, period." He sees the black poet as becoming "a positive force in the black community" by the act of "defining and legitimizing his own reality." That is, by describing the black experience as it is and in its own language, he increases the pride of the black community and reinforces blacks' realization that their own lives are valuable, meaningful, worth writing poems about. The black poet, then, Lee feels, has a special obligation. Because of his blackness he must reject topics that do not deal with the experience of being black. "You see, *black* for the blackpoet is a way of life," he says. "And, his totalactions will reflect that blackness. . . ." As a poet, the black writer's obligation is to focus on and to illuminate ordinary black life as well as to try to point the way toward a positive self-image and to mobilize the black community in general toward positive progress. This way, adds Lee, "he will be an example for his community."

Since Lee's poetry is as unconventional as his audience, it is not surprising that the critical response toward his work is varied, perhaps depending partly upon whether the particular critic is disappointed to find little conventional poetry in Lee or is pleased to find a speaker with a message to which he is so deeply committed. Helen Vendler, for example, says, "In him the sardonic and savage turn-of-phrase long present in black speech as a survival tactic finds its best poet." Theodore R. Hudson, writing for *Contemporary Poets*, agrees: "Of the strong young Black poets of the 'Black arts movement' that began in the United States in the late 1960's, Don L. Lee is one of the most powerful and persuasive in content, one of the most creative and influential in technique." But Jascha Kessler, writing in *Poetry* (February 1973), disagrees: "I've not seen poetry in Don L. Lee. Anger, bombast, raw hatred, strident, aggrieved, perhaps charismatically crude religious and political canting, propaganda and racist nonsense, yes; and utterly unoriginal in form and style; humorless; cruel laughter bordering on the insane." Although Kessler admits, "There may well be justified insanity, as there is justified homicide. . . . But poetry? Lee is deluded in thinking he has it. What he has is street language, common enough to most of us; the rest is a farago of anybody's

W. C. Williams and rehashed and rancid LeRoi Jones, mixed with editorials out of *Elijah (Muhammed) Speaks.* . . . Lee is outside poetry somewhere, exhorting, hectoring, cursing, making a lot of noise. But you don't have to be black for that, and, if you are, it's hardly an excuse.''

Lee himself feels that there are clear limits for the black poet if he wants to speak to and motivate politically the whole of the black community. For one thing, he must use the community's own language. In *Dynamite Voices: Black Poets of the 1960's* (1971) Lee criticizes another black poet for being more concerned with writing better than white poets than with speaking directly to his black readers. He warns, "Black poetry, it ain't! . . . This is a brother who is about to lose the language of his people." He observes in *A Capsule Course in Black Poetry Writing* (1975) that though "street rap" can be powerful, it can simply be trite if used for its own sake. "To exert its power . . . it must do more than copy or imitate the vocabulary of the rap. The brother who chooses this form must create an originality and a tension on the printed page. . . ." On the other hand, he thinks "mere 'protest' writing is generally a weak reaction to persons and events and often lacks the substance necessary to motivate and move people."

Not only does Lee feel that there should be constraints on language and subject; he also believes that the structure of black poetry should be unique, using short, staccato lines and omitting prosiness. He warns young black poets to avoid cliches and nonfunctional words or punctuation. Lee says American blacks are the products of a dual culture: the white European/American culture in school and the black African/American culture at home. Nevertheless, he feels that traditional white European and American literature has had little influence on contemporary poets. "The major influences," he observes, "were/are Black music, Black life style, Black churches, and their own Black contemporaries." He sees black music as the most advanced of all the black arts, and he adds that black poets' language "seemed to move in the direction of actual music." This is evident in Lee's own style and subject matter.

Lee's first book of poetry, *Think Black* (1967), was an unsophisticated little volume, perhaps partly because of his youth and partly because he wanted it to be comprehensible to a largely unsophisticated mass audience. "Back Again, Home" describes the life-style of a rising junior executive like the younger Lee who plays the game silently, submissively, unhappily. Suddenly, he resigns, lets "his hair grow," finds himself broke and hungry, but no

longer silent. Like the poet himself, he returns to the world he knows, belongs to, is comfortable in. He is finally, "Back again, / BLACK AGAIN, / Home." "Understanding but Not Forgetting" presents a litany of unforgotten affronts typical of the black experience and not unlike Martin Luther King's similar prose litany from his "Letter from Birmingham Jail." One of Lee's more powerful stanzas describes a black mother who goes out in the evening without money to get her children "something to eat, / she always came back with food. Some people / would call this prostitution but I call it— / providing for her family." Perhaps it is in images like this that the disparity between the expectations of the white reader and the experience of the black poet is most clearly illustrated.

Think Black not only describes the urban life familiar to its black readers, in poems like "Re-act for Action," but also urges blacks to work actively for their own advancement rather than passively accepting their fate. Lee explores the growth of modern black consciousness in poems like "In a Period of Growth" that use understatement to describe the development of the black attitude toward the term *black*: "like, / if he had da called me / black seven years ago, / i wd've— / broke his right eye out, / jumped into his chest, / . . . seven years ago." *Think Black*, then, touches on Lee's own rejection of the "American dream," his subsequent realization that to be black is not to be less, and his growing awareness that blacks must work together to develop their own traditions and culture rather than trying to imitate or to be assimilated into white culture.

Working together is important to Lee. He scolds younger black poets for not reading their own contemporaries, and he dedicates many of his own poems to other blacks, often using their experiences as his subject. He actively supports other black poets and artists and they, in turn, support him. His message, after all, is one of independence from whites through interdependence with other blacks. He scorns not only whites ("unpeople") but also blacks who accept any part of white society. They are not blacks ("realpeople") but merely "negroes" or "niggers," the terms used synonymously. His vocabulary often underscores his desire for black unity by combining the adjective "black" with its noun, as in "blackpeople," "blackpoetry," etc. "Whi-te," on the other hand, is often broken into two syllables, perhaps to suggest disunity, perhaps to show verbal condescension, perhaps both. He believes the black race to be inherently cooperative; the white, competitive. "The New Integrationist," the first poem in his second book, *Black Pride* (1968), declares, "I / seek / integration / of / negroes / with / black / people": the whole poem is an eight-word, eight-line thesis statement.

Lee celebrates blackness wherever he finds it. "The Self-Hatred of Don L. Lee" deplores his own former pride in his "light / brown / outer" that once opened doors of tokenism. Now instead he begins "to love / only . . . my inner / self which / is all / black." This innocence-to-experience poem mirrors the attitude shift wherein the quality of blackness itself became a source of pride rather than shame. In "The Negro" (who, to Lee, is *not* a black), Lee points out the irony of working and saving all year in order to give one's children Christmas presents, only to relinquish all credit to a white Santa. Opposing the white world wherever it is, he not only rejects fighting the white man's war in Vietnam but also making friends with whites who extend a helping hand in the battle for civil rights. "The Death Dance," dedicated to Maxine, his mother, describes a black mother scorned because of her "idiot" score on a white I.Q. test; a job in some "honky's" kitchen is the best she can manage. She works; her son dances: the stanzas alternate. Gradually the boy's dance becomes that of a frenzied warrior. The mother's dilemma is poignant; the son's rage understandable. Yet is the final, frantic death dance of revolution the answer? Whose death, one wonders? A 1968 broadside, *For Black People (and Negroes Too)*, pits Jesus, a blue-eyed blond, against Allah, the black people's god. In this battle, fought on the streets of Chicago, a white winner would be inconceivable.

Lee's third book of poetry, *Don't Cry, Scream*, continues in the same vein. Like earlier books, it had multiple printings in its first year. Lee again emphasizes black unity and solidarity. There is a preface by Lee, an introduction by Gwendolyn Brooks, three epigraphs by three different writers, and a page-long dedication to various black individuals and groups from "Ameer Baraka" and H. Rap Brown to "my oldman where-ever he is" and "all the brothers in prison." The dedication runs together, chantlike, ending with a Muslim benediction.

There is a special dedication "to all black-mothers & especially mine (maxine)." The black mother is an important and heroic figure in Lee's earlier books, and in his third book he expands his appreciation and sympathy to include the younger black woman. Poems like "The Third World Bond" and "The Revolutionary Screw" lambaste the young would-be black revolutionary who abandons his own woman to chase after a Chinese or a white woman. Even though he talks revolution, the black man is capable of using his woman as he is used by whites. Lee's black woman poignantly suffers more and stoically endures more than her man. She is the only true hero of his black culture.

According to Lee, black music is the finest black artistic achievement, and at the apex of the black musical world is John Coltrane. "Don't Cry, Scream" describes Coltrane's music as speaking directly to blacks because it grows directly out of their experience. Only a black can fully understand how it can open new dimensions to him, making his ear as sensitive and keenly developed as the blind man's. The structure of the poem is broken up with drawn-out words mimicking the sound and emotion of the music on one side of the page, normal descriptive terms on the other. Both are interspersed with longer stanzas that contrast Coltrane and the black experience with the pallid, imitative world of middle-class Negroes.

Lee's fourth book of poetry, *We Walk the Way of the New World* (1970), is also dedicated to numerous black individuals who serve as examples to the black community, among them two women, singers Miriam Makeba and Nina Simone, who are "consistently black and relevant, can u name me two brothers / blackmen that are as. . . ." The poems are divided into three sections: "Blackwoman Poems," "African Poems," and "New World Poems," but Lee says the three are interwoven because "Blackwoman is African and Africa is Blackwoman and they both represent the *New World*." His style has gradually changed and softened, as he himself notes. In "Man Thinking About Woman," he writes that he met her "the month / that my lines got longer & my metaphors softened." He writes of stoic, robust black "Big Momma" at her weekly chat with her revolutionist son, both eating from cups of soup on a newspaper tablecloth (a repeated image). Big Momma is a wise lady; Diana Ross is not because she abandons her people for the sake of her ego in "On Seeing Diana Go Maddddddddd." Although most black women, young and old, are treated sympathetically, those who err are called to task. In "African Poems" and "New World Poems," his point is quite clear. Africa is symbolic of the beautiful, the unspoiled. The poet warns Africa not to follow the same pied piper of progress that led Europe and America to pollute their skies and streams. He urges her to remain pure, pristine, a positive and reenergizing metaphor for blacks everywhere.

Lee's anger and hatred spill over onto many targets in this volume: white, middle-class Negro, Catholic, Baptist, and Jew. He is perplexed as to why the less-numerous Jews can have so much more economic and political power than the blacks. In "See Sammy Run in the Wrong Direction," he castigates Sammy Davis, Jr., for being Jewish as well as black. Black must take precedence over all else. A Muslim, Lee now sees Christianity as a white religion and Israel as "occupied Palestine." There is no gray in Lee's world, only black and white, and only black is beautiful.

Directionscore: Selected and New Poems (1971) consists of poems selected from his earlier volumes—almost all his earlier poems are included—and five new poems. Lee also includes an introduction in which he says the present New Black Renaissance in black poetry must differ from the first one of the 1920s because no lasting institutions or positive change grew out of the first. The present Black Renaissance in poetry is a political one, he believes, and can promote change if blacks take advantage of the opportunity. Blacks, he says, are negligible in America because they have no economic or political power. They are rootless, or at least they feel that way. The answer, he feels, is in black nationalism and in black education. Proper education will give blacks new power and make escape through crime and drugs unnecessary.

In February 1973, Lee had published a book-length essay, *From Plan to Planet: Life Studies: The Need for Afrikan Minds and Institutions,* and in November 1973, under the new title and name of Mwalimu (Swahili for *teacher*) Haki R. Madhubuti, he published his sixth book of poetry, *Book of Life.* Part 1 of *Book of Life* begins with a half-dozen poems written in a style similar to that of his previous books. That is, he employs street language, musical rhythms, repetition of words and phrases with jazzlike variations building to a crescendo. In his last three books his lines have grown much longer as have his poems themselves, which sometimes develop a subject over several pages. Part 2 of *Book of Life* makes a radical stylistic shift, although not an ideological one. It is a sixty-page "poem" divided into ninety numbered sections, each of which is a small semipoetic aphorism reminiscent of Confucius or R. D. Laing's *Knots* (1970) and written in standard English rather than black vernacular. Didactic, like all Lee's writing, they offer practical advice on how best to conduct one's life. Inspired primarily by Muslim or black nationalist principles, they also contain good commonsense advice. For example, he advises, "To / betray a trust / is to / cut yourself off from being / trusted." Other aphorisms recommend avoiding makeup, respecting the old, eating only natural fruits and vegetables.

Several speak to the problems Lee sees within the black communities and are constantly repeated, like drumbeats: one must not allow luxuries to become needs; one must work constantly, feverishly, to keep up with "our enemies" who "work 24 hours a day." *From Plan to Planet,* published several months earlier than *Book of Life,* presents essentially the same material in essay form. Its style also is didactic and repetitious as it persistently hammers home its message in standard English, occasional Swahili, and snatches of black vernacular.

Lee's early poetic output was prodigious and intense: six books of poetry, a book of criticism, and a book-length essay in six or seven years. During that time, he moved from being an angry young black, striking out in many directions, toward his mature voice—certainly no less angry and no less bitter, but growing steadily more convinced of the need for black nationalism, black institutions, black education, a black religion, a black cultural consciousness, and a black plan to bring it all together. Publication of his poetry, however, has drastically diminished in the last half-dozen years—his last book was published in 1973—probably because his considerable energies have turned to black education. Yet his hopes and plans for the improvement of all blacks have continued to grow and develop. To see their present shape would indeed be interesting.

—*Jerry B. McAninch*

Other:

To Gwen with Love, edited by Madhubuti, Patricia L. Brown, and Francis Ward (Chicago: Johnson, 1971);

A Capsule Course in Black Poetry Writing, includes an essay by Madhubuti (Detroit: Broadside Press, 1975).

References:

Paula Giddings, "From A Black Perspective: The Poetry of Don L. Lee," *Amistad 2,* eds. John A. Williams and Charles F. Harris (New York: Random House, 1971), pp. 296-318;

Jascha Kessler, "Trial and Error," *Poetry,* 121 (February 1973): 292-293;

Eugene E. Miller, "Some Black Thoughts on Don L. Lee's *Think Black!* Thunk by a Frustrated White Academic Thinker," *College English,* 34 (May 1973): 1094-1102;

Marlene Mosher, *New Directions from Don L. Lee* (Hicksville, New York: Exposition, 1975);

Roderick R. Palmer, "The Poetry of Three

Revolutionists: Don L. Lee, Sonia Sanchez, Nikki Giovanni," *College Language Association Journal*, 15 (1971): 25-26;

Annette Oliver Shands, "The Relevancy of Don L. Lee as a Contemporary Black Poet," *Black World*, 21 (June 1972): 35-48;

Helen Vendler, "Good Black Poems One by One," *New York Times Book Review*, 29 September 1974, pp. 3, 10.

WILLIAM MATTHEWS
(11 November 1942-)

BOOKS: *Broken Syllables* (Aurora, N.Y. & Northwood Narrows, N.H.: Lillabulero Press, 1969);

Ruining the New Road (New York: Random House, 1970);

The Cloud (Boston: Barn Dream Press, 1971);

The Moon (Baltimore: Penyeach Press, 1971);

Sleek for the Long Flight (New York: Random House, 1972);

The Secret Life (Rochester, N.Y.: Valley Press, 1972);

Without an Oar (Norfolk: Penyeach Press, 1972);

An Oar in the Old Water (Ithaca: Stone Press, 1973);

Sticks & Stones (Milwaukee: Pentagram Press, 1975);

Rising and Falling (Boston: Little, Brown, 1979).

William Matthews was born in Cincinnati, Ohio. He received his B.A. from Yale University in 1965 and his M.A. from the University of North Carolina in 1966. He married Marie Harris in 1963 (they were divorced in 1974); they have two sons. Matthews has taught at Wells College, Cornell University, Emerson College, Sarah Lawrence College, the Universities of Iowa and Colorado, and he is now director of the creative writing program at the University of Washington. Matthews also serves as vice-president of the board of directors of the Associated Writers Program, and chairman of the literature panel of the National Endowment for the Arts. He was a cofounder of Lillabulero Press and *Lillabulero* magazine, and he is a member of the editorial board of Wesleyan University Press.

Although Matthews is only thirty-seven years old, he has published approximately four hundred seventy poems in 130 different magazines, including sixty-five translations (with Mary Feeney); his work has been included in thirty anthologies, and he has published forty reviews and critical essays in twenty different periodicals. In addition to his exposure in magazines and through readings on college campuses, Matthews's influence has been felt as an editor when he coedited the magazine *Lillabulero* in the 1960s and early 1970s. *Lillabulero* became one of the more significant little magazines during that period of heightened political and poetic activity and was instrumental in elevating small-press publications to respectability in the literary community.

Matthews's work is eclectic, but from the beginning he has had a strong individual voice. He says that, early on, he was "too naive to be influenced," but one senses in Matthews a no-nonsense discrimination that has allowed him to station himself between the Brahmins and the Faustians—to take psychic risks yet survive them. His work is informed by the criticism of other poets (T. S. Eliot, Ezra Pound, Charles Pierre Baudelaire) and the likes of Gaston Bachelard, Erich Auerbach, and M. H. Abrams. He has been aligned with the poets who published in *kayak* magazine in the 1960s, whose work featured the "deep image" (Robert Bly, James Wright, W. S. Merwin, Mark Strand), and his first commercially published book, *Ruining the New Road* (1970), while an overall success, does suffer from an overreliance on metaphor and simile. In a poem such as "Cuckold" the metaphors and similes seem facile, gratuitous—Matthews's posture is almost cavalier. By *Sleek for the Long Flight* (1972), he had eliminated this tendency. Matthews does, however, employ the metaphysical conceit in an effective manner in this first book and throughout his work.

In an essay included in *American Poets in 1976*, edited by William Heyen, Matthews compares "Moving," from *Ruining the New Road*, with "Moving Again," from his most recent book, *Rising and Falling* (1979). Of the former he says, "time is like a lens opening and slicing shut. If I imagined something emblematic, in significant posture, I could get a good picture. . . . But little of life organizes itself into symbolic moments." There is, then, in poems such as this one a *tableau vivant*, what one gets in a mannerist painting. These poems also have an epigrammatic quality. By the time of "Moving Again," the poems are more expansive; time is a continuum through which he can move in any direction at will. The poems are, he says, "more lengthily epigrammatic." Referring to "Moving Again," he says, "a poem should be a large enough space that it includes several different ideas about the same situation." There is a concern with the gathering of information in this poem and others like it in the same book, most notably "Nurse Sharks."

Matthews has moved about a great deal in his life, but he shows a remarkable adaptability to the changing landscape in his work. He attributes this characteristic, in a poem such as "Moving Again," to the landscape's being "cumulative." The narrator and his sons are climbing the side of a mountain, and the location is specific. Near the end of the poem, his point of view shifts down into "the valley / of child support and lights," where he eavesdrops on a man discovering a phone number from another time and place—Illinois, to be exact. In *Rising and Falling,* such shifts are frequent and always effective.

Of his persona in "Moving Again," Matthews says, "He clearly shares certain crucial situations with me (his sons have the same names as mine); he resembles me more than anyone I know or imagine. But when I am done with a poem I walk away from it; he stays in it. In many of my poems he does not appear or appears disguised as others. . . . these imaginary selves . . . should be left behind, in some poem, on some imaginary street, whenever the continuing and moving self no longer needs them." This is one of the factors peculiar to Matthews's voice; that is, it is personal, but the "I" has developed "witness consciousness." There is a sense of catharsis in his poetry, but a catharsis that has been worked out and paid for through a deep and abiding security in Self. In *Fifty Contemporary Poets* (1977) Matthews says of his reader, "I visualize . . . a me who somehow wasn't present when I wrote the poem, and can thus read it as if it were written by someone else." This concept makes for unusual intimacy in Matthews's poems.

Ruining the New Road begins with "The Search Party," in which the narrator injects his authority by making statements such as "Reader, by now you must be sure / you know just where we are, / deep in symbolic woods. . . . The search is that of art." The authority is always in evidence, the Brechtian scaffolding omnipresent. There are several poems in this book that refer to political events of the 1960s ("The Asian War," "Newark Under Martial Law," "Why We Are Truly A Nation," "Faith Of Our Fathers," "Nothing But Bad News"), but in none of these poems do the central metaphors enter into the tension of the events. Yet these events were the prevailing climate, and one had little choice but to write about them. W. S. Merwin was highly successful in applying abstraction to these occurrences, but he had developed a consistent symbology of prophetic doom. Matthews is not comfortable with doom—or even gloom, for that matter.

Later, for one of the poems in *Rising and Falling* ("Living Among the Dead"), Matthews uses a statement from Paul Eluard as an epigraph: "There is another life / but it is in this one." Matthews's poetic consciousness exists primarily in this "other" life. In *Ruining the New Road* there are frequent references to out-of-body experiences ("The Doppelganger," "Replacing the Director," "Holding the Fort," "On Cape Cod a Child is Stolen"), and the poems begin to have night, sleep, and dreams as their predominant setting—surreal states, states of suspended consciousness.

It is not accidental that basketball and jazz are themes that appear in his books. There are two basketball poems in *Rising and Falling* ("In Memory of the Utah Stars" and "Foul Shots: A Clinic"). Of basketball Matthews says, "I've always loved . . . its particular balance between pattern and improvisation. The rift is always there, but it shifts, and the play does, too, each moving the other." This balance also exists in jazz. It is fitting that Matthews refers to these two indigenously "American" activities, for they are perfect conceits for his own creative process. In *Ruining the New Road* there are two elegies for jazz musicians ("Blues for John Coltrane" and "Coleman Hawkins, RIP"), and he includes four jazz-related poems in *Rising and Falling* ("Bud Powell," "Listening to Lester Young," "Old Records," and "Alcide 'Slow Drag' Pavageau").

The interviewer in a 1972 *Ohio Review* interview says that poems in *Ruining the New Road* deal with the "domestic—so much of one's everyday life, so much of one's psychic experience [is] in them, so much celebration." In a 1978 issue of the *American Poetry Review*, Stanley Plumly says that Matthews is "a master at redeeming the domestic cliche." Matthews somehow gets away with admitting Dagwood, Underdog, and Fruit Loops into the poems, but they are natural, unfortunately, to the American landscape. Matthews is not afraid of sentiment. He sets up his poems so that he can say, as he does in "Yes!," "I give you my love to use / and shake with fear you can't." Usually these moments of emotional vulnerability are subtly slipped somewhere into the body of the poem. He has continued to refine this quality in his work. When, in "Taking the Train Home" (from *Rising and Falling*), he says of his grandfather, "I love this dying man," the reader has little doubt as to the authenticity of this feeling because of the spell he has cast around the statement, just as in James Wright's poem "Lying in a Hammock on William Duffy's Farm," one does not doubt him when he says, "I have wasted my life." The difference is that Wright hangs the emotion out there at the end of the poem, while Matthews weaves it into the fabric.

Probably the only kind of poem in which Matthews is consistently inconsistent is the erotic poem. "The Summer Night You Can't Forget" is a poem reminiscent of D. H. Lawrence at his best, and, unlike much of Matthews's work, it is descriptive

Linda L. Fry

and linear. The poem is classically romantic, but in "Old Girlfriends" there is a tone of "male chauvinism," which, although it may be honest, is unexpected. There are slight traces of this ambivalence in all three of his books.

Sleek for the Long Flight begins with an epigraph from Theodore Roethke: "Each thing's an end of something else: / . . . Farewell, loose metaphysic skin: / I would be out: you want me in . . . ," and closes with a sign-off, "yrs, burning outward, / Bill." In comparing this volume with *Ruining the New Road*, Matthews says, "it's a less celebratory book, and in some ways it's a kind of revision. . . . if the first book celebrates . . . that perpetual recurrence of change, things being disordered, and your expectation being defeated by reality—by the second book the poems recognize the fact that many of these things happen inside the self."

The first poem, "Directions," resembles "The Search Party." The speaker addresses the reader through a conceit while accompanying him on the archetypal Quest. He is constantly shifting point of view—going in for a close-up here, pulling back for a two-shot there. Although it has a similar tone, the poem is far less literary than "The Search Party."

The forms in this book are more diverse than in *Ruining the New Road*—there are seven prose poems, two one-line poems, a prayer, an ode, a letter. Matthews is also less self-conscious of his craft. He is more comfortable in his use of sound devices, and he never breaks a line at the wrong place. Many of the poems deal with transformation (a natural outgrowth of out-of-body experiences), such as "Becoming a Woman," and here the means (or the process) and the ends have become inseparable.

The acceptance of death ("Ball and Chain" is a good example) and of karmic responsibility (as in "Marriage") become recurrent themes. He says in "Marriage": "Time to do / death's work gratefully." This sentiment is echoed in "La Tache": "suppose the task is to look on until our lives have given themselves away?," and in "Living Among the Dead" (from *Rising and Falling*) in the lines, "To help his sons live easily / among the dead is a father's great work." Now the knowledge is not something learned but that which has passed into the cells, like muscle memory. In this book almost every poem refers to night, sleep, or dreams. The vast oceanic unconscious is expanded to include the snowscape as Matthews establishes an equation between the immensity of exterior space and the intimacy of inner space.

Section 4 of *Sleek for the Long Flight* consists of two poems: "Praise" and "The Cat." Both pay homage to Pablo Neruda's odes and possibly to the Finnish epic *Kalevala*. The poems are well executed, but they do not add significantly to Matthews's canon.

In *Rising and Falling*, the poems generally revolve around suspension either in the underseascape ("Diving," "Nurse Sharks," "Eyes") or in the snowscape. Matthews makes the connection between these two settings in "Snow Falling Through Fog": "This is how we used to imagine / the ocean floor: a steady snow of dead / diatoms and forams drifting / higher in the sunken plains." This reality parallels the twilight world referred to in "Waking at Dusk," "Blue Nap," and "Bedtime." Yet the major new element that he introduces in this book is childhood. "The Party," "The Icehouse . . . ," and "Taking the Train Home" are the most obvious examples of his using childhood as a seedbed of lasting and monumental images. But this childhood is alive and whole, present and permanent. Some of his best writing is in these poems.

This collection has an increasing number of poems about death, but now death is an ally, a friendly force. The poems show a healthy nervousness about death but not the semisuicidal preoccupation one finds in much confessional poetry. Included in this group of poems are "Living Among the Dead," "Taking the Train Home," and "In Memory of W. H. Auden," all among the finest poems he has written. The Auden poem is not personal, as are the other two, but a formal elegy about public topics rather than Auden the person or Matthews's reaction to his death.

The tone and level of seriousness in these three poems are hypnotic, but in an attempt not to take himself too seriously, Matthews deliberately switches the mood in other poems by throwing in a line bordering on the absurd or by shifting the attention to something else. "Left Hand Canyon" demonstrates this technique and shows that he does have an excellent sense of humor.

Finally, there is a set of poems about the landscape of transcience, which is probably the landscape most familiar to Americans in general. This group includes "A Small Room in Aspen," "Sunday Alone . . . ," and "Four Poems About Jamaica."

With Mary Feeney as cotranslator, Matthews has, during the last few years, been translating the prose poems of Jean Follain. There is a deep reverence for objects in these poems and a consistent authority, both of which inform Matthews's work, especially in the longer poems in *Rising and Falling*. The Follain poems have been collected in *A World Rich in Anniversaries* (1979).

In the Spring 1970 issue of *Tennessee Poetry Journal*, Stephen Mooney said, "If work and love can balance the ecology of our planet . . . William Matthews will deserve our thanks. Like Gary Snyder and Wendell Berry, he knows that the poetry is in the ecology. Matthews, as I believe we shall soon see, is a man of their stature. I believe that he is the best young poet in America." Critics Stanley Plumly, Doug Blazek, Arthur Oberg, and Robert Morgan agree that he is now in the front rank of American poets. Matthews has said of Auden that he was "a wonderful combination of imagination and common sense," that he felt "We shouldn't take melodramatic or extreme postures . . . that we should mean what we say," that, in Auden, "there was a wonderful sense of responsibility." Matthews himself already reflects these same virtues. —*Ken McCullough*

Other:

Poems for Tennessee, by Matthews, Robert Bly, and William E. Stafford (Martin, Tenn.: Tennessee Poetry Press, 1971);

"Moving Around," in *American Poets in 1976*, ed. William Heyen (Indianapolis: Bobbs-Merrill, 1976), pp. 168-177;

"Nurse Sharks" [poem and commentary], in *Fifty Contemporary Poets: The Creative Process*, ed. Alberta T. Turner (New York: McKay, 1977), pp. 222-227;

Jean Follain, *Removed From Time*, translated by Matthews and Mary Feeney (Tannersville, N.Y.: Tideline Press, 1977);

Follain, *A World Rich in Anniversaries*, translated by Matthews and Feeney (Iowa City: Grilled Flowers Press, 1979).

Interviews:

"Talking About Poetry With William Matthews," *Ohio Review*, 13 (Spring 1972): 32-51;

"Interview with William Matthews," *Ironwood*, 3 (1973): 58-69;

"An Interview with William Matthews," *Words*, 2 (Winter 1974): 6-11;

"A Conversation with William Matthews," *Black Warrior Review*, 1 (Spring 1975): 57-77;

"Interview with William Matthews," *Aegis*, 3 (Fall 1975): 50-58.

PETER MEINKE
(29 December 1932-)

BOOKS: *Howard Nemerov* (Minneapolis: University of Minnesota Press, 1968);

The Legend of Larry the Lizard (Richmond: John Knox, 1968);

Very Seldom Animals (St. Petersburg, Fla.: Possum Press, 1969);

Lines from Neuchâtel (Gulfport, Fla.: Konglomerati Press, 1974);

The Night Train and the Golden Bird (Pittsburgh: University of Pittsburgh Press, 1977);

The Rat Poems (Cleveland: Bits Press, 1978);

Trying to Surprise God (Pittsburgh: University of Pittsburgh Press, forthcoming 1981).

Peter Meinke was born in Brooklyn, New York. He married Jeanne Clark in 1957, and they have four

Peter Meinke

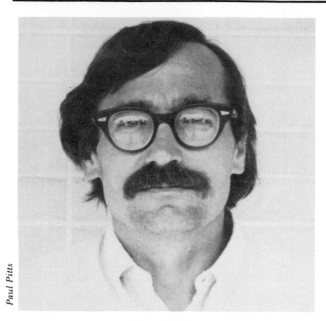

Peter Meinke

children, Perrie, Peter, Gretchen, and Timothy. Meinke received an A.B. degree from Hamilton College in 1955, an M.A. from the University of Michigan in 1961, and a Ph.D. from the University of Minnesota in 1965. He has been a visiting summer professor at the University of Sussex (1969) and Fulbright lecturer in American poetry at the University of Warsaw (1978-1979). From 1961-1966 he taught at Hamline University in St. Paul, Minnesota, returning there as poet-in-residence in 1973. In 1968 he went to teach at Florida Presbyterian College (later renamed Eckerd College) in St. Petersburg, Florida. He is currently professor of English literature and director of the creative writing program at Eckerd. Although Meinke is not well known, he is an accomplished poet of proven talent. For two decades his work has been published in such magazines as *Massachusetts Review*, *New Republic*, and *Poetry*. He has won first prize in the Olivet National Sonnet Competition (1965) and first prize in the 1976 *Writer's Digest* Poetry Contest. In 1970 he was awarded a Younger Humanist Summer Grant for work in children's literature, and in 1974-1975 a fellowship in creative writing from the National Endowment for the Arts. He has also won the Gustav Davidson Memorial Award from the Poetry Society of America (1976), and he has received a creative writing fellowship from the Fine Arts Council of Florida (1977) and a National Endowment for the Humanities summer seminar award (1977).

Meinke's first published volumes of poetry, *The Legend of Larry the Lizard* (1968) and *Very Seldom*

Animals (1969), are rhymes for children. In 1974 the Konglomerati Press brought out a limited edition of a pamphlet, *Lines from Neuchâtel*, composed of work inspired by a year in Switzerland. The best of these poems are included in *The Night Train and the Golden Bird* (1977), a book of unusual range, and Meinke's major achievement. He works slowly, and this collection represents over ten years of serious but infrequent writing that began when he was working on his Ph.D. at the University of Minnesota. His latest separate publication is a chapbook called *The Rat Poems* (1978), a sequence of twenty-four short pieces, one for each "rat" hour, beginning and ending at midnight.

As opposed to much of today's literature, which is experimental, obscure, and even at times shows a conscious disregard for its audience, Peter Meinke's poems are accessible to a broad group of readers. Sometimes bright with joy, sometimes pale with despair, they are rarely abstract or intellectual and never pretentious. As he explains in "The Heart's Location," one of the drives of his life is the search for

> a poem full of ordinary words
> about simple things
> in the inconsolable rhythms of the heart.

This goal is the same as that of Wordsworth in the preface to the 1800 edition of *Lyrical Ballads*: "The principal object, then, which I proposed to myself in these Poems was to chuse incidents and situations from common life, and to relate or describe them, throughout, as far as was possible, in a selection of language really used by men . . . and, further, and above all, to make these incidents and situations interesting by tracing in them, truly though not ostentatiously, the primary laws of our nature. . . ." Like Wordsworth, Meinke hopes to reach a broader audience than is common for his time: Wordsworth reached out to the emerging literate middle class of England at the beginning of the nineteenth century; Meinke writes in a time when serious poetry is so unpopular and unprofitable in the United States that there is hardly a poet in the country who can support himself on his writing alone. Wordsworth achieved his purpose, in part, by rejecting the "poetic" diction of Neoclassicism, Meinke by rejecting the obscure allusiveness left over from the Pound era (Pound's *Cantos* would be a good example).

The comparison between Meinke and Wordsworth soon breaks down, however: for one thing, Meinke's free-verse lyrics are formally unlike either Wordsworth's long, meditative poems or his shorter

The Coach Plays Basketball with his Students

~~PLAYING BASKETBALL WITH THE U.S. MARINES~~ warsaw 1979

At ~~46~~ 50, I suppose, it's an ~~xxxx~~ honor

they still let me play. My body remembers

what to do but ~~I can't do it anymore.~~ doesn't want to do it

The ball comes to me on a bounce. My shoulder

fakes / I swing around the first man easily

~~and~~ spot a teammate cutting to the left

and automatically whip it behind my back

for an easy lay-up. In my mind

it's complete. Only, the ball hits my back

as I do it, deflects into the wrong man's hands

and off he goes the other way, ~~for~~ an easy lay-up

for the ~~other~~ wrong side. A lifetime of smoking,

drinking, excesses to vivid to repeat

go with me on the court and everywhere.

But still, I love the game. In all my dreams

the baskets that I've made and missed return

slow motion in the dark, ~~for~~ a not-so-instant I think of heaven,

replay of those rare times when ~~body eyes~~ body eyes

~~Sometimes~~ ~~often~~, as a place / & heart conspired to work together. ——

where ~~old basketball~~ players ~~never lose their breath~~. basketball is God's elect sport

an adolescent fantasy, no doubt :

~~but float up & down some ethereal court~~ but see, they float up & down the court

soundlessly calling encouragement and praise

~~as we play at last that perfect game defeating death~~ and

~~over and over as the spinning ball / arcs through the net~~

in a dilirium ~~but~~ of the phantom body's ~~total~~ immaculate control

and the ~~mindless~~ breathless wonder of its ways.

"The Coach Plays Basketball With His Students," revised typescript

43

verses. Even more important, Wordsworth's poetry, like that of most Romantics, is devoid of humor, whereas Meinke's work is both funny ("Chicken Unlimited") and witty ("Everything We Do"). Meinke does not write "light" verse; rather, his talent is in mixing levity with gravity in a single poem. In "The Heart's Location" the reader finds a serious subject—the contemplation of suicide—treated with a humorous self-deprecation. From the very first line—"all my plans for suicide are ridiculous"—the poet's tone undercuts the seriousness of his suicidal thoughts until he laughs at his lack of nerve: "once jumped off a bridge / almost scared myself to death." In the second stanza, however, the tone changes, and the poet reaffirms his desire to live, which is linked to the personal importance of his art.

In "Cheerios," a different kind of humor arises as the poet plays with a metaphor that some Americans take literally and earnestly:

> you are what you eat & I
> I am a sexmad wheatgerm
> floating in holes of cheerios.

The poet-wheatgerm, the poem goes on to say, is produced by Kansas farm girls and boys who abandon their pitchforks just as Neptune abandoned his trident "while he rolled in the springs / with Ceres." American poetry needs this kind of humor, which turns breakfast into a romp with the gods. "Cheerios" may not be a great poem; it may not ponder the mysteries of human life; but a poet who does not always try to be "significant" is refreshing.

Meinke, however, has a serious side too. Some of his best pieces are love poems, sensitive but not sentimental. In "Surfaces" he begins by negating some of the traditional cliches of love:

> darling
> you are not at all
> like a pool or a rose
> my thoughts do not dart in your depths
> like cool goldfish.

These lines illustrate Meinke's technical control, his ability to make music in free verse. The expressions are so simple and clear that they may seem easy, but the anapestic lilt and repeated soft vowel sounds—even the uncapitalized first word—all combine to create a sincere lover's low and private voice. Writing like this is craft, not a spontaneous overflow of emotion. He ends the poem by evoking the same images of the pool and rose but with new, subtle connotations. The last lines, especially, demonstrate his sure poetic sense:

> suppose
> on the surface of a rippling pool
> the moon shone clearly reflected
> like a yellow rose
> then
> if a cloud floated over it
> I would hate the sky.

"At the Ojubo Shrine, Nigeria," a different kind of serious poem about love, separation, and art, portrays a man who is mesmerized by the clay figures of African gods he finds in the jungle. The strangeness and isolation of the setting move him to "call on the powers of darkness" to reunite him with his lover "far from this fierce place where humans carve / mad messages to the popeyed gods." The rhythm here is trochaic, hard and tense like an African drumbeat. The clear images of the jungle, the clay figures, and the intertwined, possessed artist and lover are at once exotic and mysterious yet comprehensible and moving. The tone and style of "Surfaces" and "At the Ojubo Shrine, Nigeria" are different, but both poems are examples of how well Meinke writes about love without sentimentality, one of the sure tests of a good poet.

Most of Meinke's poems are about people—strangers, friends, relatives. Family relationships are especially important to him, and he has a number of pieces about the tensions and rewards of being a father, the logical result (he has remarked in a letter) of having four children. The impression one gets from reading through *The Night Train and the Golden Bird* is that the poet and his family are typical: they misunderstand and squabble with each other, they go to Disney World and find it both magical and commercial, they worry, they support one another, and they eat a lot of fried chicken. Meinke's poetry is deeply rooted in personal experience, and whether he is writing of joy or despair, his vision is recognizable, even familiar, because it traces—returning to Wordsworth's phrase—"the primary laws of our nature." Unlike confessional poets such as Robert Lowell and Sylvia Plath, he never takes himself too seriously. If he has thoughts of suicide, as in "The Heart's Location," he finds a way to laugh about them. Even "this is a poem to my son Peter," filled as it is with the sincere regrets of a parent who has whipped his child, ends with the trace of a smile:

> I think anything can be killed
> after a while, especially beauty
> so I write this for life, for love, for

you, my oldest son Peter, age 10,
going on 11.

This quotation does not do justice to the emotional power of the poem, but it does show that at the heart of Meinke's poetry is a sense of humor that makes the pains and hazards of life more tolerable.

Although humor has the power to lighten most burdens in Meinke's world, the burdens are nevertheless present. Meinke is optimistic but not idealistic. He does not overlook social injustice, the anguish of war, the sadness of aging, or the inevitability of death. Although *The Night Train and the Golden Bird* is laced with humor, the mood of the first section ("The Night Train") is dark, especially in the opening title poem that deals with suicide without any of the humor found in "The Heart's Location." In this poem, the compartments of the night train are symbolic of what suicidal people consider to be their rushed, isolated, empty lives. The final couplet, urging the suicides on to their destiny, is as bleak as Meinke gets: "a nothing sort of place; for god's sake / get on with it: there's nothing much at stake." Yet he never repeats this despair; in the very next poem ("The Patient"), the poet, who is ill, says his disease gives meaning to his life. Although the bleakness of "The Night Train" does not reappear, ugliness and degeneration do in many forms: the "bone-bag scarecrow" ("Momia"), the decaying cities of Morocco ("Morocco"), the death of a grandmother ("Gramma"), and the despair of a war widow ("The Monkey's Paw"). These poems form the minority of his work, but, when placed next to pieces like "Cheerios" and "Chicken Unlimited," they indicate the breadth of his poetic world.

Meinke's range of subject matter is the natural result of his life-style (which has included jobs from salesman to high school teacher to professor, in places from Brooklyn to Neuchâtel to Nigeria) and writing habits (his poems begin with the notes he jots down in journals). Ideas or patterns come to him in different moods and different places. He says in an article from the *St. Petersburg Times*, 21 October 1976: "It is the job of an artist to pick out the patterns at any particular moment and communicate them. You have to be trained or ready to see it at the moment it happens. Inspiration, if that is the right word, works for me. A phrase will come to me; almost always the way I start a poem is a line pops into my head with a certain rhythm I like. I carry the phrase around, looking for an emotion to fit it."

Meinke does not write spontaneous verse. He specifically mentions rhythm as an essential part of his poetic process, but his technique includes many elements of prosody. Although he typically writes short, free-verse lyrics, he also uses traditional quatrains ("Bones in an African Cave") and the forms of sonnet (there will be a section of them in his forthcoming book) and villanelle ("The Golden Bird"). Just as he often mixes levity and gravity, so does he mix formality and informality. "The Heart's Location," for example, has the octave and sestet division of a sonnet without a regular meter or rhyme scheme. More typical of Meinke, however, is a lyric with changing stanzas, changing rhythms, and an occasional rhyme, most often at the end (as in "The Night Train" or "Vegetables"). His best poems are those that give the reader the directness and apparent spontaneity of free verse along with the aesthetic satisfaction of repeated sounds (alliteration, assonance, a variety of rhymes) and rhythmic patterns that appear for a few successive lines and then disappear again.

Meinke's poems are not always successful, but despite blemishes, his work, specifically *The Night Train and the Golden Bird*, is mature, varied, and vigorous. Meinke's next book, *Trying to Surprise God*, will be published in winter 1981 and should include poems inspired by the year he just spent as a Fulbright lecturer in Warsaw, as well as his more typical, American poems, which mix humor with the serious concerns of daily life. He has also written, in the last few years, some fine short stories, which have been published or accepted for publication in such diverse periodicals as *Sports Illustrated*, *Western Humanities Review*, and *Atlantic Monthly*; but now, at least, poetry is his surest medium. Readers will turn to *The Night Train and the Golden Bird* again and again because they know that

sometimes strange music seems
to come from it, a strain
unnatural and familiar
that speaks of love and pain. . . .

—*Deno Trakas*

Reference:

Michael Marzella, "The Poet: An Image of Nontradition," *St. Petersburg Times*, 21 October 1976, pp. 1-D, 19-D.

WILLIAM MEREDITH
(9 January 1919-)

BOOKS: *Love Letter from an Impossible Land* (New Haven: Yale University Press, 1944; London: Oxford University Press, 1947);
Ships and Other Figures (Princeton: Princeton University Press, 1948; London: Oxford University Press, 1948);
The Open Sea and Other Poems (New York: Knopf, 1958);
The Wreck of the Thresher and Other Poems (New York: Knopf, 1964);
Earth Walk: New and Selected Poems (New York: Knopf, 1970);
Hazard, the Painter (New York: Knopf, 1975).

William Meredith was born in New York City. He received his B.A. (*magna cum laude*) from Princeton University in 1940 and maintained close association with that institution for some years, as a Woodrow Wilson fellow in 1946-1947 and a resident fellow in creative writing in 1947-1948, 1949-1950, and 1965-1966. Much of his earlier published poetry takes its imagery and theme from his service in the U.S. Army Air Force (1941-1942) and in the U.S. Navy (1942-1946 and 1952-1954). Meredith has taught at the University of Hawaii and, since 1955, at Connecticut College in New London, Connecticut, where he is now Henry B. Plant Professor of English. He is not married.

Although not frequently represented in anthologies of American writing since 1950, Meredith has earned his share of plaudits and awards. *Love Letter from an Impossible Land* won the Yale Series of Younger Poets competition in 1943. He has also received *Poetry* magazine's Harriet Monroe Memorial Prize in 1944, the Oscar Blumenthal Prize from *Poetry* in 1953, two Rockefeller grants (for criticism in 1948 and for poetry in 1968), a *Hudson Review* fellowship in 1956, a National Institute of Arts and Letters Award in 1958, a Ford fellowship for drama in 1960, the Loines Award from the National Institute of Arts and Letters in 1966, the Van Wyck Brooks Award in 1971, a National Endowment for the Arts Grant in 1972, and a Guggenheim Fellowship in 1975. At present he serves as Consultant in Poetry to the Library of Congress.

Love Letter from an Impossible Land, published in 1944, emerges from a time of fascination for, but horror over, a world conflict that touches sensitive individuals profoundly. Of the thirty-three poems in the volume, the final twelve have as their focus the war as it invades the mind of Meredith, intellectual,

child of promise, embryonic man of letters. The remaining twenty-one poems make an uneven commitment to formal, codified verse inherited from the ages, but also illustrate a fierce reaction to the shock waves emanating from Ezra Pound and T. S. Eliot in London and Paris in the 1920s. Meredith was by no means singular in this reaction; his models were among the more notable of his contemporaries, such as W. H. Auden, Stephen Spender, and Muriel Rukeyser. Others among those later to be considered the first order of mid-century American poets—Robert Lowell, Theodore Roethke, and Richard Wilbur—also denied mythmaking for the development of personal idioms within the exacting confines of traditional verse forms.

There is no contradiction apparent between the lively, intellectual game—played with much convention and the big topics of Life and Death—in "A Metaphysical Sonnet" and the engrossing meditations of the title poem, "Love Letter from an Impossible Land," or "June: Dutch Harbor." Only the good fortune of survival makes the seeming growth from relative triviality to philosophic awareness possible. The juxtaposition of the occupations of a short lifetime makes the book of poems and makes it meaningful, not the relative success or failure of individual lyrics in the mode of Matthew Arnold, William Butler Yeats, Robert Frost, or Shakespeare.

Archibald MacLeish selected *Love Letter from an Impossible Land* to be published in the Yale Series of Younger Poets. In his introduction, he pointed out the "way in which the literary vehicle (for it is nothing else) of the Princeton undergraduate turns into the live idiom of a poet's speech reaching for poetry." This criticism was just when made and encouraged Meredith to further pursuit of his own voice, much more than could have any of the scant reviews that picked favorite poems from among the two distinct sections of the book.

Criticism of Meredith's work is not abundant, nor is it particularly energetic or insightful. With the poet's obvious predilection for patterned verse and his studied attention to prosodic devices and how they affect power in poetry, the tendency in secondary material is to play down the stuff of the poems, the images and rhythms, in favor of endless debate over sound and sense. No poets, Meredith included, can deny that their war consists of battle after battle to justify putting words down on paper, not merely to answer the question, "What way is best?" With the publication of *Ships and Other Figures* in 1948, Meredith may have lost sight of this fact temporarily.

Richard Howard calls the book "a retreat to modes of learning and convention," while others complain of the blurred effect of tone canceling tone, mask obscuring mask, until Meredith himself seems misplaced among the echoes of his first volume. When a career pilot no longer has a war to fight, he steadies himself with past glories or rationalizes that past contradictions still seduce him. It should not be inferred that Meredith brought more war than he could handle home with him, but *Ships and Other Figures* remains printed evidence that direct experience faded from his consideration and that he committed to posterity half-remembrances unbecoming to a man later to admit that immediacy of image and idea, spoken in the poet's own voice, are and should be the poet's object.

Certainly there are poems of originality and power in *Ships and Other Figures*, such as "A Boon." Taking blank verse to task, this poem urges no mere mask on us; it exercises nothing, instead depicts the torn edge of love with some sarcasm, humor, but mostly frankness:

> What I will ask, if one free wish comes down
> Along with all these prodigalities
> That we pick up like dollars in a dream,
> And what I urge you ask, is not that we
> Grow single in our passion without gap,
> Losing with loneliness dear differences;
> Nor lust, to burn a lifetime resinously,
> . . . .
> No, let us more ambitiously demand
> What I'd go lonely and unpaid to hold,
> The power I've heard the bravest lovers have,
> Really to aid and injure one another.
> Whereas there's no security, in dreams
> Or waking, of the things we need the most,
> The risk itself cries out to be possessed.

For the most part, however, the twenty-eight poems of Meredith's second volume overreach for their figures, count their numbers, in a predictable fashion heavy with familiarity. Particularly annoying to the new-poetry audience in 1948 may have been the anachronistic inclusion of notes, à la Eliot, at the end of the book to explain military terminology and other private difficulties. In another context, Meredith later would admit that such trappings dissipate the force or energy of a poem, which is by far more important than its *nature*, or paraphrasable meaning.

Studious, erudite, positive, honest; all these adjectives accurately describe the bulk of Meredith's production as of 1948. But the promise intimated by the twelve war poems was for an intensity more completely engaging, less academic, than these qualities. With the publication in 1958 of *The Open Sea and Other Poems*, Meredith abandoned with apparent defiance the slickly made gloss on the human condition, by now so characteristic, in favor of the slickly made poem, ripe with the evidence of private challenge. He learned more from his meters and the so often fruitless struggle with form than how to be glib. He learned concurrently the vicissitudes of life and language, how one breeds with the other to make a new whole.

Masking his voice in all manner of echoes in his first two books gave Meredith fluency and an ear more sensitive to the voices of other poets from his own and prior generations than any poet writing in 1958, except perhaps Theodore Roethke. By that time, many of his contemporaries had yielded to the allure of prosaic diction and rhythms or Beat and Projectivist theories. Thus, even the considerable achievement of *The Open Sea* met with limited enthusiasm or acceptance. Meredith's dedication to well-made poems obviously became a conviction; it is fitting that James Wright in his review of the book should compliment the editing while listing the virtues of the poems: precision, grace, and the profound depth of human feeling.

Richard Howard, in his essay on Meredith in *Alone with America*, characterizes the quiet confidence and elegant versifying now so typical of Meredith's work as the "heroism of modesty." Note, for example, these lines from "On Falling Asleep by Firelight":

> Around the fireplace, pointing at the fire,
> As in the prophet's dream of the last truce,
> The animals lie down; they doze or stare,
> Their hooves and paws in comical disuse;
> A few still run in dreams. None seems aware
> Of the laws of prey that lie asleep here too,
> The dreamer unafraid who keeps the zoo.

Equally impressive are these from "To a Western Bard Still a Whoop and a Holler Away from English Poetry":

> Of our own great poet's rage,
> Yeats', in his decorous care
> To make singing of old age
> And numbers of despair.
>
> It is common enough to grieve
> And praise is all around;
> If any cry means to live
> It must be an uncommon sound.
>
> Cupped with the hands of skill

William Meredith

How loud their voices ring,
Containing passion still,
Who cared enough to sing.

The correspondence of voice with form evident in these few lines allows Howard to say that by the time of *The Open Sea*, "Meredith insisted on play, on a response to self-hood as pleasure, on the morality of virtuosity." At ease with erudition, he shakes it, rolls it from his hand like dice, not afraid to gamble on the numbers, two to twelve. From the stylized, impersonal sonnet, "The Illiterate," to the epigrammatic "Ablutions" or his most venturesome poem in this volume, "A View from Brooklyn Bridge," in which he begins with perspectives of the actual bridge and enlarges the view to allusion and private symbolism, he offers poem after poem of compressed imagery and personalized prosody, but seldom is there an unnecessary poem, much less a failure. In a recent anthology, *Corgi Modern Poets in Focus 2*, Meredith wrote, "Chiefly I think my poverty of output stems from the conviction that an unnecessary poem is an offense to the art." *Necessary* means that one confronts what one does not understand. "Maybe that is the likeliest prescription for a work of art: a puzzle about which one has a glimmering."

For convenience, Meredith's reviewers often comment on his fascination for the sea (Dudley Fitts called him "happiest" when writing of the sea), love lyrics, or the pilot's huge loneliness in war. However, it would be more than misleading to suggest that a judgment of the body of his poetry may be reduced to a tracing of fluctuating attitudes toward different subjects or himself. There is much more relative, pictorial biography in his images but little of the confessional mode of Lowell or Anne Sexton or the therapeutic madness of John Berryman and Roethke.

The action in the mind as it responds—call it the pang of ignorance but not the object of attention—moves Meredith at this time in his life to write his poems. As he states in "The Open Sea,"

We say the sea is lonely; better say
Ourselves are lonesome creatures whom the sea
Gives neither yes nor no for company.

Big and mysterious as the sea might be, it is more objective than object, implying apprehension, meaning both psychological disturbance and the chase to capture and understand (as in "Sonnet on Rare Animals"):

It is the way with verse and animals
And love, that when you point you lose them all.

Startled or on a signal, what is rare
Is off before you have it anywhere.

Certainly Meredith's "poverty of output" is instead a rare thing among poets, a discriminating taste.

Arbitrary forms can necessitate abstraction, undecipherable allusion, and thoughts neither belonging to the poet nor honest. Conversely, at their most successful, arbitrary forms generate energy, excitement, and surprise, such as the quiet and sensitive sonnet "The Illiterate," in which Meredith forces nothing and borders on a conversational tone:

Touching your goodness, I am like a man
Who turns a letter over in his hand
And you might think this was because the hand
Was unfamiliar but, truth is, the man
Has never had a letter from anyone;
And now he is both afraid of what it means
And ashamed because he has no other means
To find out what it says than to ask someone.

. . . .

William Meredith

Layle Silbert

Afraid and letter-proud, he keeps it with him.
What would you call his feeling for the words
That keep him rich and orphaned and beloved?

The speaker of this poem has experienced the described event, a loving relationship, yet withdraws in amazement to characterize his feelings with an elegant, impersonal metaphor. As readers, we ascribe no explanation to this peculiar behavior; we simply are provoked and let our imaginations complete the characterization suggested so powerfully.

Having once faced himself and discovered his own best (most comfortable) method of expression; having modulated an awkward voice to the exigencies of language and structured verse; like a politician, having achieved incumbency with *The Open Sea*, Meredith faced further the specter to all poets: what to do and say now. By the time Meredith published the next volume of his original poems, *The Wreck of the Thresher* in 1964, he had edited a selection from Shelley's works (1962) and translated *Alcools: Poems 1898-1913* by Guillaume Apollinaire (1964). Introducing *Shelley*, Meredith seems to be picking his target for the immediate future and at the same time answering Eliot's criticism about Shelley's poor handling of borrowed philosophy, when he says: "The discoveries of a lyric poet which chiefly interest us are those concerning language and imagery. Shelley's discoveries about certain verbal effects—sounds and ideas and feelings which exist once only, incarnate in certain dispositions of English words—these are often what his poems are *about*, as is the case, it seems to me, with much great lyric poetry. What we learn from poetry is not so much the *nature* of experience as the *force* of it." If applied to Meredith's own work, no obvious discrepancy exists between these comments and interests evident in the poems published since 1944, yet all careers have special treasures that periodically must be polished and revalued according to contemporary and immediate needs.

Symptomatic of the same process of reassessment is a review Meredith wrote in 1961, "New Poetry Recordings," for the *Hudson Review*. In addition to providing the best access to the ideal version of the poem heard in the mind of the poet, a reading offers the privilege of being present when sound has its own way: "and however inadequate to that ideal music he, or we, may feel his performance to be, it has a unique authority." For Meredith, readings eliminate the need for much criticism. This is a telling opinion from a man who once glossed his own poems with notes or instructions. He says:

The most interesting readings . . . are those which project the liveliest sense of character, and a fitness of character to poem. Even where the reading is not particularly skillful or articulate . . . this rapport between person and poem is the mark of the truest poetry. The poems are *said* (to borrow again from the old master of this art, Robert Frost) by the only person who could have heard the experience in them. With the lesser poets it is not quite the same: we hear them reading poems that have occurred to them, poems they have accomplished, but there is lacking this sense of the inevitable connection between the voice and idiom on the one hand, and the character on the other.

Later he adds, "Poetry ought to be able to purge all affectation, but as a minimum it must purge affectations of speech." Although astute, this critical position is rigidly severe. Once having taken it, a poet must achieve his successes, or failures, on a higher level than before to avoid violating his own convictions.

Like his work on Shelley, Meredith's study of Apollinaire serves more as object lesson for a fertile mind than as an organic element in his poetic development. As with Pound's experimenting with alliterative lines from the Old English, while flexing an already muscular intelligence, Meredith tones his mind for the weighty job of improving his poems.

Opinions of *The Wreck of the Thresher* are mixed, but the concensus is that Meredith attains a consistently high level of performance in the twenty-three poems. He speaks in a voice finally reminiscent of the battle poems in *Love Letter from an Impossible Land*, as resonant and affecting for their ring of reality, but more profoundly mature. Despite James Dickey's objection that "He is the kind of poet who stands looking at the ocean where the atomic submarine *Thresher* went down, meditating, speculating, grieving intelligently. Things of this nature hurt him into poetry, but not poetry of great intensity. Instead, it seems muffled and distant, a kind of thin, organized, slightly academic murmur," considered reading of many of the poems confirms their intensity. Henry Taylor, in the *Hollins Critic* (February 1970), rightly identifies their limited variety of format, but he feels they stand as the first evidence of Meredith's enlarged ambition.

As with Roethke's posthumous volume, *The Far Field*, also published in 1964, Meredith enters more completely into experience, conscious of his own aging and steady bombardment by disintegrat-

49

ing social institutions. In "The Far Field" Roethke repairs to isolation and an equanimous acceptance of social chaos, while pursuing a looked-for philosophical calm: "Among the tin cans, tires, rusted pipes, broken machinery,— / One learned of the eternal." Naturalistic detail has found its way into Meredith's title poem as well:

I stand on the ledge where rock runs into the river
As the night turns brackish with morning, and mourn
                                                the drowned.
Here the sea is diluted with river; I watch it slaver
Like a dog curing of rabies. Its ravening over,
Lickspittle ocean nuzzles the dry ground,
(But the dream that woke me was worse than the sea's
                                                gray,
Slip-slap; there are no such sounds by day.)

Yet his poem is an elegy to the unfortunate waste of youth and talent, not a resignation to a private alternative expressed in conventional symbolism. It makes a thing, rather than says it, by exploring the images of a sunken ship to their appropriate depths. Unlike some of Meredith's poems in the sequential manner of Roethke (and Eliot and Berryman), this one establishes and maintains a consistent mood, moving toward its logical conclusion, which is self-deprecating to urge the reader from his lethargy over a tragic event.

Meredith has discovered the advantages of sequential presentation of related thoughts in such poems as "Five Accounts of a Monogamous Man," "Fables about Error," and "Consequences." He occasionally ranges uneasily in and around his material and does not always succeed in convincing the reader that his meditations are of sufficient consequence or assured direction. The monogamous man, "cold, grave, / Contractual as a dog," however, turns in an abstract cube of reality before the reader and is made whole, of several moods, none simple, all modern.

Robert Frost dominates selected portions of *The Wreck of the Thresher*—in name: "On Looking into Robert Frost in Kanji," in which he is invoked for his forward-thinking and positive appreciation for difficult circumstances; in mood, stanza form, and phrasing—"An Old Field Mowed for Appearances' Sake," in which Meredith plays delighted and delightful tennis with a net:

I lay the little woods in swales
To burn them as the daylight fails
For no surviving horse or cow
Is fed such crazy salad bales;

in conversational idiom and dialogue reminiscent of Frost's dramatic narratives: "Roots," wherein Mrs. Leamington, standing on a cloud, could be Frost's progenitor, or progeny, when she says: "The strangest thing would be to meet yourself. / Above ground or below I wouldn't like it." Many times in lines, stanzas, and whole poems, Meredith gives warm tribute to Frost, as much his mentor as anyone. This appreciation is particularly fitting, as by 1964 little of the artificial remains in Meredith's poems except the always meticulous design and exacting articulation now part of his own idiom.

Earth Walk: New and Selected Poems (1970) attempts to be a more faithful representation, according to Meredith's foreword. He has chosen poems of thematic interest similar to his contemporary work or "devious" in ways that still appeal. Minor editorial changes, usually rhythmical, have been made to the old poems. In the thirteen new poems Meredith loosens his syntax considerably, sliding much more consistently into meditation, yet in conversational language, without dogma, as in "Winter Verse for His Sister":

Now outside my own house at a cold hour
I watch the noncommittal angel lower
The steady lantern that's worn these clapboards thin
In a wash of moonlight, while men slept within,
Accepting and not accepting their conditions,
And the fingers of trees plied a deep carpet of decay
On the gravel web underneath the field,
And the field tilting always toward day.

For those familiar with Meredith's total production, *Earth Walk* is a just selection that as much emphasizes his variety as his quirks. Much of his best writing is here.

Most recently, in 1975, Meredith published his best book, *Hazard, the Painter*. Except for triumph over strict form, which has been relegated to a secondary position, all the finest qualities of a poet's evolving voice and personality are present. If not every poem in the sequence of masks and characterizations is equally successful, each of the sixteen contributes to the book's dynamics in a necessary way. Conceived by Meredith as a characterization of a fictional painter, Hazard, the poems arise out of an unsettled, contemporary America, a public America, that implies a breadth far too great for a lyric response. Hazard struggles with impotence, poorly timed potency, distractions, competing arts, his own pettiness, generosity, pomposity, and education, all while agonizing over his inability to come to grips with his current work, a painting of a parachutist.

In "Hazard's Optimism" the character jumps

Winter on the River

dawn

A long orange knife slits the darkness
from ear to ear. Flat sheets of Iowa
have been dropped where the water was.
A blue snake is lying perfectly still,
freezing to avoid detection — no, it is the barge-road.

noon

It's six weeks past the solstice. What
is the sun thinking of? It skulks
above the southern woods at noon.
                    Two ducks descend
on the thin creek that snakes through banks of ice.
They dream of a great flood coming
to devastate this plastic geography.
We can all remember other things than snow.

dusk

At dusk the east bank glows a colder orange,
giving back heat reluctantly. (The sickle moon
gives it back quickly.) The snake is glacier-green
where an ill-barge has latch, churned it.
Tonight unlucky creatures will die, like so many
soldiers or parents, it is nobody's fault.

midnight

The farm dogs bank at a soft crash far up-river:
the ice-breaker is coming down. We go out
in the clear night to see the lights — beacons
on the river, pharos in this sky, and a jewelled
sea-farer bringing water to the parched plain.
The hollow roar grows slower than an avalanche.
Her search-light feeling a way from point
of land to point of land, she pulls herself along
by beacon-roots. For a half-mile reach of river
she sights on us, a grove of goblins blinking
in front of their white house. Sugary rime
feathers from the bow. An emerald and a garnet
flank the twitching eye.
                    Abruptly she turns,
offering the beam of a ship that has nothing
                    to do with us.

A houseful of strangers passes, ship-noise thumping.

Down-river, other dogs take up the work.
They are clearing a path for the barges of cold
and silence which the creatures are expecting.

January 1978   William Meredith

"Winter on the River," manuscript

and lets silk support him, recreating something of his birth and vision, both necessary to the completion of his painting:

> They must have caught and spanked him
> like this when he first fell.
> He passes it along now, Hazard's vision.
> He is in charge of morale in a morbid time.
> He calls out to the sky, his voice
> the voice of an animal that makes not words
> but a happy incorrigible noise, not
> of this time. . . .

Any earned vision frets the visionary with hazards. Meredith has the wit to identify some humor in his dangling character as he concludes: "Inside the bug-like goggles, his eyes water." Sentiment, fear, the stinging wind: any or all of these make Hazard's a guarded optimism.

So often Meredith has written poems about one art form or another: music, opera, as well as poetry. In *Hazard, the Painter*, he writes not so much about the final product, the painting, but about the artist in the act of authenticating his right to paint, to mention his own name in a breath with that of Brueghel, and to know that the bold line, although earned, is not in itself all of the artist's meaning. Meredith's early volumes show the power of disparate, call them lyrical, ideas harnessed arbitrarily to form, frequently preordained. In *Hazard, the Painter*, he advances to the power of magnified focus, the single voice reverberating through broader experiences, but not with any beginning, middle, or end (as with a novelist). These poems have the sequence of necessity about them; they depict the consequential hazards of the artist as also a man, the risks of ordinary life that, if only in a modest way, make art. In "Winter: He Shapes Up" Meredith writes,

> Gnawed by a vision of rightness
> that no one else seems to see,
> what can a man do
> but bear witness?
>
> And what has he got to tell?
> Only the shaped things he's seen—
> a few things made by men,
> a galaxy made well.

Man is capable of making well, in the image of the galaxy, with so many invisible yet contending forces. He must not lose sight of his own abiding need for dignity nor his need for reserve nor the occasional joy for modest triumphs. —*Keith Moul*

Other:

"New Poetry Recordings," *Hudson Review*, 14 (Autumn 1961): 470-473;

Shelley, edited by Meredith (New York: Dell, 1962);

Guillaume Apollinaire, *Alcools: Poems 1898-1913*, translated by Meredith (Garden City: Doubleday, 1964);

Eighteenth Century Minor Poets, edited by Meredith and Mackie L. Jarrell (New York: Dell, 1968).

References:

William Rose Benét, "Seven Good Poets," *Saturday Review of Literature*, 27 (29 April 1944): 24;

Marie Borroff, "Recent Poetry," *Yale Review*, 60 (December 1970): 284-286;

John Malcolm Brinnan, "A Poet on a Painter," *New York Times Book Review*, 21 September 1975, p. 39;

David Bromwich, "Engulfing Darkness, Penetrating Light," *Poetry*, 127 (January 1976): 235;

James Dickey, "Orientations," *American Scholar*, 34 (Autumn 1965): 646-658;

Dudley Fitts, "Meredith's Second Volume," *Poetry*, 73 (November 1948): 111-116;

Fitts, "The Sweet Side of Right," *Saturday Review of Literature*, 41 (22 March 1958): 23;

G. S. Fraser, "The Magicians," *Partisan Review*, 38 (Winter 1971-1972): 474-475;

Thom Gunn, "The Calm Style," *Poetry*, 92 (September 1958): 380-382;

Richard Howard, *Alone with America   Essays on the Art of Poetry in the United States Since 1950* (New York: Atheneum, 1971), pp. 318-326;

Howard, Review of *Hazard, the Painter*, *Georgia Review*, 30 (Spring 1976): 209-211;

Thomas H. Landess, "New Urns for Old: A Look at Six Recent Volumes of Verse," *Sewanee Review*, 81 (Winter 1973): 147-150;

Ruth Lechlitner, "A New Instrument," *Poetry*, 64 (July 1944): 227-229;

Robert Mazzocco, "Undercurrents," *New York Review of Books*, 15 June 1972, pp. 31-33;

Peter Meinke, "Peter Meinke on Poetry," *New Republic*, 172 (14 June 1975): 25;

Gerald Previn Meyer, "From a Possible Land," *Saturday Review of Literature*, 31 (15 May 1948): 24-25;

John N. Morris, "The Songs Protect Us, In a Way," *Hudson Review*, 28 (Autumn 1975): 455-456;

Samuel French Morse, "Of Praise, Pain and Good

Report," *New York Times Book Review*, 27 September 1964, p. 53;

William H. Pritchard, "Shags and Poets," *Hudson Review*, 23 (Autumn 1970): 564-565;

Jeremy Robson, "William Meredith," in his *Corgi Modern Poets in Focus* (London: Transworld, 1971), pp. 117-125;

Raymond Roselip, "From Woodcarver to Wordcarver," *Poetry*, 107 (February 1966): 320-330;

Robert B. Shaw, "Poets in Midstream," *Poetry*, 118

(July 1971): 233;

Mary Shiras, "To Give Names," *Commonweal*, 67 (24 January 1958): 437-439;

Henry Taylor, "In Charge of Morale in a Morbid Time: The Poetry of William Meredith," *Hollins Critic*, 16 (February 1979): 1-15;

Louis Untermeyer, "New Books in Review," *Yale Review*, 34 (December 1944): 342-343;

James Wright, "Delicacies, Horse-Laughs, and Sorrows," *Yale Review*, 47 (June 1958): 608-610.

James Merrill

Willard Spiegelman
Southern Methodist University

BIRTH: New York, New York, 3 March 1926, to Charles Edward and Hellen Ingram Merrill.

EDUCATION: B.A., Amherst College, 1947.

AWARDS: Member, National Institute of Arts and Letters; Oscar Blumenthal Prize (*Poetry* magazine), 1947; Levinson Prize (*Poetry* magazine), 1949; Harriet Monroe Memorial Prize (*Poetry* magazine), 1951; Morton Dauwen Zabel Memorial Prize (*Poetry* magazine) for "From the Cupola," 1965; National Book Award for *Nights and Days*, 1967; Bollingen Prize, 1972; Pulitzer Prize for *Divine Comedies*, 1977; National Book Award for *Mirabell*, 1979.

SELECTED BOOKS: *Jim's Book: A Collection of Poems and Short Stories* (New York: Privately printed, 1942);

The Black Swan and Other Poems (Athens: Icaros, 1946);

First Poems (New York: Knopf, 1951);

Short Stories (Pawlet, Vt.: Banyan Press, 1954);

The Seraglio (New York: Knopf, 1957; London: Chatto & Windus, 1958);

The Country of a Thousand Years of Peace and Other Poems (New York: Knopf, 1959; revised edition, New York: Atheneum, 1970);

Selected Poems (London: Chatto & Windus / Hogarth Press, 1961);

Water Street (New York: Atheneum, 1962);

The (Diblos) Notebook (New York: Atheneum, 1965; London: Chatto & Windus, 1965);

Nights and Days (New York: Atheneum, 1966;

London: Chatto & Windus / Hogarth Press, 1966);

The Fire Screen (New York: Atheneum, 1966; London: Chatto & Windus, 1970);

Braving the Elements (New York: Atheneum, 1972; London: Chatto & Windus / Hogarth Press, 1973);

The Yellow Pages: 59 Poems (Cambridge, Mass.: Temple Bar Bookshop, 1974);

Divine Comedies (New York: Atheneum, 1976; London: Oxford University Press, 1977);

Mirabell: Books of Number (New York: Atheneum, 1978).

James Merrill's poetic career has moved steadily from accomplishment to vision; it is no extravagance to predict that his "sacred" books, when completed, will be regarded as a major poetic statement. But "sensational effects have subtle causes," Merrill once observed ("Pola Diva" in *Braving the Elements*), and the greatness of his recent work is best illuminated by the progress toward larger articulations that has been there from the start in this fastidious poet whose wit and playfulness no longer preclude openness or revelation.

Born in New York City, James Ingram Merrill attended the Lawrenceville School, and was graduated from Amherst College in 1947. For the past twenty-five years he has divided his time between Athens and Stonington, Connecticut, where he shares a house with his friend David Jackson. At the

James Merrill

beginning, his poetry was recognized for its elegance, its rococo presentation of nacreous objects or fanciful scenes; subsequently, his themes became more personal, more deeply plumbed, and the poetry was taken more seriously by critics and general readers. Four prizes from *Poetry* magazine were augmented by two National Book Awards, for *Nights and Days* (1966) and *Mirabell* (1978), a Pulitzer Prize for *Divine Comedies* (1976), and a Bollingen Prize on the strength of *Braving the Elements* (1972). The honors have accumulated as the art has matured.

Three gifts distinguish Merrill's achievement. First, he is a master of verse technique, of standard poetic forms. Second, the recognition he made in "Days of 1935" (*Braving the Elements*) that "life was fiction in disguise" has enabled Merrill to accommodate autobiographical details (which sometimes seem to come from his own life but at other times, he has warned, are hints and details from friends) to the continuing excitement of narrative. He has discovered what most lyric poets, confessional or merely personal, have yet to find: a context for a life, a pattern for presenting autobiography in lyric verse

through the mediation of myth and fable. Significantly, Northrop Frye is cited at the start of "The Book of Ephraim": the theorist who adapted Jungian ideas about myth to criticism proves that all literature is a system of interrelated correspondences. An heir of Proust, Merrill achieves a scope in poetry comparable to that of the major novelists; his great themes are the recovery of time (in spite of loss) through willed or automatic memory, and the alternating erosions and bequests of erotic experience. He focuses on what is taken, what abides, in love and time, and considers how to handle them. Third, the major phase of Merrill's career, which even astutest hindsight could not have predicted, offers his readers a model, or perhaps a metaphor, for the universe. His "poems of science" flagrantly mingle chatty seances with the dead and serious investigations of molecular biology, genetic evolution, and human history. The late work, which although still in progress must be termed epic, is clearly the cynosure of Merrill's heavenly oeuvre.

Only the elegance of Merrill's first poems points to his future. What Richard Howard deftly calls the "patinated narcissism" of *First Poems* (1951) is, in

Thomas Victor

54

The Country of a Thousand Years of Peace (1959), "literally roughed up, and the resulting corrugation of surface corresponds . . . to a new agitation of the depth." From the opening lines of the first poem, "The Black Swan," the reader can sniff the bouquet, rarefied but intense, of Merrill's language and rhythms: "Black on flat water past the jonquil lawns / Riding, the black swan draws / A private chaos warbling in its wake." There is little recklessness in *First Poems*; they are measured, reined in of feeling and, consequently, of meaning. Keatsian lushness touches Stevensesque archness in a peculiar mating of "The Eve of St. Agnes" and "The Comedian as the Letter C": "A lute, cold meats, a snifter somewhat full / Like a crystal ball predicting what's unknown; / Ingots of nougat, thumbsized cumquats sodden / With juice not quite their own" ("Portrait").

The cold perfection of these poems lacks a human center or moral wisdom. They are reticent and mannerly (in an interview, Merrill commented: "Manners for me are the touch of nature, an artifice in the very bloodstream"), but justifiably so. The holding back encourages the use of the pathetic fallacy, in a poem such as "Willow": man invests nature with meaning in order to understand his own passions. It borrows from him to clarify him; to him it was "that branches lent, though covertly, / Movements more suave, grinding what pangs there be / Into a bearable choreography." And reticence encourages equally the creation of imaginary lives for real animals in a bestiary worthy of Marianne Moore. The pelican, for instance, is assisted by "his postures foolish yet severe . . . in a courtesy nowadays / Only among artists fashionable."

In the volume's last poem Merrill alights upon an image and a subject that are to hold him throughout his career. "The House," whose first line demands an ellipsis back to the title, which is its grammatical subject, announces human fragility as a central human theme. Day is comfort, but "night is a cold house," and even "the west walls take the sunset like a blow." Houses confer meaning, not just protection; the reader learns "soberly" at dusk that "a loss of deed and structure" is his plight. Things fade and fall, ownership and actions (deeds) fail, and day is a flattering illusion, while the house of night "no key opens." The end, whether a revelation or a submission, is open and points to the potential paths that Merrill's future work may follow.

Between *First Poems* and *The Country of a Thousand Years of Peace*, David Kalstone has written, "the solitary speaker had become a world traveller," setting his subjects in various foreign landscapes. The book's primary tone is elegiac,

lamenting the early death of the poet's friend Hans Lodeizen in Switzerland, the land of the title, and trying "to drink from the deep spring of a death / That freshness [it does] not yet need to understand" ("A Dedication"). Orpheus and the Phoenix, types of rebirth, are subjects of longer poems, since Merrill wishes to reinvent Lodeizen or lead him from the millennial quiet of his Swiss grave. No one sees, however, "that starry land / Under the world . . . / Without a death" (Vergil's *"sed revocare gradum . . . hoc opus, hic labor est"*). In retrospect one can see the volume as equivalent to both Milton's *Lycidas*, as the poet is steeling himself for survival in a world indifferent to poets' voices, and to the *nekyias* (or descents into hell) of Homer, Vergil, and Dante, which ready Merrill for the grandeur of epic revelation. The ardor of seeing is the reason for following the title poem with "The Octopus," a dazzling demonstration of Merrill's metaphysical energy and prosodic daring. In alternating five- and four-stress lines, with rhymes on the first syllable of feminine endings and the second of masculine ones (e.g., *translucence / unloose, fervor / observe*), Merrill makes an elaborate comparison between "vision asleep in the eye's tight translucence" and a sleepy, caged octopus, only rarely coaxed out by the light into a waking dance, uncurling its tentacles like the arms of a Hindu god toward the object of its attraction:

> He is willing to undergo the volition and fervor
> Of many fleshlike arms, observe
> These in their holiness of indirection
> Destroy, adore, evolve, reject—
> Till on glass rigid with his own seizure
> At length the sucking jewels freeze.

The last lines summarize Merrill's early poetic stances. "Holiness" suggests the sacerdotal function of art in this century, and "indirection" recalls T. S. Eliot's remarks on the need for artistic subtlety and opacity in a modern, disjointed society.

Because of its inevitable failure, the enterprise is both sterile and disturbing. Greedy for experience and escape, vision enclosed in the eye is imprisoned like the octopus and doomed never to attain what attracts it. The predation motif, in Merrill's later poetry, will find a recognizably human corollary when it is translated into an erotic quest. Its failure is stated as Proust's law: "(a) What least thing our self-love longs for most / Others instinctively withhold; / (b) Only when time has slain desire / Is his wish granted to a smiling ghost / Neither harmed nor warmed, now, by the fire" ("Days of 1971," *Braving the Elements*).

James Merrill

At this point in Merrill's career, however, the frozen jewels of attack are thwarted in their godlike wreath of wrath as they push toward accomplishment, seizure, control. Stasis, or the cold perfection of visual luster, is accepted as second best to entrapment. Hence, all those poems about things ("The Olive Grove," "Thistledown," "A Time Piece," "Mirror," "Stones") because things, at least, are permanent. It is instructive to remember that *The Country of a Thousand Years of Peace* was published in the same year as *Life Studies*, Robert Lowell's turning volume. Although Lowell had found his major voice, Merrill still had seven years to go, but the fixation on the past and its stillness is common to both. In "91 Revere Street," Lowell announces what he and Merrill, alone among mid-century poets, were to make their obsession: in memory "the vast number of remembered *things* remains rocklike. Each is in its place, each has its function, its history, its drama. There, all is preserved by that motherly care that one either ignored or resented in his youth. The things and their owners come back with life and meaning— because finished, they are endurable and perfect." It is ironic that a critic in the *Hudson Review* singled out Merrill's volume for "scrupulously avoiding the ordinary" and for its "drier tone, discriminating and exact," while excoriating *Life Studies* as "lazy and anecdotal . . . more suited as an appendix to some snobbish society magazine." Later critical opinion would probably reverse the preference.

Merrill instinctively recognized his early limitations. In "The Book of Ephraim" (section A), attempting to decide how to form his material, he confesses "My downfall was 'word-painting,' " but he opts for poetry over fiction since "in verse the feet went bare." In the titillating seminarrative poems in *The Country of a Thousand Years of Peace*, too much is withheld, and the reader never knows exactly what is happening, or why, to whom. Cleverness, like manners, betrays. One of these poems ("A Narrow Escape") starts with a commonplace, but baffling, admission: "During a lull at dinner the vampire frankly / Confessed herself a symbol of the inner / Adventure." These lines lead to the eerie, chatty giggle at the end: "It was then Charles thought to wonder, peering over / The rests of venison, what on earth a vampire / Means by the inner adventure. Her retort / Is now a classic in our particular circle." Richard Howard has suggested, "it is not the story, not even the retort, but the notation of a world in which the retort is possible that matters to him: these poems are concerned to create a climate of opinion, a variable weather of discourse."

Another word for the poems might be Merrill's own: they are *doodles*. "The Doodler," a signature piece, exemplifies Merrill's accomplishments and warns self-consciously against his limitations. Doodles are children, "the long race that descends / From me," and also icons that grow like lichens. Inflated and comic, they are both art and preparations for it, excuses, symbols for paintings yet to come. A doodle traces the gap between intention and execution; it is an earnest, the young artist might hope, of future things. Looking at a page of designs, one confronts the equivalent of one's past, where the retrieval of meaning can be equally frustrating and fruitful: "Shapes never realized, were you dogs or chains?" Like the voices he hears in his later volumes, the art here is at first an unclear and unwilled antidote to the neat perfections of his more tightly organized poems: "Indeed, nothing I do is at all fine / Save certain abstract forms. These come unbidden." All the poet can do, in his climactic Christological year, is to look hopefully forward to future outbursts of stories, designs, and better human figures ("I have learned to do feet," he announces wryly): portraiture in which the outlines are fleshed out. Like the Phoenix, his image of rebirth and withdrawal, Merrill's poetry constantly transforms itself, preening and steadying before a possible ritual conflagration. "In the end one tires of the high flown," he says as he skims over, like Yeats, his fascination with what is difficult before lying down where all the ladders start. The bird, "keyed up for ever fiercer / Flights between ardor and ashes, / Back and forth," repeats its dazzling display until, "in the end, despite / Its pyrotechnic curiosity, the process palls." Like Roethke, Merrill learns by going where he has to go.

He goes to a new house and to his own past. *Water Street* (1962) celebrates the Stonington, Connecticut, residence; it marks, as well, a new candor about his life. In its final poem, "A Tenancy," he greets some guests and looks to his poetic future, with the fruits of his own life, the tonic of his major phase: "If I am host at last / It is of little more than my own past. / May others be at home in it." Futurity and benediction combine with a coming home, and a coming to terms.

There is a new ease in many of these poems, starting with two important reminiscences, "An Urban Convalescence" and "Scenes of Childhood," and reaching even to specimens of Merrill's earlier style, where it is deployed in the service of subjects not fully realized. "Poem of Summer's End," for example, is about the termination of a ten-year love affair, with crucial narrative detail omitted, and in its opening it shows how Merrill has absorbed the model of a poet such as Elizabeth Bishop, grafting her deceptive austerity onto the archness of his former manner. The change occurs exactly in the sardonic, un-Bishop-like third sentence:

> The morning of the equinox
> Begins with brassy clouds and cocks.
> All the inn's shutters clatter wide
> Upon Fair Umbria. Twitching at my side
> You burrow in sleep like a red fox.

The theme is like a cloak hanging on a rack instead of a human body. But upon reconsideration, the teasing vagueness of the poem is apposite to the mysteries of our lives. Who, really, are we when we love and whom are we loving? What does one see but himself in a lover's eyes? Repetition dulls experience ("Sun / Weaker each sunrise reddens that slow maze / So freely entered"), but the next turn, or path, may lead only to "the springs we started from," both a source and the bed of the opening lines.

Themes of loss and return emerge from Merrill's yearning for compensation, for accepting "the dull need to make some kind of house / Out of the life lived, out of the love spent" ("An Urban Convalescence"). In "For Proust" he weighs the need for retrenchment, as into a cork-lined room, against the requirement to "go into the world again" (Valéry's "*il faut tenter de vivre*" echoes throughout his poetry), because "over and over something would remain / Unbalanced in the painful sum of things." And, in "Scenes of Childhood," home movies are the Proustian madeleine to reawaken consciousness and to recapture a still terrifying past. Repetition, through memory, is here controlled. It may revive original feelings of dismay, or help to subjugate the dead whom it resurrects. The dead feed upon the living but are controlled by them—as Merrill will demonstrate in the prophetic books—through machines like a movie "projector" (an appropriately Freudian word). The poet realizes he is "sun and air" and also "son and heir" by comparison to his dead father. The child is father of the man, in Wordsworth's aphorism; for Merrill, the man, especially if childless, is still child himself. "The loved one always leaves," he remarked in "For Proust," but memory restores what life often denies.

The motifs of recollection and repetition are enlivened by Merrill's mirrors, which reflect a major concern: exactly how much does a resemblance replace, transform, or surpass its original? In "The Water Hyacinth" the poet looks down at a dying woman's body: "I watch your sightless face / Jerked swiftly here and there, / Set in a puzzling frown. / Your face! it is no more yours / Than its reflected double / Bobbing on scummed water." He tries to correct her jumbled details from stories so long repeated that he knows them by heart, his inheritance from the woman who is now confused by chronology and circumstance. The "craft" to take her where she is going is storytelling, a barge to the next world. The water hyacinth of the title, a rootless new arrival sixty years earlier, has now vividly congested the river on which she rode during her honeymoon. These legacies from parents to children, or from one's past selves to his present one, become in Merrill's later work the commerce between the dead and the living. In "A Tenancy," although repetition enhances (it spurs his creativity), it also diminishes: "The body that lived through that day / And the sufficient love and relative peace / Of those short years, is now not mine. Would it be called a soul?"

Bodily decrepitude is wisdom: Merrill's poems from the mid-1960s onward enact Yeats's great theme. In *Nights and Days* (1966), the first prize-winning volume, the soul is formed by the days of experience and the nights of imaginative recall, by the witty Cavafian manner (Constantin Cavafy, 1863-1933, the Alexandrian poet whose clarity of characterization and multileveled diction are models for Merrill's), and by the acceptance of those illusions on which human life depends. Another word for illusion is myth, and in the long poems, seminarrative, semimeditative, semilyric (Ezra Pound's description of his *Cantos*), which Merrill begins here and in which he finds his truest voice, one can appreciate Ernst Cassirer's remarks about the necessary filters through which one experiences reality in the modern age:

> No longer can man confront reality immediately; he cannot see it, as it were, face to face. Physical reality seems to recede in proportion as man's symbolic activity advances. Instead of dealing with things themselves, man is in a sense constantly conversing with himself.
>
> He has so enveloped himself in linguistic forms, in artistic images, in mythical symbols or religious rites that he cannot see or know anything except by the interposition of the artistic medium.

Induction, subterfuge, fiction: these are Merrill's equivalents to Stephen Dedalus's silence, exile, and cunning. They explain his precision of manner and passion for manners, as well as the occasional reticence in even the autobiographical poems. As he said in an interview: "You hardly ever need to *state* your feelings. The point is to feel and keep your eyes open. Then what you feel is expressed, is mimed back at you by the scene. A room, a landscape. I'd go a step further. We don't *know* what we feel until we see it distanced by this kind of translation." Or, as he puts it in a mock-lecture in "Days of l964," "Form's what affirms." Art and life, in other words, sustain one another; they are never rival dispensations.

Merrill's two great themes—Time and Eros, and the relations between them—flower in this volume. "Time" (as the title of the poem elliptically slides into the first line) . . . is . . . "Ever that Everest among Concepts." It is measured by the tedium of the daily round, a son caring for a dying father and playing endless games of Patience, and by the heroic effort to gain independence, the pinnacle of the mountain: "Arriving then at something not unlike / Meaning relieved of sense, / To plant a flag there on that needle peak / Whose diamond grates in the revolving silence."

Love, the energies of masking and unmasking in the erotic life, is the arena where illusion and reality perform their ritual matings and combats. In "Days of l964" the poet in Greece is both foreign and surprisingly comfortable because the stranger is always thought a god in disguise. The Homeric world lives in a modern, comic suit, and Aphrodite is reborn as Kyria Kleo, the poet's cleaning woman, who masks despair and age with the prostitute's cosmetics and tight clothing, at the same time revealing precisely those ravages of time she is so desperate to conceal. In love himself, the poet thinks the maid *"was* Love," glistening with pain and love, which are twins, not opposites. He pays her generously because "Love [the goddess as well as his current affair] makes one generous," although, ironically, she is trolloping on the hills in search of more. Is love, deity or emotion, an illusion? Kleo's makeup is "the erotic mask / Worn the world over by illusion / To weddings of itself and simple need." All oppositions are united at the end:

If that was illusion, I wanted it to last long;
To dwell, for its daily pittance, with us there,
Cleaning and watering, sighing with love or pain.
I hoped it would climb when it needed to the heights
Even of degradation, as I for one
Seemed, those days, to be always climbing
Into a world of wild
Flowers, feasting, tears—or was I falling, legs
Buckling, heights, depths,
Into a pool of each night's rain?
But you were everywhere beside me, masked,
As who was not, in laughter, pain, and love.

Through memory, the past clarifies. Distance confers a perspective on life's slowly evolving experiences. So it is in "The Broken Home," which proves that growing up is just another word for displacement and that all homes are broken but recoverable through memory. Guiding himself through recollections of childhood, the speaker recalls his parents, "Father Time and Mother Earth, a marriage on the rocks," who, like one's past, determine one's present. Returning to his old house, now a boarding school, where he hopes someone, at last, may learn something, the poet poignantly but wittily combines a memory of his old Irish setter and Wordsworth's clouds surrounding the setting sun at the close of the Intimations Ode as a symbol of mortality and wisdom: "or, from my window, cool / With the unstiflement of the entire story, / Watch a red setter stretch and sink in cloud." The puns on "setter" and "story" demonstrate the depth of Merrill's wit. Kalstone writes, "All conversational ease and, at the end, outrageous humor, Merrill's wit allows us momentary relaxation and then plants its sting . . . [it] is there to reveal patterns that vein a life: a precarious and double use of ordinary speech." Just as the ordinariness of daily life covers depths of passion and moment, so the virtuosity of Merrill's diction reveals possibilities in speech that the reader may not have previously considered. In fact, he once referred to his language as " 'English' in its billiard-table sense—words that have been set spinning against their own gravity."

The Fire Screen (l966) marks a defensive retreat, in middle age, from ardors and passions better enjoyed when young. Even grand opera, about which a series of poems revolves, seems too strenuous to confront, as he acknowledges half-jokingly in "Matinees," where the real thing, whether art or life, seems "too silly or solemn": it is "enough to know the score / From records or transcriptions / For our four hands." Sometimes, even, "it seems kinder to remember than to play." The fire screen of the title is a protection, which in its French translation, *contre-coeur*, applies equally to love's flames. Merrill's prose footnote to "Mornings in a New House" shrugs cavalierly at the Brünnhilde-like protection offered by the fancy screen: "Oh well, our white heats lead us no less than words do. Both have been devices in their day." One's "household opera," the heroic passions unknown to children, develops in time and is recorded by memory. Life imitates art, however, as a child, confronting Wagnerian passion at the Met, must thereafter arrange for his "own chills and fever, passions and betrayals, / Chiefly in order to make song of them."

The defensiveness against debilitating passions in life and art is reflected most stunningly in the book's longest poem, "The Summer People," a

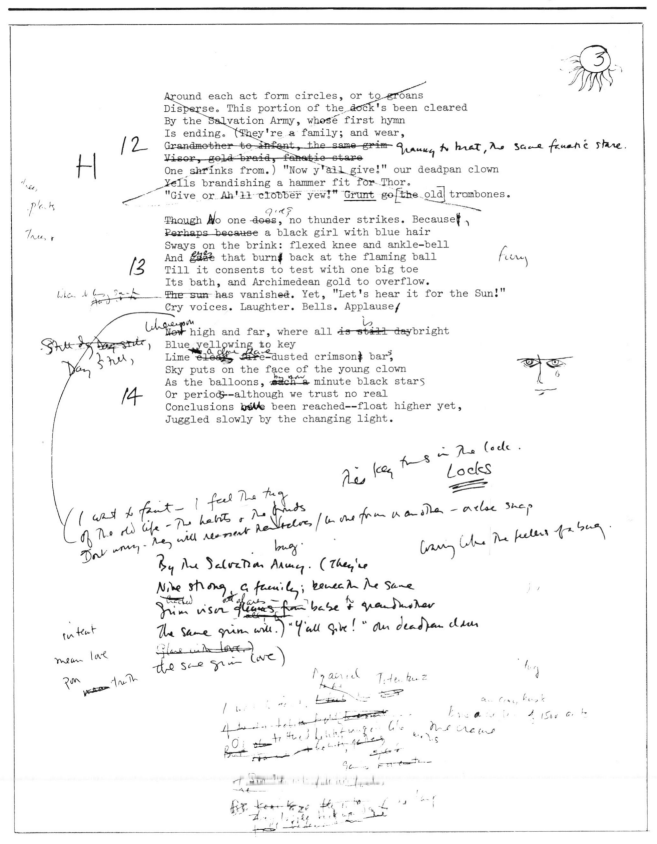

Around each act form circles, or to groans
Disperse. This portion of the dock's been cleared
By the Salvation Army, whose first hymn
Is ending. (They're a family; and wear,
~~Grandmother to infant, the same grim~~ *granny to brat, the same fanatic stare.*
~~Visor, gold braid, fanatic stare~~
One shrinks from.) "Now y'all give!" our deadpan clown
Yells brandishing a hammer fit for Thor.
"Give or ~~Ah'll~~ clobber yew!" Grunt go the old trombones.

~~Though~~ No one ~~does,~~ *gives,* no thunder strikes. Because,
~~Perhaps because~~ a black girl with blue hair
Sways on the brink: flexed knee and ankle-bell
And ~~eyes~~ that burns back at the flaming ball   *fiery*
Till it consents to test with one big toe
Its bath, and Archimedean gold to overflow.
~~The sun~~ has vanished. Yet, "Let's hear it for the Sun!"
Cry voices. Laughter. Bells. Applause.

Whereupon Now high and far, where all ~~is still~~ *is* daybright
Blue yellowing to key
Lime ~~clear, fire~~-dusted crimsons bars,
Sky puts on the face of the young clown
As the balloons, ~~each a~~ minute black stars
Or periods--although we trust no real
Conclusions ~~have~~ been reached--float higher yet,
Juggled slowly by the changing light.

Their key turns in the locks.
Locks

(I want to faint — I feel the tug
of the old life — the habits & the friends
Don't worry — they will reassert themselves / in one form or another — or else snap
bug.   *crazy like the feelers of a bug.*

By the Salvation Army. (They're
Nine strong, a family; beneath the same
grim visor glances from babe to grandmother
The same grim will.) "Y'all give!" our deadpan clown

intent
mean love   *Glare with love*
truth   *the same grim love*)

James Merrill

ballad of chilling and disingenuous simplicity that dramatizes an aphorism from Merrill's experimental novel, *The (Diblos) Notebook* (1965): "After a certain age, the heart gives itself, if at all, too easily: the gift can be taken back." A quartet of summer residents in a fishing village enthusiastically welcomes a mysterious millionaire into their midst. He, his cat, and his Japanese houseboy assume year-round residency and enchant their adopters. After one of them is bitten by the cat, who is then destroyed, the millionaire, Jack Frost, leaves for the Orient, the summer people lose their infatuation, the house and garden fall into disrepair, and the houseboy dies. It is an uneventful narrative, with an eerie disjunction between style and subject. The narrator comments upon this spookiness:

> The meter grows misleading,
> Given my characters.
> . . . .
> For figures in a ballad
> Lend themselves to acts
> Passionate and simple.
> . . . .
> But I have no such hero,
> No fearful deeds—unless
> We count their quiet performance
> By Time or Tenderness.

The weirdness is like that of Edward Gorey or the macabre textures of pornography, a tone Merrill captures well in the postcard section of "The Thousand and Second Night" (*Nights and Days*). In this suspended narrative, isolated events in the lives of the summer people are intersected by the mysterious stranger who comes from and returns to nowhere. Origins and ends are equally fathomless. The blessings of summer—dinners, musicales, amusing distractions—are magical and illusory; underneath lurks something sinister, evoked even in the halting rhythm of the ballad stanza:

> Andrew at the piano
> Let the ice in his nightcap melt.
> Mendelssohn's augmentations
> Were very deeply felt.

How? By whom? Such questions are no more to be answered than the mysteries of the heart's extensions to, and withdrawals from, a visitor from somewhere beyond. Only transience abides.

Even the title of *Braving the Elements* suggests tactics for survival, new attempts at heroism through exposure. Often, the poems begin with the enervation following upon a physical or emotional

crisis (Richard Saez has shown the similarity of this strategy to Proust's), which increases sensitivity. At the same time, one can see clearly Merrill's metaphysical mind in poems that elaborate a many-stranded conceit into a fugal pattern. "Willowware Cup," for example, works through the association, amplification, and cross-referencing of art, politics, and biology, in an updating of Yeats's "Lapis Lazuli," a commentary on the interweavings of art and life. Levels of diction touch smoothly, like layers on the ocean floor; technical vocabulary from pottery or genetics mixes happily with the pseudoserious (on the cup, an aged parent "must by now be immensely / Wise, and have given up earthly attachments and all that") or the archly cryptic. ("You are far away. The leaves tell what they tell.")

In his middle age, Merrill becomes more aware of the constancy beneath the surface of change. A proud, strutting Athenian, the classical ideal still glowing through the debased, modern flesh, extra kilos, and a moustache, is his old friend Strato ("Strato in Plaster"), just as Kyria Kleo both was and was not Love. The title seems to refer to a statue, but the reader learns soon that it is about a broken arm. The trick is legitimate since the poem deals with the ways man tends to stabilize the past and how life always resists art's attempts at finality. People are never, yet somehow always, what they used to be. The return to a new beginning is eternally the same, as in "After the Fire," when Merrill visits his Athens apartment after a conflagration to learn that "everything changes, nothing does." Kleo is still a whore, her son Noti still cruises for lovers; all become parodies of what they once were. Even objects are merely "translated," and nothing ever fully disappears since in Merrill's universe, as in Freud's, a divine economy keeps everything moving and useful. ("Life, like the bandit Somethingopoulos / Gives to others what it takes from us.") Total disappearance is impossible; there is only displacement and shifting. Love is not wholly wasted, only metamorphosed by its own mysterious laws.

Denial of love, Merrill's compulsive fear as a child of a broken home, finds imaginative consolation in "Days of 1935," which revolves around a double fantasy: that of the adult for childhood innocence and bravado and that of the child for attention through victimization. The young boy dreams he is kidnapped by a pair of Bonnie and Clyde look-alikes, movie stars right out of central casting or from the pages of the Lindbergh case. They are coarse, sexual creatures but also parent substitutes. He spins out tales for Jean all afternoon, realizing that he is Scheherazade and she the real child, and that the whole escapade, now separate from, now connected to, life past and present, proves that there is neither end nor beginning. The child returns to normal life after the supposed capture of the criminals; the adult recalls a Proustian moment when the child goes off to bed as his parents prepare for a party:

> She kisses him sweet dreams, but who—
> Floyd and Jean are gone—
> Who will he dream of? True to life
> He's played them false. A golden haze
> Past belief, past disbelief . . .
> Well, those were the days.

Life is fiction in disguise, he knew even as a child; the poet teaches that fiction is equally life transformed and feeling translated.

Divine Comedies begins Merrill's supreme fiction, a self-mythologizing within an epic program of what J. D. McClatchy has called, varying Coleridge, "The Other Life within Us and Abroad." At last Merrill's masters combine with graceful fluency in a confection entirely his own: the reader finds Proust's social world, his analysis of the human heart and the artist's growth; Dante's encyclopedia of a vast universal organization; and Yeats's spiritualism, for which the hints in the earlier volumes gave only small promise. Added to these are the offhand humor of Lord Byron and W. H. Auden, a Neoplatonic theory of reincarnation, a self-reflexiveness about the process of composition, and a virtual handbook of poetic technique. "The Book of Ephraim," the volume's long poem, is chapter one of Merrill's central statement.

Traditionally, a poet writes one great epic for which his entire career is a preparation. The half-dozen smaller poems surrounding "The Book of Ephraim" like chapels around a great cathedral adumbrate the larger work's concerns. "Chimes for Yahya," like "Verse for Urania," echoes Milton's Nativity Ode; it also reworks Yeats's "The Second Coming" and revives Merrill's concern with surrogate fathers, the Near East, the collision of cultures, and inheritance and bequests. The impressive "Lost in Translation" pinpoints, more succinctly than any of Merrill's other short poems, the issues of loss and possession. Recalling a childhood jigsaw puzzle with one missing piece, Merrill is led to consider as well his vain attempts to retrieve a translation by Rilke of Valéry's "Palme": "So many later puzzles had missing pieces" that he finds compensation in cosmic housekeeping:

> But nothing's lost. Or else: all is translation

> And every bit of us is lost in it . . .
> And in that loss a self-effacing tree,
> Color of context, imperceptibly
> Rustling with its angel, turns the waste
> To shade and fiber, milk and memory.

Poetry, said Robert Frost, is what is lost in translation; Merrill's poem proves the adage wrong, since loss through translation is the motive for the poem itself.

Memory and vision are the milk of instruction in "The Book of Ephraim," as the poet pieces together past and present, with occasional sidelong glances at an unfinished novel he once worked on and with information about the universe supplied by his psychopomp, the poem's title character. The medium is a Ouija board, on which he and David Jackson have been experimenting since 1955, the second year of their Stonington tenancy. Their familiar spirit turns out to have been a Greek Jew, coincidentally from a broken home, who died in 36 A.D. He instructs "JM" and "DJ" through the twenty-six capital letters of the board. (The poem's twenty-six sections begin with the letters of the alphabet in sequence.) Ephraim is a smiling, chatty schoolmaster, less stern than Dante's Vergil (another major difference between Dante's and Merrill's universes is that the latter lacks a hell) and an epitome of worldly wit and skepticism who chides when necessary ("WILL / U NEVER LEARN LOOK LOOK LOOK LOOK YR FILL / BUT DO DO DO DO / NOTHING"), but more frequently adopts an affable, cooing tone. ("U ARE SO QUICK MES CHERS I FEEL WE HAVE / SKIPPING THE DULL CLASSROOM DONE IT ALL / AT THE SALON LEVEL.") Ephraim gilds the philosophic pill, as Merrill does the poem: "huge tracts of information / Have gone into these capsules flavorless / And rhymed for easy swallowing." A good thing, too, since JM and DJ, as stand-ins for their own reading audience, go in fear of abstractions: they have already slept through

>   our last talk on Thomist
> Structures in Dante. Causes
> Were always lost—on us. We shared the traits
> Of both the dumbest
> Boy in school and that past master of clauses
> Whose finespun mind "no idea violates."

"The Book of Ephraim" is as worthy of Henry James as of Dante. In Heaven and Earth, the stage is set for a congregation of sociable spirits, with Ephraim as guide to what is past and passing and to come. The dramatis personae (section D) include friends, family, strangers, and fictional characters, striated and structured in manifold relationships. Every living person is the earthly representative of some otherworldly patron, who may not, however, intervene for him (only when there is "SOME POWERFUL MEMORY OR AFFINITY" may a spirit interfere with earthly arrangements, as Plato was permitted to do for Wallace Stevens). Borrowing from the most shadowy of Orphic legends, filtered through Plato and Vergil, Merrill invests his living souls with repeated incarnations, and he arranges the otherworldly spirits upon a ladder of nine stages of patronage ("with every rise in station / Comes a degree of PEACE FROM REPRESENTATION"), which provoke the return of the taken-leave-of senses "LIKE PICTURES ON A SCREEN / GROWN SOLID THAT AT FIRST ARE MERELY SEEN."

Lacking a conventional plot, the poem wheels steadily down parallel paths: speculation, lyricism, self-analysis, history, fiction. Aware of the potentially absurd wrongheadedness of it all (Auden once demurred at how embarrassing Yeats's experiments were), Merrill sensibly steps back occasionally to behold the strangeness of his poem and the world it mirrors. His skepticism, like Ephraim's heuristic methods, is an educational tool: one is readier to accept the spiritualism for the very doubts with which it is offered. In a visit to a psychiatrist (section I), JM proffers the old Wildean epigram, "Given a mask we'll tell the truth," to the fear that he and DJ are engaged in a harmless "folie à deux." What are they to make of "these odd inseminations by psycho-roulette?" His answer: "Somewhere a Father Figure shakes his rod / At sons who have not sired a child?" is certainly a reasonable Freudian explanation. Or, there may be an alternative, Jungian one: Ephraim's "lights and darks were a projection / Of what already burned, at some obscure / Level or another, in our skulls." Yeats's spirits told him they came to bring metaphors for poetry, and one may choose to take Ephraim's fables as a fictive construction, remembering, as Stevens says, that God and the imagination are one, or, as Jung would have it, that God and the unconscious are one:

He was the revelation
(Or if we have created him, then we were).
The point—one twinkling point by now of thousands—
Was never to forego, in favor of
Plain dull proof, the marvelous nightly pudding.

The poem can never say who is the creator, who the creation: perhaps we are all characters in some superplot by divine powers, or perhaps they are projections of our deepest desires. The mirror on the

book's dust jacket reminds the reader of Merrill's habitual doubling: an abiding image is now a major theme.

The admixture of worldly wit and spiritual revelation resolves itself in fanciful moments: e.g., Mozart is "A BLACK ROCK STAR / WHATEVER THAT IS," assures Ephraim; he was allowed rebirth instead of promotion because "HE PREFERS / LIVE MUSIC TO A PATRON'S HUMDRUM SPHERES" (n.b., Mirabell corrects this misinformation in the next volume). More important than his wit, however, is the sureness of Merrill's tone in the poem. "The Book of Ephraim" is encyclopedic as much by virtue of calibrations along a tonal scale as by the scope of its information. Merrill admits to having cared for music long before literature, and in a 1968 interview he used a word for tone that might explain his sympathy with the disembodied visitors he never sees: " 'Voice' is the democratic word for 'tone.' 'Tone' always sounds snobbish, but without a sense of it, how one flounders." "The Book of Ephraim" is a literal and figurative sounding of depths and scaling of heights throughout the universe and within its microcosm, the human voice.

Both "The Book of Ephraim" and its book-length sequel, *Mirabell: Books of Number*, dispel the earlier charges against Merrill's "mere" artfulness. (After Merrill won the Bollingen award, a *New York Times* editorial criticized the foundation for making an award in troubled times to a genteel poet.) They add depth to Stevens's phrase about the "essential gaudiness of poetry," because their essential vision is elaborate, comic, deliberate, and spacious. Merrill asked in the 1968 interview: "How can you appreciate the delights of concision unless you abuse them?"

The "GREAT GENETIC GOD" who figures dimly in "The Book of Ephraim" as a kind of Shavian Life Force, seeing to the gradual improvement of the universe and the human species, is more centrally located, but still offstage, in *Mirabell*. Ephraim (section P) says that he has seen souls from before the flood, nuclear in origin, compared with whom he is merely a shadow. In section U a new message is cut off: "MYND YOUR WEORK SIX MOONES REMAIN." This is the voice of Mirabell, which now, in his own book, overwhelms all the others: JM's, Ephraim's, plus the added commentaries of W. H. Auden and Merrill's Greek friend Maria Mitsotaki, both recently gone, his spiritual parents, "father of forms and matter-of-fact mother," whose common sense keeps DJ and JM from despair after their communications with the angels. The voices blend in harmonious chorus, a music corresponding to a new focus away from the individual self.

The self begins its path toward opacity in "The Book of Ephraim." In sections W and X, as life and poem approach closure, Merrill opens himself to change: "So Time has—but who needs that *nom de plume*? / I've—we've modulated. We've grown autumnal, mild." He compares the Jacksons, crazy and quarrelsome but still "serenely holding hands" in old age, with his own condition: "Already I take up less emotional space than a snowdrop." We are all different selves: "Young chameleon, I used to / Ask how on earth one got sufficiently / Imbued with otherness. And now I see."

The twentieth century has destroyed what D. H. Lawrence called the old stable ego; otherness is *Mirabell's* theme, the condition of its world. Ultimately, all of one's former lives run together (MM tells JM that "AS WITH THE OLD LOVES ONE FORGETS A FEW"). No longer is the poem's form the abecedarium used in "Ephraim"; here, discreteness and repetition nod toward Ludwig Wittgenstein's decimal arrangements. There are ten chapters, numbered from 0 to 9, each with ten similarly numbered sections. The living and the dead, a great society, meet on the Ouija board, the dead spirits anchored by the living (hence the importance of Cabel Stone, the spirit Merrill contacted even before Ephraim: Stone was his first cable to the other world), who accumulate and internalize knowledge. Heaven is "BOTH REALITY AND A FIGMENT OF THE IMAGINATION," a machine that Auden says "MAKES THE DEAD AVAILABLE TO LIFE." And although JM feels he is merely a "vehicle in this cosmic carpool," he is again reminded by Auden "WHAT A MINOR / PART THE SELF PLAYS IN A WORK OF ART." Fact is fable; creation is merely the correct reception and interpretation of signals; the universe is a whole organism in which the angel Michael says, at the book's end: "GOD IS THE ACCUMULATED INTELLIGENCE IN CELLS SINCE THE DEATH OF THE FIRST DISTANT CELL. / WE RESIDE IN THAT INTELLIGENCE."

Mirabell's voices sing solo or in chorus; its technique serves its vision. "You sound like E," says JM, "maybe you are E?" To which Mirabell makes the cryptic reply: "WE ARE U YOU ARE WE EACH OTHERS DREAM." The new spirits speak in fourteeners, the older ones in decasyllables, Merrill and fellow mortals in a variety of living human speech. Who could guess that the tea-tabling opening lines—"Oh very well, then. Let us broach the matter / Of the new wallpaper in Stonington"—

would expand to major discoveries or even follow from the epigraph drawn from Laura Fermi's memoir of her husband's atomic experiments: "They were the first men to see matter yield its inner energy, steadily, at their will." The occasion for the new book is the death and burial in Athens of David Jackson's parents. Having been out of touch with Ephraim for some time, DJ and JM contact him for "sense, comfort, and wit," as compensation for loss. But the new voice intervenes, demanding "poems of science." In "The Book of Ephraim," the poet felt initially inadequate to his task; here, he positively balks at what he always considered boring and obfuscating matters. But he plunges in, asking, "Why couldn't Science, in the long run, serve / As well as one's uncleared lunch-table or / *Mme X en culotte de Matador?*" Proton and neutron become metaphors for poetry, repeating an eclogue and "orbited by twinkling flocks."

"The Book of Ephraim" took twenty years to write; the whole of *Mirabell* was composed in Stonington during the summer of 1976. The former work was prologue, long in coming; the main body is assembled in a period of intense concentration. Ephraim was the first leader, witty and frivolous because his listeners were; the new voice, initially a number and named Mirabell by the heroes halfway through, is more serious, befitting their new maturity and higher station on the ladder of spiritual perfection. Mirabell and his peers serve God Biology (there is another god named Chaos—the universe seems more Manichean or Lucretian than previously); they are fallen, for having once trifled with creation (the result was black holes), but were forgiven, and must now "WARN MAN AGAINST THE CHAOS," which began in 1934 with atomic fission and threatens the 500-million-year-old greenhouse of nature. They appear, according to the choral report of Auden, Maria, and Ephraim, as bats (the figures on Merrill's new carpet and also a skeptic's way of seeing anything as sense-defying as these spirits).

The lesson of the universe may be briefly put. God Biology is a good, although distant, force, working eugenically with a very few souls (a biological version of spiritual election) who are cloned and recloned in his Research Lab for the gradual improvement of the race. The majority of lives is animal in nature and returns to the great genetic pool for general use. Nothing has ever been lost, except the souls of people killed at Hiroshima, and there are almost no mistakes (RNA = REMEMBER NO ACCIDENTS), which troubles Merrill's liberal belief in human choice and freedom:

"All, all, it sinks in gradually, was meant / To happen, and not just the gross event. / But its minutest repercussion." Or, as Maria says of heaven: "ONE / BIG DATING COMPUTER MES ENFANTS GET WISE: / TO BE USED HERE IS THE TRUE PARADISE."

Apparent freedoms that entrap are but half the picture. As a poem of instruction, *Mirabell* both explains and dramatizes the symbiotic relationship between worlds, the accessibility of the dead to the living. Dependence is all; the main metaphor, harmony, is another word for the high hum of spiritual commerce. Mirabell is like Keats's Moneta, the priestess of history who makes futurity pastness, but he is also Merrill's creation. One is chosen to serve or to create, and Mirabell is as much JM's servant as God's. The ego is as fluid as the atom. Mind and nature are wedded, as Wordsworth announced in his own epic plans: the result is the universe as we know it, or an image of the relationship between the conscious and unconscious minds.

Just as Mirabell is an information bank, JM is the receptacle without which the angelic knowledge would lodge useless, unrealized. The role of the scribe is to speed acceptance of God's work. This is nothing new in Western literature, but Merrill emphasizes the mutuality of scribe and master. The angels lack two humanizing gifts, language and feeling. For these they depend upon the living (the bats are just a little vampirish). Metaphor may be vulgar or negative, but the alternative, within a heavenly sphere, is pure formula. Since language is of human origin, God B has no words for his own power and grace: "Who, left alone, just falls back on flimflam / Tautologies like *I am that I am* / Or *The world is everything that is the case.*" The complex mathematical truths of the angels, both frightening and incomprehensible, must be translated by the scribes into their own "vocabulary of manners." Early in the book, Mirabell, still known as 741, is granted feeling to love his translators. His own identity, and certainly his name, depend on humanization: "I HAVE ENTERED A GREAT WORLD I AM FILLED / WITH IS IT MANNERS?" Eternity, as Blake wrote, is in love with the productions of Time.

If the gift to Mirabell in this exchange is a human name, the price to his spellers is loss of individuality. Just as souls are cloned and reborn (Ephraim's system of patronage, the reader learns now, was a simplification, a fussy bureaucracy still part of God's lab), the progress toward revelation is marked by the breakdown of identity. JM and DJ merge with MM, WHA, and 741, five souls and five elements, into a psychic atom around the nucleus of the two living men. Completeness is loss of personality, as Mirabell pronounces in tones of Wallace Stevens:

JM THE STRIPPING IS THE POINT YR POEM
                    WILL PERHAPS
TAKE UP FROM ITS WINTRY END & MOVE STEP
                    BY STEP INTO
SEASONLESS AND CHARACTERLESS STAGES TO
                    ITS FINAL
GREAT COLD RINGING OF THE CHIMES
                    SHAPED AS O O O O O

Merrill wants to know why God has chosen him and Jackson, homosexuals, for his work. Why not heterosexuals like Hugo or Yeats? The answer is a tongue-in-cheek, semipornographic self-defense:

> Erection of theories, dissemination
> Of thought—the intellectual's machismo.
> We're more the docile takers-in of seed.
> No matter what tall tale our friends emit,
> Lately—you've noticed?—we just swallow it.

Homosexuality, assures Mirabell, was a late product (4,000 years ago) to encourage poetry and music. In another neat twist, Merrill realizes that this quartet was chosen because, like the spirits themselves, they are childless. Likewise, type is set backwards but appears correctly on the page. Reversion, or inversion, when set straight, is correctness, and creation is "a reasoned indirection."

The continuing fascination of Merrill's sacred books lies in observing this typesetting in process. The end of *Mirabell* readies the reader for the next volume, as he learns from Michael that Mirabell has been promoted for his instruction of JM and has been promised, like Ephraim, that he will be able to stay in touch. One may assume that in future volumes his voice will be another in the heavenly chorus. Intelligence increases; nothing is lost; enlightenment proceeds; Mirabell is replaced by Michael, "FOR HE WHO KNOWS THE MYSTERIES, IS HE NOT BEYOND THEM?" In Merrill's world, continual and surprising revelation is our anchor to sanity.

Interviews:

Ashley Brown, "An Interview with James Merrill," *Shenandoah*, 19 (Summer 1968): 3-15;

Donald Sheehan, "An Interview with James Merrill," *Contemporary Literature*, 9 (Winter 1968): 1-14;

David Kalstone, "The Poet: Private," *Saturday Review*, 55 (2 December 1972): 43-45.

References:

Morris Eaves, "Revision in James Merrill's *(Diblos) Notebook*," *Contemporary Literature*, 12 (Spring 1971): 156-165;

Richard Howard, *Alone with America   Essays on the Art of Poetry in the United States Since 1950* (New York: Atheneum, 1971), pp. 327-348;

David Kalstone, *Five Temperaments* (New York: Oxford University Press, 1977), pp. 77-128;

J. D. McClatchy, "Lost Paradises," *Parnassus*, 5 (Fall / Winter 1976): 305-320;

Judith Moffett, "Masked More and Less Than Ever: James Merrill's *Braving the Elements*," *Hollins Critic*, 10 (June 1973): 1-12;

Richard Saez, "James Merrill's Oedipal Fire," *Parnassus*, 3 (Fall/Winter 1974): 159-184;

Henry Sloss, Review of "The Book of Ephraim," *Shenandoah*, 27 (Summer 1976): 63-91;

Sloss, Review of "The Book of Ephraim," Part 2, *Shenandoah*, 28 (Fall 1976): 83-110.

W. S. MERWIN
(30 September 1927-)

SELECTED BOOKS: *A Mask for Janus* (New Haven: Yale University Press; London: Oxford University Press, 1952);

The Dancing Bears (New Haven: Yale University Press, 1954);

Green with Beasts (London: Hart-Davis, 1956; New York: Knopf, 1956);

The Drunk in the Furnace (New York: Macmillan, 1960; London: Hart-Davis, 1960);

The Moving Target (New York: Atheneum, 1963; London: Hart-Davis, 1967);

The Lice (New York: Atheneum, 1967; London: Hart-Davis, 1969);

The Carrier of Ladders (New York: Atheneum, 1970);

The Miner's Pale Children (New York: Atheneum, 1970);

Asian Figures (New York: Atheneum, 1973);

Writings to an Unfinished Accompaniment (New York: Atheneum, 1973);

The First Four Books of Poems: A Mask for Janus, The Dancing Bears, Green with Beasts, The Drunk in the Furnace (New York: Atheneum, 1975);

The Compass Flower (New York: Atheneum, 1977);

Houses and Travellers (New York: Atheneum, 1977).

William Stanley Merwin was born in New York City and grew up in Union City, New Jersey, and in Scranton, Pennsylvania. In 1947 he received an A.B. in English from Princeton University. He worked as a tutor in France, Portugal, and Majorca from 1949 to 1951, teaching Robert Graves's son in Majorca for part of that time. In 1956 and 1957 he was playwright-in-residence for the Poets' Theatre in Cambridge, Massachusetts, and in 1962 he served as poetry editor for the *Nation*. He was an associate at the Théâtre de la Cité in Lyons, France, for the term of 1964-1965.

For both his poetry and translations Merwin has received a number of awards, grants, and fellowships throughout his career, which include the following: publication of *A Mask for Janus* in the Yale Series of Younger Poets, 1952; a *Kenyon Review* fellowship, 1954; a National Institute of Arts and Letters Award, 1957; an Arts Council of Great Britain play-writing bursary, 1957; a Rabinowitz Research Fellowship, 1961; *Poetry* magazine's Bess Hokin Prize, 1962; a Ford Foundation grant, 1964; a Chapelbrook Foundation Fellowship, 1966; *Poetry*'s Harriet Monroe Memorial Prize, 1967; a National Endowment for the Arts Grant, 1968; the P.E.N. Translation Prize for *Selected Translations 1948-1968*, 1969; a Rockefeller Foundation grant, 1969; a Pulitzer Prize for *The Carrier of Ladders*, 1971; a Guggenheim Fellowship, 1973; an Academy of American Poets Fellowship, 1974; and the Shelley Memorial Award, 1974.

As can be seen from the foregoing, Merwin has earned a steady stream of formal recognition and encouragement. Since the publication of his first book of poetry in 1952, he has produced an impressive body of work, showing himself to be one of the most prolific of American poets. Yet he has presented no major critical statement on the art, or state, of contemporary poetry, and he has avoided becoming the figurehead or mentor of a new school. Indeed, he has for the most part remained in the background and has allowed his work to speak for itself. When he has come forward, it has been to discuss in general terms the nature of poetry. In his introduction to *Asian Figures* (1973), for instance, he lists what he considers to be some characteristics of poetry: a tendency toward irreducibility, immutability, and "finality of utterance." A poem is an attempt at self-containment, an attempt to develop something complete in itself. Merwin's critical comments, however, tend to be not a prescription for other poets, but a description of what he has found poetry to be.

Perhaps it is because his poetry is such a personal and private experience—and its presence

W. S. Merwin

("before words") so inherent—that he can let his poetry speak for itself and leave other poets to make their own statements. But what does his poetry say? What are some of the themes with which Merwin is concerned? Certainly, one of the themes that has held his attention from the beginning is the question of identity. In much of his earlier poetry he deals directly, and in his later poetry more subtly, with the power through which words create order and thus identity and life. Early on he is concerned, in a shamanistic sense, with the name that discloses the essence of a thing, that illuminates the thing-in-itself. In dealing with this theme, Merwin for the most part hearkens back to a time when man knew such names, and he laments the loss of this knowledge. Paralleling this flaw, and inextricably connected to it, is man's loss of intimacy with the rest of creation. Alienation, man's plight as a creature out of touch with his creatureliness, is another of Merwin's major themes. Still another, bound up in this estrangement, is the plight of the rest of creation in the face of man's alienation. Not only is man isolated, but he isolates in his drive to dominate and to use. Merwin addresses again and again the fact that humanity is not living very well either with itself or with the world around it. Yet another subject into which he delves is the craft of writing poetry, or of discovering it. For Merwin poetry is not so much what one sees on the page as what one finds in the silences behind the words; it is something preexistent to which words provide only clothing on the lowest level and only a poor, and often inaccurate, key on the highest.

In his first book, *A Mask for Janus* (1952), Merwin explores many of man's universal themes. Dressing them out in the substance of myth and presenting them in traditional prosodic forms, he deals, for example, with the concept of the birth-death-rebirth cycle, with the ideas of journey and discovery, and with the motifs of magic and belief. On first reading one is perhaps hard put to find anything new in this poetry, and the language itself seems to add to the task. Sometimes stilted and awkward, sometimes beautiful, the language hearkens back to that of Homer, and its rhythms tend to body forth the musty odor of another age and time. In spite of all signs to the contrary, though, Merwin is not in the business here of paraphrasing old tales. He is involved rather in a double process. On the one hand, he uses these tales as convenient structures for presenting his vision of the times, and in the process he links present and future to a past that many too often consider irrelevant. On the other hand, he is busy at the personal task of putting these structures

to bed, of clarifying his vision, and of finding a language peculiar to that vision.

Two significant poems in *A Mask for Janus* are "Anabasis (I)" and "Anabasis (II)." Superficially, these are poems about sea voyages that have come to an end in the stagnant, lifeless waters of a strange and

Thomas Victor

nightmarish landscape. On another level, however, they are about the individual's journey from innocence to disillusionment and death, and about mankind's journey from the innocence and order of myth and legend to the mythless disorder of the present day. They speak of losing touch with God, with that which can anchor man and give him order. Man is caught in dire straits, and the mechanics alone of religion will not bring him out. There is no salvation unless one can fully believe, but one cannot believe, the poems say, except perhaps through the delusions of an old man's sleep. The bleak message of these poems is that man has been sentenced to drift aimlessly toward death. Then he will lose what little identity time has left to him, even "The uncertain continent of a name." "Carol of the Three Kings"

66

provides a contrast. It has a simple beauty, presented as though narrated by one of the magi. With its positive tone of adoration, it indicates that Merwin's vision is diverse enough to overcome the bog and mire of nihilism. It is not a mawkish poem; it does not fall into sentimentality; even though the subject, the nativity of Christ, is loaded with potential for such a flaw. The poem is clear and direct, and it indicates, even at this early stage in his career, the wide range and flexibility of Merwin's sensitivity.

The Dancing Bears (1954) is notable not only for the beauty of its language but also for the apparent facility with which he turns old myth to new uses. Of special interest are three poems, each entitled "Canso," and a fourth entitled "East of the Sun and West of the Moon," where Merwin uses the basic story of Psyche and Cupid as a vehicle for discussing the questions of belief, order, and identity. It is a story of love between a peasant girl and a prince, who, until the spell is broken, can appear to his love only as a white bear. Of course the spell is eventually lifted and the lovers are united, but until this happens they know each other only incompletely in a world that is unchanging and therefore unreal. It is a world in which nothing is what it seems. All is lifeless in a "perfect," prefabricated existence where neither life nor love can be effective because both must evolve from life that is by its nature imperfect.

The key line in the poem is "All metaphor . . . is magic." Metaphors, or signs, give meaning and order, and therefore life. The meanings of the poem are multifold, but three are especially significant. The first is that life can thrive only where it can also fail to thrive; death is life's natural counterpart. The second point, which is expressed clearly in the last line of the poem, is that creation, for all practical purposes, has no existence, no meaning, apart from the existence of man. The third is that man's identity depends on the mask he chooses, the mask in which he can believe. In focusing to an identity, the mask limits what is shown of the multifarious being behind it, and in this sense it hides something. But as it simplifies this same variety into an essential identity with which one can live, the mask unmasks meaning. Man's identity then, to borrow the title from Merwin's first book, is "a mask for Janus." It both hides and discloses and, in the process, makes life possible.

In *Green with Beasts* (1956), Merwin seems to have found a new power. Instead of using ready-made myths to weave relatively tame narratives that give the reader only a spectator's role, Merwin is now, in some of these poems, weaving his own myths in which the reader is more a part of the fabric. In

these poems, too, he brings the reader face to face with the mystery that surrounds him: the world and his place in it. This result is due partially to the mechanics of the poetry: the concrete imagery, the incantatory repetition, and sometimes the juxtaposition of concrete "things" with an insistence on their abstract nature. These elements, as used in "Leviathan" or in "The Prodigal Son," draw the reader into the poem and tend to hold him fixated until the poem ends. This heightened involvement is further enhanced in some cases by the nature of the subject matter itself, which often comes from the Judeo-Christian tradition. Here Merwin gives new life to stories with which many readers have grown up, stories that have grown stale, because all they could give has been drained by years of interpretation.

In "The Prodigal Son" and in "The Annunciation," for instance, the poet takes two familiar stories and creates an air of awe and wonder. In the first poem the imagery and the repeated insistence on "emptiness," "distance," and "waiting" lures the reader by degrees into experiencing the dreamlike aridity and the unmoving pain of loss and separation. The resultant expectancy of the son's returning home is so overwhelming by the end of the poem that the last line provides a cathartic release. Merwin creates a nearly objective atmosphere in "The Prodigal Son" and involves the reader to an extent that would be intolerable without this release.

In "The Annunciation," the speaker tells about the mystical experience she has had as if she were speaking directly to the reader. It becomes clear as the reader attends to her story, as he becomes absorbed in it, that she is trying to tell of something so beyond her daily experience that she cannot put it into words. The language is colloquial, and the story is told with the repetition, backtracking, and layering-on of imagery that are commonly part of any effort by one human to express the ineffable to another. The reader is drawn in precisely by this difficulty she is having in telling her story. Presumably God has no such trouble in communicating, for between God and man there is a directness of relationship that not only refuses to yield to words but also makes them unnecessary. After an experience such as the speaker's, one is left with wonder at having known something more real than that which he sees around him. It is as if a dream were so real, so immediate, as to make the waking world seem dreamlike. This is the situation of the speaker in "The Annunciation," and the only "name" she will find for her experience is living itself. He to whom she will give birth is the expression of, is the "word" for, her experience.

Other poems from *Green with Beasts* are also significant. "The Mountain," "Backwater Pond: the Canoeists," and "Tobacco" bring to bear different aspects of Merwin's whimsical sense of humor, while "White Goat, White Ram" and "Dog," among other poems, show Merwin's drive to shake the reader out of complacency by giving him new perspectives on a world that he has, apparently mistakenly, thought to be familiar. Further, Merwin often pays homage to simplicity and to quiet determination, as in "The Station," "In the Heart of Europe," and "The Fishermen." Finally, "Learning a Dead Language" provides instruction for pursuing the poet's craft; Merwin sees poetry as something that exists even before it is given words, and this poem is about learning to be in touch with the mystical "language" that gives true meaning.

Of the poems in *The Drunk in the Furnace* (1960), the first dozen are about the sea. By and large the sea is presented as threatening and awesome; there is nothing relaxing or rejuvenating about a voyage on the open sea. Such a voyage, to the contrary, is fraught with imminent peril. If the voyager does not go down to his death, as in "The Portland Going Out," if it is not a matter of sons, fathers, and brothers being lost, as in "Sea Wife," then perhaps it is a matter of spiritual or mental loss, of being so bewitched by the sea that the voyager knows neither where he is going nor why, as is the case in "Odysseus." Or perhaps the sea takes such a hold on him, as in "Sailor Ashore," that the voyager is drawn back into its treacherous maw by the illusion that being on land provides less safety from the sea than being on the sea itself. Even man's attempts at ruling the sea, at safeguarding himself against its treachery, seem to turn on him, seem to create meanings that he does not feel at home with. In "Fog-horn" and in "Bell Buoy," for example, these two manmade devices have been in some way confiscated by the sea and have become alien to man. Rather than putting him at ease, the "fog-horns" and "bell buoys" he devises to keep nature at bay are by nature assimilated and turned against him. These devices then usher him, contrary to his plans, toward the something he has been trying to escape. It could be that this something is menacing, that man cannot survive a meeting with it. It could also be that such a meeting would mean greater life. Whatever the case, these poems suggest that man cannot know the outcome. What he can know is that he is alienated from this something, and all life itself seems to pull him toward it, seems eager to reclaim him.

In *The Drunk in the Furnace* as a whole, man is given rather short shrift. For the most part, he has little more than petty, bigoted, and self-serving motives for his actions. "Fable" is a telescopic view of man's malice toward man and of man's rationalization for his actions. All of the poems about relatives, with the exception of "Grandmother Watching at the Window," depict narrow and unpleasant people. In the one exception where love is admitted, it is clear that the love brings a heavy price—loss and pain. There is a cynicism here, as also in the title poem, in "Grandfather in the Old Men's Home," and in others, that compares with the cynicism of Mark Twain. It is almost a bitterness over the starvation of spirit and the small-minded heavy-handedness that characterize the narrowly religious. There is also in this bleak vision, as presented in "Small Woman in Swallow Street" and in "The Native," a resounding disgust over the debasement to which man so often succumbs. If *Green with Beasts* takes the reader toward a heaven, whether external or internal, then *The Drunk in the Furnace* takes him into a hell and offers little hope of getting out.

With *The Moving Target* (1963), Merwin begins a new journey, a more personal journey through pain and disorder. It is as if he has run head-on into the alienation of self, into the vapid chaos of false identity, of prefab identity, which holds man dangling in meaninglessness. There is a clearer effort here to discover the self and to lay it open, to see if the heart really ticks or only pretends to. There is despair, poignant because it is presented with such an air of intimacy and with no pretense to knowing the answers that each must find for himself. Finally, there is a new style, given more to allusion and to personal symbols.

In "Acclimatization," as with most of the poems in this book, speaker, poet, and reader share a common plight, a common question. In this world, in this society and time, in which dehumanization is prevalent, what does man have that is essentially him? If he has offered himself to the faceless "them" of "Acclimatization," he has done so thinking, in his naivete, that the return would compensate for loss of self. The speaker of the poem has found out too late that it will not. He has been acclimatized to "the empire," and in the process he has lost the means for living outside of it. "They" gave him their empty rewards, welcomed him into their fold, and took his self-sufficiency, his wholeness, his dignity. Even the ability to cry, the most elemental form of complaint, is denied him and is replaced by a fake and useless eye. The poem ends on this sinister note with no indication that relief is forthcoming.

About two-thirds of the way through the book,

"To Dana For Her Birthday," manuscript

beginning with "The Crossroads of the World etc.," the obscurity of the poetry becomes nearly impenetrable. Before this point Merwin has already used such private emblems as "mirror," "bell," "hand," and "stone," but he has presented them in a relatively straightforward, logically sequential language (as in "Second Sight" and "Bread and Butter"). Now the rhythms become choppy and discordant, and there is no punctuation to prepare the reader for the sudden changes in line of thought. The imagery is surrealist, created by forcing together elements that in daily usage are incompatible.

The world, interior as well as exterior, that Merwin presents in "The Crossroads of the World etc." is one of spiritual alienation and loss of contact with the life-giving meanings of past, present, and future. Further, it is a world in which the self has become disoriented. Man is shut off from himself, and the future is only emptiness, denoted by the pointlessness of throwing food into "empty cages." There is no place for him in the future; the present, "talking to itself," passes him by; and the past is an enigma of locked "dead doors" for which he has no key. Even his shadow, which should declare his substantiality, has deserted him. The shadow—identity, self—is a "lost garment" separated from its owner, and the poem expresses no hope that the shadow can ever be reclaimed.

Perhaps Merwin is merely trying to shock the reader into action. While most of the poems in the latter third of the book speak in the flat tones of despair and hopelessness, the last two poems, "Spring" and "Daybreak," speak of a resurrection of hope. In the first, the speaker promises an "answer" and light ("There's light in my shoes"). In the second, the locked doors have been replaced by "An open doorway." Such positiveness does not deny the truth of the more pessimistic vision, but it indicates a need to stand back from the battle. "Spring" and "Daybreak" provide a rest.

While in *The Moving Target* Merwin struggles with the torment of alienation from self, in *The Lice* (1967) he seems to resign himself, albeit uneasily, to this alienation. Here the question, quite often, concerns man's relationship to the rest of creation and the irresponsibility he has shown in this relationship. In poem after poem ("The Gods," "Fly," "December Night," "The Finding of Reasons," and "The Last One," to mention a few) Merwin exposes callousness, self-importance, self-deception, and abuse of power. "For a Coming Extinction" speaks in a chillingly sardonic tone of the rapacious gluttony with which man is driving his fellow creatures to extinction. The irony is that

man sees this shameful devastation as an index of his importance. He thinks he rules, although in truth it is not a matter of ruling or of dominating. For modern man, survival is a question of mothering, of husbandry.

In "The Finding of Reasons" man is depicted as having misused his talents, his gifts, so that they desert him. He blindly feeds his own doom. In "The Last One" the outrage reaches such a peak that nature can stand it no longer. In a steadily rising crescendo of terror, the shadow of the last tree turns on him and devours him. The shadow, of course, is the night man brings upon himself. In "The Gods" and in "December Night," man is dispossessed. The earth is not his, and it can go on without him. The "single prayer" that nature offers makes no mention of him.

Although the situation seems exceedingly desperate, the desperation becomes a little less emphatic when Merwin focuses on himself. Mankind as a whole is an overwhelming subject. The picture is too grand; it obscures the little things, and it is the little things that give rise to hope. "For the Anniversary of My Death" and "Looking for Mushrooms at Sunrise" at least imply that hope is possible. Speaking out of an intimacy that says the reader is not alone, these poems are important because they point up one man's sensitivity. Mankind may be cruel and unfeeling, but mankind as a being does not exist. Individuals exist, and although many are insensitive, some are not. Only in such knowledge as this can hope grow.

In *The Carrier of Ladders* (1970), one sees the burgeoning of a greater maturity. In *The Lice* there were two distinct voices: the broad, loudspeaker voice screaming the foibles of mankind and the seemingly quieter voice that expresses Merwin's own personal bewilderment. In *The Carrier of Ladders* these voices are merged; the realization has come home that mankind is oneself. As in "Night Wind" and in "Midnight in Early Spring," it is no longer a matter of "us-and-them," but only of "us." These two poems, together, suggest that something beyond man calls him home, or awaits his return, awaits the completion of his grief. In spite of himself it will free him, will answer the prayer he can neither ask nor remember, the prayer that time must have held hidden. Salvation is out of his hands, and his blindness is so enrooted that, without help, he will not even know why the salvation is granted. There is the possibility, implied in "Midnight in Early Spring," that the entire game may be played from beginning to end without his ever having known the rules or the goal.

In "Psalm: Our Fathers" Merwin more directly avows his share in the life of man, in the dark complexity of being human. The "I" of the poem is each reader, Merwin included. All share an inheritance that cannot be shed, for any attempt to deny it in any one respect means a fulfillment of it in another. Life is an enigma, a glass both empty and full, a room both dark and light, and the only true denial would be the denial of life as a whole, death inclusive. This, though, is not permitted. What man has is all he has, and although he has not chosen it, he is stuck with it; there is nothing else to choose. One may not have chosen to be, may tell himself that he is not, "the son of love," but one cannot escape it as fact, any more than one can escape being brother to the "hangmen." "Psalm: Our Fathers" is a powerful hymn rooted firmly in this realization.

How far the integration has gone may be seen in less comprehensive poems such as "The Old Room" and "The Removal." The first poem, spoken in the first person, is about the futility of trying to deny involvement in the slaughter of the Jews. All the speaker of the poem can say is, "It is not me," but by making this weak disclaimer he, by default, casts his vote with the murderers and increases the number of the dead. Either he accepts with full being the heinous nature of such humanity or he shares in its creation. Every breath that does not work to prevent its recurrence works to bring it about. It is because of this and because all are in the same boat, says Merwin, that the guilt must sit among man and a share of the pain must be his.

In the second poem, "The Removal," which presents in poignant vignettes the victimization of the American Indian, Merwin alternates between first and third person points of view. In the first and fifth segments the Indians tell their own story, and it is the reader's story as well. He is made to experience the Indians' degradation, their dispossession. In the other segments, told in the third person, the distance between the reader and the victim leaves the reader in the uncomfortable role of spectator, of persecutor. With an eloquence and rhythm of speech that seem directly derived from Indian oratory, Merwin convinces the reader that he has, at the very least, allowed the devastation. In the last segment he even brings about guilty relief at no longer having to face the victim.

Clearly, with *The Carrier of Ladders* Merwin has come more to grips with the burden of life. The realizations that make for maturity have somewhat tempered the ambitions of youth. Like the speakers in "The Piper" and "Envoy from D'Aubigne," Merwin has become more aware of his limits, more

in touch with his true needs. Such awareness makes possible the childlike gentleness of "Little Horse," the powerful irony of "The Judgment of Paris," and the self-universalization of "The Forbears," of "The Old Room," of "Psalm: Our Fathers."

In *Writings to an Unfinished Accompaniment* (1973), Merwin peers deeper into the heart of his quest, a quest for the source that gives life and meaning. Perhaps because this search leads into that which is nameless and timeless, many of these poems achieve an obscurity, a density, that is exceedingly formidable. They are laden with a symbolism that is for the most part private to Merwin and with an imagery that is often misleading. Yet one begins to see that in his use of imagery Merwin is laboring to make his vision fresh and immediate, rather than merely to tell about it. In order to do this he must disorient the reader, must shake him out of his old habits of seeing to give him a new way of knowing the world and himself. In one poem after another, Merwin succeeds in jarring the reader loose from his moorings, whether the theme is the end of man, man's search for home, for union, for completion, man's bondage to time and division, or the tyranny of habit. In "Habits," in which Habit is personified, Merwin presents a chilling view on this latter theme. Man is so parceled out by his habits that the only self he has is a discordant concoction that obscures and discards the true self. The speaker is dismembered by his habits. They take his eyes, his ears, and his "tongues" and feed him their view of reality. The irony is in the speaker's feeble attempt to deny that habit has a hold on him while he admits that it shapes his ability to perceive. In fact habit is so powerful that even occasional vision of its deadening effect, of its link by little deaths to man's final death, brings too little impetus to overcome it. In "Habits" Merwin laments the habit-bound nature of life. In contrast to the pessimism of this poem, "A Door" (the fourth of four poems with this title) presents some hope. This poem is about the hardening of heart common to a technological age. It is also about the day of darkness when all communication of feeling and need will seem to have died, when no comfort will be forthcoming from fellow humans. Although "A Door" creates an atmosphere of near despair, in its last lines there is hope expressed in the statement that even in such straits, even in the pervasive droning of division, someone will be in touch with "a silence" and may hear the voice calling him home.

In other poems, too, such as "The Way Ahead" and "A Purgatory," there is hope expressed, although obliquely. The first of these two poems is a prophecy of devastation followed by the coming of "a light." The first two stanzas imply that, when man is the only creature left, some of mankind (who have not known their true purpose before) will be recast, reconditioned, to prepare them for the new vision. As the poem unfolds, it is stated that nature has "wanted" this "new light" and is prepared for it. Also, the poem implies that man has wanted it, although probably unwittingly—knowing that he hungered, but not for what food. Neither does Merwin say just what this "new light" will mean nor of what it will consist, but he implies that man was made for it, that it will bring him home. In "A Purgatory," also, the coming of clear vision is proclaimed. This purgatory, which is probably earthly life, means a consignment to perception that is continually shifting until one finally sees. Man pursues a vision that is elusive and that persists in sinking away into the shadows. His yearning for it grows from emptiness and despair and out of the futility of thwarted communication. It may be, however, that Merwin is speaking of a search that will begin in some afterlife. The final implication is that the search cannot stop until "the eye . . . sees."

In *The Compass Flower* (1977), Merwin's most recent book of poems, the poet strikes a mellower note. No longer is he so stridently chastising, although it is clear that he has not lost a sense of man's plight. "The Heart," "The Estuary," "Vision," "Robin," and "The Helmsmen," for example, show man consigned to darkness, or at least to semidarkness. Merwin still perceives man as moved and preserved by an unknown power, although man would like to believe in his freedom. This insistent focus on man's own value as a supposedly independent being becomes laughable (and pitiable) when one considers his desperate attempts at communication and the fact that he cannot, or will not, communicate fully with others ("The Helmsman"), much less with the unknown ("Vision"). Merwin has not lost sight of this situation, but it is less a matter of concern in this volume of poems. Instead of pounding endlessly on a door that seems forever locked, he has gone out by another that is always open.

This new passage has led to an imagery and focus reminiscent of classical Chinese poetry in its seemingly simple and direct portrayal of life. For the most part, he has discarded his private emblems, and he has apparently realized that the mystery of life is best told by telling life itself. He has reached a plateau of freedom from which he can express wonder without the ambivalence or cynicism often apparent in his earlier work. In such poems as "The Shuttles," "The Love for October," "Spring Equinox Full Moon," "On the Mountain," "Summer Doorway," and "Kore," he unabashedly celebrates life and love. In "Guardians" even fear, as a necessary adjunct to life, is honored and accepted. Indeed, acceptance is the keynote for many of these poems.

"Kore," a poem of twenty-four segments, each headed by a letter of the Greek alphabet, is a paean to the timelessness of life and love, both of which are as fully able to be experienced now as ever they were. "Kore" is a simple love poem, ostensibly addressed to a specific person, but the poem is also more universal than that. *Kore* is a Greek term meaning "maiden," usually applied to prototypical statues of the female form from the archaic period of ancient Greece. Rather than representing a particular person, these statues were apparently made as celebrations of feminine youth and beauty in general. In ancient Attica the name given to Persephone, whose periodic return from the underworld marked the end of winter and the rejuvenation of the earth, was also Kore. In Merwin's poem it is noteworthy that Kore is absent from her lover "in the flowerless month of the door god"—that is, January—and that she causes a stirring in the veins of trees. The loved one in this poem is the spirit of life, of periodic rebirth, and is also the unchanging spirit of the past, a primum mobile, that is here in the present. In other words, this spirit links past, present, and future, and Merwin here proclaims himself in touch with it, with the source and force of life. "Kore" brings to the fore Merwin's sense of the beauty and sanctity of life. More than this, "Kore" rejuvenates man's own yearning to be fully in touch with that which completes him.

From the first of his career as a poet, Merwin has steeped himself in other cultures and other literary traditions, and he has been praised as a translator. This eclectic background has given him a sense of the presence of the past, of timelessness in time, that comes across emphatically in his poetry. Without some understanding of this background the reader cannot fully appreciate Merwin's poetry. Moreover, without such appreciation one cannot comprehend the thrust of Merwin's poetic and philosophical development. He has come a long journey to reach the point at which he can say as he does in "Gift" (from *Writings to an Unfinished Accompaniment*), that one has to trust in what is given to him if he is to trust in anything.

—*Eric Hartley*

Translations:

The Poem of the Cid (London: Dent, 1959; New York: Las Americas, 1959; New York: New American Library, 1962);

Some Spanish Ballads (London, New York & Toronto: Abelard-Schuman, 1961); republished as *Spanish Ballads* (Garden City: Doubleday, 1961);

The Satires of Persius (Bloomington: Indiana University Press, 1961);

The Life of Lazarillo de Tormes (Garden City: Doubleday, 1962);

Sebastien-Roche Nicolas Chamfort, *Products of the Perfected Civilization* (New York: Macmillan, 1969);

Jean Follain, *The Transparence of the World* (New York: Atheneum, 1969);

Pablo Neruda, *Twenty Poems of Love and a Song of Despair* (London: Cape, 1969);

Antonio Prochia, *Voices* (Chicago: Big Table, 1969);

Selected Translations 1948-1968 (New York: Atheneum, 1969);

The Song of Roland (New York: Random House, 1970);

Osip Mandelstam, *Selected Poems* (London, Melbourne & Toronto: Oxford University Press, 1973; New York: Atheneum, 1974);

Pablo Neruda, 1904-1973, ed. Nathaniel Tarn, translated by Merwin and others (New York: Dell, 1973);

Sanskrit Love Poetry, translated by Merwin and J. Moussaieff Masson (New York: Columbia University Press, 1977);

Euripides, *Iphigenia at Aulis*, translated by Merwin and George E. Dimock, Jr. (New York: Oxford University Press, 1978);

Selected Translations, 1968-1978 (New York: Atheneum, 1979).

References:

Kenneth Anderson, "The Poetry of W. S. Merwin," *Twentieth Century Literature*, 16 (1970): 278-286;

James Atlas, "Diminishing Returns: The Writings of W. S. Merwin," in *American Poetry Since 1950—Some Critical Perspectives*, ed. Robert B. Shaw (Chester Springs, Pa.: Dufour, 1974), pp. 69-81;

Alice N. Benston, "Myth in the Poetry of W. S. Merwin," *Poets in Progress*, [23] (1962): 179-204;

Cheri C. Davis, "Radical Innocence: A Thematic Study of the Relationship Between the Translator and the Translated in the Poetry of W. S. Merwin and Jean Follain," Ph.D. dissertation, University of Southern California, 1973;

Davis, "Merwin's Odysseus," *Concerning Poetry*, 8 (1975): 25-33;

Davis, "Time and Timelessness in the Poetry of W. S. Merwin," *Modern Poetry Studies*, 6 (1975): 224-236;

William Frawley, "Merwin's Unpunctuated Verse," *Notes on Contemporary Literature*, 7 (1977): 2-3;

Lucy Frost, "The Poetry of W. S. Merwin: An Introductory Note," *Meanjin*, 30 (1971): 294-296;

Jan B. Gordon, "The Dwelling of Disappearance: W. S. Merwin's *The Lice*," *Modern Poetry Studies*, 3 (1972): 119-138;

Harvey Gross, "The Writing on the Void: The Poetry of W. S. Merwin," *Iowa Review*, 1 (1970): 92-106;

Richard Howard, *Alone with America Essays on the Art of Poetry in the United States Since 1950* (New York: Atheneum, 1969), pp. 349-381;

H. T. Kirby-Smith, Jr., "Miss Bishop and Others," *Sewanee Review*, 80 (1972): 483-493;

Anthony Libby, "W. S. Merwin and the Nothing That Is," *Contemporary Literature*, 16 (1975): 19-40;

Daniel Liberthson, *The Quest for Being: Theodore Roethke, W. S. Merwin, and Ted Hughes* (New York: Gordon, 1977);

Laurence Lieberman, "The Church of Ash," in *Contemporary Poetry in America: Essays and Interviews*, ed. Robert Boyers (New York: Schocken Books, 1974), pp. 256-266;

Frank MacShane, "A Portrait of W. S. Merwin," *Shenandoah*, 21 (1970): 3-14;

William J. Martz, *Distinctive Voice: Twentieth Century American Poetry* (Glenview, Ill.: Scott, Foresman, 1966);

Richard E. Messer, "W. S. Merwin's Use of Myth," *Publications of the Arkansas Philological Association*, 1 (1975): 41-48;

Cary Nelson, "The Resources of Failure: W. S. Merwin's Deconstructive Career," *Boundary 2*, 5 (1977): 573-598;

Theodore K. Quinn, "W. S. Merwin: A Study in Poetry and Film," Ph.D. dissertation, University of Iowa, 1973;

Jarold Ramsey, "The Continuities of W. S. Merwin: 'What Has Escaped Us We Bring with Us,'" *Massachusetts Review*, 14 (1973): 569-590;

Thomas P. Roche, Jr., "Green with Poems," *Princeton University Library Chronicle*, 25 (1963): 89-104;

Vern Rutsala, "The End of the Owls: W. S. Merwin, *The Lice*," *Far Point*, 2 (1969): 40-44;

Reed Sanderlin, "Merwin's 'The Drunk in the Furnace,' " *Contemporary Poetry*, 2 (1975): 24-27;

Henriette Seyffert, "Three Contemporary Translator-Poets: W. S. Merwin, W. Barnstone and J. Wright," Ph.D. dissertation, Indiana University, 1971;

Brian Swann, "The Poetry of W. S. Merwin: *The Carrier of Ladders*," *Annalidi Cá Foscari*, 12 (1973): 135-147;

John Vogelsang, "Toward the Great Language: W. S. Merwin," *Modern Poetry Studies*, 3 (1972): 97-118;

Evan Watkins, "W. S. Merwin: A Critical Accompaniment," *Boundary 2*, 4 (1975): 187-199.

HOWARD MOSS
(22 January 1922-)

BOOKS: *The Wound and the Weather* (New York: Reynal & Hitchcock, 1946);

The Toy Fair (New York: Scribners, 1954);

A Swimmer in the Air (New York: Scribners, 1957);

A Winter Come, A Summer Gone: Poems 1946-1960 (New York: Scribners, 1960);

The Magic Lantern of Marcel Proust (New York: Macmillan, 1962; London: Faber & Faber, 1963);

Finding Them Lost and Other Poems (New York: Scribners, 1965; London: Macmillan, 1965);

Second Nature (New York: Atheneum, 1968);

Writing Against Time: Critical Essays and Reviews (New York: Morrow, 1969);

Selected Poems (New York: Atheneum, 1971);

Chekhov (New York: Albondocani Press, 1972);

Travel: A Window (New York: Albondocani Press, 1973);

Instant Lives (New York: Saturday Review Press / Dutton, 1974);

Buried City (New York: Atheneum, 1975);

A Swim Off the Rocks (New York: Atheneum, 1976);

Tigers and Other Lilies (New York: Atheneum, 1977);

Notes from the Castle (New York: Atheneum, 1979);

Critical Conditions (New York: Atheneum, forthcoming 1980);

The Palace at 4 A.M. and The Folding Green (New York: Flying Point Press, forthcoming 1980).

Poet, critic, editor, satirist, and playwright, Howard Moss has established himself as one of the most important figures in American letters during the second half of the twentieth century. In his wide-ranging critical essays, from his editorial office at the *New Yorker*, and throughout his generally traditional volumes of poetry, his practice and opinion have provided a benchmark in creativity for poets for over three decades.

Howard Moss was born in New York City and grew up in Rockaway Beach in the borough of Queens. His parents were David Leonard and Sonya Schrag Moss; his father immigrated to the United States from Lithuania. Moss attended the University of Michigan in Ann Arbor from 1939-1940; but he transferred to the University of Wisconsin in Madison in 1940 and received his B.A. from there in 1944. His other formal education included a summer at Harvard University in 1942 and postgraduate work at Columbia University in New York in 1946.

After college, Moss worked for one year (1944) for *Time* magazine, first as copyboy and then as book reviewer. From 1944 to 1946 he was an instructor in English at Vassar College in Poughkeepsie, New York. After one year as fiction editor of *Junior Bazaar*, Moss joined the editorial staff of the *New Yorker* in 1948, and in 1950 he became poetry editor there, a position he still holds. In 1957 and 1964 he served as a judge for the National Book Awards. Also, he has been an adjunct professor of English, in 1975 at Barnard College in New York and in 1977 at Columbia University.

Moss's poetry has been highly acclaimed. In 1944 *Poetry* magazine awarded him the Janet Sewall David Award. In 1968 he won an award from the National Institute of Arts and Letters, and he received a grant from the Ingram Merrill Foundation in 1972, the same year in which he received the National Book Award for his *Selected Poems*. He is a member of P.E.N., the Authors Guild, and the National Institute of Arts and Letters. He has served as a judge for the Brandeis University creative awards and the University of Michigan Avery Hopwood Awards.

His first book, *The Wound and the Weather* (1946), was published when he was only twenty-four. Like most first books by young poets, this volume received mixed critical attention. The poems exhibit a range of successes and weaknesses. Generally, the poems are strict, formal, and regular; the language ranges from stiff or static to accomplished and smooth. Even in these early works, Moss shows that he is able to turn a sonnet without falling prey to its rhythm. However, at other times the syntax becomes wrenched to accommodate a form or a rhyme. The poems exhibit throughout a skillful consistency of metaphor (as in "The Frozen Lake"); they present a set of images that are often startling and unique ("Such movement could erase Manhattan"); they carry a mature feeling for wit, both in rhyme (such as *hosanna/cabana* in "Waterwall Blues") and in context (*bed/bored* in "An Answer Questioned"). What undercuts the full success of *The Wound and the Weather*, however, is the tendency of some of the language to echo the all-too-familiar, for whatever the reason (as in a line from "Around the Fish: After Paul Klee," "Waiting, the Fisher King sat down. . . ."). Likewise, there is an occasional passage that shows too clearly the hand of some influence, as in these lines, ringing of Wallace Stevens, from "Waterwall Blues": "the spinster tree / Unwound its green hosanna." Also, Moss has a tendency in these poems to rely upon abstraction, as in these lines from "The Shore Remembered":

he could not foretell
What innocence confounds the sea; for this no opiate,
No predatory wish, no magic lance,
But the darkling single diver finding hell.

Strangely enough, however, it is this use of abstraction that precipitates one of the major strengths of *The Wound and the Weather*, for Moss attempts to redeem the abstract through unusual or startling language and contexts. The results are mixed; and there are attendant difficulties of personification, as in "the flying earth / Impatient for entombment" ("Death of a Grandmother"). Nevertheless, the effects can be powerful; such lines as "Rejecting you, the weather and the house / Have myths to finish" ("The Arrow") and "A skull is therefore Mexico" ("A Portrait") indicate an understanding of the judicious use of the surreal.

In various ways *The Wound and the Weather* anticipates subsequent volumes. The settings of the poems range from the Midwest with its frozen lakes, to the ocean, to New York City with its buildings and crowds and alleys. The subjects treated are mundane, such as airplane travelers; classical, such as *Othello*; and traditional, especially death, which seems to be the preoccupation of the last third of the volume. Finally, the poems propose a wistfulness—a desire to escape the city, to belong to the open land and its animal populations, a longing to return to the ease of childhood, and a wish for freedom from such human escapades as war and such necessities as death.

Layle Silbert

Howard Moss

In his second volume, *The Toy Fair* (1954), Moss continues in the directions signaled by *The Wound and the Weather*. For the most part, the lines remain iambic; the language continues to be wry, clever, witty; the content is intellectual. The landscapes are also the same here, with the notable exception of a few pieces, such as "Bermuda" and "Venice." The wistfulness continues. What makes these poems more successful, though, is technique. In *The Toy Fair* the lines flow more smoothly; the language proceeds easily, rhythmically, yet without the dominating insistence of the rhythm. In short, Moss has learned to control the rhythms. The result of this progress is what Howard Nemerov called "one of the most accomplished collections of lyric poetry to appear since the war" (*Atlantic Monthly*, September 1954).

There is also an emotional maturing evident in *The Toy Fair*. Abstractions notwithstanding, Moss is able to survey his universe, see it objectified in "A Gothic, empty skyscraper, / Sad as a winter roller coaster" ("Cry from Montauk"), and still be able to note that "Love is the only place we live." In the finely drawn "Animal Hospital," he employs the short line (iambic trimeter) and quick rhymes to link sound and meaning more skillfully; and in the end the reader is convinced that "All loss is human then, / Even animal pain." This understanding of the meaning of human loss, however, is just another aspect of love; and Moss confronts this subject fully in perhaps the finest poem in the volume—and certainly one of his most frequently anthologized pieces—"Elegy for My Father." A mixture of grief, guilt, loss, and impotence, the poem offers no easy incantations; the final vision is of the "whirling vacuum" of death's waters. However, by the end of the volume, in "Venice," he asks, "Is it true, we think, our sorry otherness / Is to fall in love with beasts whose beauty ruins us?" The answer given is one of growth and understanding: "Those beasts are everywhere, though Venice says / Lions to be golden must be painted gold."

A Swimmer in the Air (1957) shows Moss's continuing progress as a poet, in both theme and style. As is indicated in the opening poem, "A Summer Gone," he is concerned with the passing of time, obviously related to death and change. The stuff of these poems is, again, drawn from "everyday" life: marriage, animals, rain. As in the first two books, the poems are witty, often elegant, generally sophisticated, and well crafted. Moss exhibits an unabated love for wordplay, as in "Horror Movie." But in the "serious" poems—not those, as Donald Justice (*Poetry*, October 1957) points out, in which the wit "disintegrates into a willfully cute fooling around with the sounds of words"—his lyric gift lends itself to the successful treatment of the book's major themes and subjects: the memories of a summer at the seaside; love, the need to feel, and the knowledge that those "Who give love freely may all things receive" ("The Falls of Love"); and the certainty of death, the dominant impression of "A Winter Come."

In a column for the *American Poetry Review* (March-April 1979), Moss states that "Conscience and consciousness are the two great subjects of literature. That's why murder and love are so omnipresent." His own poems do not deal so much with murder as he might indicate; however, they do focus to a large extent upon love in its various forms. Therefore, it is not surprising that his fourth book, *A Winter Come, A Summer Gone: Poems 1946-1960* (1960), is dominated by poems of love. Representing what Moss selected as his best work from the three previous volumes, these poems embody the characteristics that have come to be associated with his poetry. As Karl Malkoff points out, Moss "sees

connections between the human universe and the cosmos as a whole; [and] he depends upon wit and intellect rather than spontaneous rhythms to perceive underlying harmonies." Including only six poems from *The Wound and the Weather*, but sampling more generously from the other two collections, Moss has brought together poems that are elaborate and urbane, essentially written in a high style; the best of them are nostalgic and musical; the weakest of them are those predicated on wryness and wit. Considering the volume for the *Yale Review* (Autumn 1960), Thom Gunn calls some of the poems "slickness or empty gesturing," but he finds others "modest and moving" and adds that some of Moss's poetry is "superior to that of most of the rest of his generation." Most of the weaker inclusions are the earlier poems. In addition to the previously published poems, Moss has included fourteen new poems. In these more recent pieces he shows an increased willingness to stretch fixed forms so that, while still continuing with essentially the same themes and sources, his technique has become sharper. Also, among these new poems is the long poem "King Midas," which was set to music as a song cycle by Ned Rorem in 1961. Throughout this and most of the other poems, the poet is nostalgic, singing of things lost and of love.

It is evident from the title of his next book— *Finding Them Lost and Other Poems* (1965)—what direction the poems will take. Certainly, earlier poems have treated the sense of loss and deprivation, but from the first line of the first poem here, Moss sets a dominant tone: "Finally, from your house, there is no view." The vision is limited and apocalyptic; the dominant sets of images are those of light and darkness, of stillness and motion, of life and death (culminating in the fine translation of Paul Valery's "Le Cimitiere Marin"). Yet, despite the sense of loss, the vision of the apocalyptic seems almost optimistic. In "The Pruned Tree," the narrator says, "Shorn, I rejoice in what was taken from me." Likewise, "September Elegy," despite the bleakness of its title, posits the optimistic note that "the water birds / Depart, but some things never disappear." It is a measured and mature understanding of the rhythms of the universe—mirrored in the sea that Moss is repeatedly drawn to, the sea that beckons to him and Valery beyond the confines of the cemetery—that enables him to know that "on two crossed sticks, on stone, / By thorn or beak, in anguish, Gods are born" ("At the Fire Fountain"); and the same knowledge allows him to recognize that "in time, the dead start growing" ("The Silences").

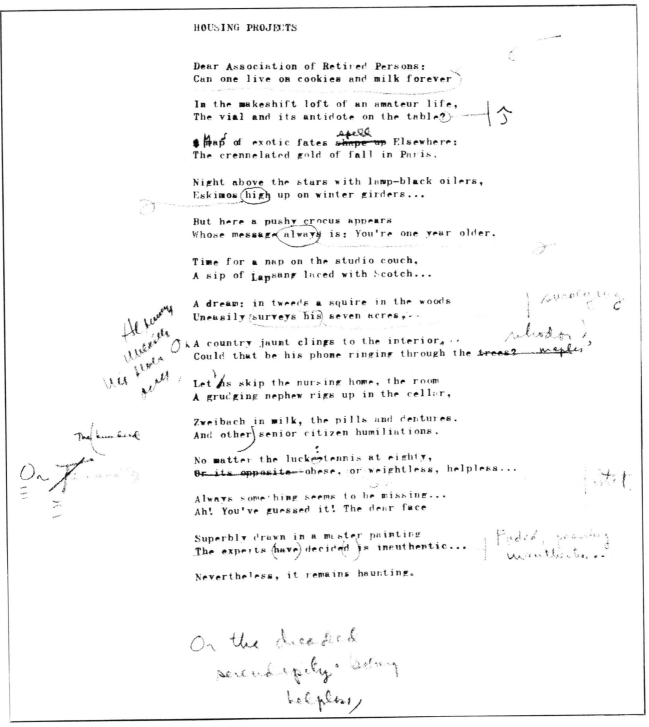

HOUSING PROJECTS

Dear Association of Retired Persons:
Can one live on cookies and milk forever

In the makeshift loft of an amateur life,
The vial and its antidote on the table?

A map of exotic fates shape up Elsewhere:
The crennelated gold of fall in Paris.

Night above the stars with lamp-black oilers,
Eskimos high up on winter girders...

But here a pushy crocus appears
Whose message always is: You're one year older.

Time for a nap on the studio couch,
A sip of Lapsang laced with Scotch...

A dream: in tweeds a squire in the woods
Uneasily surveys his seven acres,

A country jaunt clings to the interior,
Could that be his phone ringing through the trees?

Let us skip the nursing home, the room
A grudging nephew rigs up in the cellar,

Zweibach in milk, the pills and dentures.
And other senior citizen humiliations.

No matter the luck, tennis at eighty,
Or its opposite—obese, or weightless, helpless...

Always something seems to be missing...
Ah! You've guessed it! The dear face

Superbly drawn in a master painting
The experts have decided is inauthentic...

Nevertheless, it remains haunting.

"Housing Projects," revised typescript

Rightfully, *Finding Them Lost* received more unqualified critical acceptance than any of the preceding four books. Here Moss shows that he has mastered the lyric. His language and lines are clear and concise; his view of the natural world, his eye for detail (as in the tightly wrought "The Snow Weed," for example) are at home in these poems, which are, for the most part, shorter than his previous ones. His technique and sensibility are, in short, more refined.

In an interview for the *New York Quarterly*, Moss acknowledges that in *Finding Them Lost* he was consciously trying to escape from his "usual methods." The final result of this effort is a group of poems called "Lifelines." He calls these poems "attempts to get certain people I knew down on paper"; and he acknowledges that from this period his poetry begins to change.

Three years later, in 1968, he published a volume of poems whose title reflects this change, a change in both technique and author: *Second Nature*. These poems reveal his interest in the theatre, attempting to combine such dramatic elements as rhythm (or music) and the spoken language. The result is the conversational tone of such poems as "Sands" ("You'd be surprised / How the body endures / Suffering," and "I'm sorry I said that") and "Front Street" ("O.k. O.k. We'll go back to the house. / A false alarm? / What a child you are!"). Suddenly, it seems, his rhythms are looser, approaching free verse; but the language still remains tight, and the rhythms are still dominated by the insistent iambic, despite the critics who heard in the poems a "flat, often prose-like statement."

As in the previous volumes, Moss treats the theme of death (which is, in fact, another way of looking at the book's title), relying on such images as dryness, rock, and hot wind. He also turns to the nature of art, particularly in such overt poems as "Piano Practice." As always, he is unafraid of literary echoes, as he shows so blatantly in "The Love Songs of Horatio Alger, Jr." However, as Richard Howard points out, the true "second nature" of this volume "is this poet's second nature, which this poet, rather, sees as *our* second nature"; it is a vision from the outside, the same as he began in his "Lifelines."

After the publication of a book of criticism (*Writing Against Time*, 1969), Moss's next volume of poetry was his *Selected Poems* (1971). Choosing with even more discretion than he did for *A Winter Come, A Summer Gone*, he pulled together a strong collection of early verse complemented by seven previously uncollected poems. For example, the book includes only three poems from *The Wound and the Weather* and ten each from *The Toy Fair* and *A Swimmer in the Air*. The bulk of these works, then, comes from the handful of new poems in *A Winter Come, A Summer Gone*, and the two volumes that followed it; in short, these are the poems published during the 1960s, those that mark Moss's "new" directions. Yet the sampling of earlier poems allows the reader to see, and to feel, Moss's progress as a poet and craftsman; it shows the widening understanding and feeling of an accomplished writer as he achieves his "second nature." For this range and accomplishment, *Selected Poems* received the National Book Award.

In his next major volume of poetry, *Buried City* (1975), Moss returns overtly to one of the major sources of his earlier poetry. Here, New York City provides the images as, in the title poem, an archaeologist from some future time excavates to discover our civilization; what he finds, as the last line indicates, is an everlasting sameness: "They say the snow will bury us this year." Again, as in the preceding volumes, Moss is preoccupied with death and its attendant mutabilities of change, loss, and the passing of time. In regard to the latter, *Buried City* expands his thematic concerns to embrace the process and problems of aging, as witnessed in such poems as "The Old Poet" and "Morning, Night, and Very Late." Also, the poems stress the importance of memory, here often mingled with love: "I loved them once, those towering hotels / On lower Fifth" ("Memories of Lower Fifth"). And, continuing a theme from *Second Nature*, this volume also considers art and its relation to reality. All in all, though, it is a volume of concrete forms and precise lines, generally dealing with those themes that are threaded through his other volumes.

Moss's two subsequent volumes, *A Swim Off the Rocks* (1976) and *Tigers and Other Lilies* (1977), deserve brief mention. The former is a volume of light verse, apparently composed throughout Moss's career. The range is nonetheless interesting, for the poems range from the surreal ("The Private Elevator," for example) to pure romps to satires on various obnoxious social types. In other words, it is light verse, but it is not offhand or unimportant. *Tigers and Other Lilies*, however, is a different endeavor: a juvenile book of poems about plants that have animals in their names. Generally the poems are interesting and often fun, but occasionally their language and weight carries them beyond the range of their adolescent audience.

With a few exceptions, criticism of Moss's poetry has been limited to occasional commentaries, particularly reviews. He is frequently cited, always respected, yet seldom confronted. At times obscure, his poetry is never unapproachable. He has his masters: Stevens (the lush language and the love of wordplay) and W. H. Auden (controlled and urbane). His themes have remained relatively constant, as have the sources of his imagery and settings. He is ever concerned with the beauty and bleakness of the city, with the passing of time, with change and permanence, with loss and gain (of love, of friends, of life), and with death. But his poetry has not been static; and more and more he has moved toward the concrete from his initial abstractions. He has never given up underlying traditional rhythms, but in the later volumes his poems have begun to exhibit more flexibility, stretching the confines of the line and adding the dramatic value of the conversational. —*Stephen Gardner*

Plays:

The Folding Green, Cambridge, Mass., Poets' Theatre, 1958; published in *The Palace at 4 A.M. and The Folding Green*;

The Oedipus Mah-Jongg Scandal, New York, Cooperatives Theatre Club, 30 April 1968;

The Palace at 4 A.M., East Hampton, N.Y., John Drew Playhouse, 8 September 1972; published in *The Palace at 4 A.M. and The Folding Green*.

Other:

Keats, edited with an introduction by Moss (New York: Dell, 1952);

The Nonsense Books of Edward Lear, edited with an

introduction by Moss (New York: New American Library, 1964);

The Poet's Story, edited with an introduction by Moss (New York: Macmillan, 1973);

"From a Notebook," *American Poetry Review*, 8 (March-April 1979): 12-14.

References:

Richard Howard, *Alone with America Essays on the Art of Poetry in the United States Since 1950* (New York: Atheneum, 1969), pp. 382-395;

Laurence Lieberman, *Unassigned Frequencies: American Poetry in Review, 1964-1977* (Urbana: University of Illinois Press, 1977), pp. 133-139;

Karl Malkoff, *Crowell's Handbook of Contemporary American Poetry* (New York: Crowell, 1973), pp. 219-220;

William Packard, ed., *The Craft of Poetry: Interviews from "New York Quarterly"* (Garden City: Doubleday, 1974), pp. 265-293;

Richard Schramm, "A Gathering of Poets," *Western Humanities Review*, 26 (Autumn 1972): 393-395.

Howard Nemerov

Robert W. Hill
Clemson University

BIRTH: New York, New York, 1 March 1920, to David and Gertrude Russek Nemerov.

EDUCATION: A.B., Harvard University, 1941.

MARRIAGE: 26 January 1944 to Margaret Russell; children: David, Alexander Michael, Jeremy Seth.

AWARDS: Bowdoin Prize (Harvard College), 1940; *Kenyon Review* Fellowship in Fiction, 1955; Oscar Blumenthal Prize (*Poetry* magazine), 1958; Second Prize, Short Story Competition, *Virginia Quarterly Review*, 1958; National Institute of Arts and Letters grant, 1961; Golden Rose Trophy (New England Poetry Club), 1962; Consultant in Poetry, Library of Congress, 1963-1964; Arts Award, Brandeis University, 1963; election to the National Institute of Arts and Letters, 1965; National Endowment for the Arts Grant, 1966-1967; St. Botolph's Club (Boston) Arts Award, 1967; Theodore Roethke Memorial Prize for

Poetry, 1968; Guggenheim Fellowship, 1968-1969; Academy of American Poets Fellowship, 1970; Frank O'Hara Memorial Prize (*Poetry* magazine), 1971; Levinson Prize (*Poetry* magazine), 1975; election to the American Academy of Arts and Letters, 1976; Pulitzer Prize for *The Collected Poems of Howard Nemerov*, 1978.

BOOKS: *The Image and the Law* (New York: Holt, 1947);

The Melodramatists (New York: Random House, 1949);

Guide to the Ruins (New York: Random House, 1950);

Federigo, or the Power of Love (Boston & Toronto: Little, Brown, 1954; London: Gollancz, 1955);

The Salt Garden (Boston & Toronto: Little, Brown, 1955);

The Homecoming Game (New York: Simon &

Schuster, 1957; London: Gollancz, 1957);

Mirrors and Windows (Chicago: University of Chicago Press, 1958);

A Commodity of Dreams and Other Stories (New York: Simon & Schuster, 1959; London: Secker & Warburg, 1960);

New and Selected Poems (Chicago: University of Chicago Press, 1960);

Endor: Drama in One Act (New York & Nashville: Abingdon, 1962);

The Next Room of the Dream: Poems and Two Plays (Chicago: University of Chicago Press, 1962);

Poetry and Fiction: Essays (New Brunswick, N.J.: Rutgers University Press, 1963);

Journal of the Fictive Life (New Brunswick, N.J.: Rutgers University Press, 1965);

The Blue Swallows (Chicago & London: University of Chicago Press, 1967);

A Sequence of Seven with a Drawing by Ron Slaughter (Roanoke, Va.: Tinker Press, 1967);

The Painter Dreaming in the Scholar's House (New York: Phoenix Book Shop, 1968);

The Winter Lightning: Selected Poems (London: Rapp & Whiting, 1968);

Stories, Fables & Other Diversions (Boston: Godine, 1971);

Reflexions on Poetry & Poetics (New Brunswick, N.J.: Rutgers University Press, 1972);

Gnomes & Occasions (Chicago: University of Chicago Press, 1973);

The Western Approaches: Poems, 1973-75 (Chicago: University of Chicago Press, 1975);

The Collected Poems of Howard Nemerov (Chicago: University of Chicago Press, 1977);

Figures of Thought: Speculations on the Meaning of Poetry and Other Essays (Boston: Godine, 1978).

Among important mid-century American poets, Howard Nemerov is perhaps the most disarming. Hardly a disparaging claim has been made against his work that he has not acknowledged or preempted. As he says in "Attentiveness and Obedience" (1966): "The charge typically raised . . . has been that my poems are jokes, even bad jokes. I incline to agree, insisting however that they are bad jokes, and even terrible jokes, emerging from the nature of things as well as from my propensity for coming at things a touch subversively and from the blind side, or the dark side, the side everyone concerned with 'values' would just as soon forget." His low-key emotional display, his serious intellect, his habitual irony, his precise, dispassionate

language, his tendencies to sententiousness, conventional modern paradox, and convoluted syntax, as well as his dark joking, are all subjects of his own commentary in prose, poetry, and interview. But that is often the technique of the humanist intellectual: to affirm values (perhaps sententiously), to observe and analyze human weaknesses (perhaps equivocally and cynically) and strengths (by means of paradox, and thus often ironically), and to perform some positive, if ultimately ineffectual, act in the blank face of the universe.

Born in New York City, Howard Nemerov was reared to a state of mind that was sophisticated, disciplined, and dutiful. After graduating from Harvard in 1941, he served in the Royal Canadian Air Force from 1942 to 1944, becoming a flying officer, and later turned to the U.S. Army Air Force (1944-1945) to achieve the rank of first lieutenant. After the war, Nemerov taught at Hamilton College, Bennington College, Brandeis University, the University of Minnesota, and Hollins College before being appointed Poetry Consultant at the Library of Congress (1963-1964). Since that time he has been a distinguished professor on the faculty of Washington University in St. Louis. From 1946 to 1951 he served as associate editor for *Furioso*, developing his skills as a keen-witted reviewer of contemporary poetry.

Partly because of Nemerov's experience as a critic and as a practicing poet, to read *The Collected Poems of Howard Nemerov* (1977) is in some ways to chronicle the development of twentieth-century American poetry. Heavily influenced by William Butler Yeats, Wallace Stevens, Allen Tate, and T. S. Eliot, among others, Nemerov has moved from the self-conscious erudition and high-cultural didacticism of the modernists, through the brooding sensibility of those who took the measure of the vapid optimisms of post-World War II American dreams, to what Peter Meinke has called his "philosophy of minimal affirmation." Nemerov stops short of the "radical innocence" of a poet like William Stafford, although more lately he aspires to clarity and simplicity not so far from the let's-be-understood approach of the 1960s and 1970s.

Modernism taught the aesthetic utility of allusion but also gave the easy mythopoeia, the obtrusive or casual *esotērikos*, the sleek rails under carloads of academic freight: a tradition that spawned cheap top-hatted hoboes who could sling a hash of references and not say anything that mattered. The witty, withering skepticism of Howard Nemerov cut its way through the fog of others' tones and techniques, but that same hard-eyed scrutiny of the world will likely never render him a wide popular audience.

For Nemerov, what has mattered ever since *The Image and the Law* (1947) is the imaginative apprehension of an indifferent or threatening world, with wit exercised as a tool to control and make bearable his insights—no superficial efforts mounted merely to coax the reader toward cleverly poised homilies. A genuine existential belletrist, Nemerov focuses on the self in a social world of order and disorder and in a natural world of implacability. He is moral and intellectual by impulse, not by reason of external religious or political causes. Whatever uncertainties he has appear genuine, and—except in matters of taste, where he is adamant and exemplary, level and persistent—they are pervasive. Unlike the myriad poets of extravagant malaise, ennui, and angst, Nemerov maintains a dignified, authentic, existential posture.

Despite the persistence of certain themes and attitudes, Nemerov's poetry has changed in particular stylistic ways. In 1966, he edited a volume entitled *Poets on Poetry*, whose plan was to ask poets to respond to a few questions about their literary theories and practices. Nemerov reluctantly included his own essay, "Attentiveness and Obedience" (later collected in *Reflexions on Poetry & Poetics*, 1972), in which he explains the evolution of his career:

> Stylistically, I began under the aegis of notions drawn . . . chiefly from T. S. Eliot. Along with many other beginners, I learned to value irony, difficulty, erudition, and the Metaphysical style of composition after the example of John Donne. . . . I think the direction of my development was away from all these things considered as technical devices; I now regard simplicity and the appearance of ease in the measure as primary values, and the detachment of a single thought from its ambiguous surroundings as a worthier object than the deliberate cultivation of ambiguity.

A poem like "Style" shows Nemerov's intelligent clarity—capable of the apt (if not always surprising) metaphor, allusive but also explaining enough to serve even the reader who has never heard of Flaubert before this poem:

> Flaubert wanted to write a novel
> About nothing. It was to have no subject
> And be sustained upon style alone,
> Like the Holy Ghost cruising above
> The abyss. . . .

In "The Beekeeper Speaks . . . And Is Silent" he again uses enough allusion to establish significance (with only a hint of condescension) ameliorated by the casual tone and diction, despite the titillating shock of bare-armed beekeeping. Not really stoic, this poem is about risk rather than endurance, but without the abandonment that, say, James Dickey can call upon. Even as it sometimes comes perilously close to indulging in a parody of Robert Frost for language ("Outside the human, too, it gets a knowledge"), "The Beekeeper Speaks . . . And Is Silent" concludes with high and proper diction in the mouth of a speaker whose mortal self-awareness is intensified by contemplating "anaphylactic shock":

> The bloodstream is a venom in itself,
> Sometimes I think to hear it hum in me.
> . . . .
> I have felt myself become at first a bee,
> And then the single-minded hive itself,
> And after that the blossoming apple tree
> Inside the violation of the swarm—
> Until I am the brute and fruitful earth,
> Furred with the fury of the golden horde,
> And hear from far upon the field of time
> The wild relentless singing of the stars.

These lines demonstrate that clarity need not be flat: the good sense of the poem is heightened more than tranformed, for Nemerov's proclivities are not toward mystical transmutation. "I have felt myself become . . . ," says the beekeeper, but his verbs indicate the historical past, over which he has the control of retrospect. The world is not altered in Nemerov's poems: it is engaged and, insofar as possible, explicated.

The simplicity, ease, and focus that Nemerov lately espouses are, in fact, abundant in his earliest books, *The Image and the Law* and *Guide to the Ruins* (1950). The trouble with recognizing the fact, however, has been that those are not habitually considered as "Nemerov poems": they are poems of easeful common sense, not of intricate intellectualizing or aggressive wit, of the vernacular with a minimum of posturing. For instance, in "The Place of Value," a poem disparaged by F. C. Golffing as possessed of "conceptual confusion, . . . where a plea for relevance is made in the most irrelevant terms: the neurotic individual versus the healthy statistician [one wonders when, in modern art, statisticians are thought of as 'healthy'], fortuitous versus expiatory death . . . ," Nemerov speaks plainly and forcefully,

A CHRISTMAS STORM

All day, all night, the cold water comes down
at the will of heaven, freezing where it hits,
glazing the windshields and the roads and walks,
(you wanted a world without friction? here...)
sheathing the lines, the branches and the...
in leaden insulations uniform
across the counties and the towns, until
connections give and power lines come down
and limbs that had sustained the horizontal
a hundred years unstrained crack with the weight
of stiffened wet and short transformers out
until ten thousand homes cut suddenly off
go dark and silent, and the cold comes in
slowly at first, then faster, drifting through
the window frames ghostly, and under doors,
while night comes on and provident families
remember where the candles and lanterns were
from last year, and other families don't;
while lucky families light fires, and others don't
but bundle up in blankets or skid downstreet
to the mercy of the neighbors or their kin,
and cars caught out are paralyzed at hills,
and it is clear from portable radios
as from a look outdoors that the relentless rain
will go unrelentingly on till it relents.

Which it does do at last next day at dawn,
when sunrise lights the splendor of the world
in radiant brocades and faberge'd
drainpipes and eaves and shrub and brilliant fans
of bush and tree and grass the region 'round;
where every twig is ... being itself,
its outline in transparent ice, and then
the halo of that in light, as in the great
museum of mind the million crystal trees
light up at once their diamonded display,
their crystal magnificence, their candelabra
of silver winking ruby and emerald and gold
according to the sun and shifting wind,
giving away the treasures of the world
before the powerful and the poor alike.

8 i 79

"A Christmas Storm," revised typescript

perhaps to the confusion of ambiguity-hunting critics:

> The way MacLane died, they set
> His feet in a bucket of drying
> Cement and let him off the bridge
> Late one night. He screamed once,
> An adequate criticism and his best
> Epigram. It was a private fight.

Often a poet, fairly or unfairly, becomes best known for only a few of his poems: certainly a case could be made with Nemerov for "The Goose Fish," from *The Salt Garden* (1955). The work is proof of the vigor that can be accomplished in tight poetic form, with rhyme, as long as the impulse is toward image and the unusual insight of some experience. Employing the fashionably coy, oblique near-rhymes so dear to the hearts of those moderns who study to evade sameness and convention, Nemerov makes his way through lovers, the beach, the moon, the zodiac, and one stark staring image which comments upon the whole round world. "Memento mori," admonished the Middle Ages, and the grinning skull delimited the optimism and the keenest sensibilities of men for centuries. The noncommital stare of Nemerov's dead fish ("He might mean failure or success"), interpreted as comedic by the lovers, invokes aestheticians like Oscar Wilde, who think that the world of nature is subject to art, that men impose their perceptions and their interpretations. Thus, nature has no meaning—it is utterly ambiguous—of itself. Man and his consciousness are what give meaning to the universe.

As Nemerov notes in "Attentiveness and Obedience," there were

> two marked changes in my poetry. The first has to do with the natural world, which I came to rather late, having been born and raised in the city. . . . The second change is harder to speak of; it involves a growing consciousness of nature as responsive to language or, to put it the other way, of imagination as the agent of reality. . . . I do not now, if I ever did, consent to the common modern view of language as a system of conventional signs for the passive reception of experience, but tend ever more to see language as making an unknowably large part of a material world whose independent existence might be likened to that of the human unconscious, a sleep of causes, a chaos of the possible-impossible, responsive only to the wakening touch of desire and fear—that is, to spirit; that is, to the word.

In "The Goose Fish," the crucial matter is less that the people *perceive* the striking figure of the goose fish than that they perceive it as *lovers*. Their perceptions and their desires enact one another; their experiences have been heightened only moments before the discovery of the fish ("the swift tide of blood / That silently they took at flood"), and their version of reality is bound up in force ("lovers who a little while / Before had thought to understand, / By violence upon the sand"), but that force is modulated through love: their version of the world is an ongoing one, one of "optimism" and of the "comedian," however "unfinished" he or they might be. Nemerov's wit is never more restrained than in this poem: the tone of the punster who hopes that everybody gets the joke but who realizes that everybody thinks that he got it first, or better than anyone else; the particular excitement of the satirist who disguises his target and his mode just enough to flatter the intelligence of the reader but not enough to hide the thing beyond a moment's pause in the timing of cognition. Phrases like "So finished a comedian" and "That rigid optimist," as they refer to the dead fish in the sand, lead the reader to understand that bald commentary, the putting-upon of qualities when no empirical evidence can ever be in nature, are the glory and the frustration of the metaphysician and, insofar as he is metaphysical, the poet.

In the early poem, "Europe," Nemerov's metaphysical tendency is explicitly paradoxical and dialectical: "Saint and demon [who] blindly stare / From the risen stone." Here, as the poet tries to give images to the culture of Europe from which he, an American, has sprung, Nemerov affirms that no one answer is possible. Even saints and angels serve, it seems, to impede the pious efforts of human beings; and yet, the poem recalls somewhat the Great Chain of Being, the medieval idea of universal hierarchy, the cosmos headed by God and toed by inanimate objects like stones and dust. In stanza 3, Nemerov sets up an impressive group of images to collect and focus the reader's attention upon the broad historical span as well as the intellectual and physical preoccupations of the historical folk he talks about:

> The people knit Assyrian brows
> Like statues on the rack;
> They all have eaten up their cows
> And drink their coffee black.

In tough, clever Nemerovian terms, religiosity is put forward with the images of Fertile Crescent religion largely based on fertility emblems and rituals. Assyrian art is recalled as the reader imagines sculpture and bas-reliefs of ancient monuments; and the people's intensity, their religious and societal fervor, are depicted as the results of torture ("on the rack"). The core of religious symbolism is touched when the second half of the stanza beckons the reader to the present time, in which people have "eaten up their [sacred] cows" in the interests of pragmatism and "reasonableness." Finally, the stanza reiterates the anxiety of "knit Assyrian brows" in modern terms. The people "drink their coffee black": they feel the need of stimulation; they seek their energies and significant impulses as compulsions, something laid on or packed in from the outside. The poem turns to call for new heroes, new modes of expression and affirmation:

> New eucharists we must call down
> To fill our empty rooms:
> New heroes stagger into town
> Under their heavy tombs.

It is more than ironic—it is almost direct commentary—that the book *The Image and the Law* appeared in 1947; thus the "new heroes," the "new eucharists" are likely to evoke the specific "new" political/military rulers of post-World War II Europe. It is perhaps another characteristic of Nemerov that his "relevant" poems, his statements of current necessity or mode, always seem rationally to struggle for the balance between actually saying outright and most subtly concealing until the poem surprises the reader into assent or acquiescence. The sunbeam streak of intelligence is always evident (the moonglow of imagination which might blend disparate elements to sublime coherence is much less so).

One effort, in another early poem, to reach into some imaginative dream-world is "The Frozen City." The work is heavily influenced by W. B. Yeats, not so much in form or style as in subject matter and in a decidedly religious quality of the language. While Yeats went about his way inventing new religion and culling the cabala for hints and signs, Nemerov's poem shows him to be a critic of the secularizers: coming from the Jewish tradition, his sense of the decline of religion is not so easily pacified by new contrivances as Yeats's was. But the connections Nemerov feels with the seers of the past are clearly modern, clearly attached with threads of the naturalistic mode, the beliefs in touchable things rather than in the untouchable:

> Visionary and not believed
> Is no longer the position
> Nor the prerogative of

> Saints, mystics, and the holy poor.
> Rather on reefers and coke
> I expound to the multitude
> Traumatic aggrandizements
> Of my person in triplicate
> At least; for this receiving
> The indifference of belief
> From those who love the miracle
> And let the doctrine go.

Section 1 of the poem ends with an isolated line, "I enter upon my song and dance," recalling the flip colloquialism that indicates skepticism or outright disbelief: "The salesman did a song and dance about a little old lady from Pasadena who owned this car before." Such ironic use of the traditional Orphic analogues to poetry serve to make the reader suspicious of the authority of the dream in section 2:

> I saw by moonlight New York
> Which was called in my dream
> The Island of God. . . .

The city in the dream is in fact frozen: "My eyes, from the abysmal / Heaven of the dream's stance, / Detected no commerce or action." Echoing Yeats's "Sailing to Byzantium," the speaker observes,

> This was, as the dream understood,
> The artifice of eternity
> Produced by efficient suffering
> And the total wish for death. . . .

The blame of such catastrophe is placed obliquely, ironically, on "committees" and "organizations of ladies," but the hard language of the poem sometimes appears oddly dislocated when side-by-side with satiric understatement:

> The rape of God's attention
> Employed the methods commenced
> By the superior saints, with only
> A hint of economic condescension
> And the irony of the best people.

When the speaker turns to show the reader "The people awaiting death," the sympathies are obvious at first, but then the poet reveals that they have acquiesced in their condition. The dream persuades him that "these are dying / Into grace by an act of the will." The message of the frozen, static scene appears to be wholly cynical, that the rich and the poor, the weak and the powerful, all are reprehensible in their participation in the spectacle of human misery. All persons lust, covet, and seek after themselves, even as they observe themselves festering in their city. The poet stops the scene until he can momentarily order things, perceive things; then he notes,

> Then in my dream the blind
> Mercy of the Lamb was loosed
> Upon the moral world: the sun
> Burned Heaven with monstrous
> Innocent speed. The dead arose,
> And began with spastic hands
> To gather money from the streets. . . .

When the dream is ending, the speaker notes Blake and Augustine, his aesthetic, religious, mystical guides in the course of this infernal dream, as their "glacial / Eyes, frozen by their last tears," close the dream, from which the poet awakens to observe about him "the usual noises" of humanity untouched by his perceptions, his metaphysical excursions. The city as it moves is still frozen, and the loss of spiritual impulsion is evident. The poet earlier in the poem says, "as / All words are prayer, all words / Are meaningless, by the last fiat / Of the last secular council," and the here-we-go-again sense that emerges at the end—when the poet has awakened to the perpetually disappointing real world with perpetually self-serving people—has a kind of pleasure in itself but without any hope of altering the miserable conditions set forth in the poem.

Part of the hopelessness of the poem's subject matter is also subtly conveyed in the overtly "signifying" purpose of the poet as he thinks about his own dream: "Some, while / I watched, died (their heads / Rolled off, this signifying / An abdication of the will)." Such obtrusive allegorizing suggests, of course, that Nemerov is intelligently in control of the meanings he is embodying in the poem, but it also suggests that the effort to make meaning has taken on a kind of shrill pitch that the allegorizing medievalists, for instance, never even thought of: when the general consent is that all nature reveals "the signature in all things," the poet need not force himself to say the obvious. If, in the twentieth century, the poet must point out, as if to children, the easily seen and thus suppose that the reader's sensitivities are dulled or are so out of balance that the poet must strain so, then the commentary on the state of the modern, secular world is hard indeed.

In "The Truth of the Matter," Nemerov dodges the purely aesthetic uses of language to confront the efforts of the public media to report and to direct opinions of the masses. His observation (reminiscent of "What's black and white and read all over?—The newspaper!"), that black on white is what allows the reader to read is not very startling; the lines sound the trudging tones of a poet who explains more than he

shows; Nemerov even resorts to the tedious "one": "When one reads it is / As much the black as the white that / One reads, construing the letters." There is a point at which a reader can perceive the poet's ironic use of such too-proper, too-stiff pronouns, but this poem's best lines are so clearly superior to the mincing correctness of these lines that the possibility of effective irony is lost. When Nemerov writes,

> The head of a great sugar refinery
> Has died of diabetes. That sounds right:
> The citizen considers divine justice,
> Reads further of the Ministers at Paris:
> A person with a flaming sword has been
> Arrested in the rain, in Schenectady. . . ,

the reader is driven to the conclusion that the spirited and various mentality of this poet cannot be on track all the time and that "The Truth of the Matter" as a title might lead any poet into rounds of polemical cuteness which no single good stanza can derail. The poem ends lamely, "The pale, / The staring faces, twirl around and go down." Perhaps the strongest offering that this poem makes is in its second stanza, where "Words show that these faces have shuddered / Instantaneously from, say, Madrid." The language act is shown to be of considerable importance in simply identifying where the pictures were taken, where the subjects live, but more significantly, the lines show that the discriminations that are possible, perhaps even necessary, to words are at the same time disintegrative; that is, the pictures indicate that people look much the same, enough that their troubles as they might be reported from any city might be indistinguishable from the troubles—the news—reported from, say, Madrid. The universality of human experience, then, is the subject of "The Truth of the Matter," as much as the specifying and identifying capacities of words.

Chad Walsh, reviewing *The Blue Swallows* (1967), has written that "Nemerov resists the lures of current poetic bandwagons and continues on his way, becoming steadily and more certainly what he has always been: a civilized, often melancholy, frequently wry observer of himself and all things about." But Nemerov also has done best what the fashion called for; that is, he has been attuned to the fashions of poetry throughout his career, and he has been the best practitioner of the art of accommodation to the modes of a day. This is not to derogate his work; rather, it is to point out how adaptable and how various his own talents are, to tell that his sense of how poetry is made is so complete and so swiftly responsive to the times that his tones of voice, his subject matter, and his carefully preserved aesthetic core work together to give him access to many modes that would not be available to most poets, no matter how long a career they should have. Nemerov has written in formal, loose, dramatic, prose-fictional, and prose-essay styles; and those various forms, that prodigious repertoire allow him to speak in the multifarious ways of the eclectic twentieth-century poet. He is a man, like W. H. Auden, for instance, who could take hold of the particular events and customs of a special time, and make poetry that extends to include other times and unexpected people as readers.

Despite the reputation Nemerov has of the too-easy quip, the too-learned, stiffly perceptive dark wizard, many of his poems from his early career possess the very simplicity and clarity that he has lately admired. In "In the Glass of Fashion," for instance, he writes,

> I am asked why I do not
> Stop writing about death
> And do something worth while.
> To write about what would be
> Not to write about death?

The sense of the question is momentarily ambiguous because of the preservation of "would be" in the line with the infinitive phrase "to write about what." If the cut had been made as follows, "To write about what / Would be not to write about death?," the arrangement might have helped clarify the syntax by forcing a slight pause at the line-end instead of hoping for the reader to supply the necessary caesura as the line is actually written. Nonetheless, after setting the question, Nemerov proceeds to write about various "whats" that might not be about death: terror, smiling, distant catastrophes ("the laugh / That was appropriate for Spain / Will do for Shanhaikwan" sounds very like E. E. Cummings's charitable Cambridge ladies who were ignorantly "knitting for the is it Poles?"). By the time the reader reaches the end of the poem, though, the casual tone of the opening appears flat, and such flatness is the demise of many a poetic closure:

> But the verities, I say again,
> Continue to repeat themselves in
> Precisely the same manner; and the
> Resemblance to death is inescapable.

In his monograph, *Howard Nemerov* (1968), Peter Meinke pays special attention to the use of stone as monuments of death and stasis in Nemerov's poetry, but such associations are not the only ones. Stones are substance; they are fundamental; they are inanimate but corruptible, subject to erosion and

then to the trim-and-serve demolition of lichens and accident; they are weapons and they are defenses; they become dust and the dust is us. Meinke is right in that Nemerov does use stone (or, in one case, "a bucket of drying / Cement") to figure forth the ossified value systems and expectations of society (Nemerov must approve of Shelley's "Ozymandias," for its disparagement of inordinate human pride). In "The Place of Value," for example, the character MacLane is taken by Nemerov and, as a kind of allegory, sucked dry by the meaning-seeking poet. It is much like the "signifying" that Nemerov noted about himself in his dream of "The Frozen City":

> What shall I say? That the world
> Is set in its hardening history
> Like MacLane, to scream going down?
> Or that MacLane was like
> MacLane and no one else, and he
> Is dead and there is no other,
> Unique and unimportant?

What happens, of course, to MacLane in this poem is that he dies; "MacLane made concrete equivalence / And died of relevance and justice / By his lights." As the reader looks on his case, he sees that the embodying of values always means the "necrocytosis" of "the greatest state," that all, singly or collectively, are inextricably woven into a network which includes the sloughing-off of cells, the shifting of single persons, of single events past fixed values, past our hopeful aspects, past our desires for commiseration and mercy, past the needs of our peculiar selves: values become our own buckets of cement, without sequence, without the possibility of retreat when the drop is made, without the luxury of reconsidering "in committee" when the final responsibility—examined or unexamined—comes to call. The bucket is values, and its effect is certain, fragmentary with regard to mere syntax, irrevocable as to individual consequence, unpredictable as to all its ramifications: "In a bucket of cement / Cohesiveness, weight, stability. / It is a private fight." Unlike the rest of mankind, however strange and sinister his death may be, no matter how *outre* and how atypical his death may seem to the rest of the average world, MacLane died with some clear apprehension of his values, of how those values revert to justice when they are played out and how those values hold the world together after he is gone:

> The rest of us,
> Amazed mice, face the neurosis
> Of the continual choice on which
> All depends; or play the hopeless

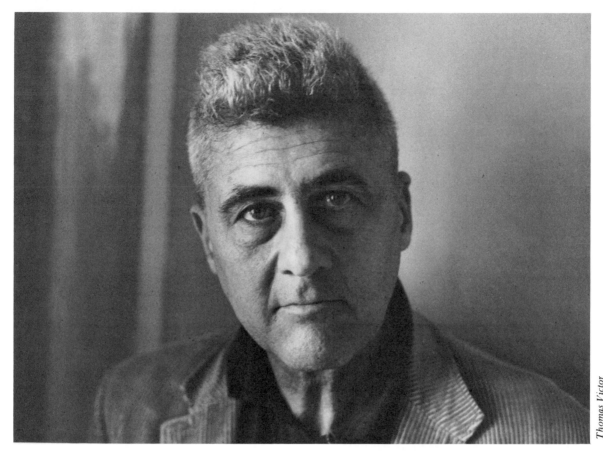

Thomas Victor

Howard Nemerov

Shell game against the cheerful
Healthy statistician, who knows
"Pretty well" the final result.

Such health as this statistician possesses is the infuriating average, the description of "norm-al" persons, the persons whose values are implicit—not explicit—in their actions, and those actions are quantified somewhere beyond the range and the knowing of those persons. MacLane, however bizarre his end, knows where he stands, where he falls, screams, and dies. When Nemerov uses the word *hopeless*, he expects the reader not to think only of the usual sense, that all is doomed, that the end is implacable, that some terrible conclusion is inevitable. Rather, he wants the Dantesque sense also to be attached, that the given condition is without hope—as with the virtuous pagans in Limbo—not that something terrible and irreversible is going to happen, but that man's very existence is devoid of hope.

However, stone is not always a hopeless thing for Nemerov. In "Autumnal," another early poem,

he uses that image to describe love (the poem is dedicated at the end, ". . . for my wife"). With a solemn and dignified first line, "October: the falling leaves resume the earth," the poem takes as its starting point the fact of aging, the certainty that the one who is loved will invariably fall like the leaves:

Fading the flesh delineates the bone,
Indicts your face, a precious artifact,
That so your legal beauty may be known.

The poem plays back and forth with the permanence and the transience of all physical things, particularly with stone, but the ultimate word is that

Love might construct a form so true, so tense
As to survive its own antithesis,
Achieving an ironic permanence

With, for a pulse, repetitive despair.

The poem is typical in some ways of Nemerov, with a kind of dignity attached to the observation of paradoxes; the dialectic impulse which seems to control many of his poems is specifically signaled by the reference to "antithesis," and the concluding stanza makes the reader understand the venerable New Critical tensions in a way that is not often done. Here the poet is able to combine his abstraction, love, with his images of stone in the midst of corruptible nature, and then to control the whole poem through an image of religious reverence which gives a kind of credence to the sacred love (called "legal" earlier in the poem) so calmly and so convincingly portrayed:

> Love is the form of stone, statue and law
> As far locked from corruption of the sun
> As Buddha smiling in the seamless rock.

The leaves become the earth; the earth, the rock; the rock, the Buddha; all the images together to fashion an image for a poet to speak of his sacred, legal love of his wife. The poem has a kind of *solempne* that Chaucer (or C. S. Lewis) might have celebrated, the serenity and pleasure of high, serious purpose.

Many Nemerov poems begin with fragments, with all sorts of fragments, from the abstract to the concrete. "A Chromium-Plated Hat: Inlaid with Scenes from Siegfried" begins, "Greatness. Warmth, and human insight. Music." But greatness begins with eight lines of fragments before the first complete sentence. The poem is one of those that seems a calculated answer to some of the critics of Nemerov who insist that he lacks warmth and pursues only intellectual virtues. It shows humor, a sort of pleasant diversion over the pretensions of the intellectual community, the high-culture crowd who place the value of their "masterpieces" above the simplest human decencies. One hesitates to recall how avidly "cultural" the high-officer Nazis were during the Third Reich: what Nemerov refers to in this poem is the necessity of keeping things in some kind of perspective that allows the reader to know about the things that matter most. The whole turn of the conclusion of this poem to the experience and interests of the old man precurses (perhaps) the ideas of Theodore Roethke in, say, "Meditations of an Old Woman" (1958) or "North American Sequence" (1964), in which the speakers are deliberately placing the activities and procedures of their long lives in righteous light, their lives so nearly over now that they must come to understanding and not just accept the allegations of virtue and priority made by the general public or by any particular school of thinking. The time comes ultimately for a man or a woman to consider what thoughts are worthy and what deeds are commensurate with personal ideals: the tracts of ideologues and the tracks of the ordinary are not in themselves enough justification; they must be tested, and Nemerov, with this poem about art,

this contemplation—however humorously intended—comes to speak of good living and human decency. He is unapologetic about speaking of "truth" and other abstractions, for he embodies their general realities in the specific postures and pursuits of people:

> Greatness. Warmth, and human insight. Music.
> But greatness. The greatness of Socrates
> And Dante and Alexander Woollcott, and the
> True charm of Horatio Alger, Jr. Also,
> The greatness of eighteen-year-old girls,
> The warmth of retired corporation lawyers,
> The impossibility of having enough books
> About truth. The important thing is
> The relation of truth to our time to Kitty Foyle.
> In addition, music. It is good to have music,
> But not at the expense of greatness:
> Better to be truly great and unmusical.
> If you are merely musical you are probably
> Not one of the great authors.
> . . . .
> To sum up, the truth of the matter is,
> Quoting William Lyon Phelps, "There is
> No masterpiece like *Lohengrin*, that
> Masterpiece," and it may be better anyhow
> To have human warmth than greatness:
> Like Grandpa, who sat by the fire all
> Winter long, in a buffalo rug with fleas.

The poem is not a great poem, a masterpiece, but it does try to tell the truth. It begins in fragmentary perceptions, proceeds to listing the speaker's experiences of various qualities called virtuous, and concludes with the perhaps ironic picture of an old man engaged in warmth. The point of greatness is that it so often is inhumane; no less so is the judgment of greatness exercised by one upon another. In the succeeding poem in *The Image and the Law* for instance, "History of a Literary Movement," the speaker is obviously in conscious pursuit of literary greatness, finding himself in concert with the other members—his friends—of a particular school or movement. Despite, however, their comradeship, the friends (if the speaker of this poem is typical of the group, and he seems to be) are also judging one another as to their relative chances at greatness. Grumbach, in the poem, comments that "There have been / Other great men. Only man / Is important, man is ultimate," a reflection that the speaker of the poem chooses to dismiss: "He was a fat man. / Fat men are seldom the best / Creative writers." Later, he refers to his closest friend in the group, Impli, who, "though one of my / Dearest friends, can never, / I have decided, become great." The implication is that the narrator feels himself to be superior to the other characters in the poem to the extent, perhaps, that he will think of himself as the only one who shall "become great." But the aspiration to greatness is undercut again and again in Nemerov; the needs to sacrifice certain human qualities, common human relationships, friendships, to the hard judgments that must be made in the interests of self-elevation; these terms are often too much for the warmth, truth, and love to persist which finally are the standards by which Greatness—even *Lohengrin* or *Siegfried*, such heroic perfections—must be measured. The fragmentary observations the poet makes are bound to be ordered by the poem; but if the ordering is finally to the detriment, the extinction, of the truly fragmentary wonders, the virtues, of living, however great the ordering, it must be questioned. James Dickey has said in *Sorties* (1971) that it may be better to be stupid and ordinary; Nemerov says, "it may be better anyhow / To have human warmth than greatness."

Nemerov's poems are not primarily motivated by narrative impulse, as in the case of James Dickey, but by a technique of perceiving reality which depends upon certain careful exclusions, certain calculated counterpoises; he extols "the power of poetry to be somewhat more like a mind than a thought" ("Poetry and Meaning," 1973). A Nemerov poem typically deals with a single, unified subject (perhaps an anecdote, if the narrative impulse strikes), but it is not deflected from a purpose of screening-out, of paring-down. Nemerov's technique is rewarded by the ironic and the paradoxical precisely because the intellect can handle a few identifiable aspects of any subject, but the Nemerov poem has few epic pretensions—perhaps he longs for that in some of the verse dramas; perhaps he aspires to more breadth and depth in his prose fiction or in his essays. But, despite his humanity and obvious skill, the impression lingers that the Nemerov poems are to a certain extent predigested, as though all ramifications are anticipated, as though the need for order in so bleak and dangerous a world as Nemerov portrays for the most part is so insistent that the poems cannot be allowed to seep away into uncharted boundaries, nor to roam like wild animals in some wilderness of the general understanding such as the public's experience, wider than that of the single poet. The surprises in Nemerov are most often those of wit—they do not startle the reader into entirely new insights about his precarious existential condition. Rather, the discoveries are frequently of the order of the eighteenth-century aspirations, to say "What oft was thought, but ne'er so well expressed." The divisions of the mind are for most of Nemerov's poems fairly clear. One may not know precisely what apprehensions are contained in the unconscious, for example, or precisely what possibilities lie at the threshold of action or articulation, but it is certain for Nemerov that the process of thinking-about and then verbalizing is the most direct route to comprehension and thus of domesticating the terrors of the Out Yonder. Or of the In Here. When the intellect of Howard Nemerov allows itself to fly loose, as in a dream, it produces a quasi-medieval dream ("The Frozen City") or it lingers at the feet of a given legend ("Cain" and "Endor"), but exercises of the human intellect are not enough to evoke and thus to deal with the frightening swamp of the nonrational. "A sense of humor," says every Miss America candidate, every over-aged game-show contestant, every movie star or political candidate (personally interviewed as to his / her philosophy of life). But what the reader learns from Nemerov's poetry is that the humor of the dark is often the humor of the grave; it is despair, not affirmation, and however Nemerov tries to work himself and his poetry up to the orderly consideration of things, his tone, his perceptions, his neatly packaged ironies and paradoxes are sometimes too neat; again and again he gives images for the laws he perceives. Again and again he replicates their decay.

To review many poetic careers, one finds that the best way to organize is to see the first part in some evolutionary relationship to the last. But with Nemerov's work, as with many people's lives, the salient observations emerge in the 1960s, especially in the poems of *The Next Room of the Dream* (1962) and *The Blue Swallows* (1967). The radicalization of the nation during that time could hardly have failed to touch somewhere the sensibilities of a poet whose trademark is his dark, satiric intelligence. With *New and Selected Poems* (1960), Nemerov was displaying the collected, rather conventional fifties-ish poems on religion, art, and easily satirized social customs. In that volume he included a final section, "Early Poems" (with all the modest derogation that that term implies), of only seven poems from his first two books. None of those poems is like the clear, homiletic, unforced detachment "of a single thought from its ambiguous surroundings" proposed by Nemerov as his goal and aesthetic guide in 1966. The times from the 1940s to the early 1960s required the poet to practice and to espouse such virtues as Nemerov has identified as the Eliot-Donne-Empson mode. Only after the 1960s began to break open in their peculiar way (by 1966 and *Poets on Poetry*) did

Howard Nemerov

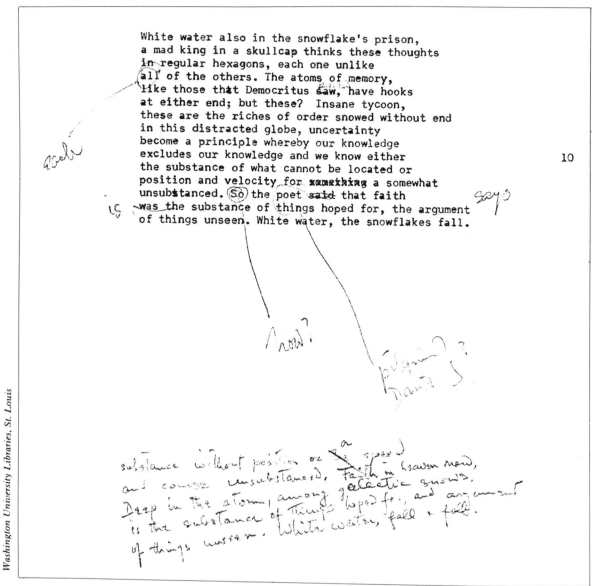

"Runes," revised typescript

Nemerov decide to shift away from those intellectual intricacies and involutions to the "newer" style he describes in his essay. The fact is, though, that Nemerov was less accurate than one might have thought. The ease, the clarity, the directness, the isolation of the single important idea in the midst of such tumultuous nature and society as man has perceived in the twentieth-century version of Renaissance, are all qualities that can be observed in his earliest published works. Rather than coming to a new understanding of techniques, Nemerov may more appropriately be said to have developed a mode that was evident in his youthful twenties.

The true intellectual rarely seeks complexity; rather, he tries to penetrate the complex scene and circumstances to the end of making things clearer for himself and others. The elegant principle, that is the goal, the divine order, the singleness of genius. But Nemerov remains skeptical even of his own affirmations: "if my poetry does envision the appearance of a new human nature, it does so chiefly in sarcastic outrage, for that new human nature appears in the poetry merely as a totalitarian fixing of the old human nature, whose principal products have been anguish, war, and history" ("Attentiveness and Obedience"). The equivocation that is detectable in Nemerov's poems is also evident in his prose, for he seems to want a better world than we have, even as he recognizes the necessities of natural and social law. He speaks admiringly of muses, imagination, the unconscious, but he continues to insist upon the orderly, coherent control over things of this world. It is as though he acknowledges the source of power in those faculties that are least subject to direct rational manipulation. As Peter Meinke has observed,

> One reason Nemerov speaks effectively to this age is that his poetry attempts to come to terms with science: not just psychology, as in the *Journal [of the Fictive Life]*, but "hard" science. . . . His general position seems to be that science is "true," but never quite accounts for our lives (though it tries): science lacks "blood" and "mystery"; it misses the essential:
> For "nothing in the universe can travel
> at the speed of light," they say, forgetful
> of the shadow's speed.

Nonetheless, whatever darkness is perceived, whatever clarity is met by ambiguous reflection, whatever difficulties are stirred by making words to bear any weight of experience, as Boyers points out, through Howard Nemerov's best poetry "we learn . . . to respect our own best faculties, as we understand how [his] characteristic probity of mind is finally indistinguishable from self-respect."

Other:

Longfellow, Selected Poems, edited with an introduction by Nemerov (New York: Dell, 1959);

Comment on "Runes," in *Poet's Choice*, ed. Paul Engle and Joseph Langland (New York: Dial, 1962), pp. 186-187;

Owen Barfield, *Poetic Diction*, introduction by Nemerov (New York: McGraw-Hill, 1964), pp. 1-9;

"The Two Gentlemen of Verona: A Commentary," in William Shakespeare, *The Two Gentlemen of Verona*, ed. Charles Jasper Sisson (New York: Dell, 1964), pp. 1-10;

Marianne Moore, *Poetry & Criticism*, edited by Nemerov (Cambridge, Mass.: Adams House & Lowell House Printers, 1965);

"The Swaying Form: A Problem in Poetry," in *To the Young Writer: Hopwood Lectures*, second series (Ann Arbor, Mich., 1965), pp. 105-121;

Poets on Poetry, edited with a preface and an essay by Nemerov (New York: Basic Books, 1966);

"Composition and Fate in the Short Novel," in *Perspectives in Contemporary Criticism*, ed. Sheldon Norman Grebstein (New York: Harper & Row, 1968), pp. 120-132;

"On the Resemblances Between Science and Religion," in *The Rarer Action: Essays in Honor of Francis Fergusson*, ed. A. Cheuse and R. Koffler (New Brunswick, N.J.: Rutgers University Press, 1971), pp. 333-339;

"Poetry and Meaning," in *Contemporary Poetry in America: Essays and Interviews*, ed. Robert Boyers (New York: Schocken, 1975), pp. 1-15;

"Exceptions and Rules," in *Evolution of Consciousness: Studies in Polarity*, ed. Shirley Sugerman (Middletown, Conn.: Wesleyan University Press, 1976), pp. 42-47.

Periodical Publications:

POETRY:

"Inventory and Statement: a Declaration," *Harvard Advocate*, March 1940, p. 16;

"Poem," *Harvard Advocate*, March 1941, p.10;

"Notes on a New England Winter," *Kenyon Review*, 2 (Autumn 1941): 408;

"To the Memory of John Wheelwright," "On the Flight into Egypt," *Vice Versa*, 1 (January 1942): 20-22;

"No More of Sanctity," *Decision*, 3 (February 1942): 23;

"Sigmund Freud," *Poetry*, 62 (August 1943): 261;

"Poem of a Death," as S. J. Canbrode, *Furioso*, 2 (Summer 1947): 35;

"Various Vacations, Vacancies," "Full Small Ballad," *Touchstone*, 1 (November 1947): 32-33;

"Last Letter, with Snapshots," *Touchstone*, 1 (December 1947): 9;

"Landscape in America," *Furioso*, 3 (Winter 1947): 45;

"To a Friend Gone to Fight for the Kuomingtang," *Partisan Review*, 16 (December 1949): 1220;

"The End Crowning the Work," *New Yorker*, 26 (2 December 1950): 84;

"Reflection," "Sonnet," *Furioso*, 6 (Spring 1951): 58;

"Dissertation 2, Canzone 1, First Ode from the *Convivio*, by Dante," translated by Nemerov, *Wake*, 10 (1951): 98-100;

"Gyroscope Top," *New Yorker*, 28 (19 April 1952): 76;

"Moralities," *Poetry*, 80 (July 1952): 199;

"Forecast," *New Yorker*, 31 (11 February 1956): 38;

"A Mobile of a Carved Wooden Fish," "A Speckled Stone Mirror," "The Battenkill in Winter," *Poetry*, 88 (Spring 1956): 286, 384-385;

"Reactionary History," *Nation*, 183 (10 November 1956): 414;

"Witch of Endor," *Nation*, 184 (23 March 1957): 258;

"To Certain Wits," *Silo* (May 1958): 5;

"Tragedy in Garden City," *Nation,* 190 (23 April 1960): 365;

"Politics," *Nation,* 191 (29 October 1960): 336;

"The Ground Swayed," *Silo* (Spring 1962): n. pag.;

"Prometheus at Radio City," *Poetry,* 100 (June 1962): 143;

"An Interview," *Carleton Miscellany,* 3 (Fall 1962): 7;

"Nobody Ever Said," *Shenandoah,* 12 (Spring 1963): 10;

"Dangers of Reasoning by Analogy," *Polemic,* 11 (Winter 1966): 41;

"Retirement on the Subjunctive Plan," *Harvard Advocate,* Spring 1969, p. 15.

FICTION:

"Justa Little Smile," *Harvard Advocate,* April 1940, p. 17;

"The Native in the World," *Harvard Advocate,* July 1941, p. 7;

"Gerhart Otto," *Harvard Advocate,* September 1941, p. 17;

"Exchange of Men," as J. Cross, with W. R. Johnston, *Story,* 29 (November 1946): 9-17;

"From a Novel as Yet Untitled," *Furioso,* 6 (Summer 1951): 11;

"Unbelievable Characters," *Esquire,* 163 (September 1959): 141; reprinted in *Best American Short Stories, 1960,* ed. David Burnett (Boston: Houghton Mifflin, 1960), pp. 218-229;

"Escapist," *Virginia Quarterly Review,* 28 (Spring 1962): 263-275;

"Digressions Around a Crow," *Carleton Miscellany,* 3 (Spring 1962): 38;

"The Idea of a University," *Reporter,* 29 (10 October 1963): 46-50;

"The Nature of the Task," *Virginia Quarterly Review,* 42 (Spring 1966): 234-243.

NONFICTION:

"A Defense of, and a Proposal of Some Advantages to Publishers," *Furioso,* 2 (Fall 1946): 38-49;

"The Instruments of Irony," review of *Selected Poems,* by John Crowe Ransom, *Furioso,* 2 (Fall 1946): 65-66;

Review of *William Blake: The Politics of Vision,* by Mark Schorer, *Furioso,* 2 (Fall 1946): 67-68;

Review of *All the King's Men,* by Robert Penn Warren, *Furioso,* 2 (Fall 1946): 69-70;

"The Agon of the Will as Idea," *Furioso,* 2 (Spring 1947): 29;

"Low Thought," review of *Bend Sinister,* by Vladimir Nabokov, *Furioso,* 3 (Fall 1947): 82-84;

"The Phoenix in the World: An Essay on *Love's Parable* by Robert Penn Warren," *Furioso,* 3 (Summer 1948): 36-40;

"The Poets," *Kenyon Review,* 10 (Summer 1948): 501-507;

"Introduction to Your Career as an Author," *Furioso,* 2 (Spring 1949): 39-45;

"Passion and Form," review of "The Diary of a Writer," by F. M. Dostoevski, *Hudson Review,* 2 (Autumn 1949): 477-480;

Review of *Sleep in a Nest of Flames,* by C. H. Ford, *Poetry,* 77 (July 1950): 234-238;

"High Thought," review of *A Rhetoric of Motives,* by Kenneth Burke, *Furioso,* 5 (Fall 1950): 72-76;

Review of *The Little Blue Light,* by Edmund Wilson, *Furioso,* 5 (Fall 1950): 71-72;

"Football," *Furioso,* 6 (Spring 1951): 66-68;

"Contemporary Poets," *Atlantic Monthly,* 194 (September 1954): 66-68;

"Sansom's Fictions," *Kenyon Review,* 17 (Winter 1955): 130-135;

"Poems of Elizabeth Bishop," *Poetry,* 87 (December 1955): 179-181;

"The Nature of Novels," *Partisan Review,* 24 (Fall 1957): 297-307;

"Meditations," *Carleton Miscellany,* 1 (Winter 1960): 33-34;

"True Moments in American Academic History," *Carleton Miscellany,* 2 (Winter 1961): 127-129;

"Other Vision," *American Scholar,* 35 (Autumn 1966): 720-723;

"The Mind's Relation with the World: Two Ways of the Imagination," *Graduate Journal,* 7 (Spring 1967): 375-397;

"Howard Nemerov on Ben Belitt," *Voyages* (Autumn 1967): 29-30;

"On Going Down in History," *Christian Century,* 85 (27 November 1968): 1500-1501;

"An Occident Symposium," *Occident,* 3 (Summer 1969): 101-113;

"On Poetry and Painting, with a Thought of Music," *Prose,* 3 (1971): 101-108;

"Speculation Turning to Itself," *Prose,* 3 (1971): 89-99;

"The New Oxford Canon," *Parnassus,* 1 (1973): 150-151;

"The Dream of Dante," *Prose,* 9 (Fall 1974): 113-133;

"Poetry and History," *Virginia Quarterly Review,* 51 (Spring 1975): 309-328;

"Thirteen Ways of Looking at a Skylark," *Poetry,* 126 (August 1975): 294-305;

"Thoughts on First Passing the Hundredth Page of *Finnegans Wake,*" *American Scholar,* 44 (Autumn 1975): 653-655;

"Speaking Silence," *Georgia Review,* 29 (Winter 1975): 865-881;

"What Will Suffice," *Salmagundi,* 28 (1975): 90-103;

"A Word from the Devil's Advocate," *Parnassus*, 4 (1975): 131-136.

Interviews:

Donna Gerstenberger, "An Interview with Howard Nemerov," *Trace*, no. 35 (January 1960): 22-25;

John Hopkins, "Poet Writes Because He 'Can't Not,' " *Collegian* (University of Vermont), 17 April 1964, p. 3;

Harry James Cargas, "An Interview with Howard Nemerov," *Webster Review*, 1, no. 1 (1974): 34-39;

"An Interview with Howard Nemerov," *Salmagundi*, no. 31-32 (1975): 109-119.

References:

Julia A. Bartholomay, *The Shield of Perseus: The Vision and Imagination of Howard Nemerov* (Gainesville: University of Florida Press, 1972);

Robert Boyers, "Howard Nemerov's True Voice of Feeling," *American Poetry Review*, 4, no. 3 (May/June 1975): 4-9;

Hayden Carruth, "In Their Former Modes," *New York Times Book Review*, 28 April 1968, p. 7;

James Dickey, *Babel to Byzantium: Poets & Poetry Now* (New York: Farrar, Straus & Giroux, 1968), pp. 35-41;

Ann B. Dobie, "The Poet as Critic, *The Stillness in Moving Things: The World of Howard Nemerov*," *Southern Review*, 12 (Autumn 1976): 891-894;

Bowie Duncan, ed., *The Critical Reception of Howard Nemerov: A Selection of Essays and a Bibliography* (Metuchen, N.J.: Scarecrow Press, 1971);

R. W. Flint, "Holding Patterns," *Parnassus*, 3, no. 2 (Spring/Summer 1975): 27-34;

David Galler, "Excellence and Victimization," *Carleton Miscellany* (Summer 1968): 110-114;

Robert D. Harvey, "A Prophet Armed: An Introduction to the Poetry of Howard Nemerov," in *Poets in Progress*, ed. Edward Hungerford (Evanston, Ill.: Northwestern University Press, 1967), pp. 116-133;

Anthony Hecht, "Writers' Rights and Readers' Rights," *Hudson Review*, 21 (Spring 1968): 207-217;

James Kiehl, "The Poems of Howard Nemerov: Where Loveliness Adorns Intelligible Things," *Salmagundi*, no. 22-23 (Spring/Summer 1973): 234-257;

Mary Kinzie, "The Signatures of Things," *Parnassus*, 6 (Fall/Winter 1977): 1-57;

Ross Labrie, *Howard Nemerov* (Boston: Twayne, 1980);

Peter Meinke, *Howard Nemerov* (Minneapolis: University of Minnesota Press, 1968);

William Mills, *The Stillness in Moving Things: The World of Howard Nemerov* (Memphis: Memphis State University Press, 1975);

Douglas H. Olsen, "Such Stuff as Dreams: The Poetry of Howard Nemerov," in *Imagination and the Spirit: Essays in Literature and the Christian Faith Presented to Clyde S. Kilby*, ed. Charles A. Huttar (Grand Rapids, Mich.: Eerdmans, 1971), pp. 365-385;

Paul Ramsey, "To Speak, or Else to Sing," *Parnassus*, 4, no. 2 (1976): 130-138;

Julia Randall, "Genius of the Shore: The Poetry of Howard Nemerov," in *The Sounder Few: Essays from the Hollins Critic*, ed. R. H. W. Dillard, George Garrett, and John Rees Moore (Athens: University of Georgia Press, 1971), pp. 345-357;

Raymond Smith, "Nemerov and Nature: 'The Stillness in Moving Things,' " *Southern Review*, 10 (1974): 153-169;

Robert Stock, "The Epistemological Vision of Howard Nemerov," *Parnassus*, 2 (Fall/Winter 1973): 156-163;

Chad Walsh, "Poetry is Alive and Well in 1967 A.D.," *Book World*, 1 (24 December 1967): 6;

Gloria L. Young, " 'The Fountainhead of All Forms': Poetry and the Unconscious in Emerson and Howard Nemerov," in *Artful Thunder: Versions of the Romantic Tradition in American Literature in Honor of Howard P. Vincent*, ed. Robert J. DeMott and Sanford E. Marovitz (Kent, Ohio: Kent State University Press, 1975), pp. 241-267.

Papers:

There is a collection of Nemerov's papers in the Washington University Libraries, St. Louis.

JOHN FREDERICK NIMS
(20 November 1913-)

BOOKS: *Five Young American Poets*, by Nims and others (Norfolk, Conn.: New Directions, 1944);
The Iron Pastoral (New York: Sloane, 1947);
A Fountain in Kentucky and Other Poems (New York: Sloane, 1950);
Knowledge of the Evening: Poems, 1950-1960 (New Brunswick, N.J.: Rutgers University Press, 1960; London: Paterson, 1960);
Of Flesh and Bone (New Brunswick, N.J.: Rutgers University Press, 1967).

John Frederick Nims was born in Muskegon, Michigan. He married Bonnie Larkin, also a writer, in 1947. Five children were born to them, but one died when very young. Nims attended DePaul University in Chicago and graduated from Notre Dame University in 1937 with majors in English and Latin. He returned to Notre Dame for his M.A. in English and, after receiving it in 1939, began work as an instructor there while also undertaking further graduate work at the University of Chicago in comparative literature. Since receiving his Ph.D. in 1945, he has taught at a number of universities both in this country and abroad. He is currently teaching at the University of Illinois at Chicago Circle, where he can be near the office of *Poetry* magazine, of which he became editor in January 1978. His honors include a variety of prizes and grants, and he has been on the staffs of many writers' conferences.

Nims began to write and publish poetry while still in college, and, following World War II, he was praised highly as a young poet of great promise. His widely commended skill with words has combined well with his knowledge and scholarly assurance to produce a number of much-appreciated translations. All of his work demonstrates his remarkable craftsmanship. He has not written as much as one might wish about his own work, the work of others, and the art of translation, but his essays and introductions dealing with these subjects are intelligent, readable, and valuable.

Just as pastoral poetry affects the manner and matter of country life in order to express the poet's thoughts, so do the poems of *The Iron Pastoral* (1947) use city life as vehicle. They reveal not only the poet's wit, his wordplay, and his wonder, but also his sense of a need for ethical and moral order. Although he is not a devotional poet, Nims's Catholicism is apparent. "He does not write," Richard O. Shaw comments, "of a 'religious' experience as such, but begins from the intellectual-artistic approach of the Catholic Renascence in the novel." Nims is no Carl Sandburg in love with Chicago, but he regards this city often with affection and amusement, occasionally with dismay, and always as an expression of something beyond itself. Dudley Fitts describes these pastorals as more than first-rate reportage, "valuable as that may be: they are moralities, and in their moral passion lies their peculiar strength."

Nims's subjects in *The Iron Pastoral* are often places: a penny arcade, a poolroom, a magazine stand, an airport, an all-night lunchroom; but they include things as well—insects, the dollar bill, a Christmas tree, a Colt automatic. Image piles upon image in many of these poems, often excessively; Nims frequently thrusts upon his reader more than the reader can handle, and the result is sometimes confusion. Meter and rhyme are a shaping force in these poems and (in one way or another) all of his poetry. "Poetry," he has said in an article for *Delos* (1970), "is less a matter of *what* is said than of *how* it is said." His method is to describe and, from that description, to infer. He does this in language that is bright, often dazzling, anything but cliche-ridden. He is occasionally too insistent on using the colloquial, but this device helps to create the effect for which he is looking, displaying what Fitts calls a "healthy, vulgar wit."

A Fountain in Kentucky (1950) does not depart radically from the matter and method of *The Iron Pastoral*, but it does represent a higher level of development. Unlike *The Iron Pastoral*, the poems here are not held together by an obvious theme; each of the four sections has its own unity. Neither are all the poems integrated with the title, except perhaps obliquely. The title poem is one of Nims's many descriptive poems, depicting a cast-iron fountain in the square of a Kentucky town, its paint flaking from age and neglect. At poem's end, there is the suggestion that its tritons still have mythic power; century makes contact with century. Despite their seeming disparity, the poems in this volume are loosely joined through their involvement with past and present; time may not be their intended theme, but in various ways it touches on the subjects of them all.

Nims's technical acuity is under better control in this second volume. Images are less packed, more sharply focused; wordplay is less contrived; and his gift for metaphor shows more truly. He is a poet able to see things and, through words, make the reader see them. He is less often able to make the reader experience things, but when he does, there is the ring of reality. That ring of reality is particularly notable in "The Masque of Blackness," which is among

Nims's most highly praised poems. James Dickey calls it "one of the most memorable, moving, and *believable* elegies in English." A narrative-sonnet sequence in ten parts based upon the poet's actual loss of his young son, this poem uses Shakespeare's

Layle Silbert

metaphor "all the world's a stage" to give it shape and to distance emotion. Nims's ability with languages becomes apparent in this volume, which includes two elegant translations of Horatian odes as well as occasional words and phrases in Latin and Greek.

It is perhaps no surprise that Nims's next volume was a translation, *The Poems of St. John of the Cross*, published first in 1959, revised in 1968, and again revised in 1979. Nims has received no higher praise than for this work, perhaps demonstrating how aptly it uses his strongest qualities. In these translations (which are printed with Spanish text on facing pages so that the reader may readily compare their fidelity to the original) Nims is both intellectual and poet, but both mind and craft are

subordinated to religious sensibility. Glauco Cambon, writing in *Poetry* magazine, speaks of the challenge these poems offer:

> The sixteenth-century mystical poet, long recognized as one of the highest spirits of Christendom, presented to his translator a formidable problem. The burning immediacy of his erotic imagery, transposed to the religious level as happens with Saint Catherine of Siena, shines though the crystal molds of rigorous meters derived from Dante, Cavalcanti, and Petrarch. The incantation of vowel-play, as Mr. Nims remarks in his excellent Notes, is essential to the total impact; and he accordingly decided to recast the phrasing of the Spanish text in such a way as to be able to reproduce in English its rhythmical, metrical, and alliterative effects. The result is often remarkable; acrobatics of the highest class, possible only to a resourceful stylist motivated by love of poetry.

These acrobatics are second always to the power of emotion experienced and created by the Spanish mystic. The language of these translations is fluent and colloquial; it carries the reader quite easily on its ecstatic tide. Published in the same year was Nims's translation of Euripides' *Andromache*, which was included in *The Complete Greek Tragedies* published by the University of Chicago Press. The collection as a whole was highly praised, and Nims's work was singled out for favorable comment in a number of reviews.

Nims also participated in the compilation of a remarkable work, *The Poem Itself* (1960), edited by Stanley Burnshaw, with Nims, Dudley Fitts, and Henri Peyre serving as associate editors. This volume contains the original texts of a variety of French, German, Italian, Portuguese, and Spanish poems, accompanied by literal renderings and explanatory discussions. The book was born out of its editors' frustration with the losses that occur in the process of translation. Since meaning in poetry may be created as much by sound as by sense, the original poems are present with their own rhythm and rhyme, but literal translations and commentary help the reader unschooled in the refinements of each language to understand the poems more fully. Nims was in charge of the Italian section and contributed to both the Italian section and the Spanish section.

Knowledge of the Evening: Poems, 1950-1960 also appeared in 1960. A National Book Award nominee, it takes its title (admired by James Dickey)

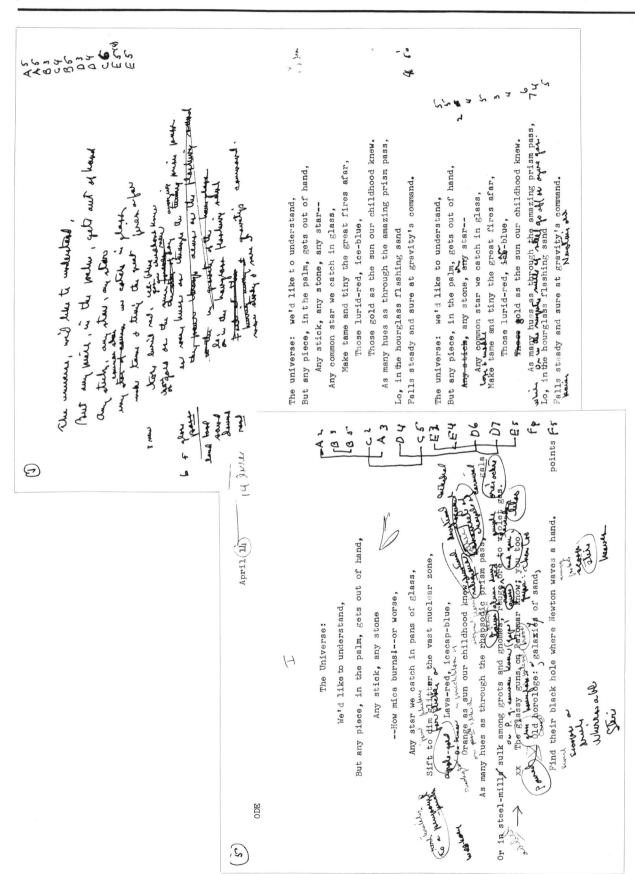

Harvard Phi Beta Kappa poem, 1978, revised typescript

from St. John of the Cross, who saw knowledge of the evening as praise of God for created being and for the knowledge of Him that one derives from the evening as distinct from daylight knowledge of God in Himself. Many of these poems reflect Nims's European experience in the decade from 1950 to 1960, a period during which he taught in Milan, Florence, and Madrid, either on grants or as visiting professor. The language itself also reflects this experience. Each section and several of the poems are marked by epigrams in various foreign languages, and Nims's erudition is also revealed in the poet's references to art, history, mythology, and geography. Usually the poems are well worth the trouble of tracking down their many allusions.

Like *A Fountain in Kentucky, Knowledge of the Evening* is notable for an elegy, "The Evergreen," an eleven-part sequence of brief stanzas in which questions are posed and answered. The voice that speaks is both choked and calm as it tells of "A little boy's thistledown body," a child lying in "a crazy-quilt of fever," the speaker remembering most "a way of death with fingers." The poem is touching, but never sentimental, not even when its Christian orientation comes through at the end:

> *But the boy below?* What's here is
> Gear in a sea-chest only.
> Stowed for a season, then
> Pleasure-bound on the deep.

There is perhaps another quality shared by this book with the earlier one, a quality suggested by "A Fountain in Kentucky" in the earlier volume and in many of the poems of this volume, particularly those set in Europe, a land deeply imbued with the life of the past. Robert Lewis Weeks speaks of that quality as the "double vision of past overlying the present," a kind of consciousness of the presentness of the past. In "Etruscan Tomb," the echoing song is "Alive oh alive," chanting to the reader how the past remains, and this chant lies behind and within the words of many other poems as well.

Nims is still the capable technician, still playing with words and attempting new things with them. Many of these poems display not only his pyrotechnics but greater ability than before to create poems meant to be read aloud. He has always had a great respect for sound, which he feels should lead to sense rather than follow from it; poetry is first of all perceived, he once said, as a sound-continuum. Still, the importance of sound is greater than ever in this collection. Perhaps the work in translation of this decade and the conscious effort to correlate rhythmic effects in English with those of another language

enhanced his sensitivity to the sound of his native tongue. Whatever the cause, these poems almost demand vocalization.

Nims's next published work was not a translation of his own but an edition of the Arthur Golding translation of Ovid's *Metamorphosis* (1965). In his introduction, "Ovid, Golding, and the Craft of Poetry," Nims admits to reservations about the beauty of the work, but he makes a case for its other claims on the reader's attention:

> It is certainly the most famous translation of Ovid into English. It was the English Ovid from the time of its publication until about a decade after the death of Shakespeare in 1616—the Ovid, that is, for all who read him in English during the greatest period in our literature. And in its racy verve, its quirks and oddities, its rugged English gusto, it is still more enjoyable than any other *Metamorphosis* in English.

The textual apparatus of this work is clearly the product of a first-rate scholar, and Nims's poetic sensibilities as well are at work in his comments.

The attention to classical poetry in this book and in Nims's other work makes itself felt in *Of Flesh and Bone* (1967), a collection of just over sixty terse, compact, epigrammatic pieces that both look and sound different from his other work. While *A Knowledge of the Evening* explores fully the uses of half-rhyme and of suggested rhyme ("ghosts and tokens storm like / gulls"), these brief poems rhyme in straightforward fashion, usually in sets of two, although occasionally in sets of three. Between / magazine, why / die, few / adieu, way / stay—these are the rhyming sets of the first two poems. Lines are end-stopped, and sentences are brief, clipped, often occurring two and even three to a line. Influenced in many ways by *The Greek Anthology* (compiled between the fifth century B.C. and the sixth century A.D.), these poems display Nims's wit in a new vein.

Time, in the sense that it brings inevitable death, is still his theme in *Of Flesh and Bone*. The title itself sets a dichotomy: flesh is life with all its attendant pain and pleasure, while bone is bare death, giving structure to life. One poem, "Love and Death," speaks directly of that necessary structure:

> And yet a kiss (like blubber)'d blur and slip,
> Without the assuring skull beneath the lip.

The book itself represents the opposition of elements. The poems with their biting wit are the flesh given shape by the poet's knowledge of time's exigencies. They are tough, disillusioned, aware of human frailty. The opening poem sets the mood:

> Few things to say—two maybe. Girls, know why?
> You craze the air with pleasure. And you die.

Sappho to Valéry: Poems in Translation was published first in 1971 and again in 1979 in a revised and augmented edition. It contains seventy-one poems by twenty poets writing in nine languages: Catalan, Provençal, French, German, Galician, Spanish, Greek, Latin, and Italian. Like the *Poems of St. John of the Cross*, originals and Nims's translations appear on facing pages so that his work supplements, but does not replace, its sources. The structure of the book and the poems themselves display his high regard for the language of the originals, a regard that becomes even more impressive in his accompanying essay, "Poetry: Lost in Translation?," earlier published in *Delos*. "The greatest infidelity," Nims says, "is to pass off a bad poem in English as representing a good one in another language." In order to show his reader "how the poem goes," he must first show him a poem. Imitations are not what he has in mind, but rather,

> To write poems that will show to some degree what certain poems in another language are *like*. One cannot translate a poem, but one can try to reconstitute it by taking the thought, the imagery, the rhythm, the sound, the qualities of diction—these and whatever else make up the original—and then attempt to rework as many as possible into a poem in English.

This effort involves setting up a constantly shifting set of priorities; in order to claim some qualities, others must be sacrificed, but "with the all-important whole forever in mind." Nims's poetic theories help him to set his priorities. "Words are suggested as much by rhythm as by the argument," he says; the form of the poem exists before the ideas. Since form determines subject, the translator must give it his first attention. The whole process is comparable to exsanguination, in which the blood of an organism is drawn out to be replaced by new blood: "In the process of translation, certainly the lifeblood of the original is drained away; the poem will survive only if the translator has living blood of his own to supply."

The background for the kind of meticulous translation that Nims advises must come from more than classroom study of the language involved. He suggests that the translator discuss his poem with someone who has known from childhood the language in which it is written. These discussions are additions to, not replacements for, actual experience with the language. Late learners are blunderers, he says, and must make use of whatever resources are possible in order to catch all the nuances of a line of poetry: "Almost nowhere is hubris more conspicuous than in translating poetry; everyone thinks he knows more than he knows."

Western Wind: An Introduction to Poetry (1974) is essentially a college textbook, but it is of value to the general reader as well. Nims's experience as a teacher is evident in his comments, which gracefully lead the reader to the poems. A revised edition is planned. *James Shirley's "Love's Cruelty"* (1980), a volume of the Renaissance Drama series, is an edition of the 1640 quarto volume with notes and introduction. Nims is also presently at work on an anthology for the general reader and on a collection of his more recent poems.

These more recent poems mark a new direction in his work, a direction apparent most particularly in "The Observatory Ode," the Harvard Phi Beta Kappa poem for 1978, which sees in modern discoveries about the universe a new myth. "No heat like this," he writes, "No heat like science and poetry when they kiss." This kiss is the central image as well of a group of forty related poems, a kiss that stands for the union of disparate yet complementary elements. It is the kiss with which God breathed life into man, the kiss of nuclear fusion, the kiss of all loves, human and divine.

John Frederick Nims has had a distinguished career, claiming both academic and poetic achievement. His poems have met with a range of critical response, but whatever the critic's stance, it is nearly always Nims's poetic technique that evokes most comment. That technique, combined with his meticulous scholarship, is also the grounding for his much-praised translations. Still active as poet, teacher, and editor, Nims is the author of a number of fine poems sure to live on in anthologies and the translator of substantial works that will be read for years to come. —*Holly Mims Westcott*

Other:

"Notes," in *Mid-Century American Poets*, ed. John Ciardi (New York: Twayne, 1950), pp. 119-125;

"Dedalus in Crete," in *Dedalus on Crete: Essays on the Implications of Joyce's Portrait* (Los Angeles: Saint Thomas More Guild, Immaculate Heart College, 1956);

The Poem Itself, edited by Nims and others (New York: Holt, Rinehart & Winston, 1960);

"Yeats and the Careless Muse," in *Learners and*

Discerners: A Newer Criticism, ed. Robert Scholes (Charlottesville: University Press of Virginia, 1964), pp. 31-60;

Ovid's Metamorphosis: The Arthur Golding Translation 1567, edited by Nims (New York: Macmillan, 1965);

"The Poetry of Sylvia Plath: A Technical Analysis," in *The Art of Sylvia Plath: A Symposium*, ed. Charles Newman (Bloomington: Indiana University Press, 1970), pp. 136-152;

Western Wind: An Introduction to Poetry, edited by Nims (New York: Random House, 1974);

James Shirley's "Love's Cruelty," edited by Nims (New York: Garland, 1980).

Translations:

The Poems of St. John of the Cross (New York: Grove, 1959; London: Calder, 1959; revised edition, New York: Grove, 1968; revised again, Chicago: University of Chicago Press, 1979);

Andromache, in *The Complete Greek Tragedies, Euripides III*, ed. David Grene and Richard Lattimore (Chicago: University of Chicago Press, 1959; Cambridge: Cambridge University Press, 1959);

Sappho to Valéry: Poems in Translation (New Brunswick, N.J.: Rutgers University Press, 1971; revised edition, Princeton: Princeton University Press, 1979).

Periodical Publications:

"Homage in Measure to Mr. Berryman," *Prairie Schooner*, 32 (Spring 1958): 1-7;

"The Classicism of Robert Frost," *Saturday Review*, 46 (23 February 1963): 22-23, 62;

"The Greatest English Lyric?—A New Reading of Joe E. Skilmer's 'Therese,' " *Studies in Bibliography*, 20 (1967): 1-4; reprinted in *The Overwrought Urn*, ed. Charles Kaplan (New York: Pegasus, 1969), pp. 56-69;

"Poetry: Lost in Translation?" *Delos*, 5 (1970): 103-126;

"Helen Chasin: An Appreciation," *New Republic*, 175 (9 October 1976): 35-37.

References:

John Ciardi, "John Frederick Nims and the Modern Idiom," *University of Kansas City Review*, 14 (Winter 1947): 105-110;

Glauco Cambon, "Immediacies and Distances,"

Poetry, 95 (March 1960): 379-381;

James Dickey, *From Babel to Byzantium: Poets and Poetry Now* (New York: Farrar, Straus & Giroux, 1968), pp. 168-170;

Dudley Fitts, "Corydon, 1947," *Poetry*, 71 (December 1947): 149-152;

Richard O. Shaw, "Sanctity and the Poetry of John F. Nims," *Renascence*, 13 (Autumn 1960): 84-91;

Robert Lewis Weeks, "The Opening of Doors," *Prairie Schooner*, 35 (Winter 1961-1962): 285-286;

Richard Wilbur, Review of *A Fountain in Kentucky and Other Poems*, *Poetry*, 77 (November 1950): 105-107.

JOYCE CAROL OATES
(16 June 1938-)

SELECTED BOOKS: *By the North Gate* (New York: Vanguard Press, 1963);

With Shuddering Fall (New York: Vanguard Press, 1964; London: Cape, 1965);

Upon the Sweeping Flood and Other Stories (New York: Vanguard Press, 1966; London: Gollancz, 1973);

A Garden of Earthly Delights (New York: Vanguard Press, 1967; London: Gollancz, 1970);

Expensive People (New York: Vanguard Press, 1968; London: Gollancz, 1969);

them (New York: Vanguard Press, 1969; London: Gollancz, 1971);

Anonymous Sins and Other Poems (Baton Rouge: Louisiana State University Press, 1969);

The Wheel of Love and Other Stories (New York: Vanguard Press, 1970; London: Gollancz, 1971);

Love and Its Derangements (Baton Rouge: Louisiana State University Press, 1970);

Wonderland: A Novel (New York: Vanguard Press, 1971; London: Gollancz, 1972);

The Edge of Impossibility: Tragic Forms in Literature (New York: Vanguard Press, 1972; London: Gollancz, 1976);

Marriage and Infidelities: Short Stories (New York: Vanguard Press, 1972; London: Gollancz, 1974);

Angel Fire (Baton Rouge: Louisiana State University Press, 1973);

A Posthumous Sketch (Los Angeles: Black Sparrow Press, 1973);

The Hostile Sun: The Poetry of D. H. Lawrence (Los Angeles: Black Sparrow Press, 1973);

Do With Me What You Will (New York: Vanguard Press, 1973; London: Gollancz, 1974);

Miracle Play (Los Angeles: Black Sparrow Press, 1974);

The Hungry Ghosts: Seven Allusive Comedies (Los Angeles: Black Sparrow Press, 1974; Solihull, U.K.: Aquila, 1975);

Plagiarized Material, as Fernandes (Los Angeles: Black Sparrow Press, 1974);

The Goddess and Other Women (New York: Vanguard Press, 1974; London: Gollancz, 1975);

New Heaven, New Earth: The Visionary Experience in Literature (New York: Vanguard Press, 1974; London: Gollancz, 1976);

Where Are You Going, Where Have You Been? Stories of Young America (Greenwich, Conn.: Fawcett, 1974);

The Seduction and Other Stories (Los Angeles: Black Sparrow Press, 1975);

The Poisoned Kiss and Other Stories from the Portuguese, as Fernandes (New York: Vanguard Press, 1975; London: Gollancz, 1976);

The Assassins: A Book of Hours (New York: Vanguard Press, 1975);

The Fabulous Beasts (Baton Rouge: Louisiana State University Press, 1975);

The Triumph of the Spider Monkey (Santa Barbara: Black Sparrow Press, 1976);

Childwold (New York: Vanguard Press, 1976; London: Gollancz, 1977);

Crossing the Border: Fifteen Tales (New York: Vanguard Press, 1976; London: Gollancz, 1978);

Night Side: Eighteen Tales (New York: Vanguard Press, 1977; London: Gollancz, 1979);

Son of the Morning: A Novel (New York: Vanguard Press, 1978);

Women Whose Lives Are Food, Men Whose Lives Are Money (Baton Rouge: Louisiana State University Press, 1978).

Joyce Carol Oates was born in Lockport, New York. She completed her B.A. at Syracuse University in 1960, and she was awarded an M.A. by the University of Wisconsin in 1961. On 23 January 1961 she married Raymond J. Smith. From 1961 to 1965 she was an instructor in English at the University of Detroit, and from 1965 to 1967 she was an assistant professor at the University of Windsor. In 1968 she won the Rosenthal Foundation Award of the National Institute of Arts and Letters for her second novel, *A Garden of Earthly Delights*, and in 1970 a National Book Award for her fourth novel, *them*. Oates presently teaches at Princeton University.

More frequently known for her fiction than for her poetry, Oates had her first collection of stories, *By the North Gate*, published in 1963. The title is taken from a poem by Rihaku in which the north gate is the boundary between civilization and savagery. The existence of savagery in civilized society is one of the predominant themes of both Oates's poetry and fiction. In all of her works, social form becomes merely a disguise for the undercurrents of psychological, and often physical, brutality. Since the publication of these stories (followed in 1964 by her first novel, *With Shuddering Fall*), Oates's critical acclaim has grown steadily. At the age of forty-two she is one of the premier women writers in America, and her productivity has shown no sign of diminishing.

Throughout Oates's poetry the struggle to maintain the identity of the self is associated with domination of women by men. Men define women, and the attempt of women to escape this imposed definition leads to love affairs that are more often psychological warfare. Her poems, short lyrics told in a confessional mode, are outbursts of the inner self against the pressure of relationships that threaten to consume it. They are intensely personal insights seeking a public language that will allow the self to maintain its wholeness in a chaotic and demeaning world.

Oates's first volume of poetry, *Anonymous Sins and Other Poems*, did not attract much attention when it first appeared in 1969, although Robert French remarked that "the volume is charged with a nervous excitement that draws the reader irresistibly into its fictions." As seems to be common in the consideration of novelist-poets, critics tend to regard Oates's poetry in terms of her previous works of fiction. There is some justice to the practice in regard to her first poetic work: the language is somewhat prosaic, and the poems owe more to their ability to startle with discord than to any power to captivate. Repeated themes—horror, isolation, love, violence, and suffering—unify what is otherwise a disjointed effort.

Most of the poems are indeed anonymous confessions of sins, told by narrators whose transgressions are violent wrenchings of the psyche. The volume begins with images of an accusatory world—accusing both the present and the past. It is a claustrophobic world, one of rush hour traffic and blaring radios that inundate the consciousness and make the skin itch for relief. Side by side with language that is occasionally flat and abstract are some of the most startling images in contemporary poetry, images that begin in the commonplace and end in horror, as in "A Married Woman's Song":

I need help. Marriage auspiciously
Drapes you in white, and then
     rapes you with hung
Bodies of broken birds.

Her imagery focuses on the human anatomy—skin, bones, eye sockets, the rind and pulp of the human body—as a symbol of a humanity at war with its soul. From this focus comes a surface whose grotesquerie is as likely to alienate as it is to entice.

If *Anonymous Sins and Other Poems* attracted little notice, her next volume of poetry, *Love and Its Derangements* (1970), was more widely received, although the attention was not always favorable. Arthur Oberg believes that "If Miss Oates wishes to move poetry toward something that is more readable and available, terrible costs to the language are involved." In contrast, Jerome Mazzaro says that the volume "provides an important interesting alternative to what, since Ezra Pound's *Homage to Sextus Propertius*, has become a narrow, near monotonous attack on the misuses of language." Indeed, the language is somewhat less abstract here than in her first volume, but one is not sure that there is much difference. Like the poems of *Anonymous Sins*, those of *Love and Its Derangements* are short, intense vehicles for often violent inner perceptions, clearly accessible, but sometimes at the expense of genuine lyricism.

The emphasis of *Love and Its Derangements* is clearly on the derangements, although the work ends positively with a series of poems entitled "A Landscape of Love." From love's passionate beginnings, there is a breaking apart in which the love is repeatedly lost in the trivia of the mundane world—in thoughts of suicide, in violent angers, and in psychological struggle. The lovers continually dive into the pool of their feelings, only to be cast back up by the depths. Always there is a fear of being trapped and typed to the detriment of the self's conception of its own identity. Despite the obstacles, however, there is an even stronger desire to maintain the struggle for love in the face of what seem to be impossible odds. The landscape of love at the end of the volume is certainly meant to represent a victory, but one wonders if the victory is earned.

The victory in *Angel Fire* (1973) is indeed warranted, however, as Oates offers poetry that demonstrates her true lyrical gifts. The lines are surer, sharper, and less abstract than in her previous poems. They have, in fact, the sensual quality of D. H. Lawrence, from whom she takes the epigraph for the volume: "Ours is the universe of the unfolded rose / the explicit / the candid revelation." Such is the nature of her enterprise. The first section, "Lovers' Bodies," moves from the physical features of the human anatomy to its reverberations in the spiritual, psychological, and emotional life. Like the poems of the first section, those of the second, "Domestic Miracles," represent brief moments of epiphany. Common events of everyday life, such as merely moving about the house or driving on a mountain highway, suddenly reveal entire landscapes that have become invested with psychological meaning and new perceptions. The angel fire itself, the heat of a celestial light in a desert world, purifies and gives new life and understanding. The third section, "Revelations," begins with the realization of the ultimate aloneness of human beings. In an impersonal world, the self struggles to maintain its separate identity, yet tries simultaneously to identify with the external world and to become one with it. The ultimate victory over these forces, which tend to pull the self apart, comes, not through some

Layle Sil—et

Joyce Carol Oates

newfound peace, but through a terror that returns the self to wholeness, as in "The Secret Sweetness of Nightmares":

> Yet the nightmare redeems
> for it is everything you have accomplished
> leading up close behind you
> shallow footprints
> it is in the finite shape
> of your body as it lies, private
> sweetened by a terror
> no chaos
> can interrupt.

The Fabulous Beasts (1975), perhaps Oates's most accomplished work, begins in a winter world of the soul. Images of snow and ice predominate as the attempt to communicate meets with pain and silence. Yet the silence itself becomes a bond between people that draws them closer together than any language. We are united in mutual suffering, Oates suggests, that is beyond the capabilities of language to eradicate or alter. There is in this work a feeling that one must return again and again to the beginnings, back beyond the common language to the common soul.

The isolation, the suffering for an identity, the love, and the pain all culminate in *Women Whose Lives Are Food, Men Whose Lives Are Money* (1978). As the title suggests, women are devoured, and men spend themselves freely to consume women. Of all Oates's works, this is her darkest. The poems move from a preoccupation with social roles through a series of transformations that are accompanied by horror. In "The Resurrection of the Dead," the third section of the volume, the soul angrily demands the things of the earth as well as the things of the spirit. The result is a soulless America crowded with useless consumer objects, an America where "immense with appetite we hurry to devour / cockleshells and periwinkles and tiny moons are shattered / beneath our feet."

Throughout Oates's poetry there is an undercurrent of the social criticism that finally appears on the surface in *Women Whose Lives Are Food, Men Whose Lives Are Money*. The claustrophobic world of her earlier collections seems inevitably to lead to this indictment of materialism as she moves from the anonymous sins of individuals to the even more anonymous sins of an entire society. On the whole, her poetry is not the strength of her canon. Certainly, she has a flair for lyricism, and her images often startle the reader into sensibility, but the subject matter is often too conventional and the language flat and abstract. —*Alex Batman*

Other:

Scenes from American Life: Contemporary Short Fiction, compiled by Oates (New York: Random House, 1973).

References:

Robert French, "The Novelist Poet," *Prairie Schooner,* 44 (Summer 1970): 177-178;

Jerome Mazzaro, "Feeling One's Oates," *Modern Poetry Studies,* 2 (1971): 133-137;

Arthur Oberg, "Deer, Doors, Dark," *Southern Review,* new series 9 (Winter 1973): 243-256.

FRANK O'HARA
(27 June 1926-25 July 1966)

BOOKS: *A City Winter and Other Poems* (New York: Tibor de Nagy Gallery, 1952);

Oranges (New York: Tibor de Nagy Gallery, 1953);

Meditations in an Emergency (New York: Grove, 1957);

Jackson Pollock (New York: Braziller, 1959);

Second Avenue (New York: Totem / Corinth, 1960; London: Centaur, 1960);

New Spanish Painting and Sculpture (New York: Museum of Modern Art, 1960);

Odes (New York: Tiber Press, 1960);

Lunch Poems (San Francisco: City Lights Books, 1965);

Love Poems (Tentative Title) (New York: Tibor de Nagy Editions, 1965);

Robert Motherwell (New York: Museum of Modern Art, 1965);

Nakian (New York: Museum of Modern Art, 1966);

In Memory of My Feelings: A Selection of Poems, ed. Bill Berkson (New York: Museum of Modern Art, 1967);

Two Pieces (London: Long Hair Books, 1969);

The Collected Poems of Frank O'Hara, ed. Donald Allen (New York: Knopf, 1971);

Belgrade, November 19, 1963 (New York: Adventures in Poetry, 1973);

The Selected Poems of Frank O'Hara, ed. Donald Allen (New York: Knopf, 1974);

Hymns of St. Bridget, by O'Hara and Bill Berkson (New York: Adventures in Poetry, 1974);

The End of the Far West (Wivenhoe, U.K.: Ted Berrigan, 1974);

Art Chronicles 1954-1966 (New York: Venture / Braziller, 1975);

Standing Still and Walking in New York, ed. Donald Allen (Bolinas, Cal.: Grey Fox, 1975);

Early Writing, ed. Donald Allen (Bolinas, Cal.: Grey Fox, 1977);

Poems Retrieved, ed. Donald Allen (Bolinas, Cal.: Grey Fox, 1977);

Selected Plays (New York: Full Court Press, 1978).

Frank O'Hara was a leading member of the so-called New York School of poets, a group that included John Ashbery, Barbara Guest, Kenneth Koch, and James Schuyler and received its name from its association with the leading abstract-expressionist painters in New York City during the 1950s—although O'Hara's personal reputation, following his death in 1966 at forty years old, and the significance of his achievement in that brief time, have extended his recognition beyond that of any group.

He was born in Baltimore, Maryland, but moved at an early age to Grafton, a suburb of Worcester, in central Massachusetts. While growing up, he was a serious music student and wished above all to be a concert pianist. O'Hara writes: "It was a very funny life. I lived in Grafton, took a ride or a bus into Worcester every day to high school, and on Saturdays took a bus and a train to Boston to study piano. On Sundays, I stayed in my room and listened to the Sunday symphony programs." After service aboard a destroyer in the South Pacific during World War II, he entered Harvard (the illustrator Edward Gorey was his roommate), first majoring in music, but changing to English and deciding to be a writer. His first published work was some poems and stories in the *Harvard Advocate*. While living in Cambridge, he met poets John Ashbery, who was on the editorial board of the *Advocate*, and V. R. "Bunny" Lang. On occasional visits to New York, he met Kenneth Koch and James Schuyler, as well as the painters who were likewise to be so much a part of his life, notably Larry Rivers, Jane Freilicher, Fairfield Porter, Grace Hartigan, Joan Mitchell, Michael Goldberg, Willem de Kooning, Franz Kline, and Jackson Pollock. He was the first of the young New York poets to write regular art criticism, serving as editorial associate for *Art News*, contributing reviews and occasional articles from 1953 to 1955. He had a long association with the Museum of Modern Art in New York, beginning as a clerk at the information and sales desk in the front lobby, later becoming an assistant curator at the museum, and in 1965, despite lack of formal training, associate curator.

O'Hara's work was first brought to the attention of the wider public, like that of so many others of his generation, by Donald Allen's timely and historic anthology, *The New American Poetry* (1960), but it was not until O'Hara's *Lunch Poems* was published in 1965 that his reputation gained ground, and not until after his sudden death that his recognition increased. Now his reputation is secure as an important and even popular poet in the great upsurge of American poetry following World War II. He did not cultivate academic alliances or solicit editors and publishers. Painter John Button remarks: "When asked by a publisher-friend for a book, Frank might have trouble even finding the poems stuffed into kitchen drawers or packed in boxes that had not been unpacked since his last move. Frank's fame came to him unlooked-for." His recognition came in part because of his early death, the somewhat absurd and meaningless occasion of that death (he was run down by a beach taxi at a vacation resort), the prominence and loyalty of his friends, the renown of his own personality, and above all the exuberant writings themselves. His casual attitude toward his poetic career is reminiscent of the casual composition of many of the poems themselves. One of his most favored poems, "Poem (Lana Turner has collapsed!)," was written on the Staten Island Ferry en route to a poetry reading, and his most important statement of poetics, "Personism," was written in less than an hour while the editor who requested it was on his way across town to pick it up. Kenneth Koch touches upon this particular quality of O'Hara's genius—his natural-ness: "Something Frank had that none of the other artists and writers I know had to the same degree was a way of feeling and acting as though being an artist were the most natural thing in the world. Compared to him everyone else seemed a little self-conscious, abashed, or megalomaniacal." When this quality entered his verse, his work was most undeniably and thoroughly effective.

During his lifetime, O'Hara was as much known as "a poet among painters," part of a group of such poets who seemed to find their inspiration and support from the painters they chose to associate with, writing more art reviews and commentary than literary opinion. (O'Hara published only two book reviews: one of poetry collections by friends Chester Kallman, John Ashbery, and Edwin Denby; the other of John Rechy's *City of Night*, 1963.) His own art criticism, the major portion of which has been collected as *Art Chronicles* (1975), helped to

Frank O'Hara

Frank O'Hara

encourage the painters he liked best and maintain the public awareness of them, although in itself it is nowhere as brilliant as, for example, Ranier Maria Rilke's writings on Rodin or Charles Baudelaire's on the Salon of 1846. Professional critics found it unhelpfully subjective or, in Hilton Kramer's words, "poetical." It is important to note, however, that it is O'Hara's poetry itself that is most painterly, making the best judgment of painting, while participating in the actual techniques of abstract art.

The extent, the sheer volume of his writings, came as a surprise to many of even his closest friends. Most wondered where he had found time to do it all. Ashbery writes in his introduction to the 590-page *Collected Poems* (1971), patiently gathered and carefully edited by Donald Allen: "That *The Collected Poems of Frank O'Hara* should turn out to be a volume of the present dimension will surprise those who knew him, and would have surprised Frank even more. Dashing the poems off at odd moments—in his office at the Museum of Modern Art, in the street at lunchtime or even in a room full of people—he would then put them away in drawers and cartons and half forget them. Once when a publisher asked him for a manuscript he spent weeks and months combing the apartment, enthusiastic and bored at the same time, trying to assemble the poems. Finally he let the project drop, not because he didn't wish his work to appear, but because his thoughts were elsewhere, in the urban world of fantasy where the poems came from." During his lifetime, although he had published more than a hundred poems in scattered magazines and in a few limited editions, there was no sizable representative collection by which to gain a proper and continuous sense of the work, no serious critical studies of his writings like Marjorie Perloff's, and few enough reviews. Before the *Collected Poems*, and later *The Selected Poems of Frank O'Hara* (1974), there were only two slight volumes readily available; other books were printed in editions of less than five hundred copies, one in only ten copies, and thus were inaccessible to most serious readers.

O'Hara's poetry, as it developed, joined the post-Symbolist French tradition with the American idiom to produce some of the liveliest and most personable poetry written in the 1950s and early 1960s. He incorporated Surrealistic and Dadaistic techniques within a colloquial speech and the flexible syntax of an engaging and democratic postmodernism. His special subject was the active sensibility's encounter with the world about it, through extravagant fantasy, a ready wit, and a detailed realism of feelings. The result, a unique blend of elements, has earned him a memorable place in American poetry. He hastened the development of an art form hitherto little practiced in English (*The Waste Land*, for example, is never designated as authored by both Ezra Pound and T. S. Eliot) that was to become popular in the later 1960s and 1970s among younger poets—the collaboration: writing poems with Ashbery, Koch, Bill Berkson; creating "translations" from the French; producing a series of lithographs with Larry Rivers, collages with Michael Goldberg, comic strips with Joe Brainard, "Dialogues for Two Voices and Two Pianos" with composer Ned Rorem, a movie with painter Alfred Leslie. He was the subject of portraits by many of his artist friends—an indication of not only his association with painters, but the esteem the artists held him in. His early death only contributed to his legend and kept alive his memory until the publication of his collected writings, beginning with *Collected Poems* in 1971, confirmed for many what a few, mostly his friends and fellow poets, already knew—that he was an immensely gifted poet, worth taking seriously and sharing.

The collection of his poems by Donald Allen and the arrangement of them in chronological order make it possible to discuss his work in the order of its development. (Two subsequent volumes prepared by Allen, one containing O'Hara's earliest poems, mostly from notebooks and unpublished manuscripts among his papers, and the other poems overlooked or unavailable at the time of his compilation of the complete poems, supplement the *Collected Poems*.)

O'Hara's earliest poems exhibit much of the promise and brilliance later fulfilled. It might be pointed out, however, because of the somewhat casual method of composition he later became celebrated for and the colloquial air or ease of those poems themselves, that O'Hara was from the start a skilled and knowledgeable poet, well aware, if not always respectful, of the long tradition of the craft. A survey of his *Early Writing* (1977), written between 1946 and 1950 while O'Hara was still a student at Harvard, reveals a striking diversity of forms that includes ballads, songs, a blues (so-called), a madrigal, musical exercises such as a gavotte, a dirge (complete with strophe, antistrophe, and epode), and even more exotic forms such as the French triolet. There are also an imitation of Wallace Stevens (with a touch of Marianne Moore) entitled "A Procession for Peacocks," a strict sonnet, a litany, poems in quatrains, in couplets, heroic couplets, poems with faithful rhyme patterns, and various prose poems. His most persistent interest, however, was the image, in all its suddenness, juxtaposed with an equally unlikely image, following techniques not of imagism but those perfected by the French Surrealists. This period of experimentation and learning (although the imitations and parodies continued) advanced into an interest in post-Symbolist French poetry, especially that of Guillaume Apollinaire and later Pierre Réverdy, along with the big-voiced, roaring surrealism of Vladimir Mayakovski. At the same time, O'Hara's innate Americanness was encouraged by writers such as William Carlos Williams and Moore, together with the colloquial W. H. Auden, whom he felt to be an "American" poet in "his use of the vernacular." He was alert to all developments in his chosen art. A 1952 lecture offered at the abstract-expressionist meeting place in New York called The Club even indicates a surprisingly early familiarity with Charles Olson's "Projective Verse" essay (1950), before it became widely known later in the decade.

Among the poems of this early period, "Oranges" stands out. A series of twelve prose poems (originally nineteen) written while he was home from Harvard during the summer of 1949, they are less the "pastorals" of their subtitle than a decidedly anti-Arcadian surrealistic parody beginning: "Black crows in the burnt mauve grass, as intimate as rotting rice, snot on a white linen field." About twenty copies of the poems, with a painting by Grace Hartigan on the cover, were later published on the occasion of an exhibit of Hartigan's *Oranges* paintings. The poems themselves do not even mention the word of the title, a cleverness the poet was well aware of. He gives an account of the series in his more justly famous "Why I Am Not a Painter," written in 1956:

> One day I am thinking of
> a color: orange. I write a line
> about orange. Pretty soon it is a
> whole page of words, not lines.
> Then another page. There should be
> so much more, not of orange, of
> words, of how terrible orange is
> and life. Days go by. It is even in
> prose, I am a real poet. My poem
> is finished and I haven't mentioned
> orange yet. It's twelve poems, I call
> it ORANGES.

Two other poems written at Harvard—the "Poems" beginning "At night Chinamen jump" and "The eager note on my door"—although among his earliest and having the same daring imagery as the surrealist poems, are exceptional as well for their narrative and dramatic poise. They remain among his finest, and he readily included them in later collections.

Following his four years in Cambridge, O'Hara went to the University of Michigan on the advice of John Ciardi, his creative writing teacher at Harvard, to compete in the Hopwood Awards, winning an award in writing for his manuscript, "A Byzantine Place," and a verse play, *Try! Try!* (later produced by the Poets' Theatre in Cambridge, Massachusetts, which he helped found). He missed the activity of New York and returned in 1951, working briefly as private secretary to photographer Cecil Beaton and then at the Museum of Modern Art. It was during this period that the New York School took its distinct shape, the name parodying, according to poet Edwin Denby who was there, the School of Paris, "which also originated as a joke in opposition to the School of Florence and the School of Venice." O'Hara himself describes the milieu in a memoir of the painter Larry Rivers: "We were all in our early twenties. John Ashbery, Barbara Guest, Kenneth Koch and I, being poets, divided our time between the literary bar, the San Remo, and the artists' bar, the Cedar Tavern. In the San Remo we argued and gossiped: in the Cedar we often wrote poems while listening to the painters argue and gossip. . . . An interesting sidelight to these social activities was that for most of us non-Academic and indeed non-literary poets in the sense of the American scene at the time, the painters were the only generous audience for our poetry, and most of us read first publicly in art galleries or at The Club. The literary establishment cared about as much for our work as the Frick cared for Pollock and de Kooning. . . ."

Frank O'Hara

O'Hara's poems at this time were still heavily surrealistic, as exemplified by "Memorial Day 1950" and "Chez Jane"—perhaps the best of them—and "Easter," which prefigured the more ambitious *Second Avenue* (1960) with its catalogue of random juxtapositions. In "Easter," the images are fully nonreferential, or referential to their own reality alone: "The razzle dazzle maggots are summary / tattooing my simplicity on the pitiable." Only the accustomed syntactic structures prevail—subjects, predicates, clauses—supporting the progression that becomes a tramp of alien, automatous images over an otherwise familiar bridge. It is a liberating experience for a few moments, before a certain saturation and fatigue overcomes the reader. No great, widely cherished, and lasting poem in English has ever been written entirely in the surrealistic mode. Surrealism is, finally, an exploration, a sortie against the limits, a frontier, rather than—except in dream or madness—an organic, living reality. When the images expand out, however, and a narrative occurs, as in "A Terrestrial Cuckoo" from this same time, the results are delightfully comic:

> What a hot day it is! for
> Jane and me above the scorch
> of sun on jungle waters to be
> paddling up and down the Essequibo
> in our canoe of war-surplus gondola parts

This is O'Hara at his best, combining his unique voice and personality with the most far-flung word montages.

Among the early poems, *Second Avenue* in eleven parts is easily the most ambitious. It was written in the spring of 1953 but not published in book form until 1960. The artist Larry Rivers recalls how this "long marvelous poem" was written in his "plaster garden studio overlooking" the avenue of the title, with the poet finishing it between poses for a sculpture Rivers was making of him. Kenneth Koch, who also had some role in the poem's composition, finds it "among the wonders of contemporary poetry," and Albert Cook, the first of the academics to recognize O'Hara, finds it "too perfect of its kind, which it has invented, to induce anyone's strictures." Most readers, however, have found difficulty with it. Perloff calls it O'Hara's "most Byzantine and difficult poem," while even Ashbery in his introduction to the *Collected Poems* speaks of "the obfuscation that makes reading 'Second Avenue' such a difficult pleasure." O'Hara sensed some of the difficulties and later offered a few thoughts concerning the poem in a letter to a reader or editor who had apparently found it obscure. In his letter he identifies some of the components, including a derisive portrait of "a poetry critic and teacher," a description of painter Grace Hartigan at work, and "a true description of not being able to continue this poem and meeting Kenneth Koch for a sandwich while waiting for the poem to start again." He also insists: "actually everything in it either happened to me or I felt happening (saw, imagined) on Second Avenue"—even though the landscape is neither recognizable nor significant on its own terms. Koch writes elsewhere that the poem "is evidence that the avant-garde style of French poetry from Baudelaire to Réverdy has now infiltrated American consciousness to such an extent that it is possible for an American poet to write lyrically in it with perfect ease," although when he states that the poem's language resembles William Carlos Williams's in being "convincing and natural," nothing could be further from accuracy. Koch also suggests the chief persona of the poem is "a sort of Whitmanian I," though this is hardly discoverable.

Second Avenue is a poem of brilliant excess and breakneck inventiveness, beginning: "Quips and players, seeming to vend astringency off-hours, / celebrate diced excesses and sardonics, mixing pleasures, / as if proximity were staring at the margin of the plea. . . ." For most readers, however, this is language in love with itself. The poem is dedicated to Mayakovski, one of O'Hara's great heroes (though an early draft is inscribed to Willem de Kooning), and certainly the images throughout are as wide ranging and as startling as Mayakovski's, but they arrive more rapidly and with less continuity, jostling for the reader's attention, a bewildering admixture. Moreover, they do not have Mayakovski's large, carrying, unifying voice. O'Hara himself explained: "where Mayakovsky and de Kooning come in, is that they both have done works as big as cities where the life in the work is autonomous (not about actual city life) and yet similar." Here, the result is a highly mosaicked, patterned surface. "The verbal elements," by the poet's own insistence, "are extended consciously to keep the surface of the poem high and dry, not wet, reflective and self-conscious." But it is perhaps the most difficult of all accomplishments in art, the texture of surface appearance. "Perhaps," O'Hara continues, "the obscurity comes in here, in the relationship between the surface and the meaning, but I like it that way since the one is the other (you have to use words) and I hope the poem to *be* the subject, not just about it."

This last statement is, in effect, a succinct definition of nonrepresentational art—and in that sense, *Second Avenue* is a perfect embodiment of the techniques of abstract expressionism, the series of strokes that in their totality alone completes a form. There is a cinematic "sleet" of images, colored vaguely by the city's lights and shapes glimpsed from the window on Second Avenue, falling with such rapidity that the dissolves occur before the gestalt-making powers of the mind can focus them. These images are, in the poem's own words, "diced essences"—sharply cut and full of chance. "Butter. Lotions. Cries. A glass of ice. Aldebaran and Mizar, / a guitar of toothpaste tubes and fingernails, trembling spear"—they are hardly full-bodied; rather, subliminal phantoms, too fleeting even for associations. The poem is too energized to be a failure, but without a guiding narrator and propelled by change and chance alone, it is all, by now, dead dada, an example of the limits of the surrealistic mode in O'Hara's early poems. The poem might be said to be, in light of the manner of composition and success of the later poems, overworked. One need only compare the "Poem" beginning "Now the violets are all gone, the rhinoceroses, the cymbals"—the same catalogue of disparate objects—to see how, when the personality takes over, a true, more shareable lyricism flowers. Perloff wisely points out that when the two strands are merged—the surrealistic, with its endless variety and high-spirited inventiveness, and the personal, the spoken American, the colloquial narrative with its charming persona—O'Hara attains his triumph.

As long as the succession of rapid-fire discontinuous images does not extend beyond tolerance, and, further, when there is some attempt to relate those images to an order of reality beyond themselves, O'Hara's surrealism works. In "On Rachmaninoff's Birthday," beginning "Quick! a last poem before I go / off my rocker," the final line—"You'll never be mentally sober"—comments on the previous assortment of images and relates to the initial "I," rounding out the poem while adding a dimension of self-reflection and conscious control to an otherwise indulgent randomness. Or where the images are consistent, added to with like elements, as in "Romanze, or the Music Students" beginning:

> The rain, its tiny pressure
> on your scalp, like onto
> passing the door of a tobacconist.
> "Hello!" they cry, their
> noses glistening. . . .

—almost like an animated cartoon—this is the cleverness that makes O'Hara most appealing.

The lyrical/narrative "I," the "I" with verve and personality, the distinctive O'Hara persona, the "I" of what he himself called his "I do this I do that" poems, makes its appearance as early as "Music," written in 1954. There, too, the persona is set upon a representational landscape of Midtown Manhattan, where landmarks are called by name, as they exist in public reality (the Equestrian statue, the Mayflower Donut Shoppe, Bergdorf Goodman's, Park Avenue itself). Just how personal and lyrical this "I" is can be seen in "To the Harbormaster," one of the finest modern love poems (written for Larry Rivers). Other poems from this period concern images of a different order, including movie stars such as James Dean, both a symbol and victim of popular culture, to whom no less than four poems are dedicated. There is also the mock-heroic "To the Film Industry in Crisis," addressed "to you, / glorious Silver Screen, tragic Technicolor, amorous Cinemascope, / stretching Vistavision and startling Stereophonic Sound, with all / your heavenly dimensions and reverberations and iconoclasms!"; continued later with the equally amusing "Ave Maria," beginning: "Mothers of America / let your kids go to the movies!" A meditative poem like "Sleeping on the Wing" from 1955 is a further advance and indication the poet's personality has fully emerged; specifically, that he is aware of the precious advantage, indeed the great comfort, of undisguised human "singularity," which he knows to be "all that you have made your own." Interestingly, despite all the appearances of a prolonged, considered meditation, the poem was actually composed with great rapidity, increasingly typical for O'Hara, a sign perhaps of the confidence, embodied by Li Po, of the poet come into his own. James Schuyler remembers: "The day this was written I was having breakfast (i.e. coffee) with Frank and Joe [O'Hara's roommate Joe LeSueur] at 326 East 49th Street, and the talk turned to Frank's unquenchable inspiration, in a teasing way on my part and Joe's. The cigarette smoke began jetting from Frank's nostrils and he went into the next room and wrote SLEEPING ON THE WING in a great clatter of keys."

"A Step Away From Them" from 1956 is classic O'Hara, at least as he has come to be known, the first of his so-called lunch poems, beginning:

> It's my lunch hour, so I go
> for a walk among the hum-colored
> cabs. . . . A
> Negro stands in a doorway with a
> toothpick, languorously agitating.
> A blonde chorus girl clicks: he
> smiles and rubs his chin. Everything

suddenly honks: it is 12:40 of
a Thursday. . . .

The poet is immersed in his mode, his *monde*. Not a hair of a word is out of place; there is nothing garish, not a single grotesquerie—except what might naturally be there (if at all). The same with his poem of determined optimism to painter Joan Mitchell ("Poem Read at Joan Mitchell's"), where happiness is "the least and best of human attainments," or the cohesiveness of "Platinum, Watching TV, Etc," preserved in *Poems Retrieved* (1977), or the equally expansive poem to another painter friend entitled "John Button Birthday." These are all poems written when O'Hara was most at home in his world and at the full strength of his style. They are followed by a series of *Odes* (1960) and continue into his most successful years, 1959 and 1960. When he wrote them, it was another dawning in American poetry and he one of the chief instigators, as he knew himself in his "Poem Read at Joan Mitchell's," when he writes: "tonight I feel energetic because I'm sort of the bugle, / like waking people up. . . ."

One of the highlights of O'Hara's collected works is *Odes*, all written in 1957-1958 and originally published in a highly priced and very limited edition (in a series with similar collections by the other principal "New York School" poets, Ashbery, Koch, and Schuyler). The most impressive of these are "Ode to Michael Goldberg ('s Birth and Other Births)" and "Ode: Salute to the French Negro Poets." The long ode to Goldberg, whose silk-screen prints adorn the edition, is more like the Romantic— specifically Wordsworthian—ode than any of the others. It concerns the growth of both the poet's mind and his role (as poet), autobiographically moving through memories of childhood toward a confrontation with mortality. The poem is neither a celebration nor congratulatory (it is not, despite the title, a birthday poem for the painter but was written during the three months after his birthday). It commemorates the persistence of mortality, the repeated births that make up a life, rather than any Wordsworthian intimation of immortality. It begins with memories first of Baltimore (O'Hara writes of his affinity for the magnolias and tulip trees mentioned in the poem in autobiographical fragments published in *Standing Still and Walking in New York*, 1975), then of Grafton, where aesthetic as well as sexual awakening occurred:

> Up on the mountainous hill
> behind the confusing house
> where I lived . . . there,
> the wind sounded exactly like
> Stravinsky

> I first recognized art
> as wildness, and it seemed right,
> I mean rite, to me. . . .

(The allusion to *The Rite of Spring* is obvious enough.) The poem proceeds through recollections of his personal life, including wartime days in the South Pacific, and psychosexual hints, to the present that must be faced, where "too much endlessness" is "stored up, and in store," awaiting. It is not his alone, but the human and historical condition. There are repeated reminders of the "darkness" at the center of life, but even as that darkness occurs it appears "a glistening / blackness in the center / if you seek it. . . . capable of bursting / into flame or merely / gleaming profoundly." Amidst all, the poet has been selected to bear like Prometheus "the gift of fire" to a "foreign land," a "temporary place of light, the land of air" (O'Hara is that noncommittal). It is this land toward which the poem moves, concluding with almost a historical imperative:

> a barque of slaves
>   who soon will turn upon their captors
> lower anchor, found a city riding there
>   of poverty and sweetness paralleled
> among the races without time,
>   and one alone will speak of being
> born in pain
>   and he will be the wings of an extraordinary liberty

The poet has never been more Romantic. "Ode to Michael Goldberg" is one of O'Hara's more exploratory poems, one in which there is a sustained effort to face the meaning of his own life and to see that life in larger philosophical reflections. Still, he resists oversimplification and insists on discontinuities. Toward the end he offers this quote and potential hope:

> "the exquisite prayer
> to be new each day
> brings to the artist
> only a certain kneeness"

—not *newness*, not *keenness*, but an absurd *kneeness*. It might even be a Platonic joke. The artist is brought down to his knees, not just by the prayer for creative novelty, one of the values necessary for his art, but he is reduced to a certain futility and awkwardness. Rebirth is frustrated, or at least not very convenient. Ironies and apparent contradictions abound: "you pull a pretty ring out of the pineapple [a grenade] / and blow yourself up"; everything is simultaneously "all right" and "difficult"; "wit" and "austerity" are shared; we fall sobbing to the floor with both "joy" and "freezing."

Even at the end, in the city of the future, almost a new world, "poverty" and "sweetness" persist as parallels. Certainly this is a "realistic" view of the world; the only romantic thing in it is the poet himself, those "wings of an extraordinary liberty."

The "Ode to Michael Goldberg" should answer any charges that O'Hara cannot sustain a theme or a poem. Drawn from the full flood of childhood memory, it courses up through "A couple of specifically anguished days" of the present which "make me now distrust sorrow, simple sorrow / especially, like sorrow over death." It is perhaps his most encompassing poem, most ruminative, intro-spective, almost uncharacteristically somber, and contains the darkness at the very quick of his soul that obviously haunted him and that he lived with so cheerfully and so well.

Resonance and great rolling tones are evident in the opening lines of "Ode: Salute to the French Negro Poets":

From near the sea, like Whitman my great predecessor,
                                                    I call
to the spirits of other lands to make fecund my
                                                    . . .

It is a voice of majesty, announcing a large theme.

```
              PERSONAL POEM


        Now when I walk around at lunchtime
        I have only two charms in my pocket
        an old Roman coin Mike Kanemitsu gave me
        and a bolt-head that broke off a packing case
        when I was in Madrid the others never
        brought me too much luck though they did
        help keep me in New York against coercion
        but now I'm happy for a time and interested

        I walk through the luminous humidity
        passing the House of Seagram with its wet
        and its loungers and the construction to
        the left that closed the sidewalk if
        I ever get to be a construction worker
        I'd like to have a silver hat please
        and get to Moriarty's where I wait for
        Leroi and hear who wants to be a mover and
        shaker the last five years my batting average
        is .016 that's that, and Leroi comes in
        and tells me Miles Davis was clubbed 12
        times last night outside BIRDLAND by a cop
        a lady asks us for a nickel for a terrible
        disease but we don't give her one we
        don't like terrible diseases, then

        we go eat some fish and some ale it's
        cool but crowded we don't like Lionel Trilling
        we decide, we like Kenneth Koch we don't like
        Henry James so much we like Herman Melville
        we don't want to be in the poets' walk in
        San Francisco even we just want to be rich
        and walk on girders in our silver hats
        I wonder if one person out of the 8,000,000 is
        thinking of me as I shake hands with Leroi
        and buy a strap for my wristwatch and go
        back to work happy at the thought possibly so
        it would probably be only the one person
        who gave me a blue whistle from a crackerjack box
```

Don Allen

Print Scene

Frank O'Hara

1959

"Personal Poem," revised typescript

The diction is quite self-consciously exalted, proper to an ode, compared to the breezy familiarity ordinarily expected of O'Hara: Love is "traduced" by shame; "reticence" is paid for by a poet in his blood; "fortuity" is in the love we bear. He even forgoes his tendency to wisecrack, before the seriousness of his intended theme: "here where to love at all's to be a politician," he writes, threatening sarcasm, and continues with a mocking rhyme, "as to love a poem / is pretentious, this may sound tendentious but it's lyrical." The drift into smartness ("it's lyrical") is checked, however, and the poem is restored to seriousness, even gravity, by what follows—"which shows what lyricism has been brought to by our fabled times"—and elevated diction like "cowards are shibboleths" and "one specific love's traduced." This ode is actually one of O'Hara's most directly political poems, mounting almost to a rhetoric of defiance: "blood! blood that we have mountains in our veins to stand off jackals / in the pillaging of our desires and allegiances...." The poem is formal even in its line arrangement—a series of long waves of couplets. There is not one drop of silliness or playful avoidance, as he continues: "for if there is fortuity it's in the love we bear each other's differences / in race." It is almost a somber poem, certainly stately, as it moves in assured and measured cadences to its end: "the only truth is face to face, the poem whose words become your mouth / and dying in black and white we fight for what we love, not are." It is a comment on racial relations in his own America at the beginning of the Civil Rights era, an important political and social statement; he is turning his back on the "terrible western world" to invoke such anticolonialist poets as Aimé Césaire. It may even be called a noble poem, and how often is O'Hara thought of in those terms?

The year 1959 was probably O'Hara's best, when one of his most famous poems, "The Day Lady Died," was written. It is a tribute to the jazz singer Billie Holiday. Told in completely paratactic order, with nothing revealed ahead of time, the powerful realization of an ending is suspended until events occur in the natural narrative of their existence. It begins with a (possibly) feigned and protracted preoccupation with cultural paraphernalia and quotidian distractions and transactions, but moves with suddenness to testify to the sanctity of human life and talent, and the eternality of art that is literally, mimetically, breathtaking. It moves through a series of choices until there aren't any, until the poet arrives face to face with the unchosen, the uninvited but inevitable, irreversible wonder of loss. Names abound—"Bastille," "Easthampton," "an

ugly NEW WORLD WRITING to see what the poets / of Ghana are doing these days," "Miss Stillwagon," "Verlaine"—but "hers" never is (only hinted at in the title, with her own title, Lady Day, reversed). Time likewise is held up, or too freely given at the beginning—

It is 12:20 in New York a Friday
three days after Bastille day, yes
it is 1959 and . . . I will get off the 4:19 in Easthampton
at 7:15 . . .

—but then held suspended, as up a sleeve, until the end, and released when most appropriate, in the natural order of events:

then I go back where I came from to 6th Avenue
and the tobacconist in the Ziegfeld Theatre and
casually ask for a carton of Gauloises and a carton
of Picayunes, and a NEW YORK POST with her face
                                                        on it

and I am sweating a lot by now and thinking of
leaning on the john door in the 5 SPOT
while she whispered a song along the keyboard
to Mal Waldron and everyone and I stopped
                                        breathing. . . .

Death silences the trivia. The last line is a perfect example of shared syntax, the merging of object into subject (at precisely "everyone") in the flux of events in the continuous postmodernist universe. Writing in the simultaneous present, the poet has total control over both time and timing—the arrival (or denial) of images, the coming (or postponing) of a conclusion.

O'Hara's level of accomplishment remained at its peak through 1961, through a series of love poems—later published as *Love Poems (Tentative Title)* (1965). Poem after poem is of a high order of achievement—"Rhapsody," "Adieu to Norman, Bon Jour to Joan and Jean-Paul," "Joe's Jacket," "You Are Gorgeous and I'm Coming," "Personal Poem." These are all poems with the identifying characteristics of an O'Hara poem, all the same quick-stepping, name-dropping, vivacious, uninhibited narrator (name-dropping because utterly at home in his surroundings, and in the poem). Artists and their creations continue to decorate the poems as comfortably as they do a sunken living room. They are the flora and fauna of O'Hara's urban landscape and heighten the authenticity of the poet's world as much as Gary Snyder's invoking a specific shrub such as manzanita. Surrealism is at easy reach, but not overshadowing; there is care for what Olson called the "dailynesses," varied rhythms, syncopation gained by restricting punctuation, an organic syntax, the trust to natural speech (although still very much the speech of a dashing sophisticate), the informed chatter, the management of time in a poem like "Fantasy," the recurrent optimism of "Poem (Khrushchev's coming)." The series of love poems to dancer Vincent Warren—including "Les Luths," "Poem (Light clarity avocado salad)," "Having a Coke With You," and "Steps"—are all affirmative, delicate, precise, poems of frontal immediacy, heartfelt, with feeling no longer hidden behind a bravado of brilliant images and discordant segments. O'Hara moves out of the modernist mode of dada, surrealism, cubism, and into the postmodern advantage: a variety of techniques, which actually incorporate the salient gains of modernism while losing nothing of the flexibility and possibility of openness, the "going on your nerve" of "Personism." At its worst or most excessive, his style lapses into giddiness, or what Howard Snedcof accurately identifies as "camp," citing Susan Sontag's definition of the phenomenon with its "peculiar relation to homosexuality." Sontag observes that "homosexuals have pinned their integration into society on promoting the aesthetic sense. Camp is a solvent of morality. It neutralizes moral indignation, sponsors playfulness." She also notes that "Camp taste is, above all, a mode of enjoyment, of appreciation—not judgment. Camp is generous. It wants to enjoy. . . . Camp taste is a kind of love, love for human nature. It relishes rather than judges, the little triumphs and awkward intensities of 'character. . . .' " While surely not limited to camp, these qualities are indeed dominant in O'Hara's poems from the start. They also happen to be the reason for their great success.

His last major effort was a long poem entitled *Biotherm* (after a brand of suntan lotion the poet happened on). Despite Perloff's high praise for it (a "great" poem) and despite the influence it had on younger poets such as Ted Berrigan and Ron Padgett (specifically, their collaborative *Bean Spasms*, 1967), it is not a very satisfying poem, being too dispersed and, finally, too obscure. It was composed over an extended period of time, from August 1961 to January 1962. O'Hara wrote to Donald Allen: "I've been going on with a thing I started to be a little birthday poem for B[ill] B[erkson] and then it went along a little and then I remembered that was how Mike's Ode ["Ode to Michael Goldberg"] got done so I kept on and I am still going day by day (middle of 8th page this morning). I don't know anything about what it is or will be but am enjoying trying to keep going and seem to have been able to keep it open

and so there are lots of possibilities, air and such." It is less airy than drafty, however, with amusing strokes but an overall smudge without the rhythms of Pollock or similar developers of the "all-over" action "field." To choose from the poem's interior:

on Altair 4, I love you that way, it was on Altair 4 "a
                              happy day"
I knew it would be
yes to everything
          I think you will find the pot in the corner
where the Krells left it
          rub it a little and music comes out
the music of the fears
          I reformed we reformed each other
being available
          it is something our friends don't understand
if you loosen your tie
          my heart will leap out
like a Tanagra sculpture
          from the crater of the Corsican "lip"
and flying through the heavens
          I am reminded of Kit Carson
and all those smiles which were exactly like yours
but we hadn't met yet. . . .

The poem simply evades our attention and will not cohere.

It is not possible to say what direction O'Hara's work would have taken if he had lived—perhaps more social satire or a mock epic like Edward Dorn's *Gunslinger*, tighter and with more theatre in it than *Biotherm*. Given the nature of subsequent political and social events, he might have become the Juvenal of his day. It is unlikely he would have abandoned poetry, despite the slowdown in production during the last years (he wrote only three poems the last year and a half of his life) and his increased responsibilities in the art world (he was to be appointed a full curator at the museum), since he had always said poetry was his life. More likely his growing recognition among young poets would have spurred him further, at the same time inspiring a greater sense of responsibility among the many who followed his lead. —*George F. Butterick*

Bibliography:

Alexander Smith, Jr., *Frank O'Hara. A Comprehensive Bibliography* (New York: Garland, 1979).

References:

Charles Altieri, *Enlarging the Temple: New

Directions in American Poetry During the 1960s (Lewisburg, Pa.: Bucknell University Press; London: Associated University Presses, 1979), pp. 108-122;

Bill Berkson and Joe LeSueur, eds., "Homage to Frank O'Hara," *Big Sky*, no. 11-12 (1978);

Paul Carroll, *The Poem in Its Skin* (Chicago: Big Table, 1968), pp. 157-168;

Albert Cook, "Frank O'Hara, We Are Listening," *Audit*, 4 (1964): 34-35;

Susan Holahan, "Frank O'Hara's Poetry," in *American Poetry Since 1960, Some Critical Perspectives*, ed. Robert B. Shaw (Cheadle Hulme, U.K.: Carcanet, 1973), pp. 109-122;

Richard Howard, *Alone with America Essays on the Art of Poetry in the United States Since 1950* (New York: Atheneum, 1969), pp. 396-412;

Anthony Libby, "O'Hara on the Silver Range," *Contemporary Literature*, 17 (Spring 1976): 240-262;

Thomas Meyer, "Glistening Torsos, Sandwiches, Coca-Cola," *Parnassus*, 6 (Fall-Winter 1977): 241-257;

Charles Molesworth, " 'The Clear Architecture of the Nerves': The Poetry of Frank O'Hara," *Iowa Review*, 6 (Summer-Fall 1975): 61-74;

Lavonne Mueller, "Frank O'Hara: Going the Full Length," *West Coast Review*, 8 (October 1972): 25-29;

O'Hara supplement, *Panjandrum*, no. 2 & 3 (1973);

Marjorie Perloff, *Frank O'Hara: Poet Among Painters* (New York: Braziller, 1977; Austin: University of Texas Press, 1979);

Harold Robert Snedcof, "The Achievement of Frank O'Hara," Ph.D. dissertation, Brown University, 1970.

Papers:

Manuscripts and letters in the Bill Berkson papers, as well as letters and manuscripts to Donald Allen, are in the Literary Archives, University of Connecticut Library, Storrs.

MARY OLIVER
(10 September 1935-)

BOOKS: *No Voyage and Other Poems* (London: Dent, 1963; Boston: Houghton Mifflin, 1965);
The River Styx, Ohio, and Other Poems (New York: Harcourt Brace Jovanovich, 1972);
The Night Traveler (Cleveland: Bits Press, 1978);
Sleeping In The Forest (Athens: Ohio Review Chapbook, 1979);
Twelve Moons (Boston: Little, Brown, 1979).

At the onset of her career as a poet, Mary Oliver seems almost literally to have followed in the footsteps of Edna St. Vincent Millay, whose lyrical manner influenced Oliver's early work. Both were "country bred," studied at Vassar, and found an artistic refuge at Provincetown, Massachusetts, combining a love of bohemia with a passion for nature. From the early 1950s, Oliver occasionally stayed at Steepletop, Millay's upstate New York farm, as a friend and assistant to the poet's sister.

Oliver's first poems attempt to achieve a timeless poetic idiom that seems grave and elevated compared to the colloquial and ironic tones often adopted by other "nature poets" such as May Swenson, Maxine Kumin, or Robert Frost. While

Christopher Ricks complained that Oliver's first volume of verse displayed "the mannerisms . . . but not the genuine unprized talent" of Millay, *No Voyage*, which was first published in England in 1963, received generous praise from critics such as Carl Johnson, Philip Booth, and James Dickey. The latter described her poems as "graceful and self-assured, serene even when they treat the ordinary agonies of life . . . richly complex without throwing complexities in the way of the reader." The title poem, "No Voyage," won first prize from the Poetry Society of America in 1963. For subsequent work, she received the Devil's Advocate Award from the Poetry Society of America (1968), a National Endowment for the Arts Creative Writing Fellowship (1972-1973), the Shelley Memorial Award (1970), the Alice Fay di Castagnola Award (1973), the Ohioana Book Award (1973), the Journalism Award from *Commonweal* (1978), the Cleveland Arts Prize for Literature (1979), and a Guggenheim Fellowship (1980). Her work has been acclaimed by Stanley Kunitz, Robert Demott, and Joyce Carol Oates, among others. She has just begun to give readings and workshops on the college circuit; her first academic post has been a Mather Visiting Professorship at Case Western Reserve University (winter/spring 1980).

Born in Cleveland, Ohio, the daughter of a

teacher, Edward William Oliver, and Helen M. Vlasak Oliver, Mary Oliver studied at Ohio State University for one year and then spent a year at Vassar. For the last decade or so she has made Provincetown, Massachusetts, her permanent home. The title of her first book, *No Voyage*, may be somewhat misleading, since the poems range in locale from abandoned farmland in Ohio to New England landscapes, London, and the River Ayr in Robert Burns's Scotland. But no matter where the poet happens to roam, the poems themselves are rooted in an intense and almost mythical sense of heartland America, the spiritual center of the poet's imagination. As she writes in "Country Bred,"

> Being country bred, I am at ease in darkness;
> Like everything that thrives
> In fields beyond the city's keep, I own
> Five wooden senses, and a sixth like water.

Because her intuitive sense of nature's dark forces is wedded to a keen sense of the real, her poetry, like Frost's, sometimes seems deceptively simple, its conventional forms masking an uncommon vision. Observing that there is "no vanity, no pretentiousness, and no false sense of urgency . . ." in Oliver's poetry, Carl Johnson concludes that "in the moderation of her stanzas there is residual strength, and . . . the simplicity and discretion of a mature mind." Despite a few lapses, *No Voyage* represents the best tradition of the lyric, moving the reader not by startling images, but by the secure mastery of feeling and form, as the concluding stanza from "Swans on the River Ayr" testifies:

In Ayr I linger on the cobbled bridge
And watch the birds. I will not tamper with them,
These ailing spirits clipped to live in cities
Whom we have tamed and made as sad as geese.
All swans are only relics of those birds
Who sail the tideless waters of the mind;
Who traveled once the waters of the earth,
Infecting dreams, helping the child to grow;
And who for ages, seeing witless man
Deck the rocks with gifts to make them mild,
Sensed the disaster of their uncaught lives,
And streamed shoreward like a white armada
With head reared back to strike and wings like knives.

If many of these first poems seem Keatsian in their controlled lyrical flights, her next volume, *The River Styx, Ohio, and Other Poems* (1972), seems Wordsworthian in its attempt to reclaim and redeem the past through memory and myth. While Stanley Kunitz notes that Oliver's "tender evocations of an Ohio childhood read like an elegy for a lost

heritage," understatement and self-restraint keep Oliver's work from becoming merely nostalgic or sentimental. "Learning about Indians" portrays an Indian named White Eagle, or Mr. White, who dons war paint and feathers for the extracurricular amusement of school children, then reverts to a "shabby salesman's suit" and drives "Tires screeching, out of the schoolyard into the night." In "Going to Walden," the point of the poem is the poet's refusal to play tourist: the "slow and difficult / Trick of living . . ." is "finding / Walden / where you are." Despite the appeal of myths and symbols, whether they happen to be swans, old world memories, or magical-sounding places like Walden or the River Styx, Ohio, Oliver also insists on the counterpoise of the real. In her struggle to "make peace with the fact," she recognizes that the most difficult voyage is inward.

In *The Night Traveler*, published as a chapbook in 1978, Oliver becomes much more daring in her explorations of the mythic dimension. Her opening poem, "Sleeping on an island," announces her intention to "take off the five senses / Like five masks" and plunge into the unconscious depths where "sleep at the bottom / Shines like oil . . . Fish are moving / Like flames under the water." This is the shadowy and luminous world one associates with Galway Kinnell and Theodore Roethke, what Oliver calls "entering the kingdom." Her Virgil on this journey into the psychic underworld is "the Night Traveler," a presence composed of "bits of wilderness . . . Twigs, loam and leaves . . ." that mediates between the natural and human, opening up the poet to the rich world of the senses. The themes of the poems—birth, decay, death, and dreams—are timeless, but the voice is personal and engaging. Noting that each of the twenty-six poems is "carefully, beautifully, constructed around an image out of nature, or out of the poet's family life," Joyce Carol Oates sees that the poems depict the tensions of living in "two worlds, that of the personal and familial, and that of the impersonal and inhuman." In both worlds, the individual must cope with loneliness and the inevitable waning of natural power. In one of her most beautifully realized poems, "Blackleaf Swamp," Oliver echoes Frost and at the same time achieves a voice distinctively her own.

I'm going to Blackleaf Swamp.
I'll be back tomorrow,
Maybe.

I want to see

The hunting owls ride by
All glassy-eyed and gloomy.

I want to see
Pools where the striped snakes cool
The burden of their backs.

. . . .

If I am a woman, and tame,
Does it mean I cannot be
Part bird, part beast?

And if this is so, why does a wing in the air
Sweep against my blood
Like a small sharp oar?

And if I am alive, but must die,
Is it not proper to study
Darkness and trees and water?

Along the shore
The grass is so green and fine,
It feels like the love of my mother.

The unexpected turn at the end of the poem, the motherly green of the grass, suggests Whitman, another poet who yearned to transcend the merely human and "study / Darkness and trees and water." Like her Romantic and Transcendentalist predecessors, Oliver wishes to reconcile the worlds of humans and animals, adults and children, even though such a reconciliation means the extinction of self-consciousness. In "Winter Sleep" she wants to "winter with the drowsy she-bear" and thus express her sisterhood with this great shy beast. "The Family" actually concerns "the dark things of the wood" who are "the family / We have run away from." Although returning to one's animal heritage means sacrificing one's human ego, it also promises renewal and regeneration, "the secret / castle of honey" in the "one tree / . . . tall as a lighthouse" ("Messages"). Most of her family poems are elegiac, grieving not only for lost relatives but also for the lost world of childhood. In "Stark Country Holiday," the onset of old age and arthritis not only ruins their mother's piano playing, but it reminds the family that "Dreams of our childhood warp and pall, / Caught in the dark fit of the world."

The compelling poems in this volume deserve the high praise of Archibald MacLeish, Joyce Carol Oates, and Robert Demott, who aptly remarked that "Oliver charts a world not fashionably surreal but authentically mythic in its dimension." Her latest book, *Twelve Moons* (1979), is even more audacious in its mythic scope. Containing fifty-one poems (several of them published first in previous volumes), *Twelve Moons* explores natural cycles and processes, equating them with what is deepest and most enduring in human experience. Many more poems now focus on specific animals ("Mussels," "The Black Snake," "The Fish," "Turtles," "Bats," "Sharks," "Two Horses," "Raccoons") or plants ("Aunt Leaf," "Looking for Mushrooms," "The Black Walnut Tree," "Winter Trees"). There are also twelve "moon" poems, each intimating a different phase of experience ("Pink Moon—The Pond," "Flower Moon—How She Travels," "Wolf Moon," "Snow Moon—Black Bear Gives Birth") and also recalling a time when lunar cycles were supposed to influence human affairs. Although each of her previous books had a thematic unity, *Twelve Moons* presents the most integrated and ambitious vision that Oliver has yet attempted.

Ultimately, her vision of nature is celebratory and religious in the deepest sense: as the opening line of "The Fawn" avows, "Sunday morning and mellow as precious metal / the church bells rang, but I went / to the woods instead." Nature is, in Baudelaire's phrase, a "living temple" where the poet can discover the joy and terror, the sustaining truths and feelings that conventional religion and modern society seem unable to provide. These spare, subtle, and dynamic hymns to the natural forces within and without us testify to Mary Oliver's ability to sing in the wilderness and make us listen.

—*Anthony Manousos*

References:

Philip Booth, Review of *No Voyage, Christian Science Monitor*, 15 April 1965, p. 9;

Robert Demott, Review of *The Night Traveler, Western Humanities Review*, 23 (Spring 1979): 185-186;

James Dickey, Review of *No Voyage, Virginia Quarterly Review*, 41 (Summer 1965): lxxxiv;

Carl Johnson, Review of *No Voyage, Commonweal*, 81 (19 March 1965): 794;

Joyce Carol Oates, Review of *The Night Traveler, New Republic*, 179 (9 December 1978): 28-29;

Christopher Ricks, Review of *No Voyage, New Statesman*, 66 (27 September 1965): 414;

Hugh Seidman, Review of *Twelve Moons, New York Times Book Review*, 21 October 1979, p. 24.

Charles Olson

George F. Butterick
University of Connecticut

BIRTH: Worcester, Massachusetts, 27 December 1910, to Karl Joseph and Mary Hines Olson.

EDUCATION: B.A., Wesleyan University, 1932; M.A., Wesleyan University, 1933; Harvard University, 1936-1938.

MARRIAGE: Common-law marriage to Constance Wilcock; children: Katherine. Common-law marriage to Elizabeth Kaiser; children: Charles Peter.

AWARDS: Guggenheim Fellowships, 1939, 1948; Wenner-Gren Foundation grant, 1952; Longview Foundation award for *The Maximus Poems*, 1961; Oscar Blumenthal Prize (*Poetry* magazine), 1965.

DEATH: New York, New York, 10 January 1970.

SELECTED BOOKS: *Call Me Ishmael* (New York: Reynal & Hitchcock, 1947; London: Cape, 1967);

Y & X (Washington, D.C.: Black Sun Press, 1948);

In Cold Hell, In Thicket (Dorchester, Mass.: Origin, 1953; San Francisco: Four Seasons, 1967);

The Maximus Poems / 1-10 (Stuttgart: Jonathan Williams, 1953);

Mayan Letters, ed. Robert Creeley (Palma de Mallorca: Divers Press, 1953; London: Cape, 1968);

The Maximus Poems / 11-22 (Stuttgart: Jonathan Williams, 1956);

O'Ryan 2 4 6 8 10 (San Francisco: White Rabbit, 1958); enlarged edition, *O'Ryan 12345678910* (San Francisco: White Rabbit, 1965);

Projective Verse (New York: Totem Press, 1959);

The Maximus Poems (New York: Jargon/Corinth, 1960; London: Cape Goliard, 1970);

The Distances (New York: Grove; London: Evergreen, 1960);

A Bibliography on America for Edward Dorn (San Francisco: Four Seasons, 1964);

Proprioception (San Francisco: Four Seasons, 1965);

Human Universe and Other Essays, ed. Donald Allen (San Francisco: Auerhahn Society, 1965; New York: Grove, 1967);

Selected Writings, ed. Robert Creeley (New York: New Directions, 1966);

'West' (London: Cape Goliard, 1966);

Maximus Poems IV, V, VI (London: Cape Goliard, 1968; London: Cape Goliard / New York: Grossman, 1968);

Pleistocene Man (Buffalo: Institute of Further Studies, 1968);

Letters for Origin 1950-1956, ed. Albert Glover (London: Cape Goliard, 1969; New York: Cape Goliard / Grossman, 1970);

The Special View of History, ed. Ann Charters (Berkeley: Oyez, 1970);

Archaeologist of Morning (London: Cape Goliard, 1970; New York: Grossman, 1973);

Additional Prose, ed. George F. Butterick (Bolinas, Cal.: Four Seasons, 1974);

The Post Office (Bolinas, Cal.: Grey Fox Press, 1975);

The Maximus Poems: Volume Three, ed. Charles Boer and Butterick (New York: Grossman, 1975);

In Adullam's Lair (Provincetown, Mass.: To the Lighthouse Press, 1975);

Spearmint & Rosemary (Berkeley: Turtle Island, 1975);

Charles Olson and Ezra Pound: An Encounter at St. Elizabeths, ed. Catherine Seelye (New York: Grossman, 1975);

The Horses of the Sea (Santa Barbara: Black Sparrow Press, 1976);

The Fiery Hunt and other plays (Bolinas, Cal.: Four Seasons, 1977);

Some Early Poems (Iowa City: Windhover Press, 1978);

Muthologos: The Collected Lectures and Interviews, ed. Butterick (Bolinas, Cal.: Four Seasons, 1978-1979);

Charles Olson & Robert Creeley: The Complete Correspondence, ed. Butterick (Santa Barbara: Black Sparrow Press, 1980-).

Charles Olson has come to be recognized in the few years since his death as a major shaper of a postmodern American poetry, the chief successor to Ezra Pound and William Carlos Williams. He was a leading voice of the so-called Black Mountain Poets (which included Robert Creeley, Robert Duncan, Edward Dorn, and Joel Oppenheimer among others), named for the experimental college with which all were at one time or another associated. His place in literary history seems assured by such achievements as his epic series, *The Maximus Poems* (1953-1975), the theoretical manifesto "Projective Verse" (1950), essays such as "Human Universe" (1951), his deeply felt study of Herman Melville, myth and America, *Call Me Ishmael* (1947), his energetic letters, as well as his acknowledged influence on an entire generation of poets. Indeed, one critic—Warren Tallman in his preface to *The Poetics of the New American Poetry* (1973)—speaks of "Olson's generation" the way Hugh Kenner has referred to "the Pound Era."

Olson's background reflects diverse interests and experience, and somewhat explains why he did not publish his first poem until his mid-thirties. Although born and raised in the central Massachusetts industrial city of Worcester, where his father was a mailman, he spent summers in Gloucester on the coast, which became the focus of his most important work, *The Maximus Poems*. He was a champion orator in high school, winning a tour of Europe as a prize. He chose Wesleyan over Harvard on the advice of his high-school debating coach, continuing there for an M.A., writing a thesis on Melville and tracking down Melville's personal library as part of his research. He eventually went to Harvard for further study in a newly begun American Studies program, completing all course work for the Ph.D.; but he left without the degree after receiving a Guggenheim Fellowship in 1939 for a book on Melville (the 400-page draft was abandoned but emerged after World War II in remarkably different form as *Call Me Ishmael*). During the war he was assistant chief of the Foreign Language Division of the Office of War Information, until resigning in protest against bureaucratic meddling and inefficiency. He served the Democratic Party's National Committee as adviser and strategist (for which service he was offered significant governmental posts), but he withdrew abruptly from partisan politics to become exclusively a writer (see his poem "The K"). It was the second time he turned his back on promising careers—that of a traditional scholar-academic and that of national politics— valuing more his independence. In 1948 he was convinced to take a temporary teaching position vacated by his friend Edward Dahlberg at Black Mountain College, returning there to teach regularly in 1951 and to serve as rector of the school until its closing in 1956. Thereafter he returned to Gloucester and preoccupation with the *Maximus* series, remaining by choice in relative isolation and poverty, until accepting a teaching post at the State University of New York at Buffalo, where he was a most effective teacher as he had been at Black Mountain. He taught again, briefly, at the University of Connecticut until overtaken by cancer. He died two weeks past his fifty-ninth birthday, having completed *The Maximus Poems* a month before. Writing autobiographically, he described himself not so much as a poet or writer but as "an archeologist of morning," and the phrase has stayed.

His first book was not poems but a remarkable study of Melville and the writing of *Moby-Dick, Call Me Ishmael*, for which he has been much praised. Published in 1947, it has been republished three times by different publishers. It has been seen as a continuation of the line of writings on American literature beginning with D. H. Lawrence's *Studies in Classic American Literature* (1923) and including Williams's *In the American Grain* (1925) and Dahlberg's *Do These Bones Live* (1941). Among the qualities it shares with Olson's poems, however, is the brisk, confident, efficient style, seen in its famous opening paragraph: "I take SPACE to be the central fact to man born in America, from Folsom cave to now. I spell it large because it comes large here. Large, and without mercy." There are also striking images, such as "a sun like a tomahawk . . . a river north and south in the middle of the land running out the blood," and other forms of compression, including the incorporation of live facts whole into the narrative, the condensing of information (for a book of less than one hundred printed pages, Olson investigated every book in the Library of Congress on the American whaling industry), the technique of montage or juxtaposition. And, thematically, there is the preoccupation with America ("we are the last 'first' people"), the delving into myth, and not least, the final chapter on the new, "prospective," post-Ahabian hero, directly anticipating Maximus.

Among his earliest poems, "The K" and "La Préface" most notably hint at the scope and concerns to come, while others of such balanced delicacy as "Pacific Lament" and "Lower Field—Enniscorthy" already strain against tidiness and, although quite formal, take advantage of rhythm and rhyme to freely move against the "closed" universe Olson will reject in "Projective Verse." In "Pacific Lament," an elegy for an acquaintance drowned in wartime submarine service, within the strictness of narrow lines the syntax follows the spirals of the boy's descent, mimetic of the fall of a body lost at sea. (It was, in fact, later danced by one of the students at Black Mountain.) The effect is enhanced by careful curtailment of line, omission of punctuation, and occasional rhyme. Above all, the sense is of free invention within control. "Lower Field—Enniscorthy," part of a larger "Enniscorthy Suite" written while Olson was on vacation at a friend's estate in Virginia, is similarly composed in free lines, but with advantageous placement of words for their ultimate effect:

> A convocation of crows overhead
> mucks
> in their own mud and squawk
> makes of the sky
> a sty

Somewhat stiffly formal and not yet the "open field" of "Projective Verse," it nevertheless has interesting allowances, tolerances. The landscape is sharp-edged and nonromantic. Prevalent monosyllabic words contrast with occasional polysyllables, and attention is paid to sounds (in the subsequent line, "A bee is deceived"). It is a picture only, having no narrator, sharing Williams's nominalism and trust in the phenomenal world. It is a careful presentation of a natural world free from human presence and interference, a "peaceable kingdom" although with lurking dangers or unpleasantness (the sheep are like soldiers, an "ambush" is possible, the crows "muck" and make of the sky a "sty," a bee mistakes a rotten stump for honeycomb, the path is "undisciplined"). There is a trust in language to represent reality, even in the deliberate flatness of the end—

> Report: over all
> the sun

—the staring camera's eye, the photorealism, tough-minded and unsentimental, the documentary impulse characteristic of the later poems.

"The K," appearing in *Y & X* (1948), a book of coordinates, is among Olson's very first poems, written in early 1945 when he was nearly thirty-five. It contains the same mixture of personal and cultural reference that will characterize almost all his poems. An early version, written while the (not yet declared) poet was on a working vacation with the Democratic National Committee at its winter headquarters in Key West, is entitled "Telegram" with significance. It was written in response to offers to keep Olson engaged in national politics through a position in the coming administration. The poem begins with his rejection of the offers by quoting another statesman in the words of another poet (Brutus in Shakespeare's *Julius Caesar*) in order to reclaim his personal freedom:

> Take, then, my answer:
> there is a tide in a man

> moves him to his moon and,
> though it drop him back
> he works through ebb to mount
> the run again and swell
> to be tumescent I.

And although this "tumescent I" is not yet a "Maximus," the poet suggests that finally the artist's concerns are more elemental than a Caesar's:

> Our attention is simpler
> The salts and minerals of the earth return
> The night has a love for throwing its shadows around
> a man
> a bridge, a horse, the gun, a grave

Such language is as symbolic as Olson's was ever to get.

Most of the other poems in *Y & X* are considerably energetic and Yeatsian in their imagery, though not sufficiently distinct to have gained the poet special regard. But "La Préface," written in the spring of 1946, is of unusual power. Again, it is both specifically autobiographical and of the widest cultural import. It can be read just as its title proposes, as preliminary to the work and new life ahead. It marks the poet's—as well as mankind's—entry into the postwar, post-Holocaust, indeed, postmodern age. Reminders of earlier voyagers are given, with Odysseus heard in the concentration camps ("My name is NO RACE") and Dante ("in vita nuova") superimposed on present horrors in that most dead of times following the worst war and cruelty experienced by man. Man now is led ahead by the survivors of Hitler's death camps, Pleistocene survivors, who represent both the end of modern man and a new beginning for the future. The theme of rebirth and openness (and the mode of same) begins following references to the Tarot and other traditional symbols for birth:

> Draw it thus: (   ) 1910 (
> It is not obscure. We are the new born, and there are
> no flowers.
> Document means there are no flowers
> and no parenthesis.

The year is the poet's first or actual birth, the open parenthesis the possibility to come. There is a pointing ahead, at the end of that time of global war and genocide, and a newborn hope in the courage and persistence of those who survived:

> Mark that arm. It is no longer gun.
> We are born not of the buried but these unburied dead
> crossed stick, wire-led, Blake Underground

Charles Olson

Charles Olson

The Babe

the Howling Babe

The poem is as allusive and deeply private in its reference as any of the later poems, but also as rewarding, with the same desire to represent an age, to speak on behalf of man-at-large (Maximus) as well as the poet himself. It may be the first—in theme and style—postmodernist poem.

Olson's first grand poem was "The Kingfishers," written in early 1949. It is a richly complex poem in which the historically conscious mind faces the upheavals of history and displacement of cultural values. It was originally part of an even longer poem, titled at one stage "The First Proteid," indicative of the ambitiousness of the effort (another portion was extracted and similarly published separately as "The Praises"). "The Kingfishers" prefigures the *Maximus* series in scope and concerns, and it might well be read as an introduction to Olson's major work. When it was first published, both Robert Creeley and William Carlos Williams responded with enthusiasm. Critics have since acknowledged it to be one of Olson's most significant poems, indeed one of the most important of the entire postwar period. It certainly was conceived on an impressive scale—balancing the

West against the East, weighing the present by the past. The principle of its composition is juxtaposition, not of images as in surrealism but of whole continents of fact, metaphysics, and cultural evocation. There are a series of separate movements, with little narrative intervention or overt causal relationships, in which the assembled blocks of information are permitted to speak for themselves and, in their dialectic, build a base for the narrator to speak personally, in the final section, as a response to the terms of the proposition with which the poem opens.

There are three sections in all (and four parts within the first section), with the Roman numeral *I* omitted to encourage direct entrance into the poem. It begins with the rallying proposition—

What does not change / is the will to change

—a modification of the Heraclitean doctrine of flux (which is continued in the body of the poem using Heraclitus's own words as presented by Plutarch) by the injection of human will (and responsibility), which some readers have given a Hegelian or Marxist interpretation. It is, in any case, a heroic call, enough so that Adrienne Rich titled one of her collections with reference to it (*The Will to Change*,

1971). The emphasis, due to the fulcrum of the solidus or slash, falls ultimately on the "will"—a function not allowed by Heraclitus, who also said "a man's character is his fate." The will is the human element in the successive ebb and flow of history that makes up the poem, the intention that holds the poem together in tension. The structure of the opening line, divided as it is, is paradigmatic for the poem as a whole. The will holds the blocks of thought and historical example in balance, allowing the associations from which the argument emerges to flow freely.

The opening section continues as if to illustrate or further the initial proposition, with a story of birds put back in their cages after a night of neglect told from personal experience. It is the start of a train of associations, leading to a recollection of the previous night and a party the poet had attended in Washington, in which the care of birds again figured, only on a wider cultural scale. One of the guests, an artist, bemoans the loss of value from the past: "The kingfishers! / who cares / for their feathers / now?" It is not clear at that point whether the "blue" and "green" birds previously mentioned are to be taken as symbolic or even as varieties of the kingfishers of the poem's title, or just what symbolic properties the birds of the title do have, other than as emblems of cultural loss. Any tendency to treat the kingfishers themselves as exclusively symbols, however, is disabused in the next section of the poem, with a description of the bird in the most ornithological terms straight from the *Encyclopaedia Britannica*, while a brief account of their legendary qualities is followed by the statements: "The legends are / legends. Dead, hung up indoors, the kingfisher / will not indicate a favoring wind, / or avert the thunderbolt." Symbols, nonetheless, are introduced in what follows—a mysterious, cultic *E* that has been "rudely" cut on "the oldest stone." This appears side by side, spliced, with a passage concerning Mao Tse-tung, whose revolution has just triumphed in China and whose victorious words are quoted in French (how, in fact, they were reported to Olson).

The entire poem is rich with allusions and documentary borrowings, but because the allusions are unfamiliar or distant from their sources (Mao's words quoted in French), they appear to be more symbolic and less referential than in fact they actually are. The documentary nature of the juxtapositions is given a narrative life of its own. The *E*—it can be known, though hardly from the little evidence the poem has to offer—is a primitive form of the Greek epsilon as it appears carved on the

stone *omphalos* at the temple of Apollo at Delphi; a symbol, in other words, of the source and navel of the Western world. It is perhaps enough for the reader that a sense of ancient mystery and elemental value is present in the *E*, but it does help to know that the stone is also representative of the essential West in the contrast with the East. The revolutionary present and perhaps (in 1949) future, located in the East, are contrasted with the past of the West. The contrasts will continue throughout the poem—East and West, past and present, light and darkness, the "primitive" and "civilized." There are not only the treasured kingfisher feathers of the ancient Khmers but the European destruction of the indigenous American civilization, the newest West (summarized in the catalogue of Montezuma's treasure as reported at the Spanish court); the control of data flow according to modern cybernetics; the metaphysics of change as discussed by Neoplatonists; reference to Dante among other representatives of the West; and borrowings from Pound and Arthur Rimbaud, Olson's modernist predecessors who brought the poet to the brink of his own position—that of "archeologist of morning," hunting among the ruins of the past (and, sadly, the present), which might contain correctives for the present and directives for a future, though not necessarily a future of improvement or progress.

The dialectics of the serially opposed sections continue up to the concluding portion, in which the poet at last steps forth fully, the "I" for the first time dominating the facts in curiously formal quatrains:

> I am no Greek, hath not th'advantage.
> And of course, no Roman:
> he can take no risk that matters,
> the risk of beauty least of all.

"But I have my kin," he continues, "if for no other reason that . . . I commit myself, and"—now echoing Pound in *Guide to Kulchur* (1938)—"given my freedom, I'd be a cad / if I didn't." He then moves to invoke Rimbaud, whose "taste for the earth and stones" he shares, concluding, not negatively as T. S. Eliot had, but as the "archeologist of morning" who would himself in less than two years go to the Yucatán to dig among the Mayan ruins:

> I pose you your question:
>
> shall you uncover honey / where maggots are?
>
> I hunt among stones.

Given the fact of change—and there is enough evidence amassed throughout the poem of the movements of civilizations, their decline and rising like young kingfishers, or phoenixes, out of old "dripping, fetid" nests—the poet cañ do nothing better than embrace change, though not passively, mindlessly. He commits his will to the search, to the act of history, the activism of "finding out for oneself," which is central to his philosophy. The final line is not to be taken as despair or a futile scrabbling among the rubble of an Eliotic waste land. It is the highest-willed engagement, a commitment to change itself, if that is what is necessary.

The poem moves with the methods, although not yet the full, spoken immediacy of a Maximus. Guy Davenport has called it "the most modern of American poems" and again "the essential poem in the Projectivist School of poets." Although rooted in its attack on *The Waste Land*, which it seeks to challenge and surpass, it begins to put into practice the techniques and attitudes of postmodernism and projective verse. The technique is still basically that of Eliot's juxtaposition, Pound's ideogrammatic method, Sergei Eisenstein's montage. The difference is that Olson, while conscious of inheritance from his predecessors, seeks to advance beyond them, beyond history as accumulation and symbol, and into the fact of change, the instant by instant engagement, the openness where all things are possible.

"The Kingfishers" is followed in time and significance by "In Cold Hell, In Thicket," title poem of Olson's first important collection of verse (after *Y & X*) and the first poem fully to put into practice the kinetics and the "breathing of the man who writes" as outlined in "Projective Verse," which he had been working on throughout that period. Written in May 1950, it is a long meditative poem of a civil war raging within the poet, a hell of indecision. Olson had been reading Dante at the time, but the *Inferno* supplies only the lightest touches—besides the title and perhaps the separated, celestial "beloved," only one reference deep within to "selva oscura," the dark woods Dante must emerge from to begin his quest. Rather, it is a secular hell:

> hell now
> is not exterior, is not to be gotten out of, is
> the coat of your own self, the beasts
> emblazoned on you

The lines are tormented by commas and parenthetical interjections, echoing the speaker's doubts and anxieties. There is a battlefield within that must be crossed, just as the field of the poem is to be traversed. The poem moves through a series of questions, probings of the deepest sort, culminating in the basic one: "Who / am I?" Man is at war to find his identity, as the poet continues: "Who am I but by a fix, and another, / a particle, and the congery of particles carefully picked one by another"—the realization, as in "Projective Verse," that man is an "object" (rather than egoistic "subject") in a "larger field of objects." The poem, in fact, in many ways is illustrative of or a commentary on the "objectism" presented in "Projective Verse"—surprisingly not recognized in all the criticism written on it. Whereas in the essay, Olson offers "objectism" as "a word to be taken to stand for the kind of relation of man to experience which a poet might state as the necessity of a line or a work to be as wood is, to be as clean as wood is as it issues from the hand of nature, to be shaped as wood can be when a man has had his hand to it," and he again writes, "It comes to this: the use of a man, by himself and thus by others, lies in how he conceives his relation to nature, that force to which he owes his somewhat small existence," in the poem he writes:

> that a man, men, are now their own wood
> and thus their own hell and paradise
> that they are, in hell or in happiness, merely
> something to be wrought, to be shaped, to be carved,
>   for use, for
>
> others
>
> does not in the least lessen his, this unhappy man's
> obscurities, his
> confrontations

Salvation lies only in the precise use of oneself: "By fixes only (not even any more by shamans) / can the traceries / be brought out." Life, by the fact of birth, is a field to be entered:

>   this at least
>   is a certainty, this
>   is a law, is not one of the questions, this
>   is what was talked of as
>   —what was it called, demand?

Life is to be faced without heroics or histrionics. By the end, the poet is resolved that he will live "without wavering," even though "forever wavers" and he too "will forever waver." It is a final acceptance, the only certainty possible, this struggle to be as "precise as hell is, precise / as any words, or wagon, / can be made."

Olson had begun his celebrated *Maximus* series in 1950, shortly before "In Cold Hell" was written, but it did not become apparent to him until 1953 that it was to be a major work, the vehicle into which he would pour his greatest effort. Meanwhile, he visited

I, MAXIMUS, OF GLOUCESTER, To You

Off-shore, by islands, hidden, in the blood
jewels and miracles, I, Maximus,
a metal hot from boiling water, tell you
what is a lance, who obeys the figures of the present
dance

1
the thing lie
around the bend of the nest
(second, time slain, the bird! the bird!
there! (strong) thrust, the mast, flight

                                        (o the birds, the kylix)
                                    D Anthony
of Padua, sweep-low, o bless
the roofs, the old ones, the gentle steep ones on whose ridge-poles
the gulls sit, from which they depart,
                                    And the flake racks
of my city!

2
love is form, and cannot be without
important substance (the weight
say, 58 carats, each one of us, perforce,
goldsmith's scale:
                    feather to feather added
                    (and what is mineral, what
                    is curling hair, the string
                    you carry in your nervous beak, these
                    make bulk, these,
                    in the end,
                    are the sum
                            o my lady

                            (o my lady of)

                            good voyage,

                                in whose arm,

                            with whose left arm
no boy, but a carefully carved wood, a painted face and schooner,
a delicate mast, a bow-sprit for

                        forwarding

"I, Maximus, of Gloucester, To You," revised typescript

the Yucatán, following his instincts, to dig among Mayan ruins (until his money ran out), and wrote his indispensable essay "Human Universe," while continuing to develop the fundamentals set forth in "Projective Verse." He stretched out in an assortment of long, often long-lined poems over the next ten years, many of which had as much influence as the *Maximus Poems* themselves. There was the proud declaration, written with "the power of American vocables," to the young German poet and editor, Rainer M. Gerhardt, entitled "To Gerhardt, There, Among Europe's Things" (followed in 1954 by a majestic elegy to Gerhardt, "The Death of Europe," upon learning of his suicide). There was also the wrathful "Letter for Melville 1951," sounding like the crack of doom. Most of the important poems of this period are included in *The Distances* (1960), a volume of selected poems that Donald Allen helped the poet put together. These include "A Newly Discovered 'Homeric' Hymn," "As the Dead Prey Upon Us," "The Lordly and Isolate Satyrs," "Variations Done for Gerald Van De Wiele," and "The Librarian"—all written while the *Maximus Poems* were in abeyance. All move in the poet's familiar discursive patterns and with far-ranging associations, yet always propelled and directed by the unusual force of his intensity. The chief theme continues to be man's life on the largest terms—including psychological and mythological—seen even in the exquisitely formed "Variations Done for Gerald Van De Wiele," a series of spring poems composed for a student at Black Mountain. These precisely lyrical variations based on a passage in Rimbaud's *A Season in Hell* (1873) show a fine ear and sense of modulation, while working within, instead of pushing, the limits of language. In the 1960s, Olson's notable poems include the deftly controlled mobile, "The Red Fish of Bones," the sweeping "Across Space and Time," and the *'West'* sequence. The rest of the poet's energies went into the *Maximus* poems and the private struggles of living.

Among the poems written at Black Mountain in the mid-1950s, the "Newly Discovered 'Homeric' Hymn," dedicated to the historian of Greek religion, Jane Harrison, and drawing upon her account of the Athenian ritual of the *Chrythoi* or "pots," begins engagingly:

Hail and beware the dead who will talk life until you
　　　　　　　　　　　　　　　　　　　are blue
in the face. And you will not understand what is
　　　　　　　　　　　　　　　　wrong,
they will not be blue, they will have tears in their eyes,

they will seem to you so much more full of life
than the rest of us. . . .

The poem continues in haunting but stately long lines, concluding—typical of the seriousness of Olson's regard for the archaic—

　　　Fall off! The drink is not yours,
it is not yours! You do not come
from the same place, you do not suffer as the dead
　　　　　　　　　　　　　　do . . .
　　Beware the dead. And hail them. They teach you
　　　　　　　　　　　　　　drunkenness.
You have your own place to drink. Hail and beware
　　　　　　　　　　them, when they come.

—rounding out the hymn, so that it, too, is a vessel of instruction. It is a poem of utmost credibility, not mere decorative imitation. The discrepancies and near contradictions we are warned against, present throughout the poem, protect an ancient mysteriousness.

"As the Dead Prey Upon Us" is the first of several poems whose sources were literal dreams. A visitation occurs, an appearance by the poet's deceased mother, almost like the ghosts in the "Newly Discovered 'Homeric' Hymn." (The same haunting by the deceased mother, four and six years after her death, occurs in "Moonset, Gloucester, December 1, 1957" and "O'Ryan 6": "What a man has to do, he has to / meet his mother in hell.") The poem seems to confirm all the primitive senses of the restlessness of departed souls. The poet's mother returns in the life of his sleep, and the poem is filled with unsought images and the elasticity of dream. Strands of dream matter are interwoven like the automobile tires presented in the dream, "masses of rubber and thread variously clinging together." One of the functions of the poem—and the creative imagination—is to sort the strands. There are memories of his mother in her Gloucester cottage and of her neighbor, the "Indian woman" (in reality, of Indian ancestry), who with the poet enables a "blue deer" to walk and talk:

　　　and we helped walk it around the room
　　　because it was seeking socks
　　　or shoes for its hooves
　　　now that it was acquiring

　　　human possibilities

And although the poem begins with all the abruptness characteristic of a dream (the poet's car "had been sitting so long unused. / I thought the tires looked as though they only needed air. / But suddenly the huge underbody was above me . . ."), in the poem, as opposed to the dream, the poet has a certain control. His imagination fuses a narrative; his intensity burns through with such extraordinary lines as:

> The vent! You must have the vent,
> or you shall die. Which means
> never to die, the ghastliness
>
> of going, and forever
> coming back, returning
> to the instants which were not lived
>
> O mother, this I could not have done,
> I could not have lived what you didn't,
> I am myself netted in my own being
>
> I want to die. I want to make that instant, too,
> perfect
>
> O my soul, slip
> the cog

It is one of Olson's most dynamic and unshakable poems:

> the nets of being
> are only eternal if you sleep as your hands
> ought to be busy. Method, method
>
> I too call on you to come
> to the aid of all men, to women most
> who know most, to woman to tell
> men to awake. Awake, men,
> awake

The strands, the entangling nets of dream, which at first had seemed so extraneous to the main burden of the poem, are actually quite useful in resolving it at the end, when the poet flatly announces that the automobile—source of much trouble and uncertainty (dreamed strangeness)—"has been hauled away." Despite the occasionally confusing dream time, which presses the reader to the verge of disorientation, the force of the poet drives through. Accepting the raw offerings of the unconscious mind, at the same time infusing dream with enormous lyrical capability, it is one of Olson's most powerful separate poems.

Another dream poem written at Black Mountain, "The Lordly and Isolate Satyrs" from 1956, offers an expansive mythopoeic experience, a choreography of archetypes, in which modern-day motorcyclists suddenly appearing on a beach are transformed into symbols of completeness: "the Androgynes, / the Fathers behind the father, the Great Halves," dimensionally larger than we are. And the result is such that

the boy-town the scene was, is now pierced with angels
> and
> with fire. And winter's ice shall be as brilliant in its
> time as
> life truly is, as Nature is only the offerer, and it is we
> who look to see what the beauty is.

Then there is that near-*Maximus*, "The Librarian," whose final lines,

> Where
> is Bristow? when does 1-A
> get me home? I am caught
>
> in Gloucester. (What's buried
> behind Lufkin's
> Diner? Who is
>
> Frank Moore?

—which Edward Dorn has called "my reunion with the nouns and questionings" of his own life—had visitors wandering the streets of Gloucester searching for Lufkin's and digging, reports had it, behind the building at night by the beams of flashlights, unaware the diner had long since been moved from its original location! It is the most *Maximus*-like of the out-of-series poems, even beginning with an echo of the opening lines of the first *Maximus* letter, and it ostensibly might have been included in the series; but undoubtedly because of the personal and confusing nature of its messages, coming especially at a time when the poet realized the focus of the poem must be on the facts of the place Gloucester, it was withheld and published apart. It, too, was originally a dream (which accounts for some of the discrepancies in the actual landscape).

Finally, moving into the 1960s, called by some the Age of Aquarius, "Across Space and Time" is a poem from the midst of Olson's most productive *Maximus* period and similar in scope to others in the sequence, although completely without the figure of Maximus and, again, not focused on Gloucester. It is another long poem of cultural expanse reminiscent of "The Kingfishers," but more concentrated and systematized; again on the widest scale, here not only historical, with the sweep of invading peoples, the great Indo-European creation of the West, but cosmological and zodiacal:

> horsemen from the Caucasus
> came in with Aries to shake the dead temple world
> and awake self and reason, the soft Aries people who
> ride
> horses backward, brilliant riders who only know the
> back

Charles Olson

is an engine of will to be sacrificed if the sons
will have wives, they ride on into battle until all
is divided between flesh and soul and Greece
is the measure of what they were worth. . . .

So many of the poems seek to answer the question, raised in "In Cold Hell" on a personal level, Who are we as a species? This is Olson's mightiest contribution, one that raises him beyond most of his contemporaries.

Olson would be a formidable poet by these poems alone, but his most important work is *The Maximus Poems*, that long series of epic intent in the tradition of Pound's *Cantos* and Williams's *Paterson*. The poem, in three volumes, is focused on the city of Gloucester, Massachusetts, which serves as microcosm to the larger America. Its theme is the development of a hero through the celebration of a place. It is a series of more than three hundred separate but interrelated poems in all, begun in the spring of 1950 and continued—with greater intensity at some times than at others—over the almost twenty years Olson was most active as a poet. Although it had roots in previous proposals for a long poem on the development of Western man (as discussed in Butterick's *Guide to the Maximus Poems*), the series began spontaneously, almost casually (in light of the extent of its commitment), as a letter to Olson's friend and surrogate in Gloucester, poet Vincent Ferrini (the designation "letters" appears throughout the first volume, as an ordering device, but only occasionally thereafter). Too vast in scope to be at all times carefully orchestrated, it remains one of the most complex poems in the language. The poet chooses for his hero the name (or title) Maximus, meaning "Greatest," derived in part from a little-known eclectic philosopher of the second century A.D., Maximus of Tyre, whose associations with his city make possible analogues between the modern world and the ancient, and in part, undoubtedly, from the unlimited possibilities such a name offers in itself.

Although Olson was born in Worcester, most of the poet's happiest and most significant memories were of Gloucester, where he summered with his parents. Following the close of Black Mountain College, he returned to live in Gloucester among the fishermen of Fort Square in a second-story cold-water flat overlooking the harbor. Thirty miles northeast of Boston, Gloucester was in the nineteenth century one of the leading fishing ports in the world. The city, which was founded in 1623 by settlers, mostly fishermen, from Dorchester, England, is on Cape Ann, an area of great natural beauty and variety, home of the intrepid fishermen Olson grew

up among and admired, daily pitting their lives against the full North Atlantic. What made Gloucester a model or source of possibility for Olson was that he conceived of it as actually an island in the Atlantic, separated from the mainland (and mainland culture) by the Annisquam River, a tidal estuary that connects Gloucester Harbor with Ipswich Bay in the north. Until the mid-1960s its regular population (not counting the summer influx) had remained the same for nearly seventy years. It enabled Olson to offer an image of a city, a *polis*, in his words, a "redeemable flower that will be a monstrance forever, of not a city but City." For instance, he writes among his notes: "The interest is not in the local at all as such—any local; and the choice of Gloucester is particular—that is the point of the interest, particularism itself: to reveal it, in all possible ways and force, against the 'loss' of value of the universal." For the poet, through Maximus of Tyre, namesake of his hero, Gloucester is the twentieth-century analogue to the Phoenician city of Tyre, which was the last holdout against Alexander the Great's conquest of the known world. Tyre was captured only after Alexander laid seige to the city and constructed a causeway or mole, comparable to the present highway Route 128 (completed in 1959 during the course of the poems), which encircles Boston and ends in Gloucester, bringing with it mainland values or the corruption of true value. That is why the first volume, published in 1960, concludes: "as the mainland hinge / of the 128 bridge / now brings in / what, / to Main Street?"

Olson explores Gloucester as a historian and archeologist rather than a sociologist. He knew every corner and rock pool, talked himself into each cranny, as his neighbor Mrs. Tarantino well knew: "You have a long nose, meaning / you stick it into every other person's / business, do you not?" Most often the tone is stalwart, upholding, defiant:

> Holes
> in my shoes, that's all right, my fly
> gaping, me out
> at the elbows, the blessing
>
>   that difficulties are once more

—although when the "difficulties" are the continuously unrectified excesses of a people, the tone can be darker, especially toward the end:

> Hunched up
>   on granite steps in the part dark Gloucester
>   and ghettoes gone cities and an infantile people
>   set loose to recreate what was ground
>   and is now
>   holes.

124

Olson sought redemption through knowing. He sought to restore to America its "city on a hill," built out of sound like Amphion's Thebes by the power of poetry alone.

The theme of the poem in all its variety may be conveniently summarized from the maps on each of the covers of the three volumes. The first, a U.S. Coast and Geodetic Survey of Gloucester and its harbor, suggests the very particular attentions of the poems, the streets and beaches delineated, the real-life topography of buoys in the harbor, the city-hall tower, the twin cupolas of Our Lady of Good Voyage Church, chimneys (like that of the LePage's glue factory), the salt marshes and mud flats, all very much as present-day and quotidian as "April Today Main Street." The second map shows the earth when it was most nearly one—mythologically, geologically, perhaps even culturally—a rendition of the archaic earth according to current theories of continental drift; here, before the land masses separated, the mythological names of the supercontinents and seas reflecting the mythological dimensions of the volume. And finally, on the last volume, edited from among Olson's papers after his death, is a map purported to have been drawn from the deck of the flagship *Arbella* by John Winthrop, a hero of the poems, on his 1630 voyage to found the *polis* of Boston, a "city upon a hill"—in Winthrop's own words from the deck of the same ship—a model city, shining or "glowing" for all to see, like Glowceastre, Gloucester in its earliest form. It is also a personal chart, just as so much of the volume is deeply personal, and an example of history as *'istorin*, finding out for one's self, drawn (a drawing) from one man's "eye-view" like that of Gloucester artist Fitz-Hugh Lane, whose presence also continues to be felt in this volume. The complexities are inexhaustible, the relationships endlessly rewarding.

The poem itself begins with Maximus (in absentia, projected) addressing his city:

> Off-shore, by islands hidden in the blood
> jewels & miracles, I, Maximus
> a metal hot from boiling water, tell you
> what is a lance, who obeys the figures of
> the present dance

—a mythical, even alchemical, hero with special knowledge and powers; clearly no mere man alone. He addresses his city to correct abuses and restore value, in all urgency and righteousness:

> that which matters, that which insists, that
>   which will last,
> that! o my people, where shall you find it, how, where,

> where shall you listen
> when all is become billboards, when, all, even silence,
>   is spray-gunned?

That will be one goal of the poem, to awaken Gloucester to itself; but equally, to awaken Maximus to all his own possibilities. As the poem progresses, the persona becomes more a person, until Maximus and Olson are all but indistinguishable. The poet moves simultaneously to create a model (a "monstrance") city together with a hero who must be "an image / of man." Gloucester must be possessed by single-minded investigation. Maximus's governing principle is *'istorin*, the Herodotean historian's "finding out for oneself." The poem explores the chosen territory to its deepest, most archaic roots, during which time the identity—and personality—of Maximus is developed. The focus on Gloucester is ever-narrowing, down to local records from the city-hall vault, drawing the reader into the city's concerns and into Maximus's consciousness until the two are interchangeable. The early poems are mostly concerned with the heroic fishermen and the early settlement at Gloucester Harbor, where the poet himself would take up residence two-thirds through the volume. The archaic makes its first appearance toward the end of volume one with the urging, "start all over" (Maximus has just said "the present is worse," meaning *pejorocracy*, a term derived from Pound, rules). "Step off the / Orontes" (the river north of Tyre), he continues, "onto land no Typhon [the "blue monster" that eventually becomes the Gloucester sea serpent] / no understanding of a cave [such as that ancient one of Trophonius, center of mysteries, or the Corcyrian, home of Zeus] a mystery Cashes [a fusing pun: both the fishing bank in the North Atlantic over which the *Rattler* of a later poem plunges, and Mount Casius overlooking the Orontes, where Zeus and Typhon fought]." As patience reveals, it all ties in, coiled, interlocking, "entwined / throughout / the system." *The Maximus Poems* welcome and reward such close readings. The lines are thick with allusions. In a poem of this size and scope, it takes a while for the recurrent patterns to emerge; but once the reader is alerted, they are readily enough perceived for their own sake.

The second volume turns its "Back on / the Sea," away from the harbor settlement, and moves inland to Dogtown, an area of wilderness at the heart of Cape Ann. Formerly the site of a settlement (the eighteenth-century cellar holes are still very much in evidence) but abandoned to widows, witches, and their dogs, it is part moor, strewn with boulders left by the retreating ice, which puts Maximus in touch with the most primordial elements of creation. A crucial poem is the third of four long ones addressed to Dogtown. It is untitled except for a line from Hesiod's *Theogony*, but known from its setting and its opening lines as "Gravelly Hill." Within it the poet seeks to identify the boundaries or divisions of the world into Earth, Heaven, and Hell, during the course of which Maximus *becomes* the hill. The poet is high up, "sitting there like / the Memphite lord of all Creation," and with the sense of the "bowl" of light at the top of Dogtown carried over from the previous "Cow of Dogtown." The same voice that has earlier said, "I have had lunch / in this 'pasture'" and "It is not bad / to be pissed off / where / there is *any* condition imposed," now continues to speak as the hill itself, "leave me be, I am contingent, the end of the World / is the borders / of my being," as the poet and his place merge to one.

It is immediately apparent in this volume how the range of the poem opens up. Passages from Hesiod and the Norse Eddas stand side by side with Algonquian tales of the wife who lusted after a serpent in a pond or the witch who each Sunday has a liaison with a mountain. Alfred North Whitehead, with his grand cosmology and philosophy of process, and Carl Jung, with his archetypism and theory of libidinal energies, more evidently offer guidance to the poems. Parallels and relationships are exposed and explored. Olson often objected that Pound had not gone back far enough in the *Cantos*—that the Renaissance had "boxed" him in. He, characteristically, on the other hand, seeks the very sources of civilization. The poems in this volume reach back to the continents before they drifted apart, back to Cape Ann depressed by the weight of the ice upon her mass, back beyond the Homeric and Hesiodic Greeks and the Phoenicians of Tyre and into the ancient Indo-European homeland, to the migrations of the Western hero, the archetype in which Maximus participates (summarized in the poems "ALL MY LIFE I'VE HEARD ABOUT MANY" and "Peloria"), various predecessors of Maximus such as Manes and Odysseus and Herakles-Melkaart, and monsters like the legendary Gloucester sea serpent or bulls both archetypal and real enough to gore a six-foot-seven Gloucester sailor (exactly Olson's height) to death. Amid poems of such clear and extricable individual power as "Maximus to Gloucester, Letter 27," "Maximus, at the Harbor," "A Later Note on Letter #15," "The Gulf of Maine," "I am the Gold Machine," "Civic Disaster," are studded briefer "tesserae," the poet

called them, some only a line or two long. In their compression they must serve to summarize an entire area of thought or layer of history, no matter how it challenges the reader. Through all, Maximus continues to be the voice of responsibility, of authority, of self-possession. Only in the third volume is the true extent of his vulnerability revealed.

With the third volume, with Gloucester in transition all around him ("fake gasoline station / and A & P supermarket / construction") and with the loss of his own personal center (his wife suddenly killed in an automobile accident in 1964, a sense of isolation in Gloucester, intermittent moves from Buffalo to London to Connecticut), the poems become increasingly personal. Redemption is sought as much for the man as for the city. The spiritual quest is highlighted by the poem whose title is, literally, an almanac entry: "A 3rd morning it's beautiful   February 5th," a meditation upon the landscape of Gloucester and specifically one "floating" island in the harbor outside the poet's windows, with a lighthouse on its snowy banks "looking / humpy and sorely bedraggled like America / since after the Civil War." The poem is fraught with digression and details that slow the reader while supplying a sufficient dimension to the focus of the meditation—too sudden, actually, to be a meditation, more a vision. While gazing at the island ablaze in the winter sun, the poet is struck with a realization summarized by an alchemical test he had been reading in Jung: simply, the "mystery / of creation" that in matter alone lies perfection, that matter can transform the spirit, and that neither matter, Ten Pound Island, Gloucester, nor the earth itself is "prison" for the soul of man. The poem is a great liberating one, itself a spiritual exercise, which the reader must follow in all its peregrinations to attain its value.

There are other poems of similar beauty and magnitude in the volume, specifically "West Gloucester," "Enyalion," "Cole's Island," "The Festival Aspect," "Maximus of Gloucester," "The winter the *Gen Starks* was stuck," "When do poppies bloom," "Hotel Steinplatz," and "Celestial Evening," which are among the finest in the series and ought not be overlooked. Among many possible readings of the poems, one might speak of a "Maximusizing" of Olson, together with an "Olsonizing" of Maximus (similar to the overall structural pattern of *Don Quixote*). If in the "Gravelly Hill" poem the Maximusizing of Olson is complete, in the final poems there is the Olsonizing of Maximus. As it becomes apparent that the vulnerabilities (already referred to in "Maximus to Himself" in volume one) are not going to diminish or be overcome, the voice of Olson speaks more from the heart than the mind and even wavers (wavers as "forever wavers" in "In Cold Hell"), his throat "tight from madness of isolation & / inactivity," hungry "for every thing." And although with the next to last poem there is accomplished "the initiation / of another kind of nation," the final poem of the series reads, with no ease of resolution: "my wife   my car   my color   and   myself." Nothing more. It is as if once again he has learned "the simplest things / last."

All the volumes contain poems of immediate accessibility, their power undiminished even when removed from context; but the majority gain from one another incrementally. Randomness is only temporary; there is solidity beyond. Call it belief—in man, in the species—it is irrepressible, unwarranted, genetic, and always welcome. Names accumulate values and dimension as they recur, and eventually patterns emerge. It is not a poetry to be possessed easily, but there are enough rewards bestowed by startling images and direct wisdom to encourage the reader to persist.

Olson's initial reputation was confounded by warring impressions, the overstated claims of his enthusiasts with concomitant senses of threat and bemusement on the part of the doubtful or aloof. He had been described by early critics who had lost sight of the American tradition from Ralph Waldo Emerson, Melville, and Walt Whitman, as an "aging beatnik" and a Poundian imitator. Antagonism was strongest from that part of the academic and literary establishment that felt itself most exposed, rejected, or ignored. His reputation held firm among a small body of fellow poets, including Robert Creeley and Robert Duncan, in the 1950s, and extended to a widespread, if young and enthusiastic, audience in the 1960s, here and in England. Following his death, academic recognition accrued, his work became the subject of books, numerous articles, and dissertations, as well as being included in textbooks and the major anthologies. He is one of the most difficult of recent poets, both because of the scope of his proposals and his own eccentricities—his refusal to simplify, the demand he makes on the reader no less than on himself (including "the secret of secrecy . . . that the work get done"). He is also one of the most thought-bearing of recent poets, one who has extended the domain and responsibility of poetry— or returned it to the Homeric and Hesiodic sense—to

include cosmology, geography, history in the sense of finding out for oneself, spiritual transformation, as well as the self-generating exuberance language has in and for itself.

Olson is of interest not for his poetry alone but for his thought about poetry, about the function of the mind, the limits of the Western "universe of discourse," the uses of the past, the value of the local, and the glory of the unreconstructed individual. His essay "Projective Verse" rallied and focused the energies of the new poetry while forwarding the line of Pound and Williams. He was among the first to see the larger intellectual consequences of the new poetry and the first to use the term *postmodern* in its current significance. His writings have a pedagogical cast, simultaneously exploratory and insistent, often daring, at times angry or didactic, like a fist brought down upon a table. He troubled himself with the larger issues of the universe, often moving ahead rather than waiting for the language to follow. His writing by its very nature can never be popular, save perhaps for the small memoir of his father entitled *The Post Office* (1975) and, to a lesser degree, *Call Me Ishmael*, which is considered a minor classic. But his poetry and essays will always attract a steadfast core of readers who seek a poetry that extends thought and language beyond aestheticism and beyond self-expression.

Bibliography:

George F. Butterick and Albert Glover, *A Bibliography of Works by Charles Olson* (New York: Phoenix Bookshop, 1967).

References:

Robert Bertholf, "On Olson, His Melville," in *An Olson-Melville Sourcebook, vol. I: The New Found Land, North America*, ed. Richard Grossinger, *Io* 23 (Plainfield, Vt.: North Atlantic Books, 1976), pp. 5-36;

Charles Boer, *Charles Olson in Connecticut* (Chicago: Swallow Press, 1975);

Boundary 2, special Olson issue, 2 (Fall 1973-Winter 1974);

George F. Butterick, *A Guide to the Maximus Poems of Charles Olson* (Berkeley: University of California Press, 1978);

Donald J. Byrd, "Charles Olson's *Maximus*: An Introduction," Ph.D. dissertation, University of Kansas, 1971;

Byrd, "The Open Form of Charles Olson's

Maximus," *Athanor*, 6 (Spring 1975): 1-19;

John Cech, Oliver Ford, and Peter Rittner, *Charles Olson in Connecticut: Last Lectures as heard by John Cech, Oliver Ford [and] Peter Rittner* (Iowa City: Windhover Press, 1975; Boston: Northeastern University Press, 1977);

Cech, "Olson, Teaching," *Maps*, 4 (1971): 72-78;

Ann Charters, *Olson/Melville: A Study in Affinity* (Berkeley: Oyez, 1968);

Paul Christensen, *Charles Olson: Call Him Ishmael* (Austin: University of Texas Press, 1978);

Christensen, "Charles Olson's 'Maximus': Gloucester as Dream and Reality," *Texas Quarterly*, 20 (Autumn 1977): 20-29;

Robert Creeley, *A Quick Graph: Collected Notes & Essays*, ed. Donald Allen (San Francisco: Four Seasons, 1970), pp. 151-194;

Guy Davenport, "Scholia and Conjectures for Olson's 'The Kingfishers,' " *Boundary 2*, 2 (Fall 1973-Winter 1974): 250-262;

Donald Davie, "The Black Mountain Poets: Charles Olson and Edward Dorn," in his *The Poet in the Imaginary Museum*, ed. Barry Alpert (New York: Persea Books, 1977), pp. 177-190;

L. S. Dembo, "Charles Olson and the Moral History of Cape Ann," *Criticism*, 14 (Spring 1972): 165-174;

Edward Dorn, *What I see in the Maximus Poems* (Ventura, Cal.: Migrant Press, 1960); reprinted in *Kulchur*, 4 (1961): 31-44;

Martin Duberman, *Black Mountain An Exploration in Community* (New York: Dutton, 1972);

Robert Duncan, "Notes on Poetics Regarding Olson's 'Maximus,' " *Black Mountain Review*, 6 (Spring 1956): 201-211; revised, *Review*, 10 (January 1964): 36-42;

Vincent Ferrini, "A Frame," *Maps*, 4 (1971): 47-60;

John Finch, "Dancer and Clerk," *Massachusetts Review*, 12 (Winter 1971): 34-40;

Robert von Hallberg, *Charles Olson: The Scholar's Art* (Cambridge: Harvard University Press, 1978);

Karl Malkoff, *Escape from the Self: A Study in Contemporary American Poetry and Poetics* (New York: Columbia University Press, 1977);

Maps, special Olson issue, 4 (1971);

Ralph Maud, "Charles Olson: Posthumous Editions and Studies," *West Coast Review*, 14 (January 1980): 27-33;

Thomas F. Merrill, " 'The Kingfishers': Charles Olson's 'Marvelous Maneuver,' " *Contemporary Literature*, 17 (Autumn 1976): 506-528;

Paul Metcalf, "Big Charles: A Gesture Towards Reconstitution," *Prose*, 8 (Spring 1974): 163-177;

Charles Molesworth, "Charles Olson and His Forces," *Georgia Review*, 30 (Summer 1979): 438-443;

OLSON: The Journal of the Charles Olson Archives (Storrs, Conn.), no. 1-10 (1974-1978);

Sherman Paul, *Olson's Push: Origin, Black Mountain, and Recent American Poetry* (Baton Rouge: Louisiana State University Press, 1978);

Marjorie Perloff, "Charles Olson and the 'Inferior Predecessors': 'Projective Verse' Revisited," *ELH*, 40 (Summer 1973): 285-306;

J. B. Philip, "Charles Olson Reconsidered," *Journal of American Studies*, 5 (December 1971): 293-305;

Martin L. Pops, "Melville: To Him, Olson," in *Contemporary Poetry in America*, ed. Robert Boyers (New York: Schocken Books, 1974), pp. 189-220;

Jeremy Prynne, "On Maximus IV, V, VI," *Iron*, 12 (1971), n. pag.;

M. L. Rosenthal, *The New Poets: American and British Poetry Since World War II* (New York: Oxford University Press, 1967), pp. 160-173;

Rosenthal, "Olson / His Poetry," *Massachusetts Review*, 12 (Winter 1971): 45-57;

Gavin Selerie, *To Let Words Swim Into the Soul: An anniversary tribute to the art of Charles Olson* (London: Binnacle Press, 1980);

Charles F. Stein, "The Secret of the Black Chrysanthemum: Charles Olson's Use of the Writings of C. G. Jung," Ph.D. dissertation, University of Connecticut, 1979;

Rosmarie Waldrop, "Charles Olson: Process and Relationship," *Twentieth Century Literature*, 23 (December 1977): 467-486;

Jonathan Williams, "AM-O," *Parnassus*, 4 (Spring-Summer 1976): 243-250.

Papers:

Olson's extensive papers, including his personal library, are in the Literary Archives, University of Connecticut Library, Storrs.

GEORGE OPPEN
(24 April 1908-)

BOOKS: *Discrete Series* (New York: Objectivist Press, 1934);

The Materials (New York: New Directions / San Francisco Review, 1962);

This in Which (New York: New Directions / San Francisco Review, 1965);

Of Being Numerous (New York: New Directions, 1968);

Alpine: Poems (Mount Horeb, Wis.: Perishable Press, 1969);

Seascape: Needle's Eye (Fremont, Mich.: Sumac Press, 1972);

Collected Poems (London: Fulcrum Press, 1973);

The Collected Poems of George Oppen (New York: New Directions, 1975);

Primitive (Santa Barbara: Black Sparrow Press, 1978).

George Oppen has had one of the most unusual careers of any American poet. He published his first collection of poems in 1934, but his second did not appear until 1962. He did not even write during this interim, partly because of his involvement in political activism and partly because of the necessity to flee from the consequences of his actions. Since returning to his poetry, Oppen has firmly established himself as an important artist; he won the Pulitzer Prize for *Of Being Numerous* in 1969.

Oppen was born in New Rochelle, New York, and grew up in a well-to-do family in San Francisco. In 1926, he briefly attended what is now Oregon State University, where he met Mary Colby. After they stayed out all night on their first date, she was expelled and he was suspended. He voluntarily left school soon afterward. Mary Oppen writes in her autobiography, *Meaning a Life* (1978), "We had learned at college that poetry was being written in our own times, and that in order for us to write it was not necessary for us to ground ourselves in the academic; the ground we needed was the roads we were travelling." They were married in Dallas in 1927 on a brief stopover while hitchhiking to New York.

The Oppens moved to France in 1929. Mary Oppen writes:

> The United States at this time was a place in which one did much better not to admit being an artist or poet or writer, especially if one believed in oneself. We did believe in ourselves, and we believed in each other, but we could not yet demonstrate our work because we had done very little. Writers, poets and artists who were important to us were not yet recognized in the United States, and we needed to find our generation, to meet the poets and artists of our times and to find a way of life in which the poetry we felt within us could come out of our lives.

In France, they began To Publishers and published Ezra Pound, William Carlos Williams's *A Novelette and Other Prose (1921-1931)* (1932), and *An "Objectivists" Anthology* (1932) edited by Louis Zukofsky, whom they had met in New York and who did the editorial work on the books they published. *An "Objectivists" Anthology* is now considered an important document in the history of American poetry; the volume includes poems by Oppen, Zukofsky, Pound, Williams, Charles Reznikoff, Carl Rakosi, Kenneth Rexroth, and T. S. Eliot. The Oppens' enterprise quickly failed because American booksellers considered their paperback books to be magazines and refused to stock them.

The Oppens returned to New York in 1933, and the next year Oppen's *Discrete Series* was published by the Objectivist Press, the short-lived successor to To Publishers. Then in 1935, according to Mary Oppen, "we decided to work with the Communist Party, not as artist or writer because we did not find honesty or sincerity in the so-called arts of the left. . . . We said to each other, 'Let's work with the unemployed and leave our other interest in the arts for a later time.' Few in the Party or in the Workers Alliance knew anything of our past, and in a short time we were no longer thinking of Paris or of To Publishers, or poetry or of painting." The Oppens spent the rest of the decade as organizers for the Workers Alliance in Brooklyn and later in Utica, New York.

Shortly after the birth of their daughter Linda, the Oppens moved to Detroit, where Oppen worked in a factory until he was drafted in 1942. He spent three years in the army and received multiple wounds from a shell explosion just before V-E Day. After the war, he first built houses in the Los Angeles area and then made cabinets for hi-fi sets. But in 1950, the Oppens fled to Mexico because of FBI harassment; they faced the possibility of going to jail for refusing to inform on their friends. In Mexico City, Oppen operated a furniture factory with a Mexican partner. He began writing poetry again shortly before returning to the United States in 1958.

Discussing the long gap in his writing career, Oppen says, "In a way I gave up poetry because of the pressures of what for the moment I'll call conscience. But there were some things I had to live through, some things I had to think my way through, really; it was the whole experience of working in factories, of having a child, and so on. . . . Hugh Kenner interrupted my explanation to him of these years by saying, 'In brief, it took twenty-five years to write the next poem.' Which is the way to say it." According to Oppen, "During those years I was perfectly aware of a lot of time before me and I at no time thought I wasn't a poet. I don't remember saying it clearly to myself, but I never felt that I would never write a poem again."

There has been, according to Oppen, a "tremendous misunderstanding" about what *objectivist* means. "People assume it means the psychologically objective in attitude," he says. "It actually means the objectification of the poem, the making an object of the poem." This method is applied throughout *Discrete Series* (1934), as in "Drawing," which describes the poem as an object:

> Written structure,
> Shape of art,
> More formal
> Than a field would be.

Oppen's subjects are also frequently objects, presented in an elliptical style, as in "Party on Shipboard":

> Tug against the river—
> Motor turning, lights
> In the fast water off the bow-wave:
> Passes slowly.

In discussing the significance of the title of the volume, he explains his style: "A discrete series is a series of terms each of which is empirically derived, each one of which is empirically true. And this is the reason for the fragmentary character of those poems. I was attempting to construct a meaning by empirical statements, by imagist statements."

When Oppen returned to poetry after a quarter century, he remained concerned with the object, but the poems in *The Materials* (1962) are more lucid than the earlier ones. "Workman" begins,

> Leaving the house each dawn I see the hawk
> Flagrant over the driveway. In his claws
> That dot, that comma
> Is the broken animal: the dangling small beast knows
> The burden that he is: he has touched
> The hawk's drab feathers. . . .

The objects in these poems have more associations built around them, more feelings involved in their presentations. In "From a Photograph," what is important is not just the object, the image, but the emotions captured in the image:

> Her arms around me—child—
> Around my head, hugging with her whole arms,
> Whole arms as if I were a loved and native rock,
> The apple in her hand—her apple and her father, and
> my nose pressed
> Hugely to the collar of her winter coat. . . .

The older Oppen clearly has a wealth of experience from which to draw his art, and several poems in *The Materials* are autobiographical, mixing memories of the past with thoughts about the present, as in "Birthplace: New Rochelle":

> An aging man,
> The knuckles of my hand
> So jointed! I am this?

In "Survival: Infantry," he recalls the emotions of the war: "We were ashamed of our half life and our misery: we saw that everything had died." Although Oppen claims his art is nonpolitical, a strain of antiwar, antibomb feelings runs through several of these poems. "Time of the Missile" ends,

> My love, my love,
> We are endangered
> Totally at last. Look
> Anywhere to the sight's limit: space
> Which is viviparous:
>
> Place of the mind
> And eye. Which can destroy us,
> Re-arrange itself, assert
> Its own stone chain reaction.

Equally concerned about more mundane matters, he asks, in "Tourist Eye," "Why are the office / Buildings, storehouses of papers, / The centers of extravagance?" Throughout his poetry of the 1960s and 1970s, Oppen expresses dismay at what man has allowed himself and his objects to become. Yet he is not entirely pessimistic; "The Source" is one of several poems to find something positive amid the squalor of our impersonal days in a city slum:

> —In some black brick
> Tenement, a woman's body
>
> Glows. The gleam; the unimaginable
> Thin feet taper down
> The instep naked to the wooden floor!
>
> Hidden and disguised
> —and shy?

The city's
Secret warmth.

This in Which (1965) continues Oppen's exploration of the emotions associated with the commonplace. His calm, deliberate approach to poetry causes him always to notice each possible side of an object, a person, a feeling. Joy can be experienced even when one expects the unusual but finds the ordinary; "Boy's Room" opens,

> A friend saw the rooms
> Of Keats and Shelley
> At the lake, and saw 'they were just
> Boys' rooms' and was moved
>
> By that. . . .

But close observation more often brings pain, as in "Street," a poem about the poor:

> It is terrible to see the children,
>
> The righteous little girls;
> So good, they expect to be so good. . . .

Too frequently what Oppen observes are signs of civilization's continuous decline; in "The Bicycles and the Apex," he notes "that slums are made dangerous by the gangs / And suburbs by the John Birch Societies." Oppen, the machinist, the cabinetmaker, looks, in this same poem, at the "mechanisms" and finds these "gadgets" that man once "loved" have become "Part of the platitude / Of our discontent." In "A Narrative," he finds man's activities increasingly misdirected:

> Wolves may hunt
>
> With wolves, but we will lose
> Humanity in the cities
> And the suburbs, stores
>
> And offices
> In simple
> Enterprise.

Oppen's poetry represents a search for values, and he often finds them in the natural world. In "Psalm," one of his best poems, he observes wild deer in a forest; the poem ends,

> The small nouns
> Crying faith
> In this in which the wild deer
> Startle, and stare out.

In a sense, Oppen's poetry is a kind of search for faith, a faith found in and taking the form of his art.

Of Being Numerous (1968) includes his two longest and most highly regarded works: the title poem and "Route." He says that the entire collection "asks the question whether or not we can deal with humanity as something which actually does exist." "Of Being Numerous," an expansion of "A Language of New York" from *This in Which*, is a meditation on life in the city, on being an individual or being a part of the community at large. Oppen sides with the virtues of isolation, referring frequently to the shipwrecked Robinson Crusoe:

> We are pressed, pressed on each other,
> We will be told at once
> Of anything that happens
>
> And the discovery of fact bursts
> In a paroxysm of emotion
> Now as always. Crusoe
>
> We say was
> 'Rescued'.
> So we have chosen.

Oppen prefers the individual, the thinker, the lonely perceiver:

> To dream of that beach
> For the sake of an instant in the eyes,
>
> The absolute singular
>
> The unearthly bonds
> Of the singular
>
> Which is the bright light of shipwreck.

As usual with Oppen, the poem is filled with meditations on his art:

> One must not come to feel that he has a thousand
>   threads in his hands,
> He must somehow see the one thing;
> This is the level of art
> There are other levels
> But there is no other level of art.

Here Oppen defines himself as an artist: "I am one of those who from nothing but man's way of thought and one of his dialects and what has happened to me / Have made poetry." In "Of Being Numerous," writes Rachel Blau DuPlessis, Oppen shows that "we are at home in the world and that we do have something to hold to. This discovery is made again and again in Oppen's poetry and is one of his major themes; one might even say it is his major consolation."

Oppen says that "Route," which extends the themes of "Of Being Numerous," deals with "learning that one is, after all, just oneself and in the end is rooted in the singular, whatever one's absolutely necessary connections with human history are." Man's sense of isolation is announced throughout "Route":

> I might at the top of my ability stand at a window
> and say, look out; out there is the world.
>
> Not the desire for approval nor even for love—O,
> that trap! From which escaped, barely—if it fails
>
> We will produce no sane man again.

Oppen is also still concerned with defining his style:

> Clarity, clarity, surely clarity is the most beautiful thing
> in the world,
> A limited, limiting clarity
>
> I have not and never did have any motive of poetry
> But to achieve clarity.

Oppen's art reaches its apex in *Of Being Numerous*; in his collections since then, his striving for clarity has not been as successful. The poems in *Seascape: Needle's Eye* (1972) represent a return to the more fragmentary style of *Discrete Series*. "Some San Francisco Poems," however, are still concerned with the search for the humanity amid the objects:

> One writes in the presence of something
> Moving close to fear
> I dare pity no one
> Let the rafters pity
> The air in the room
> Under the rafters.

The bewildering search for faith also continues, as in "Myth of the Blaze," one of twelve new poems in *Collected Poems* (1975): "I believe / in the world / because it is / impossible." In *Primitive* (1978), Oppen examines the natural world, language, and how they mingle to form poetry. His style is repetitive as he presents a word, a group of words, or an image and pauses to reflect on its significance, approaching it constantly from all sides. Two poems, "If It All Went Up in Smoke" and "The Natural," even share the same ending:

> help me I am
> of that people the grass
>
> blades touch
>
> and touch in their small
>
> distances the poem
> begins.

For Oppen, the end of one poem is always the beginning of the next, and they all flow together to form one epic vision of man's humanity and inhumanity, his relation to all the things in his world and mind, alternately joyous and despairing.

Some critics have complained that Oppen's poetry is too abstract, too concise, too impersonal, too humorless (there is absolutely no humor in his works). Irvin Ehrenpreis's objections are typical: "sparseness has little power by itself. When Oppen rejects the common privileges of a poet, he not only adds little excitement to his language; he also risks bathos. The elliptical character of his style barely distinguishes it from the cryptic. When one receives his insights, they often sound like those of Pound and W. C. Williams, and though truly felt are unsurprising. . . . I wonder whether by resisting the lure of abundance he has not been left with a style that is pinched and thin."

Nevertheless, Oppen has always had enthusiastic advocates. Ezra Pound's preface to *Discrete Series* ends, "I salute a serious craftsman, a sensibility which is not every man's sensibility and which has not been got out of any other man's books," and in reviewing the volume, William Carlos Williams praised its "craftsmanlike economy of means." More recently, Diane Wakoski has stated a view completely opposite that of Ehrenpreis: "He has that rare art of saying, simply, what he thinks, feels, sees, means, in just a few words. Oppen, at his best, makes us see how many Victorian cobwebs are still wrapped around both our thinking processes and the language which expresses them."

Louis Simpson expresses a similar sentiment: "Reading Oppen I am aware of all that has been excluded by a very discriminating mind in order to arrive at significant life. The mind, moving toward clarity, sheds those matters that are, as Gatsby said, 'just personal.' As it begins to know itself, the mind moves, and thought is felt as movement, along the line. We experience the life of the mind in its physical reality, the movement of verse." Theodore Enslin writes, "In great measure, Oppen is a conscience of our time, no less a poetic conscience than a moral one. There is sadness, and there is an inexorable admonition in that voice—perhaps anger, though the anger is never shrill, is always touched with kindness." To Charles Tomlinson, Oppen is simply "the most human of poets."

—*Michael Adams*

Interviews:

L. S. Dembo, "George Oppen," *Contemporary Literature*, 10 (Spring 1969): 159-177;
Charles Amirkhanian and David Gitin, "A Conver-

sation with George Oppen," *Ironwood*, 5 (1975): 21-24;

Kevin Power, "Conversation with George and Mary Oppen, May 25, 1975," *Texas Quarterly*, 21 (Spring 1978): 35-52.

References:

Cid Corman, "Together," *Parnassus*, 4 (1976): 83-95;

L. S. Dembo, "The Existential World of George Oppen," *Iowa Review*, 3 (Winter 1972): 64-91;

Dembo, "Individuality and Numerosity," *Nation*, 209 (24 November 1969): 574-576;

Rachel Blau DuPlessis, "George Oppen: 'What do we believe to live with?' " *Ironwood*, 5 (1975): 62-77;

Irvin Ehrenpreis, "The State of Poetry," *New York Review of Books*, 22 January 1976, p. 4;

Theodore Enslin, "If it Fails—" *Ironwood*, 5 (1975): 59-61;

Serge Fauchereau, "Three Oppen Letters with a Note," *Ironwood*, 5 (1975): 78-85;

Michael Hamburger, *Art as Second Nature: Occasional Pieces 1950-74* (Cheshire, U.K.: Carcanet Press, 1975), pp. 153-156;

Hugh Kenner, *A Homemade World: The American Modernist Writers* (New York: Knopf, 1975), pp. 163-188;

Kenner, "Poems Made Like a Choir, Each Part Joined and Tested," *New York Times Book Review*, 19 October 1975, p. 5;

Mary Oppen, *Meaning a Life* (Santa Barbara: Black Sparrow Press, 1978);

Ezra Pound, "Preface: *Discrete Series* by George Oppen," *Stony Brook*, 3-4 (Fall 1969): 21;

Carl Rakosi, "A Note on George Oppen," *Ironwood*, 5 (1975): 19;

Charles Reznikoff, "A Memoir," *Ironwood*, 5 (1975): 29;

Louis Simpson, "Poetry in the Sixties—Long Live Blake! Down With Donne!" *New York Times Book Review*, 28 December 1969, p. 18;

Charles Tomlinson, "An Introductory Note on the Poetry of George Oppen," *Ironwood*, 5 (1975): 12-18;

Tomlinson, "Objectivists: Zukofsky and Oppen, a Memoir," *Paideuma*, 7 (Winter 1978): 429-445;

Diane Wakoski, "The True Art of Simplicity: An Appreciation of George Oppen," *Ironwood*, 5 (1975): 31-34;

William Carlos Williams, "The New Poetical Economy," *Poetry*, 44 (July 1934): 220-225;

Paul Zweig, "Making and Unmaking," *Partisan Review*, 40 (1973): 273-276.

JOEL OPPENHEIMER
(18 February 1930-)

BOOKS: *Four Poems to Spring* (Black Mountain, N.C.: Privately printed, 1951);
The Dancer (Highlands, N.C.: Jonathan Williams, 1951);
The Dutiful Son (Highlands, N.C.: Jonathan Williams, 1956);
The Love Bit and Other Poems (New York: Totem / Corinth, 1962);
The Great American Desert (New York: Grove, 1966);
Sirventes on a Sad Occurrence (Madison, Wis.: Perishable Press, 1967);
In Time: Poems 1962-1968 (Indianapolis & New York: Bobbs-Merrill, 1969);
On Occasion: Some Births, Deaths, Weddings, Birthdays, Holidays, and Other Events (Indianapolis & New York: Bobbs-Merrill, 1973);
The Wrong Season (Indianapolis & New York: Bobbs-Merrill, 1973);
Pan's Eyes (Amherst, Mass.: Mulch Press, 1974);
The Woman Poems (Indianapolis & New York: Bobbs-Merrill, 1975);
Acts (Driftless, Wis.: Perishable Press, 1976);
names, dates, & places (Laurinburg, N.C.: Saint Andrews Press, 1978).

Joel Oppenheimer was born in Yonkers, New York, and raised there, in a neighborhood a short walk from the New York City line. He attended Cornell University and the University of Chicago before finding himself at Black Mountain College, where he studied writing with M. C. Richards, Paul Goodman, and especially Charles Olson, while beginning a long association with fellow Black Mountain writers Edward Dorn, Robert Creeley, Jonathan Williams, Michael Rumaker, and Fielding Dawson (later associates included Paul Blackburn, Allen Ginsberg, LeRoi Jones, Frank O'Hara, and Gilbert Sorrentino). Having actually been a student at Black Mountain from 1950 to 1953, taking courses with Olson and having his work published in the *Black Mountain Review* edited by Creeley, Oppenheimer is one of those writers most legitimately a part of the group known in recent literary history as the Black Mountain Poets, and he is included as such in Donald Allen's famous anthology, *The New American Poetry* (1960). His writing is hardly restricted to representing a literary movement, however, and his subsequent reputation as a poet is as much a result of his life and literary activities in New York as it is due to his Black Mountain connections.

Joel Oppenheimer

He has lived in New York City itself since 1953, working for fifteen years in print shops (as printer, typographer, production manager) before becoming director of the St. Mark's Poetry Project in 1966, one of the liveliest series of readings and workshops on the East Coast, and of New York's Teachers and Writers Collaborative. Since 1969 he has had a regular column in the *Village Voice*—on sports (baseball), politics, the seasons, occasional literary-cultural matters, over-coffee musings—a domestic Joseph Addison or Richard Steele—and he is poet-in-residence (Distinguished Visiting Professor of Poetry) at the City College of New York. For almost ten years he has lived in Westbeth, a federally sponsored artists' and writers' community rehabilitated from the old experimental laboratories of the Bell Telephone Company in Greenwich Village. The ambiance of his poems is even more typically New York than that of the self-consciously called "New York School" poets such as Frank O'Hara, although Oppenheimer's preoccupation and chief accomplishment has not been the evoking of place but the exploration of interpersonal relationships—sexual, marital, family, between friends. He summarizes his interests himself in "A Long Testament" (published in *Mulch* magazine, Spring 1972):

> myself i can think of
> nothing but the interpersonal
> relationship. each man at it
> his own way.

Early influences were E. E. Cummings, the first poet whom he read and to whom he still pays tribute by his use of lowercase letters. Also influential—at least for his early poems, those of the 1950s—was Robert Creeley, who shared his sense of the personal. The most pervasive and persistent influence, however, has been William Carlos Williams, to whom he was introduced at Black Mountain (at least the Williams of the *Collected Earlier Poems* [1951] and *Pictures from Breughel* [1962] rather than of *Paterson*, which Oppenheimer felt was "a magnificent and futile failure"). And it was not Charles Olson's own poetry as much as Olson the teacher that significantly affected him, instructing him to discover his own voice and, specifically, to allow the full natural "discursiveness" of that voice to enter the poems.

One of the most immediately noticeable characteristics of Oppenheimer's poetry, even before one gets to the content, is the absence of uppercase letters—a manner derived in part, as suggested, from Cummings, but also consistent with his own poetics.

It is true for his prose as well, whether his stories as collected in *Pan's Eyes* (1974), his "sort of a baseball book" *The Wrong Season* (1973), or, until recently (when the publisher insisted otherwise), his *Village Voice* column. He responds to the issue in a 1974 discussion of poetics: "I don't think they [capital letters] serve any functional purpose. In general they seem to me to get in the way of a flat line, and I suppose if I had to talk that way I'd say that I don't want the words to get in the way of the poem." He argues, "a cap on a proper noun . . . implies there are improper nouns," and he adds: "I also like the visual look of it. On my typescripts, I'll type the title in spaced capitals—single space between each of the letters and a triple space between the words because I like that appearance. So I'm not against capitals as letter forms. I guess I'm against miscegenation between capitals and lower case letters." Finally, he offers still another reason: "having made that determination that I liked the way it worked in the

134

poem, in about 1955 when I was just beginning to get published a little bit consistently, the shift key on my typewriter broke, so the decision was made by God."

Oppenheimer's are mostly short-lined poems, with enjambment but little syncopation or other pyrotechnics of the line. The poems are nevertheless gently rhythmic, unfolding from the live flow of speech. He trusts to a simple vocabulary (the words do not "get in the way of the poem") and—especially in the later work—a consistent, undistorted, unambiguous syntax. It is a leisurely pace; some might find it languid, a strolling conversation or gentle monologue. Effects are cumulative and often not reached until several lines have passed. The poet is concerned with direct communication; so much so, there are even moments when he writes, "what i mean to say is. . . ." He is certainly not unaware of life's (and art's) complexities, however, and some of the best poems have faint brushes of irony or satire. Still, simplicity is his trust. The ear is not startled awake by the beat of an opening alliteration, no paradox is immediately issued to be eventually resolved, images are not used to lure the reader along. The desired effect is achieved by repetition and sincerity, rather than a shock of image (or summarizing by image) or lyric exaltation. There is an unhurried mildness, an unstudied repose—grace, it might be called—to the poems. That, along with their inherent warmth, the perception and defense of such human values as independence, fairness, tolerance, frankness, are their most admirable qualities.

Among his first published poems, "The Dancer," fully in the manner of Williams and Olson—written in tribute to dancer Katherine Litz and published by Jonathan Williams, with a drawing by Robert Rauschenberg—indicates the company it was possible to keep at Black Mountain. Oppenheimer himself has found (in his interview with Whitney Jones) more care and craftsmanship in the lines in the earlier volumes, *The Dutiful Son* (1956) and *The Love Bit* (1962), while the collections *In Time* (1969) and *On Occasion* (1973) are more discursive—not only in syntax but also in the range of material, the free sliding between private feelings and public concerns, personal relationships and political issues—very much like the 1960s themselves. He writes in "The Innocent Breasts":

> we are all, we know
> now, bone-pickers after
> darwin, rag-pickers after
> marx, brain-pickers
> after freud—we are

> trying to reconstruct
> our history.

The poems in *The Dutiful Son* and *The Love Bit*, more so than the later poems of direct address, are obliquely evocative. Metaphors are sketched, not scored; they are seldom hardened into mirror shards as in imagism. Ornament, when necessary, is worn lightly. Skill is evident early, in the effective parallels and repetitions of "The Bus Trip" and "The Bath." "The Rain" and "The Gardener," both first published in the *Black Mountain Review*, show the influence not only of Williams but Creeley, whose poems and stories Oppenheimer had immediately responded to when Olson read them in class. "The Rain" follows its own fall, the quiet grace of its emotion supported by the delicacy of its firm but narrow structure. These poems explore and celebrate the young poet's immediate world as it begins to form around him. There are poems to his new wife, to his wife as mother of their first child, poems for the second child, for the family of four, for himself as father. Gradually, the solid simplicity of pride in possession of "The Bath"—

> what he is most pleased about is
> her continuing bathing.
> in his tub. in his water. wife.

—gives way (as culturally, historically it would anyway) to much quicker-paced poems. The acuity is seen in the title poem of *The Love Bit* itself, the snap of language, hip and alert, evident not only in the poem's end but—in the catalogue of color images—in the ability to pull in images at will from far afield:

> the colors we depend on are
> red for raspberry jam, white
> of the inside thigh, purple as
> in deep, the blue of moods, green
> cucumbers (cars), yellow stripes down
> the pants, orange suns on ill-
> omened days, and black as the
> dirt in my fingernails.
> also, brown, in the night,
> appearing at its best when
> the eyes turn inward, seeking
> seeking, to dig everything but
> our own. i.e. we make it crazy or
> no, and sometimes in the afternoon.

It is a poem directly comparable, if not owing, to those in Creeley's *For Love* (compare the structure of "The Invoice"). It wears its style appropriately, fully deserving to be title poem of the volume. In "Blue

Joel Oppenheimer

Funk," the encouragement is jazz, as is evident by the title. Lines are deliberately "flattened," flatted like a blue note. There are careful repetitions and a keen delicacy but with sentimentality muted like a trumpet. Indeed, along with Williams and Creeley, trumpeter Miles Davis is an acknowledged influence: "You know those tiny little phrases that Miles was blowing," Oppenheimer reminds his audience in discussing the early poems at Kent State.

In his two later and larger collections, *On Occasion* and *In Time*, he has proven himself master of the occasional poem, one of the most accessible and therefore popular poetic modes. (In many ways his column for the *Village Voice* is a logical extension, though on a lower, less essential frequency.) He has written well of what he means by an "occasional poem" in his prefatory note to *On Occasion*, which (unlike *In Time*) stretches over the full extent of his poetic career from 1950 on:

> goethe says somewhere that occasional poetry
> is the highest form of art; when it succeeds i
> incline to agree with him—by success i mean
> when the poem moves past the personal
> impetus for writing it, but preserves the solid
> air of that impetus; in other words, that the
> poem, hopefully, may be meaningful far
> beyond the immediate situation.
>
> occasional poems also indicate, for me, a
> "usefulness" for poetry as a function of life
> and a benefit to society that belies popular
> rumor.

There are poems in both volumes addressed to Ezra Pound, Frank O'Hara, LeRoi Jones, Charles Reznikoff, Edward Dahlberg, Malcolm X, Marilyn Monroe, and to women he has known (including the delightful "Ladies of Westbeth"), two excellent elegies for Williams, another for Olson. "The Polish Cavalry" is his tribute to Olson, written the day after his death, in which images of various battles are mixed along with a personal acknowledgment of a younger poet to his teacher, the "son" to his "father." It is a fitting memorial to a poet who appreciated the facts-as-events of history:

> what i am trying to say is
> that you brought two generations
> to life, and you'll have to
> live with that. you always did move
> like a grampus and you still do.
> the polish cavalry at least had lances.
> what you've got only your sons and
> your grandsons know. . . . i'm sorry
> i have to speak in different images,

> but you told me a long time ago
> to speak in my own, and i believed
> that. . . .

There are also fine poems for his great-grandparents ("An Anniversary") and upon the marriage of young friends ("A Wedding"), and a particularly effective elegy for the son of Paul Goodman, killed in a mountain-climbing accident ("For Matthew, Dead"). Battles are waged ("The Only Anarchist General") and sometimes won ("Come On Baby"). As in a poem for his father's birthday ("For My Father, One Year Older"), "he remembers everything life / is, and shouldn't be—he knows / by now it is, in general, unfair—and / yet. . . ." There is always the "and yet" in Oppenheimer, the irrepressible. Sometimes he hurries the opportunity and creates his own occasion; the poem, thus begun, responds to itself, and this response resonates. This is as much a source for discursiveness as a superabundance of material pressing in, or the inability or reluctance to subordinate one experience to another.

"A Treatise" reflects the poet's other major concern after human relationships—politics and history, which are actually the study of human relationships on the larger scale. Here the subject is the effect of the city on man, as it has persisted for over seven thousand years. His is very much the anarchist's view: "what else the / concentration camp but / the perfection of the / city, what else the SS / but the perfection of / the state, what else / the factories and stores / but lesser gas chambers. . . ." Momentum is gained in the poem by progressive parallels, cohesion by strategic recapitulations. Also in *In Time* is a long, impassioned indictment of the United States, titled by its date of composition, "17-18 April, 1961." It is one of the first of the waves of poetic protests (along with those by Ginsberg, Olson, and Dorn) against American expansionism and "dreams of empire" that culminated in the Vietnam War and corporation rule, at the expense of the nation's own dreams and premises:

> i am just reminding you you did not
> want to listen when allen yelled at you
> like jeremiah, you did not listen when
> charles patiently explained to you what
> you had done to gloucester, you don/t
> listen even now when ed tells you how
> it is about charitable clothes. . . .

Even more effective, because it offers values that transcend politics—or more precisely, that are the essence of politics—is "A Poem for Children" from *On Occasion*. Written in 1970, during a time of

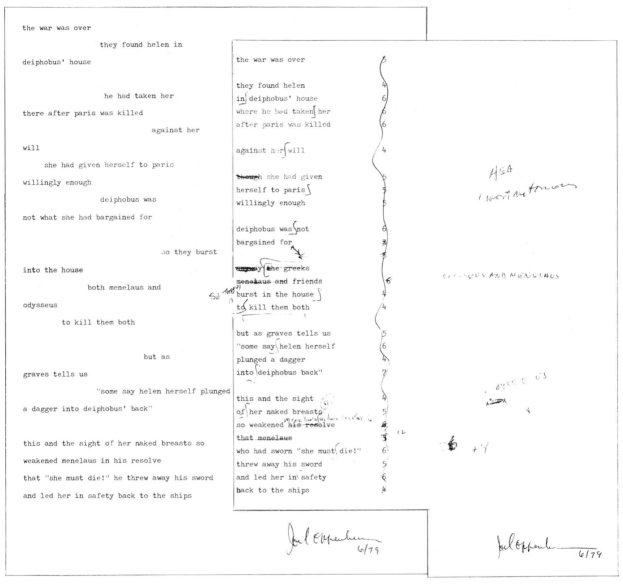

Work-in-progress, revised typescripts

confrontation—with his own infant son in mind as well as the newborn children of two of his literary friends, poets Paul Blackburn and Tom McGrath—it challenges the threats to individual liberty then evident in American society. Images of police, their weapons and helicopters at People's Park in Berkeley, site of just one notable clash of the popular will with emblematic powers, intrude in the poem as they do in the world the poet is seeking to make for the young:

> what we are saying is
> these children, born, are not going
> to eat shit; i have a better hope for
> it than ever—tom mcgrath is over

fifty! paul blackburn is over forty! joel oppenheimer is over thirty! they are breeding children! those children will have children to learn from! they will be immune from teargas! they will come happily! even when young! they will be able to like tits without being hung up on them! they will recognize cops in one-fifth of a bartender's time! they will even know how to play in parks! they will even know how to shoot down helicopters over the parks!

It is a poem for the future of the young, and one of the

few Oppenheimer poems in which exclamation points appear, in which the voice or the line is raised from its "flatness."

Perhaps "A Sirventes on a Sad Occurrence," first published separately in 1967, may be singled out as his finest poem. It is also one that brings into play all his best qualities—heartfelt sympathy, the patient telling, a winsome personality, accurate inflections of speech (in this case, especially, a New York Jewish or Yiddish idiom), the utter naturalism, a true democratic spirit. His authority comes from his deeply shared sense of humanity. The poem begins with the poet, in all good cheer, setting out down his tenement stairs for work on a spring day, when he inadvertently comes upon an old neighbor, a "great grandma," who has been incontinent, involuntarily defecating on her way up the stairs to her apartment. Her daughter, "older than / my mother," has gone back to the apartment to get something to wipe up the mess: "don/t / tell, mrs. stern, the daughter screams, / i/ll be back, right away i/ll clean, / don/t tell. . . ." The poet continues:

> what can she possibly
> tell, old woman, that you are old,
> that you have had your children, they
> have had theirs, they, theirs, and
> you are still here, your world
> still exists, where does she fit in?
> —as if there weren/t already
> shit in the world, and you invented
> it. what further indignities to
> allow besides inventing shit?

Conscious of the paradox of coming face-to-face with old age and its weakness in the flush of spring vitality, the poet has already announced his intention: "i will write / against that which is in us to / make age an embarrassment in the / season of coming alive." He captures the simple drama of the moment of encounter:

> and on top of it, as you clung to
> the bannister at the top step, almost
> around, fifteen feet from your
> door, to face me suddenly, coming
> down from one flight up, my hat no
> longer swinging but over my head,
> over my thin bearded face, my god
> the moan then, even your daughter
> scared by it, i thought you were
> dying /til i found out the truth. . . .

He goes on to uphold the woman's honor while efficiently allowing the narrative to reveal the full circumstances:

> this is a
> natural act, why will you
> fear me for it, i see each day
> more shit than you could ever
> dream of making, screw your
> daughter, let mrs. stern watch
> out for her own steps, i am just
> standing here waiting for you
> to pass, too late now for me
> to go back up the stairs, i have
> just discovered what the fact is
> much too late, and will stand quietly.

This is the poet in his most necessary role—willing to speak up for human dignity, to defend and extol man's humanity amidst vast creation, to raise man from his embarrassment to the acceptance of human frailty and the celebration of an underlying common nobility. He concludes by gently rebuking the old woman:

> this is the east
> side, guns crack, people snort
> their noses full of life, and you
> are dying because you shat
> upon these steps? and were faced
> with me? old lady, act your age.

It is a voice of tender scolding, one that warms and chastens our own hearts.

The poet's next book, *The Woman Poems* (1975), a "loosely sequential series" written over 1973 and 1974, can be seen as a furtherance of his concern with relationships, especially sexual relationships, now in their fullest psychological complexities. It is a series of poems honoring and exploring the Great Mother in her various manifestations, specifically the four chief ones of Good Mother, Death Mother, Ecstasy or Dancing Mother, and Stone or Tooth Mother, which Oppenheimer had encountered in Robert Bly's *Sleepers Joining Hands* (1973), deriving ultimately from Erich Neumann's classic, *The Great Mother* (1955). Oppenheimer comments during a reading of the poems in 1975: "I read the essay [by Bly] and got terribly excited and that's really what the book grew out of except that I was faced with a choice, which was either to write the poems or to do all the research. I chose to write the poems." In one sense, he had been researching the subject all his life. The poems range from the obviously Oedipal "Mother Poem" to those of explicit sexual fantasy such as "Dirty Picture Poem" or "Fantasy Poem" itself. The lovely personal tribute to his wife's breasts in "The Innocent Breasts" in *In Time* becomes a celebration of the Feminine and her specific attributes in the more boldly titled "Your Tits Poem," which concludes with a celebration of the "goddess of nine breasts" whom he will continue to attend.

It was a curious volume to bring out in 1975, in the midst of ardent feminism in the United States and especially in New York, yet a perfectly appropriate one, being both elemental and elementary. There is a paternal, at times patriarchal, quality to the poems—to the dismay, conceivably, of some women readers—but the timeless sincerity of them is beyond question or reproach. One of the best and an example of his welcome naturalism is "Father Poem," which the poet begins by announcing, "i have fathered / four sons, they surround / me in an age of / women," and in which he describes himself as a victim of the wars of life and between the sexes:

> like always and always,
> i will be defeated, they
> will carry me ball-less and
> regal into the house of
> the dead where i will
> pay for this sin, having
> fathered only sons. . . .

"But," he continues,

> this is in me rock-
> like, to do the wrong
> thing, to pick the
> wrong time. it is
> obduracy, pride, a
> need to go the wrong way.

Yet he surpasses self-pity with pride in his sons and the happily exaggerated prospect of being brought to his "golden throne" by them: "defeated, regal, honored. / when i get there i / will have a drink and / let them do the fighting." He concludes wryly: "the fathers of daughters / cannot say this." As with so many of his poems, this one is characterized by a generous good humor rather than dogmatism or a brittle and infernal cleverness.

Occasional poems continue in his *names, dates, & places* (1978), a collection of poems written throughout the 1970s, its title alone evidence of its concerns. There is the vignette of a brief meeting on the street—the poet in red hat encountering a woman in red cape, making it a "red letter day"—its obligation to Williams given in the title, "Spring and Some" (a variation of Williams's *Spring and All*, 1923). Also included is "The New Year," which interestingly enough was revised, its discursiveness somewhat compressed, from its first appearance as "Signs and Portents, Omens, Bodings, and Good

and Bad Beginnings as Seen for the New Year" (1975)—mostly leaving out some of the topicality, such as "abe beame [then mayor of New York] asked / his wife which coat to / wear to his swearing-in, / whereas i chose mine with / firmness of purpose" or changing "nixon remains, but then, / so do i" to "the world remains but so do i." The revisions, however, make the poem neither more nor less effective, since both versions succeed by going on at a happy length listing in detail a great many of the poet's accomplishments and resolutions, his keeping "up-to-date at least this far," concluding with the mild and cheerful irony that the year is only "two days old." It is such self-knowledge rather than righteousness that most gives Oppenheimer his appealing modesty.

"Cacti," written in November 1975, is an example of another discursive poem—half-narrative, half-lyric. The longest lines are only five words, and there are occasional repetitions or recapitulating statements, usually direct narrative addresses ("i told you / i am not complaining"), with occasional light sound arousals such as "at the rear / of all these plants / rearing proudly." The poem itself is actually an extended metaphor—perhaps even imitating the spare, spiky, elongated length of the varieties of cacti described—in which the plants stand for the poet himself, persistent when given a little water, or love, once a month.

The separately published *Acts* (1976), likewise, is a long poem with a single central metaphor, in this case arising from a newspaper account of the death of "the first human cannonball" and his reported lifelong ambition to have been a painter. It similarly is divided into "stanzas," or spaced sections according to sense, rather than seeking syncopations and varieties of rhythm. Form, typically in these poems, is underplayed; sense through talking is everything. As Donald Phelps points out, Oppenheimer is a monologist rather than a declaimer or riddler. It is not that there are no complexities. Indeed, every sense is that his life has suffered from them (then gained). But the complexities and contradictions can be told at length just as effectively—only differently—rather than by fierce compression or gnarled and violent upheavals of the line. There are not the breath lengths or phrasing of Olson or Creeley, each stanza is a sentence, so there is no rhythmic modulation other than that of simple speech, no syncopation gained by syntactical maneuvers, no acidic twists of irony. Oppenheimer's poetry is completely within the tradition of Williams and what he himself calls a "flat" line, not the full Whitmanian majesty or bardic lengths of Ginsberg or elegance of Robert Duncan, the campy speed of O'Hara, the pared subtleties of Creeley, the demands of Olson. He emphasizes the simplicity in Williams, at times at the expense of the terror (the Williams who was aware of love's "stain" or intricate "cruelty" or who knew the beckoning "descent").

In 1975 Oppenheimer sought to extend his exploration of relationships and extend the form of his poems in a promising although uncompleted series tentatively called "The Man Discovered Through the Kitchen Window," three sections of which were published in the magazine *Credences*. These allowed the poet to write about himself in the third person—he being the man "discovered through the window," each time while washing the dishes, by a neighbor called "the Realist Painter" (a real-life artist living across the Westbeth courtyard who "has been known to call down and bitch about the rareness of the roast beef or inquire what's in the third container of Chinese food")—all of which poses fascinating complexities to be explored, such as the artist (any artist) as voyeur, the problem of the representation of reality, life beyond the framed moment, all the basic concerns of the imagistic arts. The opening poems succeed well, although regrettably the series was never sustained. "My circumstances changed," Oppenheimer tells Whitney Jones, "I was no longer doing dishes and then going right into writing. Now I do the dishes and take the kid over to school and then stop and have coffee and then get back. So that kind of energy is hard to sustain over that hour in between."

Oppenheimer's latest work continues the rambling meditation and honest, earned wisdom that he has consistently sought, seen most successfully in the gently unfolding "Houses." The occasion is a visit to the home of his first wife for the marriage of their first son. Showering in preparation for dressing, he recalls her habit of long baths when they were first married, and he quotes from a poem, "The Bath," written for her twenty-three years earlier. The present poem is a long pondering, more rumination than reminiscence ("don't misunderstand me / i am not speaking / of romance / or rekindled love / or even second chances"), a tender accounting of how over the years the poet has come to peace with the knowledge:

> the house i've fought
> my way through to get to
>
> this house which is
> not so clean and neat
> as yours

> i am a man
> i need a woman's touch
> might be the pity of it

(This is the closest Oppenheimer comes to splayed or shared syntax—still within natural speech rhythms.)

> but i've learned to build
> without it
>   but now can see
> how pleasant such things are
> and where they come from
> in me
>   that is what
> i did not know
>   and what
> i now do know
> and will remember.

It is utterly convincing, neither overly solemn nor self-aggrandizing; one has no reason to doubt his sentiment. It is a time of rest, of release from the high-wired tensions and energy thrusts of another order of poetry. It is not sublime or ecstatic, but welcome and usable. The pleasure in all such poems is their sense of resolution, a fitting end. Oppenheimer has said in an interview: "A friend of mine . . . says that every human life has a kind of logic: it consists of 'a beginning, a muddle, and an end.' I thought that was good enough to put in a poem. The 'muddle' is one of my favorite themes."

Oppenheimer's laconic, unhurried view suggests an essential sameness, an unchanging quality to human nature that, like heartbreak or sexual confusion, must be treated with patience and deliberate regard. His discursiveness, then, is deliberateness. Controlled but unforced, he prefers straight talk to a savagery of indifference or surrealistic strewing of illusion or entertainment. The reader is held, swayed, by a gentle caring voice. There is no effort to plunge the reader, held like Achilles by the heel, into a purifying fire of confusion. Rather, the implication is that life is confusion enough, suffering is suffered enough; let man be acknowledged, celebrated—or condemned—directly. This is Oppenheimer's special wisdom. He has qualities of a mild or lesser sage. Life-wise and folk-simple is his approach—straight from the heart, and most revivifying.

All indications are that Oppenheimer, who lives deeply in and for the occasion of the present, will continue to write occasional poems, with periodic extensions into the discursive monologue as the subjects arise. He will continue to be known and thanked for his dependable sense of humanity and his imaginative coping with all that troubles our own most intimate selves. He is evidence that the Williams inheritance can be shared and participated in and that it is a most viable, strongly American tradition. —*George F. Butterick*

Periodical Publications:

"Charles Olson 1910-1970," *Village Voice*, 15 January 1970, p. 9;

"The Inner Tightrope: An Appreciation of Robert Creeley," *Lillabulero*, 8 (Winter 1970): 51-53;

"Beginning the Portrait"; "The Concierge"; "Rinsing His Teeth," *Credences*, 2 (July 1975): 5-12;

"Cacti," *St. Andrews Review*, 4 (Spring-Summer 1977): 55-63;

"Houses," *Chicago Review*, 30 (Winter 1979): 89-99.

Interviews:

"Interview with Poet Joel Oppenheimer," *Noiseless Spider*, 1 (Spring 1972): 2-5;

William L. Owens, "Joel Oppenheimer at Storrs, Conn.," *Credences*, 2 (July 1975), 13-25;

"Three Versions of the Poetic Line," *Credences*, 4 (March 1977): 55-60;

F. Whitney Jones, "An Interview With Joel Oppenheimer," *St. Andrews Review*, 4 (Spring-Summer 1977): 45-54.

Bibliography:

George F. Butterick, *Joel Oppenheimer: A Checklist of His Writings* (Storrs: University of Connecticut Library, 1975).

References:

Robert Bertholf, "On The Great American Desert and The Woman Poems," *Credences*, 2 (July 1975): 26-35;

Maxine S. Combs, "A Study of the Black Mountain Poets," Ph.D. dissertation, University of Oregon, 1967, pp. 167-172;

Robert Creeley, " 'An intensely singular art,' " in his *A Quick Graph: Collected Notes & Essays*, ed. Donald Allen (San Francisco: Four Seasons, 1970), pp. 202-206;

Karl Malkoff, *Crowell's Handbook of Contemporary American Poetry* (New York: Crowell, 1973), pp. 243-245;

Donald Phelps, "The Simple Ecology of the Soul," *For Now*, 11 (1970): 28-31.

Papers:

Oppenheimer's papers are in the Literary Archives, University of Connecticut Library, Storrs.

GIL ORLOVITZ
(7 June 1918-10 July 1973)

BOOKS: *Concerning Man* (Pawlet, Vt.: Banyan Press, 1947);

Keep To Your Belly (New York: Louis Brigante / Intro, 1952);

The Diary of Dr. Eric Zeno (San Francisco: Inferno Press, 1953);

The Statement of Erika Keith, and Other Stories, Poems and a Play (Berkeley: Miscellaneous Man, 1957);

The Diary of Alexander Patience (San Francisco: Inferno Press, 1958);

The Papers of Professor Bold (Eureka, Cal.: Hearse Press, 1959);

Something to Tell Mother (London: American Letters Press, 1959?);

Selected Poems (San Francisco: Inferno Press, 1960; London: Barrie & Rockliff, n.d.);

The Art of the Sonnet (Nashville, Tenn.: Hillsboro Publications, 1961);

The Middle Sex (New York: Beacon-Signal Books, 1963);

Left of Sex (New York: Universal Publishing, 1964);

Five Sonnets (Lanham, Md.: Goosetree Press, 1964);

Milkbottle H (London: Calder & Boyars, 1967; New York: Dell, 1968);

Couldn't Say, Might Be Love (London: Barrie & Rockliff, 1969);

Ice Never F (London: Calder & Boyars, 1970);

More Poems (Fredericton, New Brunswick, Canada: Fiddlehead Poetry Books, 1972).

Gil Orlovitz was born in Philadelphia, Pennsylvania. His grandfather was the chief rabbi of Lithuania, and his father, who also had an extensive knowledge of the Talmud, warned Orlovitz about relying too heavily upon art as a basis of life. His mother, Orlovitz explained, showered upon him a combination of "babble, love, and lox." An English teacher introduced him to the arts of prosody, which he absorbed to the exclusion of other school subjects. He attended Temple University in Philadelphia for a short while and then was in the U.S. Army Air

Gil Orlovitz

Corps for four years during World War II. After the war, he attended Columbia University, studying dramaturgy under Hatcher Hughes and also taking courses in comparative religion and philosophy. From there he went to study with Erwin Piscator at the Dramatic Workshop in New York. Little is known about his first wife, Betty, with whom he had no children. He married Maralyn Marquize in 1952. They had three children. Orlovitz worked as a radio monitor, in the import-export trade, and as a

Gil Orlovitz

researcher for Standard Oil of New Jersey. After three Off-Broadway productions of his plays in the early 1950s, he worked in Hollywood as a staff screenwriter for Columbia Pictures and then as a free-lance television writer. He returned to New York in late 1958 because of his father's illness. Until the end of his life he held editorial positions with New York publishers, including a job as softcover book editor at Universal Publishing and Distributing Corporation from 1960 to 1969.

Gerald Stern reports that Orlovitz belonged to no literary cliques. He was mostly nonpolitical and also uncalculating. Although Orlovitz had many close friends, he seems not to have been intimate with any other well-known poets. He judged his contemporaries harshly. Yet he was a prolific and serious writer whose work deserves greater critical

attention and a wider audience. His novels, *Milkbottle H* (1967) and *Ice Never F* (1970), were long in finding publishers, and their disillusioning reception may have contributed to Orlovitz's drinking problem, which complicated his final years. Robert Nye found *Milkbottle H* to be "a major work of fiction by any standards," and Ken Sullivan commented that it "is a no-novel, and Gil Orlovitz is a no-novelist, which is to say a writer, and essentially a poet, whose explosive, sprawling, non-stop prose insists constantly on its own self-sufficiency." Its technical virtuosity made analysis a difficult process, and the novel was virtually ignored by American reviewers. Orlovitz also failed to find a major publisher for his poetry; hence most of it was produced in small editions that were also largely ignored.

Both in his poetry and in his public comments, Orlovitz maintains a position of superiority that, while partly justified, tends to antagonize. "It will ultimately be found," said Orlovitz, "that the extent and depth of my esthetic is so fabulous and of such variety and texture and sheer wonder that my work will be adjudged second to none at any time in the history of art." According to poet Hale Chatfield, Orlovitz believed that America has "so far produced two poets worthy of the name: Emily Dickinson and himself, and he rates himself as America's best novelist since James and Melville."

Gerald Stern, in an appreciative article, points out a number of reasons why Orlovitz's poetry is difficult to write about. First, there is no common, overriding attitude about the poetry. Some reviewers have lumped Orlovitz with the surrealists, others with the Beats. But the general lack of critical response has inhibited the formulation of a critical position. Second, Orlovitz's audience is "unfathomable." That is, while his work is familiar to many older readers of poetry, many young readers of poetry have never heard of him. Another difficulty has to do with the shifting moral stance of the poems. Likening Orlovitz and his poetry to a country not on the map, Stern suggests that while they exist, they have not been clearly defined. Orlovitz's wild energy makes mapping difficult, and the constantly shifting boundaries of subject and attitude confuse the geography. There is a persistent element of turmoil in the poetry, of inchoate ingredients that have not yet stabilized and are incapable of being frozen. Yet for all the difficulties, Orlovitz's voice is one of the most unique in contemporary American poetry. It is full of despair, satire, song, lyricism, obscenity, and love. His tendency to pun will try any reader's patience, and his quick shifts of metaphor and point of view can stymie the most attentive.

The reader of Orlovitz's poetry should not look for linearly developed ideas. Nor should he attempt to explain the sense in prose. Just as one cannot paraphrase a painting or a piece of music, Orlovitz's verse defies cognitive referential associations. According to Orlovitz, in an "informal remarks" section of *The Statement of Erika Keith* (1957), "I seek to make the reader capitulate to the world of my images." The following lines are from "Sonnet On Man" in *Concerning Man* (1947):

Terror at days gougeout whores man ice beneath
his sheets of flesh, pays her shriek, cower, shrivel,
she strumpet of obsess he courts at a dervish swivel,
what screaming succulence of ripe wind on hells heath,
how grind his cells in glaciers of devouring teeth,
what a shadowing skulk of her he does as though
his magnitudinous grandeur must be raped
to get him space to conceive what he has aped.

Orlovitz shares with Gertrude Stein the ability to depict advancing time in the constant succession of the present moment, a repetitive explosion of images. By juxtaposing contrary verbal patterns, he creates a verse of "constantly flowering surrealistic paradox." His intent is simple: to transmit through image the paradoxes of experienced phenomena. Understanding the poetry, then, does not depend on the rational-intellectual level, but on the feeling level. For Orlovitz, symbols in poetry do not simply connote reality; they are pieces of reality themselves, as in these lines from "Mug Manhattans Swinging Doors" in *Keep To Your Belly* (1952):

spaghetti fog
springs knives like eels
streetcorners slouch
in satin blouses

skyline rabbis
read river scrolls
by bridges torahs
throw in the toll

If such a group of words can evoke a corresponding image in the reader's mind, an experience has been created.

Orlovitz seeks to infuse his poetry with a sense of drama, insisting that poetry requires a constant play of tensions. "To exclude tensions," he says in *The Statement of Erika Keith*, "is to exclude art and to make for a product which will slide past the reader as an indifferent record of a value-system making negligible contact." To give an impression of lack of conflict is fatal to the poem and results in hackneyed metaphors. For Orlovitz the complex and the complicated are beautiful. From such ferment he creates exciting verse, as in these lines from "Index (#9)" in *The Diary of Dr. Eric Zeno* (1953):

of sticky luminescence had been wonder a
lemondrop halfconsumed by
the ghost of a childstongue hovered away on a sled like
a child

I had walked in a sifting sensitive stupor
blue butterflies unpinned flew masks
at the corners of my mouth spittle little stars
the night is a
nursery rhyme

Orlovitz is not concerned with the traditional resolution to dramatic presentation. He is just as likely to leave the reader suspended, awaiting a nonexistent climax, and his response to the frustrated or bewildered reader is: "Enjoy yourself: there is a certain marvel, I think we may admit, in suspension without the preconception of a rope." Because he feels no obligation to settle everything in neat comprehensible forms, he flouts the established rules of symmetry, especially in his sonnets, as these lines from "#65," in *The Art of the Sonnet* (1961), testify:

The great sea confessing to the wrack and remnancy,
crossed by no cavil, tossing up no holycup
for sprinted soul and ghostthrowing crucihook,
breaks broodbread with body, breaks, whole harrow
veiled
in moonteeth on the sunnolent shore.
What ruminant landman's strident rib can pour
gunnels of lung over the rachet of cries?
preach from polypous pulpits to the galegunned eyes?

The reader should not try to apply traditional criteria to this kind of verse. Rather, the experience of daily events should serve as guide. The metaphor of the poem is the experience. Orlovitz is in rebellion against the modern artistic trend to write *about* phenomena. His intent is to make the phenomenon itself one of symbols. He writes:

Analogically: That a given substance becomes differentiable from other substances, its constituents form relationships and behaviors of those relationships which render its events distinctive from the events of other substances. . . . To seek the substance of an image, I too will seek to utilize other substances to make the distinctive relationships and their behaviors of an *image-substance*.

Gil Orlovitz

The reader knows little about substances other than that they exist; he can experience them without truly understanding them. But complete understanding is not necessary in order to react strongly. It is sheer nonsense, Orlovitz maintains, for art to be logical. Great art is often puzzling and irritating.

Yet Orlovitz is not defending impenetrability. Symbols in the work of art could have their sources in the unconscious evolution of the artist's whole organism, and a good deal of time may have to elapse before it is possible to identify the tenor of the symbols of the evolutionary act, but all this just constitutes a difficulty in understanding a work. Orlovitz hopes that his position will be clarified when he remarks that "the perceiver of an art's substances must sense the event of a phenomenon; otherwise the art has no merit, and has failed."

Orlovitz wrote poems in many forms, but the majority were sonnets, lyrics, satires, and masques. His hundreds of sonnets are scattered throughout his work and make up a number of sequences. The tight control of the form is wrenched by Orlovitz's dynamic and often weird juxtaposing of image and thought. The sonnet's traditional limitations in form often become, in Orlovitz's idiom, a surprisingly explosive package, and one suspects that he dearly loved to outrage the reader's sensibilities by manipulating an art nearly as old as Western poetry.

The lyrics, in their quiet beauty, are unearthly lulls in a world of passion. Orlovitz could speak the language of love with the best poets, as in these lines from "If You Should Feel Troubled in the Night," in *Couldn't Say, Might Be Love* (1969):

If you should feel troubled in the night,
wake me, tell me, let me know.

If a cry so catch you by the rib,
that you had thought fed, and quieted, quite long ago,
wake me, tell me, let me know.

In his satires, Orlovitz takes on all the miseries of modern life. Here his tendency to pun is most acute and his dissatisfactions are most clearly expressed. Note these lines from "The Rooster":

the rooster crows in my belly
an old hangout for the billiard cues of the morning
and table-hopping hail hail the ganglias all here
after sunset like a mouthwash last yesterlight
and the white tails of the gorillas on television
and that liberal politician stumping for twilight
    supremacy
down by that old
      shill

    stream
As I buttonholed the Ancient Auctioneer
how goes America going
      going

As is usual with other Orlovitz poems, the reader of the satires is given, in David Ignatow's words, "an impression of absolute willful disorder." His satires exhibit certain traits of stream of consciousness and an immersion into nightmare, combining elements of the Beatles' "Lucy in the Sky with Diamonds" and Lautréamont's *Les Chants de Maldoror* (1868). "The Rooster" ends thus: "WHEN IT LAUGHS IT DISPLAYS URANIUM-FILLED / Tombstones / the bones / of contemporary saints / CROW / ROOSTER / CROW / going / going / Forest Lawn? / NO! / ELECTRONOLAUGH!"

Orlovitz's biographical masques begin with *The Diary of Dr. Eric Zeno, The Diary of Alexander Patience* (1958), and *The Papers of Professor Bold* (1959). In these, successively, "The errant ganglia of a Western Christian psychoanalyst, a self-confessed but unreliable stoic, and a somewhat rococo academician are brought to book." In "The Diary of Matthew Parson" (1960), an ordained American minister ruminates upon religious attitudes not confined to any one sect and exercises upon them "a wit at some expense to dogma, and altogether at the expense of himself." "M'sieu Mishiga" (1960) predicates a psychologically nonclassifiable lunacy on the part of its hero. "With this operating attribute," Orlovitz tells the reader, "the major principles of sanity, as our *Zeitgeist* has them, are put to the test and protest." Finally, "The Letters of Great Ape" (1960) employs the conceit that literacy on this lower evolutionary level is possible. A great ape of above-average intelligence, residing at some distance from his superior genus but provisionally accepted therein, expresses himself at length in correspondence with typical representatives of human society, whose replies the author sees fit to withhold.

Gil Orlovitz sets before the reader of contemporary poetry a paradoxical challenge. His original variations of tone, direction, and meaning demand an open mind and a willingness to set aside preconceived notions. Although some of his metaphors may be farfetched and his symbols unconnected (even seemingly random), they coalesce in the realm of feeling on the frontiers of what is possible, what is beckoning, in American poetry today. Orlovitz deals with but never accepts the tragedies of life. Some of his subjects may be unpleasant, but in the words of Alfred Kreymborg,

Gil Orlovitz "never evades the responsibility of opening his body and mind to the deepest wound."
—*William Mattathias Robins*

Plays:

The Case of a Neglected Calling Card, New York, Dramatic Workshop, 1952; published in *The Statement of Erika Keith*;
Noone, New York, Provincetown Playhouse, 1953;
Stefanie, Philadelphia, Central Players of the YMCA, 1953; New York, Amato Theatre, 1954;
Todt and Thor (reading), New York, Gallery East, 1955.

Screenplay:

Overexposed, by Orlovitz and James Gunn, Columbia Pictures, 1956.

Other:

"Some Autobiographical Words," *Literary Review*,

2 (Winter 1958-1959): 197-199;
The Award Avant-Garde Reader, edited by Orlovitz (New York: Award Books, 1965).

Bibliography:

Guy Daniels, "Notes Toward a Bibliography of Gil Orlovitz," *American Poetry Review*, 7 (November-December 1978): 31-32.

References:

Henry Birnbaum, "The Poetry of Protest," *Poetry*, 94 (September 1959): 408-413;
Hale Chatfield, "Literary Exile in Residence," *Kenyon Review*, 21 (1969): 545-553;
Robert Nye, "Paradox Made Manifest," *Scotsman*, 8 April 1967, p. 1;
Gerald Stern, "Miss Pink at Last: An Appreciation of Gil Orlovitz," *American Poetry Review*, 7 (November-December 1978): 27-31.

GUY OWEN
(24 February 1925-)

BOOKS: *Cape Fear Country and Other Poems* (Lake Como, Fla.: New Athenaeum Press, 1958);
Season of Fear (New York: Random House, 1960; London: Gollancz, 1962);
The Guilty and Other Poems (Lanham, Md.: Goosetree Press, 1964);
The Ballad of the Flim-Flam Man (New York: Macmillan, 1965);
The White Stallion and Other Poems (Winston-Salem, N.C.: J. F. Blair, 1969);
Journey for Joedel: A Novel (New York: Crown, 1970);
The Flim-Flam Man and the Apprentice Grifter (New York: Crown, 1972);
The Flim-Flam Man and Other Stories (Durham, N.C.: Moore Publishing, 1980).

Guy Owen was born in Clarkton, North Carolina. He holds a B.A. (1947), an M.A. (1949), and a Ph.D. (1955) from the University of North Carolina. Owen has taught at Davidson College, Elon College, Stetson University, and he is currently professor of English at North Carolina State University. He has also been writer-in-residence at Appalachian State University and the University of North Carolina at Greensboro. Owen has received a Bread Loaf Scholarship (1960), the Henry Bellamann Foundation Literary Award (1964), a Yaddo Fellowship (1968), the Roanoke-Chowan Poetry Cup in 1969 for *The White Stallion*, and the Sir Walter Raleigh Award in 1970 for his third novel, *Journey for Joedel*, which was also recommended for the Pulitzer Prize in 1971.

In his work as a novelist, poetry editor, and poet, Owen has remained consistently interested in the landscape and people of the South, particularly eastern North Carolina. His novels, *Season of Fear* (1960), *The Ballad of the Flim-Flam Man* (1965), *Journey for Joedel* (1970), and *The Flim-Flam Man and the Apprentice Grifter* (1972), are set in the downstate tobacco country where he grew up. These novels range in tone and mood from Gothic melodrama to folkloric comedy to understated sensitivity, but Owen's mythic Cape Fear country serves as the setting for them all. That regional literature, particularly about the rural South, is currently out of vogue does not seriously disturb or discourage Owen, as he indicates in an interview with John Carr: "I don't consider myself a

Guy Owen

"For James," manuscript

regionalist. I write about the South because I grew up in the South. I sent my nerve ends out, and they didn't encounter icebergs or igloos or ivory hunters. They encountered tobacco patches and cotton fields and tobacco barns. . . ." This southern rural landscape and the way it shapes character can still, despite its present liabilities, yield genuine art in the hands of a writer who knows his subjects as well as Owen does, for as T. J. Fleming says in his review of *Journey for Joedel*, Owen "takes us back to the hard, lovely land, to the language of work and reward that are still the fundamentals of our experience" (*New York Times Book Review*, 5 July 1970).

Owen's work as an editor of poetry has for more than twenty years been an important stimulus to southern literature. Owen began editing *Impetus* in 1958 at Stetson University, and in 1964, after he and the magazine moved to North Carolina State University, it became *Southern Poetry Review*, which he continued to edit until 1975. One of the roles that Owen intended *Impetus* and *Southern*

Poetry Review to perform was to provide an alternative outlet for young southern writers unable to break through the built-in prejudices of the New York publishing industry. This intention was realized in a way that proves such a venture is not doomed to mere regionalism, for under Owen's editorship the magazines published poems by such writers as A. R. Ammons, Fred Chappell, Donald Justice, David Madden, Doris Betts, and James Dickey. The consistently high quality of work by both well-known and lesser-known poets published in *Southern Poetry Review* led Louis Rubin, Jr., to call it "a leading organ for the promulgation of poetry in the South, and one of the very best poetry magazines in the United States." Owen has also edited or coedited several anthologies of poetry, among them *New Southern Poets* (1974), *Contemporary Poetry of North Carolina* (1977), and *Contemporary Southern Poetry* (1979); and he was coeditor of the magazine *North Carolina Folklore* from 1966 to 1972.

Owen's first collection of poems, *Cape Fear Country* (1958), is divided into two sections, "The Bitter Thread," containing poems of a generally academic tone, and "Cape Fear Country," containing poems that take aspects of the rural South as their subjects. The poems in the first section display too frequently a straining after rhyme, a somewhat artificial choice of subject matter, and a self-conscious literariness, as in these lines from "To a Pregnant Student":

> I could never make you quick. Your sullen feet
> Scraped in and out my door;
> A stone beneath the waters of my wit
> You slouched, bovine and bored.

In some poems, though, Owen indicates a distrust of intellect and literary form as interferences in perception and experience of the world. "Plato Obtrudes" deals in a direct way with the potential of literature not only to color but to obscure perception of the actual:

> Images gash the eyes; the pupils scar
> as from the touch of jewels.
> The dusts of metaphors accrue
> until all sight fails
> before this native pond, that naked tree.

In other poems Owen introduces the imagery of blood and bone to achieve a sense of violence and the elemental that provides a fruitful balance with the artificiality of form. This kind of imagery is used successfully in "It is Not the Sea," "This Pain I

Prize," "Child of Earth," and "Identity" to suggest the risk inherent in daily life, an attitude most forcefully expressed in these lines from "Identity":

Each day cuts like the quick knives thrown
    By side show men. They leer
And flick their blades close to the whining bone
    Leveling nose and ear.

The poems in the second section of *Cape Fear Country* are exclusively concerned with rural subjects, and in them the sense of risk in everyday life takes on a heightened authenticity. The ruralism in Owen's best poetry, like that of Robert Frost, whose influence is strongly felt here both in form and approach, is not simply the overly pretty pastoralism toward which this subgenre too frequently tends. Rather, Owen is very much aware of the elements of threat in the daily lives of semisubsistence farmers, and he is equally aware of the strength and creativity meeting such threats requires. In "On Castration Day" the experience of observing the castration of farm animals is overwhelming to a young boy as he runs away terrified from what the adults find humorous:

I lunged along the pasture lane,
My groin swelling with the pain,
Through bleeding briars that cut my hand
To sprawl, alone, and utterly unmanned.

Similarly, in "The Field of Bread" and "Hawk" the tenuousness of agrarian existence is emphasized by the passing shadows of birds of prey, competitors for the same food supply as the humans in the poems. But if this kind of life is harsh, it is also capable of beauty, as in "Arrowhead" when a farmer, while plowing, turns up the artifact that he calls a "stone-heart flower." He begins to imagine the man who made it:

Perhaps he spied and loved the stone—
    He blessed it with his art—
And sure in flight, it cleaved the bone,
    And graced the stricken heart.

Owen's second book of poetry, *The White Stallion and Other Poems* (1969), includes both new poems and slightly revised versions of several poems from *Cape Fear Country*. Again, as in the earlier volume, the best poems are those of the rural life that allow Owen to examine a culture with which he is deeply familiar but which is rapidly being transformed and eradicated by urbanization and industrialism. This change is felt in many of the poems as a genuine sense of loss for a dying culture; they are, in effect, elegies for the subsistence-farming

life. Some poems in this elegiac mood, particularly those that confine themselves to static descriptions of abandonment such as "Deserted Farm," "Old Barn," and "Burnt Farmhouse," sometimes tend toward sentimentality. In other poems, though, Owen captures dynamically the human creativity and inspiration that are lost with the death of the farming life. In several such poems he sees man's role as an agent through which the forces of nature speak. In "My Father's Curse," the delicacy of this creative role is balanced against the roughness such a life inevitably includes:

Yet though he raged in bitter brew
    Thick oaths that belled his throat,
God rammed His springing juices through
    And fleshed Himself in fruit.

Owen creates a similar balance in "Poem to a Mule, Dead Twenty Years" when the speaker first imagines the mule sold to a processing plant and now "in the guts of hounds / circling the sedge, threading the trees at night," but then, to temper the threat of that vision, he remembers the acts of creation they performed together:

Guy Owen

147

but I would have it known
how once we commanded dead fields
and they answered, gold or green.

Many of the poems in *The White Stallion*, like some of the best poems from *Cape Fear Country*, deal with the threat and risk of rural life that, as Owen suggests, reside as much on the psychological level as on the physical level. In "The Fallen Scarecrow," for example, an old farmer superstitiously seeks omens in the falling of his double, the scarecrow wearing his cast-off clothes. "The Encounter" examines a somewhat less illogical kind of threat, that of walking alone in the woods and feeling an unidentifiable, possibly dangerous, presence:

Oh, I knew the things it was not
And tolled them one by one. But what
It *was* would give no further sign—
Or if it did, I couldn't divine
The hint, not with thrush at ear.

The sense of danger in the rural life is best expressed in "Pastoral," a poem set in a countryside where not lambs but "only the wind bleats at the door, / breathing windfalls," a land of owls, nettles, sumac, and crumbling barns where "for nightingale, one crow, my familiar, / humps on the burnt-over knoll." Amidst this decaying landscape the speaker is able to say, "It is against these I risk myself, / and go on risking. . . ." Here the threat of the dying rural life becomes as abstract as fear of the dark; to live in the country is to be in jeopardy.

Although Owen's best poetry concerns the landscapes and people of his native region, he is not, of course, limited to exclusively southern subjects. *The White Stallion* also includes several poems about university teaching, a series of "Imaginary Epitaphs," and a comic poem titled "Jonathan Edwards," among many others. Two of the best of the nonsouthern poems are "The Hanged Pazzi Conspirator," based on a da Vinci sketch, and "The Beggars," based on Brueghel. Although Owen does not attempt in "The Beggars" the kind of rhythmic and emotional analogue to the painting that William Carlos Williams so brilliantly achieves in his *Pictures from Brueghel* (1962), he does capture the viewer's response to this disorienting vision of suffering:

Our eyes, unless they blur with pitying,
Must vault this pain. They do, they run
These red brick walls to fields, and leap to seize
The green and tender prophecies of Spring.

Owen has published only a few poems in

anthologies since *The White Stallion*, and he has indicated that lack of stylistic growth in his poetry as opposed to his fiction has been a determining factor: "I don't know if this isn't one of the reasons I'm not writing very much poetry right now: I look at it and I don't find the kind of growth I want there. And I think if you can't grow, it's best to stop." But if Owen's production of poetry has drastically decreased, he has certainly not been idle. In the years since the appearance of *The White Stallion*, he has edited three poetry anthologies and a collection of criticism, and he has published two novels and a collection of short stories. He also has a novel forthcoming. This kind of energy has made Owen a vital force in the literature not only of his native North Carolina but of the South. —*Charles Frazier*

Other:

Southern Poetry Today, edited by Owen and William E. Taylor (Deland, Fla.: Impetus Press, 1962);

Essays in Modern American Literature, edited by Owen, Richard E. Langford, and Taylor (Deland, Fla.: Stetson University Press, 1963);

Southern Poetry Review: A Decade of Poems, edited by Owen (Raleigh, N.C.: Southern Poetry Review Press, 1969);

North Carolina Poetry, edited by Owen (Raleigh, N.C.: Southern Poetry Review Press, 1970);

Modern American Poetry: Essays in Criticism, edited by Owen (Deland, Fla.: Everett/Edwards, 1972);

New Southern Poets: Selected Poems from Southern Poetry Review, edited by Owen and Mary C. Williams (Chapel Hill: University of North Carolina Press, 1974);

Contemporary Poetry of North Carolina, edited by Owen and Williams (Winston-Salem, N.C.: J. F. Blair, 1977);

Contemporary Southern Poetry, edited by Owen and Williams (Baton Rouge: Louisiana State University Press, 1979).

References:

John Carr, ed., *Kiteflying and Other Emotional Acts* (Baton Rouge: Louisiana State University Press, 1972), pp. 236-262;

Victor Dalmas, "Guy Owen and the World of Cape Fear Country," *St. Andrews Review* (Spring-Summer 1975): 43-50;

Daphne Euliss, "Folk Motifs in Guy Owen's *Journey for Joedel*," *North Carolina Folklore*

Journal, 24 (November 1976): 111-114;

R. T. Rundus, "American Pastoral: The Novels of Guy Owen," *Pembroke Magazine,* no. 3 (1972): 15-20;

Richard Vela, "This Native Pond, That Naked Tree: The Realities of Guy Owen," *South and West,* 11 (Winter 1973): 14-20;

R. B. White, "The Image of Sexual Repression in *Season of Fear,*" *North Carolina Folklore Journal,* 19 (March 1971): 80-84.

ROBERT PACK

(19 May 1929-)

BOOKS: *The Irony of Joy,* in *Poets of Today II,* ed. John Hall Wheelock (New York: Scribners, 1955);

Wallace Stevens: An Approach to His Poetry and Thought (New Brunswick: Rutgers University Press, 1958);

A Stranger's Privilege (Hessle, Yorkshire, U.K.: Asphodel Books, 1959; New York: Macmillan, 1959);

The Forgotten Secret (New York: Macmillan, 1959);

Then What Did You Do? (New York: Macmillan, 1961);

Guarded by Women (New York: Random House, 1963);

Selected Poems (London: Chatto & Windus, 1964);

How to Catch a Crocodile (New York: Knopf, 1964);

Home from the Cemetery (New Brunswick: Rutgers University Press, 1969);

Nothing But Light (New Brunswick: Rutgers University Press, 1972);

Keeping Watch (New Brunswick: Rutgers University Press, 1976);

Waking to My Name: New and Selected Poems (Baltimore: Johns Hopkins Press, forthcoming 1980).

Robert Pack was born in New York City. He earned a B.A. from Dartmouth College in 1951 and an M.A. from Columbia University in 1953. Pack has participated in the Poetry Workshop of the New School for Social Research and the Bread Loaf Writers' Conference. He has also been editor of *Discovery* magazine. He has received a Fulbright fellowship (1956), a National Institute of Arts and Letters Grant (1957), a Borestone Mountain Poetry Awards first prize (1964), and a National Endowment for the Arts Grant (1968). Married to Patricia

Powell, Pack has taught at Barnard College and is currently professor of English at Middlebury College in Vermont.

Pack's fidelity to traditional poetic conventions marks his as a distinct voice among contemporary American poets. For a quarter of a century, while others have turned to experimentation and escape, Pack has continued to write a quiet, orderly, almost peaceable poetry. His measured phrases; his subtle, controlled repetition; his preference for stanzaic uniformity—all more characteristic of another age—have become the staples of his verse. Yet the reader who fails to see beyond this formality will miss the pleasure of Robert Pack, for Pack is essentially a personal poet who, as Harold Bloom has suggested, "has taken as his own the hard enterprise of hallowing the commonplace."

Pack embraces a wide range of subjects, but his best work treats the very private world of his own family. Memories of his father's death, the awesome rituals of child rearing—even speculations on his own physical demise—are topics that inspire him. In many poems—"Prayer to My Father While Putting My Son to Bed," for example—the poet transcends the fixed limits of physical death to join several generations in a single, poignant, poetic statement. In others, the mere routine of domesticity becomes the object of Pack's sense of humor and his fanciful imagination. "Breakfast Cherries" is a humorous account of the beginning of a typical day, and Pack imagines himself "the breakfast poet," living in a world of ripe fruit in porcelain bowls, singing birds, and grumbling children. Always, however, his laughter is guarded, and even the most comic poems may have ominous conclusions: "The children are quarreling, / cherry-pits in their kisses, / orioles in their ears. Join me, be with me, hold on, / we have everything to lose."

Although Pack's subject matter varies widely, his poems rarely fail to assert, even dignify, the human element. In poem after poem, he defines and redefines his own place within the scheme of creation, establishing often a pact of mutual protection and admiration between himself and nature. In "Preparing for Winter," the poet recognizes his role as a benevolent, life-sustaining force within his personal domain: he plants winter grass, he splits and stores wood for his fire, he wraps his fruit trees to prevent the rabbits from gnawing their trunks. In another, earlier poem ("Parable"), the poet discovers that his pact with nature is indeed mutually beneficial. Conscious of his own mortality, he warns the animals of their physical frailties only to find himself disregarded. In the end, however, it is

Robert Pack

Robert Pack

the poet who receives a kind of consolation, perhaps because the animals are by nature aware of what he tries to tell them:

> Within the darkness of my indecision,
> Within the introspection of my dying,
> I stopped still as I could and did not move,
> And the animals came forth and licked my hands.

In poems inspired by an apparent violation of the pact—that is, when the poet realizes his inability to help another creature—the reader feels, with Pack, a profound personal sympathy. In "At the Concert," a mentally deficient young woman attending a musical performance with her mother evokes the poet's pity by waving a childish good-bye to the orchestra at the concert's conclusion. "The Children," one of Pack's few politically inspired poems, is an emotionally charged treatise against the senselessness of warfare and again finds the poet disturbed and shaken by his own helplessness.

The seriousness that characterizes much of Pack's work does not find its way into all of his poems. Indeed, Pack possesses a delightful comic sense and is capable of playful verbal architectonics. "The Frog Prince: A Speculation on Grimm's Fairy Tales" appears to have no other motive than to imagine the comic conclusion to a rather bizarre fable:

> And in the morning when the mother
> Came and saw them there in bed,
> Heard how a frog became a prince;
> What was it that her mother said?

And in "Ballad for Baby Ruth (or *How to Burst Joy's Grape*)," Pack mingles several physical appetites into a truly funny poem of verbal irony:

> And here is a honey-do gumdrop kiss
> Forever yours until our teeth decay,
> And here is my vanilla bean,
> And here is my milky way!

Both delight and despair are represented in the poems that comprise Pack's first collection, *The Irony of Joy* (1955). Published in the second volume of the Scribners *Poets of Today* series, with Norma Farber's *The Hatch* and Louis Simpson's *Good News of Death and Other Poems*, *The Irony of Joy* is an inconsistent but admirable first work. Several poems in the volume lack the depth of insight and maturity that characterize the majority. "A Song of Dark," "The Wood is Round," and "Cyclic" are short, lyrical pieces that do not compare favorably with his stronger poems. "On the Death of Dylan Thomas" is a moderately successful but disappointing appreciation of the Welsh poet. On the whole, however, *The Irony of Joy* is impressive. "To Gunner Henrick Nilson," engendered by a *New York Times* article recounting the harpooning of a fifty-six ton white whale, is a memorable poem that displays Pack's capacity for haunting lines: "Moby Dick is dead," the poem begins, immediately establishing a strikingly nightmarish tone. And the ending, no less direct, reverberates: "And the white mirror, broken, reassembles / on the ocean floor: drowned Ahab trembles." "On the Seventh Anniversary of the Death of My Father," while not the best of Pack's imagined dialogues with his deceased parent, marks the beginning of the poet's treatment of a subject that throughout his career has yielded some exceptional poems.

This first book is important because its poems exemplify an ethic that has been the shaping force behind much of Pack's work, both early and late. In an introduction to *The Irony of Joy*, John Hall Wheelock cites a section of Pack's essay by the same title, which provides considerable insight into the poet's concerns:

> Poetry is important only in that it promotes
> the conviction that despair, suffering and

150

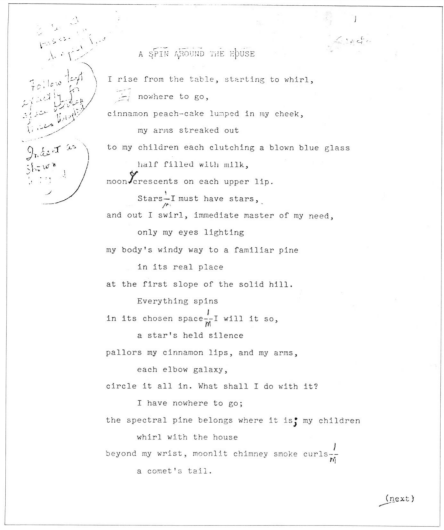

A SPIN AROUND THE HOUSE

I rise from the table, starting to whirl,
    nowhere to go,
cinnamon peach-cake lumped in my cheek,
    my arms streaked out
to my children each clutching a blown blue glass
    half filled with milk,
moon crescents on each upper lip.
    Stars—I must have stars,
and out I swirl, immediate master of my need,
    only my eyes lighting
my body's windy way to a familiar pine
    in its real place
at the first slope of the solid hill.
    Everything spins
in its chosen space—I will it so,
    a star's held silence
pallors my cinnamon lips, and my arms,
    each elbow galaxy,
circle it all in. What shall I do with it?
    I have nowhere to go;
the spectral pine belongs where it is; my children
    whirl with the house
beyond my wrist, moonlit chimney smoke curls—
    a comet's tail.

(next)

"A Spin Around the House," corrected typescript

death are necessary—though to be combated—and that mortal life is rich. For life, like poetry, is irony: a paradoxical attempt to transcend the very limitations without which human existence is impossible. . . . That sorrow and happiness are one, that death and life are one, is the meaning of moral possibility; it is the necessary irony of our poetry, and the necessary irony of our joy.

The interdependence of disparate emotions is indeed evident in this first collection. The lighter poems treat the theme almost comically: the companion poems, "A Cage in Search of a Bird" and "A Bird in Search of a Cage," are examples. The cage, speaking in the first poem, knows that, while his prisoner "can't get out," others most assuredly "can't get in." The captured bird in the second poem also finds a certain comfort in its imprisonment: "And if a friend should stop to talk, / Reminding me

of what is past, / And ask the meaning of my song, / I'd say that only cages last."

This same sense of irony is also employed in the more serious, more ambitious poems. "To the Family of a Friend upon His Death" says in verse what Pack has written in his prose essay. The poem begins straightforwardly—"No consolation for despair will do"—and continues toward a bitter but moving conclusion:

> You want his life. Somewhere some still eat
> Their bread in happiness, abundant breath;
> And you must know your early joy depended
> Necessarily upon his death.

Apart from demonstrating a continued interest in form, the two subsequent collections, *A Stranger's Privilege* (1959) and *Guarded by Women* (1963), indicate clearly Pack's use of personal experience, both real and imagined, in his poetry. Some of the

151

poems are bound contextually to situations outside the reader's realm of experience, but they are by no means esoteric. Pack draws from his experiences emotions common to all. "The Friend," from *A Stranger's Privilege*, is addressed to an individual whose participation in war has altered his thinking. But the poem is not about war; it is about a state of emotional separation that occurs when friends discover a disparity of experiences and interests. At the conclusion of the poem, even amid familiar surroundings, the friend becomes a stranger:

> The cat is huddled on the window-sill
> While winds are blowing in the apple tree;
> The milk is splashed and leaping from the pail.
> Your smile disturbs with its felicity.
> Who are you anyway, what do you want with me?

Similarly, "Grieving on a Grand Scale," from *Guarded by Women*, recounts a waking nightmare of a loved one's death, and again Pack manages to transcend the strictly personal. Realizing the real possibility of loss, the poet imagines more, and the universality of grief, here expressed in particulars, becomes the thematic focus of the poem.

Pack's imagined experiences are not limited to a world of possibility. Especially in these earlier collections, the fable, the parable, and what one writer has termed the "moral nursery rhyme" account for a surprising, and engaging, portion of the poems. "The Monster Who Loved the Hero" and "The Shooting" present comically grotesque situations wherein the narrator speaks with a matter-of-fact, childlike innocence that is disturbing in its straightforwardness. Equally gripping are the biblically inspired poems such as "The Creation" and "A Letter from Hell." The first is an imagined account of the experiences of Eden's first inhabitant, the second a fictionalized message from a darker world. The latter poem concludes with a haunting line that reminds the reader of Pack's earlier assumption that pain and pleasure are inseparable: "Heaven will not begin when hell will end."

When *Home from the Cemetery* appeared in 1969, several reviewers commented on the work's "new directions." If there exists a turning point in Pack's verse, it begins with this collection. But the directions are not really new; they are merely more noticeable, more clearly defined. The comic-satiric sense that informed much of Pack's earlier work realizes its full potential in such poems as "The Last Will and Testament of Art Evergreen," which Anne Sexton called "one of the great American poems," and "Burning the Laboratory," a truly delightful poem. Likewise, Pack's ironic juxtaposition of life

and death asserts itself with renewed emotional force in the book's final section, where he places the title poem, "Home from the Cemetery," alongside the touching "Welcoming Poem for the Birth of My Son."

"The Last Will and Testament of Art Evergreen" is a comic tour de force that manages to rattle the foundations of art itself. Throughout the poem's thirty stanzas, Art Evergreen prepares his will, bequeathing portions of himself—his eyes, his ears, his record collection ("A—M remaindered by divorce")—to a series of former wives and other relations, one of them a son who spends his time learning Greek nouns in a "wine-dark attic." While the duly unappreciative family members appear to go about their artless business, the poem's central figure digresses his way through his estate ("There are flowers in my room. Did you think I was nowhere writing this?") as the narrator chides him ("Damn you, Art, get on with your will"). That Pack is able to sustain this pleasantly absurd pose during the course of a long work is a remarkable feat. More important is the poem's implicit recognition that art is at times a contrivance and a temporary means of surviving in a world that, like Art Evergreen himself, is systematically coming apart.

Except in the truth that a certain newness comes in with each exploration of an already familiar ground, Pack's most recent collections, *Nothing But Light* (1972) and *Keeping Watch* (1976), are not innovative. They are, in essence, rededications to a life, to a world, to a belief established long before. In short, *Nothing But Light* and *Keeping Watch* reemphasize everything that is a part of Pack's personal mythology. "Were It Not," the opening poem of *Nothing But Light*, is in fact an invitation to all the cherished familiarities of the poet's world: "Nothing can spoil this now / you are all / Every one of you / all all are invited / This warm morning / to my house."

This "house," according to Mona Van Duyn, is a "large, peaceable, fenced domain where birds and beasts may still, though tentatively, come near; where the familial, the domestic, still succeed, though effortfully, in gentling the only enemy, Time." In these latest collections—these most recent additions to the house—there are trees to be cared for ("Pruning Fruit Trees"), animals to be watched after ('Preparing for Winter"), human life to be protected ("My Daughter"). There is laughter in the morning ("A Spin Around the House") and fear at night ("The Screech Owl"). And in the poems written about his parents and his children, there is that inevitable linking of family past and family present.

If there is a move toward anything new in these collections, it is perhaps a tendency to lessen the distance between the poet and the reader, to abolish, as it were, any narrative facade and allow the poet's voice to come through with clarity and directness. "Maxims in Limbo" is a gathering of one hundred and one brief, unobscure revelations. "I write these crazy poems / in order to live / a saner life," reads one; "The happy poet proclaims / the circle, wishing only / for what he has," says another.

What Pack has, and has had through twenty-five years of writing, is a small, well-defined world to which he turns for inspiration, for protection, for peace. It is a circular world, like that depicted in "The Ring," the closing poem of *Keeping Watch*, where a slight turn of a wedding ring turns back time, where reflections from the gold band are, too, reflections of other lives and other loves. We look forward, in anticipation, to another twist of the ring.
—*Stephen A. Parris*

Other:

The New Poets of England and America, edited by Pack, Donald Hall, and Louis Simpson (Cleveland: Meridian, 1957);

The Mozart Librettos, edited and translated by Pack and Marjorie Lelach (Cleveland: World, 1961);

New Poets of England and America: Second Selection, American poets section edited by Pack (Cleveland: Meridian, 1962);

Poems of Doubt and Belief: An Anthology of Modern Religious Poetry, edited by Pack and Tom Driver (New York: Macmillan, 1964);

Literature for Composition on the Theme of Innocence and Experience, edited by Pack and Marcus Klein (Boston: Little, Brown, 1966);

Short Stories: Classic, Modern, Contemporary, edited by Pack and Klein (Boston: Little, Brown, 1967).

RON PADGETT
(17 June 1942-)

SELECTED BOOKS: *Some Things*, by Padgett, Ted Berrigan, and Joe Brainard (New York: "C" Press, 1964);

In Advance of the Broken Arm (New York: "C" Press, 1964);

Sky (London: Goliard, 1966);

Bean Spasms, by Padgett and Berrigan (New York: Kulchur Press, 1967);

Bun, by Padgett and Tom Clark (New York: Angel Hair Books, 1968);

Great Balls of Fire (New York: Holt, Rinehart & Winston, 1969);

The Adventures of Mr. & Mrs. Jim and Ron, by Padgett and Jim Dine (New York: Grossman, 1970; London: Cape, 1970);

Sufferin' Succotash, by Padgett and Brainard, with *Kiss My Ass*, by Michael Brownstein (New York: Adventures in Poetry, 1971);

Back in Boston Again, by Padgett, Clark, and Berrigan (New York: Telegraph Books, 1972);

Antlers in the Treetops, by Padgett and Tom Veitch (Toronto: Coach House, 1973);

Oo La La, by Padgett and Dine (New York: Petersburg Press, 1973);

The World of Leon, by Padgett and others (Bolinas, Cal.: Big Sky, 1974);

Crazy Compositions (Bolinas, Cal.: Big Sky, 1974);

Toujours l'amour (New York: Sun Press, 1976);

Arrive by Pullman (Paris: Générations, 1978);

Tulsa Kid (New York: Z Press, 1979);

Triangles in the Afternoon (New York: Sun Press, 1980).

Ron Padgett was born in Tulsa, Oklahoma. He received his A.B. from Columbia University in 1964 and was given the Boar's Head Poetry Prize and the George E. Woodberry Award in 1964. He studied in Paris as a Fulbright fellow in 1965-1966. From 1968 to 1970 he helped edit the *Paris Review*. Other awards Padgett has received are the Gotham Book Mart Avant-Garde Poetry Prize in 1964, Poets Foundation grants in 1964 and 1969, and grants from the New York City Academy of Arts and Letters in 1966 and 1971. Besides participating in numerous readings, Padgett is actively involved with The Poetry Project at a church in Manhattan's East Village, St. Mark's In-the-Bowery, well known for its poetry readings and for providing a forum for established and aspiring poets. Still acting as its editor, Padgett started The Poetry Project *Newsletter* in January 1973.

Since 1969 he has been associated with the Teachers and Writers Collaborative, a group of artists who work in public-school classrooms to introduce art and writing to children. He coedited their publication, *Whole Word Catalogue 2*, in 1976. In December 1973 he was a cofounder of Full Court Press, established as an alternative to the large or commercial press. Full Court has published works by Allen Ginsberg and Frank O'Hara, among others.

Some early magazine appearances of Padgett's poetry in 1960 and 1961 were published under the

Ron Padgett

pseudonym Harlan Dangerfield. Moreover, Padgett and Tom Veitch once used each other's names on various pieces out of mischief. Besides translating, editing, teaching, and lecturing, Padgett continues to write poetry. *Tulsa Kid* appeared in the fall of 1979, and another volume, *Triangles in the*

Pat Padgett

Afternoon, has just been published. At present he is editing "The Selected Letters of Frank O'Hara," which will be published in 1981. He resides with his wife and son in New York City, retreating to the mountains of Vermont during the summer.

Padgett is usually placed among the poets known as the New York School. Like most writers, he does not see himself in any "school," but by living in New York City and having been a student of Kenneth Koch at Columbia University, he has inherited the attitudes of Koch, John Ashbery, and Frank O'Hara, who revolted against the academic poetry of the 1940s and 1950s. In the preface to *An Anthology of New York Poets* (1970), Padgett and David Shapiro defend the individuality of each of the poets whose work is included: "Perhaps we do protest too much, but this is to prepare ourselves for the gruesome possibility of the 'New York School of

Poets' label, one which has been spewed forth from time to time by some reviewers, critics and writers either sustained by provincial jealousy or the bent to translate everything into a manageable textbookese."

Padgett shuns classification, although his poems reflect Dadaism and Surrealism in which the alogical world of the imagination becomes a suitable subject for poetry. The poems defy explanation and specification, appearing incoherent on the surface, but once the surface is penetrated, the private world of the poet emerges. Ron Padgett brilliantly transforms mundane experience into the subject of poetry, through subtle humor, wordplay, and a childlike fascination with the world.

Padgett has often collaborated with other writers and artists. The technique follows in a tradition initiated by the French Surrealists. Where the Surrealists seemed to need a collection of artists, poets, and musicians to convey their private visions to a public unable to decipher their message, Padgett's efforts are spoofs of his forerunners. Padgett calls *Some Things* (1964), created with poet Ted Berrigan and artist Joe Brainard, "a fugitive work." It contains fifteen unbound photocopied leaves of ink drawings captioned with suitable phrases, so indecipherable that it seems to be parodying works usually considered unacceptable by established publishers. *Bean Spasms* (1967), with the same collaborators, is less zany than *Some Things*. Yet Michael Benedikt notes, "One pictures its authors getting together for pleasant evenings and throwing off these pieces as a sort of by-product." In two hundred pages the collaborators included poems, fiction, letters, interviews, photographs, drawings, and whatever else came to mind, with one artist's idea provoking another artist's reaction to it. In *Bun* (1968), Tom Clark and Padgett create a stream-of-consciousness poem. The unity of the piece is not found in a message or a recurrent motif, but in the fact that the poets react and respond to each other's ideas. The reader can envision the connections between the poets and their thoughts, suggested by the gaps of space on the printed page. The poem comes alive after the initial invitation from one poet to the other: "Hello. May I be alive in your dream of unconsciousness?"

Padgett's collaborations with artists have been whimsical games, as in *Sufferin' Succotash* (1971), done with Joe Brainard. Brainard's comic-strip frames and Padgett's play on the word *sensation* create a humorous adventure. With Jim Dine, Padgett is most successful in *Oo La La* (1973) and *The Adventures of Mr. & Mrs. Jim and Ron* (1970), in which themes in pictorial images are echoed in parallel poetic images. In *The Adventures of Mr. & Mrs. Jim and Ron* the reader observes the marriage of two artistic minds, rambling with them through their world of images.

In the collaboration with Tom Clark and Ted Berrigan, *Back in Boston Again* (1972), the poets contribute their own account of a trip to Boston, focusing on the seemingly insignificant moments of the journey. Humor informs these subtle, simple recollections as the bizarre and ordinary are made significant simply because both have been recorded in a collection of prose poems. An account such as Padgett's anecdote about his experience with the waitress in Woolworth's, where he orders a chocolate frappe, eventually discloses the author's true concern—why the word can be pronounced "frap" or "fra-pay." The reader enters each narrative at the moment the poet digresses into significant minor details that made the trip memorable. Three characteristics of Padgett's unique style are clear in this collaboration: his interest in language, his mask of naive bafflement, and his digression from the general to the specific.

These collaborative experiments show that Ron Padgett has an ability to play games with his free-flowing imagination, allowing him to grab an image and take off with it. In his poems written without collaborators, his poetic vision is more apparent. For him, as with the Surrealists, the imagination is intriguing, almost beguiling, with its storehouse of ideas. From dreams come a plethora of images, and no matter how incoherent they may appear (since they are creations of the imagination), they make excellent subjects for the artist. Padgett seeks in the mundane something that will excite the imagination: banal, trite, everyday words and phrases of language can be exciting. He looks at the world with awe, appearing to observe life for the first time with uncalculating eyes. Language for him is an intricate system. It can entangle and confuse; it can be humorous; its manipulation can be a game; it can be simple, ordinary, common, and yet poetic. His style emerges as he breaks through the boundaries of the real world. Many of his poems begin in chaos and end in order, for he takes a panoramic sweep of the universe, the world, the city, or an idea, and through a complex network of language, focuses on a detail. He sets his mind at ease while he orders his world, allowing the reader to sigh with relief that there is a way out of the convoluted maze of images.

In Advance of the Broken Arm (1964) is a collection of Surreal-Dada poems, showing Padgett in the early stages of exploring his imagination and playing with puns. Imagery overflows the pages, along with word games—"Later you beat me to a pulp magazine." The entire collection connects disparate images from a world where nothing exists the way it should. The prose poem *Sky* (1966) exemplifies how simple language can become poetic. The poem says little—"The sky is nothing." Its nothingness suddenly becomes overwhelming to the poet who observes nothing in it. Eventually, through simple statements consisting of very simple words, the reader is brought down to earth, to observe with the narrator the immense nothingness. *Sky* is Padgett's precise statement of his version of existentialism.

Great Balls of Fire (1969) shows Padgett as an ingenious manipulator of language. From the metaphorical title, to the allusions to *round, balls, cycles,* to the poem title "Around Paris," and even to the fact that the first poem of the collection, "Detach, Invading," is also the last, the volume is clever with the convolutions. Padgett's play with language in "Some Bombs" initially appears incoherent but when it is read aloud, one realizes it approximates by means of English words the sound of mispronounced French words. The auditory distortion in this poem emphasizes the difference between spoken and written language. Where there is ambiguity in the sound of the spoken word, there is also discrepancy in the meaning of words in a sentence. The exhaustive listing in the poem "The Complete Works" consists of five pages of one-line alliterative puns and sentences with incomplete ideas.

Padgett's ability to fragment reality begins to emerge in two poems of this collection. "Poem for Joan Inglis on Her Birthday" focuses on an interior scene, capturing a moment of life. In the case of this poem, title and poem appear unrelated, because Joan Inglis is never described. What is described, instead, is a man having just experienced "the happiest scene of his life," poised before a mirror in a bedroom. The reflection of objects in the room is staged against the "hurricane violence" of a wind rising outside. Glancing in the mirror, the man notices the stasis inside juxtaposed to the chaos outside. A moment in the man's life, or the small bedroom within vast nature, or Joan Inglis's birthday, are insignificant details, yet they are significant calms in a world of flux. "Strawberries in Mexico" begins in the hustle of New York City, digresses through streets and buildings in the poet's mind, and ends with reorientation and relief for the reader as the poet examines the books he just purchased: "One a book with a drawing / By Apollinaire called 'Les fraises au Mexique' /

Disgruntled Man

~~Because I realize~~
that people ~~are making fools of themselves,~~
~~does that make me any better?~~

~~I'll leave out the transi~~tion.

I brush ~~my~~ *th* hair located on the right side of my head,
I brush it beautifully,
thinking of you. Then
I notice that the hair on the left side
is standing slightly higher than the right,
and ~~so that~~ my head appears to be lopsided.
I don't want it to look that way.
So I begin to brush down the left side,
grimly, with a sense of purpose
devoid of pleasure
that drips down the well wall
toward some deep, dark and cool pool
only in which peace is reflected.

~~And~~ soon my head is in balance,
But it has become a head brushed for bad reasons,
and I do not like the face I see.
A man disgruntled
with the way he brushed his hair.

21 Sept 1975
Lancaster, S.C.

"Disgruntled Man," revised typescript

'Strawberries in Mexico.' " The moment becomes significant in the midst of the chaotic activity of life.

"16 November 1964" is one of the best poems in this early collection. The poem details a day in the life of a poet as he takes a walk to observe, experience, and record "the sudden illumination of the trivial." As the poet later reflects on the events of the day, he concludes: "There must be something in a soda bottle / That we can understand, though I don't know what. Just as there must be / Something of value" to everything he has recorded.

Reception of *Great Balls of Fire* was mixed. David Lehman felt that "Padgett displays a genuine and admirable sensibility," but that in "Some Bombs" he tends to verge on being "too cute, too gimmicky, too instantly avant garde." Louis Martz found wit in the Italian Odes, which are mock translations. Reed Whittemore classified the poetry with a marvelous metaphor: "It is a poetry of the Supermarket, with the poet throwing anything and everything into his basket, rolling it forth and saying, as if we had an obligation to care, 'look what I found!' "

Crazy Compositions (1974) appears on the surface to be exactly what the title implies. But a closer examination of the two poems in the volume reveals a poet trying to create order and to communicate. "Big Bluejay Composition" represents the poet, bombarded with images, in the act of composing, much as a photographer might take pictures of various subjects to create a composition. What emerges is a photographic montage where fragments of objects or brief glimpses of action are captured. In the poem, the poet's mind swarms with a multitude of impressions, symbolized by a reappearing blue jay, as he feels inspired to write "Compositions in harmony." There are, however, too many interferences with any possible harmonious impression, especially with the soaring flight of the blue jay. With a "Click— / the bluejay fluttered on its shoulder" and the anticipated montage vanishes. In "Crazy Otto" the poet is concerned with bringing the idea down to the plane of earthly language so that words mean what they say. Words are the means of communication, but with so many languages "you can't get through to a foreigner / by simply speaking your own language." You must mean what you say, not be a Gutzon Borglum who:

> sits saying over and over
> I—Love—You
> only he says it in a tone of voice which implies
> that it is
> not he who loves you
>   and, well
> Blue turns to gray.

His words are meaningless because he speaks untruths. The poet suggests that the words will become meaningful when "truth catches up with them."

Padgett reiterates the general problem of the artist, but embellishes *Crazy Compositions* with his own style, which he perfects in *Toujours l'amour* (1976). The childlike view of the world is a recurrent theme, but now the poet is less bewildered. His free-flowing images and associations are less fragmented and chaotic than in previous volumes as they move from a broad spectrum to the narrow. The poems begin with significant statements, sweeping the reader into the poet's world in anticipation of some great observation, only to end insignificantly. The wisdom of the poems is in the paradoxes of their conclusions—because no definite meaning is specified, the poems encourage more meaning. "Sides" begins in just this way, seeming to be a poem about observing women, but it moves into a discussion of how topics for poems pulsate in the poet's head. Remembrance of the past is the theme of

"Wilson '57," where the poet, in remembering classmates from junior high school, catalogues minute details about his friends. In "Radio" the subtlety of Padgett's wit surfaces as, baffled by the advanced technology and versatility of radios, he expresses the thrill of hearing news and entertainment from stations all over the world. The poem moves into a list of radio messages, which are no better than the sensational yellow journalism of the local newspapers. "June 17, 1942," by engulfing the reader in the speaker's obsession with self-pity, elicits humor rather than sympathy:

> I'm off my theme
>   lost the original impulse
>   which was about pity
>   wanting everyone to pity me
>   because I'm a miserable dumbbell

"Tell us, Josephine" strays from a description of a man and a woman in a nightclub to the poet's daydream of flying a plane, emphasizing details and captured moments. The poet describes the man, wearing a "blue and white tie" and a "gray suit," in a frozen tableau with the woman, dressed in "black silk / That sheathes her body." He goes on to describe the landscape as he sees it from a plane:

> pleasure at being alone
>   up so high all silver and blue
> Over pink and gray cloud patches that blur to
>   orange wisps over there
> And down to a rather artificial-looking purple
>   beyond that.

These poems exemplify Padgett's technique of intensifying trivial details. Furthermore, the poems of *Toujours l'amour* restate his concern about language. Where "Crazy Otto," republished in this collection, recognizes that, because of the mutability of words, meanings can never keep up with them, "Louisiana Perch" makes an alternate suggestion. Comparing the connotations of words to an attractive waitress, the poet finds their beauty superficial and ephemeral. He concludes, "great words are those without meaning"—articles, prepositions, conjunctions.

> The rest are fragile, transitory
> like the waitress, a
> beautiful slender young girl!

The poem abandons its meaning, becoming something other than its title states. "Louisiana Perch" is representative of Padgett's poetic theories—nothing can be signified, because once it is, it loses its significance, and its meaning changes. Yet, in the

Ron Padgett

most insignificant is the significant, in the most meaningless, meaning. Ron Padgett never ceases from exploring the mystery of the commonplace while giving pleasure as he illuminates the trivial.

—*Caroline G. Bokinsky*

Other:

Tom Veitch, *Literary Days*, edited by Padgett and Ted Berrigan (New York: "C" Press, 1964);

Guillaume Apollinaire, *The Poet Assassinated*, translated by Padgett (New York: Holt, Rinehart & Winston, 1968);

An Anthology of New York Poets, edited by Padgett and David Shapiro (New York: Random House, 1970);

Pierre Cabanne, *Dialogues with Marcel Duchamp*, translated by Padgett (New York: Viking, 1971);

Blaise Cendrars, *Kodak*, translated by Padgett (New York: Adventures in Poetry, 1976);

Valéry Larbaud, *The Poems of A. O. Barnabooth*, translated by Padgett and Bill Zavatsky (Tokyo: Mushinsha, 1976);

The Whole Word Catalogue 2, edited by Padgett and Zavatsky (New York: Teachers & Writers Collaborative / McGraw-Hill, 1976).

References:

Michael Benedikt, Review of *Bean Spasms*, *Poetry*, 113 (December 1968): 206-207;

Tom Clark, Review of *Bean Spasms*, *New York Times Book Review*, 31 March 1968, p. 32;

Jonathan Cott, "The New American Poetry," in *The New American Arts* (New York: Horizon, 1966);

David Lehman, Review of *Great Balls of Fire*, *Poetry*, 119 (January 1972): 226-227;

Louis I. Martz, "New Books in Review," review of *Great Balls of Fire*, *Yale Review*, 59 (Summer 1970): 554-556;

Aram Saroyan, "Good-Bye to the 1960's," *Village Voice*, 24 January 1977, pp. 73-74;

Gilbert Sorrentino, "Toujours l'amour," *New York Times Book Review*, 19 September 1976, p. 8;

Reed Whittemore, Review of *Great Balls of Fire*, *New Republic*, 161 (31 December 1969): 23.

LINDA PASTAN
(27 May 1932-)

BOOKS: *A Perfect Circle of Sun* (Chicago: Swallow, 1971);

On the Way to the Zoo (Washington, D.C. & San Francisco: Dryad, 1975);

Aspects of Eve (New York: Liveright, 1975);

The Five Stages of Grief (New York: Norton, 1978).

Linda Pastan was born in New York City to Jacob L. and Bess Schwartz Olenik. She took a B.A. from Radcliffe in 1954, an M.L.S. from Simmons in 1955, and an M.A. from Brandeis in 1957. Married to Ira Pastan since 1953, she has three children. Pastan has won the *Mademoiselle* Dylan Thomas Poetry Award and the Poetry Society of America's di Castagnola Award.

Pastan's first book, *A Perfect Circle of Sun*, appeared in 1971 as the forty-fourth volume in the Swallow Press New Poetry Series. It is a solid accomplishment. In these poems she exhibits, as Janet Bloom observes, "an easy, strong, and direct rhythm; and a gift for observation," qualities that, along with her ability to create memorable images and her penchant for examining life's unpleasant emotions, characterize her subsequent verse. Pastan considers one of the seasons in each of this collection's four sections. Her purpose is not to comment finally on nature, although she does that; rather, she examines the human moods and realities that correspond to the various seasons.

The poems in "January, 7 A. M.," in keeping with the winter season, address various aspects of mortality. Somber throughout, Pastan considers a slumbering second son's vulnerability; a vision of an empty family home; a father's death; and a woman staring through a train's window at dusk, only to see her own ghostly reflection. The best of these poems are "At the Gynecologist's," in which Pastan portrays a woman with her legs in the stirrups, riding toward death; "Distances," about distance between a husband and wife, one of her dominant themes; "Notes from the Delivery Room," in which she argues that children should grow into life as do beets or turnips so they will return easily to the earth when dead; and "Dirge," a poem about occupational deaths, but especially about poets' inescapable urge to seek death, as illustrated by Dylan Thomas, Sylvia Plath, Hart Crane, Randall Jarrell, Delmore Schwartz, and Weldon Kees. With precise diction, sharp imagery, and controlled mood, these economical poems address aspects of death without a hint of the maudlin or the banal.

With spring comes life, and Pastan focuses on April, the kindest month, to show humanity in the process of becoming. She portrays life growing from death in four substantial religious poems ("At Bingham Falls, Vermont," "At the Jewish Museum," "Adam Remembering," and "Passover"), but superior to them are the secular ones. "Skylight," for example, describes a woman captured in a windowless room of artifice, but she is saved from sterility and suffocation by the skylight that permits her to see nature and to "sit in a perfect circle of sun." As spring evolves from winter, so will this woman journey from her entrapment into nature and into life. But even better is "Early Walk," a poem that gives its name to this second section. It is a love poem about a husband and wife whose separate activities and interests keep them apart more than they would like. Their marriage is strained. They go for an early-morning walk and pause to kiss. Behind her he sees leaves turning green, and behind him she notices rosebuds almost ready to blossom. While each sees a different aspect of nature, they both observe the birth of spring. They hope that their marriage will grow out of coldness, out of death, into the intimate relationship they once had. Spring predictably functions as a season of hope.

Pastan's summer is not what one expects. She portrays a boy listening to the whistle of the last train ever to pass his house, ponders parents' influence on their second son, who will finally reject them, laments (in her only overtly political poem) the sacrificing of young men in battle in 1966, and quietly mourns the loss of a husband. Pastan examines the nature of summer most fully in "Camouflage." Here a woman notes that summer is not always what it seems; it is like the chameleon that "turns from simile / to metaphor and back to lizard. / Summer is only camouflage." She sees old trees under new leaves and clay under topsoil. Beneath the summer's radiance rests decay. That reality reflects this woman's marriage:

> We say the waves like rosaries,
> hour on hour, and later
> flat against the sand
> turn beach colored ourselves.

Husband and wife appear bronzed and healthy, but their relationship is tense. Pastan frequently observes that pleasing exteriors conceal death's roots.

In the last section, "October Funeral," Pastan deals with events in September, October, and November, capturing perfectly the mood of each. Most successful is "September." Here a woman notes

that the wind causes her expectations to "blow out of reach," and she admits that she has difficulty breaking "the habit of beginning." In anticipating winter she notes that "things seem transfused / with new blood— / turning the woods red." There is an energy, a vitality in those first days leading to death. After averring that "we have been dying all our lives," Pastan concludes "Each Autumn" with one of the best images in her early poems:

> Listen
> to the first snow fall from the ruined branch
> with the same sound as earth
> thrown into a new grave.

"Each autumn seasons us for death," she writes, and she elucidates that theme fully in this marvelous poem. She ends her book with "Journey's End" ("How hard we try to reach death safely") and "A Dangerous Time" (referring to November), poems acknowledging the inevitability of death.

Pastan was wise to structure her first volume on the cycle of the seasons. That topic forces a poet to address certain issues, but it also challenges one to search for new ways to interpret and relate familiar material. She does just that in her impressive first book of verse.

On the Way to the Zoo (1975) is a thin volume of seventeen poems treating the human condition through animal imagery. As in her first book, here the poet is introspective, even melancholy. An untitled poem establishes the theme of Pastan's second collection:

> *I have pulled teeth*
> *from the shaggy mouth*
> *of a lion,*
> *making him no more*
> *than an angry man.*
> *Yet deep in sleep's thicket*
> *I hear a roar*
> *and am afraid.*
> *. . . . .*
> *Somewhere, real animals wait*
> *inside their smells.*

She sees that animals are not so dangerous as commonly believed, but she suspects that she has yet to confront seemingly innocent animals, humans, that are in fact dangerous.

Pastan's animals are not the fearful beasts of the jungle. While she uses snakes and a fox, most of her animals—snail, dog, donkey, rooster, squirrel, duckling, hummingbird, turkey, turtle, and chimpanzee—are not physically threatening, although she employs them to express powerful human emotions. For example, in "To an Adolescent Son" a woman sees her son, with a bedroll on his back, as a snail. Certainly he resembles that animal outwardly, but his mother sees that, like a snail, he is moving slowly yet steadily away from her. He is leaving childhood for adulthood, and she cannot hinder his progress, although she wishes to.

Two poems near the end of the volume treat the difficulty of loving well, which is one of Pastan's major themes. In "To Her Lover" she examines the regenerative qualities of a eucalyptus, a snake, and a whidah bird; but while they replace their lost parts naturally, a woman refuses to restore herself by returning to her lover grown cold:

> If there is a lesson here
> I will not learn it,
> though you amputate my arms
> almost sadly
> from around your neck.

If he removes her arms, she will not grow new ones; she will not pursue him. She would rather suffer considerable emotional pain than offer herself to a man who does not accept her. She chooses self, integrity, and independence over faithfulness to an unresponsive man.

Pastan continues that sentiment in "Departures," a poem of awareness and self-deprecation in which a woman sees herself yearning for her remote husband, just as her dog pursues a squirrel:

> My dog barks under an empty tree
> long after the squirrel has gone.
> . . . .
> And I stand gazing up at you
> who long ago stopped loving me,
> while that foolish dog still barks.

Not only is this image fresh and appropriate, but the poem illustrates woman in the process of acknowledging her individuality, her ability—and need—to stand as a complete, independent being. Hardly a radical feminist, Pastan writes eloquently in these two poems about a woman's refusal to tolerate a man's emotional abuse.

Pastan has numerous humans qua animals confront a woman on the way to the zoo. Once there the woman learns, in the title poem, that "It is always the day / after the holiday," that pleasure is difficult to locate and sustain. A child will leave home and a lover will grow cold; similarly, the innocent chimpanzee in the zoo will die "grieving" for freedom. But people are not free either, for the laughter that they direct at the imprisoned chimps "climbs / the cage of our ribs." Humans are also encaged, and they will grieve lest they gain emotional freedom.

Another, larger volume of Pastan's verse appeared in 1975. *Aspects of Eve* was her first book to bear the imprint of a major New York publisher, Liveright. It is an ambitious volume in three sections, each titled with one of these lines from Archibald MacLeish's "Eve's Exile":

> Space within its time revolves
> But Eve must spin as Adam delves
> Because our exile is ourselves.

The lines inform the volume. In it Pastan suggests that woman is responsible for her own anguish, even though it is encouraged by society in general and by men in particular.

As in her first two books, the dominant mood of Pastan's third volume is predominantly quiet and even melancholy. The opening section deals mostly with death; it also contains some love poems. Pastan treats death sensitively and movingly, although she approaches it not religiously or even especially philosophically but rather stoically, acceptingly. In "A Real Story," for example, she writes about a woman visiting her ninety-five-year-old grandfather as he approaches death. When she was young, he told her stories about chickens saved providentially from becoming soup. But she was not content with his tales; she demanded "a real story," whereupon he avoided her by reading a newspaper that he held between them. Now, as an adult in her dying grandfather's presence, she attempts to cheer him by saying that he will soon be better. He knows that he will not recover, and he pulls the sheet

> over his face,
> raising it between us
> the way he used to raise
> the Yiddish paper
> when we said
> enough chickens
> tell us a real story.

She has become the storyteller, the fabricator, the soother; he has become the one demanding truth. Time does not stop, and death is inevitable.

In "Go Gentle," one of her best poems, Pastan presents a woman reflecting on her dying father. As in the grandfather poem, this woman's relationship with her father has become reversed since her youth. She obviously loves him deeply and wishes that he would quit fighting for life, so as to avoid undue suffering:

Remember when you taught me
how to swim? Let go, you said,
the lake will hold you up.
I long to say, Father let go
and death will hold you up.

Pastan excels in expressing succinctly and expertly life's deepest and most difficult-to-express emotions.

The section entitled "But Eve Must Spin as Adam Delves" (i.e., man dictates woman's actions) contains poems on various topics, including mythical heroes and the challenge of writing verse. Here Pastan's most successful poems concern the difficulty of sustaining passionate relationships, women's traditional dependence on men, and women's ability to stand independent of men. In "Swimming Last Summer" she comments on a husband's coldness toward his wife. In summer they swam together in a warm lake and had to dive deep to find coolness. But the poem's present is January, and his eyes

become glazed and cold,
your thoughts of me more sluggish than
some winter-dazed trout
swimming as close to bottom as it dares.

He does not satisfy her; she attempts to regain his attention with her "remembered body / for bait." If he does not desire her, however, she will probably remain frustrated. Woman is at man's mercy. Although she may choose not to be dominated, such a decision will cause her anguish.

This woman is also unhappy with other aspects of her life. She is one who, in "Knots," has been taught to be a patient, accepting spouse. But despite her patience, she is frustrated. She is a woman of energy and talent who feels so trapped within her family that she has "dreamed of knotting / bedsheets together / to flee by." Her rage is silent, but it is rage nonetheless.

Finally, in "Aspects of Eve," Pastan resolves many of the conflicts expressed in this section. In two short sentences she acknowledges women's original indebtedness to Adam, but she avows that the sexes are different, that one is not superior to the other, and that women should not be forced into male molds. Girls

grow into something
quite different
knocking finally
as a bone knocks
on the closed gates of the garden—
which unexpectedly
open.

Women are women; men are men. Women are as eager to experience life's complexities as are men, and, after repeated knocking, the gates open before them. In dominating women men have disserved both women and themselves.

Pastan illustrates that MacLeish is correct in noting society's demand that "Eve must spin as Adam delves," but she suggests that women are

Linda Pastan

ultimately responsible for their own plight. She makes this point repeatedly in "Because Our Exile is Ourselves," the volume's concluding section. Here she examines a woman's fear of reality and, therefore, her inability to confront it. In "Hurricane Watch," for example, a woman lives passively on life's periphery. The hairs on her arms are controlled by the wind; she is at the mercy of outside forces:

I rise and fall
with the barometer,
holding on for my life.

She lives in "a storm cellar / of flesh," reading her palm, hoping to avoid life's harshnesses. "Eclipse" presents a similar idea. This poem tells of a woman's

Linda Pastan

reaction to the sun's eclipse, but Pastan uses the sun to symbolize man and his governance of life and the moon to represent women. So when the moon eclipses the sun, when woman gains control over man, this woman cannot witness the event directly:

> Afraid of a truth that could blind
> I turn my cold shoulder to the sun
> and catch its shadow in a cardboard box. . . .

Because her culture values men more than women, she is afraid to acknowledge the truth that women are as powerful as men. To her seeming relief, the sun returns "like a swallowed sword"—with all the male sexual dominance that image suggests—and the universe returns to its previous order. But the woman reflects on the event and concludes that

> It is not chaos
> I fear in this strange dusk
> but the inexplicable order of things.

She is finally ready to assume the risks that freedom entails. No longer is she content with sexual stereotyping or with accepting men's supposed superiority over women. By the end of the volume Pastan has examined women's entrapment and finds that they are ready for freedom. Eve may assert her independence from Adam.

Pastan's most recent volume, *The Five Stages of Grief* (1978), is her most accomplished. The collection is divided into five parts, each representing one stage of grief: denial, anger, bargaining, depression, and acceptance. Kenneth Pitchford has observed that these stages "describe the different phases a terminal patient goes through in coming to terms with the fact that she or he is dying." Some of these poems treat physical death; collectively they document a spiritual—but not religious—death. Pastan's basic concern is with how a woman should respond to a cold husband. The independent woman who emerges at the end of *Aspects of Eve* does not continue to develop in this collection; rather, she finally accepts her plight within marriage.

The poems in "Denial" establish the somber mood that dominates the volume. A woman has an argument with her husband and attempts unsuccessfully to avoid him. She acknowledges her failures as a poet, feels comfortable with them, and stores some of her verses for a time when she will have lost the requisite sensitivity for writing good poetry. This woman is angry, to be sure, but she does not blame others entirely for her plight. She is self-analytical; she reveals her faults.

In "Funerary Tower," a woman, at age forty,

reflects on the past and notices that she has changed little since childhood. The season is autumn (a "season of salt"), a time when falling leaves expose a tree's structure. That revelation of the tree's essence reminds her of an event in childhood with her father. He told her, lovingly and tenderly, what good bones she had, but she withdrew from him impatiently. Now he is dead, and she and her mother visit his grave. The older woman tends to the grave, but the younger one is impatient and cuts short her mother's activity. The daughter concludes that "We carry our childhoods / in our arms," and she understands—if she does not entirely accept—her impatient nature. She sees herself accurately. If she has little patience with her parents, surely she will not accept indifference from a husband, but that is exactly what she has to confront and resolve.

After denying her parents and, implicitly, her anguish, this woman becomes angry. She sees that women have no place in men's activities and that men are free to betray their wives. A woman's plight is difficult. What is she to do when her husband and children evaluate her every action? She presents this problem in the wryly amusing "Marks," wherein a husband gives his wife an A for cooking, an incomplete for housework, and a B-plus for lovemaking. Her son says that she is an average mother; her daughter, believing in the pass/fail option, gives her a passing grade. Frustrated, the woman decides to save herself by leaving the family. But she does not leave, nor does she commit suicide, which she ponders. She settles for quiet, for solitude, for restrained anger. Unable to gain emotional freedom, she concludes, "Go away, / all of you" (in "Exeunt Omnes"). This woman has few options. Bound by commitment and guilt to continue as the family's mortar, she can begin to express her anger, but she cannot remedy its cause.

Since she is trapped, she decides to bargain, to offer some part of herself in exchange for peace, warmth, and understanding. But she has little to bargain with (and perhaps that is why the poems in this section are less satisfying than in the others). In "March," she observes that the oaks have finally lost the leaves that they have retained "fiercely," and Pastan uses that image to symbolize a woman's friends who are divorcing. Divorce is obviously a possibility for this woman and her husband, but she feels ambivalent about it and finally implores him not to leave her:

> Don't leave now
> We have almost
> survived
> our lives.

She is at his mercy. Perhaps she will become comfortable in their strained relationship.

Her bargaining obviously fails, and depression follows. The woman recounts a twenty-fifth high-school reunion ("We have all / turned into / ourselves") and comments on a blaring New York radio station ("I pick up the siren call / of WNYC"), but she is affected most by the quiet that accompanies her depression. She likens her plight to the silence of the snow falling in a shaken paperweight (artificial nature), and she also sees her predicament reflected in real, undiluted nature. She perceives her depression in the fog as it disperses and in the monotony of the moon. Most significantly, she notices a similarity between her face and the "jagged pieces" of ice on a lake. Not only does she see herself in nature, but when she asks nature what love is, she discovers that "Silence is answer enough." Her love has turned to silence; silence pervades her life.

She soon accepts her fate, as time urges one to do. She becomes an old woman rocking in a chair, accepting her grief; she accepts the death of a friend; she accepts her decision, years ago, to marry. In "Love Letter," one of Pastan's shortest and most poignant poems, the woman finally accepts her husband:

> in the cold battle
> of breath
> yours forms
> the only cloud
> on which I can rest
> my head.

Even though their relationship has been strained to the point that it is no longer satisfactory to the woman, she can find comfort only with her husband, with the familiar, with the imperfect. She has accepted her plight. But that is not the end of her difficulty. Her response to grief is cyclical and infinite, not linear and finite. The title poem suggests that acceptance is not the speaker's final attitude toward grief. She learns that "Grief is a circular staircase." She has lost love, and once she attains acceptance through these five stages, she will repeat them time and again. Her fate is similar to Sisyphus's.

So ends Pastan's fourth and best book of verse. Here and in her other work she carefully examines life's deepest emotions. While some of her early poems suggest the possibility of happiness, and some collected in 1975 indicate women's ability to stand alone independent of men, she concludes, in *The Five Stages of Grief*, that a woman can probably

only accept her plight. Pastan deserves serious attention for her finely wrought dark comments on the human condition. Not spectacular, she is a solid poet whose work speaks to all of mankind. Her verse will endure. —*Benjamin Franklin V*

Other:

"A Note," *Voyages*, 2 (Spring 1969): 68;
"Roots," in *American Poets in 1976*, ed. William Heyen (Indianapolis: Bobbs-Merrill, 1976), pp. 212-223;
"Old Woman," in *Fifty Contemporary Poets: The Creative Process*, ed. Alberta T. Hunter (New York: David McKay, 1977), pp. 249-251.

References:

Janet Bloom, "A Plea for Proper Boldness," *Parnassus*, 1 (Fall-Winter 1972): 130-132;
Joseph Garrison, "Heart and Soul: Two Poets," *Shenandoah*, 24 (Summer 1973): 92-93;
Roderick Jellema, "The Poetry of Linda Pastan," *Voyages*, 2 (Spring 1969): 73-74;
Kenneth Pitchford, "Metaphor as Illness: A Meditation on Recent Poetry," *New England Review*, 1 (1978): 104-108;
Peter Stitt, "Violence, Imagery, and Introspection," *Georgia Review*, 33 (Winter 1979): 928-930.

SYLVIA PLATH
(27 October 1932-11 February 1963)

SELECTED BOOKS: *The Colossus* (London, Melbourne & Toronto: Heinemann, 1960; abridged edition, New York: Knopf, 1962);
The Bell Jar, as Victoria Lucas (London, Melbourne & Toronto: Heinemann, 1963; New York, Evanston, San Francisco & London: Harper & Row, 1971);
Ariel (London: Faber & Faber, 1965; New York: Harper & Row, 1966);
Crossing the Water (London: Faber & Faber, 1971; New York, Evanston, San Francisco & London: Harper & Row, 1971);
Crystal Gazer and Other Poems (London: Rainbow Press, 1971);
Winter Trees (London: Faber & Faber, 1971; New York, Evanston, San Francisco & London: Harper & Row, 1972).

Sylvia Plath

In "Three Women," the final poem of *Winter Trees* (1971), Sylvia Plath speaks through the voice of a woman in a maternity ward, whose words provide a fitting statement for the poet's singular fixation with annihilation:

A power is growing on me an old tenacity.
I am breaking apart like the world.
                              There is this blackness,
This ram of blackness. I fold my hands on a mountain.
The air is thick. It is thick with this working.
I am used. I am drummed into use.
My eyes are squeezed by this blackness.
I see nothing.

Composed during the last year of Plath's life, "Three Women" foreshadows the poet's self-asphyxiation in February 1963. In all of the poems written during the two-year period immediately preceding her suicide, including those in *Ariel* (1965) and *Crossing the Water* (1971), Plath expresses her anguish with her experiences as a writer, a wife, and a mother. She had come to see her life dominated by forces beyond her control, by ungovernable and meaningless pain brought on, in many cases, by her own depression.

In 1940, when Plath was eight years old, her father died after a long, painful illness, and the memory of this loss was to stimulate much of the violent father imagery of *The Colossus* (1960) and *Ariel*. By the time she entered Smith College in Northampton, Massachusetts, on an academic scholarship, she had already had prose and poetry accepted by the *Christian Science Monitor* and *Seventeen*, and while in school she continued to publish in *Seventeen* and served on the editorial board of the *Smith Review*, a student literary publication.

In the next two years Plath won several poetry prizes as well as *Mademoiselle* magazine's College Board fiction contest, which allowed her to work as a guest editor for one issue of the magazine. She continued to publish poems in various outlets before suffering acute depression that resulted in her subsequent hospitalization and suicide attempts. She later chronicled this period of her life in *The Bell Jar* (1963), an autobiographical novel published, under the pseudonym Victoria Lucas, one month before her death. In many respects *The Bell Jar* forms the backdrop for recurring motifs in Plath's poetry. "Three Women," for instance, is a thematic outgrowth of a particular situation described in the novel. The protagonist's observations as she is led through a maternity delivery room by a young medical student prefigure her own hospitalization later in the novel, while her description of the effects of sodium pentothal provides a framework for understanding Plath's preoccupation with psychological and physical pain:

I thought it sounded just like the sort of drug a man would invent. Here was a woman in terrible pain, obviously feeling every bit of it or she wouldn't groan like that, and she would go straight home and start another baby, because the drug would make her forget how bad the pain had been, when all the time, in some secret part of her, that long blind, doorless and windowless corridor of pain was waiting to open up and shut her in again.

The Bell Jar chronicles the trauma of Plath's life during her years at Smith College. But in spite of her bouts with depression, Plath excelled academically, and in the spring of 1955 she graduated *summa cum laude* and attended Cambridge University on a Fulbright scholarship. The following spring she married poet Ted Hughes and returned to teach at Smith in 1957. During the next two years, until she returned to England in December of 1959, Plath taught at Smith, worked on preliminary drafts of *The Bell Jar*, and tried with little success to have her first collection of poems, *The Colossus*, accepted for publication. In 1960, in England, Plath's first child was born and her poetry book was published by William Heinemann.

The initial reception of her first book of verse was unsatisfying for Plath. John Wain, writing in the *London Times Literary Supplement*, called it "clever, vivacious poetry, which will be enjoyed most by intelligent people capable of having fun with poetry and not just being holy about it." Other critics, notably P. S. Hurd and Thomas Blackburn, spoke respectively of "the adroit fashioning of metaphor and simile" and the "fine handling of language and vitality of observation," but no one praised the underlying passion of the poems. Plath wanted more than an affirmative nod toward her technical expertise with words and wit, and the lackluster reviews were hardly strong enough forces to pull her from the ensuing psychological trauma brought on by what she considered to be exhaustive efforts to write while raising a family.

In the two and one-half years preceding her death, Plath completed *The Bell Jar* as well as most of the poems included in her posthumous books. During this time, she suffered a miscarriage, then an appendectomy, and then became pregnant with her second child. The subject matter of many of her poems is taken from these hospital experiences, and the predominant theme is death. Her obsession with annihilation results from a finely developed sense of self-importance; her poems are an outgrowth of an untiring egocentrism, much as Walt Whitman's stem from his conscious celebration of living. In an extensive passage published in Charles H. Newman's collection, *The Art of Sylvia Plath* (1970), Anne Sexton tells of Plath's obsession with talk of dying and suicide:

> Suicide is, after all, the opposite of the poem. Sylvia and I often talked opposites. We talked death with burned up intensity, both of us drawn to it like moths to an electric light bulb. Sucking on it! . . . as if death made each of us a little more real at the moment. . . . We talked death and this was life for us, lasting in spite of us, or better, because of us, our intent eyes, our fingers clutching the glass. . . . I know that such fascination with death sounds strange (one does not argue that it isn't sick—one knows it *is*—there's no excuse), and that people cannot understand.

The "richness" to which Sexton alludes manifests itself in the poems of *The Colossus*. Plath recognizes the state of her existence and knows the "Colossus" will never be pieced together entirely:

> I shall never get you put together entirely,
> Pieced, glued, and properly jointed.
> Mule-bray, pig-grunt and bawdy cackles
> Proceed from your great lips.
> It's worse than a barnyard.

The poet's consciousness is totally fragmented in *The Colossus*, and recognizing the practical implications of such a state—insanity or death—she tries to piece together the figure that haunts her. But Plath seems to know intuitively that no glue is strong enough to hold the human mind forever in place, particularly when the psyche is forced to undergo the pain at the heart of the poet's writing.

The theme of disembodiment is mirrored in *The Bell Jar*, in which Plath's protagonist is led through a training hospital where medical students are offered prizes for "persuading the most relatives of dead people to have their dead ones cut up whether they [the students] needed it or not, in the interest of science." The cadaver image is sustained through the novel as a reminder of the girl's concern with suicide—"and pretty soon I felt as though I were carrying that cadaver's head around with me on a string, like some black, noseless balloon stinking of vinegar."

In many respects, Plath echoes French Existentialists Jean-Paul Sartre and Albert Camus, as well as twentieth-century German philosopher Karl Jaspers in their attacks on the brutal nature of modern life. Each laments man's state in the "scheme of things" that makes individuals into pieced-together robots. The ego is shattered by technology and man is faced with nothingness, the void that informs him that meaning exists only in death. The last stanza of "The Colossus" might be read as an ironic mockery of T. S. Eliot's closing lines in *The Waste Land* (1922), where there remains at least the hope of redemption. For Eliot, man can shore up his ruins and begin to fish for some sort of meaning and order. Plath, however, entertains no such optimism:

> Counting the red stars and those of plum-color.
> The sun rises under the pillar of your tongue.
> My hours are married to shadow.
> No longer do I listen for the scrape of a keel
> On the blank stones of the landing.

Plath recognizes in man's condition a potential for destruction and pessimism that is not balanced by an alternative concept of hope. Her hours, "married to shadow," are measured by the bleakness of a meaningless landscape and the expressionless despair of "the blank stones of the landing."

In "All the Dead Dears," perhaps the darkest of the poems in *The Colossus*, Plath writes of a skeleton in the Cambridge museum. The poem illustrates her near obsession with death:

> How they grip us through thin and thick,
> Those barnacle dead!
> This lady here's no kin
> Of mine, yet kin she is; she'll suck
> Blood and whistle my marrow clean
> To prove it. As I think now of her head,
> From the mercury-backed glass
> Mother, grandmother, great grandmother
> Reach hag hands to haul me in,
> And an image looms under the fishpond surface
> Where the daft father went down
> With orange duck feet winnowing his hair—

The images of the family return to haunt the poet; the "barnacle dead" reach out to pull her inside the "mercury-backed glass." Plath's theme revolves around the death of the poetic imagination, which is pictured as essentially female in nature. A conglomerate of images merges in the poem: the dead reaching out to haul the living into the grave with them, the women physically joined by blood and death, the father figure looming evil above the rest, the young poet mutilated and bled by some unnameable destructive force. Although the images and allusions are far-reaching, they are never dispersed. Each connects with another, and the effect is that of terror and blind power.

Plath's dominating concern for death, her own death in particular, ultimately surfaces as the controlling force of her poetry. Even in poems where death is not the stated theme, the implicit darkness of nonexistence hovers in the background. In "Watercolour of Grantchester Meadows," the setting is rimmed by an undertone of bleakness, and the pastoral landscape is interrupted by latent hysteria:

> Droll, vegetarian, the water rat
> Saws down a reed and swims from his limber grove,
> While the students stroll or sit,
> Hands laced, in a moony indolence of love—
> Black-gowned, but unaware
> How in mild air
> The owl shall stoop from his turret, the rat
> cry out.

The "moony indolence of love" is disturbed by black gowns, gowns that reek of ritualistic unconcern. The vegetarian rat, about his constant business, is eclipsed by the carnivore. Only the poet hears the rat "cry out."

During the five months preceding her suicide, Plath wrote almost the entire body of poems that were to be collected two years later and published as *Ariel*. The poems are personal testaments to the loneliness and insecurity that plagued her, and the desolate images suggest her apparent fixation with self-annihilation. The violence of the *Colossus* poems is continued in *Ariel*, and the suicidal themes become frighteningly direct, as in "A Birthday Present": "And the knife not carve, but enter / Pure and clean as the cry of a baby, / And the universe slide from my side."

In *Ariel*, the everyday incidents of living are transformed into the horrifying psychological experiences of the poet. The domesticity of the situations serves as an ironic backdrop to the tragic elements of nearly every poem. "The Bee Meeting," for example, concerns some people who are watching a beekeeper move virgin bees away from the queen. It is a simple job, but one that, when viewed from Plath's unique poetic perspective, acts as a symbol for human isolation and suffering. Initially, the poet is "nude as a chicken neck" without the protective gear necessary to approach the hives. Until she dons her smock, hat, and veil, she is in danger of being stung. However, the physical danger is no more menacing than the isolation that begins to take shape in the poet's imagination. As the poem progresses, she begins to identify with the queen bee, who will undoubtedly die when the other bees are released the following year. Toward the close of the poem, she anticipates her own death in her questioning: "Whose is that long white box in the grove, what have they accomplished, why am I cold?"

The undercurrent of violence in "The Bee Meeting" surfaces in Plath's most famous poem, "Daddy." The death of Plath's father when she was a child is of considerable importance to her writing, but the "daddy" of the poem is by no means a representation of her own father. Images of mutilation recur throughout the poem, but whereas the persona of "The Colossus" attempts to piece together the inhuman figure that haunts her, in "Daddy" the poet's own image is dichotomized before it is pieced together "with glue":

> I was ten when they buried you.
> At twenty I tried to die
> And get back, back, back to you.
> I thought even the bones would do.
>
> But they pulled me out of the sack,
> And they stuck me together with glue.

The power of "Daddy" supersedes human hope. When there is an attempt at redemption, the necessary method is savage violence:

> If I've killed one man, I've killed two—
> The vampire who said he was you
> And drank my blood for a year,
> Seven years, if you want to know.
> Daddy, you can lie back now.
>
> There's a stake in your fat black heart
> And the villagers never liked you.
> They are dancing and stamping on you.
> They always knew it was you.
> Daddy, daddy, you bastard, I'm through.

In this pivotal poem the violence is not dissolved but only transferred to the villagers, people whose fear has turned to hatred and inhuman brutality. The Poles and Jews and gypsy women turn on the Nazi "panzer-men," but there clearly is no redemption, only dominance replaced by revenge.

"Tulips," one of the few *Ariel* poems written more than two years before Plath's death, recalls the time she spent in a hospital recovering from an appendectomy. As in the great majority of her poems, the protagonist is isolated and despairing, but the tone of the poem is reflective. The frenzy of "Daddy" is replaced by thoughtful acquiescence to the pain and fear of living. The speaker, a hospital patient, is intent on surrendering her individuality to the faceless world around her: "I have given my name and my day-clothes up to the nurses / And my history to the anaesthetist and my body to / surgeons." The attending nurses are anonymous creatures likened to birds:

The nurses pass and pass, they are no trouble,
They pass the way gulls pass inland in their white caps
Doing things with their hands, one just the same as
                                                    another,
So it is impossible to tell how many there are.

The poet apprehends herself as an inanimate object, content to let others control her: "My body is a pebble to them, they tend it as water / Tends to the pebble it must run over." In allowing the nurses to "run over" her, the poet rejects her individual ability to bring about her own convalescence, a decision that foreshadows Plath's decision to kill herself.

A brief, ironic respite from Plath's obsession with death occurs in "Black Rook in Rainy Weather," a moving poem in the tradition of Robert Frost's skeptical verse and central for understanding her posture in *Crossing the Water*, a second posthumous volume published in 1971. In particular, the poem is clearly reminiscent of four Frost poems—"Design," "For Once, Then, Something," "Dust of Snow," and "The Most of It." The parallel images and the stance taken by the poet in Plath's poem point to the close proximity of the two poets' skeptical perspectives. Plath questions the feasibility of universal order, as Frost does in "Design." She employs the same questioning stance as the poet figure in "The Most of It." There is concern for the brief epiphany brought on by a commonplace occurrence, which is Frost's concern in "A Dust of Snow." And the poet of "Black Rook in Rainy Weather" becomes aware of the fleeting nature of truth, much like the poet figure of "For Once, Then, Something."

In Plath's "Black Rook in Rainy Weather," the poet figure watches a rook arranging its feathers in the rain, and her observation prompts speculation on the nature of poetic inspiration. She begins with her stated cynicism:

I do not expect miracle
Or an accident

To set the sight on fire
In my eye, nor seek
Any more in the desultory weather some design,
But let spotted leaves fall as they fall,
Without ceremony, or portent.

The poet figure is alone, and as her honest musings begin to unfold, her cynicism is replaced by the innocent desire to receive "some backtalk from the mute sky," some primitive "original response" that will help her hallow "an internal / Otherwise inconsequent / By bestowing largesse, honour, / One might say love." Here Plath is not speaking of the indolent love witnessed in "Watercolour of Grantchester Meadows"; instead, she is after a kind of primordial inspiration, a sign that will link her perception to some nameless and sympathetic deity. The rook offers an instant of belief in life, but the final ironic lines undercut the hope that has momentarily lodged in the poet's mind:

I only know that a rook
Ordering its black feathers can so shine
As to seize my senses, haul
My eyelids up, and grant

A brief respite from fear
Of total neutrality. . . .
. . . .
. . . Miracles occur,
If you care to call those spasmodic
Tricks of radiance miracles. The wait's begun again,
The long wait for the angel,
For that rare, random descent.

As in "Daddy" and "The Colossus," Plath patches together "a content of sorts," a content much like Frost's attempt to achieve momentary stays against confusion. The kind of miracles that occur to Sylvia Plath are simple, fleeting epiphanies, ridden with nuance and uncertainty. They are little more than "spasmodic / Tricks of radiance," as brief as they are unpredictable.

The theme of annihilation operates again in *Winter Trees* (1971). In "Brasilio," for instance, where the idea of sacrifice becomes a thematic focal point, Plath reacts to the conglomeration of mechanistic and spiritualistic power:

O you who eat

People like light-rays, leave
This one
Mirror safe, unredeemed

By the dove's annihilation,
The glory,
The power, the glory.

The poet's religious imagery suggests the theme of redemption, a redemption accompanied by death at the hands of a sadistic deity. There is no human glory, no salvation except death.

The desire *not* to be redeemed translates into

Plath's obsession with individual purgation, at both the spiritual and intellectual levels. The man is not redeemed by "the dove's annihilation" because the redemptive power is not centered in a loving deity. Instead, each individual is subjected to dominance by pure power, amoral and staggering in its scope and intensity. In the face of such awesome strength, the poet appears incapable or unwilling to establish a stable viewpoint from which to study the situation. Such ambivalence stems from a perception of reality colored by fear, fear of something "other," something beyond comprehension in both its loving and its hating potential, akin perhaps to the malevolent force in E. E. Cummings's *The Enormous Room* (1922), the pervasive fear in the works of Kafka, or the faceless angst of the existentialist writers.

Sylvia Plath's desperate need to "talk death" is the underlying power of her poetry. As Anne Sexton points out, death seemed to make her "a little more real at the moment," and this perception of reality translates itself into poem after poem. One discovers in Plath's work an indulgence in ego so pervasive as to warrant the ego's own destruction. She is a twentieth-century Emily Dickinson who has left the silent insanity of a New England home and ventured into a world of existential despair. More primitively vocal than her nineteenth-century counterpart, Plath reacts to violence and fear in bursts of guttural emotion, as in "Daddy":

> Ich, ich, ich, ich,
> I could hardly speak.
> I thought every German was you.
> And the language obscene
>
> An engine, an engine
> Chuffing me off like a Jew.

Characteristically, as in "The Colossus," Plath sees her own mind as a "mouthpiece of the dead." At her most articulate, meditating on the nature of poetic inspiration, she is a controlled voice for cynicism, plainly delineating the boundaries of hope and reality. At her brutal best—and Plath is a brutal poet—she taps a source of power that transforms her poetic voice into a raving avenger of womanhood and innocence.

Plath's legacy is one of pain, fear, and traumatic depression, born of the need to destroy the imagistic materialization of "Daddy." The horrifying tone of her poetry underscores a depth of feeling that can be attributed to few other poets, and her near-suicidal attempt to communicate a frightening existential vision overshadows the shaky technique of her final poems. Plath writes of the human dread of dying. Her primitive honesty and emotionalism are her strength. —*Thomas McClanahan*

References:

Eileen M. Aird, *Sylvia Plath* (New York: Barnes & Noble, 1973);

A. Alvarez, *The Savage God* (New York: Random House, 1972);

Edward Butscher, *Sylvia Plath, Method and Madness* (New York: Seabury Press, 1976);

David Hobrook, *Sylvia Plath: Poetry and Existence* (London: Atholone Press, 1976);

Ted Hughes, "Notes on the Chronological Order of Sylvia Plath's Poems," *Triquarterly*, 7 (Fall 1966): 81-88;

Judith Kroll, *Chapters in a Mythology: The Poetry of Sylvia Plath* (New York: Harper & Row, 1976);

Ingrid Melander, *The Poetry of Sylvia Plath; A Study of Themes* (Stockholm: Almquist & Wiksell, 1972);

Charles H. Newman, ed., *The Art of Sylvia Plath* (Bloomington: Indiana University Press, 1970);

Cameron Northouse and Thomas Walsh, *Sylvia Plath and Anne Sexton: A Reference Guide* (Boston: G. K. Hall, 1974);

Nancy Hunter Steiner, *A Closer Look at Ariel: A Memory of Sylvia Plath* (New York: Harper's Magazine Press, 1973).

STANLEY PLUMLY
(23 May 1939-)

BOOKS: *In the Outer Dark* (Baton Rouge: Louisiana State University Press, 1970);

Giraffe (Baton Rouge: Louisiana State University Press, 1973);

How The Plains Indians Got Horses (Crete, Nebr.: Best Cellar Press, 1973);

Out-of-the-Body Travel (New York: Ecco Press, 1977).

Stanley Plumly's poetry focuses on psychological dramas involving those people and events—an alcoholic father, a long-suffering mother, a series of failed marriages—central to his life. These figures and experiences haunt the poet's inner self, creating a darkness reflective of the human and natural worlds beyond the self. Plumly's first book, *In the*

Outer Dark (1970), bears an especially appropriate title, for it suggests the relationship of the writer's two worlds: the somber realities of the outer world force the poet into the equally harsh, equally dark recesses of his own inner world. *Giraffe* (1973) further clarifies Plumly's central subject—the artist and his aesthetic process, the poet's attempts at love and marriage, the son's relationship with his father. *Out-of-the-Body Travel* (1977) reveals a narrowed but even more intense field of vision. This book concentrates almost exclusively on the separate figures of the writer's mother and father, suggesting as well the ways in which their union has influenced the poet's own expectations for marriage. A small chapbook, *How The Plains Indians Got Horses* (1973), contains poems included in the second major collection.

Stanley Plumly, the son of Herman and Esther Plumly, was born in Barnesville, Ohio. The writer's father, who died at the age of fifty-six of a heart attack brought on by his chronic alcoholism, dominates the poet's work: "I can hardly think of a poem I've written that at some point in its history did not implicate, or figure, my father" (*Iowa Review*, Fall 1973). His mother, as she appears in the poetry, personifies the silently suffering witness of her husband's downfall. Following Plumly's birth, the family moved from farm work to carpentry jobs and back to farm work in Virginia and Ohio. Plumly graduated from Wilmington College, a small work-study school in Ohio, in 1962. While he was in college, his writing talents were recognized and encouraged by the playwright-poet-teacher Joel Climenhaga. Plumly received his M.A. from Ohio University in 1968 and did course work toward a Ph.D. at the same university. He has taught at numerous institutions including Louisiana State, Ohio, Princeton, and Columbia Universities, and the Universities of Iowa, Michigan, and Houston, as well as at the Bread Loaf Writers' Conference in 1978 and 1979. Among his awards for poetry are Ohio University's Baker Fund Award (1972); the Delmore Schwartz Memorial Award for Poetry (1973); a Guggenheim Fellowship (1973); a National Endowment for the Arts Grant (1977); nominations for the National Book Critics Circle Award (1978) and the William Carlos Williams Award (1979) for *Out-of-the-Body Travel*; and the Pushcart Prize (1979-1980) for "Wildflower," which appeared in *Antaeus* in 1978. He served as poetry editor of the *Ohio Review* and the *Iowa Review* and since 1975 has been contributing editor of the *American Poetry Review*.

Plumly's first volume, *In the Outer Dark*, illustrates the poet's remarkably early realization of his aesthetic vision. The central figure of this work is the artistic self from which other subjects extend like satellites. The writer attempts to connect with the outer world beyond himself but finds in that world only the still moments of silence and darkness. Since his movement outward results in such isolation, the poet is eventually forced back into himself, into the world of his own inner dark.

In the Outer Dark frequently presents Plumly's poetic method in terms of painting. The writer suggests that no matter how full of life and sound it may be, the painting or poem is finally static and silent; its vision is produced whole in the mind and then meticulously transferred onto the canvas or page. The poet marvels at Georges Seurat's passion for working all day and night, plying his "science of dot / loving dot." Immediately following his poem about the pointillist painter, Plumly presents two works that attempt to duplicate Seurat's method of creating precise images through externally accurate concrete details and then transforming these images, through the artist's personality, into impressionistic statements. "Inside the Drop of Rain" focuses upon the movement "inside the mind's rainfall" of a minute particle of dust trapped within a drop of water; the writer then imagines himself inside that drop with his "inverted feet already / turning to snow." "Study in Kore" emphasizes another drama in miniature as the poet looks into the smallest unit of the eye to find his source of art:

> I become the image
> quick in that point of light,
> the all-too-literal photography
> of your eyes, twice-fixed
> and clearly there
> to float back into
> the seeing mind,
> transfixed in the imagination
> to the sight I have become.

This statement announces the poet's creative method: the detail recorded and transformed through the imagination is recalled later to create a poem.

The writer's method is further dramatized in "Deer Park in Winter," a poem that also demonstrates the overwhelming silence filling the outside void, that world beyond the self:

At dawn they stand bird still in the snow,
in odd pairs, ears tense to the winded silence,
Not even the cold cries.

The red sun rises in their eyes.

They shiver within the knowledge of its presence:
wherever they step now

they must step in shadow.
Heads lifted, they listen to the dark from a sun's
                                                distance,
as now they watch it rise

into the sky's
fields. Tonight they will pasture in sleep's indifference;
with warm noses plow the snow.

Much of this scene depends on the poet's eye, which functions like the painter's. In its movement back and forth from darkness to light to darkness, from cold to warm to cold, from dawn to light to night, the poem illustrates major motifs in this volume.

Employing his recurrent Whitmanesque image of the "houses and rooms" of the self, Plumly travels, in "At Palmer House," from the outward, still darkness into his own inner dark: "As always, we have / wandered in from the outside / of ourselves, silent, empty- / handed, the shy way that deer / enter another part of the forest." The poet attempts to overcome pervasive emptiness, silence, and darkness through touch, through love, as he seeks to share his personal isolation with another, as in "Between Flesh and What Follows":

> when I put my hands
>
> all over you, there is still
> that darkness between the touch,
> the blind breath still
>
> between the teeth.
> Even the talk
> that love makes making love
>
> is darker by the silence after.

Touch serves as a potential means of connecting not only the outer and inner worlds of the self but also the two isolated lovers; however, the emptiness that occurs after lovemaking creates a darkness and silence that cannot be diminished by love.

The most compelling subject of *In the Outer Dark* and, indeed, of all Plumly's major collections is the poet's father. This figure assumes many roles in Plumly's works: he is the carpenter who builds the houses and rooms that function as metaphors for the self's interior; he is the fisherman who dances in his long boat, which becomes in the poet's dreams a ceremonial craft transporting the older man toward death; he is the violin player who gives sound to his inner song of agony; and he is the farmer who must stay drunk in order to withstand the gruesome process of slaughtering his cattle. The father is, in

many respects, a version of the ruined artist, the creative man who destroys himself a little bit at a time. Yet the poet keeps his father alive through dreams and memories:

> I remember my father used to get so drunk I thought he was going to fall off the planet. He was a bull in his body. He ran into, over things. Once set in motion, his momentum seemed a natural, terrible force. As a child I would lie awake in bed long into the early morning listening and waiting for him to come home. He was always late and always drunk, but he always came home. And as it was a dark house, he invariably seemed to break into it. My father's house. In those waiting, and wasted, hours I lost the secret of sleep.

In his difficult sleep the poet escapes from the body to return to his psychological origins, and as he sleeps, he moves as if underwater into the viscous silence of dreams. Water, usually associated with the subconscious, figures as an important medium throughout Plumly's works, and sleep becomes a kind of middle ground between the living and the dead. The sleeper assumes the posture and the loss of consciousness associated with the dead, and in so doing he recalls and resurrects the dead to life. "Now That My Father Lies Down Beside Me," for instance, depicts the father and son together as they "lie in that other darkness, ourselves." The younger man cannot touch or see his father, but "I dream we lie under water, / caught in our own sure drift." The poet achieves a kind of communion with his dead father in this spiritual drift of the two selves. The proximity of the two—one somnambulistically alive, the other dead—causes a physical constriction within the writer so that he can "barely breathe" as, of course, his father cannot at all. Yet, instead of being made fuller from such a meeting, the speaker feels much more keenly his inner emptiness once he awakens. Ironically, however, in his dreams and memories of the dead and dying, the poet seems more alive than when he is awake and oppressed with the ennui, the angst of empty houses and rooms marking his own personal isolation.

The deep affection the writer feels for his lost father provides the impetus for some of Plumly's most moving lyrics. In "One Song," for example, he wishes to bury his father standing up, "arms lifted like a tree." He would have his father's hands bloom into flower and watch him "grow back / into the world, back into me / . . . I want to bury bones to where they bend, not break." The memory of his father does bend constantly in the writer's mind; death does not break their bond, a bond increasingly examined in the next two books of poetry.

Giraffe demonstrates the writer's careful focusing of his poetic vision. This volume is divided into three parts, and each section concerns one of the writer's major subjects—his creative method, his attempts at marriage, and his emotional connections with his doomed father. Each of the three parts is marked by an appropriate emblem from the outer

Thomas Victor

Stanley Plumly

world; the giraffe, the heron, and the horse, respectively, become symbols for the poet, for love relationships, and for the father. The metaphor of water appears in almost every poem as well, suggesting the connection of the outer world with the poet's subconsciousness; water becomes either the medium by which the writer approaches life through the imagination or the vehicle for transporting him to death, for "to die / is to drown."

The first section concentrates on the poet's method of creation. He attempts to escape from the body, the physical self, in order completely to immerse himself in the realm of the imagination.

Traveling to the subconscious and to memory is an essential feature of his method. In "Walking Out," for example, the writer wishes to "undress utterly" and leave behind his body, to become pure imagination, while walking to the water's edge on his hands; those who follow after him will "imagine flight": "I would be silence . . . I would be totally absent from myself . . . I would forget, myself entirely . . . But I would still be walking, if I could, / out of body, leaving behind, in a wake / of absence, clothes, fingerprints, words." Plumly views this kind of draining of the self from the body, the poem from the man, as a possible cause of Randall Jarrell's suicide. As the poet's page fills, his life seems to ooze out of his body. The transfer of the poem from the body to the page drains the life from the writer, and he becomes "a man about to walk out of his shadow / into the speed of light . . . a man saying out loud, I give you back this / gift, having already put it down."

In the second section, "Heron," the love poems chronicle the failures of touch. "Three Wives," for example, carries the slightly comic but painful lines about those with whom the writer has attempted marriage: "Table and chair. / This is no marriage / but an arrangement." In "Light," the wives again make brief appearances and perform "the laying-on of hands" according to their separate identities. The light is intended to help one "to be understood"; however, the physical act designed to heal one's spirit succeeds only in bringing one "back / from whatever dark to whatever body is." In "Pull of the Earth," the writer holds to a much more confined expectation in touch:

And if in sleep I sometimes
reach for you, across
whatever distances
we dream, across the distance

I am dreaming now,
against silence
and the body's fear of falling,
if I reach across this space—

barely the width of one of us—
and you turn to me,
your full face pale
and perfect as a moon,

dream or real, as the blind
know braille, I follow
that face, its body,
and hold what I can.

As the poet suggests in his first volume, to touch

Stanley Plumly

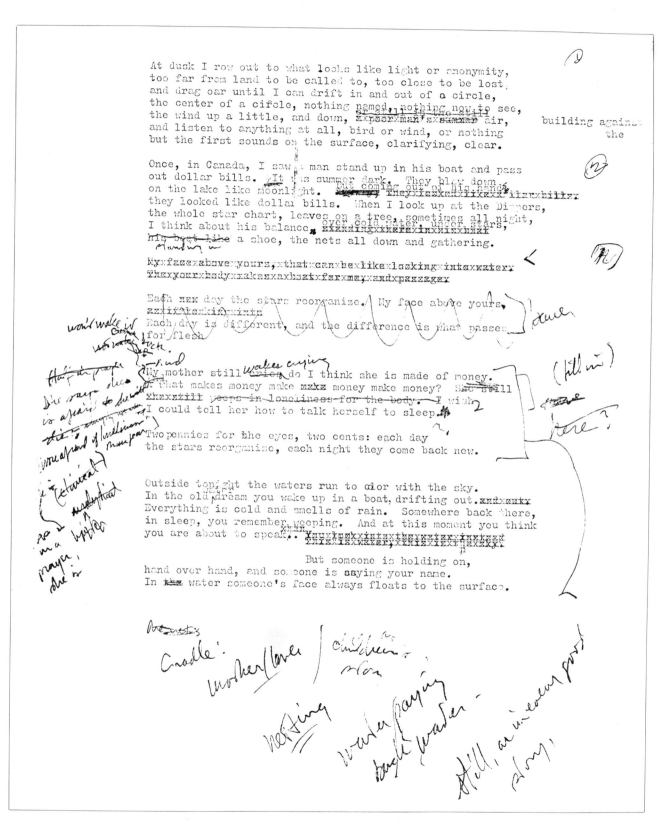

At dusk I row out to what looks like light or anonymity,
too far from land to be called to, too close to be lost,
and drag oar until I can drift in and out of a circle,
the center of a circle, nothing named, nothing now to see,
the wind up a little, and down, ~~xxpoorxmanxsxsummer~~ air,
and listen to anything at all, bird or wind, or nothing
but the first sounds on the surface, clarifying, clear.

building against
the

Once, in Canada, I saw a man stand up in his boat and pass
out dollar bills. It was summer dark. They blew down
on the lake like moonlight. ~~But coming out of his hands~~
they looked like dollar bills. When I look up at the Dippers,
the whole star chart, leaves on a tree, sometimes all night,
I think about his balance, over cold water, under stars,
~~hisxbxxtxxikex~~ a shoe, the nets all down and gathering.

~~Myxfacexabovexyours,xthatxcanxbexlikexlookingxintoxwater.~~
~~Thexyourxbodyxmakesxaxbxxtxforxmexandxpassage.~~

Each new day the stars reorganize. My face above yours,
~~xxiffixxkixxinix~~
Each day is different, and the difference is what passes
for flesh

My mother still ~~cries~~ wakes crying do I think she is made of money.
What makes money make ~~mxkx~~ money make money? She still
~~xkxxxxiii peeps in loneliness for the body.~~ I wish
I could tell her how to talk herself to sleep.

Two pennies for the eyes, two cents: each day
the stars reorganize, each night they come back new.

Outside tonight the waters run to color with the sky.
In the old dream you wake up in a boat, drifting out. ~~andxoutx~~
Everything is cold and smells of rain. Somewhere back there,
in sleep, you remember weeping. And at this moment you think
you are about to speak. ~~Youxlookxintoxthexwaterxinstead~~
~~ThisxisxwaterxxThisxiexthexwaterx~~

                    But someone is holding on,
hand over hand, and someone is saying your name.
In ~~the~~ water someone's face always floats to the surface.

Untitled typescript, revised

172

someone is to share a still moment; yet this touching results in the awareness of being made both fuller and emptier within the self. One transmits through touch the hope of diminishing his personal darkness and emptiness. This leaving of the body is transmitted to another self, who brings to the relationship similar expectations of ridding the self of one's private agonies. When the two selves meet in that middle ground of love, they are for a moment made fuller by each other. Once the touching is completed, however, they return to their separate selves, finding themselves much more keenly aware of their own private darkness, just as the poet is drained when he has completed the poem.

The third section of *Giraffe* is "Horse," an important metaphor for the writer's father. This emblem of beauty, strength, and virility suggests the deep affection the poet feels for his father, who died while the writer was in Europe on his Guggenheim grant in 1973-1974. With his father's death an actuality rather than an inevitability, Plumly's poems dramatically reflect this change. In "By Heart" the poet again recalls his father in his dreams, but now the poetry assumes a painful realism that does not occur in such poems as "One Song."

> In my dream I see you
> dressed out on a table,
> filled with the clinician's blue light—
> ....
>
> This is always like a memory.
> And, Father, I know you know
> these lines by heart.
>
> In every sleep I dream your death.
> I lie down and you lie with me.
> In every room this is still
>
> your house, your history.
> And if in the morning I rise
> like a ghost, outside it is still
>
> winter and sun bright, and snow
> like the memory of a long rain.

In "Counting Coup" the writer goes through the agonizing process of returning for his father's funeral, and in "Summing Up," like "Counting Coup," he adds up the qualified accomplishments of a life now ended:

> These now are the final figures of my father:
> he lies in state in the long boat
> of his own body
> he is perfectly alone
> his arms are tucked into a ceremony

> of sleeves   his face is soft
> he looks like a governor
>
> I have come back a thousand miles for this

The father's death forces the writer into a more intense examination of his own life as he tries to decide its meaning. As "One of Us" suggests, the poet thinks about the future and about "how the mind, all alone, / makes it up in order to deal / with what is coming"; the mind of the writer attempts to create his own future.

Out-of-the-Body Travel demonstrates what the mind "makes up" from the remnants of the past. As the title suggests, the poetic process of evaluation and recreation takes place as the self moves out of the physical body to travel, through dreams and memories, the harrowing landscape of the subconscious mind. Once again the writer probes his most important family relationships; marriages, past and present, are touched upon, but the mother becomes an increasingly important figure in this book, and the most significant subject remains the writer's dead father. By concentrating his focus on his parents, Plumly has created his most compelling and artistically accomplished book of poetry to date.

The mother in *Out-of-the-Body Travel* is a lonely figure trapped in the isolation of her marriage: "the woman in the doorway / who used to call / my name in the summer, / ... the woman who loved / clean floors and rain / on the streets after dark— / who knelt at my ear, / night after night, / whose story / could break your heart / if you listened, the woman / with her forehead pinned to the wall." She is in fact often remembered as standing in a doorway calling the speaker's name at supper time; the image carries in its ordinariness a brief epiphany into the woman's sad loneliness. "Linoleum: Breaking Down" illustrates the quietly desperate process of the mother's breaking down. When she wakes in the morning, she gathers her children around her as she complains of sore arms or legs; she lies on the cold linoleum while her heart races: "And we would lie down with her, my sister / and I, and she would tell us not to worry, / that it was all right, this is what happens, / like a bruise above the heart." Yet, when she urges her children to talk to her, she has nothing to say. Her silence embroils her children in the emotional quagmire of the suffering wife of an alcoholic who tacitly enlists her progeny as solace against the bruises she endures in her life. The scuff marks on her floor gradually cause the linoleum to crack and break; the bruises on the mother's heart cannot be washed away by the rain she loves, and the emotional cracks that run throughout her life cannot be healed. Her husband refers to her as a "weeper," and in "Anothering," the poet agrees: "for days she carries / a weight, like water, / around inside her, as she carried that other, my sister, / for months. In there, she says, / where it's empty." The primary cause for her personal agony is her husband; in "The Iron Lung," she stands " in a doorway / telling my father to die or go away."

The poet's view of marriage is formed by that of his parents, a union marred by emotional pitfalls and ultimate estrangement. In "Brothers & Sisters" the writer alludes to a family photograph as he wonders about the woman who was once aloof and beautiful and about her marriage to his father:

For years now their faces have run together. My father's
lives in my mother's as if by blood. Brother and sister.
She looks down at me from the dream as through a
                                    mirror.
She has the face of a child, somebody small, lunar.
Somebody's always standing by the bed. Sleep is the
                                    story
in which the child falls to the dead, rises, and is loved.

Like the pained union of his father and mother, the poet's marriages, mentioned only briefly but significantly in this volume, reflect emotional estrangement:

I gave my word. And broke it. I gave
it again, broke it again, gave it a third time,
and broke it. So much for honor among wives.

Although this slightly comic shrug toward wives seems to dismiss his earlier marriages, the writer, in "For Hope," uses his fourth wife's name as a rather optimistic omen in giving his word again in marriage and in his art: "This woman you love, in whose face shines / your own, like an oath of sun— Heart, / you say to her, my word, silence is golden." The "word" is expressed not through verbal promises but through silence. Communications between a man and a woman—as witnessed by the poems concerning the writer's mother and father— are certain to be difficult; each partner in a marriage has his or her private self, his or her complex history of relationships, and these elements must affect the marital union:

I lie down in yours with others. Freud says
every fuck is a foursome. I love
you. But the bodies are piling up.
And the girl wanders back and forth
between rooms. There's a dead planet out

there for each of us. That's why we fill
the earth with rooms and lie down together.
That's why I lie down in you with others.

This mocking "Sonnet" clarifies the serious dilemma the poet perceives in one's attempts to share his private self—and all that is cast in its dreams, memories, and subconscious—with another private self and its personal history. The probabilities for failure in such a connection are great.

The most compelling figure in this volume is again the poet's dead father. He is a man who plays the violin, "this finest of furniture," and causes a roomful of relatives to become aware that "this was / drawing of blood . . . They saw even in my father's / face how well he understood the pain / he put them to ." The suffering the father causes others is caught within himself as well. When he must, for instance, slaughter his cattle, as in part 2 of "Out-of-the- Body Travel," the father laments the act: "And in one strike he brings the hammer / down like mercy, so that the young / legs suddenly fly out from under it . . . / he is the good angel Chagell . . . The violin / sustains him." In "Such Counsels" he must stay drunk "a week in a day" to carry out this performance. The image of the father's hammer striking to kill turns horribly on himself in "Horse in the Cage." As the poet dreams about his father's death, he remembers how the man had hit a horse in the face and

    In my dream the horse
rocks in a cage too small, so the cage swings.

I still wake up dreaming, in front of a long face.
That day I hugged the ground hard.

Who knows if my heartbroken father was meant
to last longer than his last good drunk.
They say it's like being kicked by a horse.

You go down, your knees hug up.
You go suddenly wide awake, and the gate shuts.

Perhaps the most significant account of the father concerns the effects of the man's death. In an uncharacteristically long poem, "After Grief," Plumly develops perhaps the most important of his surrealistic dreams about his father as he envisions the man climbing out of his coffin as he wakes among the dead:

    I remember how even near the end
    you would go out to your garden
    just before dark, in the blue air,
    and brood over the failures
    of corn or cabbage

or the crooked row
but meaning the day had once more
failed for you.

. . . .

All this recorded in the dream unending.

The first death was the death of the father.

. . . .

This is the dream that holds the planet
in place.

And you, my anonymous father,
be with me when I wake.

The final lines of the poem suggest two possible roles for the father figure: he may be with his son in the latter's memory when the son awakens from his dream, or he may be there to greet his son as the younger man encounters his first moments of afterlife. In either case, the father exercises an ever-present influence upon the poet.

Stanley Plumly's three major collections of poetry are deeply moving artistic accomplishments. He avoids the potential sentimentality inherent to his subject matter by offering emotionally authentic accuracy. His technical maturity is impressive, but his emotional honesty is his most outstanding quality. His art depends on the uncomfortable revelations of a man nakedly facing the truths of his own psychological character. And because of his great power, Stanley Plumly is a poet of major talent and voice. —*Ronald Baughman*

Other:

"On Stanley Plumly's Poems," by Plumly and Maura Stanton, in "A Symposium of Young Poets," ed. Michael Ryan, *Iowa Review*, 4 (Fall 1973): 54-126;
"The One Thing," in *American Poets in 1976*, ed. William Heyen (Indianapolis: Bobbs-Merrill, 1976), pp. 254-261.

DAVID RAY
(20 May 1932-)

BOOKS: *X-Rays, a Book of Poems* (Ithaca, N.Y.: Cornell University Press, 1965);
Dragging the Main and Other Poems (Ithaca, N.Y.: Cornell University Press, 1968);
A Hill in Oklahoma (Shawnee Mission, Kans.: BkMk Press, 1972);
Gathering Firewood: New Poems and Selected (Middletown, Conn.: Wesleyan University Press, 1974);
Enough of Flying: Poems Inspired by the Ghazals of Ghalib (Calcutta, India: Writers' Workshop, 1977);
The Tramp's Cup (Kirksville, Mo.: Chariton Review Press, 1978);
The Mulberries of Mingo and Other Stories (Austin, Tex.: Cold Mountain Press, 1978).

David Ray was born in Sapulpa, Oklahoma. In 1970 he married, and he and his wife Judy have four children. He was educated at the University of Chicago, receiving his B.A. in 1952 and his M.A. in 1957. Besides being the author of six volumes of poetry, Ray is a teacher, editor, and writer of fiction and literary criticism. He has taught English at Wright Junior College in Chicago (1957-1958), Northern Illinois University (1958-1960), Cornell University (1960-1964), Reed College (1964-1966), and Bowling Green State University (1971). Since 1971 Ray has been on the faculty at the University of Missouri, where, in addition to teaching, he edits the literary quarterly *New Letters*. He has been a visiting lecturer at the University of Iowa (1969-1970) and Syracuse University (1978-1979), and he has given readings on numerous college campuses, at the Poetry Center in New York, at the Library of Congress in Washington, D.C., at the Sorbonne in Paris, and for the BBC radio in England. His work has been widely anthologized and has appeared in popular magazines such as *Harper's* and the *New Yorker*, as well as in numerous literary journals. Among his awards are the *New Republic* Young Writer's Award (1958), the Kossuth Award of the Hungarian Freedom Fighters (1963), the *Kansas City Star* Poetry Prize (1974), and a Woursell fellowship from the University of Vienna, which allowed him to live abroad from 1966 to 1971. Recently he was awarded an editorial fellowship by the National Education Association for his work in developing *New Letters*.

Ray's poetry, which reflects the free verse and "American idiom" of William Carlos Williams, is unpretentious and unembellished. His subjects are wide-ranging, from Goethe to grampa, Pamplona to Sapulpa, sculpture to chiggers. His approach is always direct—he never drifts into obscurity—but his many successful poems transcend the common communication of emotions and impressions. A Ray poem is like a broad, midwestern field from which, out of the tall grass, he pulls the unexpected. He is like the searcher in "Archeology" who digs through the ruins of a run-down farm and finds "the rusty three-pronged / pitchfork . . . that linked Grampa / to the sea." He discovers the small artifacts that link common people with the mysteries of life.

At the age of thirty-three, Ray had his first volume, *X-Rays, A Book of Poems* (1965), published. As he has pointed out in *Contemporary Poets*, the title is significant, and not just because of the pun on his name: "I like the comparisons that have been made of my poems to x-rays or to found objects, as my poems are attempts to render verbal equivalents of what happens inside me or in persons or things I have found in the world and which have given me and sometimes them a different context through my finding them." Behind this comment lies Williams's theory of objectivism, which holds that a poem is more than an effort to copy an object in nature; the poem is a new object, a verbal construct that the poet has created out of his perceptions. The principal concern is with the integrity of the aesthetic object made by the poet rather than with any material object. To emphasize theory, however, is to misrepresent Ray's attitude toward poetry. Like Williams, Ray knows that a poem is not significant simply because it is informed by a coherent theory. In "W.C.W.," Ray says Williams knew that a poet does not always have to write great poems, that his work will be flawed, just as life is flawed. This observation reveals the characteristic honesty of Ray's poetry.

Although *X-Rays* is not his best collection, it has a few pieces that illustrate the simple power of Ray's objectivism. One of the best is "X-Ray," which begins:

> Strangely
>> my mother's sad eyes
>> did not show up
>> on the X-ray
> though I had long since
> swallowed
>> all her sorrows. . . .

Behind the ribs of this poem hides a timid passion, which the reader often finds in Ray. The external object of the poem is an x-ray, cold and scientific; but the aesthetic object is a picture of the poet's psyche, specifically the psychological imprints left by a despondent mother and promiscuous father. The tone is melancholy, threatening to sink into bitterness after the second stanza but rising at the end

to a tentative triumph. The theme of a childhood with uncaring parents recurs in Ray's poetry and fiction. Commenting in *Fifty Contemporary Poets* (1977) on a long poem entitled *Orphans*, he has explained the importance of this theme in his life and work: "*Orphans* is an expression resulting from years of concern with an experience, namely that of having been placed, after a series of very inadequate foster homes, where my sister and I endured such indignities as being locked out of homes, starved, etc., in an institution called The Children's Home in Tulsa. This unforgettable (unforgivable) experience, considering that my mother and other family members were perfectly capable of keeping us, seemed the capping indignity of a childhood defined by poverty and total rejection by both parents, the father by absolute desertion, and the mother by periodic acceptance alternating with abandonment."

From the consistent autobiographical background of Ray's poetry, the reader can piece together a characterization of the author. The scenes in *X-Rays* and other books are primarily rural—a boy picking greens with his mother or drinking from a gourd or worrying about chigger bites—and the reader finds that Ray feels comfortable on farms, in fields. Occasionally he lashes out against what he perceives to be the demons of technological progress (as in "Deathlace," a poem about carbon monoxide), and the reader sees David Ray the activist who, along with Robert Bly, has founded American Writers Against Nuclear Energy. His political convictions, however, appear rarely in his work, with the exception of *Dragging the Main* (1968). Usually he is more confessional than political, and the subjects that rise out of his personal experience have to do not with ideology but with falling in and out of love, teaching an English class, and getting drunk on Jack Daniels.

Ray's second book, *Dragging the Main and Other Poems*, is his most political: roughly a third of its poems include criticism of government, war, or technological society. The concerns of political poetry are usually dogmatic rather than aesthetic, and dogma rarely makes good poetry. Ray's work is no exception. Lines like the following from the third stanza of "Some Notes on Vietnam" are clumsy in their prosaic statements:

> It is time to honor the old Fascists.
> So *Life* looks up Mama Mussolini
> and adores her steaming spaghetti.

When, in the next stanza, Ray focuses on the ordinary person, the inductee rather than the

David Ray and family

general, when his dogma is implicit rather than explicit, when his aim is compassion rather than satire, his poetry is better.

Ray is at his best and most subtle when portraying the emotions involved in a sexual relationship, whether they be love, fear, or despair. In the fine title poem of the book, he describes an encounter between a man strolling around town in the evening and a woman who is "dragging the main." When she glances at him, he says,

> I thought the love that had
> Once thrown me away was sneaking up
> On four tires and about to say
>
> You get right in here.

He continues to walk, and she continues to drive, passing him again and again. The poem fully captures the braking/revving rhythm of their game; its images suggest the sexual teasing of their encounter. Finally, the woman stops, rolls down her window, and speaks:

> She said it wasn't love stinging my face
> But only the pure cars of America that
> Were dragging the main, looking for fools
> Who want to hold even the lights of Main

Street, and the sweetness of a face.

"Dragging the Main" is successful not only for its description of a modern American ritual but for the persona's honest acceptance of the lesson that sexual excitement is not love.

In 1972 Ray had a small book of fourteen poems entitled *A Hill in Oklahoma* published. All but two of these poems were later included in *Gathering Firewood: New Poems and Selected* (1974), a significant volume with a broad range of subject matter and technique. Some of the new pieces are very short—two, three, or four lines. Other poems are relatively long, sixty lines and more, but the typical piece is a free-verse lyric of between ten and thirty lines. Ray's technique is based on conversational diction and accessible images rather than on tricks of prosody. Communication is important to him, and he has the courage, working with a genre in which simplicity is suspect, to say plainly what he means. In "Speaking" he questions himself on the matter of clarity:

> Have I made the mistake
> of trying to be too
>   transparent
> to some human being?
> ....

177

David Ray

Ralph Eugene Meatyard's Pictures

All nature is a meatyard
and sometimes the soul is caught
As it leaps aside,
a swipe of paint against
a clapboard barn,
or bushes he once,
~~caught in a boy,~~
got lost in,
or a lady with legs, crossed arms
And ~~I think too~~
~~of~~ Abelard
~~who~~ believed that all
God permitted was good
and that God would not
undo the good,
and then they came to take away
his woman and his manhood
~~and~~ if the best
God could do
was take away the best
love ~~that ever man~~ found
in ~~less than~~ a thousand years,

one's scholastic logic /might

~~have needed revis~~ed —
*But the meaning of de faith
is to believe
& to an artist
to go on to the end
as if one were to end*

David Ray

"Ralph Eugene Meatyard's Pictures," *revised typescript*

178

Everywhere behind us, grieving
waters. . . .

The last two lines quoted show Ray at his most ambiguous, reacting seriously to a criticism of his poetic transparency; but this ambiguity is unusual for him. The poem's beginning, direct and conversational, is much more typical. Ray's opening lines are almost always prosaic, as if he is afraid that obscure verse will intimidate the reader. He is careful, however, to make his poems more than broken prose, and after a conversational opening, his poems condense, the images intensify, and the mood resounds deeper and deeper.

This aesthetic strategy is perhaps most evident and most successful in his poems of European travel. "In Heraklion" provides a good example of this developing intensity, here achieved by evoking the myths of the Minoan Empire. The beginning is literal, until the speaker mentions "riches" in line 4:

When we counted out the few coins in our purse
at the hotel desk
and found out we had enough to take a bath
they did not guess what riches we took with
us. . . .

Then the poem recalls the lovers' visit to Knossos, site of the ancient Cretan civilization, and by the end of the poem, the two people have entered the myth of King Minos:

so they didn't try to take you away
from me and it was easy
to pay for a room and watch my
princess sink into the ancient pool.

Gathering Firewood has many fine poems like this one that combine simple descriptions of simple events with the complex mysteries of love, death, and time.

Ray's next book, *Enough of Flying* (1977), is a sequence of love lyrics inspired by the *Ghazals of Ghalib* (Urdu poems by the Indian poet Mirza Ghalib, which Ray read in the English translations produced by the collaboration of Aijaz Ahmad and seven American poets and published by Columbia University Press in 1971). *Enough of Flying* is an unusual collection of eighty-six short poems that are not, strictly speaking, *ghazals* (poems of five or more independent couplets) but that are sometimes haikulike and sometimes epigrammatic in their statements. Lyric 78, for example, compares two lovers with insects and ends with a brief, joyful image like a haiku:

as our wings dry,
a giant leap or two
fluttering.

Many of the shorter poems have the quick flash of beauty leading to a smoldering development of meaning that is the mark of good haiku. Other pieces rely on direct statement, such as "How can we recover our strangeness / to each other?" (lyric 48) and "We have been the most fantastic / places together" (lyric 6). A few of the longer poems have the conversational rhythms and tones of Ray's more typical work and would not seem out of place in *Gathering Firewood*. Lyric 57, presenting lovers as metaphoric gladiators, is similar in approach to "In Heraklion," although it lacks the unity and intensity of the latter. *Enough of Flying* is not one of Ray's more successful books; although it has some fine passages, overall its poetry is insubstantial. Read one right after another, the pieces begin to sound alike. To Western sensibilities, in general, haiku and other very short lyric forms seem minor, incapable of greatness simply because there is a limit to how much can be said or implied in three or four lines. Ray's intention, however, is not to strive for greatness but to "provide glitterings from the facets of that diamond, love," and *Enough of Flying* does just that.

Ray's latest work is his best. *The Tramp's Cup* (1978) is a book of voyages: most of its poems seem to have been written or inspired during the travels of the Ray family through Mexico, England, Italy, Greece, Morocco, and back to Missouri. As is true in *Gathering Firewood*, the poems with foreign locations are usually his most satisfying because different cultures provide Ray with rich traditions and myths. The poet makes the same use of native materials in a few fine poems such as "Archeology" and "Dragging the Main," but usually his rural America pieces offer little more than regional color. On the other hand, when Ray is in Heraklion, Crete, or Uxmal, Mexico, his objective, foreign perception finds the symbols (Minoan ruins, phallic temples) that characterize the history and culture of a people.

The poet of *The Tramp's Cup* seems caught in a dilemma: he is a happily married, accomplished, middle-aged man traveling with his family—his personal world is secure—but what he sees, what he feels he ought to write about, are the "rats of Venice," the lonely widow on an English train, or gypsy women "quite hopelessly" washing clothes. The theme of the title poem, which is also an implicit theme in the whole volume, is that perfect

David Ray

contentment may be possible only in the life of a tramp, the simple life of a man without job, home, property, or responsibilities. Ray describes the advantages of his life-style in the ending of "The Tramp's Cup":

> All one really needs
> is to keep out
> the damp.
> He had learned that well
> and had not an enemy
> in the world, had nothing
> to fear, nothing
> to lose, nothing
> to stop loving him.
> And thus his cup of tea was sweet.

Because he enjoys and believes in this itinerant life-style, Ray is contented in the voyages of *The Tramp's Cup*; for this reason, the poems about poverty, hardship, and loneliness do not quite ring true. However, poems such as "A Dance on the Greek Island," which is about the carefree Greek spirit, are consistent with Ray's vision and show the poet at his best and most mature. *The Tramp's Cup* is a relatively large volume of approximately one hundred poems, and although there are many pieces that fail, there are more than enough that delight the reader and justify his respect for Ray's poetry.

Ray has recently completed fellowships at Yaddo and the Millay Colony, where he has been working primarily on a novel entitled "The Orphans of Mingo." He is not a newcomer to fiction, having published a volume of short stories, *The Mulberries of Mingo* (1978), and several other stories in magazines. But even though he is concentrating on fiction for the time being, he is too fine a poet to leave poetry for very long. Contemporary poetry needs clear, honest voices like that of David Ray.

—*Deno Trakas*

Other:

The Chicago Review Anthology, edited by Ray (Chicago: University of Chicago Press, 1959);
From the Hungarian Revolution, edited by Ray (Ithaca, N.Y.: Cornell University Press, 1965);
A Poetry Reading Against the Vietnam War, edited by Ray and Robert Bly (Madison, Minn.: American Writers Against the Vietnam War, 1966);
Richard Wright: Impressions and Perspectives, edited by Ray and Robert M. Farnsworth (Ann Arbor: University of Michigan Press, 1973);
"Orphans" [poem and comments], in *Fifty Contem-*

porary Poets: The Creative Process, ed. Alberta T. Turner (New York: McKay, 1977), pp. 252-260;
The Jack Conroy Reader, edited by Ray and Jack Salzman (New York: Burt Franklin, 1979).

References:

Hayden Carruth, "Poetic Tradition and the Individual Talent," *Harper's*, 258 (May 1979): 89;
Elliott Coleman, "Priceless Catch," *Nation*, 208 (17 March 1969): 345-346.

ISHMAEL REED
(22 February 1938-)

BOOKS: *The Free-Lance Pallbearers* (Garden City: Doubleday, 1967; London: MacGibbon & Kee, 1968);
Yellow Back Radio Broke-Down (Garden City: Doubleday, 1969; London: Allison & Busby, 1971);
Catechism of D NeoAmerican Hoodoo Church (London: Paul Breman, 1970);
Conjure Selected Poems, 1963-1970 (Amherst: University of Massachusetts Press, 1972);
Mumbo Jumbo (Garden City: Doubleday, 1972);
Chattanooga (New York: Random House, 1973);
The Last Days of Louisiana Red (New York: Random House, 1974);
Flight To Canada (New York: Random House, 1976);
A Secretary to the Spirits (New York: NOK, 1978).

Ishmael Reed was born in Chattanooga, Tennessee, the son of Bennie and Thelma Coleman Reed. At age four he moved with his mother to Buffalo, New York, where later he attended the University of Buffalo (now the State University of New York at Buffalo) between 1956 and 1960. He married, but later divorced, Priscilla Rose, and he has a daughter, Timothy Brett. He presently lives in Berkeley, California, with his wife, the choreographer Carla Blank.

In New York City during the early 1960s he started writing "visionary poetry" and associated with writers in the Umbra Workshop, "the institution," Reed says, "which began the current inflorescence of 'Black Poetry' as well as many other recent Afro-American styles of writing." In 1965 he cofounded the *East Village Other,* an early example of the "New Journalism" that incorporated the work of artists and writers into "collage newspapers."

After leaving New York in 1967, Reed settled in Berkeley, California, and taught writing at the University of California. Although he was denied tenure in 1977, he continues to lecture, consult, and conduct writing courses. The denial of tenure, coupled with conflicts over his teaching while he was a visiting professor at the University of Washington in Seattle in 1969-1970, incited his bitterness against white-dominated university academia. Much of his fiction and poetry reflects this cynicism.

Reed's interest in publishing led to his establishment on the West Coast of the Yardbird Publishing Company with Al Young; the company publishes works of different ethnic groups in the *Yardbird Reader.* Young and Reed felt that American publications reflected only a single culture in a country consisting of many cultures. The company is named for Charlie "Yardbird" Parker whose jazz renditions captured in music the same free spirit the editors espouse for literature. The publishing interest expanded into Reed, Cannon and Johnson Communications Company, which publishes novels and produces the *Steve Cannon Show,* an audio-cassette magazine containing interviews, jazz concerts, "soap opera," and poetry. Reed hopes that the company may some day support the television shows of Afro-American and nonnative American producers in a field otherwise closed to them.

As an active promoter of Afro-American artists, Reed helped organize in 1965 the American Festival of Negro Art, the first major Afro-American cultural organization. He is also interested in helping students and aspiring writers. Students from his writing courses, with his help, are working on publishing a national anthology of student writing.

For his fiction and poetry Reed has received several awards. In 1974 he received a National Endowment for the Arts Grant and in 1975 a Rosenthal Foundation Award for *The Last Days of Louisiana Red* as well as a Guggenheim Fellowship. In 1973 both his book of poetry *Conjure* (1972) and his novel *Mumbo Jumbo* (1972) were nominated for National Book Awards. *Chattanooga* (1973) was recommended for a Pulitzer Prize in the same year.

Reed might be viewed as a pioneering American defining a true American literature. Just as William Butler Yeats, a writer whom he admires, created a myth by reviving his native Irish culture, so Reed wants to reshape America's sense of its own heritage.

Americans, he feels, do not know where their cultural origins lie. A nearsighted view leads them back to England, but the American tradition is eclectic, made up of a combination of numerous groups, and not just the one tradition that, in Reed's opinion, has grown stale. To distribute the literature of ethnic Americans to bookstores around the country, Reed has formed the Before Columbus coalition, which he hopes will help America rediscover its diverse literary heritage.

For many writers who work in several genres, one genre may be used as practice for the other. With Reed, this is not the case. He enjoys all forms of writing and is equally proficient in all. In the introduction to *Shrovetide in Old New Orleans* (1978), he states: "I can't say which form, fiction, poetry, or the essay, requires the most discipline. . . . I'd say I get the most kicks out of writing poetry; fiction is the second most fun; the essay is the ditch-digging occupation of writing." Although Reed may enjoy writing fiction and poetry, its entertainment for the reader is often overshadowed by the author's cynicism and bitterness. Whereas many black writers express a black consciousness directed to a black brotherhood, Ishmael Reed goes a step beyond conventional black aesthetics to embrace America's eclecticism and thereby to create a mythology that incorporates all subcultures comprising the one *American* culture.

According to Reed's mythology, the cycles of history are recurrences of the conflict between oppressor and oppressed. Taking early Egyptian culture as a point from which all subsequent cultures evolved, he fabulates his version of the repeating cycles of history, only changing the figures that represent protagonists and antagonists. While the novels tend to explain the myth in narrative form, the poems capture glimpses of segments of a cycle. For instance, while the novel *Mumbo Jumbo* traces the pattern in history, going back four thousand years to Egypt, some of the poetry in *Catechism of D NeoAmerican Hoodoo Church* (1970) recalls America's Wild West, one part of the cycle.

Because the American culture has African, West Indian, American Indian, European, and Oriental origins, it is conglomerate. The perfect American aesthetic Reed envisions will not evolve on its own because, he feels, American cultural patterns have become entrenched in a European tradition, which stifles free-flowing ideas. Reed wants to act as a catalyst and "stir things up a bit," to start the reaction that will eventually produce the true national literature. Since inciting critical contro-

Ishmael Reed

versy has always been Reed's aim, he challenged the established literary scene with his first novel, *The Free-Lance Pallbearers* (1967). Although reviewers did not give it great praise, it was the beginning of his development of his myth theme, fragments of which appear in his poems, works Reed uses to vent his ire. In his four volumes of poetry, he experiments with different techniques, moving from the oral tradition of black writing captured in the first volume, *Catechism of D NeoAmerican Hoodoo Church* (1970), into the more formal diction of social commentary in the last, *A Secretary to the Spirits* (1978).

In *Catechism of D NeoAmerican Hoodoo Church*, with "Badman of the guest professor," Reed satirizes the pretentious language of college professors by writing the poem in black slang. "I am a cowboy in the boat of Ra" places the ancient Egyptian deity in the American West. Ra, the sun god, who symbolizes Reed's sense of spiritual freedom, and the cowboy, who symbolizes America, together will "unseat Set," the figure who is suppressing freedom. "Catechism of d neoamerican hoodoo church" assails those who criticize him and best explains the basis of Reed's ideas for a cultural

rebirth. He calls for a new American art based on the aesthetics of hoodoos—"free spirits who / need no / monarch." This art will encourage freedom of expression for the individual—"WHAT WILL WORK / FOR YOU." The establishment belongs to the white man who will now pay the "tab" for oppressing blacks, mere "junk beneath yr feet." Reed sees himself as the necromancer, carrying a black cat, casting the spells to "end two thousand years / of bad news." He was rightfully named *Ishmael*, an outcast from the established system who could survive and endure.

Conjure contains not only the poems of *Catechism of D NeoAmerican Hoodoo Church* but also additional poems that echo the musical and rhythmical quality of the black dialect. Although the poems attain lyrical excellence, Reed's anger permeates the poetry. His statement in the introduction to *19 Necromancers From Now* (1970) illuminates his purpose and indicates the source for the title *Conjure*: "The Afro-American artist is similar to the Necromancer. . . . He is a conjuror who works JuJu upon his oppressors. . . ."

Reed explains in the foreword to *Conjure* that four of the poems were put to music but were turned

Ishmael Reed

182

down by record companies because they were full of "black magic." "Betty's Ball Blues" and "Mojo Queen of the Feathery Plumes" describe sorceresses casting spells over their men. "The Black Cock" is dedicated to Jimi Hendrix, whom Reed calls a natural "HooDoo." His music "crows" to the "torture" blacks have lived under. "The Wardrobe Master of Paradise" designs clothes "from ancient patterns," not "the phony / trends." Use of rhyme and regular meter sets these four poems apart from others with similar themes but less regular form.

Besides poems berating Reed's adversaries, there are those relating to his myth. "The Neo-HooDoo Aesthetic" reiterates the call for creative freedom. It is written as a recipe with no specific measurements because "The proportions of ingredients used depend / upon the cook!" "Neo-HooDoo Manifesto" is a prose poem defining the nature of "Neo-HooDoos," the people Reed feels manifest the spirit of Haitian voodoo in which they have their origins: "Neo-Hoodoo believes that every man is an artist and every artist a priest. You can bring your own creative ideas to Neo-Hoodoo."

Because he believes that American literature should encompass the various American cultures and their origins, Reed must reestablish identity with his roots. The poems in *Chattanooga* pertain to the city where he was born and involve the artist's recapturing his past. Unlike the social protest poems of *Conjure*, these poems are personal. For example, Reed offers several poems on lost loves, and as his birthday approaches, he comments on his advancing age. In other poems his figures of speech suggest analogies to his emotions. Most noteworthy is the last poem of the volume, "Jacket Notes," where he confesses, "Being a colored poet / Is like going over / Niagara Falls in a / Barrel." Reed's anger exudes from between the lines. Without being sentimental, he metaphorically bemoans his plight—the difficulty of being a black poet when everything is against him: the barrel maker does not think he will make it; the tourists watch him, hoping he will fall on his face. Even nature seems to be against him because "A mile from the brink / It begins to storm."

Although the volume ends with a sense of defeat, the speakers of other poems seem to gain strength in fighting against their foes. Returning to Chattanooga helps the poet to regain his self-confidence, despite his initial shock on seeing the area for the first time after a long absence. "The Katskills Kiss Romance Goodbye" describes the poet's reaction to a city changed with time. Progress has altered the neighborhoods; women are liberated; the militant men are now placid. Facing the reality

of these changes is difficult but important for the poet. The first poem, "Chattanooga," discloses the importance of his idealized memories of his place of birth. The city symbolizes all he has conquered: a woman he has possessed, a battle he has won, or odds he has overcome:

> Chattanooga is something you
> Can have anyway you want it
> The summit of what you are.

Reed notes that, historically, Chattanooga has represented pinnacles of different sorts to others. During the Civil War, it was an important stronghold to General Grant; to the Cherokee, it was "a rock that / Comes to a point." To the black poet, obsessed with the importance of freedom, his Southern origins represent a link to his slave forefathers. He sees that having once been enslaved, attaining freedom is much more meaningful—"To get to Chattanooga you must / Go through your Tennessee." Chattanooga transcends its earthly location to symbolize the essence of freedom. Without criticizing or blaming anyone for his misfortunes, Reed speaks in this poem as poet of mankind. Unfortunately, Reed fails to write another poem like "Chattanooga."

The poetry in the most recent collection, *A Secretary to the Spirits*, returns to the tone of verbal tirade that characterizes Reed's social protests. In these poems, he no longer employs the device of black dialect written as it is pronounced; the rhythm of the earlier poems is missing. In its place is more emphasis on the power of language as social commentary, scathing assaults on the established system.

"Poem Delivered Before Assembly of Colored People Held at Glide Memorial Church, Oct. 4, 1973 and Called to Protest Recent Events in the Sovereign Republic of Chile" berates Richard Nixon. Compared to him, writes Reed, Hitler is a "Kindergarten aide." "The Return of Julian the Apostate to Rome" suggests the cyclical pattern of history in Reed's myth by juxtaposing ancient Rome's corruption against that of today. In contrast to the poems criticizing society, "Sky Diving" depicts the poet in a reflective mood. Metaphorically linking a skydiver, a shooting star, and a successful poet, Reed realizes that "brilllance" will quickly be extinguished. Thus, he must anticipate his decline and "Learn how to fall." "A Secretary to the Spirits" restates Reed's idea of his ability to endure and rise, in this case, from "errand boy for the spirits" to "Secretary to / the Spirits." With dedicated work, he hopes to become a spiritual leader. *A Secretary to the Spirits* is an experiment in collaboration between Reed and the artist Betye Saar. Both artist and poet envision a multicultural art. In their collaborative efforts, they have successfully unified two forms into one harmonious unit. Saar's Egyptian collages make visual the historical origins and repeating cycle of history that Reed suggests in the poems.

Read as a whole, Ishmael Reed's poetry is full of wrathful indignation at white racists and blacks who are sycophants to white expectations. Although he has honest intentions, his anger is occasionally a detriment in his writing. Furthermore, his purpose, to stimulate "new" literature written in response to his satire, is often precluded by the very intensity of his criticism and his vituperatively humorous depiction of the facts of history. Reed's search for new art forms is more noteworthy in his fiction than in his poetry. Even if he cannot define or create the true multicultural American literature, he will force readers into an awareness of the need for it by inciting literary controversy. —*Caroline G. Bokinsky*

Other:

19 Necromancers from Now, edited by Reed (Garden City: Doubleday, 1970);

Yardbird Lives!, edited by Reed and Al Young (New York: Grove, 1978);

Yardbird Reader, volumes 1-5, edited by Reed

(Berkeley: Yardbird Publishing, 1971-1977);

Shrovetide in Old New Orleans (Garden City: Doubleday, 1978).

Interviews:

John O'Brien, "Ishmael Reed," in *The New Fiction*, ed. Joe David Bellamy (Urbana: University of Illinois, 1974);

Ishmael Reed, "The Writer as Seer: Ishmael Reed on Ishmael Reed," *Black World*, 23 (June 1974): 20-34;

Cameron Northouse, "Ishmael Reed," *Conversations with Writers*, volume 2 (Detroit: Bruccoli Clark / Gale, 1978).

References:

George Lamming, Review of *Conjure, New York Times Book Review*, 6 May 1973, pp. 36-37;

Neil Schmitz, "Down Home with Ishmael Reed," review of *Chattanooga, Modern Poetry Studies*, 5 (Autumn 1974): 205-207;

Schmitz, "Neo-HooDoo: The Experimental Fiction of Ishmael Reed," *Twentieth Century Literature*, 20 (April 1974): 126-140;

Schmitz, "The Poetry of Ishmael Reed," review of *Conjure, Modern Poetry Studies*, 4 (Autumn 1973): 218-221.

Adrienne Rich

Anne Newman
University of North Carolina at Charlotte

BIRTH: Baltimore, Maryland, 16 May 1929, to Arnold Rice and Helen Jones Rich.

EDUCATION: A.B., Radcliffe College, 1951.

AWARDS: Yale Series of Younger Poets prize for *A Change of World*, 1951; Guggenheim Fellowships, 1952, 1961; Ridgely Torrence Memorial Award (Poetry Society of America), 1955; Grace Thayer Bradley Award (Friends of Literature) for *The Diamond Cutters*, 1956; National Institute of Arts and Letters Award, 1960; Phi Beta Kappa poet, College of William and Mary, 1960; Bollingen Foundation grant for translation, 1962; Amy Lowell Traveling Fellowship, 1962; Bess Hokin Prize (*Poetry* magazine), 1963; Phi Beta Kappa poet, Swarthmore College, 1965; Phi Beta Kappa poet, Harvard University, 1966; Litt.D., Wheaton College, 1967; Eunice Tietjens Memorial Prize (*Poetry* magazine), 1968; National Endowment for the Arts Grant, 1969-1970; Shelley Memorial Award, 1971; Ingram-Merrill Foundation grant, 1973; National Book Award for *Diving into the Wreck*, 1974.

SELECTED BOOKS: *Ariadne, A Play in Three Acts and Poems* (Baltimore: J. H. Furst, 1939);

Not I, But Death, A Play in One Act (Baltimore: J. H. Furst, 1941);

A Change of World (New Haven: Yale University Press, 1951; London: Oxford University Press, 1952);

The Diamond Cutters and Other Poems (New York: Harper, 1955);

Snapshots of a Daughter-in-Law: Poems, 1954-1962 (New York & Evanston: Harper & Row, 1963; London: Chatto & Windus / Hogarth Press, 1970);

Necessities of Life: Poems, 1962-1965 (New York: Norton, 1966);

Selected Poems (London: Chatto & Windus / Hogarth Press, 1967);

Leaflets: Poems 1965-1968 (New York: Norton, 1969; London: Chatto & Windus / Hogarth Press, 1972);

The Will to Change (New York: Norton, 1971; London: Chatto & Windus, 1972);

Diving into the Wreck: Poems, 1971-1972 (New York: Norton, 1973);

Poems: Selected and New, 1950-1974 (New York: Norton, 1975);

Of Woman Born (New York: Norton, 1976; London: Virago, 1977);

The Dream of a Common Language: Poems, 1974-1977 (New York: Norton, 1978);

On Lies, Secrets, and Silence: Selected Prose 1966-1978 (New York: Norton, 1979).

Adrienne Rich has made significant contributions as a critic, a scholar, and a teacher; but she speaks most importantly as a poet. Her work sustains her belief that "Poetry is above all a concentration of the *power* of language which is the power of our ultimate relationship to everything in the universe." Her poetry is remarkably integrated with other dimensions of her life, and changes in form and tone from volume to volume reflect changes in her personal life and consciousness. Rich grew up in Baltimore, Maryland. Her father, a physician, encouraged her to read and to write, and she was sensitive to his criticism and praise. Two pieces of juvenilia (a three-act play and poems published when she was ten; a one-act play published when she was twelve) are indications of the early support for Rich's interest in writing. She graduated with honors from Radcliffe College in 1951, the same year her first collection of poetry was published. In 1953 she married Alfred H. Conrad, an economist teaching at Harvard University. Their three sons, David, Paul, and Jacob, were born in 1955, 1957, and 1959. During this period Rich continued to write and publish poetry. In 1966 the family moved from Cambridge, Massachusetts, to New York City when her husband began teaching at City College of New York. Rich began her own teaching career, which

has included positions at Swarthmore College, Columbia University, Brandeis University, and City College of New York. After her husband's death in 1970, Rich continued to live in New York City, and taught at various times at City College, Brandeis University (as Hurst Visiting Professor), and Douglass College. Since 1976 she has lived with the writer and historian Michelle Cliff, and in 1979 they left New York, moving to western Massachusetts. Rich has published nine volumes of poetry and a considerable body of nonfiction prose. She is recognized as one of the best contemporary American poets and has received a number of prizes and awards, including the National Book Award for Poetry in 1974, which she rejected as an individual award but accepted as cowinner with Audre Lord, in the name of all women.

Rich's early poetry emphasizes the ways in which one copes with frustration and pain by imposing the mind and will upon the emotions to control experience, and her traditional forms and language express this attitude toward life. But she has come to believe that language has been subverted from its true purpose, to give a sense of personal and communal fulfillment, and has become instead a manipulative tool of destructive forces in society. Her sense of urgency for change that will reconstitute language and restore its life-giving power becomes a driving force and a major principle of form in her poetry. As Rich's vision centers upon women as the hope for survival of the world—a world that she sees as having denied to women the validity of their emotions, the wisdom of their nature, and the strength of their unity—her style gradually becomes more open and personal, and in her latest works it reaches visionary power.

A Change of World (1951), published when Rich was only twenty-one, was selected by W. H. Auden for the Yale Series of Younger Poets. In his introduction to the collection, Auden praised her mastery of form, delicacy, and restraint from striving for intense individuality. Other critical comments support Auden's evaluation, finding this volume remarkable for so young a poet. In a 1971 essay, "When We Dead Awaken: Writing as Re-Vision," Rich herself comments upon her early poetry: "I know that my style was formed first by male poets: ... Frost, Dylan Thomas, Donne, Auden, MacNeice, Stevens, Yeats. What I learned chiefly from them was craft." She practiced the craft she learned from the major models of her college days with skill and grace, speaking chiefly through personae or using other distancing techniques, following the prevalent poetic ideal of objectivity that was intended to

Adrienne Rich

express the universal through restraint of open, personal emotion. Her major themes, too, were among the most often employed of the time: the poems in *A Change of World* concern sterility and loss in modern life. Art itself, isolated and pure, is seen as the primary source of fulfillment and protection in a world of threatening change. Several poems directly concern the effort to confine and control emotion through aesthetic form. "At a Bach Concert," for example, reveals Rich's concept of poetry at this period of her life, as she defines it through an analogy to music: "A too-compassionate art is half an art. / Only such proud restraining purity / Restores the else-betrayed, too-human heart." In "Storm Warnings," a directive for living with "weather abroad" and "weather in the heart," the speaker draws the curtains and lights "candles sheathed in glass." This fragile protection is the "sole defense against the season." Both poems are early examples of Rich's skill in using extended metaphor to define ideas and emotions, a technique that is effective throughout her canon.

Two other poems that deal with defense against inner turmoil are portraits of women engaged in handiwork. Even this early in her work, Rich extends the meaning of this traditional activity beyond its usual implication of passive, patient acceptance. In "Mathilde in Normandy" the woman waits for men who are away at war:

> Say what you will, anxiety there too
> Played havoc with the skein, and the knots came
> When fingers' occupation and mind's attention
> Grew too divergent.

Here the pattern has been distorted by violent activities that divert the mind. All handiwork images—weaving, knitting, embroidering—become increasingly important in Rich's poetry as a major metaphor for life-forces. She sees life as a fabric, with the individual strands becoming part of a complex pattern that can be made beautiful through conscious effort. But the pattern, she sees, may have many false starts and distortions; strands must frequently be pulled out, mistakes unraveled; and the sense of loss and pain must be accepted as part of the life-weaving process. Breakage, then, may be necessary and constructive, leading to birth or rebirth; or destructive, leading to sterility or death. Images of wounds, blood, cutting instruments, and fire carry both possibilities and are defined in context as either life-giving or life-denying. Consistently on the life-giving side, however, are natural images related to earth and sea, as opposed to images of dryness related to restrictive power systems of society.

Early in her career Rich was not fully aware of the real nature of her conflicts, and the pattern of images and motifs that begins to develop here is partially unconscious. As she says in reference to another poem in this collection that includes the handiwork image as a symbol of subdued creative energy:

> poems are like dreams: in them you put what you don't know you know. Looking back at poems I wrote before I was twenty-one, I'm startled because beneath the conscious craft are glimpses of the split I even then experienced between the girl who wrote poems, who defined herself in writing poems, and the girl who was to define herself by her relationships with men.

The portrait of the woman in "Aunt Jennifer's Tigers" is presented with economy through the tension of opposing images: the condition of Aunt Jennifer herself,

> Aunt Jennifer's fingers fluttering through her wool
> Find even the ivory needle hard to pull.
> The massive weight of Uncle's wedding band
> Sits heavily upon Aunt Jennifer's hand.

is poised against her choice of subject for the tapestry: "The tigers in the panel that she made / Will go on prancing, proud and unafraid." Rich's further comments on this poem give insights into both the form and intention of much of her earlier poetry:

> It was important to me that Aunt Jennifer was a person as distinct from myself as possible—distanced by the formalism of the poem, by its objective, observant tone. . . . In those years formalism was part of the strategy—like asbestos gloves, it allowed me to handle materials I couldn't pick up bare-handed.

Thus her first collection, which has been justly praised for its fine craftsmanship, has many echoes of her masters and muted notes of her personal voice.

Rich's second volume, *The Diamond Cutters and Other Poems* (1955), continues in much the same tone and style; again the major theme is the need for caution and control in art and life. The title poem proposes as a model the diamond cutters' techniques of cutting and polishing the gem: "Be serious, because / The stone may have contempt / For too-familiar hands," and "Respect the adversary, / Meet it with tools refined, / And thereby set your price." The form of the poem, like the art it defines, is delicate and controlled.

A number of the poems, written while Rich was

TRANSCENDENTAL ETUDE
(FOR MICHELLE CLIFF)

This August evening I've been driving
over backroads fringed with queen anne's lace
my car startling young deer in meadows——one
gave a coarse intake of her breath and all
four fawns sprang after her
into the dark maples.
Three months from today they'll be fair game
for the hit-and-run hunters, glorying
in a weekend's destructive power,
triggers fingered by drunken gunmen, sometimes
so inept as to leave the shattered animal
stunned in her blood. But this evening deep in summer
the deer are still alive and free,
nibbling apples from early-laden boughs
so weighted, so englobed
with already yellowing fruit
they seem eternal, Hesperidean
in the clear-tuned, cricket-throbbing air.

Later I stood in the dooryard,
my nerves singing the immense
fragility of all this sweetness,
this green world already sentimentalized, photographed,
advertised to death. Yet, it persists
stubbornly beyond the fake Vermont
of antique barnboards glazed into discothèques,
artificial snow, the sick Vermont of children
conceived in apathy, grown to winters
of rotgut violence,
poverty gnashing its teeth like a blind cat at their lives.
Still, it persists. Turning off onto a dirt road

from the raw cuts bulldozed through a quiet village
for the tourist run to Canada,
I've sat on a stone fence above a great, soft, sloping field
of musing heifers, a farmstead
slanting its planes calmly in the calm light,
a dead elm raising bleached arms
above a green so dense with life,
minute, momentary life——slugs, moles, pheasants, gnats,
spiders, moths, hummingbirds, groundhogs, butterflies——
a lifetime is too narrow
to understand it all, beginning with the huge
rockshelves that underlie all that life.

No one ever told us we had to study our lives,
make of our lives a study, as if learning natural history
or music, that we should begin
with the simple exercises first
and slowly go on trying
the hard ones, practicing till strength
and accuracy became one with the daring
to leap into transcendence, take the chance
of breaking down in the wild arpeggio
or faulting the full sentence of the fugue.
—And in fact we can't live like that: we take on
everything at once before we've even begun
to read or mark time, we're forced to begin
in the midst of the hardest movement,
the one already sounding as we are born.
At most we're allowed a few months
of simply listening to the simple line
of a woman's voice singing a child
against her heart. Everything else is too soon,
too sudden, the wrenching-apart, that woman's heartbeat
heard ever after from a distance,

· 72 ·

· 73 ·

"Transcendental Etude," corrected proof

187

Adrienne Rich

traveling in England and Europe on a Guggenheim Fellowship in 1952-1953, are about famous places. These, and even less exotic spots, are viewed through the detachment of the tourist, though the particular scene may act as backdrop for a subdued expression of pain in a fallen world. "A Walk by the Charles" is a fine poem of this type in which the visual and musical renditions of landscape combine with philosophical contemplation.

The language of the poems is often dependent upon literary allusion and authority, and the style upon her mentors, as are these lines from "Lucifer in the Train" with their echoes from Wallace Stevens (specifically "Sunday Morning"), but without Stevens's creative vitality:

> Once out of heaven, to an angel's eye
> Where is the bush or cloud without a flaw?
> What bird but feeds upon mortality
> Flies to its young with carrion in its claw?

That Rich is able to echo different models is evident in this book. For example, in two monologues she skillfully maintains the conversational tone within the iambic pentameter form, but the Frostian manner is so marked that it becomes distracting. In these poems, she reveals the marriage relationship as the center of the problem: the woman speaking in "The Perennial Answer" responds to her frustration with a destructive, neurotic energy; the woman in "Autumn Equinox" with quiet acceptance of her diminished expectations of life.

The Diamond Cutters has been recognized for strengths similar to those of Rich's first volume; but mixed with the strong praise are hints of disappointment—questioning whether she is growing as a poet or settling into, and for, an achieved style with too much facility and overdependence on models. Rich's own reaction supports this doubt: "By the time that book came out I was already dissatisfied with those poems, which seemed to me mere exercises for poems I hadn't written." That she refused to continue writing in a form she had outgrown is clearly demonstrated in her next book.

During the eight years between the publication of *The Diamond Cutters* and *Snapshots of a Daughter-in-Law* (1963), Rich had heavy responsibilities as a wife and the mother of three young sons. Looking back at her feelings during that period of her life, she says:

> I was writing very little, partly from fatigue, that female fatigue of suppressed anger and loss of contact with my own being; partly from the discontinuity of female life. . . .

> . . . I felt . . . guilt toward the people closest to me, and guilt toward my own being.

The sense of frustration, guilt, and suppressed anger is a major theme of this third collection.

Some of the poems, such as "The Knight," are traditional in structure, close to the style of her first books. "The Knight" is an effective poem, but Rich is still distancing her personal voice, identifying here with the masculine side (which she feels society has defined as the creative aspect of the individual). But the poem does express the conflict between her burden of enervating responsibilities and her creative side, as well as the need to free herself from poetic conventions:

> Who will unhorse this rider
> and free him from between
> the walls of iron, the emblems
> crushing his chest with their weight?

Poems later in the book show that Rich has broken out of her armor. The change reflects, to a degree, the trend in American poetry in mid-twentieth century to move away from meter, set stanzas, and rhyme to a more open form, consistent with the move away from objectivity to speaking in the more personal voice. Rich's breakthrough in poetry, however, is also closely connected with the growing consciousness of herself as artist and woman. As she says:

> In the late fifties I was able to write, for the first time, directly about experiencing myself as a woman—Until then I had tried very hard *not* to identify myself as a female poet. Over two years I wrote a ten-part poem called "Snapshots of a Daughter-in-Law" (1958-60), in a longer looser mode than I'd ever trusted myself with before. It was an extraordinary relief to write that poem.

In this poem and many later ones in the volume (Rich begins dating her poems in this collection), she clearly begins to deal more directly with experience. Her form is modulated to portray the dynamics of the inner world; the "instrument" of form, one might say, has shifted from that of the diamond cutter who produces beautifully polished, set pieces to that of the photographer who tries to catch the unposed portrait. In "Snapshots of a Daughter-in-Law" form and rhythm tend to reproduce the thought patterns of the woman, although as Rich has said, she was not yet able "to use the pronoun 'I'—the woman in the poem is always 'she.' " Still, dropping the initial capital letter in each line, increasing enjambment, using speech cadences in place of formal meters, limiting the use of rhyme, and varying stanza lengths increase the personal tone.

The "snapshots" center upon a relationship in which a woman is bound by expectations that make her not only the passively wounded, but also the active wounder of other women, as she identifies herself through masculine approval. The focus of consciousness in the poem is a young woman who is aware of the forces that limit her and other women; and there is a gradual progression from her feelings of restriction, helplessness, and subdued rage toward a hope for change. The poem begins with a picture of the mother-in-law, her "mind now, mouldering like wedding-cake," "crumbling to pieces under the knife-edge / of mere fact." The tone is a mixture of sympathy and outrage toward the woman who is an accomplice in this denial of her own life. In the next section the young woman realizes that she too is losing her personal identity, and her inner voice, the "angel," incites her to rebellion. But numbed by the endless round of meaningless tasks, she cannot heed the voice. Section 3 is a distressed recognition of the division of women against each other: "All the old knives / that have rusted in my back, I drive in yours." Other sections show anger at the role of woman as object, which Rich sees as the imposed ideal of our society; for instance: "she shaves her legs until they gleam / like petrified mammoth tusk"— devastating lines showing the self as lifeless, extinct. This stifling role leads to an urgent plea for all women to realize the demeaning effects of being praised for mediocrity, for "slattern thought styled intuition," that the accepted role promotes. Two sections recognize Emily Dickinson and Mary Wollstonecraft as women who, through remarkable courage and control, did not settle for mediocrity. These examples lead to a vision of the modern woman who will break out of the reductive pattern of relationships and expectations: "Well, / she's long about her coming, who must be / more merciless to herself than history. / Her mind full to the wind." One senses in "Snapshots of a Daughter-in-Law" the relief of which Rich has spoken and the release into new concepts of form. This poem also indicates the true beginning of her open treatment of relationships between women, a subject that becomes increasingly important for her. "A Woman Mourned by Daughters" deals with a natural relationship that Rich thinks has been subverted in a patriarchal society. Mothers, she feels, tragically deny their own feminine wisdom and wound their daughters in preparing them to fit into a masculine, power-based society. In this poem, the daughters bear a heavy burden of love and hate as the mother leaves them only "solid assertions" of herself: "teaspoons, goblets, / seas of carpet." "Sisters" combines the sense of estrangement with the recognition of past bonds. The focus in this collection, then, is a consciousness of the difficulty of a woman's maintaining a sense of personal identity or a sense of community with other women.

The poems are filled with expression of pain and loss, but only occasionally do they lapse into self-pity or sentimentality, as in "Peeling Onions," where the emotion seems somewhat contrived, with a note of facile cleverness that appears with less and less frequency in Rich's work. In several poems toward the end of the book, Rich begins to view her situation with more optimism but with no illusions about the risk involved in breaking out of old patterns. In "The Roofwalker" she considers her condition (the woman is now "I"): "exposed, larger than life, / and due to break my neck"; then questions: "Was it worth while to lay— / with infinite exertion— / a roof I can't live under?" There is a hint of exhilaration in the question itself, no matter what the implied answer may be. And in "Prospective Immigrants Please Note" she proposes the definite alternatives of opening the door to discovering the self or of compromising with the existing situation; but "The door itself / makes no promises. / It is only a door." That Rich herself has chosen to open the door is evident in the poems of this collection.

Rich's assurance in handling a new style is illustrated in her next collection, *Necessities of Life* (1966). In many of these poems she demonstrates a new acceptance of moments of release and celebration in ordinary, sensuous life—moments that lead to a reintegration of body and mind. The strong title poem describes this process of becoming the self:

> Piece by piece I seem
> to re-enter the world: I first began
>
> a small, fixed dot, still see
> that old myself, a dark-blue thumbtack
>
> pushed into the scene,
> a hard little head protruding
>
> from the pointillist's buzz and bloom.
> After a time the dot
>
> begins to ooze. Certain heats
> melt it.

Using an analogy to Postimpressionist painting, Rich shows the gradual diffusion of the psyche, which is followed by the sense of having been "wolfed almost to shreds" by the lives of others. Then comes the beginning of reintegration through the senses, the ability

> now and again to lay
> one hand on a warm brick
>
> and touch the sun's ghost
> with economical joy,

which brings forth a promise to the self to "dare inhabit the world / trenchant in motion as an eel, solid / as a cabbage-head." These realistic images of eel and cabbage defy illusion but incorporate the hope that "practice" will make her "middling-perfect." "In the Woods" begins, " 'Difficult ordinary happiness,' / no one nowadays believes in you," and ends with the speaker's amazement at her own ability to accept the moment of sensuous release: "If I move now, the sun / naked between the trees / will melt me as I lie." The release that brings body and mind together extends to the unconscious mind in "The Trees," with its compelling immediacy of dream imagery as the struggle to become a part of the life-force continues: "The trees inside are moving out into the forest," and

> The leaves strain toward the glass
> small twigs stiff with exertion
> long-cramped boughs shuffling under the roof
> like newly discharged patients
> half-dazed, moving
> to the clinic doors.

Throughout her work, Rich battles against illusions but recognizes dreams as a deep part of reality. Yet the struggle to keep in touch with the elemental forces, the "necessities of life," is never easy, as the closing lines of "Like This Together" imply:

> Only our fierce attention
> gets hyacinths out of those
> hard cerebral lumps,
> unwraps the wet buds down
> the whole length of a stem.

As the opening up to life takes place, anger against forces that deny life increases; and Rich begins to speak her anger as well as her joy more openly. When this anger is directed through a sustained experience such as that in "Night-Pieces: For a Child," it can be powerful emotionally and aesthetically. Less successful is "Open Air Museum,"

which begins with the question, "What burns in the dump today?," and is followed by a stream of images that do not coalesce to lead convincingly into lines such as "Oh my America / this then was your desire?" This is one of the few poems in the book in which Rich does not seem to be speaking in her personal voice, and she is most universal when she relates events through her own sense of experience. This collection also includes a group of translations of modern Dutch poems, and although these translations have been praised for their lively and sensitive qualities, the importance of the volume lies in Rich's original poems.

Reactions to her next book, *Leaflets* (1969), have been more mixed. In fact, they range from the conviction that *Leaflets* marks a decline in Rich's career, to high praise of her new vision of the changing world and the changing self. Both critical stances can find supportive evidence in the poems. In the late 1960s, Rich was becoming increasingly active in protest movements. The cover of the book, a collage of windblown and torn newspaper columns, photographs, tickets, and other "leaflets" of the time—concerning the Vietnam War, student unrest, Black Power, and so on—indicates the emphasis upon major issues of the 1960s. Rich's sense of conviction and urgency is strong, so strong that at times statement and moral judgment overpower aesthetic awareness. The long title poem, for example, is a pouring out of grief and anger in a rush of images that touch a number of specific issues. Strong images induce "this seasick neon / vision, this / division"; but the poem does not sustain this intensity and is marred by prosaic statements such as "your tears are not political / they are real water." The compulsion to break through the barriers to communication ("I want to hand you this / leaflet streaming with rain or tears / but the words coming clear," "I want this to reach you," "*Tell me what you are going through*") is the driving force of "Leaflets" and many other poems in the book. In "The Demon Lover": "Only where there is language is there world," and in "Implosions": "I wanted to choose words that even you / would have to be changed by." Her sense of urgency for personal and political communication increases her awareness of the inadequacy of language as an instrument for survival in a violent world.

Part 3 of *Leaflets*, Rich explains in an introductory note, was written after she had read translations of the *ghazals* of the Urdu poet Mirza Ghalib, who lived from 1797 to 1869 and was also "writing in an age of political and cultural break-up." Although Ghalib's structure and metrics, she says, are stricter than hers, she has "adhered to his use of a minimum five couplets to a *ghazal*, each couplet being autonomous and independent of the others." Many of the couplets are rather prosaic statements; others have a crisp imagery that gives them epigrammatic force. They are, as are many other poems in the book, uneven in quality; but writing them helped Rich discover a new concept of juxtaposition, of circling around a thought (here the "political and cultural break-up"), in place of careful linear, logical progression.

The Will to Change (1971) continues to combine personal and political commitment, centering on the pressing need for the act of will to change the self and the world. Again, aesthetic quality is uneven, but Rich's sense of identity is clearer. She says of the strong poem "Planetarium": "at last the woman in the poem and the woman writing the poem become the same person." Here, through the voice of the astronomer Caroline Herschel, Rich makes her own direct statement of commitment for her art as an instrument for change:

> I am an instrument in the shape
> of a woman trying to translate pulsations
> into images   for the relief of the body
> and the reconstruction of the mind.

She expresses her anguish about a language that has been used to support tyranny; for example, in "The Burning of Paper Instead of Children": "knowledge of the oppressor / this is the oppressor's language," "yet I need it to talk to you," and "there are books that describe all this / and they are useless." Rich turns hopefully to modern film as a model for the "reconstruction" of "the oppressor's language." She was fascinated with the films of Jean-Luc Godard and other New Wave filmmakers who experimented with the handheld camera, fast zooms, rapid panning, freeze frames, and jump cuts. With this freedom and flexibility, thematic meaning comes through rapid images that build to motifs, rather than through more traditional narrative. Rich adapts this film method as a poetic form to express her concept of change, and she uses the metaphor of film itself extensively in the collection. In "Images for Godard," for example:

> the mind of the poet is the only poem
> the poet is at the movies
>
> dreaming the film-maker's dream but differently
> free in the dark as if asleep
> free in the dusty beam of the projector

> the mind of the poet is changing
>
> the moment of change is the only poem.

The long poem "Shooting Script" incorporates some techniques of modern film in an adapted form of the *ghazal*. Part 1 shows the tragic limitations of language, beginning with "We were bound on the wheel of an endless conversation" and ending with the wounds of separation in this passionate rush of images:

> Picking apart the strands of pain; a warp of wool dipped in burning wax.
>
> When the flame strikes to a blue bead, there is danger; the change of light in a flickering situation.
>
> Stretched on the loom the light expands; the smell of a smell of burning.
>
> When the change leaves you dark, when the wax cools in the socket, when I thought I prayed, when I was talking to myself under the cover of my darkness.
>
> Someone who never said, "What do you feel?"

Part 2 sees hope for breaking out of the impasse of "a poetry of false problems, the shotgun wedding of the mind, the subversion of choice by language." The "alternative" is "to purge the room with light to feel the sun breaking in on the courtyard." Film has been a valuable tool, but it also has become too static, too far removed from reality:

> Whatever it was, the image that stopped you, the one on which you came to grief, projecting it over & over on empty walls.
>
> Now to give up the temptations of the projector; to see instead. . . .
>
> . . . the initial split, the filaments thrown out from that impasse.

In her next book Rich makes the direct plunge into experience, as the title *Diving into the Wreck* (1973) indicates. This collection was cowinner of the National Book Award for Poetry, and most critical reactions strongly support the choice. Rich begins the book with a restatement of the necessity for new language, new vision, and new action. In the opening poem she defines specifically what she sees as the root of the problem; in "Trying to Talk with a Man," language has become a destructive force and his "dry heat" "feels like power." In "When We Dead Awaken" the betrayal of the earth and the

Adrienne Rich

betrayal of women by this power become synony-
mous, and "Here in the matrix of need and anger,"
"words / get thick with unmeaning." What saves
Rich's anger from being more bitter is that it so
clearly comes out of her conviction of the necessity of
change for the benefit of all humanity and that it
includes an optimism about possibilities for change
brought about by the common language and love of
women:

> fellow-creature, sister,
> sitting across from me, dark with love,
> working like me to pick apart
> working like me to remake
> this trailing knitted thing, this cloth of darkness
> this woman's garment, trying to save the skein.

She feels that "never have we been closer to the
truth," but she refuses to see the truth in any
devitalized, idealized way: "the faithfulness I can
imagine would be a weed / flowering in tar, a blue
energy piercing / the massed atoms of bedrock
disbelief." Rich's consciousness has now rejected
any temptation toward protective retreat or false
compromise; as she says in "Waking in the Dark":
"A man's world. But finished. / They themselves
have sold it to the machines." Her conviction of an
ending opens up a vision of a new beginning, a new
freedom:

> Clarity,
>   spray
> blinding and purging
> spears of sun striking the water
> the bodies riding the air
> . . . .
> the water opening
> like air
> like realization.

The full "realization" comes in the title poem,
where the dive is the controlling metaphor. The
purpose of this journey of discovery is to explore
"the wreck and not the story of the wreck," "to see the
damage that was done," and to find "the treasures
that prevail." It is, then, a dive into the unconscious
to touch the dark, powerful, elemental forces of
life—and to bring the knowledge back into the
conscious mind. But here, as always, Rich is aware of
the difficulty and pain involved in any entry into the
depths of experience. The diver prepares with the
standard equipment of the conscious mind: she reads
the "book of myths" for directions and carries a
camera for recording and a knifeblade for protection.
And she is dressed in "body armor," but the "absurd

flippers" and mask are armor for discovery, different
from the burdensome mail of her earlier poem "The
Knight." The diver must descend the ladder alone,
crawling "like an insect," with no one to tell her
"when the ocean / will begin. / First the air is blue
and then / it is bluer and then green and then /
black." She learns to turn her body "without force /
in the deep element." After this letting go, this
relinquishing of the old self, she can see the wreck—
the "damage" that has been done to the individual
psyche and the world:

> This is the place.
> And I am here, the mermaid whose dark hair
> streams black, the merman in his armored body
> We circle silently
> about the wreck
> we dive into the hold.
> I am she: I am he
>
> whose drowned face sleeps with open eyes.

Once there she touches the primal forces of life and
finds the "treasures" of full realization and
commitment, as the conscious and unconscious
parts of the mind are unified in the androgynous
image. The diver accepts the side of herself that is
part of the collective heritage of man, and the poem
reaches the visionary power of a mind that has
tapped the depths of the unconscious. The
incantatory rhythms, repetitions, and multilevel
imagery add to the mythic feeling of this journey of
discovery.

Having realized this integration of the psyche,
Rich expresses with new power, in later poems in the
book, both anguish and anger at distorted
communication. Note these lines from "The
Phenomenology of Anger":

> I hate the mask you wear, your eyes
> assuming a depth
> they do not possess, drawing me
> into the grotto of your skull
> the landscape of bone.

After the full awakening, she cannot go on sharing
the dry inner landscape in which even nightmares
are limited to argument and fact: in "August,"

> His mind is too simple, I cannot go on
> sharing his nightmares
>
> My own are becoming clearer, they open
> into prehistory.

Poems: Selected and New, 1950-1974 (1975)
contains poems that Rich chose from her seven

earlier collections, several earlier poems not previously published, and twelve new poems written in 1973 and 1974. This is a valuable collection; it includes most of the best poems and, read chronologically, gives a true sense of her development as a poet. The new poems continue to express the major themes of *Diving into the Wreck*. For example, in "The Wave" is this vision following the discovery of the self:

Layle Silbert

Thinking of the sea I think of light
lacing, lancing the water
the blue knife of a radiant consciousness
bent by the waves of vision as it pierces
to the deepest grotto.

Blue has become for Rich the color of creative thought and action. It may be in conjunction with sharp instruments, as is "the blue knife" here; or elsewhere, as "blue energy," "hyacinths like blue flame," and other images of burning that are related to strong, positive life-forces. But in the long poem "From an Old House in America," the vision is retrospective. The visitor to the "old house" thinks

of the women, "mostly inarticulate," who have lived there. In several remarkable, brief portraits, she imaginatively reconstructs their lives from the simple, ordinary things they have left behind. But the burden of history fills her with painful empathy for these women whose full creative potential has been denied to them and with admiration for their courage in trying to hold together the fabric of their lives.

Rich's historical awareness that appears in this poem, the last one in the book, is extended in *Of Woman Born*, published two years later in 1976. In this prose work of almost three hundred pages, Rich traces the concept of motherhood as it has developed in a patriarchal society. Some critical reactions to the book are almost vehement, claiming Rich's perspective has been clouded by a rage that has led her into biased statements and a strident style. Others, who have read it with more sympathy, call it scholarly and well researched and insist that it should not be read quickly for polemics. Rich has commented on her feelings about writing the book:

> I have seen massive sculpturelike weavings, of jute, hemp, and wool, in which many varicolored strands are quickly visible like vines or striations; but when you come closer and try to touch this or that strand, your hand enters a dense, bristling mesh, thick with knotted and twisted filaments, some harsh and rough to the fingers, others surprisingly silky and strong. In writing *Of Woman Born*, and in thinking about motherhood ever since, I have felt a similar sensation, of elemental exploration and of complex discovery.... For motherhood is the great mesh in which all human relationships are entangled, in which lurk our most elemental assumptions about love and power.

Her style in *Of Woman Born* reveals her deep sincerity; she is speaking to a wide audience and speaking with conviction. Throughout the book, passages from her journals support her thesis with the authority of personal experience combined with many examples based on extensive research. One of the most moving sections of the book—and one closely related to her poetry—concerns the history and practices of delivering babies. In the two chapters titled "Hands of Flesh, Hands of Iron" and "Alienated Labor," delivery by the midwife and delivery by the male obstetrician become, for Rich, important polarities. She compares the experience of childbirth with the midwife in attendance (her care and support easing the process of birth and promoting a sense of continuity) to the hospital delivery that tends to force the birth (with attention and concern limited to the moment of completion). The midwife becomes a symbol for Rich; she sees her own poetry now as an instrument that, like the midwife's hands, gives calm and intimate direction. In her latest collection of poetry, this concept of woman as instrument, easing the natural birth into the fabric of life, becomes the experience of transcendence.

The poems in *The Dream of a Common Language* (1978) are a vision of being one with all life, with faith that this vision can be fulfilled and with hope that men may learn the art of survival from women. Rich's poetry has moved beyond anger into a tone of quiet celebration. The male personae and distancing "she's" of the early poems and the strong personal "I" of later ones are both replaced here by the communal "we" of shared love. For Rich herself, the sense of communion has come through the way of lesbian feminism, but her personal choice does not lead to any intent to impose it on others. Rather, it leads to a greater insistence upon the freedom of choice for each individual in the discovery of personal fulfillment. With her choice has come the sense of joy in being alive, as a few lines from "Twenty-One Love Poems," the middle section of the book, show: "We want to live like trees, / sycamores blazing through the sulfuric air, / dappled with scars, still exuberantly budding." The image of the woman's hands that "might piece together / the fine, needle-like sherds of a great krater-cup" brings together the fragments of civilization:

Such hands might carry out an unavoidable violence
with such restraint, with such a grasp
of the true range and limits of violence
that violence ever after would be obsolete.

"Power," the first poem in the book, speaks of Madame Curie, who dies from the effects of radium, of which she had discovered the healing power: "denying / her wounds / denying / her wounds came from the same source as her power." Rich herself has given up this kind of denial; she has learned to accept wounds as a necessary part of achievement, and she feels that pain can be transcended through this acceptance. In the moving poem "Phantasia for Elvira Shatayev," she thinks of the women's climbing team led by Shatayev and imagines their pain's being transcended in a moment of total unity before their death by freezing: "*A cable of blue fire*

ropes our bodies / burning together in the snow." Blue flame, symbolic here of creative unity, transforms death into a part of the life pattern. The speaker in "A Woman Dead in Her Forties" grieves over her former silence when, following the conventions of a society that makes death a fearsome and isolated experience and also forces silence about women's love for each other, she withholds this sense of communion: "we never talked at your deathbed of your death."

"Sibling Mysteries" depicts a kind of psychic death—the denial of the elemental mysteries. Earth images are strong (as they are throughout the book) and frequently contain erotic overtones. The daughters in the poem, as children, have been in touch with "the planetary rock!" Later, they have "passed bark and root and berry / from hand to hand, whispering each one's power." But the mother has forfeited her own natural love and power and sends them "weeping into that law" where they will dwell in "two worlds / the daughters and the mothers / in the kingdom of the sons." But in "Nights and Days" the possibility of change brings forth a vision: "The stars will come out over and over / the hyacinths rise like flames" as "the rivers freeze and burn." The vision must be fulfilled through gentleness, as the quality is defined in "Natural Resources":

gentleness is active
gentleness swabs the crusted stump

invents more merciful instruments
to touch the wound beyond the wound
....
I have to cast my lot with those
who age after age, perversely,

with no extraordinary power,
reconstitute the world.

Consistent with Rich's concept of form as a continuing language, the individual poems take on additional strength and meaning in the context of the book, where they become like strands whose images and ideas reinforce the pattern. This is true of "Transcendental Etude," the final poem, which is an important poem in itself and attains even greater visionary strength in context. The poem begins quietly. The woman driving alone on an August evening startles a doe and her fawns and thinks about the fruitfulness of nature, her "nerves singing the immense / fragility of all this sweetness, / this green world" that "persists stubbornly." "A lifetime," she thinks, "is too narrow / to understand it all." She realizes how unprepared we are for this study, and

Rich introduces the study of music as the metaphor for how we should progress: to begin with the simplest exercises and slowly move to the hard ones, "practicing till strength / and accuracy become one with daring / to leap into transcendence." But, rejecting the temptation to become virtuosos, "competing / against the world for speed and brilliance," we must cut away the "old force" and "disenthrall ourselves" because

> the whole chorus throbbing at our ears
> like midges, told us nothing, nothing
> of origins, nothing we needed
> to know, nothing that could re-member us.

With the cutting away of useless knowledge there comes a new awareness of unity, "a whole new poetry beginning here." The poem closes with the beautiful section in which a woman is quietly transformed into a mythic figure as her composition becomes a hope for all mankind:

> Vision begins to happen in such a life
> as if a woman quietly walked away
> from the argument and jargon in a room
> and sitting down in the kitchen, began turning in her
> lap
> bits of yarn, calico and velvet scraps,
> laying them out absently on the scrubbed boards
> in the lamplight.

To the pattern the woman adds "small rainbow-colored shells," "skeins of milkweed," "the dark blue petal of the petunia," and other fragments from the natural and animal world.

> Such a composition has nothing to do with eternity,
> the striving for greatness, brilliance—
> only with the musing of a mind
> one with her body, experienced fingers quietly pushing
> dark against bright, silk against roughness,
> pulling the tenets of a life together
> with no mere will to mastery,
> only care for the many-lived, unending
> forms in which she finds herself,
> becoming now the sherd of broken glass
> slicing light in a corner, dangerous
> to flesh, now the plentiful, soft leaf
> that wrapped round the throbbing finger, soothes the
> wound;
> and now the stone foundation, rockshelf further
> forming underneath everything that grows.

In this image of the woman, Rich brings together the

major images of her poetry, her concepts of language and form, and her feminine consciousness, with visionary power. Reviewers of *The Dream of a Common Language* recognize this power and praise the reconciliation that allows Rich to speak freely and compassionately in a language that is universally applicable. This is an important book that combines vital thematic and aesthetic awareness.

In *On Lies, Secrets, and Silence: Selected Prose 1966-1978* (1979), Rich traces her personal and political development. The selections not only illuminate her ideas about poetry but also reveal additional integrated aspects of her life. For example, as a literary critic, in essays on Emily Dickinson, Anne Bradstreet, Charlotte Brontë, and other women writers, she brings a strong new feminine perspective; in the long essay "Toward a Woman Centered University" she gives a penetrating analysis of the contemporary university system; and in several pieces she makes a passionate appeal for the unity of women in the feminist ideal. Her personal comments preceding each selection give the book a sense of the continuity of her experiences and developing ideas. Still, it is through her poetry that Rich communicates most convincingly.

In her essay on Emily Dickinson, Rich defines her concept of the dual, but inseparable, role of the true poet:

> Poetic language—the poem on paper—is a concretization of the poetry of the world at large, the self, and the forces within the self; and those forces are rescued from formlessness, lucidified, and integrated in the act of writing poems. But there is a more ancient concept of the poet, which is that she is endowed to speak for those who do not have the gift of language, or to see for those who—for whatever reasons—are less conscious of what they are living through. It is as though the risks of the poet's existence can be put to some use beyond her survival.

Rich herself continues to strive toward this ideal, and as much as any poet of our time, she has succeeded in integrating the gift of language and the sense of mission. She has taken the risks, and at times the note of urgency overpowers her commitment to aesthetic mastery. But Rich's increasing confidence in her newer tone of strong, calm vision indicates that she is approaching her ideal of the poet who speaks as a seer in a "common language."

Other:

Poems by Ghalib, translated by Rich and others (New York: Hudson Review, 1969).

References:

Robert Boyers, "On Adrienne Rich: Intelligence and Will," *Salmagundi,* no. 22-23 (Spring-Summer 1973): 132-148;

Albert Gelpi, "Adrienne Rich: The Poetics of Change," in *American Poetry Since 1960,* ed. Robert B. Shaw (Cheadle, Cheshire, U.K.: Carcanet Press, 1973), pp. 123-143;

Barbara C. Gelpi and Albert Gelpi, eds., *Adrienne Rich's Poetry: A Norton Critical Edition* (New York: Norton, 1975);

Randall Jarrell, "New Books in Review," *Yale Review,* 46 (September 1956): 100-103;

Erica Jong, "Visionary Anger," *Ms.,* 2 (July 1973): 31-33;

David Kalstone, *Five Temperaments* (New York: Oxford University Press, 1977), pp. 129-169;

Judith McDaniel, *Reconstituting The World: The Poetry and Vision of Adrienne Rich* (Argyle, N.Y.: Spinsters Ink, 1979);

Alicia Ostriker, "Her Cargo: Adrienne Rich and the Common Language," *American Poetry Review,* 8 (July-August 1979): 6-10;

Helen Vendler, "Ghostlier Demarcations, Keener Sounds," *Parnassus,* 2 (Fall-Winter 1973): 5-10, 15-16, 18-24.

Theodore Roethke

Keen Butterworth
University of South Carolina

BIRTH: Saginaw, Michigan, 25 May 1908, to Otto and Helen Huebner Roethke.

EDUCATION: A.B., University of Michigan, 1929; M.A., University of Michigan, 1936; Harvard Graduate School, 1930-1931.

MARRIAGE: 3 January 1953 to Beatrice O'Connell.

AWARDS: Guggenheim Fellowship, 1945, 1950; Eunice Tietjens Memorial Prize (*Poetry* magazine), 1947; Levinson Prize (*Poetry* magazine), 1951; Ford Foundation grants, 1952, 1959; Pulitzer Prize for *The Waking,* 1954; Fulbright grant, 1955; Bollingen Prize, 1959; National Book Award for *Words for the Wind,* 1959; Shelley Memorial Award, 1962; Litt. D., University of Michigan, 1962; National Book Award for *The Far Field,* 1965.

DEATH: Bainbridge Island, Washington, 1 August 1963.

BOOKS: *Open House* (New York: Knopf, 1941);
The Lost Son and Other Poems (Garden City: Doubleday, 1948; London: Lehmann, 1949);
Praise to the End! (Garden City: Doubleday, 1951);
The Waking, Poems: 1933-1953 (Garden City: Doubleday, 1953);

Words for the Wind (London: Secker & Warburg, 1957; Garden City: Doubleday, 1958);
The Exorcism (San Francisco: Poems in Folio, 1957);
I Am! Says the Lamb (Garden City: Doubleday, 1961);
Party at the Zoo (New York: Crowell-Collier, 1963);
Sequence, Sometimes Metaphysical (Iowa City: Stonewall Press, 1963);
The Far Field (Garden City: Doubleday, 1964; London: Faber & Faber, 1965);
On the Poet and His Craft, ed. Ralph J. Mills, Jr. (Seattle & London: University of Washington Press, 1965);
The Collected Poems of Theodore Roethke (Garden City: Doubleday, 1966; London: Faber & Faber, 1968);
Theodore Roethke: Selected Poems, ed. Beatrice Roethke (London: Faber & Faber, 1969);
Straw for the Fire. From the Notebooks of Theodore Roethke, 1943-63, ed. David Wagoner (Garden City: Doubleday, 1972);
Dirty Dinkey and Other Creatures: Poems for Children, ed. Beatrice Roethke and Stephen Lushington (Garden City: Doubleday, 1973).

The motif of the journey is more crucial to the poetry of Theodore Roethke than to that of any other major American poet since Whitman. Perhaps it is more important to Roethke than it is to Whitman. Certainly it is more coherent. Whereas Whitman's journey, if it can be called that, is outward, in all directions, until the fragmented poet achieves reintegration by becoming the cosmos itself, Roethke's is a simple journey, a journey from beginning to destination. But to say that it is simple is not to imply that it is easy. The journey, as it is recorded in *The Collected Poems* (1966), is that of a modern-day *Pilgrim's Progress*, fraught with its own temptations of vanity and pride, its own sloughs of despond. But Roethke's journey is essentially more difficult than Christian's. For Christian there is a road, worn, and thus defined, by those who have gone before him, and always in the distance stand the Delectable Mountains to mark his destination and draw him onward. For Roethke there is no such well-defined path, nor are there signposts or prominences to indicate his destination. His journey is through a wilderness, a particularly American wilderness, and although the general direction of the journey is never in question, Roethke must make his groping way relying on his instincts or intuitions, "feeling" and learning by the very act of "going" itself, as he was to articulate the process in his poem "The Waking." Nevertheless, Roethke's quest is a religious one, just as Christian's is. In America, however, the order of European Christianity has given way to a pantheistic paganism, the structure of which is as uncertain as that of Nature itself. The American pilgrim makes his way westward through the wilderness toward discovery and self-realization: this is the movement of both Roethke's poetry and his life.

Roethke's journey is also an evolutionary one, essentially that described and speculated on by his contemporary Loren Eiseley in *The Immense Journey* (1957). In his second published book, *The Lost Son* (1948), Roethke returns to his evolutionary past, where he joins the worms, slugs, and snails in the slime of primordial existence. From that point, Roethke's poetry moves forward, through the realization of his kinship with the higher animals, through the realization of his own humanity (in *The Waking*, 1953, and *Words for the Wind*, 1957), and finally to the transcendence of spiritual man in *The Far Field* (1964). It is a movement from unconscious life, through various stages of intermediate consciousness, to the highest forms of self-realization man is capable of.

These statements about the radical nature of Roethke's journey may seem to imply that he discarded tradition, particularly the Old-World traditions, in his work. In a sense that is true:

although *Open House* (1941) is certainly traditional, *The Lost Son, Praise to the End!* (1951), and parts of *The Waking* are an entirely new kind of poetry, invented by Roethke. Although in the later poetry, from *The Waking* through *The Far Field*, he adopts traditional poetic forms from both the Old World and American past, it appears as if Roethke were reinventing these forms rather than copying or imitating them. This is instructive, for in *Open House* Roethke is most definitely imitating tradition. As technically correct as these first poems are, Roethke himself understood their lack of distinction and vitality. Consequently, he rejected the tradition he felt was stultifying him in order to redefine poetry itself. Thus the development of his work is a journey also—this time a technical one, which parallels and reinforces the physical and spiritual journeys the poetry depicts.

Of course, even when Roethke's poetry is most radical, as in *The Lost Son*, he never really escapes tradition. No poet of value ever does that: he cannot escape the poetic traditions any more than he can escape the traditions of the language in which he is writing. As Jenijoy La Belle has shown in *The Echoing Wood* (1976), Roethke's poetry is filled with echoes, paraphrases, and even direct borrowings from his poetic forebears. The lines of *The Lost Son* and *Praise to the End!* often suggest Wordsworth, Blake, Whitman, and others. Nonetheless, the radical readjustment and synthesis of traditional elements that Roethke effects in these poems give the impression of an entirely new kind of poetry that has broken with tradition. This is Roethke's genius. It is, in that way, much like the genius of Eliot, Picasso, and Stravinsky. A number of critics have praised this originality in *The Lost Son* and *Praise to the End!* Many feel that these books contain his best poetry and have criticized the later work (which calls attention to its relationships and debts to tradition), as imitative and unoriginal. These critics have failed to see that the later poetry is no less original for its formality. In fact, the originality of *The Lost Son* is only one step in the process that leads to *The Far Field*: it is a step that was necessary before Roethke could return to and revitalize those aspects of tradition he found still valid. The process is that of American history itself: in escaping Old World tradition Americans have been forced to invent new forms. Often they have found, however, that they merely reinvented old forms, readjusted perhaps, but essentially the old forms. Americans have revalidated those forms because they seemed appropriate, necessary to the conditions of a new existence. More important, in reinventing them, Americans have revitalized them. These principles are applicable to Roethke's poetry. Of all our major poets, Roethke—in his initial imitation of tradition, his subsequent departure from and final return to it—seems more representatively American, even, than Walt Whitman himself, who represents, of course, only the initial stages of the process.

Theodore Roethke was born in Saginaw, Michigan. His father, Otto Roethke, had immigrated to America from Germany as a child with his family in 1872. On arriving in Saginaw, the Roethkes bought twenty-two acres of land on which they established a market garden. Those were the days of the Michigan timber boom; consequently there was a great demand for fresh produce. The Roethkes prospered; and when Roethke's grandfather had made sufficient money, he built a greenhouse so that he could enter the florist business, which also prospered. After the grandfather's death, Otto Roethke and Roethke's Uncle Karl took over the management of the business. In 1906 Otto Roethke married Helen Huebner, another German immigrant, and they took up residence in a house on Gratiot Avenue, where Roethke was born two years later. When Roethke was two years old, Otto built his own house adjacent to the one in which they had been living, just in front of the greenhouse, so that he would always be nearby to tend his flowers. As a child, Roethke followed his father about his work and was given small chores of his own. Thus, Roethke almost literally grew up among the plants of the greenhouse. His experience of this vegetable world affected him deeply: the greenhouse itself was to become the central image of *The Lost Son* and *Praise to the End!* Also on the property, beyond the greenhouse, was a large field, where Roethke often played as a child. This field, too, became an important image in his poetry.

The intense and painful introspection of his adulthood, which is so evident in his poetry, grew from a tendency established very early in his life. Roethke's playmates during these years seem to have been his cousins Violet and Bud, for June, Roethke's sister, was five years younger than he. Although Violet has recalled her relationship with Roethke fondly, she was two years older and had different interests. Bud was only six months older than Roethke, but he was much larger and seems to have bullied his younger cousin. Or, at least, Roethke found him threatening, for he developed an intense dislike for Bud that lasted most of his life. Also, Roethke was a frail and sickly child who had to spend a good deal of each winter indoors recovering

from the effects of influenza and bronchitis. As a result he became retiring, shy, and he turned inward upon himself.

At five, Roethke was sent to the John Moore School, where he took the usual course of math, reading, composition, and, because of the large German population, an hour of that language each day. He was an intelligent child and appears to have gotten on well in school, although he retained almost none of the German he learned during these years.

In 1921 Roethke entered Arthur Hill High School in Saginaw. During his freshman year he distinguished himself by giving a speech on the Junior Red Cross, which was published and later translated into twenty-six languages for international distribution. Although filled with the usual platitudes and cliches, it was quite a good piece of writing for a thirteen-year-old boy. This recognition also whetted his ambition. He already knew that he wanted to become a writer, although he had not yet considered becoming a poet. At the time, he later recalled, he wanted to be a prose writer; so he began studying essayists, such as Walter Pater, Thoreau, and Emerson, and short-story writers. But not all of his time during these high-school years was devoted to reading, writing, and his other studies. He also joined a high-school fraternity, most of whose members were athletes—with a reputation for drinking. To further his image of the all-around man, Roethke took up tennis. He had little natural ability and moved about the court awkwardly, flying into rages at himself whenever he made a mistake. Nevertheless, through hours of practice, he became a good enough player to enter several city and state tournaments—and later he would coach two college tennis teams.

During Roethke's second year at high school, his father died of cancer, a "kink in the bowels" as the doctors said. Outwardly, Roethke accepted the event calmly, probably because he had been prepared for it by the long illness that preceded Otto's death. However, as Roethke's mature poetry suggests, the loss had a deep and lasting effect on him. His attitude toward his father had been ambivalent. On the one hand, Otto had often been a hard taskmaster, demanding perfection from his son and belittling him when he failed to live up to standards. Consequently, Roethke resented his father as a threat to his own individuality and ego; at times this resentment seems to have been intense. On the other hand, Roethke could admire the life-giving quality in Otto, not just as his own progenitor, but as the gardener who could bring plant life from the soil, who devoted his life to the perpetuation of life. Also, even the young Roethke must have sensed that his father was responsible for the order of his world. In "The Lost Son," which is written from the point of view of the child, the father's arrival is associated with order (*ordnung*). In "My Papa's Waltz" Roethke captures the earthy vitality of Otto, and also something of his own joy, and bafflement, as the victim of his father's exuberant energy. Later, in "Otto," written forty years after his father's death, Roethke objectively records the vitality, order, and contradictions in his father's character.

But these poems represent the reflections of Roethke the mature poet. The adolescent Roethke adjusted quickly to his father's death. As the oldest child and the only male, he was now head of the family. He continued to work diligently at school, and even became something of a leader among the youths of the Presbyterian Church. During his senior year he announced to his mother that he wanted to go to Harvard, but she insisted that he go to nearby University of Michigan at Ann Arbor. That summer, 1925, Roethke worked for the Heinz pickle factory in Saginaw (where he would work each summer during his undergraduate years), an experience that he used later in the poem "Pickle Belt." In the fall he entered the University of Michigan, the first member of this family to attend college.

Roethke did well in college and seems to have enjoyed his four years as an undergraduate (although he was to say later that he hated all the years of his schooling, high school through Harvard). Now at 6' 2 ½", 190 pounds, he bought a gorgeous coonskin coat and sometimes walked about campus as if he were a great hulking bear, a self-image that he was to cultivate further in later years and use in some of his poetry. He also began to develop the image of himself as a tough guy who had connections among the Chicago underworld. Indeed, he did go occasionally to a speakeasy near Detroit where gangsters and smugglers (it was the height of Prohibition) hung out. And though in later years Roethke bragged about his experiences with gangsters, this seems to have been the extent of his ventures into the underworld.

On campus, Roethke entered into the social life, joining Chi Phi fraternity and playing intramural tennis. His real interest, however, was in training himself to be a writer. He took a general course of study, but concentrated on literature and language. He had four courses in German, two in French, two

in Polish, one in Sanskrit (in translation) and twelve in English composition and literature. He did well in all these courses, and was elected to Phi Beta Kappa during his senior year. In his study of Roethke's notebooks, Allan Seager discovered that it was also during these undergraduate years that Roethke began writing poetry, although he did not tell his friends and teachers about it.

After graduation in 1929, Roethke entered the University of Michigan law school. But his effort seems to have been half-hearted, for his mind was not suited to the study of law. In fact, Roethke enrolled in only one class, Criminal Law, and received a D in that. In February 1930 he withdrew from law school and entered the graduate school to pursue a master's degree in literature. Roethke did well in these studies, but his real interest had turned to writing poetry, rather than studying it as a scholar. He was serious about his poetry now and frequently talked about his favorites among the moderns: Elinor Wylie, for her lyricism, and E. E. Cummings, for his courage in experimentation. In June 1930 three of his poems appeared in the little magazine the *Harp*. Rather bad poems, they were at least a start.

Roethke continued his studies at Michigan during the summer of 1930; in the fall, however, he entered Harvard Graduate School, where he would, as he said, study under "men he could respect." There he showed three of his poems to Robert Hillyer, who praised them and suggested that he submit them to reputable magazines. Two of them were accepted, "The Conqueror" by *Commonweal* and "Silence" by the *New Republic*. He also studied under the great English critic I. A. Richards, who seems to have helped Roethke shape his own concept of his role as poet and gave him direction in pursuing his career. Probably, Roethke would have continued his graduate work at Harvard; perhaps he would have gone on to earn a Ph.D., as he had intended, but the Depression was affecting Roethke's family as it was the rest of America, and he was forced to withdraw from school and find a job. He sent out several applications for teaching positions and was accepted by Lafayette, a small Presbyterian college in Pennsylvania.

Roethke stayed at Lafayette for four years. There he got a reputation for his eccentricities and hard drinking, but his students found him informal and stimulating, a natural teacher. He was so well liked by his students that they petitioned the college to retain him when he was to be released in 1935. But he had been kept already two years beyond the normal tenure for an instructor, and was let go with excellent recommendations by his department head. He had also been the college's tennis coach for two years and director of public relations: he was excellent at both jobs.

Socially this had been an important period in Roethke's life. He fell in love with Mary Kunkel, the daughter of a biology professor at Lafayette College. They talked of marriage, but Roethke was in no position to take on that kind of responsibility and they drifted apart. But other friendships formed during his years at Lafayette were to have a permanent influence on his career as poet. Poet Rolfe Humphries offered intellectual friendship, understanding criticism, and encouragement. Humphries also introduced Roethke to Louise Bogan, whom Roethke admired a great deal, and whose poetry he had studied seriously along with that of Elinor Wylie and Leonie Adams. In Stanley Kunitz, Roethke found a most sympathetic spirit. Roethke had studied and admired his poetry so much that he sought out Kunitz on his farm in Bucks County, Pennsylvania. Immediately, they struck up a friendship that was to last the rest of Roethke's life. Kunitz saw Roethke's potential as a poet and offered him helpful criticism. But Roethke's academic duties and social life did not take up all his time. He continued to devote a great deal of it to writing poetry. His colleagues remember that he always carried his notebook around, in order to jot down ideas and lines as they came to him. This was a habit Roethke started early and kept up all his life. (At his death he left behind 277 notebooks.) From these notes he built his poems. During 1932-1934 he published nineteen poems in such magazines as *Poetry*, *New Republic*, and *Saturday Review*.

From Lafayette, Roethke went to Michigan State College in Lansing. Again, students found him to be an exciting teacher. But Roethke was drinking very hard that fall, and he began to behave erratically from time to time. In November he had a mental breakdown, the first of a series that was to plague him the rest of his life. He was admitted to a local hospital for treatment and remained there until mid-January 1936. Then he went home to Saginaw to recuperate, assuming that he would resume his teaching position in the fall. But later in the spring he learned that he had been replaced during his absence and would have to find another job.

During the spring Roethke resumed writing poetry (for he seems to have stopped during the turmoil of the previous fall) and applied for jobs at several colleges. He was accepted at Pennsylvania State. Here he fell in love again, this time with a

librarian, Kitty Stokes, and began to live an active social life. He even took up cooking and fancied himself a gourmet, and he again became the college tennis coach. Roethke's life at Penn State seems to have been fulfilling. With Kitty Stokes's encouragement and help in typing his work, Roethke devoted much of his time and energy to his poetry. By 1939 he felt that he had enough poems for a book. Stanley Kunitz helped him arrange the poems and suggested the book's title. The manuscript went to several publishers before it was accepted by Alfred A. Knopf, who published it as *Open House* in March 1941. Always neurotic in his craving for approval, Roethke waited anxiously for the reviews. When they came, they were nearly all favorable, and by such people as W. H. Auden, Louise Bogan, Yvor Winters, Rolfe Humphries, Elizabeth Drew, and Babette Deutsch. Roethke's career as a poet was launched.

Open House is indeed a volume that shows poetic promise: the reader can see here a talented craftsman, a poet who knows well the tradition of his art; but it is obvious, in retrospect, that Roethke had not yet found his themes or his proper manner. Among the forty-seven poems there is a great variety of forms and tones. And there is the echo, sometimes an obvious imitation, of poets he had been reading and admired. For instance, "No Bird" and "Genesis" are obviously imitations of Emily Dickinson's short lyrics, and as Jenijoy La Belle has pointed out, "No Bird" seems to be Dickinson's epitaph. There are also echoes of and allusions to such poets as Donne, Blake, Hopkins, Robinson, Frost, Eliot, Auden, Wylie, and Bogan. There are several very good poems, such as "For an Amorous Lady," "Academic," and "The Bat," which foreshadow the humorous poems in *Words for the Wind* and the children's poems of *I Am! Says the Lamb* (1961). Several poems deal with his father's death, one of which, "The Premonition," suggests the manner he was to develop in *The Lost Son*. But if there is a recurring theme in *Open House* it is Roethke's expressed desire to shed the past and the poetic traditions he felt stultifying him. "Feud" states the case: "The spirit starves / Until the dead have been subdued." "Prognosis" puts it a different way: "Though the devouring mother cry, 'Escape me? / Never—' / And the honeymoon be spoiled by a father's ghost." In "The Auction" Roethke foresees success in escaping the past: "I left my home with unencumbered will / And all the rubbish of confusion sold." In "Sale" the strategy is to sell all the furniture and bric-a-brac inherited from past generations. Thus from this heterogeneous collection of poems, this confusion of styles, the reader hears Roethke's voice crying for release. He senses the need to escape his poetic forebears and create his own individual style. Significantly the volume ends with the poem "Night Journey." The train on which the narrator has embarked is heading west—away from tradition, toward purification and renewal.

After the publication of *Open House*, Roethke became dissatisfied with his job at Penn State, where, he said, his abilities and accomplishments went unrecognized. Although Roethke was still without a large reading public, he was now known by the literary community. Among his new acquaintances were Robert Frost, Bernard De Voto, Morton Zabel, F. O. Matthiessen, and Henry S. Canby. He received further evidence of his recognition when he was invited to give one of the Morris Gray readings at Harvard in the spring of 1942. Always one to seize the main chance to further his career, Roethke set the wheels in motion to acquire a Guggenheim Fellowship, with the support of Canby, Stanley Kunitz, and Rolfe Humphries. Although Roethke's name was not on the list for 1943, he had contingency plans underway. The previous year he had applied for a position at Bennington College, where he thought the atmosphere would be much more congenial to his career as a poet and teacher. He was accepted, and in the spring of 1943, taking an indefinite leave of absence without pay from Penn State, moved to Bennington, Vermont.

Indeed, Bennington was a different kind of school. Although only thirteen years old, it had brought together a distinguished faculty, and it carefully screened the girls who were admitted. Moreover, the faculty was not hierarchical: all the members were considered equals, and the classes or seminars were run informally, as if the students were the intellectual equals of their teachers. This was a new challenge for Roethke. At first he appears to have been intimidated by it, but that only drove him on to perfect his teaching techniques. He developed courses on verse forms and the analysis of poetry that were thought by many to be the best literary courses in the school. Roethke drove himself, as well as his students. They were fascinated by his earnestness and vitality; many have said that Roethke made them believe poetry was the most important activity in life. Because of Roethke's magnetism a number of intimate relationships developed between Roethke and his students. In fact, one of his affairs was brought to the attention of the administration by the girl's parents, and nearly caused his dismissal: in all probability he would not have been rehired by the college in 1947, but he left of his own accord.

While at Bennington, Roethke established several important relationships with his colleagues. Mary Garrett, the dean of the school, assumed the essentially motherly role that Mary Kunkel and Kitty Stokes had played before her. Leonie Adams, whose poetry Roethke had admired for some time, was also on the faculty. She helped in shaping his courses, and they talked about poetry. But most important, Roethke became friends with Kenneth Burke, whose apartment was in the same cottage as his. Burke was perhaps the most erudite man Roethke had ever known and a discerning critic. Roethke read him several of his new "greenhouse" poems: Burke knew immediately that Roethke had struck the right vein and told him so. With the encouragement of his new friends and colleagues, Roethke threw himself into a fit of poetic creation that was to produce the major poems of *The Lost Son*. Unfortunately this frenzy of activity was the result, or the cause, of another of Roethke's manic states. A period of depression followed in the winter of 1945. He was taken to a hospital in Albany where he underwent shock treatments. When he was released from the hospital in January, he returned to Saginaw to recuperate under the care of his mother and sister. Fortunately, Roethke had applied for a Guggenheim Fellowship in 1945 and this time had received it: thus he could remain in Saginaw without having to worry about returning to work.

Roethke resumed work on his poetry during the spring while he was recovering his strength. He had finished nearly all the poems he needed for a second volume; he worked steadily through 1946. By February 1947 the poems were completed, and fearing that he would not be rehired at Bennington, he returned to Penn State to teach the spring semester. That summer he went to Yaddo, where he became friends with Robert Lowell. Also during the summer he was accepted for a teaching position at the University of Washington in Seattle. In September he went west.

Roethke had been disappointed in Knopf's handling of *Open House*: they had not advertised the book properly, and had failed to bring out a second printing, even when the first small printing of 1000 copies had been sold out. In the meantime he had established contacts at Doubleday; consequently when the manuscript of *The Lost Son* was completed in the spring of 1947, he sent it to them, and it was accepted. Because of delays caused by Roethke's stipulations about typography, binding, and publicity, however, publication was delayed until March 1948. Again Roethke waited anxiously for the reviews; this time they were even more laudatory than those for *Open House*. This was original poetry, and the reviewers recognized it as such.

Indeed, *The Lost Son* is *original* poetry in several senses of the word. First, it is original in the sense that nothing like it had ever been written before. Secondly, its rhythms, for the most part, are of a primal nature: they suggest the unmeasured rhythm and energy of unconscious life. And further, the poems are original in that they are about a return to the very sources of life itself. Most of them deal with plant life and animal life of a very low order. The first section of the book contains a series of poems about life in the greenhouse based on Roethke's childhood memories. "Cuttings," "Root Cellar," and "Forcing House" are concerned with the first stirrings of life in the dank and dark underground. The other poems of this section deal with activities and events in the greenhouse itself. The second section contains contrasting poems of a more traditional nature, such as the much anthologized "My Papa's Waltz" and "Dolor." The third section returns to the world of unconscious life. And the fourth section contains four long poems all concerned with the evolution from the darkness of the primitive vegetable and animal world toward the light of the human world. The most important poem in the book, the title poem, "The Lost Son," is found in this fourth and final section. In it the themes and method of the book find their most complete expression.

"The Lost Son" is a stream-of-consciousness poem. Roethke is projecting himself back into his own psyche as an adolescent at the time of his father's death. In the first section, "The Flight," the trauma of the father's burial at Woodlawn Cemetery causes the boy to flee reality. His flight is into the natural world looking for strength and answers to his questions about existence; but nature is enigmatic; it offers only riddles without answers. As the boy looks more desperately, he regresses into a child's sensibility, represented by the nursery rhyme stanzas at the end of the section. In the second section, "The Pit," the regression continues. The "Pit" is the dark fecund female principle: the womb, in which life is unconscious and chaotic. In the next section, "The Gibber," the boy reemerges from the pit, but still he is lost in the world. The death wish then asserts itself as autoeroticism, but he is called back into the rational human world by material concerns, represented here by "money." In "The Return" he makes his way through the darkness toward light: the coming of dawn and the rational order his father had imposed upon his world, the world of the

greenhouse. In the final section, "It was the beginning of winter," the boy sees that although the answers have not come to him yet (because it is an "in-between time"), the light, the "Lively understandable spirit," which in childhood was manifest in his father, will come again. He need only be patient and wait.

The poem has often been interpreted in terms of Freudian psychology; and certainly it has Freudian elements. But it is more comprehensible in terms of Jungian psychology. The patterns and movements of the poem are archetypal in nature: the death of the father; the descent into the depths (here into the evolutionary-genetic abyss of the self); the return to the world of light; the return of the father (here connected with the sun god); and the promise of renewal. These patterns are as old as myth itself, for they rise from the collective unconscious. The narrator is both Telemachus and Odysseus (for both are really two aspects of the same psyche).

There are two short poems in *The Lost Son* that help to explain one of the basic ideas or attitudes of the book: man's relationship to his evolutionary past. "Night Crow" suggests that certain images can conjure up analogical images from our collective unconscious, or even perhaps from a genetically transmitted memory. "River Incident" implies that our evolutionary past is present in our bodies; thus we can "feel" or intuit this past, since it is in our bones, flesh, and blood. It is precisely this past that Roethke explores in *The Lost Son*. This past also allows man to establish an intuitive rapport with the natural world. There has never been another Western poet who has achieved the same kind of feeling of oneness with nature in his poetry that Roethke has. Thoreau's, Whitman's, and their transcendentalist forebears' sense of communion with nature is spiritual, in that all partake of the Godhead, and quite different from Roethke's literal and concrete kinship. Before Darwin, Western man's belief in his superiority to the natural world would not allow him to feel that oneness. And even in the period after Darwin, evolution was only a novel idea for most people. But now many have had time to absorb the implications of evolution; they can feel, rather than merely understand, their relationship to the rest of nature. Roethke was the first poet to give intense expression to this new attitude.

Roethke had already moved to Seattle when *The Lost Son* was published. At first his feelings about the city were ambivalent. He liked the natural beauty of the area and especially the riot of plant life about him. He also liked the easy, informal campus life; there were none of the pretentions of dress and manners that he had found in the East. On the other hand, Seattle was a provincial town—a bourgeois town run by matriarchs who had just stepped out from under the hairdryer, he said. But Roethke soon settled into a routine of life and was happier than he had been in any of his previous teaching positions. He was required to teach only two classes; he found the students good; and within his first year he was made a full professor. Again he was popular with his students. Among these students were several who were to become poets in their own right: Carolyn Kizer, David Wagoner, James Wright. Furthermore, Roethke got on well with the administration. Robert Heilman, who was made department head in 1948, became one of Roethke's most loyal supporters. Also, Roethke found almost upon arrival in Seattle a replacement for Mary Garrett and Kitty Stokes as a mother figure in Jerry Lee Willis, a widow, who was also a teacher in the English department.

Under these favorable conditions Roethke worked hard at both his teaching and his poetry. His serious work was on the poems that would make up *Praise to the End!*, but he was also writing a sequence of children's poems about animals that were published as *I Am! Says the Lamb* in 1961 (some of these poems appeared as early as 1950 in the magazine *Flair*). During the summer of 1949 Roethke went to Saginaw, where he could work uninterrupted. He concentrated intensely on his poetry throughout the vacation. When he returned to Washington in September, his friends saw that he was obviously in a highly agitated state. In October, he had to be taken to the local hospital, from which he was transferred in November to a sanitarium. Roethke remained there recuperating and working on his poetry until March 1950. Since he was on leave without pay from the university and his expenses were heavy, Roethke applied for another Guggenheim Fellowship, which was granted in the spring of 1950. That summer Roethke went east to Yaddo; in September he bought his first automobile and drove it cross-country to Seattle. Now recovered from his illness, he returned to teaching for the fall semester. Sometime this year he finished the poems for *Praise to the End!* and sent the manuscript to Doubleday. They accepted the book and it was published in November 1951.

The title of the volume is taken from Wordsworth's *The Prelude* (I). It consists of thirteen long poems, nine of which were retained in *The Collected Poems*. Although reviews of the book were generally favorable, the reviewers expressed no sense of surprise, of discovery, as they had in reviews of *The Lost Son*, for *Praise to the End!* is really a

continuation of the mode and themes of its predecessor. The volume explores further the child's sensibility, which has not been separated by self-consciousness from the world about it. In fact, it is a world in which there is a fluid movement between the conscious and the unconscious. It is a world of extraordinary immediacy—if the reader is willing to give himself over to it. But it is also a myopic and cloying world, especially the poems of the first section. Those of the second section, "Praise to the End!" and "I Cry, Love! Love!" in particular, open up the perspective a bit more. The narrator begins to reveal what he has learned in this immediate world of *things*. The "thingy spirit," a primitive spirit of energy and light that pervades primordial life, has revealed itself to him; and the reader senses that by the end of the volume the narrator is ready, and willing, to leave the world of plants and animals and inanimate things. He has absorbed all he can from it and is prepared to enter the conscious world of the adult. But, when at the end of "I Cry, Love! Love!" he says, "We never enter / Alone," the reader realizes the narrator will not leave the world behind entirely: he will carry it with him as an integral part of his being.

Roethke now had three volumes of poetry and a reputation. In 1951 he received *Poetry* magazine's Levinson Prize. In 1952 he was awarded a Ford Foundation grant, which he had applied for so that he would have time to read in philosophy and theology, as well as work on his poetry. And in the spring of 1952 his friend Dylan Thomas visited the Seattle campus. There he stated that Roethke was the best poetry reader in America. (Roethke cherished this praise from the master reader himself and often repeated it.) Roethke was now at the height of his career, and he no longer had to worry about money as he had in the past. In June he went to Saginaw to see his family and work undisturbed, away from the distractions in Seattle. He remained in Saginaw most of the fall. In December he went to New York to give a poetry reading. There he ran into one of his former Bennington students, a beautiful woman, Beatrice O'Connell from Winchester, Virginia. She was now living in New York teaching art in a public school in Harlem. They began to see each other daily; their courtship was short: they married within a month, on 3 January 1953.

For their honeymoon, the Roethkes went to Europe, where W. H. Auden had lent them his villa at Ischia. They stayed at the villa from early March through May, living a relaxed if somewhat primitive existence. Here Roethke worked on poems that would later go into *Words for the Wind*. From

Ischia, they went on to Rome, to Geneva, then on to Paris. In July they crossed the channel to England, where they remained until the first week in August. This was the first time Roethke had left the North American continent. He did not like the anxieties travel caused him and refused to do much sightseeing, but he enjoyed the social life, for he got to see many of his old acquaintances and make a number of new literary friends. In August they returned to America, visited Saginaw, and arrived in Seattle at the beginning of September. There they rented a house on the shore of Lake Washington and settled down to married life.

In September 1953 Doubleday brought out *The Waking*, a selection of Roethke's poems, written between 1933 and 1953. It also included eight new poems. The first of these—"O, Thou Opening, O," "A Light Breather," and "The Visitant"—continue in the mode of *The Lost Son* and *Praise to the End!* However, in "The Visitant" the form of a woman materializes briefly amidst the natural world: she seems to be the idealized female spirit who will lead the narrator out of his "thingy" world and into the social world where he can find his place in relationship to other human beings. And certainly the other new poems in the collection manifest an entirely different world from that of the first three. For instance, the often anthologized "Elegy for Jane," in which Roethke expresses his sense of loss at the death of a student, is quite conventional in terms of its manner and sentiment. The two most successful poems in the collection, however, are "Four for Sir John Davies" and "The Waking"— perhaps the greatest poems Roethke ever wrote. In the first, a four-part poem, Roethke is having a good time with his jokes and wordplays, yet he still deals with serious metaphysical concepts. The initial idea for the poem was suggested by Davies's "Orchestra," but Roethke combines a number of other ideas and allusions here. (Particularly, Roethke pays his homage to Yeats, whom he had studied for some years and to whom he owed a great deal in developing his methods of composition.) The central concern of the poem is the relationship between the ideal and the material world. The "Dance" of the first section refers to the dance of life (done to the cadence of song). "The Partner" of the second section is the real woman who comes as a fulfillment of the female spirit of "The Visitant." She draws the narrator into a social context and lifts him above the animality of his baser nature. But she eventually does more than that, for in the Western tradition of Romantic love she is an earthly embodiment of the ideal. Ultimately, like Dante's Beatrice, she leads the narrator into the realm of ideality. Thus, through love, the narrator transcends the material world and redeems his own fleshly nature. The whole poem builds in strong, even iambic cadences toward the final couplet—one of the greatest in all poetry—"Who rise from flesh to spirit know the fall / The word outleaps the world, and light is all." It is the climactic expression of the theme that has been developed throughout the poem. But whatever one says about it seems totally inadequate to explain its precision and power. "The Waking" is an entirely different kind of poem. The theme is particularly modern: now that man can look back on the long evolution of life on earth and the development of human culture, he sees that the belief of the Enlightenment in his ability to control his destiny through the exercise of rational thought and will misses the mark considerably. Man has evolved through a long process of trial and error; his civilization has evolved in much the same way. And yet there seems to be an intuition, or spirit, that pervades the world: it, rather than rational thought, is the force that leads man's progress. In "The Waking" Roethke applies this idea to his own life. He "thinks by feeling" and "learns by going." He is not sure where he will end up, but he has faith that intuition will direct him to his proper destination. The tight, repetitive villanelle form reinforces the feeling that a purposeful fate is at work in his life.

In November 1953 Roethke had a minor mental breakdown, probably the result of the unsettling effect of travel during the past year, and of his intense emotional life with Beatrice. The precipitating event seems to have been the death of Dylan Thomas on 5 November. Roethke recovered quickly, however, and was home with his wife for Christmas. In February he suffered another shock when his mother died. It had been a bad fall and winter, but good news came several weeks later: he had won the Pulitzer Prize for *The Waking*.

During the next year the Roethkes remained in Seattle, moving their residence twice. Roethke continued his teaching and worked hard at his poetry. He had, however, in retrospect, decided that he liked to travel, particularly since it allowed him to escape from the routine of teaching. He applied for a Fulbright grant to go to Italy and was awarded one for the academic year 1955-1956. In September the Roethkes took passage to Gibraltar and toured southern Spain. From there they went to Madrid, to Barcelona and then along the French Riviera to Italy, where Roethke was to teach at the Magistero in Florence. It was a teachers' college, and Roethke was unhappy with his students, because he could not get them to "hear" English poetry. But he liked being abroad well enough, for he tried to get his Fulbright extended for the next year to teach at Bedford College in London; his application, however, was turned down. In April Roethke delivered several lectures in Rome, and in the following month he gave two lecture-readings in Austria. In July, on their way home, the Roethkes stopped in Paris, where they met René Char. Roethke had admired his poetry, and now he found he liked the man as well. In August, before embarking for America, the Roethkes spent two weeks in England being entertained by old friends such as Stephen Spender, William Empson, and Dame Edith Sitwell. Roethke had enjoyed this European tour much more than the first. This time, he could travel without anxiety. And now he was sure that his work was respected and admired on both sides of the Atlantic.

In September 1956 Roethke resumed teaching at the University of Washington. The year went well, and during the summer the Roethkes purchased their first house—on the shore of Lake Washington where Roethke had lived when he first came to Seattle. In September 1957, however, he began to show symptoms of another mental breakdown. It was serious this time: he was hospitalized for three months. Nevertheless he recovered soon enough to return to his teaching duties in the spring. In the fall of 1958 Doubleday published *Words for the Wind* (forty-three new poems and a selection of the best work from his earlier volumes). The critical reception was overwhelmingly favorable, and for the volume he received a number of awards the following year; among them, the Bollingen Prize and the National Book Award. Roethke's ego, which always craved adulation, and had often felt slighted in the past, was elated by this well-earned recognition and praise: it was evident that he was a major poet—maybe *the* major poet.

The new poems of *Words for the Wind* are divided into five groups. The first contains several humorous pieces and children's verses. Roethke delighted in this kind of poetry all his life; only T. S. Eliot was his peer at writing it. The second group is love poems. They continue and develop the theme of "Four for Sir John Davies": the relationship between the ideal and the real in the loved woman. As in *The Waking*, the woman appears first as an idealized vision (in "The Dream"). The vision then assumes material form in the lover. The first benefit the lover brings is to draw the narrator out of the abyss of himself and into the objective world, a world that gains completion by the conjunction of two opposites: the ideal descends to take palpable form in

the woman as the animal nature of the man is drawn upward to meet it. The release in the narrator from the constrictions of self-love brings a great joy, which he shares with the lover: "I bear, but not alone, / The burden of this joy" ("Words for the Wind"). The problem is that the narrator may love the ideal rather than the real woman. The lover realizes this and says, "O love me while I am, / You green thing in my way!" He does, but he also realizes her spiritual value as an ideal. And finally, as in "The Swan," she redeems him through the transcendence of their love: "She sighs me white, a Socrates of snow."

One of the most famous of the love poems is "I Knew a Woman." Some critics have found its sentiment and exaggeration embarrassing. Certainly the poem is hyperbolic and sentimental. But the sentiment is beautifully balanced with humor: as the awkward lover moves about his primum mobile, the reader laughs but also senses the lover's earnestness and feels the power of love. It is one of the most successful love poems in the language. "The Sensualists," from this section, is different in tone from the others. Here love has been degraded by the carnality of the lover, who has forgotten the ideal. Roethke seems to have included it, and placed it strategically, as a contrast and balance to the other love poems.

The third group of poems, "Voices and Creatures," represents a return to the natural world: both its ugliness and its grace are evoked. "The Beast" presents the narrator's desire to enter nature (or to be at one with his own animal nature), and his regrets about his inability to do so, for he is now part of the conscious, rational world of man.

The fourth division is a single poem, "Dying Man," written in memory of W. B. Yeats. It, like the love poems, represents an attempt to reconcile the life of the spirit with the life of the flesh, but in a much broader context—much like Yeats's "Sailing to Byzantium."

The final section, "Meditations of an Old Woman," is written in memory of Roethke's mother, and was begun shortly after her death in 1954. In actuality it seems to be an attempt to merge his and his mother's identities, to articulate for her those thoughts she could never have articulated herself. It carries forward the themes of the love poems and "Dying Man" to a pantheistic reconciliation to death. "Meditations" certainly is indebted to Yeats's Crazy Jane poems, but it owes a debt also to Wallace Stevens's "Sunday Morning."

In January 1959 Roethke had another mental breakdown and was admitted to Halcyon Sanitarium in Seattle. He continued to write poetry, and he was well enough to resume his teaching duties for the spring quarter. During the fall, however, he took leave without pay, having once again won a Ford Foundation grant. In the spring of 1960, the Roethkes went to New York, where Roethke gave several readings. In June they embarked for another trip to Europe. They went to Paris and Brittany, but Roethke's real object on this trip was to visit the country of Yeats and Joyce. In July they flew to Dublin. They toured the country and visited Yeats's widow. In November they went to London, where they stayed through the winter. There Roethke gave several readings and appeared on the BBC, as he had on his last visit in 1956. In March they flew back to America, in time for Roethke to teach for the spring quarter, and for the publication of his book of children's poems *I Am! Says the Lamb.*

Roethke remained in Seattle for the last years of his life, teaching, working on the poems that would appear posthumously as *The Far Field*, and making frequent trips to receive awards and give readings. In June 1962 he was presented an honorary Doctor of Letters degree from his alma mater, the University of Michigan. In October he gave a reading for the Seattle World's Fair. By the summer of 1963, he had completed the first draft of the manuscript for *The Far Field*. He intended to revise it further, but on 1 August, while swimming in a friend's pool, he had a coronary occlusion from which he could not be revived. He was buried beside his mother and father in Oakwood Cemetery in Saginaw. At the time of his death Roethke's reputation was high in both America and Europe. Many considered him the best American poet of his generation. Since his death there has been a steadily increasing interest in his poetry both by critics and the reading public. Most have placed him in the top rank of all American poets. Had he lived another ten years, he might have received the Nobel Prize he so coveted during the later part of his life.

In 1964 Doubleday published *The Far Field* in the form Roethke had left it. The first, and best, section, "North American Sequence," contains six meditative poems. In tone and form they are indebted to Whitman, Eliot (of "Ash Wednesday" and *Four Quartets*), Stevens, and Robinson Jeffers. But no one save Roethke could have written them. Here the persona returns to the natural world; it is not, however, the same world of *The Lost Son* and *Praise to the End!* For between these two immersions, the poet has spent his time both in the social world and the philosophical and spiritual world of ideality. In the process the natural world

has become objectified: it is no longer the subjective, internalized natural world of *The Lost Son.* Thus, when the poet of *The Far Field* reenters nature, he is not reentering himself. Rather his desire is to become one with all things. Although he has doubts, when the natural world seems to be a meaningless abyss, the prevailing image is one of nature redeemed by a pervasive spiritual light. This is particularly true of "Meditation at Oyster River" and "The Far Field." In the final poem of the sequence, "The Rose," he sees the world imbued with such spiritual significance that he feels no need for heaven.

The second section is a group of love poems. They are not nearly so good as those of *Words for the Wind*, but significantly Roethke projects himself into the mind of the loved girl in several of them. The following section is called "Mixed Sequence." The first poem, "The Abyss," is a continuation of the themes of "North American Sequence," but in a tighter form. It is followed by miscellaneous poems, including several about his childhood ("Elegy," "Otto," and "The Chums") and several written about his European experiences ("The Lizard" and "The Storm"). The final section is entitled "Sequence, Sometimes Metaphysical." It returns to the themes of the first section, but treats them in a more formal manner. The first poem, "In a Dark Time," is concerned with how one climbs out of the abyss of self to become one with God. The subsequent poems pursue this relationship between the man, the natural world, the loved woman, and the Godhead. The sequence reaches its conclusion in "Once More, the Round," which ends:

> Now I adore my life
> With the Bird, the abiding Leaf,
> With the Fish, the questing Snail,
> And the Eye altering all;
> And I dance with William Blake
> For love, for Love's sake;
>
> And everything comes to One,
> As we dance on, dance on, dance on.

It is the fitting conclusion to the volume—and to Roethke's career: the poetic emotional and spiritual journey had come to its proper end. It is difficult to imagine where he could have gone from here.

Letters:

Selected Letters of Theodore Roethke, ed. Ralph J. Mills, Jr. (Seattle & London: University of Washington Press, 1968; London: Faber & Faber, 1970).

Interview:

Cleanth Brooks and Robert Penn Warren, eds., *Conversations on the Craft of Poetry* (New York: Holt, Rinehart & Winston, 1961), pp. 48-62.

Bibliographies:

James R. McLeod, *Theodore Roethke: A Manuscript Checklist* (Kent, Ohio: Kent State University Press, 1971);

McLeod, *Theodore Roethke: A Bibliography* (Kent, Ohio: Kent State University Press, 1973);

Keith R. Moul, *Theodore Roethke's Career: An Annotated Bibliography* (Boston: G. K. Hall, 1977).

Biography:

Allan Seager, *The Glass House: The Life of Theodore Roethke* (New York: McGraw-Hill, 1968).

References:

Richard Allen Blessing, *Theodore Roethke's Dynamic Vision* (Bloomington: Indiana University Press, 1974);

William Heyen, ed., *Profile of Theodore Roethke* (Columbus, Ohio: Merrill, 1971);

Jenijoy La Belle, *The Echoing Wood of Theodore Roethke* (Princeton: Princeton University Press, 1976);

Gary Lane, ed., *A Concordance to the Poems of Theodore Roethke* (Metuchen, N.J.: Scarecrow Press, 1972);

Karl Malkoff, *Theodore Roethke: an Introduction to the Poetry* (New York: Columbia University Press, 1966);

Ralph J. Mills, Jr., *Theodore Roethke* (Minneapolis: University of Minnesota Press, 1963);

Jay Parrini, *Theodore Roethke: an American Romantic* (Amherst: University of Massachusetts Press, 1979);

Nathan Scott, Jr., *The Wild Prayer of Longing: Poetry and the Sacred* (New Haven: Yale University Press, 1971),

Arnold Stein, ed., *Theodore Roethke: Essays on the Poetry* (Seattle: University of Washington Press, 1965);

Rosemary Sullivan, *Theodore Roethke: The Garden Master* (Seattle: University of Washington Press, 1975);

Harry Williams, *"The Edge Is What I Have"* (Lewisburg, Pa.: Bucknell University Press, 1977).

M. L. ROSENTHAL
(14 March 1917-)

SELECTED BOOKS: *The Modern Poets: A Critical Introduction* (New York & London: Oxford University Press, 1960);

Blue Boy on Skates: Poems (New York & London: Oxford University Press, 1964);

The New Poets: American and British Poetry since World War II (New York & London: Oxford University Press, 1967);

Beyond Power: New Poems (New York & London: Oxford University Press, 1969);

The View from the Peacock's Tail: Poems (New York & London: Oxford University Press, 1972);

Poetry and the Common Life (New York & London: Oxford University Press, 1974);

She: Poems (Brockport, N.Y.: BOA Editions, 1977);

Sailing into the Unknown: Yeats, Pound, and Eliot (New York & London: Oxford University Press, 1978).

Macha Louis Rosenthal, poet, critic, editor, and teacher, was born in Washington, D.C., the son of Jacob and Ethel Brown Rosenthal. He took his B.A. (1937) and M.A. (1938) degrees at the University of Chicago. On 7 January 1939, he married Victoria Himmelstein, now a senior psychiatric social worker. They have three children: David, Alan, and Laura. From 1939 to 1945, he taught as an instructor in English at Michigan State University in East Lansing, Michigan. In 1946, he was hired as an instructor at New York University, where he earned his Ph.D. in 1949. He has also done special studies at the University of Michigan and Johns Hopkins University. In 1961, he served as U.S. Cultural Exchange Program visiting specialist to Germany; in 1965, to Pakistan; in 1966, to Rumania, Poland, and Bulgaria, and in 1980, to Italy and France. In 1974, he was a visiting poet in Israel. From 1977 to 1979 he served as director of the Poetics Institute at New York University where he is still a professor of English, and he lives in Suffern, New York. He is a fellow of the American Council of Learned Societies and has twice won Guggenheim Fellowships (1960, 1964). He has contributed poems, articles, and reviews to such leading journals as the *New Yorker,* the *New Statesman, Poetry,* the *Spectator* (London), *ELH,* and the *Quarterly Review of Literature;* he has also served, from 1956-1961, as poetry editor of the *Nation,* from 1970-1978 as poetry editor of the *Humanist,* and since 1973 as poetry editor of *Present Tense.*

In his numerous critical works, Rosenthal has made many statements about the function of poets, the purpose of a single poem, and the nature of poetry, expressing such thoughts as,

> Poets are the verbal antennae of a people. The awareness they distill and convert into the dynamics of language is somehow present in the populace at large.

> What poets have to report rises from a world of experience shared with people of all conditions, people whose inward sense of life is of the same order as their own.

> A poem is the putting out of the soul to scavenge.

> I *want* each poem to be and say at least as much as the insight behind it—its dynamics to betray more than I realized.

> Poetry depends absolutely on its idiosyncratic truthfulness to the poet's own sense of reality.

> Poetry is the voice of the common life.

> Poetry, and perhaps modern poetry especially, is saturated with political consciousness.

> In poetry as in no other form of thought, all ideas are referred to the seismograph of inner awareness.

> Common speech, common awareness, are both the soil and the substance of the most absorbing poetry.

These quotations indicate a fundamental tension that runs throughout all his verse: the public versus the private voice, political consciousness versus inward states of feeling. These opposing tendencies may be seen in the subjects treated in one of his books of criticism, *Poetry and the Common Life* (1974). This study is divided into six chapters, the titles of which serve as the most succinct summary of the overall themes in his own poetry: "Poetry and Ordinary Experience"; "Memory and the Sources of Poetry"; "Musics of Awareness: Time and Space"; "Musics of Awareness: Association and Feeling"; "Politics"; "Love and Death and Private

Layle Silbert

Things." In his use of forms and techniques, he ranges from the traditional rhyme of the controlled lyric to more open metrical forms, including free verse; however, his most characteristic form is the sequence or a series of related poems. Sometimes his experiments with the visual line approach the daring. Although his diction is frequently colloquial, his language is always clear.

Rosenthal's first collection of verse, *Blue Boy on Skates* (1964), was published when he was forty-seven. The book contains thirty-four poems and one mixture of prose and poetry entitled "Footnote." Most of the poems are no longer than a page. The setting for many of the poems is the urban environment of New York City. In several ways, the title of the volume and the title poem provide clues to the character, form, and content of all the poems. *The Blue Boy* is, of course, the title of Thomas Gainsborough's striking, sensitive painting of a young boy. Rosenthal is attracted to this figure not because he believes that he still possesses the youth of Gainsborough's boy but because he feels at middle age a youthful vigor and an artist's sensitivity. The title poem, "Blue Boy on Skates (Twilight)," elaborates the metaphor in detail. Twilight is a time of romance but also the transition period between light and dark, life and death. The skating motion suggests the type of poet-artist that Rosenthal conceives himself to be, for his lyrics will stress graceful ease of motion—"I whirr away through the summer air." However, his poetic material is the recalcitrant, sometimes ugly, "stone" of the city. Thus, the creative act that results in song is fraught with tension as "the metal on the stone / does the singing." The roller-skating metaphor is not meant to trivialize the breadth of the poet's interests: although his motion is light and easy, although it only skims the surface, the artistic designs—that is, concerns and themes—encompass "little and big circles." The themes of the first volume include love, death, the sources of poetry, and the urban condition; in many poems, these concerns coalesce.

The main interest of the first volume is the poet's response to urban scenes and urban figures. Love in the city is often tawdry and sordid, if not desperate. In "Message," a modern-day Helen of Troy sends this plea: "Mack, I want you! / Come to 88 East 88 Street at once! / I love you! I need you!" Years later, the male speaker thumbs through his old address book and muses over his one-night stands: "I do not remember her name, her face, her city." The city seems to be filled with sardonic figures and social injustice. In "Three Conversations," Washington Square is viewed as a tableau whose figures include a "delegation of pot-hunting dandies," "green-lidded girls," and "the cop, shoving the drunk." The figure in "Jim Dandy" is a sardonic but urbane dandy who cruelly sported with and then deserted anonymous ladies in the park. While he cut a dashing figure about town, twirling "a gay guitar" and smoking "the sweetest cigar," he also "lay on the grass / With the head of the class / And left her all ajar." Poems about unnamed male figures capture other unattractive or disturbing aspects of the city: the competitive business executive in "Oyez!" rises "to the top like / Oil in bilge water," while an overnight visitor in a downtown hotel ("In a Hotel Bed") suffers through a surreal nightmare that begins with "the shower-thing dripping" and moves through devils bumping on the windowpane, "corpses / Dragging down corridors to laundry chutes," and the John Birchers smashing down his door.

Injustice and prejudice against different ethnic groups are portrayed through dramatic encounters in "The Intruders" and "The Enemy." In "The Intruders" irony is heaped upon irony as a cycle of retaliations is set off. The gruesome action begins when "A man came from a certain far place

(downstairs), / Saying that the people there were dying." Because the speaker feels uneasy and irritated at this interruption of his trivial activities (he's filing his nails), he reacts swiftly and matter-of-factly: "I put a bullet through his head." This action does not end the speaker's troubles but causes new ones, as "his countrymen lately / Keep setting fire to my house." The whole round of bigotry ends with the sardonic epigram, "One's always having one's personal affairs intruded on." "The Enemy" is one of the most interesting and realistic poems in the volume. Here Rosenthal presents an incident from his childhood memories—an ethnic brawl in front of the corner grocery store. Urban violence and community prejudice begin at an early age: "The enemy's a little pale guy, squats / Behind the breadbox outside the corner grocery / White-hot. . . ." That afternoon Rosenthal, the "Jewish kid," loses to Raymond and his "three staunch Christian friends" his bread and coins; years later, the mature poet forgives them all and understands the larger culprit behind the incident—"Oh, could enemies but crucify . . . foolish History!"

Other poems in the first volume deal with the larger themes of death and love. For Rosenthal, death is a certain and final state of cold inertia—like "the stars in all their silence" in the impressionistic series "The Gate"—but in such poems as "A Song of Dead Friends," "Memorial Day Inscriptions," and "If I Forget Thee," the deceased live in the region of memory, one of the sources of poetry. More important to the poet, however, is the force of love, which works to counteract both the ravages of death and disturbing, harsh aspects of the city. Three poems that rely on a love-at-a-window motif are placed strategically near the beginning, middle, and end of the collection. Humaneness, the simple thrust of love reaching out beyond self-absorption, is the saving gesture in "My Reflection in the Study Window." In the sequence poem "Liston Cows Patterson And Knocks Him Silly," the urban scene is violent and dingy; a scream is heard in "a dirty street" and the glass of the window is "soiled." Yet an unnamed woman—a threadbare Byronic delight who "walks in beauty, in that one sweater and skirt / that are all she has"—gives love and comfort to the speaker and announces his aggression: "She loves me. I touch. She touches." In the final piece ("Footnote," an admixture of poetry and prose), the speaker gazes from a window at the city below on a late winter afternoon and knows that the "faces of men are terrible because, until they are the faces of friends, they are blank." Again, love and compassion are needed to sustain the human community, and the speaker hears the message in the snorting of an old sea elephant in the distance: "BLOUAUGH! I LOVE YOU!"

Reviewers of Rosenthal's first collection of verse showed only a little love for his work. Although some praised his "lyrical incisiveness," his "clear-cut" language, his "provocative forms," his "restraint," his "candor," and his "wisdom," most wondered why he bothered at the age of forty-seven to turn from writing distinguished criticism to writing poetry. They complained that the poems were "slight in conception," marred by "excessive literary allusiveness," or, more generally, "strained," "uncommunicative," and "unmemorable." All this changed, however, with the appearance of his second volume, *Beyond Power* (1969). Generally, reviewers were impressed with the new seriousness of this volume: one called it "a serious attempt to analyze what ails us," and another noted that "it is marked by a deeper and more enriched tone." Two separate voices are interwoven throughout the volume: one is the public voice that expresses the poet's agony over Vietnam and other tragedies of the 1960s; the other is the private voice that grieves over the recent loss of his mother and brother.

The poems in the public voice are built on both form and content. Concerning the impact of Vietnam on poetry, Rosenthal has written: "There is little question that the war in Vietnam, and the sense of government as an impersonal, impervious, complex engine of destruction, has murderously colored the sense of spiritual desolation of much recent American poetry." The poetic form most appropriate to this social context is the sequence in which "the speaking sensibility" is itself "testing the social and cultural landscape, the lines of continuity with the past, and the prospects of possible reconciliation with the alienating real world at every step along the way."

Two sequence poems demonstrate these principles. The impressive "Beyond Power: A Sequence" is composed of four parts and is based on the Paris street demonstrations of May 1968. In the first part of the sequence, "Paris, 1968," the poet shows why he is interested in Paris: the setting stresses the international (as opposed to national or narrowly partisan) implications of the protests—"Songs in all languages! / The Great Babel Festival is on!"—and the scene recalls past incidents of violence in French history—"Spilt blood on paving stones called back / the brute wash of ancient powers." Although the realization is depressing, the history of tyranny and revolution is cyclical: "He reigned, fell, rose again.— / Reigns he now, or hangs?" Part 2, "The

Radiance," captures splendidly the excitement of a brief moment when hope and idealism surge. Here the young people in the streets sense the sound of a new voice and the "touch of new hands." In the face of this ritual of brotherhood, "The man of power grew silent." Tragically, the heavy irony of the final lines dispels the dream of youth: *Fraternité*, thy moment chimes. / Forgive us, we are not ready." Part 3, "Three Poets," alludes to the fates of Vladimir Mayakovski, Boris Pasternak, and Hart Crane, all of whom looked forward to a new social order but ended their lives in despair or suicide. Poetry and humane idealism are no match against "a million troops, / a million children with clenched fists, / a million tanks." Part 4, "Beyond Power," is the most affecting and sardonic of the four-poem sequence. Here the "man of power" is presented as blind to the wider perspective of the humane "crystal river" that "purifies each life" because he "sees only his own reflection." The consequences of a political leader's constricted vision are widespread in society: "Blasted are the meek, for their leaders inherit the earth." After surveying the contemporary political landscape, the speaker's spirit is left desolate, and he concludes that gestures of love are faltering, if not impotent: "I put out my hand to you. The darkness touches / upon us. It is too much for us. It is our own reflection." The unhappy tone and ironic technique are not as effective in another sequence with worldwide political implications, "Three Songs for Children." Parts 1 and 2, "London" and "God," present a fanciful world of daydream where noise and pollution problems are solved by people and cars floating magically up above the clouds, a world in which God wears many disguises but is always elusive. Not until part 3, "Civil Defense Act," is the answer to the mysterious riddle provided: the clouds are mushroom clouds and the poet has been talking about the aftermath of nuclear holocaust.

Other individual poems in *Beyond Power* employ the public voice to rage against the injustices of politics or the impersonality of history. One poem, "Lord Hee-Haw," commingles an allusion to Lord Haw-Haw, the British Nazi propagandist who was executed as a traitor, with the braying sounds of an ass. The poem is a capsule picture of some of the horrors of the 1960s, a decade replete with assassins and executioners at home—"Our true loves have all died in our arms"—and with the dehumanizing agony of Vietnam: "Napalm-blazing ghosts enkindle 'the psychopathology of every day life'; / The 'human form divine' flops in wrinkling balloons." In "To the Rulers," he makes a direct and high-pitched appeal to political leaders to "Lay down

```
                              ONCE


      "Mistress," I said to her

      whose name is body of my desire,

      "will these green days

      remain with us forever?"


      "Mistress," I said to her

      whose name is all my thought,

      "I had forgot

      the very name of Death.

      Desire for Her blew through me once like the mistral."


      A cold, forgotten voice replied,

      "Desire blew through us once like the mistral."
```

M. L. Rosenthal

"Once," typescript

arms" and withdraw from Vietnam: "He who withdraws / wins / by these souls."

A good portion of the volume's sense of spiritual desolation, however, is attributable to Rosenthal's personal grief over the recent loss of close relatives. The dedication on the first page reads "To the memory of my parents and my brother." The poems that evoke their memory, "I Strike a Match," "Winter without Danny," and "Farewell," all have winter settings in which the chill of death grips the snow-covered earth. The personal grief is overwhelming because he believes that there are no heavenly rewards beyond death; that is why the subject of immortality is treated so humorously in "Funerals Depress Me, For Some Reason," in which Jesus and Lazarus, "the sole habitants of Heaven," ironically cannot understand why none of the invited guests come to the party in the sky. But this note of humor is rare: the awareness of death evokes a private voice that is brooding and introspective. In several poems this meditative thrust is linked to the image of a mirror. Whereas the window serves as an emblem of outward-directed love in *Blue Boy*, in *Beyond Power* the mirror represents inward preoccupations, isolation, and loneliness as the poet confronts his own mortality. Thus, in the complex poem "Into the Mirror," the speaker's line of sight fluctuates between viewing the world of nature through a train window and seeing his own image reflected in that same mirror-window. Although the speaker thinks longingly of an unnamed lover, he cannot get beyond the self-absorption symbolized by his fascination with his own reflection. Furthermore, the impersonal world of nature that flies by outside provides no Wordsworthian comfort or aid: "Norfolk's green world out there flying, / it is a love-thrust takes me / into, out of, nothing." The mirror image is also essential to the three-part prose poem "The Footprint on the Mirror," a reverie that coalesces thoughts about his own death with the

211

pressing memories of his recently deceased close relatives. In part 1 the poet looks at himself in his bedroom mirror and sees both a "face perhaps enlivened by spirit" and the print of a "passing bloody foot that had cut its mark on the mirror." Was it the abstract noun Time that had moved from the room into the mirror? The answer is personal and poignant: "If a soul, it was a soul with slashed feet. And indeed, of course, it *was* my own soul, my own self, in pursuit of my own death." Part 2 opens with the injunction "Let us summon up beautiful faces." For a time, the poet can recall happy memories of friends and relatives now gone. Eventually, however, the mirror renders a stark truth, the reflection of his inner soul: "But now the faces become one face, shadowed with some inward desolation." Part 3 offers no hope of immortality through the sustaining force of love. In the boundless regions of space, earthly loved ones recede "a light year away." When all the desolation—over which man has little or no control—in both public and private spheres is tallied, one wonders whether "Beyond Our Power" would have been a more appropriate title for the volume.

In his third book of poetry, *The View from the Peacock's Tail* (1972), Rosenthal shows a new command of both form and content. This volume of thirty-four poems is the most direct expression of the poet's actual personality; ironic masks are dropped. One reviewer stated the accomplishment succinctly: "Protective irony is replaced by a more open compassion." Others hailed the "voice of seasoned wisdom," the qualities of "openness" and "gentleness," and observed that "We are exposed to the depths of the poet's concern, to that sensibility of how vulnerable is rational thought when faced by the excesses of the modern age." In this volume, Rosenthal discovered the full potentials of his characteristic poetic form—the sequence. In his essay "We Begin These Sequences Lightly," contributed to William Heyen's *American Poets in 1976* (1976), he discusses in great detail the poetic form of the sequence and how it applies to both *The View from the Peacock's Tail* and his fourth volume of verse, *She* (1977):

> The key to making a sequence is the key of immediacy. It is struck in the quick of language. It animates ideas and makes them organs of the poem's body. (A sequence is a larger body made of smaller units, self-sufficient for the most part.) . . .
>
> . . . Because it enables one to project these psychic shifts so readily, the poetic sequence is

our form of both epic and bardic poetry. It embodies cultural tasks and it assumes prophecy. Its protean landmark is the private sensibility, against which we test everything. The touchstone of reality, now more than ever before, is intensity of experience. Moments of such intensity, high points of self-confirmation by the poem's ultimate voice, are almost essential to its genuineness and conviction.

The thirty-four poems (a sixth of which are prose poems) in *The View From the Peacock's Tail* are divided into three sections, and they cover a diverse range of thematic topics: revolution, drugs, violence, love, death, and the poetic vocation. Section 1, "His Present Discontents," is a sequence in twelve parts. The source of the series is political, as he explains in his essay for the Heyen collection: " 'His Present Discontents' began coming to me during a period. . . . [when,] in the aftermath of the 'revolutionary' 1960s, I was thinking a great deal about the connections between private intensities of all sorts and the claims of the political left, from Lenin to the Students for a Democratic Society and the Weathermen. Personal crisis and social crisis always seem to reflect one another." As for the content of the sequence, he notes that it is " 'about' human murderousness, desire, the enterprise of beauty"; however, he stresses that the entire form of the sequence must be experienced by the reader because "nothing matters of all I might say unless the play of feeling, the shifting tones, and the whole growing complex of elements speak for themselves." Thus, the poems of the sequence cannot be picked apart analytically. To read this sequence is to experience the workings of the organic, associative process: the Joycean stream-of-consciousness technique harnessed to poetic form.

In section 2, "Notations of Love," the poet shifts ground from the political to the intimate. The poem "Late at Night" contains the source of the volume's title and elaborates two important metaphors that recur throughout: the peacock and the stage. The peacock is a beautiful and violent bird; the stage is the public point of intersection of raw reality ("the commonplace") and superficial appearance ("that proud shield of glory up front"). These two metaphors coalesce to define the poet's perspective and to provide the volume's title: "I'm backstage! / O unrehearsed rear of the Real, / the view from the peacock's tail!" Section 2 also contains a five-part sequence entitled "Notations of Love," in which the speaker explores from various perspectives the thoughts linked with feelings of love. In Part 1, "Your Passion Pleases Me," the anticipation of love is conveyed through the image of "a mid-March wind / all rushing past" as two lovers are suddenly drawn together on the street. Part 2, "Incredulous, Our Bodies Are Remembering," captures the postcoital moment of intense nostalgia: "Our loins are heavy, remembering / the sweet penetration, holding it." Here, however, the love act is viewed as an insular experience—"ourselves, we, essence of us / far away and present to our inner touch." In the next poem of the sequence, "In the Burning Glass," the speaker thinks of the multitude of humanity, especially the world's starving children in pain, at the very moment of amorous consummation: "in the marriage bed of our love, there bursts / before our dismayed ecstasy / the terrible human face of need—." Part 4, "Ode on a Young Woman's Confession," extends the multiple perspectives on love by presenting a prostitute and her client. Her thoughts on love are confused—"Terrible to desire someone / you detest"—and nothing comes of her relationship because it is simply a mechanical act, captured in the image of the "rocking boat." Part 5, "First Morning of January," announces the beginning of a new love cycle and serves as an encore by echoing phrases and images from the previous poems. In the final line, the birth of the human soul takes place so that "We do have speech."

Section 3 is entitled "Like Morning Light," and it elaborates the line glancingly mentioned in the prose poem "Jammed Up" in section 1: "I have a 'tragic view of life' *and* an optimistic 'nature.' " The poems in this third section explore the theme of human mortality as the poet meditates on the juxtaposition of romance and reality, passive contemplation and passionate action. The thoughts and actions of poets from the past are used as points of departure: Shakespeare in "Intermission"; Eva E., a childhood poet-friend, in "Like Morning Light"; Sylvia Plath and others who committed suicide in "Deaths of the Poets"; and W. B. Yeats in "Visiting Yeats's Tower." The final poem in the volume, "Memory: A Meditation and a Quarrel with the Master," is one of the collection's most poignant, and it continues to explore the themes of human fragility and the delicate balance between realism and romanticism. Raw reality in the forms of "blood-smeared streets of struggle" and "heaps of human skulls" continues to trouble the poet's imagination. But the memorable words of the poet's own deceased mother in the last line of the book convey the poet's ideal resolution to the problem of human mortality: "Love one another, and the Jews,

and lovely books and thoughts."

She is Rosenthal's fourth and most recent volume of verse. Although it is the slimmest of his volumes (twenty-six poems), it has received extensive treatment by one critic. Sally M. Gall discusses all of the poems in *She* and hails the volume as an "encompassing love poem, a paean to the ability of the human spirit to change despair and desolation into song, and a major addition to the genre of the modern lyric sequence."

Rosenthal provides some interesting reflections on the background of *She* in "We Begin These Sequences Lightly": "If reality touches us awake at all, it does so in many ways. Awakening to love is awakening to anonymity, to loneliness, to the absence of all that has been lost, to the terror of uncontrolled vision." And further, "My 'She' is a woman who makes me think into her childhood and her humanity. . . ." The entire volume *She* is one sequence of poems focused on an enigmatic female figure who evokes the many moods, effects, and perspectives of love; the volume's cycle of feelings oscillates between ecstasy and despair, with various intermediate stages. The ecstatic phase is captured in such poems as "Ecstasy," "From a Distance," "Intimacy," and "Incantation." The poem "Once" links Desire and Death and serves as a transitional passageway to the despair of doubting recorded in "Not Quite Metaphysical" and "The Darkest Dream." In "Night Vision (1973)" and "Through Streets Where Smiling Children," the She-figure is elevated to the status of a blithe female spirit or Beatricean goddess who nurtures hope in the poet surrounded by cruelty and violence in the urban streets of the modern world: "You wear your passion lightly, like a summer frock, / through streets where smiling children kick / each other's heads, twist each other's penises."

Rosenthal's poetry exhibits the qualities of intelligence, energy, variety, and craftsmanship. His poetic vision is sometimes personal, but never private; it is sometimes political, but never inflammatory. The poetic personality that comes through in poem after poem is that of a gentleman blessed with the characteristics of humor and wit, an honesty and generosity of spirit, and a truly humanitarian outlook. His questions are often passionately intense, but his answers are never narrowly dogmatic. In times of suffering and turmoil, his voice of mature wisdom is to be valued. His continuing experiments with the sequence form are an original and important contribution to contemporary poetry.

—*William B. Thesing*

Other:

Chief Modern Poets of Britain and America, edited by Rosenthal, Gerald D. Sanders, and John Herbert Nelson (New York: Macmillan, 1962; revised, 1970);

The New Modern Poetry: An Anthology of British and American Poetry since World War II, edited by Rosenthal (New York: Macmillan, 1967; revised edition, New York: Oxford University Press, 1969);

"Some Thoughts on American Poetry Today," in *Contemporary Poetry in America: Essays and Interviews*, ed. Robert Boyers (New York: Schocken Books, 1974);

"We Begin These Sequences Lightly," in *American Poets in 1976*, ed. William Heyen (Indianapolis: Bobbs-Merrill, 1976).

References:

Emile Capouya, "The Poetry of M. L. Rosenthal," *Nation*, 225 (1 October 1977): 311-314; 225 (22 October 1977): 409-411; 226 (21 January 1978): 56-59;

Sally M. Gall, " 'Wild with the Morning': The Poetry of M. L. Rosenthal," *Modern Poetry Studies*, 8 (1977): 119-135;

William Heyen, "Sensibilities," *Poetry*, 115 (1970): 426-429;

Theodore Weiss, "The Many-sidedness of Modernism," *TLS*, 1 February 1980, pp. 124-125.

JEROME ROTHENBERG
(11 December 1931-)

BOOKS: *White Sun Black Sun* (New York: Hawk's Well Press, 1960);

The Seven Hells of the Jigoku Zoshi (New York: Trobar Books, 1962);

Sightings (with *Lunes* by Robert Kelly) (New York: Hawk's Well Press, 1964);

The Gorky Poems (Mexico City: El Corno Emplumado, 1966);

Between: Poems 1960/63 (London: Fulcrum Press, 1967);

Conversations (Los Angeles: Black Sparrow Press, 1968);

Sightings I-IX & Red Easy a Color (London: Circle Press, 1968);

Poems 1964-1967 (Los Angeles: Black Sparrow Press, 1968);

Polish Anecdotes (Santa Barbara: Unicorn Press, 1970);

The Directions (London: Tetrad, 1970);

Poland/1931 (Santa Barbara: Unicorn Press, 1970; enlarged edition, New York: New Directions, 1974);

Poems for the Game of Silence 1960-1970 (New York: Dial Press, 1971);

A Book of Testimony (San Francisco: Tree Books, 1971);

A Poem of Beavers: Seneca Journal I (Blue Mounds Township, Wis.: Perishable Press, 1973);

Esther K. Comes to America 1931 (Greensboro, N.C.: Unicorn Press, 1974);

The Cards (Los Angeles: Black Sparrow Press, 1974);

The Pirke and the Pearl (San Francisco: Tree Books, 1975);

Seneca Journal: Midwinter (St. Louis: Singing Bone Press, 1975);

A Poem to Celebrate the Spring & Diane Rothenberg's Birthday (Mount Horeb, Wis.: Perishable Press, 1975);

The Notebooks (Milwaukee: Membrane Press, 1976);

A Seneca Journal (New York: New Directions, 1978);

B R M TZ Z H (Mount Horeb, Wis.: Perishable Press, 1978);

Abulafia's Circles (Milwaukee: Membrane Press, 1979);

Letters and Numbers (Madison: Salient Seedling Press, 1980);

Vienna Blood (New York: New Directions, 1980).

Jerome Rothenberg is a respected poet, translator of poetry, and editor whose name is often linked with that of another New York-based poet, Robert Kelly, in connection with the deep-image movement of the late 1950s. Rejecting the objective image of the Imagist poets, Rothenberg coined the term *deep image* to describe a concrete detail drawn from the poet's unconscious that operates in a context of powerful feelings and evokes a similar context in the reader when it appears in an imaginatively conceived poem; in his words, the deep image is "an exploration of the unconscious region of the mind in such a way that the unconscious is speaking to the unconscious." Rothenberg's interest in reestablishing forms of visionary poetry for the modern world has made him a leader in recent efforts to preserve and learn from ancient and primitive cultures. In addition, he is associated with the small-press movement and has founded several important poetry magazines.

Rothenberg was born in New York City, received a B.A. from City College of New York in 1952 and an M.A. in literature from the University of Michigan in 1953. He has taught at several institutions, including City College, the New School for Social Research, and the University of Wisconsin, and he is currently on the faculty in the department of visual arts at the University of California at San Diego. He is married and has one child. He has received several awards, most recently a Guggenheim Fellowship (1974) and a National Endowment for the Arts Grant (1976). He has participated in innumerable poetry conferences. Rothenberg founded the Hawk's Well Press in 1958 and the magazine *Poems from the Floating World* in 1960; from 1965 to 1969 he coedited, with David Antin, the magazine *some/thing*; he was ethnopoetics editor of *Stony Brook Poetry Journal* from 1968 to 1971. From 1970 to 1976, he coedited, with Dennis Tedlock, *Alcheringa: A First Magazine of Ethnopoetics*, and he now edits *New Wilderness Letter*.

Rothenberg's own poetry attracted relatively little attention during the early 1960s although critics did praise his intense exploration of imagery, his sensitivity, and his experiments with the musical qualities of poetry. His first volume, *White Sun Black Sun* (1960), reveals affinities with the Surrealists, particularly with the work of Garcia Lorca; the book focuses on the bleak, concrete landscape of the American city. His second book, *The Seven Hells of the Jigoku Zoshi* (1962), is a group of poems about the punishments for breaking archetypal taboos. Although the title refers to the twelfth-century Japanese *Scrolls of Hells*, the poems seem to develop Judeo-Christian concepts of morality and responsibility.

Poems 1964-1967 (1968), containing the poems previously published in *Sightings* (1964), *The Gorky Poems* (1966), and *Conversations* (1968) and two sections of poems published for the first time ("Further Sightings" and "A Steinbook & More"), drew considerable critical attention. The poems in the sections called "Sightings" and "Further Sightings" are experiments with what Rothenberg calls collage technique, in which fragments of poems are arranged in musical juxtaposition. The final product is a poem consisting of a series of single lines that are separated by a "silence equal or proportionate to the duration of each succeeding phrase." Because the content of the individual line is unconnected to that of any other line, the poem depends almost entirely on the aural effect and on the meaning that can be derived by the juxtaposition of the images. For example:

I

He hides his heart.
•
A precious arrangement of glass & flowers.
•
They have made a covenant between them, the circumstance of being tried.
•
Who will signal you? . . .

In "Sightings," the lines are separated by white spaces or by typographical bullets; in "Further Sightings," sets of lines are arbitrarily partitioned by numbers. "Conversations" is also experimental. Short lines alternate between voices, and there are questions and answers, but it is never clear whether the answers are in response to the questions or even how many speakers there are. This technique is partly intended to violate the reader's expectations and often has surprising consequences. "The Gorky Poems" were written as a result of contact with the paintings and writings of Arshile Gorky. Although Rothenberg claims no specific connection between the poems and Gorky's works, he was attracted to Gorky's surrealism and use of images and space, all of which are reflected in Rothenberg's poems. The imagery is rich, sensual, and ambiguous, as in "The Betrothal":

How they began it. Dead bodies
moved in the flowerbed, a finger stopping & turning, showing
a page & an ocean, a longboard covered with stars. *In the great night
my heart will go out*, will be scooped from me, swept thru the water. . . .

"A Steinbook & More" consists of work influenced by or written in imitation of Gertrude Stein, to whom much of Rothenberg's work is indebted. Several of the poems are modeled on Stein poems; indeed, one, in homage to I. B. Singer, is a "syllable by syllable substitution of vocabulary from Singer's novel, *Satan in Goray*, for the vocabulary that Stein was using in a poem . . . called 'Dates.'" Rothenberg experiments here with combining highly charged, emotional language (instead of Stein's "low-key, non-romantic, not highly associative" language) with Stein's methodology. The entire volume of *Poems 1964-1967* may be said to reflect Rothenberg's efforts to find satisfactory ways of structuring his poetry.

Poland/1931 is Rothenberg's most ambitious work. Published in parts beginning in 1970, it reached its final form in 1974. The title refers to

Jerome Rothenberg

Rothenberg's ancestral homeland and the date of his birth. Prefaced by a quotation from Edward Dahlberg ("And I said, 'O defiled flock, take a harp, & chant to the ancient relics, lest understanding perish' "), *Poland/1931* is a series of poems that explores the uniqueness of the Jewish experience, with particular attention to ghetto life in Europe and the Jewish immigrant in America. In an interview in 1971, Rothenberg called *Poland/1931* "an attempt to write an ancestral poetry":

> What I've been trying to do in various ways is to create through these poems an analogue, a presentation of the Eastern European Jewish world from which I had been cut off by birth, place and circumstance. . . . I have gone back towards an exploration of the reality in general, through the terms of a collective unconscious, to the particular terms of a particular people of which I have some understanding, although it is something I carry entirely in my mind. I do use aids to that understanding, to supplement the imagination and memory with whatever becomes available to me.

Among the aids he employs are literary sources such as the Bible, Yiddish literature, numerology,

primitive verse, and oral legends, as well as the *Zohar*, the Cabala, and other Jewish mystical commentaries. He employs his collage technique to create what he has called a "grab-bag," a "miscellany of the mind" that, in Kevin Power's words, "tackles the problem of establishing a coherent cultural identity in a reality defined essentially by tension and contradiction." Although *Poland/1931* is a search for identity, it never lapses into autobiography, for Rothenberg does not feel that the history of an individual is as interesting as the history of a people. His past is included in the poems, but only in the form of voices, memories, and fantasies that create an imaginative vision of shtetl life and describe the trauma of cultural assimilation. The first poem in the series, "The Wedding," is representative; in it, Rothenberg uses incantation and lists of images to bring to life an archetypal subject:

> poland poland poland poland poland
> how thy bells wrapped in their flowers toll
> how they do offer up their tongues to kiss the moon
> old moon old mother stuck in thy sky thyself
> an old bell with no tongue a lost udder. . . .

Rothenberg's interest in ancestral poetry led to his becoming a resident at the Allegany Seneca Indian Reservation in Salamanca, New York, from 1972 until 1974, an experience that resulted in, among other things, the publication of the various editions of *Seneca Journal* (1973, 1975, 1978). In these poems, he records his initiation into a new culture and associates its myths and rituals with the Jewish tradition he was raised in. The volumes also reveal Rothenberg's skill at translating and interpreting so-called primitive poetry. From 1968 to 1973 he worked as editor, commentator, and frequent translator on three anthologies of ancestral poetry that are significant contributions to literature and anthropology.

The first of these, *Technicians of the Sacred* (1968), is a collection of poems, chants, rites, "events," and legends created by the primitive tribes of Africa, America, Asia, and Oceania, and it attempts to draw parallels between primitive and modern poetry. Although some anthropologists disagree with Rothenberg's principles of selection, there is no question that *Technicians of the Sacred* is an important book because it provides access to much primitive poetry that was previously unpublished and because it emphasizes the elements common to ancient and contemporary cultures.

Shaking the Pumpkin (1972), although smaller in scope (limited, according to the subtitle, to *Traditional Poetry of the Indian North Americas*), is

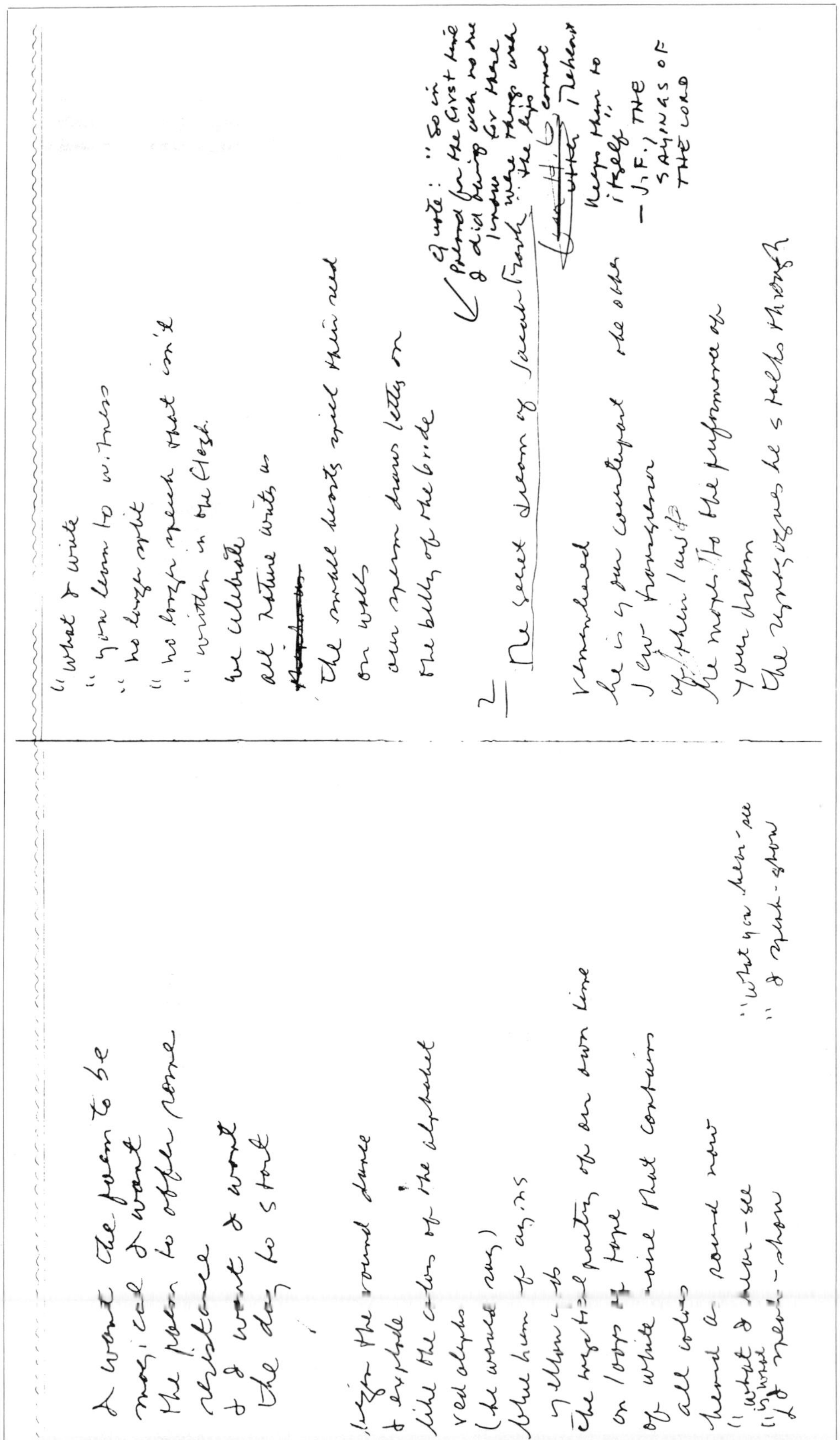

Worksheet for "The Secret Life of Jacob Frank"

a larger book and attracted a great deal of critical attention from both literary critics and anthropologists. Many readers praise the high quality of the translations, the manner in which the anthology draws analogies between traditional and modern poetries, and the astonishing range of materials included; the book has been criticized, however, for failing to place each work within its historical-cultural context and for inadequate or ambiguous commentaries. The most important aspect of the anthology is its concept of "total translation," which Rothenberg defines as "the rendering of all sounds & repetitions which the translator can be made to perceive in the original." Going far beyond mere word-for-word rendition, he presents oral poetry to the reader in such a way that the dances, movements, pauses, and interactions between performer and audience become evident. An example of a "total translation" is *The 17 Horse-Songs of Frank Mitchell*, first published in 1969 and included in *Shaking the Pumpkin*. As H. S. McAllister explains in his essay on Rothenberg's contribution to American Indian literature, Rothenberg's unique translations recreate the original aural experience for the reader. One particular selection, the first few lines of "The 12th Horse-Song," can be translated from the Navajo literally as "some are and are going to my house" repeated three times. Rothenberg's rendition is:

Some are & are going to my howinouse baheegwing
    hawuNnawu N nngahn baheegwing
Some are & are going to my howinouse beheegwing
    hawuNnawu N nngahn baheegwing
Some are & some are gone to my howinouse nnaht
bahyee naht-gwing buhtzzm bahyee noohwinnnGUUH

McAllister admits that the strangeness of the transcription is intimidating and inhibiting, but Rothenberg wants the reader to participate in the poem by reading it aloud. In this way he will achieve at least some semblance of the original Navajo chant.

Rothenberg's third major anthology, *America a Prophesy* (1973), coedited with George Quasha, draws more strongly on the thesis that modern concepts are linked to the primitive, and, subtitled *A New Reading of American Poetry from Pre-Columbian Times to the Present*, it sets out to redefine poetry as "an act of vision, charged with the immediate energies of authentic speech and shaped by its moment in history." The function of poetry, therefore, is "to interrupt the habits of ordinary consciousness by means of more precise and highly charged uses of language and to provide new tools for discovering the underlying relatedness of all

life." As in *Shaking the Pumpkin*, the anthology includes aboriginal American poetry in addition to the folklore of Afro-Americans and the poetry of radical religious sects, visionary poets of the colonial period and the nineteenth and twentieth centuries, as well as "metapoetry"—innovative uses of language that are not normally categorized as poetry, such as diaries, Aztec murals, Shaker emblem poems, and modern concrete poetry. *America a Prophesy* is, like *Shaking the Pumpkin*, important for its unusual range and juxtaposition of materials.

Since 1974 Rothenberg has completed two additional anthologies. *Revolution of the Word: A New Gathering of American Avant-Garde Poetry, 1914-1945* (1974) includes representative works of thirty poets, well known and obscure, and attempts to demonstrate that there is a link between avant-garde poetry of the early twentieth century and the experimental poetry of the 1950s. *A Big Jewish Book: Poems and Other Visions of the Jews from Tribal Times to the Present* (1978) contains materials from over two hundred sources and Rothenberg's commentaries; again, the selection and juxtaposition of materials are unique and often startling.

Rothenberg's interests and creative impulses have followed a pattern of expansion throughout his career. Beginning with poetry that draws on the poet's own unconscious for its images, he is now involved with poetry that reflects the collective unconscious of entire cultures. As Eric Mottram points out in an essay in *Vort* (1975), "Rothenberg's career in fact now shows as a fine demonstration of the essential process of poetry—the translation performance of private into public and of one culture into another." Rothenberg himself sees his role as that of a shaman, a "poet renewing his visions in each present instance." In the future, readers may expect from him more poems and anthologies that will again expand the concept of poetry.

—*Beth Fleischman*

Other:

New Young German Poets, edited and translated by Rothenberg (San Francisco: City Lights Books, 1959);

Rolf Hochhuth, *The Deputy*, adapted by Rothenberg (New York, Hollywood, London & Toronto: French, 1963);

Ritual: A Book of Primitive Rites and Events, edited by Rothenberg (New York: Something Else Press, 1966);

The Flight of Quetzalcoatl, translated by Rothenberg (Brighton, U.K.: Unicorn Books, 1967);

Technicians of the Sacred: A Range of Poetries from Africa, America, Asia and Oceania, edited by Rothenberg (Garden City: Doubleday, 1968);

Hans Magnus Enzensberger, *Poems for People Who Don't Read Poems*, translated by Rothenberg (New York: Atheneum, 1968; London: Secker & Warburg, 1968);

Eugen Gomringer, *The Book of Hours and Constellations*, translated by Rothenberg (New York, Villefranche-sur-mer & Frankfurt-am-Main: Something Else Press, 1968);

The 17 Horse-Songs of Frank Mitchell, Nos X-XIII, translated by Rothenberg (London: Tetrad Press, 1969);

Shaking the Pumpkin: Traditional Poetry of the Indian North Americas, edited by Rothenberg (Garden City: Doubleday, 1972);

America a Prophesy: A New Reading of American Poetry from Pre-Columbian Times to the Present, edited by Rothenberg and George Quasha (New York: Random House, 1973);

Revolution of the Word: A New Gathering of American Avant-Garde Poetry, 1914-1945, edited by Rothenberg (New York: Continuum / Seabury Press, 1974);

A Big Jewish Book: Poems and Other Visions of the Jews from Tribal Times to the Present, edited and translated by Rothenberg, with additional translations by Harris Lenowitz and Charles Doria (Garden City: Doubleday / Anchor, 1978).

Interviews:

David Ossman, *The Sullen Art* (New York: Corinth Books, 1963), pp. 27-32;

"Craft Interview with Jerome Rothenberg," *New York Quarterly*, 5 (Winter 1971): 8-23;

"Jerome Rothenberg, A Dialogue on Oral Poetry with William Spanos," *Boundary 2*, 3 (Spring 1975): 509-573.

References:

Barry Alpert, ed., *Vort Twenty-first Century Pre-Views: David Antin - Jerome Rothenberg* (Silver Spring, Md.: Vort Works Ink, 1975);

H. S. McAllister, " 'The Language of Shamans': Jerome Rothenberg's Contribution to American Indian Literature," *Western American Literature*, 10 (February 1976): 293-309;

Kevin Power, *"Poland/1931*: Pack Up Your Troubles in Your Old Kit Bag & Smile, Smile, Smile, from Diaspora to Galut," *Boundary 2*, 3 (Spring 1975): 683-700.

Diane Wakoski, "20th Century Music," *Parnassus*, 1 (Winter 1972): 142-147.

JAMES SCHUYLER
(9 November 1923-)

BOOKS: *Alfred and Guinevere* (New York: Harcourt, Brace, 1958);

Salute (New York: Tiber Press, 1960);

May 24th or So (New York: Tibor de Nagy Editions, 1966);

Freely Espousing (Garden City: Paris Review Editions / Doubleday, 1969);

A Nest of Ninnies, by Schuyler and John Ashbery (New York: Dutton, 1969);

The Crystal Lithium (New York: Random House, 1972);

A Sun Cab (New York: Adventures in Poetry, 1972);

Hymn to Life (New York: Random House, 1974);

The Fireproof Floors of Witley Court: English Songs and Dances (Newark & West Burke, Vt.: Janus Press, 1976);

Song (Syracuse: Kermani Press, 1976);

The Home Book: Prose and Poems, 1951-1970, ed. Trevor Winkfield (Calais, Vt.: Z Press, 1977);

What's for Dinner? (Santa Barbara: Black Sparrow Press, 1978).

Born in Chicago, James Schuyler grew up in Washington, D.C., and New York before attending Bethany College in West Virginia. After spending several years in Italy, he returned to the United States and settled in New York City, where he met Frank O'Hara, John Ashbery, and other poets of the New York School. Like them, he wrote for the magazine *Art News*. His libretto for Paul Bowles's *A Picnic Cantata*, recorded by Columbia Records in 1955, was followed by a novel, *Alfred and Guinevere* (1958). His first collection of poems, *Salute*, appeared in a limited edition in 1960, and he continued to have limited editions published while bringing out his three major volumes of poetry, *Freely Espousing* (1969), *The Crystal Lithium* (1972), and *Hymn to Life* (1974). Schuyler has also written two other novels, *A Nest of Ninnies* (1969) with John Ashbery and *What's for Dinner?* (1978), and several plays.

Generally, Schuyler's poems are concerned with the transactions of the speaker with the natural, urban, and linguistic worlds. His poetry is free of dramatic incident, grandiose mythology, and elaborate conceit, concentrating on rendering the texture and movement of quotidian existence. Although his work can be loosely associated with the Objectivist tradition of the New York Poets, it is best to approach his poetry without trying to find analogies with the poetics of other writers.

In his first major collection, *Freely Espousing,* Schuyler demonstrates his range in form, style, and subject, particularly in the title poem, where he leaps from perception to memory to self-consciousness:

> a commingling sky
>
>> a semi-tropic night
>> that cast the blackest shadow
>> of the easily torn, untrembling banana
>>> leaf
>
> or Quebec! what a horrible city
> so Steubenville is better?
>> the sinking sensation
> when someone drowns thinking, "This can't be
>> happening to me!"
> the profit of excavating the battlefield where Hannibal
>> whomped the Romans
> the sinuous beauty of words like allergy. . . .

Usually, however, Schuyler's moods are more restrained than this, for he consciously seeks to underplay his experience by simplifying his diction and by refusing to slow down to develop a sensation or a thought. In "February," for example, he records his perceptions "at five P. M. on the day before March first," using typically direct language: "A chimney, breathing a little smoke. / The sun, I can't see / making a bit of pink / I can't quite see in the blue." At the end of the poem he tries to give the day an atemporal essence, a heightened significance, only to cast it back into the flow of time that, for Schuyler, equalizes all moments: "It's the shape of a tulip. / It's the water in the drinking glass the tulips are in. / It's the day like any other."

He is a poet who does not seek poetic subjects but who stylizes the objects of common experience: "dirty socks in dirty sneakers / capless tubes of unguents among brushes and septic Band-Aids." He is a writer who does not force poetic objects to surround significant moments, as he says in the same poem, "Sorting, wrapping, packing, stuffing":

> when the great bronze bell
> sounds its great bronze bong
> it will find a lifetime jar of Yuban Instant in my right
>> hand,
> in my left, Coleman's Mustard.

Even though Schuyler's poetry is that of the observer and not the participant, his observations are

James Schuyler

not exclusively private, for he can also empathize with the public spectacle and extract what is valuable for him. Such is the case with Christmas in Manhattan in "December":

> Each December: I always think I hate "the over-
>> commercialized event"
> and then bells ring, or tiny light bulbs wink above the
>> entrance
> to Bonwit Teller or Katherine going on five wants to
>> look at all
> the empty sample gift-wrapped boxes up Fifth Avenue
>> in swank shops
> and how can I help falling in love? A calm secret
>> exultation
> of the spirit that tastes like Sealtest eggnog. . . .

This evocation of the pleasurable surface of the event without its attending crassness calls up a justification for his aesthetic detachment: "Californians need to do a thing to enjoy it. / A smile in the street may be loads." Having defended his mode of being, the speaker then puts it into practice by separating the satisfaction of hope in the present from the expectation of fulfillment in the future: "to have been so happy is a promise / and if it isn't kept that doesn't matter."

But Schuyler's best poems are those in which he uses his perceptions of the landscape to locate and establish his feelings, as in "Buried at Springs," an elegy for Frank O'Hara. The poem, which is divided into two sections, begins by associating O'Hara with a hornet: "There is a hornet in the room / and one of us will have to go / out of the window into the late August midafternoon sun. / I won." After rejecting the presence of O'Hara, the speaker begins composing a scene ("Rocks with rags / of shadows washed dust clouts / that will never bleach"), only to deny what he has created ("It's not like that at all") as the memory of O'Hara returns: "it's eleven years since / Frank sat at his desk and / saw and heard it all."

In the second part of the poem the speaker turns back to the world, and his perceptions are suffused with the memory of O'Hara. The result is not a facile pathetic fallacy but the process of searching for an objectification of an emotion: "A day subtle and suppressed / in mounds of juniper enfolding / scratchy pockets of shadow." Having established the scene visually, the speaker transforms O'Hara's hornet's threatening buzz that opened the poem:

> There is nothing
> but shade, like the boggy depths
> of a stand of spruce, its resonance
> just the thin scream
> of mosquitoes ascending.

After several more attempts to characterize the day, Schuyler closes with arresting images that do not permit the day's heavy sadness to bury its terror. It is "a faintly clammy day, like wet silk / stained by one dead branch / the harsh russet of dried blood."

In *The Crystal Lithium* Schuyler takes up similar subjects, although his style and poetics have more subtlety than in his previous work. The clue to his poetics is his conviction that "all things are real / no one is a symbol" ("Letter to a Friend: Who is Nancy Daum?"). Having stripped words of immanent and transcendental significance, he also wants to avoid having his words interpreted with the heavy baggage of traditional symbolism, a tendency that is undermined by the blizzard of ordinary, unembellished objects that fill his poems. What is important about his words is that they emerge from his dealings with the concrete world of the present. Hence, they give a sense of the substance and texture of the exterior stimulus and do not send the reader searching for historical or mythological allusions. Reality is a presence that imposes itself on the poet's

sensibility or provides the material for interpretation or transformation. However, Schuyler is interested not in synthesizing these interpretations into a new mythology but in breaking down existing interpretations to get a fresh look at the world, as he playfully puts it in "The Trash Book":

> Then I do not know what
> to pass next in the
> Trash Book: grass, pretending
> to be a smear maybe or
> that stump there that knows
> now it will never grow
> up to be some pencils or
> a yacht even.

Although Schuyler is aware of the arbitrary, conventionalized relations between words and things, he does not permit the uncertainty of these connections to force him into an easy solipsism. The poet confronts this epistemological problem directly in "Empathy and the New Year," the first part of which takes place on New Year's Eve:

> But
> what if it is all, "Maya,
> illusion?" I
> doubt it, though. Men are not
> so inventive. Or
> few are. Not knowing
> a name for something proves nothing. Right
> now it isn't raining, snowing, sleeting, slushing,
> yet it is
> doing something.

The next morning the reader watches the poet's mind's darting from present to past, from sensation to idea:

> Awake at four and heard
> a snowplow not rumble—
> a huge beast
> at its chow and wondered
> is it 1968 or 1969?
> for a bit. 1968 had
> such a familiar sound.
> Got coffee and started
> reading Darwin: so modest,
> so innocent, so pleased at
> the surprise that he
> should grow up to be *him*.

After these desultory attempts to get a grip on the new year, he arrives at a moment of understanding, at an inchoate idea that is still immersed in his perception of the empirical world: "Night / and snow and the threads of life / for once seen as they are, / in ropes like roots."

In "A Stone Knife" Schuyler insists both on the infinite significance that one can bring to an object and on its intrinsic emptiness. It is an exploratory poem in which the speaker plays with his response to a letter opener that he has just received:

> It's just
> the thing I needed, something
> to rest my eyes on, and always
> wanted, which is to say
> it's that of which I
> felt the lack but
> didn't know of, of no
> real use and yet
> essential as a button
> box, or maps, green
> morning skies, islands and
> canals in oatmeal, the steam
> off oyster stew.

When the question of utility arises, the speaker rejects this limited relationship to the object for a disengaged, aesthetic stance that never locks meaning and phenomena together:

> To
> open letters? No, it
> is just the thing, an
> object, dark, fierce
> and beautiful in which
> the surprise is that
> the surprise, once
> past, is always there:
> which to enjoy is
> not to consume.

Yet again in this volume, Schuyler is at his best in his descriptive poetry, where he skillfully manipulates syntax, line, rhythm, and diction to give each landscape its own character, a particular complicity with the speaker at a given moment. In "In January," for example, he combines long lines and complete sentences with studied diction to compose a static scene of dense images:

The yard has sopped into its green-grizzled self its new
  year whiteness.

A dog stirs the noon-blue dark with a running shadow
  and dirt smells cold and doggy

As though the one thing never seen were its frozen
  coupling with the air that brings the flowers of
  grasses.

In "A Sun Cab" the reader hurtles through the

sights and sounds of the city, as the jagged short lines keep him off balance:

> goes by below
> reflected across the street
> in a window
> four stories up
> a train
> sends up its
> passing metal roll
> through grills and gone
> the more than daily Sunday

> CRIMINAL NEW JERSEY
> THIRSTING FLESHPOTS OF NEW YORK.

Frequently in these descriptive poems, Schuyler stays with the same scene and changes the metaphoric grid through which the reader perceives it, remaking reality in each line, as he does in "Buildings":

> each building shoots (straight up)
> out of its small allotment
> all those buildings fibered together
> their flowing sap
> traffic threading
> O coral reef
> O slick and edible matter
> housed in seashell buildings. . . .

The most interesting and daring poem in this volume is the title poem, for in it Schuyler explores the peculiarities of his sensibilities and his commitment to reality, as well as the consequences of his kind of thinking for others. The touchstone of the poem is a winter beach scene that is the occasion of some of his most effective description. The speaker darts from reflection to memory to creative reengagement with reality, and the long enjambed lines that are stripped of periods do not let the reader catch his breath or order the rush of words:

The smell of snow, stinging in nostrils as the wind lifts
  it from a beach
Eye-shuttering, mixed with sand, or when snow lies
  under the street lamps and on all
And the air is emptied to an uplifting gassiness
That turns lungs to winter waterwings, buoying, and the
  bright white night
Freezes in sight a lapse of waves, balsamic, salty,
  unexpected:
Hours after swimming, sitting thinking biting at a
  hangnail
And the taste of the—to your eyes—invisible crystals
  irradiates the world. . . .

From the hangnail his thoughts leap to nail clippers, whose coldness calls up marble and then snow. This devotion to private experience threatens to make the speaker and his poetry impenetrable to others, and he faces this problem in the last part of the poem:

> we stare at or into each
> Other's eyes in hope the other reads there what he reads:
>   snow, wind
> Lifted; black water, slashed with white; and that which is,
>   which is beyond
> Happiness or love or mixed with them or more than
>   they or less, unchanging change,
> "Look," the ocean said (it was tumbled, like our sheets),
>   "look in my eyes". . . .

The problem of the inaccessibility of other minds cannot be resolved, of course; there is always epistemological tension between the perceiver and sensory input, both human and nonhuman. One can only try to objectify one's thoughts and search for faint patterns in the always-moving ocean or in the ever-shifting eyes of a lover, a poet.

In *Hymn to Life* Schuyler continues his sculpted landscapes and his stylization of ordinary experience, although he expands his range of expression. Instead of relying so heavily on the visual world to shape his emotions, he now uses memory and imagined situations to enrich his perceptions. Even though "The Crystal Lithium" demonstrates a similar reliance, it does not show the concentration to which he now puts this technique.

"So Good," a poem about his grandmother, is a fine example of how Schuyler weaves perception and memory together. The speaker begins with the world before him at the moment: "One bird / peck, pecking / on bleached winter grass." Then the March cold awakens the memory of the kiss he gave to his grandmother at her funeral, and that in turn recalls the facile consolation of his elders. Against this rationalization is pressed the image of pain being carved into his body:

> March is here
> like a granny
> a child doesn't
> like to kiss:
> the farm smell,
> a chill sweet-
> ness. He'll
> get over it.
> March will pass
> other birds

> will sing in
> other weather
> time twists my
> bent back.

Some of Schuyler's expanded range is attained by working with tightly organized, traditional subjects, and not by following the fragmented, variegated style of *Freely Espousing*. In "The Day," for example, the deathly winter moves in on the last living shape on the horizon, the "hovering late moths, / the size of big snowflakes":

> what
> were they doing
> there, so late
> in the year? Had
> they laid their
> eggs, and fluttered
> in the then still
> woods, aware of
> the coming wind,
> the storm, their
> end? But they
> were beautiful,
> there in the woods,
> frantic with life.

He is not often content to work with conventional interpretations of existence, however, and in "Buttered Greens" he takes up one of his most philosophical subjects, the problem of distinguishing man from nature. Typically, the question develops dramatically from the speaker's perception of the visual world, a development that is given density and tension by the short, elliptical lines:

> Sunshine
> makes shade
> acid blue
> leaf work
> of elms
> . . . . . .
>   In
> fields rise
> as of them-
> selves, houses.
> Don't 'tsk
> tsk' men and
> habitations
> are nature
> too. . . .

Leaves and houses become the terms for pursuing the

ways in which man and his will are at one with
nature:

> leaves which
> have not
> free will:
> have you?
> You have
> you use it
> unknowingly
> as a house
> leaf plastered
> after a storm

Frustrated by its limitations, the will, the part of man
that tries to be free from nature's flux, struggles for
permanence and significance:

> and the will
> stirs and
> turns out
> from it-
> self, housed
> in disposable
> rib cages
> (the heart
> thumps) in
> disposable
> houses, wood
> ribbed and
> glazed to
> flash back
> buttered
> green, what
> it means:
> leavings and
> the permanence
> of return

Then Schuyler takes this quest for permanence and
identifies it with natural processes:

> the year
> returns in
> its ad-
> vance to
> take again
> what it
> last took
> and what
> it takes
> brings back:
> all done
> not by
> us or for
> us but

> with us
> and within
> the body
> of a house
> the frame
> of wood or
> bone it is
> much the
> same

The best poem in *Hymn to Life*, however, is the
title poem, which exhibits the poet's range, skill, and
discernment. Although it is similar to "The Crystal
Lithium" in its loose, associative structure and in its
concern for the immediacy and movement of the
speaker's thoughts, the later poem works on a
broader canvas and with greater penetration. From
the basic scene, Washington, D.C., in the spring, the
speaker whirls the reader through other times and
settings, from his childhood tonsillectomy to
"dinner in the Fiji Room" to unspecified times when
he watched "rain that falls / through the basketball
hoop on a garage." Schuyler's principal concern is
with the elusive empirical world that resists his
attempts to ascribe meanings to it:

> A window to the south is rough with raindrops
> That, caught in the screen, spell out untranslatable
> glyphs.
> A story
> Not told: so much not understood, a sight, an insight,
> and you pass on
> Another day for each day is subjective and there is a
> totality of days
> As there are as many to live it.

He consciously avoids grand truths and
incidents, keeping his words close to sensations.
Even his occasional generalizations, such as the one
quoted above, are made in short, direct strokes that
emerge from the concrete, although they often come
dangerously close to being platitudinous. The
strength of this and all his poems is not the depth of
philosophical insight but the range, sequence, and
shape of the memories, objects, and sensations.
Frequently, the speaker is the quiet observer who
wants to make his presence felt but who is capable of
rendering only the feeling of passivity before the
power of exterior forces:

> The days slide by and we feel we must
> Stamp an impression on them. It is quite other. They
> stamp us, both
> Time and season so that looking back there are wide
> unpeopled avenues. . . .

There are also moments when reality does not flow past; rather, it invades. When a woman has a fit in a delicatessen, the speaker escapes from the store but not from the suffering:

> Not knowing how to help I left, taking with me
> The look of appeal in faded blue eyes. Between these
>   sharp attacks
> Of harsh reality I would like to interpose: interpose is
>   not the
> Word. One wants them not to happen, that's all, but,
>   like slammed
> On brakes—the cab skids, you are thrown forward,
>   ouch—they
> Come.

Such pain calls up comforting religious sentiments and explanations: however, since religion is a mythology purporting to be a certainty, it closes one off from reality. Hence, the speaker rejects it:

> Times when religion would help: "Be merciful"
>   "Intercede"
> "That which I should have done . . ." Fear and
>   superstition and some-
> Thing more. But without the conviction of a truth, best
>   leave
> It alone. Life, it seems, explains nothing about itself.

In the face of life's impenetrability, the speaker always turns back to the empirical world, where he can experience identity, even if he cannot explain it: "Open the laundry door. Press your face into the / West April chill: a life mask. Attune yourself to what is happening / Now, the little wet things, like washing up the lunch dishes."

For Schuyler, the self is not an independent entity, free from forces inside and outside the skin, so he personifies time and events to give them an active power in the creation of his identity: "Time brings us into bloom and we wait, busy, but wait / For the unforced flow of words and intercourse and sleep and dreams / In which the past seems to portend a future which is just more / Daily life." Stripped of autonomy and intrinsic meaning, the self must create its significance by hammering out the lineaments of the swirling sensations coming from the interior and exterior worlds. His empirical frontier is beneath all abstract questions, and it is the speaker's primary concern and source of satisfaction, as he says at the end of the poem:

> Winter is suddenly so far away, behind, ahead. From the
>   train
> A stand of coarse grass in fuzzy flower. Is it for miracles

We live? I like it when the morning sun lights up my room
Like a yellow jelly bean, an inner glow. May mutters, "Why
ask questions?" or, "What are the questions you wish to ask?"

It is through such skillful objectifications of his personality and perceptions that Schuyler has earned his reputation as an important American poet.

—*H. Meili Steele*

Other:

John Ashbery, ed., *Penguin Modern Poets 24,* includes poems by Schuyler (Harmondsworth, U.K.: Penguin, 1973).

References:

David Kalstone, Review of *The Crystal Lithium, New York Times Book Review,* 5 November 1972, p. 6;

Stephen Spender, "Can Poetry Be Reviewed?," review of *The Crystal Lithium, New York Review of Books,* 20 September 1973, p. 8;

Edmund White, Review of *Hymn to Life, Village Voice,* 29 August 1974, pp. 25-26.

ANNE SEXTON
(9 November 1928-4 October 1974)

BOOKS: *To Bedlam and Part Way Back* (Boston: Houghton Mifflin, 1960);

All My Pretty Ones (Boston: Houghton Mifflin, 1962);

Eggs of Things, by Sexton and Maxine Kumin (New York: Putnam's, 1963);

More Eggs of Things, by Sexton and Kumin (New York: Putnam's, 1964);

Selected Poems (London: Oxford University Press, 1964);

Live or Die (Boston: Houghton Mifflin, 1966; London: Oxford University Press, 1967);

Poems, by Sexton, Thomas Kinsella, and Douglas Livingstone (London: Oxford University Press, 1968);

Love Poems (Boston: Houghton Mifflin, 1969; London: Oxford University Press, 1969);

Joey and the Birthday Present, by Sexton and Kumin (New York: McGraw Hill, 1971);

Anne Sexton

Transformations (Boston: Houghton Mifflin, 1971; London: Oxford University Press, 1972);

The Book of Folly (Boston: Houghton Mifflin, 1972; London: Chatto & Windus, 1974);

The Death Notebooks (Boston: Houghton Mifflin, 1974; London: Chatto & Windus, 1975);

The Awful Rowing Toward God (Boston: Houghton Mifflin, 1975; London: Chatto & Windus, 1977);

The Wizard's Tears, by Sexton and Kumin (New York: McGraw-Hill, 1975);

45 Mercy Street, ed. Linda Gray Sexton (Boston: Houghton Mifflin, 1976; London: Secker & Warburg, 1977);

Anne Sexton: A Self-Portrait in Letters, ed. Linda Gray Sexton and Lois Ames (Boston: Houghton Mifflin, 1977);

Words for Dr. Y. (Boston: Houghton Mifflin, 1978).

Anne Sexton was a confessional poet; that is, she wrote poetry out of the most intimate and painful details of her life. To a certain extent every poet does this, but few have done so with the frankness and audacity of this one. Sexton presented the truth about herself, her experiences, and her psychic life in the starkest possible terms. She was strongly influenced by other confessional poets, including Robert Lowell and, in particular, W. D. Snodgrass; her friends Sylvia Plath, Maxine Kumin, and George Starbuck also played a part in her poetic development. Sexton's subject matter was often related to her mental therapy, for she was continuously under the care of a psychiatrist and was several times treated in mental institutions. Hence her poems—which in fact began as therapy—are often attempts to deal with the guilt, fear, and anxiety that were the legacy of her childhood. If the poems sometimes seem like one long psychiatric case history, they nevertheless document in a remarkable fashion the growth of a gifted and tortured sensibility, and readers undaunted by intimacy and intensity in poetry will find in Sexton's work an extraordinary aesthetic experience.

Sexton was born Anne Gray Harvey in Newton, Massachusetts. The daughter of Ralph Churchill Harvey and Mary Gray Staples Harvey, she attended the public schools of Wellesley, Massachusetts, from 1934 to 1945, the Rogers Hall preparatory school for girls in Lowell from 1945 to 1947, and Garland Junior College in Boston in 1947 and 1948. At the age of nineteen she eloped to North Carolina with Alfred Muller ("Kayo") Sexton II, whom she married 16 August 1948. In later years she lived with her husband in Baltimore and San Francisco, as well as

in the Massachusetts towns of Cochituate, Lower Newton Falls, and Weston. A beautiful woman, she occasionally worked as a model, having studied modeling on a scholarship provided by the Hart Agency of Boston. Her first child, Linda Gray Sexton, was born 21 July 1953. The following year the young mother entered a mental institution after suffering a nervous breakdown. Out of the hospital, Sexton gave birth to a second daughter, Joyce Ladd Sexton, on 5 August 1955, but was again hospitalized for mental illness the following year. The first of several suicide attempts took place in 1956, but her life took a new course when her psychiatrist encouraged her to begin writing poetry. Actually Sexton was not a complete tyro, for she had as a schoolgirl written poetry, some of which appeared in the Rogers Hall school yearbook, but her mother made a slighting remark, and Sexton abandoned it. Out of her experiences in the hospital and her anguish at seeing her children sent away to relatives would eventually come her first volume of poetry, *To Bedlam and Part Way Back* (1960).

In 1957 and 1958 Sexton participated in a poetry workshop with John Holmes at the Boston Center for Adult Education. This tentative beginning led to her attending the 1958 Antioch Writers' Conference, where she worked with W. D. Snodgrass, whose *Heart's Needle* (1959) she would always credit as a major inspiration and influence. Later that year she worked with Robert Lowell, taking his graduate poetry writing seminar at Boston University, and the following summer she attended the Bread Loaf Writers' Conference on a Robert Frost Fellowship in poetry. After the 1960 publication of *To Bedlam and Part Way Back*, the years brought increasing professional activity as she became recognized as an important new poet. She taught her craft not only at Harvard, Radcliffe, Oberlin, and Boston University, but also at high schools and mental institutions. She toured Europe and Africa, and read widely in England and in the United States. Continually under the care of psychiatrists, she was hospitalized twice more, in 1962 and 1973.

She quickly achieved international recognition. Poems from *To Bedlam and Part Way Back* and *All My Pretty Ones* (1962) were published in England as *Selected Poems* (1964), which was a Poetry Book Society selection; in 1965 she was elected a fellow of the Royal Society of Literature. The high point of her career was 1967, when she received the Poetry Society of America's Shelley Memorial Award, and her 1966 collection, *Live or Die*, received a Pulitzer Prize. In subsequent years she received honorary Phi Beta Kappa awards from Harvard (1968) and

Radcliffe (1969), and honorary doctorates from Tufts University (1970), Fairfield University (1970), and Regis College (1973). Sexton's death came when her professional stature was at its height. She had attempted unsuccessfully to take her own life in 1956, 1966, and 1970. At 3:30 P.M. on 4 October 1974 she succeeded in committing suicide by carbon monoxide poisoning in her garage.

Not counting *Selected Poems* and a collection entitled *Poems* (1968), which also includes the work of Thomas Kinsella and Douglas Livingstone, Sexton produced ten volumes of verse, of which four or five are first-rate and only one or two, the product of her last, unhappy years, are truly unexceptional. With Sexton, as with most writers, there seems to be a direct correlation between revision and quality. Her later, poorer works were often first or second drafts hurried into print, but the finely crafted poems in her first volumes reveal both discipline and an acute and intuitive sense of form. Preferring syllabics to formal meter, she would work at a poem for days until she came to "know" whether its lines should be long or short and what length its stanzas should be. Though she took particular pride in her images, her rhymes were perhaps the greater accomplishment. Of few poets can it be said that virtually every rhyme is significant, but the merely decorative rhyme is remarkably rare in Sexton.

Her first book, *To Bedlam and Part Way Back*, contains some of the best work she would ever produce, much of it the product of agonizing, months-long revision. Some of the poems in this collection concern the experience of madness and life in an asylum; others begin what would be a career-long therapeutic probing of familial relationships. In "You, Doctor Martin" the inmate of a mental hospital addresses the psychiatrist. Its opening lines—"You, Doctor Martin walk / from breakfast to madness"—have been criticized as facile, but they have the rare and surely great quality of being utterly memorable. As the poem continues, the asylum is described by the speaker as a place of regimentation, isolation, and despair. "I am queen of all my sins forgotten," she declares, echoing "all my sins remembered," the words of the allegedly mad Prince of Denmark. The progression of rhymes within individual stanzas conveys a whole picture of life in a mental hospital: *walk, talk, stalk; make, take, break; sky, eye, cry*. Each of the stanzas is run on to the next through the use of enjambment; only the last ends with a full stop and the suggestive rhyme—for a mental patient—of *self* and *shelf*.

Some of the best poems are elegies. "For Johnny Pole on the Forgotten Beach" describes a fictitious brother as a boy at the seaside and as a young man dying in a wartime beach assault. Its acceptance by the *Antioch Review* in 1959 marked in Sexton's mind a turning point; she felt that she was beginning to be published in important poetry periodicals. Even finer are two poems about the poet's spinster great-aunt, Anna Ladd Dingley, who had lived with the Harveys after retiring as a newspaper editor. "Elizabeth Gone" went through a large number of drafts before attaining its final form. It is in two parts of two stanzas each. In the first part "Elizabeth" dies; in the second she is "let go" by the grieving speaker of the poem. The rhymes, again, are particularly effective. The two stanzas of each half of the poem contain two rhymes apiece, one of which is shared, thus unifying the stanzas and making more absolute the break between the poem's two parts, which is the break between Elizabeth dying and Elizabeth dead. Another poem about "Nana," as Sexton called her great-aunt, is "Some Foreign Letters," a work admired by Robert Lowell. The poem follows "Elizabeth Gone," which ends with the poet's sorting the dead woman's things. Now she reads through letters written home from Europe in 1890, pausing to consider, from time to time, the difference between the withered old maid she has known and the sprightly girl on her grand tour so long ago. The traveler's letters are a window on the past, through which the poet sees "London . . . on Lord Mayor's Day," German castles, and amorous noblemen. But "I loved you last, / a pleated old lady with a crooked hand." "Some Foreign Letters" anticipates the poems of motherhood, daughterhood, and generation that conclude this collection, for the great-aunt lives—for the length of the poem at least—as girl and as crone in the mind of the woman in her prime who is the poet.

Another anticipation of the later poems is "Unknown Girl in the Maternity Ward," in which an unwed mother speaks to her illegitimate child, whom she will give up: "You will not know me very long." The poem seems to be a straightforward and realistic monologue, but at the end the girl says, "Go child, who is my sin and nothing more," and one hears echoes of envois from Chaucer to Pound. This "child" is also a poem, "my sin." The connection between poetry and the confession of sins will recur in later works, like "With Mercy for the Greedy" in *All My Pretty Ones*: "I was born / doing reference work in sin, and born / confessing it. This is what poems are."

The most impressive piece of work in this collection is "The Double Image," a sequence of seven poems. The poet describes two portraits, herself and her mother, facing each other on opposite walls. The "double image" becomes a metaphor for the thirty-year-old poet's split between the older generation and the younger, between her mother and her daughter. Like Shakespeare in his first twenty sonnets, Sexton shows that painting, poetry, and procreation are all image-making, but Sexton's replicating images, unlike Shakespeare's, are made relevant exclusively to the question of the poet's own problematic identity. The sequence begins with *I* and ends with *me*, and the unity of the generational selves described in the poem is underscored in the identical rhyme in its conclusion, where *me* is rhymed with itself.

All My Pretty Ones, nominated for a National Book Award, shows the poet gaining mastery. As the title of this new collection implies, these poems are about loss—loss of parents, lovers, God, even parts of the body in operations. As *To Bedlam and Part Way Back* ends with "The Division of Parts," a poem about dividing up the possessions of the poet's recently deceased mother, so *All My Pretty Ones* begins with further attempts to sort out the tangled emotions left at that death and at the death, shortly after, of Sexton's father. "The Truth the Dead Know," revised some three hundred times, according to the poet, concerns a funeral and its numb emotional aftermath. "All My Pretty Ones," which follows, is ironically titled, for Sexton's emotions toward the family she has lost are decidedly more ambivalent than those of the character in *Macbeth* who suffers a similar loss and laments his "pretty ones." This poem is primarily about the father, an alcoholic, and like the contemporary Scottish poet George MacBeth's "The Drawer," it is devoted to an inventory of the effects of the dead. It ends with the recognition that perhaps the father was not, after all, one of the poet's pretty ones. But "Whether you are pretty or not, I outlive you, / bend down my strange face and forgive you." Though one reviewer complained that "to forgive the dead is the ultimate condescension of the living," these lines and their sanguine rhyme express something central in Sexton's poetry, the need both to forgive her parents and to be forgiven by them for some nameless fault she seems always to have been convinced that she had.

As would be increasingly typical of her work, the modalities of loss seem often to have religious aspects or dimensions. In "With Mercy for the Greedy," for example, the poet identifies herself as a confessional poet in a double sense when she describes her work not merely as self-revelation, but as sacramental confession. Yet she balks at identifying herself as a believer, because "Need is not quite belief." Another poem, "In the Deep Museum," resembles D. H. Lawrence's *The Man Who Died* (1927) in that it describes Christ's regaining consciousness in the tomb and admitting that he has "lied." But where Lawrence's Christ walks out and makes a new life, Sexton's is eaten alive by rats. Both leave an empty tomb. "We have kept the miracle," says Christ in the poem, "I will not be here." Part of the bizarre effect of the poem lies in Christ's behaving like a gentle Saint Francis with the rats as they consume him in a travesty of the Eucharist. "For three days, for love's sake, / I bless this other death." A far cry from the maudlin "rowing toward God" of the later Sexton, the poem is brutally effective whether it be taken as calculated sacrilege or—as Sexton seems to have intended—as heteroclite piety. Its slyest touch, at any rate, is the hint that the voracious and unsaved scavengers are not rats at all but Christians: "Unto the bellies and jaws / of rats I commit my prophesy and fear." As early as this poem, Sexton may have been identifying herself with those rats.

The humor is less grim in the charming "Letter Written on a Ferry While Crossing Long Island Sound," a poem that begins in concrete everydayness—"at 2 o'clock on a Tuesday / in August of 1969"—and ends in a whimsical fantasy in which four nuns take flight from the deck of the ferry. Again, loss is the subject, for the speaker of the poem has just separated, perhaps finally, from someone she loves. Her misery generates the need for some miraculous escape from the painful moment, and so the poem is replete with emblems of salvation (the life preserver, the lifeboat) and of wholeness (things circular, from the life preserver to the round mouths of the nuns). The poem ends hopefully, if fantastically, with the nuns calling back "from the gauzy edge of paradise, / *good news, good news.*"

The good news is still relatively remote in Sexton's Pulitzer Prize-winning *Live or Die*, the poems of which date from early 1962 to early 1966. The volume's subject is again implicit in the title, for the poems, arranged in the order in which they were written, constitute a logbook of the poet's continual hesitation between a responsibility to life and a need for death. Prominent among these poems are reflections on the contrasting experience of the poet's own childhood and motherhood. "In the Beach House"—in which parental lovemaking, "the royal strapping," is overheard—and "Cripples and Other Stories"—in which a child's warped psyche threatens to manifest itself in ways that cannot be hidden—describe the childhood traumas that would concern this poet throughout her career. "Lovely Girl, My Stringbean, My Lovely Woman" and "A Little Uncomplicated Hymn" describe the poet's daughters in terms proving that however warped Sexton's childhood, she was capable of the warmest feelings for her own children. But always now these familiar subjects are subordinated to the mighty clash of the responsibility to live and the hunger for death, an antinomy that led one reviewer to compare the book to a fugue, its themes announced and developed contrapuntally. Although the book ends with "Live" and the resolution that title implies, one hears a greater intensity in the more numerous poems about death, which include "Sylvia's Death" (about Sylvia Plath), "Wanting to Die," "Suicide Note," and "Somewhere in Africa."

In the last, an elegy for her first poetry writing teacher, John Holmes, the poet deplores the jejune and shallow obsequies for her friend, the forms dictated by a religion he apparently did not practice. She invokes a richer ceremony presided over by a god "hidden / from the missionary, the well-wisher and the glad hand." Imagining this savage god as a woman, a "tribal female who is known but forbidden," the poet conjures a vision of Holmes in transit down some great river in Africa in this deity's "shallow boat" and apostrophizes the dead man: "John Holmes . . . lie heavy in her hold / and go down that river with the ivory, the copra and the gold." The poem ends here, but the reader knows that if Holmes goes downriver in Africa he journeys out of darkness toward some radiant and mysterious sea. "Somewhere in Africa" is one of the few poems in which Sexton, a poet with a tropism for death, hints at just what there might be to that undiscovered country.

There may be further hints in "To Lose the Earth," a somewhat obscure poem that seems to be describing death as a return to the womb, imaged as an Egyptian grotto in which a mysterious flutist plays. The flutist is a "midwife," and "At the moment of entry / your head will be below the gunwales, / your shoulders will rock and struggle / as you ship hogsheads of water." One enters in this fashion a state that is "close to being dead." But is it death or the little death that is being described in terms of this "entry"? The suggestive imagery allows both readings, and although the reviewer who described "To Lose the Earth" as "about as Freudian as a poem can get" sounded somewhat frustrated, the poem is to be praised for the evocative richness of its ambiguity.

More than one of the poems in *Live or Die* describes a kind of visceral yearning for death. "I

know at the news of your death," the poet says in "Sylvia's Death," "a terrible taste for it, like salt." In "Wanting to Die" she refers to "the almost unnameable lust" for death, the "drug so sweet" that has "dazzled" her. At the same time, however, at least in this poem, death is an "enemy," its invidiousness in curious balance with life, which is an "old wound." The poem's bleakness is relieved only by the inchoate spirituality that dictates the image of "breath," the pneuma, incarcerated in sinful flesh: "Death waits for me, year after year, / to so delicately undo an old wound, / to empty my breath from its bad prison."

The imagery of incarceration is muted in "Flee on Your Donkey," in which the mental institution to which the poet returns, "the scene of the disordered senses," is referred to as a "sad hotel." Despite its references to attempted suicide, its details of previous visits to this place, and its account of the inadequate therapy of dream analysis and hypnotic trips into the past, the poem is ultimately positive, for it ends with the speaker's resolution to leave, to flee on her donkey. Sexton worked on this poem off and on for four years; consequently it can be related to much of her other work, early and late. Versions of the poem's refrain, "O my hunger! My hunger!," and its central conceit, riding the donkey, figure in a number of other poems, notably the later "Suicide Note," in which the poet declares: "Once upon a time / my hunger was for Jesus. / O my hunger! My hunger! / Before he grew old / he rode calmly into Jerusalem / in search of death." But Sexton seems not so much to hunger for Jesus as to identify with Him. The donkey she rides out of the asylum in the earlier poem carries her toward death in the later one; the "toy donkey I rode all these years" ultimately figures in the panoply of a death wish compounded with some obscure Christ complex. Humble and absurd, each rider acquiesces in the death that waits.

The horrors of wanting to die, of the asylum, and even of the traumatic childhood are at some remove in Sexton's next collection, *Love Poems* (1969), whose sales of over 14,000 copies within eighteen months made it one of Sexton's most popular books. The turn from madness and death to love, that perennial subject of poetry, is consistent with the resolution to live at the end of *Live or Die*. The image of the carpenter, used as an analogue to the suicide in "Wanting to Die" ("suicides. . . . Like carpenters . . . want to know *which tools*. / They never ask *why build*"), is now used in "The Touch" for the lover who builds and heals and overcomes isolation. Of course not all the poems are simple celebrations of love; some, like "The Ballad of the

Anne Sexton

Anne Sexton

Lonely Masturbator," "You All Know the Story of the Other Woman," and "The Interrogation of the Man of Many Hearts," concern the unhappiness of love's often unsmooth course. Several, including "The Nude Swim" and "Loving the Killer," are addressed to the poet's husband, while others, such as "Song for a Lady," which describes lesbian lovemaking, and "Eighteen Days Without You," about waiting for a lover away on duty with the air force reserve, seem to belie—as one baffled reviewer observed—the dust jacket description of the author as a suburban, middle-class housewife with a husband and two daughters. But if some of the loves described in these poems are imaginary, one ought not to carp at a poet's transmuting emotions into little dramas whose fictitiousness is superficial: the passion, one feels, is authentic, and the eroticism manages to be both convincing and elegant. In poems like "The Breast," "Barefoot," "Knee Song," and "That Day," the figures for the body and its sexual parts are far from reticent but never coarse. The center of woman is an "eye" or a "jewel"; the phallus is an etching of red and blue veins; an erection is a "monument" that comes "forth more sudden than some reconstructed city" ("That Day").

"The Break," one of the collection's best poems, is a subtle critique of sensuality. Consisting of twenty regularly rhymed quatrains, it describes a painful and crippling broken hip suffered by the poet on her fortieth birthday. Although not exactly accident-prone, Sexton had her share of mishaps and serious operations—many of which became poems. As a child she had put her arm into the wringer of a washing machine and had lived for some time with the prospect of permanent disablement. The recurrent idea in the poems about such accidents is that external crippling will make the internal psychic crippling impossible to conceal; "would the cripple inside me / be a cripple that would show?," she asks in "Cripples and Other Stories," one of the poems in *Live or Die.* Thus when, as an adult, the poet falls down a flight of stairs and breaks her hip in two places, "the post of it and also the cup," the physical injury is viewed as merely emblematic of an emotional one, and the poem about the experience begins, "It was also my violent heart that broke." The breaking of the heart, "old hunger motor," has little to do with conventional amorous distress. It seems rather linked to the ineluctable fate of age and infertility, a fate she describes in lines hinting that for even the most confirmed sensualist, fertility somehow validates sexuality. "My one dozen roses are dead," the speaker says from her hospital bed. "They have ceased to menstruate. / . . . / And the heart too, that cripple, how it sang once."

Various kinds of emotional crippling also figure in Sexton's next and most popular book, *Transformations* (1971), in which she returns in a new way to the world of childhood and its fears. The seventeen poems in this collection are versions of fairy tales by the Brothers Grimm. Sexton's Ovidian title is a reminder that fairy tales often feature metamorphoses—of straw into gold and frogs into princes, if not maidens into laurel trees. It also points to Sexton's transforming of the idiom and moral of each tale so that it becomes a sardonic expose rather than a cozy bedtime story. But the debunking of romantic cliches—the rescued maiden, the frog who proves to be a prince, the living happily ever after—is the simpler side of these deft pieces. The poems show the real genius of their creator in their frank treatment of what Freudians would call the "submerged fantasy content" of the original tales. Sexton converts stories normally thought of as a means of exorcising childish fears into a means of therapeutically revisiting—as she had so often done, on the couch and in verse—the childish origins of adult complexes. What is truly original and horrifying about these poems is their demonstration that the fears supposedly confined to childhood can intensify rather than disappear with maturation. Small wonder, then, as J. D. McClatchy has pointed out, that in his study of the psychological significance of fairy tales, *The Uses of Enchantment* (1976), Bruno Bettelheim has occasion to cite these poems.

Sexton tells her fairy stories in language that is colloquial and hip; each begins with a prologue, its tone varying from earnest to bitter, that introduces the poet's modern angle on her subject. Thus "Rumpelstiltskin" begins, "Inside many of us / is a small old man who wants to get out." The assertion that this horrid little man is something internal prepares the reader for the psychoanalytic treatment of the familiar tale that follows. Similarly the reader learns in the opening lines of "Rapunzel"—"A woman / who loves a woman / is forever young"—that the focus of this version of the story will be on the lesbian relationship between Rapunzel and Mother Gothel rather than on the relationship between Rapunzel and the prince.

The degree of the transformation into modern and personal relevance is heightened from poem to poem. Thus in one of the first poems, "Snow White and the Seven Dwarfs," the qualification of the original fantasy is subtle and understated. At the end, after the jealous stepmother has been disposed of, Snow White marries the prince and holds court—

"sometimes referring to her mirror / as women do." The implication is that soon she will be asking it "who is the fairest of us all?" The sly last words work perfectly to suggest the archetypal and cyclic relationship between all the little Snow Whites and all their jealous stepmothers. Later the satire becomes more intense, the fantasy content of the tales less ambiguous. The prologue to "The Frog Prince" seems to be addressed to a woman psychiatrist and contains a blunt observation about the symbolism of the frog: "Frog is my father's genitals." (Barbara Swan's drawing of the frog, which accompanies the poem, manages to suggest its phallic aspect with nice subtlety.) The fairy story then unfolds, from the princess "walking in her garden" to her retiring to bed with "the sinuous frog," who turns into a prince who has to be married. "After all he had compromised her."

"Cinderella" is one of the most successful of these redactions and is often anthologized. It begins with a modern analogue: "the plumber with twelve children / who wins the Irish Sweepstakes. / . . . / That story." The nursemaid, the milkman, and the charwoman all follow, each finding sudden wealth or love or happiness or all three. "That story" is the poet's repeated, sardonic comment on these fantastic wish fulfillments. And that is the story with Cinderella, who wins her prince in the familiar sequence of events. In Sexton's transformation of the story, the "happily ever after" cliche receives the full brunt of her sarcasm:

> Cinderella and the prince
> lived, they say, happily ever after,
> like two dolls in a museum case
> never bothered by diapers or dust,
> never arguing about the timing of an egg,
> never telling the same story twice,
> never getting a middle-aged spread,
> their darling smiles pasted on for eternity.
> Regular Bobbsey Twins.
> That story.

Transformations was Sexton's last good book. There are good poems in the later books, but fewer and fewer as the poet allowed herself to become facile or strident or incoherent. Of the later collections, only *The Book of Folly* (1972) contains much work of sustained quality. J. D. McClatchy, however, considers it significant in that it marks a return to the confessional mode, abandoned or adulterated since *Live or Die*. The subjects treated are for the most part familiar, but when the poet's relations with and feeling of guilt toward her parents undergo analysis yet again, the treatment of this Electral triangle begins to wear thin. Before Sexton's mother died of cancer in 1959, she accused her daughter of giving her the disease by attempting suicide. The charge was absurd, but it did much damage, and obsessive references to Mary Harvey's agonizing death recur in volume after volume. In this one they appear in appalling images of severed breasts and bloody lactation. The preoccupation with the baleful influence of the father also figures in this collection. Even Sleeping Beauty, in *Transformations*, had not been spared this obsession. At the end of her story, an insomniac as dependent on soporific drugs as Sexton herself, she speaks from bed: "It's not the prince at all, / but my father / drunkenly bent over the bed, / circling the abyss like a shark, / my father thick upon me / like some sleeping jellyfish." In *The Book of Folly* this nightmare receives further attention in the sequence entitled "The Death of the Fathers." These poems modulate from the merely suggestive "Oysters," in which the poet, a girl, consumes this reputed aphrodisiac in the company of her father and rises from the table a woman, to the explicit "How We Danced," in which, dancing with her father, the daughter discovers that he has an erection: "the serpent spoke as you held me close." But poems like this one must strike even the most committed Freudian as overdone. A good poet seems spoiled by excessive analysis. The problem, finally, is that the reader begins to feel more pity for the maligned father than for the allegedly traumatized daughter. Yet "The Boat," another poem from the sequence, contains one of the finest moments in Sexton's poetry, a description of her family's near death when their speedboat is handled carelessly by her father. The boat goes through rather than over a wave, and the young passenger discovers that "Here in the green room / the dead are very close." Arresting the moment in the heart of the wave, Sexton makes it a moment out of time, and the effect is riveting.

Sexton's last years were apparently filled with hysteria, and the chronicle of these years is tremendously pathetic. According to Lois Ames and Linda Gray Sexton, editors of *Anne Sexton: A Self-Portrait in Letters* (1977), the poet came to demand more and more from her friends and became estranged from those who declined to give over their lives to keeping her company and soothing her fears. Late in 1973 she divorced her husband, expecting at the age of forty-five to commence a varied love life. She was disappointed and at one point even registered with a computer dating service. The poetry of these last, desperate years seems hurried; its "confessional" aspects seem a needless and ill-advised dragging of personal obsessions into the

open. But the poems of her next collection, *The Death Notebooks*, which came out early in 1974 (to what Ames and Sexton call "universally poor" reviews), are not all from this period, for she had for some time been setting aside certain poems as unsuitable for publication during her lifetime. The source of her reticence is unclear, since nothing in the volume—which she decided to go ahead and publish—is as shocking as "The Death of the Fathers" in *The Book of Folly* or even certain of the less-inhibited poems in *Transformations*. The primary problem of *The Death Notebooks* is its lack of a center, its manifest desultoriness. Unlike every preceding volume, it has no central theme or dialectic. The title notwithstanding, meditations on death do not seem particularly important—though they are here, in "For Mr. Death Who Stands with His Door Open" (in which the poet becomes the reluctant bride of death who, unlike Emily Dickinson's courtly gentleman, is fat, "middle-aged and lower-class") and in the six-poem sequence "The Death Baby." If any one mode dominates, it is the religious, seen in "Gods," "Mary's Song," "God's Backside," "Jesus Walking," and "O Ye Tongues." Some of these, notably "Jesus Walking" and "O Ye Tongues," seem genuinely pious; others reveal the religious uncertainty and ambivalence that Sexton was never able to shake completely. In "Gods" the gods of the world are sought far and wide but are finally found in the speaker's own bathroom, and the poem ends as she blithely locks the door, preparatory, one assumes, to dealing with them once and for all. In "God's Backside" the deity moons creation, and in "Hurry Up Please It's Time" the example is followed by the poet, who pulls down her pants and defecates in the face of both death and life. Of course any work of literature can be made to sound ridiculous in paraphrase, but these poems often skirt the ridiculous without ever approaching the sublime. Only occasionally is an observation couched in wit sufficient, as Dr. Johnson would say, to make it sweet: "Before there are words / do you dream? / In utero / do you dream? / Who taught you to suck? / And how come?" ("Hurry Up Please It's Time").

Even worse than the poems of *The Death Notebooks* are those of *The Awful Rowing Toward God* (1975), written for the most part in twenty days in January 1973, "with two days out for despair, and three days out in a mental hospital." She no longer revised extensively—sometimes she did not revise at all. Consequently the poems are formless, incoherent, and embarrassing, and one reads and reads without discovering anything redeeming or memorable. The book contains only occasional images as good as "death looks on with a casual eye / and picks at the dirt under his fingernail" ("After Auschwitz") and only a few lines as rhythmic as "We must all stop dying in the little ways" ("Children"). The reviews, perhaps in deference to Sexton's passing, were not so uniformly bad as those of *The Death Notebooks*, but even well-disposed reviewers like Joyce Carol Oates, Robert Mazzocco, and Ben Howard (their reviews are collected in McClatchy's 1978 book) seem compulsively to devote their comments to other Sexton volumes, as if unwilling to trust themselves with the volume in hand.

Sexton had in her last months become somewhat obsessively religious, though the religiosity seems patently a desperate grasping for stability and comfort. The theme of *The Awful Rowing Toward God*, as the title implies, is the poet's quest for religious certainty. But while the most hardened atheist can respond to the religious poetry of John Donne or Gerard Manley Hopkins, neither he nor the believer will be anything but embarrassed by these poems, which seem genuinely unwholesome, even insincere, if insincerity be defined as professing without adequate conviction. The remarkable thing is that the poetry Sexton had written during periods of extreme mental instability before had been clear and honest. With the abandonment of discipline one perceives an abandonment of the will to fight for mental equilibrium and clarity. It is a sad dissolution.

Sexton's last books were posthumous collections edited by her daughter. The poems in *45 Mercy Street* (1976) are often somewhat difficult to make out, but again the reader shares a quest for value, love, stability, forgiveness, and sanity. The book is not particularly good, although it is less distressing than the volumes immediately preceding it. The work included dates from 1971 to 1974, and while these were Sexton's last, hardest years, the poems seem if anything less bleak than those of the previous volumes. The collection is divided into four sections, from "Beginning the Hegira" to "Eating the Leftovers." The hegira, of course, is never successfully completed—and leftovers are a sad note on which to end this ninth book, the last that Sexton herself had any hand in arranging. Another section is a sequence, "Bestiary U.S.A," which contains poems describing various animals and reminds one of nothing so much as the grostesques and drolleries in the margins of medieval manuscripts. The centerpiece of the collection, the sequence entitled "The Divorce Papers," seems curiously restrained, almost elegiac; there is little violent emotion, only much

ambivalence toward the man the poet had lived with for twenty-five years. It seems likely, though, that some of the poems excluded from the volume because of "the pain their publication would bring to individuals still living" come from this sequence.

Poems have also been excluded from *Words for Dr. Y.* (1978), "the first collection of Anne Sexton's poetry from which her editorial guidance was totally absent." This volume contains sequences and odd pieces discovered in the poet's files during the preparation of *Anne Sexton: A Self-Portrait in Letters*. One section, "Letters to Dr. Y.," was originally to have been part of *The Book of Folly* and dates from the 1960s. A number of the later works reveal a promising return to form. Especially noteworthy is "The Errand," dated 2 December 1972. For the most part artfully rhymed (though one winces at the rhyming of *folly* and *by golly*), it is in eight stanzas that develop the metaphor of life as an errand the single purpose of which is to visit the "one store" kept by shopkeeper Death. Like *The Book of Folly*, *Words for Dr. Y.* also contains prose. It concludes with three "horror tales," one of which is of particular relevance to Sexton's life and poetry. The title character and narrator of "The Ghost," although never actually identified, is obviously the poet's great-aunt, Anna Ladd Dingley, the subject of "Elizabeth Gone" and "Some Foreign Letters." Her influence, qua ghost, on the life of her grandniece is not as salubrious as one might expect, given the intimacy of the two in life.

"The Ghost" is one of the rare works in which Sexton looks at herself through the eyes of another person, and the effect is refreshing. The relationship between art and personal life is perforce an intimate one for a poet like Sexton, but ultimately the distinction must be preserved, as Patricia Meyer Spacks argues in an astute discussion of *45 Mercy Street* in the *New York Times Book Review* (30 May 1976). In this review, which is reproduced in the McClatchy volume, Spacks applauds the honesty and the precision of Sexton's early work but laments the narcissism, the obsession with the self and its misery, that spoils the later: "the verse implicitly argues that anguish is self-justifying, neither permitting nor demanding the further pain of balanced self-knowledge or the illuminations of controlled imagination and poetic technique. In life we forgive sufferers the necessities of their obsessions. In literature we must ask more: acknowledging the pain that produces such work as Anne Sexton's later poems, yet remembering that art requires more than emotional indulgence, requires a saving respect for disciplines and realities beyond the crying needs, the unrelenting appetites, of the self." These remarks recall the criteria by which all of Sexton's work must be evaluated. Yet one must not discount the magnitude of this poet's suffering or forget the heroism involved in producing much good poetry in spite of anguish and despair that must have been overwhelmingly debilitating. If she eventually crumbled under the weight of her manifold sorrows, she first set a formidable example of courage in the face of adversity. She was always capable of the kind of wan optimism manifested in the epitaph she chose for herself, a palindrome of which she was especially fond: "Rats live on no evil star." Glamorous and celebrated as she was, she often saw herself as humble and despised, but "the lowest of us all," as she observes in a poem on this palindrome in *The Death Notebooks*, "deserve to smile in eternity." —*David Cowart*

Other:

"Anne Sexton Some Foreign Letters," in *Poet's Choice*, ed. Paul Engle and Joseph Langland (New York: Dial Press, 1962), pp. 274-277.

Periodical Publications:

"The Barfly Ought to Sing," *Tri-Quarterly*, 7 (Fall 1966): 89-94;

"Anne Sexton: Worksheets" [ten drafts of "Wall-flower," from *All My Pretty Ones*], *Malahat Review*, 6 (1968): 105-114;

"The Freak Show," *American Poetry Review*, 2 (May-June 1973): 38, 40;

"A Small Journal," *Ms.*, 2 (November 1973): 60-63, 107.

Interviews:

Charles Madden, ed., *Talks With Authors* (Carbondale: Southern Illinois University Press, 1968), pp. 151-179;

Beatrice Berg, "Oh I was Very Sick," *New York Times*, 9 November 1969, pp. D1, D7;

Carol Green, "A Writer Is Essentially a Spy," *Boston Review of the Arts*, 2 (August 1972): 30-37;

Charles Balliro, "Interview with Anne Sexton," *Fiction*, 1 (1974): 12-13;

Elaine Showalter and Carol Smith, "A Nurturing Relationship: A Conversation with Anne Sexton and Maxine Kumin, April 15, 1974," *Women's Studies*, 4 (1976): 115-136;

William Heyen, "From 1928 to Whenever: A Conversation with Anne Sexton," in *American

Poets in 1976, ed. Heyen (Indianapolis: Bobbs-Merrill, 1976), pp. 304-328.

References:

Rise B. Axelrod, "The Transforming Art of Anne Sexton," *Concerning Poetry*, 7 (Spring 1974): 6-13;

Lawrence S. Cunningham, "Anne Sexton: Poetry as a Form of Exorcism," *American Benedictine Review*, 28 (1977): 102-111;

Richard J. Fein, "The Demon of Anne Sexton," *English Record*, 18 (October 1967): 16-21;

Beverly Fields, "The Poetry of Anne Sexton," in *Poets in Progress*, ed. Edward Hungerford (Evanston, Ill.: Northwestern University Press, 1967), pp. 251-285;

Nancy Jo Hoffman, "Reading Women's Poetry: The Meaning and Our Lives," *College English*, 34 (October 1972): 48-62;

A. R. Jones, "Necessity and Freedom: The Poetry of Robert Lowell, Sylvia Plath and Anne Sexton," *Critical Quarterly*, 7 (Spring 1965): 11-30;

Suzanne Juhasz, "The Excitable Gift: The Poetry of Anne Sexton," in her *Naked and Fiery Forms: Modern Poetry by Women, A New Tradition* (New York: Harper, 1976), pp. 117-143;

J. D. McClatchy, ed., *Anne Sexton The Poet and Her Critics* (Bloomington: Indiana University Press, 1978);

Ralph J. Mills, Jr., *Contemporary American Poetry* (New York: Random House, 1965), pp. 218-234;

Mills, "Creation's Very Self: On the Personal Element in Recent American Poetry," in his *Cry of the Human: Essays on Contemporary American Poetry* (Urbana: University of Illinois Press, 1975), pp. 1-47;

Linda Mizejewski, "Sappho to Sexton: Woman Uncontained," *College English*, 35 (December 1973): 340-345;

Charles Molesworth, " 'With Your Own Face On': The Origins and Consequences of Confessional Poetry," *Twentieth Century Literature*, 22 (May 1976): 163-178;

Cameron Northouse and Thomas P. Walsh, *Sylvia Plath and Anne Sexton: A Reference Guide* (Boston: G. K. Hall, 1974);

Robert Phillips, *The Confessional Poets* (Carbondale: Southern Illinois University Press, 1973), pp. 73-91;

M. L. Rosenthal, *The New Poets: American and British Poetry Since World War II* (New York: Oxford University Press, 1967), pp. 131-138;

Ira Schor, "Anne Sexton's 'For My Lover . . .':

Feminism in the Classroom," *College English,* 34 (May 1973): 1082-1093;

Sol Zollman, "Criticism, Self-Criticism, No Transformation: The Poetry of Robert Lowell and Anne Sexton," *Literature and Ideology,* 9 (1971): 29-36.

LOUIS SIMPSON
(27 March 1923-)

BOOKS: *The Arrivistes: Poems 1940-1949* (Paris: Privately printed, 1949; New York: Fine Editions Press, 1949?);

Good News of Death and Other Poems, in *Poets of Today II,* ed. John Hall Wheelock (New York: Scribners, 1955);

A Dream of Governors (Middletown, Conn.: Wesleyan University Press, 1959);

James Hogg: A Critical Study (Edinburgh & London: Oliver & Boyd, 1962; New York: St. Martin's Press, 1962);

Riverside Drive (New York: Atheneum, 1962);

At the End of the Open Road (Middletown, Conn.: Wesleyan University Press, 1963);

Selected Poems (New York: Harcourt, Brace & World, 1965; London: Oxford University Press, 1966);

Adventures of the Letter I (New York, Evanston, San Francisco & London: Harper & Row, 1971; London, Bombay & Melbourne: Oxford University Press, 1971);

Air With Armed Men (London: London Magazine Editions, 1972); republished as *North of Jamaica* (New York, Evanston, San Francisco & London: Harper & Row, 1972);

Three on the Tower: The Lives and Works of Ezra Pound, T. S. Eliot, and William Carlos Williams (New York: Morrow, 1975);

Searching for the Ox (New York: Morrow, 1976);

A Revolution in Taste: Studies in Dylan Thomas, Allen Ginsberg, Sylvia Plath, and Robert Lowell (New York: Macmillan, 1978).

Born in Jamaica, British West Indies, Louis Aston Marantz Simpson grew up in the environs of Kingston, Jamaica, where he studied at Munro College, a preparatory school, from 1933 to 1940. His father was a lawyer of Scotch ancestry, and his mother was from a family of Polish Jews who immigrated to the United States at the beginning of the twentieth century. Both his boyhood in Jamaica and his European background become important material for Simpson's poetry.

When Simpson was seventeen, he moved to New York City and entered Columbia University. He was inducted into the U.S. Army as an infantryman in 1943, and he served with the 101st Airborne Division in Europe until 1945, receiving two Purple Hearts and a Bronze Star. After the war, he returned to Columbia University, receiving his B.S. degree in 1948, an M.A. in 1950, and a Ph.D. in 1959. He worked as an editor for Bobbs-Merrill Publishing Company from 1950 to 1955 and has taught at Columbia University (1955-1959) and the University of California at Berkeley (1959-1967). Since 1967 he has been a professor of English at the State University of New York at Stony Brook. Among the awards and honors he has received are an American Academy of Arts and Letters Rome Fellowship (1957), a *Hudson Review* Fellowship (1957), an Edna St. Vincent Millay Memorial Award (1960), two Guggenheim Fellowships (1962, 1970), an American Council for Learned Societies Grant (1963), a Pulitzer Prize for *At the End of the Open Road* (1964), and Columbia University's Medal for Excellence (1965).

In 1949, Simpson published, at his own expense, *The Arrivistes: Poems 1940-1949. The Arrivistes* is composed of thirty poems and two verse plays. The major theme of this book is the effect of combat on a young man who is both innocent and sensitive. The machine of war grinds through these poems and produces in the poems' speakers the concurrent emotions of terror, alienation, and absurdity. The most powerful of Simpson's war poems, "Carentan O Carentan," is found in this book. Written in ballad form, "Carentan O Carentan" tells the story of an ambush of an American infantry platoon by German soldiers. The Americans walk through a "shady lane" where lovers in more peaceful times once walked. Simpson describes the soldiers in a Frostian manner:

> Could you have seen us through a glass
> You would have said a walk
> Of farmers out to turn the grass,
> Each with his own hay-fork.

The quiet mood is broken by rifle fire from the camouflaged Germans, but the pastoral tone of the poem remains unchanged as the speaker shifts from the use of the plurals "we" and "us" to the singular "I."

> I must lie down at once, there is
> A hammer at my knee.

> And call it death or cowardice,
> Don't count again on me.

The wounded speaker calls on his leaders, his sergeant, his lieutenant, his captain, to tell him what to do. But the sergeant is "silent," the captain is "sickly / And taking a long nap," and the lieutenant is "a sleeping beauty, / Charmed by that strange tune." There is a comic and biting shock in these ironic descriptions of instant death. In the last stanza, the speaker emerges from the trance caused by the violent ambush:

> Carentan O Carentan
> Before we met with you
> We never yet had lost a man
> Or known what death could do.

Simpson has said that training for war is training to make one desire it. But the speaker of "Carentan O Carentan" does not want war; he is surprised by it. He is even more surprised by senseless wounding and death. The tone of the poem registers the absurdity of violent death in the idyllic wooded lane.

The Arrivistes also contains the frequently anthologized "Song: 'Rough Winds Do Shake the Darling Buds of May.' " This erotic lyric tells of the lust of a sixteen-year-old girl and of her first sexual experience. The last lines take up the imagery of the tournament:

> Well, I have seen
> have seen
> one come to joust
> Who has a horn
> sweet horn,
> and spear to sink
> Before he rests.
> When such young buds are torn, the best true loves they make.

The humorous love sonnet "Summer Storm" is like "Song" in its erotic intensity. The sonnet tells the story of two athletic lovers who, in their ardor, couple in every conceivable place: "bed, couch, closet, carpet, car-seat, table, / Both river banks, five fields, a mountain side, / Covering as much ground as they were able." In a park, the lovers are discovered by an outraged woman who writes an indignant letter to the newspapers. Simpson ends the poem on an introspective note: "God rest them well, and firmly shut the door. / Now they are married Nature breathes once more."

Good News of Death and Other Poems (1955) also contains many poems of love and war. To these two themes is added the exploration of the meaning of contemporary American life. The war poems of *Good News of Death* focus on the terror and humiliation of mechanized warfare. Here is the faceless soldier of "The Battle":

> Helmet and rifle, pack and overcoat
> Marched through a forest. Somewhere up ahead
> Guns thudded. Like the circle of a throat
> The night on every side was turning red.

Enemy shells burst around the soldiers, leaving the snow black with "corpses stiffened in their scarlet hoods." The final stanza personalizes the horror:

> Most clearly of that battle I remember
> The tiredness in eyes, how hands looked thin
> Around a cigarette, and the bright ember
> Would pulse with all the life there was within.

In "The Ash and the Oak," modern war is defined by contrast.

Layle Silbert

At Malplaquet and Waterloo
They were polite and proud,
They primed their guns with billets-doux
And, as they fired, bowed.

. . . .

But at Verdun and at Bastogne
There was a great recoil,
The blood was bitter to the bone
The trigger to the soul,
And death was nothing if not dull,
A hero was a fool.

The battle is fought by anonymous and hollow modern men while their noble compatriots from other ages mock them. This is not to be taken as a romantic or naive attitude toward the past. Throughout his poetry, Simpson displays a tough-minded view of history. When he is tempted by an idealized past, as he is in "The Heroes," another war poem in this collection, he blunts the urge by couching the past in terms of dreams:

I dreamed of war-heroes, of wounded war-heroes
With just enough of their charms shot away
To make them more handsome. The women moved
                                                          nearer
To touch their brave wounds and their hair streaked
                                                          with gray.

The reality is quite different from the dream. Simpson ends the poem with this ironic comment:

A fine dust has settled on all that scrap metal.
The heroes were packaged and sent home in parts
To pluck at a poppy and sew on a petal
And count the long night by the stroke of their hearts.

The most memorable love poems of *Good News of Death* are set in the past. They celebrate love affairs that have ended but are not forgotten. "A Woman Too Well Remembered" is a wistful portrait of a woman who "was the only daughter of a line / That sleeps in poetry and silences."

Then is she simply false, and falsely fair?
(The promise she would break she never made)
I cannot say, but truly can compare,
For when the stars move like a steady fire
I think of her, and other faces fade.

The American poems of *Good News of Death* initiate a new and intense interest, one that pervades Simpson's subsequent poetry. "West," set in California, explains the grandeur of the continent's last frontier and creates a vision of America as a demiparadise, as the speaker, a rancher in Bolinas, sits on his veranda watching the sprinklers irrigate his land and listening to "the peaches dropping from the trees" and "the ocean in the redwood trees":

On their red columns drowse
The eagles battered at the Western gate;
These trees have held the eagles in their state
When Rome was still a rumor in the boughs.

The promise of a new life, a new perfectible civilization, is held in the natural fruitfulness and endurance of the land, the trees, the animals themselves. Simpson contrasts this ideal—a type of American Dream—with what Americans have made of the Promised Land and the new civilization. In later poems Simpson becomes one of the most eloquent critics of American society, and he finds a symbol for his expression in the life and work of his mentor, Walt Whitman.

A Dream of Governors was published in 1959, the same year Simpson received his Ph.D. in comparative literature from Columbia University and began teaching at the University of California at Berkeley. The two binding themes of *A Dream of Governors* are life as it is practiced in America and World War II with its aftermath. In this book Simpson often draws away from traditional conventions of rhyme and meter to experiment with free verse.

More than half of the pages of *A Dream of Governors* are given to war poems. The longest of these is "The Runner," a realistic story of a soldier in the 101st Airborne Division prior to and during the Battle of the Bulge. Simpson writes that the story is fiction, but many episodes in the poem are clearly autobiographical. The central character of the poem, Dodd, is a runner who carries messages from one command post to another. During an artillery attack he is slightly wounded but carries on his duties. The soldiers are attacked by cannon, machine guns, and tanks. The weather gives them rain, snow, and mud. On one mission Dodd comes face to face with a German soldier. Fleeing in fear, dropping his rifle, he is fired at by the German. He runs across his own lines in panic, is chastised by his captain, and is made a butt of jokes by his comrades.

In a companion poem, Simpson writes, "Humankind . . . cannot bear / Too much reality. . . ." War brings the daily reality of death to the combatants. Some soldiers break. One such is the veteran in a mental hospital in "Old Soldier":

He lies remembering: "That's how it was . . ."
And smiles, and drifts into a youthful sleep
Without a care. His life is all he has,
And that is given to the guards to keep.

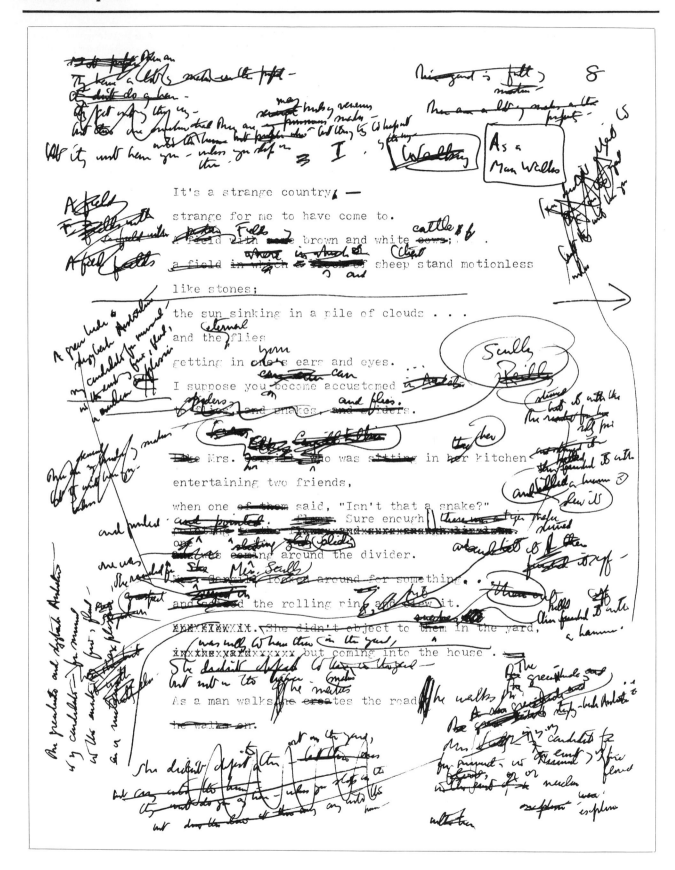

It's a strange country, —

strange for me to have come to.

A field with brown and white cows;

a field in which sheep stand motionless

like stones;

the sun sinking in a pile of clouds . . .

and the flies

getting in one's ears and eyes.

I suppose you become accustomed

to flies and snakes, and spiders.

Mrs. who was sitting in her kitchen

entertaining two friends,

when one of them said, "Isn't that a snake?"

Sure enough

coming around the divider.

looked around for something . . .

and the rolling pin it.

She didn't object to them in the yard,

but coming into the house .

As a man walks he creates the road

he walks on.

"As a Man Walks," revised typescript

238

For a brief period after World War II, Simpson suffered from what he calls "delayed battle fatigue." He spent time in a mental hospital with amnesia and feelings of despair and uselessness. He writes of his ennui at this time in "The Silent Generation."

> We lack enthusiasm.
> Life seems a mystery;
> It's like the play a lady
> Told me about: "It's not . . .
> It doesn't *have* a plot,"
> She said, "it's history."

The plight of emotionally wounded veterans is also discussed in "Against the Age."

> Our minds are mutilated—*gueules cassées*,
> They walk the night with hood and mask and stick,
> The government won't let them out by day,
> Their ugliness threatens the Republic.
> Our minds are like those violated souls
> That pass in faceless, threatening patrols.

The second section of *A Dream of Governors* is titled "My America," and it demonstrates Simpson's attempt to define America and Americans. "To the Western World" tells of America's quest:

> The treasures of Cathay were never found.
> In this America, this wilderness
> Where the axe echoes with a lonely sound,
> The generations labor to possess
> And grave by grave we civilize the ground.

In "Orpheus in America," he suggests that America's early settlers carried an Orphean vision: they left behind the hell of European tyranny and deprivation, left the desiccated old civilization, for the promise of "a greener Thrace," of "this America, this other, happy place." The story of how this new paradise has been corrupted and exploited occupies much of Simpson's later poetry.

At the End of the Open Road (1963) won a Pulitzer Prize for poetry. This book marks a change in Simpson's style. He abandons rhyme and traditional metrical patterns for a colloquial free verse, and he experiments with metaphor and image clusters. In 1974, Simpson wrote, "My earliest work was in traditional forms. I was much taken with the lyricism of the Tudor poets. At the end of the 1950's I began writing in irregular, unrhymed lines. I was attempting to write verse that would sound like speech."

He uses these new techniques to expand his criticism of American society. "In California" invokes two definers of America, Walt Whitman and Mark Twain.

Lie back, Walt Whitman,
There, on the fabulous raft with the King and the Duke!
For the white row of the Marina
Faces the Rock. Turn round the wagons here.

Lie back! We cannot bear
The stars any more, those infinite spaces.
Let the realtors divide the mountain,
For they have already subdivided the valley.

In this poem, Simpson suggests that Whitman's utopian vision for America has been corrupted (by people like the King and the Duke and the realtors) and also that Whitman's vision, despite its appeal, is untenable because of its limitlessness.

"Walt Whitman at Bear Mountain" extends Simpson's analysis of Whitman's ideas. The poem's narrator asks,

> "Where are you, Walt?
> The Open Road goes to the used-car lot.
>
> "Where is the nation you promised?"

Walt Whitman replies:

> "I am here," he answered.
> "It seems you have found me out.
> Yet, did I not warn you that it was Myself
> I advertised? Were my words not sufficiently plain?
>
> "I gave no prescriptions,
> And those who have taken my moods for prophecies
> Mistake the matter."

Simpson writes that most Americans have "turned a deaf ear" to Whitman anyway, but that certain people, a storekeeper, a dumb housewife, are "relieved" that Whitman did not really direct them to be better than they are.

Several poems in *At the End of the Open Road* are characterized by surreal, dreamlike images, many of which are based on childhood memories. The most impressive poem in this group is "My Father in the Night Commanding No." The speaker recalls his father sitting and reading, his mother crying while listening to opera from a phonograph. Memory freezes the scene:

> *They* will not change
> There, on the stage of terror and of love.
>
> The actors in that playhouse always sit
> In fixed positions—father, mother, child
> With painted eyes.
> How sad it is to be a little puppet!

The surreal poem "The Troika" relates a nightmare vision set in World War I. The speaker drives a horse-drawn troika across fields. He sees a bird and pursues it.

> I held the bird—it vanished with a cry,
> and on a branch a girl sat sideways, combing
> her long black hair. The dew
> shone on her lips; her breasts were white as roses.

At the End of the Open Road ends as it begins, with a poem about California. "Lines Written Near San Francisco" recalls the disastrous earthquake. The third section of the poem begins,

> Every night, at the end of America
> We taste our wine, looking at the Pacific.
> How sad it is, the end of America!

The frontier has run out in California, so Americans must turn inside themselves. In conclusion, Simpson again speaks of Whitman:

> Whitman was wrong about the People,
> But right about himself. The land is within.
> At the end of the open road we come to ourselves.

In 1965, Simpson published *Selected Poems*, which contains poetry from each of the previous books and twelve new poems. The new poems deal with the continuing search for the meaning of America and with the new themes of space flight, the Vietnam War, and the history of the American Indian. He again employs surreal images to give several of the new poems the substance of dreams.

The new themes are restated in *Adventures of the Letter I* (1971), where the American Indian poems tell of the dispossession of the Indians. In "The Climate of Paradise," Simpson contrasts the splendor of Mount Shasta, a seat of Indian tribal gods, with the urban "caves inhabited by Pufendorf's dwarfs." These modern citizens are "haunted by Red China"; "They're terrified they'll be brainwashed."

Whereas Simpson had written of the violence of war from the point of view of an eyewitness, in this book he assesses the violence in Vietnam from a distance. He measures the threats of "new" wars in "American Dreams":

> In dreams my life came toward me,
> my loves that are slender as gazelles.
> But America also dreams. . . .
> Dream, you are flying over Russia,
> dream, you are falling in Asia.
>
> As I look down the street
> on a typical sunny day in California
> it is my house that is burning
> and my dear ones that lie in the gutter
> as the American army enters.

In "A Friend of the Family," he expresses his fear that America is trying to extend its dominion to the new frontier of Vietnam, "expanding the war on nature / and the old know-how to Asia." In the same poem, Simpson combines his new themes in eight lines:

> Nowadays if we want that kind of excitement—
> selling beads and whiskey to Indians,
> setting up a feed-store,
> a market in shoes, tires, machineguns,
> material ecstasy, money with hands and feet
> stacked up like wooden Indians . . .
>
> we must go out to Asia
> or rocketing outward in space.

In *Adventures of the Letter I*, Simpson attacks American materialism and imperialism, suggesting that they are the major causes of the destruction of American ideals.

In the first two sections of *Searching for the Ox* (1976), Simpson writes of his boyhood in Jamaica and his young manhood in New York City. He relates in the preface the similarity between his early years in Jamaica and Albert Camus's early life in Algeria: "In the tropics where nature is everything and man is nothing, a man may decide that he alone is responsible for his life." In colloquial poems he recounts the loneliness of his boyhood and his confusion about the words and actions of his divorced parents and his stepmother. As a student in New York City, he feels alienated in a strange culture.

Many of the poems in the last sections of *Searching for the Ox* attempt a definition of the poet's task in the modern world. In earlier poems that explore and define America, Simpson finds inspiration in the poetry of Walt Whitman. In *Searching for the Ox*, he turns to Wordsworth for a similar inspiration. In an essay, "Rolling Up," he writes that Wordsworth "imagined men and women who were full of feeling, who communed silently with nature and loved one another. These people were not found in nature but in the imagination of a poet. He created a nation that he could not find. He wished to reveal the deep springs that join one man to another and constitute a real nation." In part, Simpson sees the role of the American poet in this light. The nation may be created by the artist's imagination.

In "Searching for the Ox" Simpson extends his musings on the creative ability of the poet's imagination. The imagination must have concretion, as found in Wordsworth's rustic people and in nature in the Lake District. As Simpson contemplates the work of "engineers from IBM" and men walking on the moon, he reaches a conclusion:

> And still, I must confess,
> I fear those *messieurs*, like a peasant
> listening to the priests talk Latin.
> They will send me off to Heaven
> when all I want is to live in the world.

> —*Charles Israel*

Plays:

The Father Out of the Machine: A Masque, in *Chicago Review*, 5 (Winter 1950): 3-13;

Andromeda, in *Hudson Review*, 8 (Winter 1956): 499-518.

Other:

The New Poets of England and America, edited by Simpson, Donald Hall, and Robert Pack (Cleveland: Meridian, 1957);

Thom Gunn and Ted Hughes, eds., *Five American Poets*, includes poems by Simpson (London: Faber & Faber, 1963);

An Introduction to Poetry, edited by Simpson (New York: St. Martin's Press, 1967; London & Melbourne: Macmillan, 1968);

"Rolling Up," in *American Poets in 1976*, ed. William Heyen (Indianapolis: Bobbs-Merrill, 1976), pp. 467-495.

References:

C. B. Cox, "The Poetry of Louis Simpson," *Critical Quarterly*, 8 (Spring 1966): 72-83;

Yohma Gray, "The Poetry of Louis Simpson," in *Poets in Progress*, ed. Edward Hungerford (Evanston: Northwestern University Press, 1967), pp. 227-250;

Dell Hymes, "Louis Simpson's 'The Deserted Boy,'" *Poetics*, 5 (June 1976): 119-155;

George S. Lensing and Ronald Moran, *Four Poets and the Emotive Imagination: Robert Bly, James Wright, Louis Simpson, and William Stafford* (Baton Rouge: Louisiana State University Press, 1976), pp. 133-175;

Ronald Moran, *Louis Simpson* (New York: Twayne, 1972);

Moran, "'Walt Whitman at Bear Mountain' and the American Illusion," *Concerning Poetry*, 2 (Spring 1969): 5-9;

Lawrence R. Smith, "A Conversation with Louis Simpson," *Chicago Review*, 27 (Summer 1975): 99-109.

Papers:

There is a collection of Simpson's papers at the Library of Congress.

L. E. SISSMAN
(1 January 1928-10 March 1976)

BOOKS: *Dying: An Introduction* (Boston: Little, Brown, 1968);

Scattered Returns (Boston: Little, Brown, 1969);

Pursuit of Honor (Boston: Little, Brown, 1971);

Innocent Bystander: The Scene from the 70's (New York: Vanguard, 1975);

Hello, Darkness: The Collected Poems of L. E. Sissman (Boston: Little, Brown, 1978).

L. E. Sissman died in 1976 leaving nearly three hundred pages of closely typed verse, all of it written in a twelve-year period at the end of his life. Although some of it invites the harshest strictures, the sheer volume of his output requires that considered attention be paid to it. His reputation has recently become substantially more widespread than it was before his death, partly because of a raft of poems published posthumously in the *New Yorker*. The phenomenal amount of verse produced in the full flood of his creative decade, and the publication of much of it in the *New Yorker*, have led to the general impression that his muse was possessed of a heart pregnant with celestial fire. And his early death at what appeared to be the peak of his writing career, together with his own poems about his impending death from Hodgkin's disease, has obscured the objective appraisal of his work in a wash of sentiment. Neither of these attitudes is the result of a balanced assessment of Sissman's poems.

What facts are so far known about the poet's life are mostly contained in the preface written by Peter Davison, the editor of Sissman's *Collected Poems* (1978). Born Louis Edward Sissman on New Year's Day 1928, of half-Jewish parentage in Detroit, Michigan, he was the only child of parents who, Davison says, "seem to have been peripatetic, homiletic, and remote. His mother urged him to accomplish much. Like other gifted children, he developed interests—cars, planes, technologies, and varieties of expertise—that enabled a boy to go it alone, under warily benign parental eyes." Davison speaks of Sissman's "hothouse childhood and . . . precocious youth," during which he was a Quiz Kid on a national radio program and, at the age of thirteen, won the National Spelling Bee in Washington. For this he received a $500 defense bond and an all-expense-paid trip to New York. Sissman himself has said of this experience: "My main reaction to all this was to lose my lunch more frequently than usual, a longstanding symptom of my revulsion to performing in public, and to conceive a lifelong hatred for the exploitation of the young."

This comment is contained in Sissman's book of prose, *Innocent Bystander* (1975), which is a selection of columns he wrote regularly for five years for the *Atlantic Monthly*. In it he also says of his childhood: "My parents, who were constitutionally opposed to the idea of property, fearing its potential stranglehold on their freedom, never owned a house while we lived [in Detroit]. Instead, they rented run-down but commodious buildings which could house both my father's business and our living quarters. This neatly avoided the problem of living in the suburbs and at the same time put me in more than nodding touch with the heart of a city. . . . Still, I lacked more than the merest trace of a sense of belonging until, in 1944, I made the trip east to Boston." Graduating from Detroit Country Day School, he entered Harvard that year, not yet seventeen but full grown at 6'4", 200 pounds. There his assigned roommate was, he says, "a tall, courtly, withdrawn youth who was so steeped in the Brahmin tradition that he sometimes seemed barely able to function in the real world." Aside from his roommate, Sissman was quite attached to the Irish maid who cleaned his room, "Mrs. Circassian," whom he commemorates in a poem called "A College Room: Lowell R-34, 1945." "To me she was helpful, sensible, motherly, always forgiving: a kind of foster mother in my strange home, and one who never demanded the things my real mother did. . . . I never saw any reason to reconsider my vision of Boston as bound up in those two people." As Davison says, "Boston had set its seal upon his heart, and both his life and his work would be played out mostly against its background." And so it was: except for a brief, unhappy period in New York, he lived in or around Boston for the rest of his life.

Sissman's first two years at Harvard seem to have been happy enough. "Poems written in the 1960s testify to college escapades, observations and debauches, romantic pursuits of knowledge and honor." But evidently he did too little assigned school work, and at the end of his sophomore year, in 1946, he was dismissed for what he much later told a *Newsweek* reporter were "lousy grades, laziness and insubordination. I goofed off and discovered girls." He was to be readmitted to Harvard in the spring of 1948, but in the meantime his foray into the outside world was not unprofitable. Davison says, "He got himself a job as a stack boy in the Boston Public Library, found a series of furnished rooms around Boston, and wrote home regular reports on his diet and health and regular requests for money—each request gravely particularized as to the benefits that would accrue." During this interlude, Sissman began to write poetry in earnest; from it he would return to Harvard ready to do more serious work. During the summer of 1947, he and a few of his sometime classmates founded a literary magazine, called *Halcyon*, which ran for exactly two issues. Yet it was an extremely important event in the beginning poet's literary life.

Sissman says that he and his friends started *Halcyon*, "as the preface to the first issue stated, to 'fight tooth and nail the prevailing tendency among advance-guard quarterlies to become journals of current intellectual fashion.' . . . The founding of *Halcyon* enabled us to be—and not just think ourselves—active participants in the battle Auden so accurately described: the conflict, then just beginning, between the Apollonians, dull academics, administrators, order-makers, exegetes, and the Hermetics, disorderly, idiosyncratic free creative spirits. We were, of course, in Hermes' army (no two uniforms alike), and we took second place to nobody in our broad and frequent snook-cocking at Apollo's fat Establishment. As we might not have acknowledged quite so quickly, we were also second to none in our haste to correspond and hobnob with our betters. . . . there was nothing to prevent us from swamping the great and near-great with scores of letters beseeching them for samples of their work, and that's exactly what we did." By this process, they received contributions from E. E. Cummings, Howard Nemerov, Richmond Lattimore, Oscar Williams, even Wallace Stevens, and others. Sissman goes on to say: "Sandwiched securely between James Merrill and Marya Zaturenska and set in the same size type as they, I was a happy man. And that was what it was really all about . . . the sense of being part of a tradition . . . of becoming by fiat, by our own act of linking our names in print with theirs, the legitimate heirs of Cummings and Eliot and Stevens and Pound."

One wants to believe that in these last two sentences Sissman is being entirely ironic, but his tone does not indicate that this is necessarily so. In reading Sissman's poems and prose it seems that he never fully comprehended the difficulty of writing good poetry. His use of the words *fiat* and *legitimate* here, even if it were clearly in jest (and it seems not), tends to confirm this suspicion, because he appears to take the matter so lightly. Have there been *any* "legitimate" heirs to these four poets, or *can* there be any? How could one achieve such legitimacy anyway? Only through the most imaginative and enduring labor, the highest order of genius. The mere suggestion that it can be done by "fiat" is frivolous. Sissman seems to have considered none of these questions when he chose the word, much less the question of how one could *possibly* be heir to all four of these disparate poets at once. Although this essay is a reminiscence of two decades' distance, its tone is disturbingly presumptuous, questionable even for an undergraduate and certainly not acceptable from a middle-aged poet. This point would scarcely be worth belaboring if what Steven Aronson calls the "elephantine egoism" of Sissman's poems were not such a pressing issue. But unfortunately it is: it forces itself upon the reader at every turn.

Sissman's main poetic influence, according to him, was W. H. Auden, whose work he discovered during the winter of his first year at Harvard. He has a good deal to say about this influence in his essay on Auden in *Innocent Bystander*, although the self-esteem with which he embellishes the story is embarrassing. He says that when he composed his first poems in the early autumn of 1945, he "lacked a corrective influence" that would "give my verse that astringent distancing and humane bite that characterize the best of modern poetry." According to the middle-aged man, therefore, all the Harvard sophomore needed was a "corrective influence" to be writing some of "the best of modern poetry." He goes on: "It was not until I discovered Auden that winter that I met my Influence: the stern, minatory figure that, poetically speaking, put iron in my veins, bone in my backbone, and lead in my pencil"—as if all but the last of these were accomplished facts. He continues: "I had been moved—and I daresay influenced—by both Yeats and Eliot, but it was Auden who became my closest literary kin." One wonders in what sense. "Like me, he had a boyish love of landscapes and machinery; like me, he had a predilection for the remedies of radical politics; like me, he saw the cataclysm of Europe . . . as an opportunity for romantic adventurism." Of this sentence one will want to ask: why does he not say "like him, I . . ." instead of "like me, he . . ."?

Sissman does not rest until his startling finish: "Because he [Auden] *has* lived, in his enduring influence on myself and others, it is safe to say that he *will* live. Of that I am quite sure." Does Sissman mean, as he appears to, that Auden's work will live on because it influenced Sissman's (and "others' "), because Sissman's will surely endure? Suffice it to say that Sissman's writing persona is often unpleasantly self-important; it makes the proper appreciation of his poetry difficult indeed.

After Sissman returned to Harvard in 1948, he received encouraging criticism of his poetry from his teachers, John Ciardi, Andrews Wanning, and especially Theodore Morrison, and he received Harvard's Garrison Poetry Prize. He graduated *cum laude* in 1949 and was elected class poet. Having married his first wife in 1948, he then went to New York, holding a job as a copy editor at a publishing house for a while, but he returned to Boston in 1952. He had also stopped writing poetry: "discouraged by lack of luck in publishing my verse, I stopped writing it for a pause of what amounted to ten years." In 1952 he worked as an aide in John F. Kennedy's first Senate campaign, and later held odd jobs as Fuller Brush man and vacuum cleaner salesman. Finally in 1956 he took a job as a copywriter in the Boston advertising firm of Kenyon and Eckhardt, in which he later became an executive. He followed this career the rest of his life. In 1958 he married for the second time (neither marriage produced any children) and moved with his wife Anne to the country an hour west of Boston, near the village of Harvard, Massachusetts.

"Sissman mastered the craft of advertising and proved himself capable of making a good living at a business he delighted in," says Davison. By 1969 he had risen to the rank of vice president and creative director of Kenyon and Eckhardt's Boston office, having "earned renown and prizes for his advertisements," according to an article in *Newsweek* called "Boston's Adman-Poet": "One of his best-known efforts was a promotion for a Cardinal Cushing Charity Fund exhibition football game—featuring a pose by the cardinal himself in a football helmet. A Sissman slogan—'The man you talk to is the bank'—personalized traditionally aloof Boston financial advertising and helped build client New England Merchants' into the city's fourth largest bank." It is important to realize the influence that advertising had on Sissman's poetry, for it is saturated with brand names.

In 1963, for reasons unknown, Sissman started writing poetry and prose again. "I sat down and decided to write," he says in *Newsweek*. "At first it

L. E. Sissman

was short things, then longer." Thereafter he took one day off a week to work on his poetry and a novel, which apparently was never finished. He never had any intention of quitting business, however, because advertising's practical problems always held much of his interest, "such as finding a common ground between good sense and good selling." "It's valuable," he said, "for a writer to have one foot in the world of business."

By 1965 Sissman had compiled enough material for a volume of poetry, some of it revived from college notebooks. The rate of his production was prodigious indeed, and between 1963 and 1974 he amassed a formidable amount of verse. In 1965 an event occurred that made the impulse to write all the stronger: he discovered he had Hodgkin's disease. In the remaining decade of his life, his output of poetry and prose was never slowed, except during periods of hospitalization, radiation treatments, and chemo-therapy. He had published his first book of verse, *Dying: An Introduction*, in 1968, and two more books within the next three years: *Scattered Returns* (1969) and *Pursuit of Honor* (1971). He also began writing reviews for the *New Yorker* and had *Innocent Bystander* published in 1975. After 1974 he was unable to write more poetry, but he continued to write prose until near his death in 1976. His unpublished poems were collected with those from the previous books in *Hello, Darkness* in 1978. Sissman's poetry gained quick recognition: he received a Guggenheim Fellowship in 1968, a $5000 grant from the National Institute of Arts and Letters in 1969, and was invited to deliver the Phi Beta Kappa poem at Harvard in 1971.

Howard Moss, poetry editor of the *New Yorker* who first published many of Sissman's poems, remembered him in a conversation as being "well self-educated, very mature, very worldly, not scrimmaging for reputation, very civilized, above the battle, brave in the face of cancer, sweet, generous and intelligent." Sissman trusted Moss completely in editing his poems, was nervous about his first reading at the YMHA in New York, had "beautiful manners, disliked sloppiness in anything—emotions, dress, writing." Davison recalls that when he first saw Sissman he found him to be "a long, slightly lopsided man, grave, formally dressed, extremely courteous, even owlish, so polite as to lend me confidence in my own opinions." He says that their friendship, "though more than professional, could not be described as intimate. I suspect that most of Sissman's friendships—with men at least—contained an element of wariness. Though much admired and beloved, though given to deep and

explicit courtesy and capable of conferring a sense of warm camaraderie, he was not easy to get close to.... His sense of personal privacy was acutely developed, yet it may have been linked to his artistic gift by a reverse gear, for his poetry, or at least that part of it written after 1963, had a very high autobiographical content."

One has some difficulty reconciling many of these impressions with the inflated ego that appears

L. E. Sissman

in much of Sissman's written work, ultimately supposing that in his writing he was perhaps unable to tone down properly the sense of literary importance that his rapid acceptance in certain quarters gave him, although it is true that in many poems and essays the self-importance is not merely literary. Davison's remark about the "high autobiographical content" of Sissman's poetry is quite true. It appears that Sissman automatically assumed that his autobiography in verse would be interesting. Steven Aronson says of the matter: "What a flabby bore the collective hero of these poems is! Both charm and hairline attenuated, he is life's garbageman-philosopher, a smoothly-modulated nincompoop, crunchless and without instinct. One is appalled by the sheer banality of his life ('stuffing'

244

would be a better word), and the sheer ease. He is indolent and quite simply dishonest." These are harsh words, but they are often accurate. Sissman typically writes distressingly bland reminiscences of his life ("the bone and marrow of his own past," Davison calls it)—of his childhood, his years at Harvard, a trip to New York, a weekend at Cape Cod, his medical history, literally anything that he has ever done, seen, or heard of—then strings a lot of these memories together in numbered sections and calls them something like "Pursuit of Honor, 1946" or "A War Requiem" (one of the longest poems ever published in the *New Yorker*, according to *Newsweek*). Too often a Sissman poem is a mere journalistic recording of events from an uninteresting and frequently irritating point of view, with no imaginative heightening at all. "It's a pity," says Aronson, "that these chatty and inconsequential rhymes have been mistaken by some critics for poetry with good plot."

In spite of such failings, however, Sissman has had editors and an audience who believe in him. According to Vernon Young, "Sissman earned precisely the readership he deserved, that of hardcore Manhattanites who like wised-up poems which sound sophisticated while implacably hostile to modes of sophistication not of their own kind. . . . his talent . . . was not distinguished. . . . I fear that the defence of Sissman is exaggerated. To believe that he was a first-class practitioner of urbane critical verse is not only to forget W. H. Auden but also, let me insist, John N. Morris, William Meredith, Oscar Mandel. Brevity, taste and a perfect ear are the qualifications for an epigrammatic poet who is chiefly moved by asperity towards the social setting. Sissman had a tin ear (his mindless alliterations send one up the wall); he was deficient in moral nuance; when his animosity was aroused—frequently—he was incapable of distinguishing acceptable polemic from the ugliest forms of abuse."

As for Sissman's tone, Jim Harrison makes a reasonable assessment of it in the following statement: "L. E. Sissman writes the sort of poem that helps sell thousand-dollar jade talc dispensers in *The New Yorker*. *Dying: An Introduction* simply goes on and on with the most flatulent urban humoresque, an assumption that we all must share some fey attitude toward the 'unlawfulness' of life. Often the poems remind one of a story by John O'Hara set to poetry by L. E. Sissman—those trying days at Harvard, the deliciously ironic aspects of urban lint are held up to be chuckled at. Sissman is to his credit fantastically inventive, but the inventiveness is misdirected—a solid research chemist getting

stripes into the toothpaste tube."

Similarly, Aronson entitles his review of *Scattered Returns* "Urbane Trash": "Surely there's a quiet spot this side of *Paradiso* where L. E. Sissman, the most clothes-minded poet of his generation, can set up shop. Threads seem his true calling: who else's poems these days sport girls in 'Marimekko and lavender glasses,' stout salesmen 'tailored by Weatherill,' windows that are 'Bonwit's'? Where else these days outside of tailor shops do 'baggy trouser legs' and 'outsize cloth caps' get their comeuppance?" Aronson's is the most vitriolic attack yet mounted against Sissman's poetry, but his arguments are convincing: "Sissman's is the true gift of the adman sensibility moving along in time. He loves to give us trademarks, brand-names: not a steak but a 'New York steak,' not just an apple pie but a 'Hostess Apple Pie,' not just a typewriter but a 'Smith-Corona'. . . . The adman-poet also leaves no name undropped: The Princeton Club, Grosse Pointe Country Day, the freshman crew in '43, dear old Louisburg Square (he really *is* shameless), Lüchow's." John Updike says he admires the "specificity" of Sissman's verse, and, its haughtiness aside, one must admit that it is specific—but too often in a superficial way. He does not see deeply enough. There is barely a single startling, metaphorically creative and fresh, figuratively sparked connection of new recognition in his poetry, and thus there is practically not an image in it that inspires the reader to remember it, or even remark it in passing.

Aronson does not stop there, however: "In 'Cambridge, 1963,' a poem about the death of John F. Kennedy, whose campaign aide the blurb says Sissman was, he writes:

> . . . When, earlier,
> My secretary said she'd heard that he
> Had just been shot . . .

Ah, we are meant to think, so he has a secretary! But why not 'my maid,' 'my houseboy,' or, even better, 'my tailor'? The elephantine egoism of the poems is astonishing." One fears that Aronson has Sissman dead to rights, and is dismayed that the poet was innocent enough to expose himself, in poem after poem, to the burning coals that critics do not tire of heaping upon him. As Aronson says, "these poems are tailor-made for taking pot-shots at." He also dismisses Sissman's poetic technique by citing a few of his particularly bad coinages: "The sun infects the earth with crescence," "the moderniqueness of our ways," "the solvent sun of May."

To these Aronson could have added many other

lines, such as: "My key mutters the password," "The moon's sway / As night-light laureate," "Your cool electrifying skin humming / With wattage," and, in a colossal failure of taste, this description of an operating table:

> I shuffle to the table, where
> A shining bank of instruments—
> Service for twelve—awaits my flesh
> To dine.

The truth is that he has no ear at all. "And bone saws stammer blue smoke as they bite" is absolutely the best line he ever wrote; it is quite fine, "stammer" being the best word choice in all his work. After that comes "dissolve our marriage / To our dear self, the lost boy in the burning / Building of bone" from "Getting On: Grave Expectations." Add to these as noteworthy, New York described as "that grey fret of a city over there," "skinny girls / Who tap the typewriters of summertime" and "a small-breasted race / Of long-haired daughters" in "Clever Women," as well as the following admirable lines from "Two Happenings in Boston":

> No one who
>
> Savors the sound of words like a devotee
> Of the Alliance of Arts dares do
> More than lie back and let a lurid sea
> Of tone colors ravish her hair-do.

The technique here is extremely deft and the satire is marvelous. It is a great pity that Sissman could not create this kind of gem more often. There is little else that is vivid or memorable. He wrote too much too quickly and did not refine any of it; he left it as low-grade ore. According to Sissman's obituary in the *New York Times*, " 'My mind,' he said at one point, 'is compartmentalized.' And he added, 'In advertising you learn the discipline of working against deadlines. I find this useful in writing poetry.' " Surely this is how he managed to produce such a vast accumulation of verse. It is odd that a poet's mind should be "compartmentalized," since literally everything that impinges on his consciousness should enrich the resources of his imagination. Great poems are not written against deadlines.

Sissman does have his defenders, to be sure, but none of them has been able to marshal a real case for him, and they often inadvertently betray some egregious aspect of his style. Almost every critic has remarked on the excessive preciosity of his fondness for frivolous wordplay, conceit, and allusion. Alan Williamson, for example, in lukewarmly defending Sissman, picks out one of the most questionable passages in the entire canon to illustrate this defect that he readily acknowledges: "witness a passage addressed to a friend in a mental hospital (named, of course, Noah):

> Still captain of your heart, aboard this ark
> Whose passengers are your fellow animals:
> Rough beasts who slouched to Bethlehem to die,
> Mild innocents immaculately conceived,
> Old men, all veins, who babble of green fields. . . .

In five lines, Henley, Yeats, and Shakespeare, plus two unconnected religious references on top of the basic ark conceit—and I am afraid . . . [it] . . . simply goes under." Williamson avers that "this is Sissman at his rare worst," and it is true that this is an unusually concentrated specimen. But the poet does this kind of thing too many times in his three hundred pages of collected verse. Sissman's allusions serve no other purpose than to show off an acquaintance with English literature. They do not contribute any additional depth of meaning, which is the only legitimate reason for using an allusion, and instead are merely plugged in when the poet's own words fail him. Such trivial trafficking in allusion is insulting to the very works he alludes to because he uses them for such shallow purposes.

Sissman is quite a formal poet, and he nearly always writes in a fairly regular iambic pentameter, occasionally rhymed but usually blank verse. Updike praises this blank verse and, in so doing, unwittingly returns another serious indictment of Sissman's style, namely his vocabulary, by expertly picking out some of his worst transgressions: "With 17th-century richness as a model, his blank verse displayed an aggressive if not prankish wealth of scientifically, commercially, polylinguistically exact terminology and a one-time spelling champion's rakish vocabulary—'fane,' 'virid,' 'pervigilium,' 'ennial,' 'cenereous,' 'stertorous radamacues,' 'repletive borborygmogenesis.' " One wonders if Sissman thinks he is licensed to do such things because of Auden's fascination with *recherché* words from the *Oxford English Dictionary*, but even Auden's practice is occasionally questionable, and Sissman does not have Auden's linguistic sophistication.

It is almost as if Sissman's poetry is so riddled with faults that even his defenders cannot avoid pointing them out. X. J. Kennedy says, "Part of the fun of reading him comes in recognizing particular streets, bars, hotels; and for such middle-aging readers as me, there are the reincarnations of 'the marching feet of Movietone' and other trivia of the 1940s and 1950s. Some poems wear the look of kept diaries, or scenes out of the context of a novel whose beginning and end we haven't read." Is this supposed to be praise? In the final analysis, Aronson's opinion is probably most correct about the place of Sissman's poetry in American letters: "Loaded with groggy banter and a really rather prodigal silliness, the poems . . . are full . . . of cozy vacuities and shallow prettinesses already gone a little seedy."

Sissman saw himself differently. He says in *Innocent Bystander* that he began writing reviews "after years of stumping and (I hoped) dazzling other people with anything I cared to try in verse." And he is quoted in *Contemporary Poets* as saying: "I hope to achieve some sort of universality by wedding colloquial, allusive contemporary language to traditional form. I experiment both with language and with time sequences and often invent words based on existing roots. . . . The tone of most of my verse is dry and ironic, though I don't hesitate to use the organ-like capabilities of the line of Shakespeare and Milton for large effects." (His "elephantine egoism" was such as to preclude any sense of insecurity that might have stimulated him to attempt some self-improvement.)

Is there nothing to be salvaged, then, from the considerable mass of Sissman's poetry? His single best poem is "Patrick Kavanagh: An Annotated Exequy," although the annotations are unnecessary. Aside from this, the reader may peruse "Lettermen," "The Village: The Seasons," and several of the posthumously published poems, "Getting On: Grave Expectations," "Spring Song," "The Clearing in the Woods," "Work: A Sermon," "The Better Half," "The Persistence of Innocence," and the last three poems in his last book (recommended by William H. Pritchard): "Homage to Clotho: A Hospital Suite," "Cancer: A Dream," and "Tras Os Montes." —*James Mann*

References:

Steven M. L. Aronson, "Urbane Trash," *Poetry*, 116 (April 1970): 40-42;

"Boston's Adman-Poet," *Newsweek* (13 October 1969): 97-98;

Jim Harrison, Review of *Dying*, *New York Times Book Review*, 28 April 1968, p. 6;

Anthony Hecht, Review of *Dying*, *Hudson Review*, 21 (Spring 1968): 215-217;

X. J. Kennedy, Review of *Scattered Returns*, *Nation*, 210 (30 March 1970): 378-379;

Hilton Kramer, "Late Returns," *New York Times Book Review*, 3 July 1977, pp. 3, 16;

William H. Pritchard, "Innocence Possessed," *Times Literary Supplement*, 28 July 1978, p. 847;

John Updike, "Witness to His Dying," *New York Times Book Review*, 14 May 1978, pp. 10, 47;

Alan Williamson, Review of *Hello, Darkness*, *Poetry*, 133 (November 1978): 100-102;

Vernon Young, Review of *Hello, Darkness*, *Hudson Review*, 31 (Winter 1978-1979): 686-687.

DAVID SLAVITT
(23 March 1935-)

BOOKS: *Suits for the Dead: Poems*, in *Poets of Today VIII*, ed. John Hall Wheelock (New York: Scribners, 1961);

The Carnivore (Chapel Hill: University of North Carolina Press, 1965);

Rochelle, Or Virtue Rewarded (London: Chapman & Hall, 1966; New York: Delacorte, 1967);

The Exhibitionist, as Henry Sutton (New York: Geis, 1967; London: Geis, 1968);

Feel Free (New York: Delacorte, 1968; London: Hodder & Stoughton, 1969);

Day Sailing (Chapel Hill: University of North Carolina Press, 1969);

The Voyeur, as Henry Sutton (New York: Geis, 1969; London: Hodder & Stoughton, 1969);

Anagrams (London: Hodder & Stoughton, 1970; Garden City: Doubleday, 1971);

Vector, as Henry Sutton (New York: Geis, 1970; London: Hodder & Stoughton, 1971);

The Eclogues of Virgil (Garden City: Doubleday, 1971);

A B C D (Garden City: Doubleday, 1972);

Child's Play: Poems (Baton Rouge: Louisiana State University Press, 1972);

The Eclogues and The Georgics of Virgil (Garden City: Doubleday, 1972);

The Liberated, as Henry Sutton (Garden City: Doubleday, 1973; London: Allen, 1973);

The Outer Mongolian (Garden City: Doubleday, 1973);

The Killing of the King (Garden City: Doubleday, 1974; London: Allen, 1974);

Vital Signs: New And Selected Poems (Garden City: Doubleday, 1975);

King of Hearts (New York: Arbor House, 1976);

That Golden Woman, as Henry Lazarus (New York: Fawcett, 1976; London: Sphere, 1977);

David Slavitt

Jo Stern (New York: Harper & Row, 1978);

Rounding the Horn: Poems (Baton Rouge: Louisiana State University Press, 1978);

The Sacrifice, as Henry Sutton (New York: Grosset & Dunlap, 1978);

The Idol, as David Benjamin (New York: Putnam's, 1979);

The Proposal, as Henry Sutton (New York: Charter, 1980);

Cold Comfort (New York: Methuen, forthcoming 1980).

David Rytman Slavitt was born in White Plains, New York, the son of Samuel Saul (a prominent attorney) and Adele Beatrice Rytman Slavitt. He married Lynn Nita Meyer in 1956. This marriage produced three children—Evan, Sarah, and Joshua. It ended, by divorce, in 1977. In 1978 he married Janet Lee Abrahm, a physician.

Slavitt attended Phillips Academy in Andover, Massachusetts, where he studied with the late Dudley Fitts and where he published his first poem—a parody of Whittier's "Snowbound" that Winfield Townley Scott printed in the magazine section of the *Providence Journal.* He entered Yale in 1952 and studied with Cleanth Brooks, Robert Penn Warren, Richard Sewall, and Paul Weiss. He was Scholar of the House and, among other things, followed after William F. Buckley, Jr., as anchorman on the Yale debate team. He graduated *magna cum laude* in 1956. In 1957 he took an M.A. at Columbia University and there wrote his master's essay on the poetry of Dudley Fitts, working under the tutelage of R. W. B. Lewis. Slavitt then taught for a year in the English department of the Georgia Institute of Technology before he took a job at *Newsweek.* He worked for that magazine from 1958 to 1965, in various capacities, chiefly as book critic and film critic, serving as an associate editor. In 1965 he left *Newsweek* to devote himself entirely to writing, supporting himself mostly by the publication of novels, both under his own name and several pseudonyms. In recent years he has also taught literature and creative writing at the University of Maryland and at Temple University, where he was a visiting associate professor of English.

Since the appearance of his first collection of poems, *Suits for the Dead* (1961), in the distinguished Scribners *Poets of Today* series, Slavitt has proved himself to be one of the most adroitly versatile and productive writers in America. He has built up an impressive canon including both serious and popular (and sometimes best-selling) novels and a body of work in poetry and translation that, in and of itself, would demand close and serious attention. John Hall Wheelock, editor of the *Poets of Today* series, singled out Slavitt's extraordinary virtuosity, the variety of forms he gracefully commanded, and the points of view, strategies, and stances, all held together by "one of the outstanding characteristics of Mr. Slavitt's work, his use of tone: either to mask an inner seriousness, which is then gradually permitted to assert itself, and with all the greater force, as the poem goes on; or . . . to yield us an experience on two levels." Wheelock also stressed "the brilliance and clarity of his work, its brisk pace and taut resonance of line, its sardonic counterpoint, and, above all, its dramatic tensions" as the essentially distinguishing characteristics of the young poet's work. As is often the case with the most gifted and productive poets, the future is at once discovered and mapped, with quick claims and territorial rights, in these early poems. Survival (which Slavitt sees and says, in any number of poems, is as much a matter of luck or utterly unearned blessing as anything else) and not the least diminution of interest and energy have given us a sufficient body of Slavitt's work to see and to trace some clear outlines of it.

Fourteen years after *Suits for the Dead,* Doubleday published *Vital Signs: New and Selected Poems* (1975). The sheer size and weight of the volume are impressive—and all the more so in an age that has come more and more to cultivate the trendy fashion of poetic minimalism, what poet Brendan Galvin wittily named "the poetry of inner mumbling." No minimalism, no mumbling here. There are 320 pages and some 194 poems, of which 88 are new and previously uncollected. In the section "Selected Poems," including all the work that had previously appeared (though sometimes slightly revised) in book form, the poet chooses to group them not in the more conventional manner according to chronological development, but instead by subject, theme, general and specific concern. The results of this arrangement are somewhat paradoxical. For even as the earlier poems are shown to be more similar, related, and coherent, within fairly broad boundaries, than they may have seemed to be within the context of their individual collections, the formal daring and brilliance, the technical virtuosity are all the more strikingly manifest. And this knowledge, in turn, leads toward yet another paradox. Although all of these selected poems, earliest as well as most recent, seem to be equally well crafted, equally finished, and thus for all practical purposes, to be virtually simultaneous in the making rather than the result of a steady and discernible development, nevertheless the rich variety of forms, closely juxtaposed, gives a clear impression of continuing, almost ceaseless experimentation—that quality which, commenting on *Child's Play* (1972), Adrien Stoutenberg described as the sense of witnessing "an expert juggler at work." Just so, and quite as paradoxically, the "New Poems" that occupy nearly half the pages of the book, although they also are grouped into units of general similarity—"Vital Signs," "At Home, In the World," and "Tough Characters"—are more obviously part of a deeper and darker development, going well beyond the limits of the "Selected Poems" even as they appear to derive from them. Clearly structure became particularly important to the poet when he came to survey the way he had already come and to seek to indicate, often by hints and clues and shadows, the directions he felt himself to be taking into the future.

This emphasis on structure in *Vital Signs* is perhaps the central paradox of the collection; for Slavitt had previously been quite explicitly outspoken about the relative insignificance to anyone (except the poet himself) of the arrangement of poems in order of appearance in any given individual volume. As he told critic John Graham in an interview for *The Writer's Voice*: "It's not a very high level of intellectual activity, it's about the same sort of thing as determining what order the acts ought to go on, say, an Ed Sullivan show." He also adds that "it's like arranging fruit in a basket. You put the good ones on top, and then, for the suspicious housewife, you put a couple of good ones at the bottom. The other poems, all the ones in the middle, you sit there trying to find some plausible order for that reader—there aren't very many of them, I think—but for the reader who does sit down and read the poems sequentially."

Between the publication of *Day Sailing* (1969) and *Vital Signs* came the experience for Slavitt of translating (and interpreting) Virgil's *Eclogues* and the *Georgics*, published in 1971 and 1972. Slavitt, an excellent Latinist with a solid background in classical languages and history, conceived of these translations first of all as a technical and critical challenge: "Finally, I worked out a desperate kind of attack, which was to ask of each *Eclogue*: If you were ever a living, breathing poem, what could you conceivably have been about?" He settled upon a basic theme of the *Eclogues*. "Indeed, the lit biz is a primary concern of the *Eclogues*. No writer who has raged at agents, editors, publishers, critics, other writers, or the public can fail to recognize the anguish Virgil felt, the compassion, or the hope." Borrowing from the ways of Medieval and

Bernard Golfryd

Renaissance translators, Slavitt developed a method involving sections of summary, critical interpretation, and commentary; and dramatically, and with deliberate anachronism, introducing himself, the living poet and translator, speaking directly to the present-day reader. His justification of the liberties of his method is at once straightforward and eloquent. "My hope," he writes in the preface to the *Eclogues*, "in these renditions of Virgil's exciting poems, is that by taking certain liberties, I shall have been able to convey something of the experience of the originals, the exhilarating whipsaw feeling Virgil's readers must have experienced as they translated back from the bucolic pastures and fields of Meliboeus and Menalcas and Moeris to the elegant drawing rooms of Roman literary life, and then, feeling the brittleness, the sophistication, the suffocation of Rome, yearned for something else, something better—and by that yearning made the cardboard shepherds suddenly real as only the objects of profound desire can be."

The results can be often witty and clever, often deeply moving also as these, the final lines of the ninth *Eclogue*, "Moeris": "Then Lycidas / tells him another, and Moeris . . . sighs / for the way it was when there was nothing else / to worry about but

David Slavitt

143

The hewn stone is cool to my leaning forehead,

a prop, a comfort, fortress, monument

all at once, ~~and~~ A caution -- the stone wall

against which the apothegmatic head

bangs itself to a bloody pulp. But heads

perceived the rectangular solid, imagined the wall,

and gave the stone its shape and position here.

On an ordinary evening in New Haven

with my son and daughter, I am ~~a~~ the ghostly presence

haunting them as my father haunts me.

I would fold them all in arms of stone and speak

in the stone's laconic tongue of reliable love;

144

They don't believe it, ~~as I didn't and don't,~~ ~~it isn't ever true~~

but we ~~can~~ pretend, letting what faulty love

we bear one another pass for that best we deserve

to give and get. Those moments of courtesy

like dainty insects ~~catch~~ in amber, ~~would~~ survive

as ~~the~~ data of history. Let the grubby truth

~~be~~ cart, away -- with New Haven, a grubby place

except in the mind. Drive on, and don't look back

to hobble imagination. Let ~~the~~ own haven~~s~~

be always new, and the broken down world heal

as ~~the~~ poets have taught us to think it ~~may~~. It may

if we ~~may~~ so ~~often enough~~ often and ~~loud~~ enough.

Revised typescript

250

spring and a sprung line. / But it closes in. The reception rooms are waiting / with blondes behind blond woods of expensive desks, / and further back the offices of villains. / The babble of song has turned to the last glug / of water down a drain. The plug is pulled.''

Through the *Eclogues* and next the *Georgics*, which required seven years of hard labor, Virgil grew and changed from a bright young poet, at the bright center of things in Augustan Rome, into a mature artist, wiser and sadder, deeper and more deeply serious, and unquestionably one of the greatest of poets. Those who follow after him, literally or figuratively, are likely to be taught by the same experience, as Slavitt seems well aware in these lines from his superb rendering of the most celebrated of all the *Eclogues*, the fourth—''Pollio'': ''Later, the poet of Naples / gave Virgil into the hands of St. Paul. And Dante / took Virgil with him. The dreams were close enough— / a new beginning. / But the sheep are not yet blue / nor any of those colors. And ships and planes / scurry and wreck. Plows wound the ground / and a field smells of sweat and diesel fuel . . . .''

In following after Virgil, translating and glossing him, Slavitt seems to have arrived at a darker vision of his own life and times, even as he comes to a deeper sense of both the glory and the folly of the poet's vocation. And yet the dark side was present from the first, most clearly evident in some of the longer poems of *Suits for the Dead*, historical and mythological poems like ''Jericho,'' ''Actaeon,'' and ''Orpheus.'' This quality of his work was noticed and underlined by the distinguished scholar-critic Louis Martz in a laudatory review of *The Carnivore* (1965) for the *Yale Review* (March 1966). Pointing out ''the bleak resolution'' of the book's final poem, the long and classical ''Elegy for Walter Stone,'' Martz added that together ''with a glittering wit, some fearful puns, amusing poems for and about children, and vigorous scenes in Central Park or 47th Street, there is in this volume a somber undercurrent that may at first suggest a stoical resignation, but is actually closer to a grim resentment toward death. . . . One becomes aware, gradually, of how many of these poems deal with deaths and endings: lemmings in the sea, of aging movie heroes in decaying Westerns, of Leonardo's last years, of a hated mouse killed in the kitchen, of the end of the School of Athens, of wreckers smashing gables, of fishing with grenades, of the great Theodoric's abandoned ashes, of Eskimos floating away on ice floes.'' By the time *Child's Play* appeared in 1972, others had also noticed the depth of

what Joyce Carol Oates describes (*Southern Review*, Autumn 1973) as Slavitt's ''dazzlingly accomplished poems.'' Oates uses adjectives like *harrowing* and *grim* to indicate the dark qualities of many of the poems. Yet she notes other qualities as well: ''Slavitt is cynical and detached, but at times curiously moving—he is unafraid of gentleness.'' She sensitively discerns that his is a highly original voice at a time when it may be said that originality is not at a critical premium. ''Strangely,'' she writes, ''the near-ubiquitous voice of the era seems generally absent in Slavitt. He is his own man, his own poet.''

At that stage, and to a large extent even now, Slavitt was revealed as a poet of almost brutally ironic contradictions. He is a learned and gifted metricist and an elegant formalist, whose use of many and various verse forms, both traditional and oddly and newly designed, book by book, could easily be taken as a textbook for the use of forms in contemporary American poetry. He is, in fact, as expert and as easy with his elegant expertise as the late W. H. Auden, a poet he has often celebrated (and mourned) and, in such poems as ''Another Letter to Lord Byron,'' directly challenged. Yet, at one and the same time, he is the cheerful master of the living and breathing, spoken urban-American vernacular, as fastidiously accurate with its rough-and-ready idiom and syntax as, for example, the late John O'Hara. And so, inevitably, the *things* of our times tend to appear in the context of a language that ranges easily between the colloquial and slangy and the purely elegant. Who else would begin a serious and sonorous poem, ''Homage to Luigi Boccherini,'' with this wild joking of unlikeness—''Landon to Hayden's Roosevelt, Luigi / Boccherini also ran / bows over strings / made minor music poor (I mean unmoneyed) / and died poor''? Or there is his memorable, moving elegy on ''The Death of Mozart,'' which seems to throw away its first few lines (out of twenty) before it moves to tears— ''Uraemia is painful enough without birds / chirping their heads off, warbling in thirds / while you're busy dying. A little quiet please.''

There is conflict, contradiction, within the poems—then, a dramatic clash of subject and tone, of language and form, which is structured to arrive at (usually) a surprising, yet satisfactory, denouement. If, before he had worked on and through the Virgil translations, Slavitt was chiefly unconcerned about the larger structure of whole groups of poems, he was always fascinated by the possibilities of intricate architecture within the individual poem.

Finally there is the paradox that, of all the poets of his generation, Slavitt has written most

David Slavitt

successfully, during the years at *Newsweek* and with any number of best-selling novels, for the popular, mass audience in America. Yet, unlike many poets who have been spared both that experience and the ability to enjoy it, Slavitt has always conceived of poetry as, essentially and by definition, an elite and hermetic art. No Whitman dreams of great democratic audience for him. In *The Writer's Voice* he said simply, and not entirely in jest—"One writes poems for oneself, and one's wife, and eleven friends." Talking to students at the Bennington Workshops in 1979, he said: "It's easier to be a poet [than any other kind of writer], because with poetry it doesn't make any difference. If you do not publish a poem ever, then there you are with Emily Dickinson. And that's not a bad place to be. And you can publish hundreds of poems and be there with a lot of terrible poets. And that doesn't make any difference either. . . . What you can long for is to write good poems. But this is a very risky, indeed silly ambition. And the virtue of the poetry, the goodness of the poetry, is likely to lose you more readers than it can gain you."

For some poets such knowledge and such rigorous conclusions might prove to be inhibiting. Not so for Slavitt. His most recent collection, *Rounding The Horn* (1978), shows no diminishment of talent or interest. There are explorations of some of the themes and subjects that have always concerned him, through fifty-odd poems, all in different forms. But this volume takes a turn in a new direction, seems to end something as it begins something else. "Reunion Elegiacs," written to be read at the twentieth reunion of his Yale class (1956), is there to be balanced against "Class Poem," delivered at graduation and published in *Suits for the Dead.* "Reunion Elegiacs" seems to round off something, if not to end it. But the title poem, "Rounding the Horn," presents a new form and possibility. It is a long, elaborately structured poem, twenty-four "octaves," eight-line stanzas, followed by a twenty-fifth that is a fourteen-line sonnet. These are poems of statement and meditation, each built around a central image or metaphor, each related to all the others thematically and in sequence. There are flashes of the old hijinks: "Crystal Lagoon, the Franco-Irish Bombshell / with hair the color of sand was innocent once, / a cheerleader with Coral Strand, waved pom-poms, / and shouted 'Gauguin, Go!' Those days are gone." But most often this sequence, built mainly around the metaphors of voyaging, escape, and adventure, and the weight of the aging animal self upon the ageless spirit, is more direct, sadder and simpler, the knotty complexity of thought, the snarls and pain of thinking as it happens (and *thinking* is very rare in recent verse), being caught in the tight, repetitive, shifty verse forms. The penultimate octave, "24," shows it well.

> Depression, whiskey, diarrhea, rage,
> and late at night a pouring over maps . . .
> the old symptoms return, I pace my cage
> like a jungle cat so long in the zoo, the lust
> for escape has faded away. Assume a lapse
> of diligence, a door left open just
> that longed-for moment; would he still make the try,
> or give it up, stop pacing at last, and die?

Insofar as the metaphor, or at least one level, refers to the poet and his art, Slavitt has neither given it up nor ceased to pace—sometimes even dancing—in the strict cages of his own construction. He has accomplished a great deal, more than most of his better-known contemporaries. By most definitions and standards he would have to be regarded, at his age, as a major poet of ours. And indeed a very slight change in poetic fashions, in the trends that too often pass for fluent artistry, could bring him forward to real prominence and influence. For at what he does and does well, there is no one else like him. Where he will go next as a poet while he waits for the wider recognition that he certainly deserves and just as certainly doubts that he can or ever will receive, remains to be seen. He has just completed a much longer and more complex work deriving from the ways of "Rounding the Horn." "Dozens" is a book-length poem, composed, as its title asserts, of 144 twelve-line stanzas. A half-dozen separate stories and images—scenes from urban life, life as a brief vacation in a grand hotel, terror and revolution in the streets, the disposal of garbage and waste, the life of the artist, and the private life and times of David Slavitt himself—are simultaneously juggled into a dazzling unity. Harder and tougher, more unflinching than ever, the poet's vision is nonetheless more reconciled, if neither resigned nor blithely optimistic. At the last he argues that his voice (and so ours) matters, that poetry and even this poem matter. Having visited with his son and daughter at Yale on "an ordinary evening in New Haven" (an obligatory allusion to Wallace Stevens as the ghostly Virgil of "Dozens"), the poet drives away. At least unafraid of the truth. At least maintaining the bravado to pun once more, to let the reader grin and bear it with him:

> Let the grubby truth
> be carted away—with New Haven, a grubby place
> except in the mind. Drive on, and don't look back
> to hobble imagination. Let our havens

always be new and the broken down world heal
as the poets have taught us to think it may. It may
if we say so often enough and loud enough.

—*George Garrett*

Play:

The Cardinal Sins, New York, Playwright's Unit, 1968.

Other:

"The Ageless Kittens of Cardinal Richelieu," in *The Girl in the Black Raincoat*, ed. George Garrett (New York: Duell, Sloan & Pearce, 1966), pp. 78-91;

"Critics and Criticism," in *Man and the Movies*, ed. W. R. Robinson (Baton Rouge: Louisiana State University Press, 1967), pp. 335-344;

Sexuality in the Movies, ed. Thomas R. Atkins (Bloomington: Indiana University Press, 1974), pp. 233-240.

Periodical Publications:

"Conscience of an Exhibitionist," *Esquire*, 69 (May 1968): 122-125;

"Notes toward the Destitution of Culture," as Henry Sutton, *Kenyon Review*, 118 (1968): 108-115.

Interviews:

George Garrett and John Graham, "David Slavitt," in *The Writer's Voice: Conversations with Contemporary Writers*, ed. Garrett (New York: Morrow, 1973), pp. 248-272;

Garrett and Graham, "Forms of the Public Novel: Conversations with R. V. Cassill and David Slavitt," *Contempora*, 2 (September / February 1971-1972): 13-16.

References:

George Garrett, "An Amoebaean Contest Where Nobody Loses: The Eclogues of Virgil Translated by David R. Slavitt," *Hollins Critic*, 8 (June 1971): 2-14;

Paul O'Neil, "Calculating Poet Behind a Very Gamey Book," *Life*, 64 (26 January 1968): 64-68;

John Hall Wheelock, "Introductory Essay: Man's Struggle To Understand," in *Poets of Today VIII*, pp. 13-27.

DAVE SMITH
(19 December 1942-)

BOOKS: *Bull Island* (Poquoson, Va.: Back Door Press, 1970);

Mean Rufus Throw-Down (Fredonia, N.Y.: Basilisk Press, 1973);

The Fisherman's Whore (Athens, Ohio: Ohio University Press, 1974);

Cumberland Station (Urbana: University of Illinois Press, 1976);

In Dark, Sudden With Light (Athens, Ohio: Croissant, 1977);

Goshawk, Antelope (Urbana: University of Illinois Press, 1979).

David Jeddie Smith was born in Portsmouth, Virginia. He was educated at the University of Virginia (B.A. 1965), Southern Illinois University (M.A., 1969), and Ohio University (Ph.D., 1976). He married Deloras M. Weaver in 1966, and they have three children—Jeddie, Lael, and Mary. Besides a tour of active duty in the U.S. Air Force (1969-1972), he has taught English and French (and coached football) at Poquoson (Virginia) High School (1965-1967), and has taught English and creative writing at Western Michigan University (1973-1974), Cottey College (1974-1975), as well as at Southern Illinois University, Christopher Newport College, Thomas Nelson Community College, William and Mary, and Ohio University. From 1976 to 1980 he was director of the creative writing program at the University of Utah. In September 1980, he will be a visiting professor in the English department at the State University of New York at Binghamton. His numerous awards include the John Atherton Fellowship in Poetry for the Bread Loaf Writers' Conference (1975), a National Endowment for the Arts Grant (1976), a Borestone Mountain Award (1976), and an award from the American Academy of Arts and Letters and National Institute of Arts and Letters (1979), as well as several annual poetry magazine awards—from *Sou'Wester* (1973), *Kansas Quarterly* (1973), *Yearbook of American Poetry*, *Pushcart Prize Anthology*, and *Portland Review* (all 1979). In 1969 he founded *Back Door*, a poetry magazine, and edited its first five issues (through 1972); from 1974 to 1979 he coedited the remaining issues (no. 6-no. 11/12) with Robert DeMott. Since 1979 he has served as poetry and fiction editor of the *Rocky Mountain Review*, and in 1978 he began a three-year term as a member of the board of directors of Associated Writing Programs.

From the outset of his career in the late 1960s,

when he began publishing poetry in numerous little magazines and journals, Dave Smith has worked with an exalted conception about the function and purpose of poetry that now marks him as a legitimate heir to the Romantic tradition in America—the only tradition he regards "worth prolonged consideration." His conception of poetry as a redemptive act stems from his own formative experience, explained in a recent interview with H. A. Maxson: "There are, very much alive and kicking, those people in our society who still believe, as Auden says in the Elegy for Yeats, that 'poetry makes nothing happen.' I just simply by God don't believe it. I know in my life, poetry was very near a conversion. It was very like a religious conviction had come into my life. I was drifting. Then I discovered I wanted to write poetry, and read poetry, and my life took on a shape, a direction. It may not matter very much to anyone else but it literally makes my life happen."

Out of this dignified sense of purpose and unstinting commitment to the life in art, Smith has evolved a belief in the poem as a moral act—"the song of possibility, not the dwindling record of doom," he told Maxson; and, he continued, "One of the things . . . the poem can do, is try to get at truth" by "an impulse toward a cleanness, or impulse to support life." Despite the religious language he often employs to articulate this idea, there is nothing moralistic (in the limited orthodox or sectarian definition) about Smith's poetry. His sense of aesthetic morality arises from his acceptance of the covenant implicit in the poet's commission of a sacramental duty, and the energetic necessity, as he says, "to be ambitious for art." While he has never shied away from the darker, meaner aspects of human existence (most of his finest poems actively embrace deprivation, loss, and death) in his pursuit of truths arising from human and natural mysteries, he achieves a holistic vision and tonal integrity that are essentially celebratory. "Driving Home in the Breaking Season," one of the poems in *Cumberland Station* (1976), fulfills these imperatives and announces the poetic tradition in America ("Roethke in his green war / gone like Whitman, bulldozed / like the secret river of the soul, but not ended, only / diverted, carving new banks") to be an enduring alternative to our industrial blight:

> Poetry,
> who watches you easing out along a timber stand, as I
> do,
> dreaming the feel of trunk bark,
> cradling the insults we make to God? To wake up glad

by a field alive with more than words,
the dead singing our wars remembered and
                         unremembered, is
to love your life and give it
a way to rejoice. Isn't home the same everywhere, the
                                              open
room of the sea, your hands
slippery with all the fish the fathers haul in their nets?
Damn death. Today I do not believe
a single sparrow will die but I will croak back his life.

Unlike many of his more fashionable contemporaries (for whom the poem can be an occasion to demonstrate technical or imagistic virtuosity at the expense of overt subject and heightened language), Smith's mature poetry is experiential, visionary, and frequently dithyrambic. "I am not one who cares much for form without content," he says in an essay in *Poets Teaching* (1980), "or even content serving form. But the poem whose language is indivisible from its content . . . is the balance we must honor, for it is the dynamic body of passion which both celebrates and is possibility. This dualism, like anything that matters, is complex and scarcely permits the easy resolution of flat statement."

As a result of his enormous contributions as a

poet, teacher, critic, editor, and tireless advocate for contemporary writing, Smith can be considered a major presence in American poetry. He brings to this pluralistic arena an individual sense of design, a distinctive voice, a unique notion of subject, and a considered, yet flexible, conviction in standards of excellence (based on clarity, beauty, and value), so that Peter Stitt's recent judgment of him as one of "the most talented poets we have" is both deserving and prophetic.

Smith's oracular posture fits the prevalent, but eclectic, Emersonian tradition in American poetry (he considers Emerson's essay "The Poet" the seminal theoretical statement of American poetics), both in regard to the poet's Adamic function as namer, and in his appropriation of a "husky" voice and rhetorical style. Smith is a poet of enormous receptivity, intellectual range, and linguistic resourcefulness, so it is not surprising to hear echoes of other writers in his work. Critics have rightly discerned the formative influence of James Dickey's *Poems 1957-1967*, which Smith maintains is one of the finest collections of poetry ever written by an American, and one that spoke to him "in a way no other poet ever has." If there is a confession of derivativeness in this heritage (manifested in Smith's use of spacing, violent imagery, and narrative mode, especially in *Bull Island*, 1970, and several poems in the first half of *The Fisherman's Whore*, 1974), it is outweighed by Dickey's liberating effect on Smith, particularly in guiding his realization that poetry can spring from the shared ground of Southern life, with its potential for a particular kind of human tragedy, based in ritual longing, nostalgic intimation, and rural values.

However, even this kinship requires qualification. Besides Dickey (whom he now considers less "durable and exciting"), other writers frequently cited for thematic and stylistic influence include Gerard Manley Hopkins, Thomas Hardy, Robert Lowell, James Wright ("The Pure, Clear Word," a collection of essays on Wright edited by Smith, will appear in 1981), and Robert Penn Warren. Warren's poetry and his essay "Knowledge and the Image of Man" are especially important to Smith: "I can't imagine the world without him," he told Maxson. To these authors must be added his prior assimilation of Anglo-Saxon poetry, William Faulkner's fiction, and the Bible—the latter two among the ineluctable legacies for the Southern writer. Of these three, his study of Anglo-Saxon has exerted the greatest influence on his rhetorical style, his preference for charged, heavily accented lines, and strongly stressed language. In "The Scop"

(Anglo-Saxon court poet), one of the major poems in *The Fisherman's Whore*, his conscious predeliction for the ancient rhythmical origin of poetry is apparent: "He delivered the news from each / seam he wore on his flesh, / news of wars, of death / in the snow-capped mountains, / of oceans crossed and lush lands / where the fishmongers hummed. . . ."

The legacy of the bardic tradition (John Gardner says Smith's poetry is "unpretentiously heroic"; his "noble" use of diction, mythic intimations, and "jammed and hovering stresses" produce "the fierce ring of iron on iron") resides in Smith's belief that one of the poet's most important functions is to sing, no matter how painful the occasion, inspiration, or event. His poetry has sought to release the full music of passionate but rigorously shaped language. In a recent review, "One Man's Music," he extends music's conventional meaning to include the "saying and staying power of the ruthlessly human voice courting its most precise, clear and vivid articulation *in the awareness* it must become more interesting and more special than any other form of speech."

This Emersonian-like vision of poetry as "artful thunder" is augmented by Smith's unique exploration of specific geographical landscapes and his preference for narrative structure or the architectural dimensions of "story." John Haislip says of him, "There is a *story* to tell, and he gets it told with great dispatch, the language driving forward, churning with energy and nailed down with exactitude." At its most charged, Smith's poetry embodies the rhythmical cadence of testimony, the full and imaginative awareness of human vulnerability witnessed and transfigured, as in this stanza from a magnificent poem in *Cumberland Station*, "The Funeral Singer": "My God," the speaker says, "how long does a man have to sing / to hear it be right just once . . ." and continues:

I promise even if I live to die
to get our colors in their right places, I won't
leave you alone under the vines until it's done,
until I sing like the most acute needle on earth
every note we dug out of those pressed grooves.

The literal and figurative implications of witnessing are essential to Smith's poetry, not only for the lyrical or incantatory response such a privilege creates, but also for what is revealed about his characteristic stance toward the world, and the resolution of his primary thematic preoccupation—*pietas*, the ancient commission of duty and obligation that informs the legacies passed from elders to children. Even when he inhabits the personalities of other characters (in his first three books there is a greater dependence on speaking through masks; subsuming or removing the lyrical "I" by finding suitable local or historical personages whose experiences can be envisioned by taking on their point of view), the abundant Romantic strategy of the central perceiving self (his poetry is acutely determined by eye and ear references, physical activity, natural symbolism, and light-dark imagery) invites a sacred trust between the poet and his subject. "I love poems," he writes in an essay, "Sailing the Black River," that "admit me to that private chapel of the soul where things matter, where I know what I have to encounter will make me pay for my life. . . ." Like Hart Crane, intoxication with visionary experience, energetic, active verbs, and involved syntax can occasionally obscure his intention, but it is a risk he is willing to take.

And yet Smith's testimonies should not be confused with "confessional" poetry, a genre he abhors. Whether he adopts the empathetic, invented voice, or the more personal projected voice, the speaker never asks for pity, never simply draws attention to naked suffering or self-absorption. "A Daylight Lady" (in *The Fisherman's Whore*) is an example of the former strategy. He speaks in the person of Ann Saunders who, in 1826, saved herself on a deserted ship by devouring her fiance's corpse. The subject is admittedly sensational, but by handling it with measured serenity, even the most horrific moment, when she eats the man's genitals ("Like sparrows, / for days, they filled me with your sweet praise"), is redeemed by her awareness that the entire act of cannibalism redefines "everything / the world calls love. . . ." Since *Cumberland Station*, Smith has preferred the imagined speaker, what he terms the "second self"—"a voice which serves the human need to witness all that is human . . . in language we cannot forget." In both types of voices, solipsism is averted by his awareness that human experience is inseparable from the sheer presence and elemental weight of the physical world. In "Roundhouse Voices" (*Goshawk, Antelope*, 1979), the speaker's own life as a man of words is severely tested at the funeral of an imagined uncle, a railroad man who taught him to play baseball. The final stanza exhibits the mutual exhaustion of form and content Smith demands, the rhetorical power of his voice, and caps the arching dimensions of his vision:

Do you hear the words that, in oiled gravel, you gave me
when you set my feet in the right stance to swing?
They are coal-hard and they come in wings
and loops like despair not even the Mick

could knock out of this room, words softer
than the centers of hearts in guards or uncles,
words skinned and numbed by too many bricks.
I have had enough of them and bring them back here
where the tick and creak of everything dies
in your tiny starlight and I stand down
on my knees to cry, *Who the hell are you, kid?*

Smith has always set large thematic, formal, and conceptual demands for himself as a poet. The "ambition" and "care" that Helen Vendler has recently praised have been apparent from the beginning, although his early work does not possess such mastery of language and form. All his books, however, reflect a passionate attraction to the myriad possibilities of the way poems can be written, rather than a studied subservience to a fixed model. He told Maxson he had not settled the "question of how I'm going to write the poem . . . and I don't know, deep down, that I ever want to settle it." This restiveness is precisely the factor that gives his best poems their startling power, their capacity to surprise and delight his readers, even when he is transforming such traditional forms as sonnets or dramatic monologues. Each book enacts a process of technical discovery that is itself an organic extension of the persona's metaphysical quest, and leads finally, in *Cumberland Station* and *Goshawk, Antelope*, into the presence of poems "humanly beautiful and original," some of them among the finest poems of the past decade.

Geographical setting functions powerfully in Smith's work. All of his books are the direct result of his engagement with a physical place and a specific landscape—Tidewater Virginia in the first three books, Cumberland, Maryland, and Virginia (again) in *Cumberland Station*, and Wyoming and Utah in *Goshawk, Antelope*. His major technical paradigm is a journey back to and through those literal and symbolic geographies—a generative conjunction of questing figure and primal landscape. In his first three books the speaker's function is to filter and order the memories and events that he has directly experienced, or that are vicariously available to him through local and/or historical characters. He is enamored of the tough, crusty "watermen" (self-sufficient Atlantic coast shellfishermen), especially the men of the Carmines family, who have willfully chosen a lonely, painful life on the ocean. They are mostly uneducated and inarticulate, but they possess an endurance, grace, and fatalism that Smith considers heroic. In *Cumberland Station* the journey becomes a full-fledged quest, and is much more personal. Instead of relying on passive memory, the past of the poet is immediate; its piety rooted in a familial heritage. In *Goshawk, Antelope* a much larger movement occurs. The speaker is a fictive projection of the poet, who moves inland to a primordial landscape, far from Smith's sacred Atlantic Ocean, but deeper than ever into the rock-ribbed sources of his magisterial vision.

His first collection, *Bull Island,* a limited edition chapbook of twenty-two poems, initiates Smith's poetical journey, although it is often uncertain and halting. A line from "Wharf Watch," about a dockside cat who "sprawls in satiet satisfaction," reveals his love of sibilant language but gives little promise of his later resonance. Some of these apprentice poems are marred by a blurred focus, inadequate tension, and cliched language ("Resurrection" ends "Ain't that life?"). Behind the obvious weaknesses, however, *Bull Island* is important because it demonstrates his first attempt to structure a book around a journey "back to the village" of childhood—the isolated coastal fishing village of Poquoson, Virginia—and because it initiates the search for a father figure that dominates Smith's work. From the very first, Smith conceived of poetry as a record of the integral growth of a perceptive, narrative consciousness (who is charged with keeping alive "voices that do not die / but float in the mind like images / of fathers in rural parlors"), rather than as a grab bag of discrete impressions or showy images.

Aware of the dichotomy between the allure of nostalgia and the existential demands of identity implicit in such a return, the speaker generally manages to avoid sentimentality by entering the personalities of local fishermen, embracing the meanness and deprivation of their lives, and celebrating their resoluteness and quiet heroism. In "Bull Island Waterman" his aim is realized in what Peter Stitt calls Smith's "precocious . . . plain style": "When they asked me why / I was a waterman / I told them riddles: how / I had seen my face / on the underside / of a white gull's wing / so it haunted me until / I believed some men sailed / forever through tightening circles / dreaming of getting back / to a place of beginning."

His second book, *Mean Rufus Throw-Down* (1973) (the title refers to a gifted baseball catcher whose skillful execution of the pick-off throw to second base Smith admired), contains forty-seven poems of varying length, subject, and voice. The poems alternate between those that arise from or are related to his native seacoast region, and those that are domestic or occasional in subject (and essentially descriptive in mode), including poems on his wife's pregnancy, a paean to Willie Mays, and even a comical poem on warts. Although Smith considers *Mean Rufus* a finished and complete work, he also thinks of it as a "rehearsal"—a stage in his development that provided an opportunity to work through two distinctly different kinds of poetry. His fully engaged voice emerges only occasionally here, but its delineation is increasingly apparent, as is his characteristic attention to design. He consciously structured the book by juxtaposing individual poems with contrasting tonal qualities, and by alternating the narrative poems with the shorter "image" poems.

The most successful poems confront death, and they spring from "the place of beginning" only partially explored in *Bull Island.* "Pit Carmines," an elegy for a lost waterman, whose "bones / bend stiffly at the river's push," achieves its strength through Smith's refusal to treat death sentimentally. In the book's most dramatic poem, "Dying Off Egg Island Bar," he creates "the narrative experience of a drowning man . . . not yet technically dead." The result is a startling combination of bold invention, imaginative empathy, and charged language, as the first stanza reveals:

> I hung like a man on trapeze, my arms stiffening
> into spines, my feet feathering the water as the last
> blood in my veins gives up its body heat for the cold
> precision of swimming. . . .

In a reflexive sense, "Dying" is also a birth because it marks the first time Smith successfully transferred his vast poetical energy into long rhythmic lines necessary to contain his vision. "Dying" points directly forward to a superb poem in *The Fisherman's Whore,* "Captain Carmines' Death Song" (Vernon Young calls the poem "worthy of comparison with Hopkins's 'The Wreck of the *Deutschland*' "), which shows Smith capable of handling the most radical transcendence—the body out of itself—in suitably expanded form:

> but possessed of everything   taking the chance   able to
> rise
>   to walk like a fish   glide   dance with the wind
>   the life that is longed forever.

Despite some unevenness, his third book, *The Fisherman's Whore,* marks an important advancement in execution. The second half of the book contains several gratuitous poems ("One for Rod Steiger," "Bad Man's Lament," "What Lady, He Said," and "Doubling Back with Bogart") that fit the thematic shape of the speaker's education, but not the heroic implications of the introductory epigram

Salt Lake City
1976

Between that rust-coated fence tall as my father and that hunkered
brow of iron thorns, what man on earth could get through?
In or out and no difference now I see but
then, coming down the little vale of soot, cutting
the regular road in half I did not see. I walked
with my grain lovely slugger from Louisville
out of the sun that made its soft glove on my hand
and I thought a fence like that works one way
only, to keep out whoever wants in.
so I waved like atrack boy and went in and got past the man who
hollered once that I could get to hell from there quick for stealing
but I wasn't there to steal or to get out. Neither was he.
You can't catch me lardass, I can go left and right,
I said, taking that slugger by the neck and laying down
a bunt between coal cars stunned and jerking, so safe,
in a slide on ash I heard him stop and wheeze
the words still hard as brakeshoes: Who the hell are you

kid? The fence around a yard is big when you are boy and slugging
looks easy even if your uncle whips a fat grey softball over
a cracked plate nobody owns. I have been back to the wall
for hours with that thump on bricks like a heartbeat
when ball trickles at your feet, have hit the damn thing
every fine lick I could manage and no wall did I once clear.
but the sewer stood

And who the hell is it I see now, a speck in my eye like a cinder
floating, coming through a tunnel of grey porches and down
through the vse of rock where the ash smears like hope
in lost layers? Who is it giving the finger in light
that, in memory, outgleams the best B&O high-grade globe,
where the old man gets up to do his job without hate,
knowing the kid can't be caught, so sits down to sob
and is still sobbing and sick in the staggering hours
one Christmas when the thing in the chest comes and he
recalls a morning of first love? Who is the one

drunk and dying as he leans into a grease-stained box of tools
that once fit everything like a girl's bright promise?
He knows, uncle, which way the fence is built, sees
how the barbs point in and he still wants to keep me out
but I gave him the finger, I pumped hard, and got in so you
could tell me again what it means to wait here.
for the right pitch to float down like the sun / that glows in its glove an
Them Pirates, they can come back anytime young man.
Hell, ain;t I told you age don't mean nothing?
But knowing what's what?
Alone I hear the wheeze of air compressors giving up like you,
Uncle, today is a day I did not want to see. I stand in the roundhouse
where it is black and quiet as the walls of a grave, the seep
of a hose in pits making me think of you gone worked and swirled the world
for the ball under the tools. Somewhere tracks reach back
something I can't name anymore, thumps and if that old man
came in here right now he'd see me taking the best you had
all the way to the wall and falling back, whipped, in oil

"The Roundhouse Voices," revised typescript

from *The Seafarer* ("He who goes on the sea longs for it forever").

A few poems from the previous books are published here, but, revised and rewritten, they testify to Smith's considerable growth, especially his accurate eye for details, the specificity of his language, and his accommodation of metaphor. The title poem (the watermen's boats are their "fabled whores") profits from his careful attention. Where, in the third stanza of the *Bull Island* version, the imagery is conflicting and the tone dreamy: "From the empty porches / of the sleeping village you can / hear the timid swamp reeds / rustle angrily / like lean snaking whips"; here the poem is tighter, more musical, and tonally suggestive: "Along the swing-laden / porches of whitewashed houses you / can hear the lacy swamp grass / rake angrily, bladed / now in winter's first wind." Similarly, "The Wives at Old Point Comfort" (originally "Wives of the Fishermen") is improved by more precise focus ("On the last day they wake / pressing abrasive kisses against / the nerves of their husbands. . . ." became "On the last day they wake, like knives, / all knees and ribs and teeth cutting / the fishermen free of the sheets / and the flies banging on the screens / where the summer is storming."), and a vastly deepened sense of loss ("love sticks like a skin ripped / on smoldering rocks, transparent / as fish scales, small pockets / clutching at sunlight" was transformed into ". . . she remembers loving him, turning back / at the black docks, the fish scales / everywhere, tiny jewels, egg chips / like pockets of sunlight on her legs / transparencies she must remember always").

Once again, the seagirt region ("where all roads run off / into the infinite blue border") provides the compelling ground of inspiration, meaning, and belief. "I had loosed the dead / from memory, but coming back / confused, I find them waiting / here at the sea's rattling edge" ("Among the Oyster Boats at Plum Tree Cove"). From the title poem's invocation of primal themes linking men, the sea, and their craft, to the benediction of love and transmission of legacy passed on to his daughter ("in the unimaginable dawn . . . all creation steps down safe"), Smith moves through an integrated landscape where elemental forces and spare physical actions become symbolic gestures. The venerable qualities of endurance, skill, piety, courage, and especially "grace" (as the "Old Whore"—the culminating symbol of Sea-Life-Experience—instructs the speaker in a Yeatsian monologue) are still operable in this world.

Violence too is an integral part of the lives he inhabits. The major achievement of *The Fisherman's*

Whore is the way Smith earns his world view. It is based on a belief that inscrutable presences which occur in even the meanest lives can produce ennobling effects. In "The Shark in the Rafters" he joins the symbol of malignant but fascinating force with an act of individual acceptance. The poem is written with absolute sureness, narrative direction, and imagistic clarity, so much so that it is impossible to see it as a pale echo of Dickey's "The Shark's Parlor," or to agree with Robert Kent, who says Smith's poetry "has no essential experience of its own" and is "written in language without identifiable resonance." A captured shark has killed and eaten a fisherman; the shark, "beautiful and terrible, terrible," is cut open, "and a man / begins at last to descend among them." The poem ends with the widow's tragic, haunted perspective:

> And this afternoon
> while her children plunge and dive in the light,
> a woman shall climb stairs and lie
> with only a swimmer's shadow
> on her breast, in the room
> where a clock's familiar rasp
> makes her spin and whisper
> as if to a face crusted with salt,
> a mouth cracked like summer clouds, bearing
> the white sheer teeth of the shark
> that follows her everywhere.

In *Cumberland Station*, the quest is circular—extending from the Virginia coast to the Maryland mountains and back again to the sea. It follows the route taken by Smith's ancestors, and suggests the personal, quasi-autobiographical basis for these poems that justifies the urgent quality of the speaker's voice, delivered almost entirely in first-person mode. In "Looming: An Address to Matthew Fontaine Maury," he writes:

> These are stories of outsiders choked up
> with delusions and the downhill nights of mines.
> I hope they have found a country to live in
>
> as I stand sighing over the cat's fur of the sea,
> thinking of you gone from Virginia, skidding
> like a skimmed stone in the half-light of exile.

The book is structured in three movements. Part 1 concerns familial origin and historical identity that loom in the speaker's past. The major events initiate him into an awareness of death and loss. The perspective is capacious—both national and individual. He ends one ambitious and allusive poem, "With Walt Whitman at Bear Mountain," with echoes of Whitman's "Out of the Cradle Endlessly Rocking." "I want to tell you," he says to the reader and to the ghost of Whitman:

> how progress has not changed us much.
> You can see breaking on the woods the lights
> of cars and the broken limbs glow
> in the boomed rush of traffic that chants
> *wrong, wrong, wrong, wrong.*

Near the end of the initial section he returns to the Cumberland, Maryland, railroad station (no longer standing) where his grandfather spent his life in a "ticket-seller's cage." The station is Smith's Chapel Perilous, and he is tested by its deprivation and meanness: "In this vaulted hall / I think of all the dirt passed down / from shovels and trains and empty pockets. . . . / Churning through the inner space of this godforsaken / wayside. . . ." The speaker encounters only "bad news"—the utter emptiness of existence under an industrial regime ("I dig / my fingers in my temples to bury a child / diced on a cowcatcher, a woman smelling / alkaline from washing out the soot"), and the moral bankruptcy of a society where "nobody cares / who comes or goes here or even who steals / what nobody wants." The startling, brilliant power of "Cumberland Station" is a result of Smith's unblinking view of the void, "a place I hope / I never have to go through again," and the pure passion of his language, which overcomes it.

The effects of his descent into hell linger in part 2. The middle section is a passage through various trials of the flesh and word encountered in distant places—Michigan, Ohio, Illinois, Indiana. The speaker is in exile, prey to conflicting and unresolved feelings of love and despair, doubt and joy—flip sides of the "anguish I have no word for." Except for "The Funeral Singer," "One Question, Two Seasons," and the long, free-style "Drunks," there is a distance and coldness in these poems that come from Smith's experimentation with parable. "The Delivery," "The Sex of Poetry," and "Small Song for Breadloaf" have hard edges and impenetrable surfaces. A prose poem, "The Divorce," is almost inaccessible, its satire out of context with the poignant tone of the book: "Mommy broke her / dinner plate on her forehead and said that's the last / time I eat dead trout."

Finally, the physical location shifts toward the ocean, and marks the speaker's emergence into a mythical condition, where the full knowledge of reality demands compassion, grace, and love. Salvation begins with individual courage. In "Sailing the Back River," one of the dozen or so truly brilliant poems in the book, the poet is "the pale

sailor who / glides with the music of nails through plank rot / and oil scum to sit in the toy wheelhouse of fathers." This is the place, he says,

> to honor crab song, reed's aria
> where every hour the mussel sighs *begin again.* Say
> I am water and learn what I hold as river, creek,
> lake, ditch or sewer. I am equal with fire and ice.
> We are one body sailing or nothing. My life, yours,
> what are they but hulls homing, moving the sand?

The poems are dense, evocative, intense ("exquisite" Helen Vendler says). The linked patterns of flowing images—boats, water, fish, rivers, music—capture the processional quality of Smith's vision. The lyrical apprehension of dynamic life occasionally breaks through its boundaries into a glimpse of the divine, "where every breath turns . . . reckless and pure as gull / song tuned by nothing but ribbed sealight."

In "Night Fishing for Blues," the concluding poem, Smith's mastery of narrative form (what Stanley Plumly has identified as the "prose lyric") reaches its most resonant height. The themes of history, personal initiation, and sacred benediction are gathered in this poem and carried forward with relentless energy, precision, and music. At Fortress Monroe, Virginia, near "where Jefferson Davis / hunched in a harrowing cell," the speaker comes to fish for "big-jawed Bluefish, ravenous, sleek muscle slamming / into banked histories of rock . . . great Ocean / Blues with bell-bones ringing like gongs." The tide and feeding conditions are absolutely right: "Bluefish are pouring at me in squads / . . . . I know I have waited / a whole life for this moment." He catches more than fish, however. In the intensity of the moment, a wild cast snags an elderly black woman fishing near him. They remove the hook and continue fishing, until their lines foul, "leap rigid as daguerreotypes . . . but we go on for the blue blood of / ghosts that thrash in the brain's empty room." The woman is history, the image of mortality and continuity in whom the speaker recognizes dignity, grace, and endurance. Her legacies include the right way to fish ("She wants / nothing but to fish"), the proper attitude toward nature ("Sons *they done let us go*"), and the economy of death ("We kneel . . . break their backs / to keep them cold and sweet, the woman gravely / showing us what to do"). In a moment of communal integrity, they "drink beer like family," the speaker dramatically transfigured by a vision of lambent order larger than all of them:

All the way home thousands of Blues fall from my head,
falling with the gray Atlantic, and a pale veiny light

fills the road with sea-shadows that drift in figure

eights, knot and snarl and draw me forward.

In *Goshawk, Antelope* the consequential development of Smith's consolidation of persona and landscape reaches significant new dimensions. The sustaining themes of obligation, piety, and heroism are given a new context and extended as a result of his metaphysical obsession with experience, love, and time, which "the dazzled world stands still to remember." If *Cumberland Station* is Smith's book of changes, this one is his cosmogony; where his earlier books had been carefully structured, *Goshawk, Antelope* is orchestrated.

The world imagined here is primarily a dreamed world, almost surreal in quality. "Somehow I have slipped . . . down into the root-tangles / of dream." The persona's characteristic stance is to function as witness to otherwise inscrutable events. In the opening poem, "Messenger," the speaker says, "Even now I can't see why it happens, the moment of change, / but must try to witness each particular index / of landscape and irony of promise." Peter Stitt has found a lack of correlation between style and content in this book, as if Smith's lush Southern sensibility was not right for the harsh Western landscape. What Stitt misses, however, is that while Smith's language is abundant in this book, it is not glib and loose the way some of his earlier "Southern" poems had been. The book gains its stunning and cumulative power because a new landscape challenges Smith's imagination (not only his memory) to produce poems commensurate with its enormity and sublime grandeur. Smith accepts the challenge ("Who / would not risk everything / for this?"), and in doing so is released from the burden of chronicling strictly autobiographical moments. Here he creates an entire world—landscape, persona, and experience—and invests it all with fully imagined palpability, resonant, symphonic language, and technical resourcefulness matched by few other poets his age. Here is the opening of "The True Sound of the Goshawk"; the swoop of the hawk matched in intensity by the sweep of language, the immediacy and clarity of observation:

A gathering of dust, that gray piston from the world's
first balance insinuates everything and comes
down from blue-white croppings of rock
in Wyoming. Hoofprints fade, they
do not notice how they are

filled with that small body's cold summoning, but I
see

that strange gesture which is like the swoop
of love, its corrective oscillations
without fear and beyond loneliness
that flies in my body and waits.

The title poem contains the basic antinomies of the book that occur repeatedly: Goshawk-Antelope, male-female, dark-light, death-love, action-words, change-permanence. The poem also enacts the basic technical strategy—retrospective vision generated by the adult speaker returning to childhood. The speaker sees a Goshawk fall "across my windshield, a dot at sixty, and I, half-looking for a place I had never seen, half-dreaming rooms / where blind miles of light lie on framed family faces, / saw him. . . . saw memory." The speaker watches the hawk attack a full-grown antelope: "Dark and light bucked, / clung, shredded in me until I was again a boy on a fence, / hunched across the dream contending world."

Goshawk, Antelope is Smith's most difficult and demanding book. It repeatedly takes his reader to the edge of existence where language itself is threatened with annihilation ("Come to the window and I will show the world without / dreams, starless, mouthing itself, and the apples / growing black with nothing to tell us"), yet somehow is never lost. The book's striking achievement is recorded in the speaker's struggle to find words that will not fail his message of love, his "enormous hunger." That is an arduous process, but it is utterly believable, earned, and honest. In a nearly perfect poem, "In Snow, A Possible Life," he writes, "Whoever I am, whatever words I badly use, / may we come to the pure heat of our bodies / and keep in ourselves the dark edges / no snow in this world ever softened enough." This is poetry that fulfills his own requirements to be placed in contact with sacramental energy, to hear life's true speech, and to embark on a journey as good in reflection as it was in the going.

—*Robert DeMott*

Other:

"On 'Dying Off Egg Island Bar,' " in *New Voices in American Poetry*, ed. David Allan Evans (Boston: Winthrop, 1973), pp. 215-216;

"Sailing the Black River," in *American Poets in 1976*, ed. William Heyen (Indianapolis: Bobbs-Merrill, 1976), pp. 342-363;

"Passion, Possibility, and Poetry," in *Poets Teaching*, ed. Alberta Turner (New York: Longman, 1980), pp. 173-191.

Periodical Publications:

"Chopping the Distance: On James Wright," *Back Door*, 7/8 (Spring 1975): 89-95;

"The Muse in Peril . . .," *Prairie Schooner*, 49 (Summer 1975): 178-184;

"Fifty Years, Mrs. Carter: The Poetry of John Woods," *Midwest Quarterly*, 17 (Summer 1976): 410-431;

"That Halting, Stuttering Movement," *Ironwood*, 10 (Winter 1977): 111-130;

"Recent Poetry," *Western Humanities Review*, 32 (Autumn 1978): 269-286;

"He Prayeth Best Who Loveth Best: On Robert Penn Warren's Poetry," *American Poetry Review*, 8 (January-February 1979): 4-8;

"The Child of the World: Louis Simpson's *Searching for the Ox*," *American Poetry Review*, 8 (January-February 1979): 10-15;

"Dancing Through Life Among Others: Some Recent Poetry from Younger American Poets," *American Poetry Review*, 8 (May-June 1979): 29-33;

"The Second Self: Some Recent American Poetry," *American Poetry Review*, 8 (November-December 1979): 33-37;

"One Man's Music: Some Recent American Poetry," *American Poetry Review*, 9 (March-April 1980): 40-43.

References:

John Gardner, "On Dave Smith," *Three Rivers Poetry Journal*, 10 (1977): 6-9;

John Haislip, " 'Flood, Salt, Debris, Relief': The Poetry of Dave Smith," *Sou'Wester*, new series, 2 (Spring-Summer 1974): 56-64;

Robert Kent, "Between Wild Dreams and Tame Realities, and Elsewhere," *Parnassus*, 4 (Fall-Winter 1975): 195-205;

H. A. Maxson, "The Poem as a Moral Act: An Interview With Dave Smith," *Sam Houston Literary Review*, 2 (November 1977): 64-74;

Stanley Plumly, "Chapter and Verse," *American Poetry Review*, 7 (January-February 1978): 15-19;

Peter Stitt, "The Sincere, the Mythic, the Playful: Forms of Voice in Current Poetry," *The Georgia Review*, 34 (Spring 1980): 202-212;

Helen Vendler, " 'Oh I Admire and Sorrow,' " *Part of Nature, Part of Us: Modern American Poets* (Cambridge: Harvard University Press, 1980), pp. 289-302;

Vernon Young, Review of *The Fisherman's Whore*, *The Hudson Review*, 27 (Winter 1974-75): 611-614.

WILLIAM JAY SMITH
(22 April 1918-)

SELECTED BOOKS: *Poems* (Pawlet, Vt.: Banyan Press, 1947);

Celebration at Dark (New York: Farrar, Straus, 1950; London: Hamilton, 1950);

Typewriter Birds (New York: Caliban Press, 1954);

Poems 1947-1957 (Boston: Little, Brown, 1957);

The Tin Can, and Other Poems (New York: Delacorte, 1966);

New and Selected Poems (New York: Delacorte, 1970);

The Streaks of the Tulip: Selected Criticism (New York: Delacorte, 1972);

The Traveler's Tree, New and Selected Poems (New York: Persea Books, forthcoming 1980);

Laughing Time, Nonsense Poems (New York: Delacorte, forthcoming 1980);

Army Brat, A Memoir (New York: Persea Books, forthcoming 1980).

William Jay Smith was born in Winnfield, Louisiana. He received his secondary education in St. Louis and graduated from Cleveland High School in 1935; then came a distinguished academic career highlighted by a 1939 B.A. from Washington University in St. Louis, followed by an M.A. in French (1941) from the same school, as well as studies in France and England, where he was a Rhodes Scholar at Oxford (1947-1948). During World War II he served as a liaison officer aboard a Free French naval vessel. The early postwar years established him as an important translator through his publication of the works of Valéry Larbaud (1955) and Jules Laforgue (1956). Smith's impressive literary career includes such positions as Consultant in Poetry to the Library of Congress (1968-1970), poetry reviewer for *Harper's* (1961-1964), and several appointments at American universities as poet-in-residence and professor of English. In addition, he has served a term in the Vermont House of Representatives (1960-1962) and has received numerous awards, ranging from *Poetry* magazine's Young Poets Prize (1945) to a Ford Foundation grant in drama (1964) and a D.Litt. degree from New England College (1973).

Smith's writing is as diversified as his experience. In addition to his serious verse and translations, he is the author of a play and several juvenile works, and he has edited books on French and English writers, recently adding a collection of essays to his growing list of accomplishments. The poetry itself is both scholarly and clear, at the same time light and despairing. As Smith describes it: "I am a lyric poet. . . . I believe that poetry should communicate: it is, by its very nature, complex, but its complexity should not prevent its making an immediate impact on the reader. Great poetry . . . must resound with the mystery of the human psyche." In his first book, *Poems* (1947), the tone is particularly delicate and aesthetic, recalling Wallace Stevens in some of the best, like "The Peacock of Java," which speaks of how Solomon's mariners find the fabled bird that "brings, even / To the tree of heaven, heaven." The poet speaks of how they struggle for this ineffable treasure but do not understand it:

> How they turned and on the quiet
> Water then set sail
> For home, the peacock's tail
> Committed to the legends of the sea.

This lyric resembles Stevens's focused imagism in its preoccupation with myth, the search for truth and beauty; there are technical similarities as well in the deft rhyme scheme and use of strong pentameter to drive home the final line. Yet the early Smith is more openly Romantic, and certain weaker poems ("Love, O Love, These Oceans Vast") suffer from a predictable meter and theme that Stevens usually avoids.

But the first book displays to fine advantage certain features common to most of Smith's poetry. Image and metaphor predominate, presented in verse heavily rhymed and metered. Although there is technical variety, one remembers the picture and hears the heavy sound patterns echo in his ears; one sometimes misses (as with many imagists) the struggle that adds fear and tension to the poetic experience. As Thomas H. Landess observes, "The selections from *Poems* . . . are slight by comparison with the later, more ambitious works, slight because , , , there is no Dionysian impulse straining against the boundaries, no compelling mystery that barely escapes solution."

In *Celebration at Dark* (1950), some of the best pieces from the first book are reprinted, but one sees a new lyric intensity and even some of the "Dionysian impulse" in poems like "The Girl in Glass." Here the impulse is sexual: a girl combing her hair, "Both white hands / Infiltrating copper strands," in an ageless and mythic gesture that equates her with "A mermaid in a fable." The tension is between her symbolic, eternal qualities as woman and her personal, immediate beauty, the passion of the moment as the lamp burns "coral-red." While the poet recognizes and appreciates the universal aspects of her beauty, the man in the bedroom scene realizes that he can only have the momentary and personal, saying "You've stood there long enough." This theme of ultimate loss is examined from many angles, usually with less optimism, as in "On Parting," where Smith concludes, "Love also dies; the dead have loved you best."

The strength of this collection is its fine images. In poems like "Lachrymae Christi," Smith reminds the reader of Robert Frost's "After Apple-Picking" through a perfectly rendered scene of ladders among cherry trees "All aslant the summer air." He skillfully presents his theme of the inescapable flight of time by focusing on various aspects of the setting. In *Contemporary Poets* Daniel Hoffman points out Smith's strengths as "devotion . . . to brief lyrics,

Layle Silbert

263

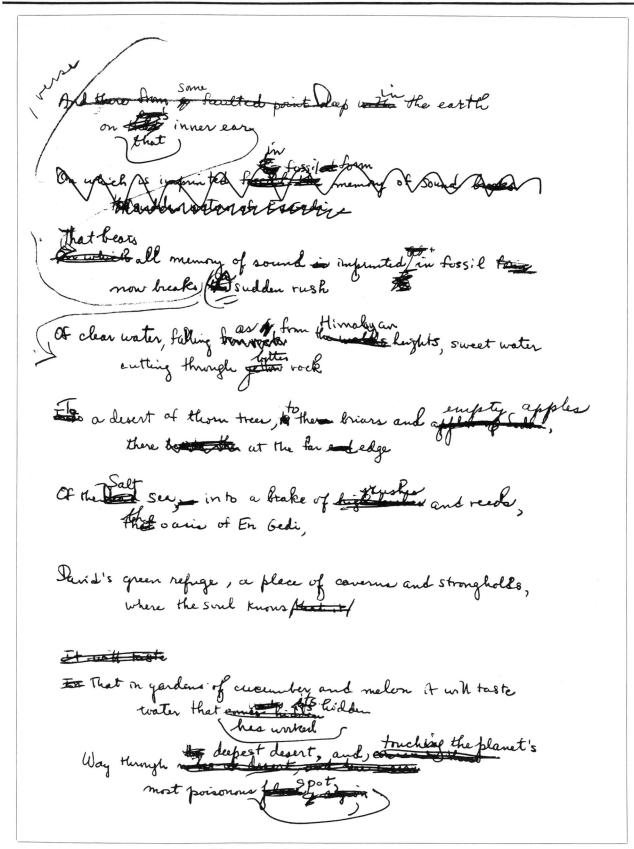

"Journey to the Dead Sea," manuscript

264

conventional forms, aesthetic distance from his subjects, and a burnished surface." This surface is often simple and complex at once, making the imagistic pieces the most memorable.

Smith's next major collection, *Poems 1947-1957* (1957), is a major treat, containing in its three sections a taste of everything the poet had attempted to date, from light verse to translations to serious poems both old and new. The scope and variety of this volume serve as a showcase for Smith's considerable talents, and the book has done much to broaden his critical and popular reputation. As James Dickey describes it: "If sensuous delight and intellectual pleasure are among the important values conferred by poetry, we stand to gain more from Smith than from all but a handful of his contemporaries . . . great good humor and playful satire . . . a strong sadness underlying these poems." While the sadness is a metaphysical constant in Smith's work, the playfulness is present in both his juvenile and adult verse, and it has drawn serious attention from critics as a technique for dealing with the aggravations of modern life. Dorothy Judd Hall explains that "laughter too is ranked high on the scale . . . for in laughter the poet finds the power to 'summon completeness and cancel confusion.' " Poems like "A Pavane for the Nursery" are serious statements disguised as children's whimsy; the humor is used thematically to gain distance from reality and thereby conjure up new perceptions, to create a plane of existence where "However is Ever, / And Ever is Now." Smith's best poems call the reader to this never-never land.

If in technique the early Smith resembles Stevens, in theme he suggests Frost. "In Memoriam Wallace Stevens" provides a hint as to Smith's intentions in form and subject matter as well as one of the reasons for his underlying despair. The last stanza says that "all the blue thoughts that he sang / Are things which must by nature fail, / But, being beautiful, are true." This sentiment suggests a Keatsian connection between Truth and Beauty, a declaration of Romantic intentions, while admitting that these things of Stevens fail "by nature," that acts of the imagination in themselves are little more than Frost's "momentary stay against confusion." The very next poem, "A Room in the Villa," uses the symbol of a mirror that, "Like some black lake, absorbs all things in silence" to illustrate how the keenest observations might only show that "the shadows wait," a possibility ironically expressed in a Frost poem like "For Once, Then, Something." This cross-pollination of poetry is exciting evidence of a

growing American literary tradition and a fertile seeding ground for future harvests.

In *The Tin Can, and Other Poems* (1966), the old themes have a new wardrobe. Still basically imagistic, still blending light and dark, these poems are written in free verse with long and sinuous lines that echo Whitman in their rambling perceptions. As Smith explains the new technique, "My recent poems have been written in long unrhymed lines because the material with which I am dealing seems to lend itself to this form, which is often close to, but always different from, prose." A new and more personal poetic intention is revealed in the title poem, which refers to the Japanese custom of personal seclusion for meditation, called going into the "tin can." This is where Smith takes the reader, in flight not from "a stewing, meat-and-fish smelling city of paper houses," but from a New England winter landscape in order to confront "the horrible, black underside of the world." This descent into the subconscious, the personal and subjective, comes through a series of surrealistic images that depict various aspects of life and individuality, often with overt echoes of Whitman's *Song of Myself*:

O bodies my body has known! Bodies my body
    has touched and remembered—in beds, in
    baths, in streams, on fields and streets—
    will you remember?

Finally, the subjective self discovers an "unseen immensity that will never be contained!" Daniel Hoffman disagrees with the contention that Smith has succumbed to the "prosier incantations" of someone like Allen Ginsberg by noting that this work is closer to the French poet Valéry Larbaud (whom Smith has translated) and calls this attempt "a new, freer prosody, in which the dark side of experience is presented in a more unmediated way" than in the former enclosed forms. Yet John Malcolm Brinnin claims that in the open form, "Smith takes chances that only now and then are lucky. Too often the center won't hold, description gets windy, self-generating, and we are left with expert maneuvers in a vacuum." While experimentation is the soul of art, the reader might find that the "slight" humorous pieces like "Dachshunds" linger in the mind far longer than the unfocused journeys of the free-verse works, which water down a linguistic intensity formally focused by meter and understatement.

In addition to the best from previous collections, *New and Selected Poems* (1970) contains two excellent new poems, "Fishing for Albacore" and

"What Train Will Come?," in which the potential of the free-verse mode seems more fully realized than in *The Tin Can*. The former, called by Landess "the best of the group," is a description of a boy's initiation into manhood and "the beauty and terror of nature" while on a fishing trip with his father. The latter, whose title is taken from an inscription found on a subway wall, is an examination by image of modern social problems. But here, rather than a slow diffusion of the reader's attention, Smith achieves a gradual intensification through the use of the underground train as a symbol of death and society's degeneration, and he achieves structural unity by using the title as a refrain. This pessimistic view, the dark imagery and bleak subject matter, might signal a future shift in theme as well as form, a departure from the early Romantic tendencies that he seems to reject:

> And through it [the tunnel] cracks spread from
> a dark center—veins like roots tunnelling
> through the ground—
>
> And my step clicks on cement, and whichever way
> I move—from whichever way the train will
> come—the way is down. . . .

The natural roots, traditional givers of life, have now become metal tracks for some express train to destruction, both personal and societal. Smith's more recent work suggests a shift from the Romantic to the prophetic, from Keats and Stevens toward T. S. Eliot and Robinson Jeffers.

Recently, Smith has been at work on three books to be published in 1980. These include another collection of new and selected poems, titled *The Traveler's Tree*, which addresses the theme of movement through space, time, and self. Also forthcoming are an autobiographical volume dealing with the poet's early life and his Choctaw heritage and a large collection of poems written over the past twenty-five years. His wide-ranging pursuits will soon take him from the classroom to residence in New York City.

Smith's is a poetic voice in the tradition of Stevens and Frost, with a personal style that transforms his subject matter into a memorable reading experience through a lively wit and a writer's eye perceptive enough to make the reader see more than he thought his vision could accommodate. In the history of American literature, Smith will be highly regarded for all his contributions, not merely as a Southerner, a translator, or one of the postwar poets; but as an innovator, a fine stylist, and one of the premier writers who are influencing the voices

only now beginning to be heard. —*Bob Group*

Play:

The Straw Market, Washington, D.C., Arena Stage, 1965.

References:

John Malcolm Brinnin, Review of *The Tin Can, and Other Poems*, *Partisan Review*, 34 (Winter 1967): 159-160;

James Dickey, *Babel to Byzantium: Poets & Poetry Now* (New York: Farrar, Straus & Giroux, 1968), pp. 74-75;

Dorothy Judd Hall, "William Jay Smith and the Art of Lightness," *Southern Humanities Review*, 3 (Winter 1968): 67-77;

Josephine Jacobsen, "The Dark Train and the Green Place: The Poetry of William Jay Smith," *Hollins Critic*, 12 (February 1975): 1-14;

Thomas H. Landess, "New Urns For Old," *Sewanee Review*, 81 (Winter 1973): 137-157;

Elisavietta Ritchie, "An Interview with William Jay Smith," *Voyages*, 3 (Winter 1970): 89-103.

W. D. SNODGRASS
(5 January 1926-)

BOOKS: *Heart's Needle* (New York: Knopf, 1959; Hessle, U.K.: Marvell Press, 1960);

After Experience (New York, Evanston & London: Harper & Row, 1968; London: Oxford University Press, 1968);

Remains, as S. S. Gardons (Mt. Horeb, Wis.: Perishable Press, 1970);

In Radical Pursuit (New York, Evanston, San Francisco & London: Harper & Row, 1975);

The Führer Bunker: A Cycle of Poems in Progress (Brockport, N.Y.: BOA Editions, 1977).

William De Witt Snodgrass was born in Wilkinsburg, Pennsylvania. He grew up in a Quaker household and was educated at Geneva College (1943-1944, 1946-1947) in nearby Beaver Falls. His education was interrupted by a hitch in the navy during World War II, and a number of his early poems deal with feelings of alienation upon his return to the United States. He completed his bachelor's degree in the Writers Workshop at the University of Iowa in 1949. He went to the workshop to master the art of play writing but found he had no gift in that direction. He remained at Iowa where he received an M.A. in 1951 and an M.F.A. in 1953, while being trained in the symbolist/metaphysical traditions of nineteenth-century French and seventeenth-century English poets.

Snodgrass has been married three times, and the trauma of his stormy marital life and separation from his children becomes a major subject in his first two books of poems. His 1946 marriage to Lila Jean Hank ended in a divorce in 1953. Cynthia Jean, the child of this marriage, is the subject of Snodgrass's first major achievement, the ten-poem grouping called "Heart's Needle." His 1954 marriage to Janice Marie Ferguson Wilson produced a second child, Russell Bruce, and at that time he adopted his wife's child by a former marriage. This marriage ended in divorce in 1966, and in 1967 Snodgrass married Camille Rykowski.

While in Iowa, Snodgrass worked as a hotel clerk and a hospital aide, but most of his employment has been in academia. He was an instructor at Cornell University from 1955 to 1957 and at the University of Rochester in 1957 and 1958. In 1958, he left Rochester to take a *Hudson Review* fellowship. When he completed the year's fellowship in 1959, he went to Wayne State University, where he taught in the English department until 1968. Since 1968, Snodgrass has been a professor of English and speech at Syracuse University.

Snodgrass's first volume of poetry, *Heart's Needle* (1959), which included collected poems and the title group dedicated to his daughter, was a smashing success. It won a Pulitzer Prize in 1960 and the British Guinness Award, and it was instrumental in getting Snodgrass a National Institute of Arts and Letters Award in 1960. For Snodgrass, the Pulitzer for his first book may have been too much too soon. He was virtually silent for a decade, although he did publish a number of poems under the pseudonym S. S. Gardons, an anagram of his last name. He used the pseudonym partly because he felt the poems were too personal and might hurt their subjects if the author's identity were known, but there is also the clear sense that Snodgrass did not find them worthy of the Pulitzer laureate.

In the "Second Selection" of *New Poets of England and America* (1962), edited by Snodgrass's friends Donald Hall and Robert Pack, "Gardons" is identified as a blue-collar, red-necked dabbler in poetry: "born in Red Creek, Texas, 1929. Works as a gas station attendant in Fort Worth. He has published in *Hudson Review*." In 1970, a whole volume of "Gardons's" poetry, *Remains*, was published. Most of it is similar to the confessional poems of *Heart's Needle*, although not nearly so even in quality. In addition to the existence of "Gardons," an indication of the effect of the Pulitzer Prize is Snodgrass's theory, put forth in several interviews, that the careers of a number of American poets, notably Wallace Stevens, have been composed of only two masterpieces: a dazzling first volume, and then after a long valley, a second peak near the end of their careers.

In 1967, Snodgrass published, with Lore Segal, *Gallows Songs*, a translation of *Alle Galgenlieder*, a collection of satirical, often surrealistic, poems by the German poet Christian Morgenstern. The translations capture the witty punning of the original as well as its wicked irony. A second volume of translations of *Six Troubadour Songs* (1977) received mixed reviews. *Choice* said "Snodgrass has translated the songs into jingly verse, which is not comparable to his own poetry," but the *Virginia Quarterly Review* called the translations "graceful, buoyant and bawdy."

A second volume of original verse, *After Experience* (1968), was widely hailed as adding to Snodgrass's reputation, but there were some complaints that it was merely more of what had already been done well enough in *Heart's Needle*. The volume included a large sampling of translations from poets like Ranier Maria Rilke, Gérard de Nerval, and Arthur Rimbaud, which were universally admired by the critics. In 1972, Snodgrass was made a member of the National Institute of Arts and Letters, and in the following year, he was elected a Fellow of the Academy of American Poets. A volume of criticism, *In Radical Pursuit* (1975), traces the development of several of his own poems as well as offering evaluations of such moderns as Theodore Roethke and John Crowe Ransom.

Snodgrass's latest volume of original poetry, *The Führer Bunker* (1977), aroused a storm of protest, chiefly because of its subject matter. The collection of monologues by the various Nazis who shared Hitler's last days was seen in many quarters as being too sympathetic to the Nazis.

When *Heart's Needle* appeared in the same year as Robert Lowell's deeply personal *Life Studies* (1959), it was inevitable that Snodgrass would be paired with Lowell as a confessional poet, especially since Snodgrass had been one of Lowell's students. Snodgrass acknowledges the debt to Lowell, but he mentions several times a remark of Randall Jarrell's: "Snodgrass, do you know you're writing the very best second-rate Lowell in the whole country?" By this, Jarrell meant that Snodgrass's early poetry overused elaborate rhetorical devices to create dense symbolic poems.

Snodgrass says that he does not find the term *confessional* useful for dealing with his poetry. The term suggests a private, often purgative, use for poetry that might fit Anne Sexton or Sylvia Plath (who was once a student of Snodgrass's). He also intimates that reading Sexton or Plath properly

Layle Silbert

W. D. Snodgrass

requires a fairly intimate knowledge of their biographies, while this is much less necessary in his own poetry. Most of his finest poetry deals not so much with the recreation of events of the past as it does with the discovery of images that objectify the emotional crises he has been through.

At the Iowa Writers Workshop, Snodgrass had been drilled in the poetry of T. S. Eliot and his doctrine of the "objective correlative." His training, therefore, taught him to displace emotion with its symbolic equivalent and then to remove the straightforward statement of the emotion. He worked this way until he discovered that Eliot's doctrine of impersonal poetry was designed largely

to hide the very personal nature of his poems. With this discovery, Snodgrass stopped burying the open statement of emotion. Snodgrass's postsymbolic poetry does not shun the objective correlative, but rather retains it along with the personal statement. This doubleness changes the symbol from a private, often obscure, sign for which the reader needs a biographical clue into an open image of the poet's emotional state.

Occasionally Snodgrass seems to be furnishing his universe with symbols rather than discovering ones appropriate to his emotion. In "Heart's Needle: 8," a series of images of eating seems artificially contrived to set up the rather sentimental last stanza:

> I crave sweets when you leave and know
> They rot my teeth. Indeed our sweet
> Foods leave us cavities.

This is too coy and clever a way to tell that the presence of his daughter causes greater hurt when she is gone. The same vice is found in "Heart's Needle: 7," where the swinging away of his daughter on a playground swing becomes a symbol of his tenuous hold on her and her love.

Far more effective is the image of the poet trying to cut his losses through the recognition that his daughter is changing so that each time he sees her he will have much less of her life to share. His metaphor for loosening his hold on her is that of a fox chewing off his own paw caught in a trap: "the paw, / Gnawed off, he cannot feel; / Conceded to the jaw / Of toothed, blue steel." The metaphor clearly expresses Snodgrass's realization that there is a wisdom in giving up part of a needed thing to preserve the rest of it.

The poems in *Heart's Needle* are mostly about memory, but only a few of them, like "Ten Days Leave" or "September in the Park," are blatantly nostalgic pieces in which the poet can hoard his memories like "gray squirrels gather together / their hoard of rich acorns." A few poems try to hide the nostalgia with an ironic toughness that seems finally more clever than felt, so that the image of home in "Returned to Frisco, 1946" is "Alcatraz, lavender with flowers."

One of the primary concerns of this first book of poems is the poet's attempt to find his proper place in the universe. His uncertainty begins in μῆτις . . . . . οὔ τις [Noman . . . No man], whose title refers to the "no man" pun in *The Odyssey*. The poet sees himself as a kind of Ulysses who is unable to take off the mask of "no man" even after his deception of Polyphemus is finished. His fear that self-assertiveness will become egotism is compounded by the worry that there is no place for a poet in the crass modern world and also by the belief that as a middle-aged man he has outgrown his youthful dreams without having replaced them with new ones. In "Home Town," the poet returns to his old haunts only to find he lacks the youthful nerve to be the hero he once wanted to be. When the opportunity arises, the speaker avoids seizing the prize and concludes: "Pale soul . . . / have you . . . / learned you are no one here?" In his critical writings, Snodgrass acknowledges that the fear of egotism is partly the result of his schooling in the symbolist/metaphysical tradition: "We had been taught that we mustn't talk directly about our feelings or use the first person singular."

As the poet finds he is being hamstrung by memory and ancient desire, he responds by reasserting himself in the present. The most eloquent statement of assertion is in "These Trees Stand," where he uses the illusion of the relative movement in the night sky to prove his actions do count. The poet notes that while the trees stand still, the heavens seem to move if he walks through the forest: "all stars traverse / This steep celestial gulf their branches chart." Although he recognizes this self-caused celestial movement as illusion, he then goes on to claim that the poet as maker, as creator, can cause the heavens to move, and he ends each stanza by naming his name, denying that he will any longer be called "no man": "Your name's safe conduct into love or verse; / Snodgrass is walking through the universe." Snodgrass has commented that he wrote this deliberately pompous-sounding line after hearing similar pomposity in Mozart. The line helped him free himself from the antiegotistical stricture of his early symbolist training.

Mere assertion of well-being is not enough for the poet: he has to analyze this well-being in terms of accomplishment, which he does in "April Inventory." He begins by inventorying his losses—of hair, of youthful sleekness, of prestige—but then he balances these by growth in personal strength and the ability to identify himself: "I taught myself to name my name, / To bark back, loosen love and crying." The poem is gently self-mocking, particularly about his lack of accomplishment as a scholar: "I learned one date. And then forgot." The playfulness, however, disappears when he insists that although one cannot choose whether he wins or loses, he can choose the game he plays and the quality of life he leads.

The fullest examination of this motif of self-identification is in "The Cardinal," the longest single poem in the collection. The poet, still trailing clouds of academia, goes off into the woods to try to write poetry, but he finds himself an alien in nature. All creatures become silent when he approaches: "The weeds sing where I leave." A cardinal appears that first annoys the poet with its strident song, which the poet takes as the voice of the encroaching man-eat-man world. The negative attitude changes to a neutral one as the poet finds the bird's voracious appetite to be a mindless Darwinian principle (Darwinism as Tennyson sees it: "nature red in tooth and claw"). There is then a further shift as the cardinal becomes an image of the spirit asserting itself, which cues the poet into doing the same thing. Both assert themselves: the bird does it by instinct, but the poet has to learn how from his observations of nature: "Each trade has its way of speaking, / each bird has its name to say." There is a valuable discussion of the genesis of "The Cardinal," along with an early draft of the poem, in the essay "A Poem's Becoming" in *In Radical Pursuit*. Snodgrass views the change of the poem from a tight symbolic structure to a looser, more personal self-analysis as typical both of the development of his own poetic career as well as the development of recent American poetry. He uses examples of the early and late Lowell to illustrate his point that many modern American poets have moved from arcane symbolism to more open personal statement.

The title piece of the book, a ten-poem cycle, shows Snodgrass at his best. The poems in the "Heart's Needle" section deal with his separation from his daughter, Cynthia, because of his divorce. In the cycle, seasonal change reflects emotional change, and there is one poem for each season from the winter of 1952 to the spring of 1955. The depth of this trauma is indicated by his revelation that one of the influences on the work was the *Kindertotenlieder*, Gustav Mahler's musical settings to songs about the death of children. Nor is the fact that this trauma takes place against the background of the Korean War lost on Snodgrass. He knows that the more he allows himself to love his child, the more he will suffer when she leaves. This leaves him with the choice of loving her more and suffering for it or loving her less, which will devalue the precious little time he has with her. When he says "I was torn by love I could not still," he is defining the conflict between these emotions as an internal cold war that is set against a time "when the new fallen soldiers froze / in Asia's steep ravines."

Snodgrass's best nonsentimental display of emotion is found in "Heart's Needle: 2," where he describes the small destructions of his child's play. The description of the way the child has destroyed the garden he has made for her is reminiscent of the equally nonsentimental elegy "Bells for John Whiteside's Daughter" by John Crowe Ransom. Ransom is a favorite of Snodgrass's, and there is an essay about him in *In Radical Pursuit*. In Snodgrass's poem, the garden is a pledge of his love that he hopes his daughter will care for every day and so remember him. The irony is that he knows her typical destructiveness will allow the garden to fall into ruin and thus destroy his pledge of love.

Although Snodgrass denies the continuing influence of John Donne, whose poetry was so heavily emphasized in his years at Iowa, "Heart's Needle: 3" is a prime example of the intellectual working out of emotion so typical of the metaphysical poets. The poem deals with the way the divorced parents of the child tend to pull the child apart for their own purposes. Snodgrass starts with an image of the parents awkwardly swinging the child between them. The child then symbolically becomes a wishbone with each parent thinking that if he can keep the child for himself he will be happy. The poem ends with a paradox reminiscent of the pair of compasses at the end of Donne's "Valediction: Forbidding Mourning." Just as Donne has the compasses describing a perfect circle even as they are closing, so Snodgrass consoles himself when he says that by giving up the child to his former wife, he is gaining not losing:

> It may help that a Chinese play
> Or Solomon himself might say
> I am your real mother.

The reference to Solomon refers to the biblical king's threat to cut in half a child whose parentage was in dispute: the real mother gave up the child rather than see it cut in half. The reference to "a Chinese play" suggests a similar incident in *The Circle of Chalk*, a thirteenth-century Chinese play that is the source of Bertolt Brecht's play *The Caucasian Chalk Circle* (1944-1945). Donne himself would have been proud of the paradox by which the good father turns himself into the "real mother" even as he gains by losing.

In *In Radical Pursuit*, Snodgrass includes an essay, "Finding a Poem," which discusses his very personal way of using symbols to produce, paradoxically, more universal poems. The poem in question is "Heart's Needle: 6," which was written for Easter season, the spring of 1954. He begins with images appropriate to the season: Easter eggs, birds, rebirth. The poem (a first draft is presented in the essay) does not work until he adds a stanza devoted to his daughter's asthma attack, which he sees as a symbolic refusal of life. This in turn leads him back to her first breath of life in the birth trauma. In the course of adding these stanzas, the poem changes from another exploration of the theme of Snodgrass's grieving over his lost daughter into a more universal affirmation of life. Like his daughter with her asthma, Snodgrass had remained emotionally motionless, refusing to breathe the air of his new daughterless life. The conclusion of the poem acknowledges that he must now go on living: "Child, I have another wife, / Another child. We try to choose our life."

The cycle ends with two poems about outings: one alone to a museum, the other with his daughter to a zoo. The museum poem, "Heart's Needle: 9," is the bleakest in the collection. The poet examines the displays of animals mummified in poses of eternal hate and sees in them images of his personal life. Instead of a "peaceable kingdom," he finds that the animals represent the quarrels between his daughter and stepdaughter, between himself and his former wife, and between himself and his daughter. But if the past is grim, the future is even bleaker. He sees in the tension of the present a future of malign, misshapen relationships represented by a shelf of fetal monstrosities: "a two headed foal . . . / the hydrocephalic goat . . . / a limbless calf." All of these are less malignant than his own trouble: "a diseased heart."

The zoo poem, "Heart's Needle: 10," rescinds some of this bitterness, but not enough to end the cycle on an optimistic note. The zoo animals are seen as prisoners living limited lives; in his relationship with his daughter, he will have to accept similar restrictions: "the coons on bread and water / Stretch thin black fingers after ours."

Many of the poems in *After Experience* continue in the same personal vein used in *Heart's Needle*. None is more typical than "Mementos 1" and "Mementos 2," both of which deal with the way the discovery of an item from the past evokes a flood of memories. In most of the personal poems in this collection, Snodgrass insists upon what he calls the poet's "tact": the refusal to wax highly emotional over personal or social trauma. For this reason, almost every one of the personal poems ends with understatement: the last line is often some small gesture that indicates a turning away from emotion. After a heartrending day with his daughter, for example, Snodgrass will conclude: "I can't remember / Your face or anything you said," or in another: "We go about our business / I have turned my back."

In his essay "Tact and the Poet's Force," Snodgrass says, "we simply do not believe any one who talks very easily about matters of great feeling or ultimate belief." The concept of "tact" is meant to guard against the twin dangers of overblown sentimentality and assertive rant, but the continual, conscious underplaying of sentiment in poem after poem strains the reader in the opposite direction. Although one could hardly object to the cooling of feelings in a single poem, the damped emotion becomes a well-honed tool rather than a felt response. When the poet, talking of his daughter, says, "We have a life at [your expense], / Now I can earn a living / By turning out elegant strophes," his irony cannot quite hide the fear that his tasteful structuring of emotion has turned his personal life into commercial capital.

The poems of toned-down nostalgia represent only one avenue taken by Snodgrass in this collection. Among the several satiric poems, "Exorcism" recalls "Six Poets in Search of a Lawyer" by Donald Hall, to whom *After Experience* is dedicated. "Exorcism," like Hall's poem, consists of a series of brief satiric portraits or "characters." Hall's portraits are stereotyped poetic poseurs; Snodgrass's are real politicians turned into types. The title refers to the poet's trying to exorcize the spirits of Secretary of State John Foster Dulles, of political influence-peddler Bernard Goldfine, and of then Vice-President Richard Nixon. In the poem they are renamed Dullard (there is also a "Dullard" in Hall's poem), "Goldfinder of the groin," and "Nixmaster of the tongue." As "Nixmaster," Nixon becomes the archetypal naysayer, but through a pun on Mixmaster, he also becomes a conniver who whips words up into a soft semblance of truth.

One of the most powerful poems in the collection is "The Examination," a surreal satire on education in which the university becomes a fantastic operating room where hellish beasts lobotomize, castrate, and cut the wings off the student so that he will learn "to fly no higher than his superiors fly." This searing indictment of academia represents a vein Snodgrass has not much mined, probably because satire violates his principle of tact. Satire assumes the superiority of the satirist to his subject, but Snodgrass, in the essay on tact, warns: "of all the ulterior motives [of poets], none is more common, none more debilitating, none more damning than the pretense to moral superiority."

Another new direction explored in *After Experience* is found in a series of poems written about paintings by the Impressionist painters Henri Matisse, Jean Édouard Vuillard, Edouard Manet, Claude Monet, and Vincent Van Gogh. The paintings are reproduced in *In Radical Pursuit*, which also includes an essay on the composition of

these poems. These illustrations are in black and white, and a student would do well to find color plates of the paintings since much of the argument of the poems deals with the use of color by the Impressionists. The series began when Snodgrass taught an adult education course in modern art, a subject in which he had no formal, and little informal, training. Out of an argument with a student about why Matisse's *The Red Studio* frightened her, Snodgrass began to formulate a theory of the relationship of color to energy in the painting. In his essay on the writing of these poems, he reveals the varied associations that go through a poet's mind. He relates the overwhelming red of the painting to a rug in his psychiatrist's office, to classical theories of the universe, and to a story of electric fences and childhood repression told by comedian Mort Sahl. These associations coalesce into a speculation that Matisse had intuited a theory of the conversion of matter into energy, not unlike Albert Einstein's. *The Red Studio* is frightening, Snodgrass argues, because the red color makes one feel the conversion of matter into energy. Matisse's "mind turned in concentrated fury, / . . . Till all environments of living are / Transformed to energy."

The Vuillard poem, although as poetry the least impressive in the series, is Snodgrass's finest piece of art criticism, probably because it deals with the subject Snodgrass knows best: the small signs and symbols of domestic crisis. Snodgrass revises the standard critical estimate of Vuillard as a minor figure using impressionist techniques to decorate domestic subjects. In "The Mother and Sister of the Artist," he shows how Vuillard uses color, texture, and composition to depict the psychological domination of daughter by mother in the painting. After describing the impressive density of the mother, he notes of the daughter that the design of her dress fabric makes her seem part of the wallpaper; she "grows too ethereal / to make a shape inside her dress."

Technically the most interesting of these poems about paintings is the one that deals with Van Gogh's *The Starry Night*. The painting has a schizoid quality: the little Dutch town is painted with the solidity of genre painters like Jacob Van Ruisdael, while the sky bursts with energy. Snodgrass captures this split with two verse forms: solid iambic lines to describe the village and, to describe the heavens, broken nonmetrical lines, often composed of isolated phrases or sentence fragments. The description of the heavens is set on the page in irregular, asymmetric clusters. Interspersed in the poem are fragments from Van Gogh's letters revealing the aesthetic theory that made this painting possible.

The group of poems on paintings provides an enlightening example of an artist in one medium examining the techniques of artists in another. The Van Gogh piece, in particular, reveals Snodgrass trying to work out analogs to the innovations of the painters. It is significant that he considers himself only an amateur as an art critic. He is intent on explaining the poems to himself as well as to the reader. On the other hand, the poems that deal with music, a subject with which he is far more comfortable than art, offer much less to the reader. There is no sense of his exploring or attempting to tame an alien medium. In "Regraduating the Lute," for example, Snodgrass works out a neat analogy between tuning a lute and refocusing his life, but the validity of this is assumed, rather than hammered out as in the poems on painting.

Of all the poems in this collection, the most important innovations are found in the title poem, "After Experience Taught Me," and in "A Visitation." Both are dialogues, in alternating strophes, between two very different voices. In "After Experience," one of the voices is that of the Dutch philosopher Baruch Spinoza, and the words he speaks are a paraphrase of the opening of Spinoza's essay, "On the Improvement of the Understanding" (1677). Alternating with the philosopher's voice is the voice of a military drill instructor teaching the art of weaponless hand-to-hand combat. The Spinoza voice teaches spiritual self-preservation, which consists of finding true happiness: "No virtue can be thought to have priority / Over this endeavor to preserve one's being." The martial arts instructor teaches how to preserve one's physical being and warns that at some point another human being may have to be destroyed to this end. At the close of the poem, the poet's voice, in a mood of Sartrean engagement, combines the two and defines the well-lived life as one so valuable that even absolute evil may be called upon to preserve it: "What evil, what unspeakable crime / Have you made your life worth?"

This abstract notion of evil reifying good is dealt with again in the other dialogue, "A Visitation," in which the spirit of Adolph Eichmann visits the poet. Snodgrass begins with Hannah Arendt's contention that "no member of the human race can be expected to want to share the earth with" the Nazi war criminal. The poet considers Arendt's statement and refutes it by denying that he, and by implication anyone, is so far above Eichmann to deny his humanity. The poem presents the problem posed in "After Experience" from a different angle. Who is it, asks the poet, that would have the strength to refuse the orders to commit an unspeakable crime? The shade of Eichmann reminds the poet that he has acted against his conscience during the war and urges that the difference between them is "Luck, friend, not character." The poet cannot refute the ghost's contention and decides that he is better off haunted by Eichmann lest he forget how easily moral philosophies can be undone when faced by the hard facts of life: "How subtle all that chokes us with disgust / Moves in implacably to rule us unaware."

Snodgrass's third volume of original poetry marks a radical departure from the personal, self-absorbed lyrics of *Heart's Needle* and *After Experience*. Only the Eichmann poem, "The Visitation," gives any indication of the new direction taken in *The Führer Bunker*. Snodgrass had been a poet concerned mostly with the problems of his own ego, but in *The Führer Bunker* he has become what Keats would call a chameleon poet as capable of being an Iago as an Imogen—or in this case, nine Iagos. What Snodgrass has created is a series of dramatic monologues spoken by the men and women who shared the bunker during Hitler's last days.

Snodgrass had been trying to write a play based on H. R. Trevor-Roper's *The Last Days of Hitler* (1947) when he was granted an interview with Hitler's master architect, Albert Speer. He was greatly impressed with Speer's intellect and began to recast his projected play into a series of monologues modeled after those of Robert Browning. The most influential of Browning's poems were the amoral self-studies like "Mr. Sludge, 'The Medium' " and "Bishop Blougram's Apology." The project is particularly attractive to Snodgrass because it allows him to change his own image as a poet, to shake once and for all the tag of confessional poet: no one is likely to confuse poet and speaker in this series of poems.

To charges that he has humanized the Nazi monsters, Snodgrass replies that they were already human before he dealt with them. Nevertheless, he admits to making the Nazis more attractive than they were in life: he removes much of Hitler's braggadocio, and he gives Joseph Goebbels a sense of humor. Snodgrass argues that his purpose is to "investigate the thought and feelings behind the public facade" of the Nazis in order to reveal the deep-seated sources of their destructiveness.

Ironically, Snodgrass's strategy of removing the masks distorts rather than clarifies the portraits he presents. By eliminating the boastful, self-justifying veneer of Hitler, for example, he removes much of the Führer's essence—the man was the mask. Snodgrass perceives a paradox in Hitler's self-image in the monologues. Hitler "sees himself as acting in a way completely free and is in a way absolutely and completely *un*free." Granting Hitler this unfreedom creates a more disturbing paradox. Snodgrass turns him into an innocent whose murderous acts are completely determined by his warped childhood and his idealistic dreams.

As Snodgrass sees it, Hitler's slightly twisted childhood develops into a dream of devouring all of Europe. The Führer remains essentially the boy who ate up half of his brother's birthday cake and fouled the rest. As a grown man, he eats up half of Europe and tries to destroy what he cannot eat. Like a spoiled child, Hitler finds fault everywhere, but sees his only fault in his overgenerosity and overkindness to friends and enemies. The faultfinding is aimed at explaining why his task has been left incomplete; there is never any sense of justifying his crimes because he never conceives he has done anything wrong.

This failure of the Nazis to wrestle with or recognize their guilt is the intellectual weakness underlying the whole collection. Each comes off as a frustrated idealist whose idealism was triggered by some youthful trauma. Joseph Goebbels is a clubfoot who finds the virtue of self-denial in his infirmity: as a cripple he has always been satisfied with less. For him, the obliteration of Europe is an idealistic nihilism, a way of destroying the old order to give place to the new. Magda Goebbels is a nymphomaniac who sees her lust as a displacement of her perfect loyalty to the Führer. Speer becomes a Promethean architect of the impossible for whom the glass-shattering, anti-Semitic riots of Krystal Nacht are the first signs of the rebel's rage against limit. His rebellious spirit was fostered in secret anger against his cold aristocratic family, while he secretly dreamed of a few warm minutes in the bosom of his porter's humble, close-knit family. Although the monologues become interesting case histories, all of the Nazis cease to be criminals and become instead Freudian victims of environment and heredity.

In *The Poetry of Experience* (1957), Robert Langbaum argues that the most interesting approach to Browning's dramatic monologue is to accept their amorality rather than impose upon them Christian morality. Langbaum's view is particularly instructive in dealing with Browning's aristocratic "villains" like the Duke of Ferrara whose murder of his Last Duchess is simply one more act of will in a world where aristocratic will is law. Perhaps when Snodgrass's Bunker poems can be viewed with the same distance as Browning's Renaissance portraits, his psychological portraits will seem less eccentric.

Despite the eccentricity of their subject matter, the poems in *The Führer Bunker* represent the most innovative and technically varied examples of Snodgrass's work. Snodgrass experiments with contrasting typefaces that express contrasting emotions, with parallel statements of the different levels of the subject's consciousness that intersect without ever being unified by the poet, and with song lyrics that counterpoint Eva Braun's rationalizations.

A number of formal variations are meant to reflect the character of the speaker. Joseph Goebbels speaks in tight couplets that reflect the crabbed spirit of the man who saw his clubfoot as a theme for renunciation (the similarity to another cripple, Alexander Pope, is intentional). Albert Speer's poems are in the shape of pyramids to indicate the expansiveness of his character, and Magda Goebbels is given intricate forms like a quartet of villanelles to represent her climb into the elegance of "the best society."

The Führer Bunker is subtitled *A Cycle of Poems in Progress.* If Snodgrass follows his usual technique of revision, he will open out the poems, destroying some of their technical brilliance in order to add depth of characterization. He might do well to leave these poems as they stand and let their fine surfaces speak for the Nazis. For example, in one of the Joseph Goebbels poems, the analyses of Goebbels's sublimation fantasies are rather amateurish as psychoanalysis, but they are brilliantly presented in a series of Christo-Freudian puns on "rock," "crows," "cock," "Peter" so that the Nazi leader ends up "robbing my Peter to play Paul." *The Führer Bunker*, one hopes, has been done. It is a promising sign that Snodgrass has published them in a state he feels is unfinished; he is too good a poet to hide his light under a bushel.

—*Jeffrey Helterman*

Other:

Christian Morgenstern, *Gallows Songs*, translated by Snodgrass and Lore Segal (Ann Arbor: University of Michigan Press, 1967);
Six Troubadour Songs, translated by Snodgrass (Providence, R.I.: Burning Deck Press, 1977).

W. D. Snodgrass

Interviews:

Philip Gerber and Robert Gemmett, " 'No Voices Talk to Me': A Conversation with W. D. Snodgrass," *Western Humanities Review*, 24 (Winter 1970): 61-71;

Robert Boyers, "W. D. Snodgrass: An Interview," *Salmagundi*, no. 22-23 (1973): 149-163;

David Dillon, "Toward Passionate Utterance: An Interview with W. D. Snodgrass," *Southwest Review*, 60 (Summer 1975): 278-290;

Paul Gaston, "W. D. Snodgrass and *The Führer Bunker*: An Interview," *Papers on Language and Literature*, 13 (Summer / Fall 1977): 295-311, 401-412.

Bibliography:

William White, *W. D. Snodgrass: A Bibliography* (Detroit: Wayne State University Press, 1960).

References:

David Farrelly, "Heart's Fling: The Poetry of W. D. Snodgrass," *Perspective*, 13 (1964): 185-199;

William Heyen, "Fishing the Swamp: The Poetry of W. D. Snodgrass," in *Modern American Poetry*, ed. Jerome Mazzaro (New York: McKay, 1970), pp. 351-368;

Richard Howard, *Alone With America   Essays on the Art of Poetry in the United States Since 1950* (New York: Atheneum, 1969), pp. 471-484;

Jerome Mazzaro, "The Public Intimacy of W. D. Snodgrass," *Salmagundi*, no. 19 (1972): 96-111·

J. D. McClatchy, "W. D. Snodgrass: The Mild, Reflective Art," *Massachusetts Review*, 16 (Spring 1975): 281-314;

Donald Torchiana, "Heart's Needle: Snodgrass Strides Through the Universe," in *Poets in Progress*, ed. Edward Hungerford (Evanston, Ill.: Northwestern University Press, 1967), pp. 92-115.

GARY SNYDER
(8 May 1930-)

SELECTED BOOKS: *Riprap* (Ashland, Mass.: Origin Press, 1959);

Myths and Texts (New York: Totem Press / Corinth Books, 1960; London: Centaur, 1960);

Riprap and Cold Mountain Poems (San Francisco: Four Seasons Foundation, 1965);

Six Sections from Mountains and Rivers Without End (San Francisco: Four Seasons Foundation, 1965; London: Fulcrum Press, 1967); enlarged and republished as *Six Sections from Mountains and Rivers Without End Plus One* (San Francisco: Four Seasons Foundation, 1970);

A Range of Poems (London: Fulcrum Press, 1966);

Three Worlds, Three Realms, Six Roads (Marlboro, Vt.: Griffin Press, 1966);

The Back Country (London: Fulcrum Press, 1967; New York: New Directions, 1968);

The Blue Sky (New York: Phoenix Book Shop, 1969);

Earth House Hold (New York: New Directions, 1969; London: Cape, 1970);

Regarding Wave (Iowa City: Windhover Press, 1969; enlarged edition, New York: New Directions, 1970; London: Fulcrum Press, 1972);

Manzanita (Bolinas, Cal.: Four Seasons Foundation, 1972);

The Fudo Trilogy (Berkeley: Shaman Drum, 1973);

Turtle Island (New York: New Directions, 1974).

Gary Snyder was born in San Francisco, California. He has married three times, the first two marriages ending in divorce. In 1950 he married Alison Gass and was divorced in 1951; in 1960 he married Joanne Kyger and was divorced in 1964. His third marriage, to Japanese-born Masa Uehara, has produced two children: Kai and Gen. In 1951 Snyder received a B.A. in anthropology and literature from Reed College and began graduate work at Indiana University. From 1953 to 1956 he studied Oriental languages at the University of California, Berkeley. Perhaps the most interesting feature of his education, and certainly the most relevant to his poetry, is the time he spent studying Zen Buddhism in Japan. He began in 1956 on a scholarship from the First Zen Institute of America and, after numerous interruptions, completed his studies in 1968. In addition to his career as a poet and a student of Zen, Snyder has spent considerable time as a manual laborer: a logger, a fire lookout, a U.S. Forest Service trail crew worker, and a seaman. As a poet he has won the National Institute of Arts and Letters Award in 1966, the Frank O'Hara Prize in 1967, *Poetry* magazine's Levinson Prize in 1968, and a Pulitzer Prize for *Turtle Island* in 1974.

Snyder's poetry bridges an ever-widening gap

between the serious critic and the less sophisticated lover of poetry, particularly the young, on whom his influence has been enormous. Early identified with Allen Ginsberg and other poets of the Beat Generation, he became the central figure, loosely disguised as Japhy Ryder, in Jack Kerouac's *The Dharma Bums* (1960). Unlike Neal Cassady, the protagonist of *On the Road* (1957), Snyder's popularity with the young is independent of Kerouac's fiction. The simplicity and cleanness of his language has made his poetry accessible to youthful audiences that often distrust more complex lyricism. Indeed, G. S. Fraser asserts that Snyder "is one of the poets whom the young enormously overrate, perhaps because they fear complexity." A similar sentiment is expressed by Robert Boyers. He believes that Snyder's poetry is "monotonous, flat and superficial, and probably for those reasons is much esteemed by a variety of people, most of them young." Nevertheless, the voices of Fraser and Boyers form a minority dissent to Snyder's critical reputation. Thomas Parkinson believes that Snyder is "a skillful poet, and his work develops steadily toward more thorough and profound insight." Abraham Rothberg, Samuel Charters, and Richard Howard all hasten to point to Snyder as the heir of the Emersonian tradition in twentieth-century American poetry.

No matter how firmly grounded Snyder's poetry is in an older American tradition, it cannot be fully appreciated without regard to his Zen philosophy. He is no dabbler in religious fads, but a man who studied seriously the workings of Zen for many years. What emerged from those studies is a poetry that is deceptively simple, rather than superficially simplistic. In accordance with the teachings of Zen, Snyder envisions the world as a network of relationships unapproachable by traditional Western logic, rather than as a conglomeration of things that can be identified, codified, and rationalized. Often the spokesman for Snyder's own thoughts—a logger, a seaman, a tramp, or anyone outside the scope of middle-class respectability—is based on the wise-man-as-clown tradition of Oriental literature.

Snyder's first volume of poetry, *Riprap* (1959), is a collection of poems on both Snyder's experiences in the backwoods of the American Far West and on his early experiences in Japan. If the lines of some of the weaker poems in the collection are often sloppier than is characteristic of Snyder's later poetry, the volume still contains some of his best and strongest poems, among them "Riprap," "A Stone Garden," and "Praise for Sick Women." The last poem is particularly important to an understanding of

Snyder's view of women in general. Snyder is fascinated by and sympathetic to the problems of the menstrual cycle, and his attitude toward women is at once intensely physical and equally intensely mystical. He may regard the menstrual cycle as part of a larger cycle of universal meaning, but despite Snyder's mysticism, neither the poem nor the women ever disappear into abstraction. Women remain closely bound to the earth, both in poetic image and in the poet's regard as he demonstrates a decided attraction for both the sexual frankness and the fertility myths characteristic of more primitive societies.

Snyder's poetry is in itself primitive, according to his own definition. "Riprap," which takes its title from a cobble of stones laid down to make a path for horses in the mountains, is one of Snyder's few poetic comments on the act of making a poem: "In the thin loam, each rock a word / a creek washed stone / Granite: ingrained / with torrent of fire and weight. . . ." In a more prosiac vein, Snyder states in *Earth House Hold* (1969): "POETRY is to give access to persons—cutting away the fear and reserve and carping of social life: thus for Chinese poetry. Nature poetry too: 'this is what I've seen.' Playing with the tools—language, myth, symbolism, intellect—fair enough but childish to abuse."

Six years after the appearance of *Riprap*, Snyder made the relationship between the primitivism of the Far West and Far East more explicit by combining the original volume with his translations of the Chinese poet Han Shan (in English, Cold Mountain) in *Riprap and Cold Mountain Poems* (1965). Han Shan, "a mountain madman" and poet of the T'ang dynasty (618-906), along with his constant companion, Shih-te, became favorites of Snyder as exemplars of the wise fool. In his preface to the translation, Snyder establishes the clear relation he sees between the Oriental folk type and the individuals he often encountered on his excursions into the wilderness. "They became immortals," Snyder says, "and you sometimes run onto them today in the skidrows, orchards, hobo jungles, and logging camps of America."

Snyder sees an even clearer point of congruence between the East and West in the American Indian and the myths he created to explain his universe. Snyder regards primitive societies as "those societies which have remained non-literate and non-political while necessarily exploring and developing in directions that civilized societies have tended to ignore." The so-called primitive society of the American Indian forms the core of Snyder's first truly unified work, *Myths and Texts* (1960). As the title suggests, the texts of civilized society are held up against the myths of primitive cultures and, not surprisingly, are found wanting.

The work is divided into three sections. The first, "Logging," is based on Snyder's early experiences working on a logging crew in the backwoods of the Pacific Coast region. The poems in this section are poems of initiation to both the physical wilderness and a wilderness of the spirit, a felling of trees necessary before one can see the forest. The second section, "Hunting," is central both in sequence and importance. The poetry, like the prayer of the hunter, becomes a magical incantation to bring good fortune. Like the hunter calling to his prey to come and give itself up to him, the poet calls on the world to open its gate and render itself to his understanding: "honey-eater / forest apple / light-foot / Old man in the fur coat, Bear! come out! Die of your own choice!" The bear, or the insight, that does not give itself up of its own choice was not meant for the man who received it. The final section, "Burning," is a trip through hell and a return to a world in which the poet's perceptions are significantly altered. Of all those perceptions, the most significant is the realization that language is inadequate to articulate the meaning that lies beyond the grasp of rational discourse.

Myths and Texts is probably Snyder's most complete work, but it will eventually have to be compared with his proposed magnum opus, *Mountains and Rivers Without End*. Its title taken from a sideways Chinese scroll painting and its structure based roughly on that of the Japanese No play, the work is eventually to comprise approximately forty sections, of which thirteen have been published to date. Six of these sections—"Bubbs Creek Haircut" (1960), "The Elwha River" (1961), "Night Highway Ninety-Nine" (1962), "Hymn to the Goddess San Francisco in Paradise" (1963), "The Market" (1964), and "Journeys" (1965)—have been collected in the short volume *Six Sections from Mountains and Rivers Without End* (1965), to which *The Blue Sky* (published separately in 1969) was added in 1970 to make *Six Sections from Mountains and Rivers Without End Plus One*. Six other sections have been published in various places so far: *Three Worlds, Three Realms, Six Roads* (1966), "Eight Songs of Clouds and Water" (*Poetry*, March 1968), "The Hump-Backed Flute Player" (*Coyote's Journal*, no. 9), "Ma" (*Coyote's Journal*, no. 10), "Down" (*Iowa Review*, 1970), and "The California Water Plan" (*Clear Creek*, November 1971). "Eight Songs of Clouds and Water" was included, with the significant exception of the section titled "The

Rabbit," in *Regarding Wave* (1969). "The California Water Plan" was included, along with "Spel Against Demons" and "Smokey the Bear Sutra," in *The Fudo Trilogy* (1973).

Many of the poems in this projected collection tend to be more political than Snyder's earlier work, some reflecting a more polemic attitude toward the destruction of the wilderness by corporate America and some more intensely concerned with the plight of the American Indian in the twentieth century. Although the scene is the American Far West, Zen philosophy appears more on the surface than before. Images of the East are woven with the natural setting of the poem, and all the images tend to rise out of nowhere and disappear again into primeval dreck, like so many passing headlights on "Night Highway Ninety-nine." Although the themes here are less traditional than in *Riprap*, particularly in the emphasis on psychedelics in "The Blue Sky," thorough evaluation of the work must wait until its completion.

While writing *Mountains and Rivers Without End*, Snyder collected his earlier works, including his translation from Miyazawa Kenji, in *A Range of Poems* (1966), and he completed *The Back Country* (also included in *A Range of Poems*, but published separately with several new poems added). *The Back Country* (1967) is a significant title in a number of ways, suggesting not only the untamed regions of the West but the so-called backward countries of the Orient and the primitive regions of the unconscious. The volume is divided into five sections: "The Far West," "The Far East," "Kali," "Back," and the translations of Miyazawa Kenji earlier included in *A Range of Poems*. The beginning section, "The Far West," establishes a clear relation between the back section of the landscape and the back regions of the mind. Coyote, the Trickster and Creator of Indian mythology, becomes a central figure here, suggesting the primitive mode in which the wilderness was apprehended by the earliest imagination to touch the American continent. More indebted to Jung than Freud for his understanding of the unconscious, Snyder's backcountry is a place of serenity free from the entanglements of civilization and social forms. The peace remains largely untapped, however, except by those in "The Far East" whose Zen philosophy has eliminated the noise of rational thought and found a center of consciousness uncontaminated by the inconsistencies of Western logic. That this serenity is achieved by accepting a way of life that most Westerners consider premodern and backward seems to be a worthwhile exchange to Snyder, whose distrust of civilized America becomes more apparent with each new volume.

"Kali," however, based on Snyder's trip to India, leads to a reconsideration of some of the aspects of premodern societies. Depressed by the poverty, the overcrowding, the squalor, and the misery he finds there, Snyder must reevaluate some of his earlier positions. India comes to represent the horror of evil, but in the nightmare of the journey, Snyder also finds acceptance. India may be horrifying, but it is also sexual and, thus, creative. Unfortunately Snyder's language, although still clear and precise, is not equal to making the creative power of the Indian subcontinent an adequate compensation for the poverty he finds. Nevertheless, he asks the reader to believe in his acceptance of the otherwise unacceptable, a belief the reader is only half-willing to grant, in order to make the fourth section, "Back," more plausible.

"Back" is simply the return to America from the sojourn in the Far East. The landscapes of this section are not so much psychologically as politically symbolic, as Snyder alters his emphasis from his feeling of oneness with the wilderness to anger about its destruction. Much of his early hope for the Pacific backcountry has disappeared, and in its place he has substituted a more realistic apprehension of the dangers facing its preservation. Action in the political arena, not withdrawal into the forest, is needed to save the wilderness.

In *Regarding Wave*, perhaps his most mature work, Snyder leaves the traditional outdoor themes of his poetry to concentrate on his newly found happiness with domestic life. Written under the influence of his third marriage and the birth of his first child, Kai, *Regarding Wave* celebrates Snyder's sense of responsibility to his family. Masa, his wife, forms the center of this complex work whose title is taken from the Sanskrit word *vak*, meaning vibrator or voice. She becomes the symbol of all forms of energy—"the earth, plants, air, animals, water, the sun"—to which Snyder offers his gratitude.

Kai, Snyder's son, is also an important feature, and many of the poems in the volume are devoted to him. There is no doubt that the birth of his first child deeply affected Snyder, who was thirty-eight at the time. Under the influence of a growing awareness that others depended on him, he completed his Zen studies and returned to the United States to teach and promote ecological reforms. "Kai Today," one of his finest poems, celebrates not only the boy's birth but also the process of birth itself as a transformation to another state of being. Although the theme is superficially Wordsworthian, as Bob Steuding points out, Snyder grounds his ideas firmly in Zen so

Gary Snyder

that Kai is not leaving a higher, more blissful state, but merely being transformed from one avatar to another. Birth is an occasion for celebration and not regret.

Snyder's family also appears in *Turtle Island*, his Pulitzer Prize-winning volume of 1974, but they are not so central to the work as the nature poetry to which Snyder returns. In technique, *Turtle Island*, which takes its title from the old American Indian name for the North American continent, is certainly Snyder's best collection. The lines are unusually sharp and clear, and Snyder shows greater certainty and control. On the other hand, the volume is by far his most blatantly polemical work, often to the detriment of the superior technique. In the preface, he says, "The poems speak of place, and the energy pathways that sustain life. . . . Hark again to those roots, to see our ancient solidarity, and then to the work of being together on *Turtle Island*."

Turtle Island contains four sections: "Manzanita" (published separately in 1972), "Magpie's Song," "For the Children," and "Plain Talk," a collection of essays on ecology. The didactic impulse of the

277

"Plain Talk" section, however, seems to dominate the entire volume. The serenity and joy that came from the personal relationship with nature now seems to be imposed by the teachings of Zen. One might reasonably argue, however, that the two cannot be distinguished. Indeed, a greater closeness to the primal world often comes with a detachment from it. Yet detachment does not negate bitterness about abuses of nature.

"Front Lines," for example, is a technically fine poem, but it is so politicized that one feels as if he had read a prose treatise rather than an excellent poem. Much the same may be said for "Spel Against Demons" (parts of which are prose), a magic incantation against the destruction of the few remaining areas of wilderness. The technique of both poems is excellent, the lines clear, the language clean, the images fresh, and the subject matter appropriate to the form, but one can never quite escape the feeling that he has been taught.

Since 1974 Snyder has devoted his time to finishing *Mountains and Rivers Without End.* Even without the completion of his magnum opus, however, his place would be assured in twentieth-century poetry, for no other contemporary poet has been quite so successful at blending Eastern and Western poetic traditions. Much of Snyder's poetry is based on the Oriental haiku—sharp, uncomplicated images that, like many Oriental paintings, form sketches that the reader's imagination must fill in. But Snyder also acknowledges his debt to D. H. Lawrence, Kenneth Rexroth, Robinson Jeffers, William Butler Yeats, and Ezra Pound. If he is more often known by virtue of his position as a spokesman for ecology and the subculture, he nevertheless remains a highly competent poet. —*Alex Batman*

References:

Robert Bly, "The Work of Gary Snyder," *Sixties,* no. 6 (Spring 1962): 15-42;

Robert Boyers, "Mixed Bag," *Partisan Review,* 36 (Summer 1969): 306-315;

G. S. Fraser, "The Magicians," *Partisan Review,* 38 (Winter 1971-1972): 469-478;

Thomas J. Lyon, "The Ecological Vision of Gary Snyder," *Kansas Quarterly,* 2 (Spring 1970): 117-124;

Thomas Parkinson, "After the Beat Generation," *Colorado Quarterly,* 17 (Summer 1968): 45-56;

Parkinson, "The Poetry of Gary Snyder," *Southern Review,* new series, 4 (Summer 1968): 616-632;

Parkinson, "The Theory and Practice of Gary Snyder," *Journal of Modern Literature,* 2 (1971-1972): 448-452;

Sherman Paul, "From Lookout to Ashram: The Way of Gary Snyder," *Iowa Review,* 1 (Summer 1970): 76-91; 1 (Fall 1970): 70-86;

Kenneth Rexroth, *American Poetry in the Twentieth Century* (New York: Herder & Herder, 1971);

Rexroth, "A Hope for Poetry," *Holiday,* 40 (March 1966): 147-151;

Bob Steuding, *Gary Snyder* (Boston: Twayne, 1976).

GILBERT SORRENTINO
(27 April 1929-)

BOOKS: *The Darkness Surrounds Us* (Highlands, N.C.: Jargon Books, 1960);

Black and White (New York: Totem Press / Corinth Books, 1964);

The Sky Changes (New York: Hill & Wang, 1966);

The Perfect Fiction (New York: Norton, 1968);

Steelwork (New York: Pantheon Books, 1970);

Imaginative Qualities of Actual Things (New York: Pantheon Books, 1971);

Corrosive Sublimate (Los Angeles: Black Sparrow Press, 1971);

Splendide-Hôtel (New York: New Directions, 1973);

Flawless Play Restored: The Masque of Fungo (Los Angeles: Black Sparrow Press, 1974);

A Dozen Oranges (Santa Barbara: Black Sparrow Press, 1976);

White Sail (Santa Barbara: Black Sparrow Press, 1977);

The Orangery (Austin: University of Texas Press, 1978);

Mulligan Stew (New York: Grove, 1979).

Gilbert Sorrentino was born in Brooklyn, New York, to August E. and Ann Davis Sorrentino. He married and was later divorced from Elsene Wiessner. He is now married to Victoria Ortiz, and he has three children: Jesse, Delia, and Christopher. He was educated in New York public schools and attended Brooklyn College (now part of the City University of New York) in 1950-1951 and from 1955 to 1957. He served in the U.S. Army Medical Corps from 1951 to 1953. He has received a Guggenheim Fellowship for fiction (1973), a National Endowment for the Arts Grant (1974), a Samuel S. Fels Award for the short story "Catechism" (1974), and a Creative Artists Public Service grant (1975). Sorrentino lives in New York City, where he teaches at the New School for Social Research.

Sorrentino has been a word craftsman for over thirty years. He began writing poetry soon after high school. While working as a clerk in a textile-factoring company in New York, he read some Walt Whitman and thought, "Well, I can do that too." And he began writing, always telling anyone who asked what he was doing that he was practicing to become a journalist, a more "sensible" career goal. His first serious piece was a story he wrote for a Brooklyn College magazine in 1950.

After his discharge from the army in 1953, Sorrentino spent three years on a 600-page novel, which, as he puts it, "will never see the light of day." Since then Sorrentino has published four experimental novels, flawed but bravely adventurous and critically acclaimed. He has served as editor and publisher of the magazine *Neon* (1956-1960), and as book editor for *Kulchur* (1961-1965), for which he wrote many critical pieces about contemporary poetry. He has worked as an editor for Grove Press (1965-1970). All in all, Sorrentino is an accomplished author who is familiar with most aspects of the writing profession. His is a voice that consistently and with ever-increasing originality stands out from the literary chorus.

Sorrentino is a poet of survival. The art of creating poetry is an effort to ward off encroaching dangers, both physical and spiritual. Much of Sorrentino's verse is necessarily bleak in tone, disciplined and tight in form, opaque in allusion, transcendent in intent. Although often witty, and brilliant with insightful flashes that illuminate personal and universal dilemmas, his poetry is all too often depressingly uncompromising. He is a poet of the moment, exploring various realities, and painting verbal pictures with somber shades.

Sorrentino's poetry is specifically urban and interior. He is a close observer and recorder of the mind. For Sorrentino the poem is not only descriptive: the poem has to be self-existent. The action should be constructed within the poem, for a poem illustrates the relationship of things to one another and the mingling of objects in a single present moment. The action is observable, yet of no special importance by itself. Most of the poems are not stories projected in time, but formations of relations among many elements in the poet's surroundings.

These self-reflective images are isolated in time and space and are what Sorrentino calls "fiction": "Reality is glass, a glass. / Clarity and a certain bright / reflection." Such solipsism is the truest reality, independent from anything outside itself. In fact, it is the "perfect fiction" of the title of his third book of verse. Such a term permits Sorrentino certain freedoms. He can present the ultimate twentieth-century confessional poem, and while the image is personal, as Henry Weinfield says, "a portion of the self which is located, cast forth, and lost within its boundaries," there is also a quality of universality that these poems explore: "there is no truth / but in dead event" ("Toward the End of Winter").

On the basis of an analogy between art and nature and on the view that human existence is compounded of dualities (body and soul, physical and spiritual, temporal and eternal), Sorrentino writes poems that contain both the grotesque and the beautiful. The poem, like life, is a combination of the comic and the serious, as in "The Man in the Moon":

Old man with whitening beard,
snapped once his fingers and the world
began, and with it, Mr Moon, no matter
what the wise ones say,

the voyeur Mr Moon, and the man
in him, with all those dirty postcards
taken of us all. To be bathed!
in milky light!

Reality as conceived by the poet is projected in verse. He is capable of such elevated flights of fancy as these lines from "Charles and Arthur":

The skies are azure: peace
a cheap boutonniere: yet and yet
this terrible metal

This terrible metal
says goodbye
for all of us.

or the whimsical gutter humor of "Beautiful Soup":

Heed the story of the man
who took the garbage out
and threw himself away.

Sorrentino's style is characterized by beautiful language, resonating lyricism, and a variety of poetic media. It is a style of vibrant, virile sound.

Sorrentino's first book, *The Darkness Surrounds Us* (1960), takes its title from Ecclesiastes 2:14, "The wise man's eyes are in his head but the fool walketh in darkness: and myself perceived also that one event happeneth to them all." This passage reflects Sorrentino's basic need to establish the boundaries of

Gilbert Sorrentino

personal identity. The poet isolates his ego in opposition to reactionary forces: "I've nothing to say / to them. And I won't write." Life is a struggle that must be got through, a working week that must be survived, a love that needs reaffirmation, a horror with which one must come to terms. The title poem defines the strategy to be employed. In "The Darkness Surrounds Us," Sorrentino shows that only through the creative act can the outside be kept distant:

> The Darkness Surrounds Us
>
> not so much perhaps,
>
> darkness: but that here
> for the moment there is no darkness
>
> and so it seems
> we're sort of blanketed with light, I might say
> even warmth.
>   And then I might say
>
> in what I know is selfishness
> throw on
> another goddam piece of wood
> hustle up some coal   the hell with that
> I mean all that   out there: let's kind of be like
>
> Indians! Because
> the darkness is all around us.

Sorrentino emphasized the importance of establishing the integrity of the ego in an interview with David Ossman: "You've got to know your place as a poet in the world—all you are is someone who reveals essence of things. If you feel that your essence is worth revealing, then that's got to be done with absolute artistry, or it's a failure."

Sorrentino's integrity is his own, but the preface to *The Darkness Surrounds Us* relates that his three great literary mentors are Ezra Pound, who taught him that verse is the highest of arts and gave him the sense of tradition, William Carlos Williams, who showed him that language can produce this sense, and Robert Creeley, who demonstrated that the attack on poetry need not be head-on.

Sorrentino's second book, *Black and White* (1964), was a gathering of material largely written in 1960-1961. While *The Darkness Surrounds Us* was, as Sorrentino put it, "the usual first book . . . they just happened to be the best poems I had over about four years," *Black and White* was an attempt to put together poems that had more or less the same tone. Sorrentino still finds the book interesting because in it he began to realize that the poem did not have to be a literal statement about anything: "It could be

itself." In an interview with Barry Alpert, Sorrentino elaborates upon his poetic credo: "You could nail a poem together that had a kind of reverberation to it—that didn't say anything, that made a kind of aesthetic whole." The poet presents a kind of "excellent article" that he has made and says, "Here this is!" Such a poem "looks fine and sounds fine and has beautiful edges to it. It's a kind of sculpted figure and it doesn't mean anything."

Sorrentino writes poetry in a rush, and as he told Barry Alpert, "if the poem doesn't come out right for me when I write it, I don't tinker with it, I usually junk it and start the poem over." Often, Sorrentino's first draft is a kind of talking to himself, because he doesn't know exactly what he wants to say. Perhaps something in the middle of the poem is the heart of the matter. So as a matter of course he sets aside the poem for a while and returns to it, possibly weeks later, to cut it or to rearrange the lines.

Sorrentino is fairly consistent in his choice of theme. In "The Transcript" from *Black and White* he continues to define himself as isolated and defiant:

> I am no tree
> no dogwood, nor
> red sumac, not
> even crabgrass
>
> am a man, a
> support but not a
> tree, feelings
> in me flow in
>
> blood and cartilage.

But this stance is in marked contrast to the next poem, "The Charm": "How can this man tell you / what skies hang over him? / How tell you / that you are in the sky / a gentle thing, a tender / thing?" This is the essential dilemma of Sorrentino's verse: how to maintain a protective shell over a compassionate heart. Both stances seem like poses, but they are more than masks through which a poet figure sees a troubled world. They are remedies to soothe the pain that rushes upon the unprepared observer. They are weapons to battle the enemy on its own terms, with subterfuge, parody, and disguise.

Sorrentino gets very close to the enemy in order to examine the danger better, as in "The Edges":

> My life is too full of faces,
> my imagination too full of gestures
> full as a garden is of leaves
>
> and colors. Various movements
> in my mind have counterpoint in reality

but I don't want that to be, the gestures
are too much for me.

As the title, *Black and White*, indicates, there is a rough dichotomy of purpose to this book. Throughout much of Sorrentino's work the imagination battles reality. The reader is made aware that the poem is an artificial construct useful for dealing with the world, making sense of it, ordering it, but ultimately temporary. Thus, as he writes in "Ars Longa," Sorrentino can be grateful to his creations for their momentary support, and also hostile to their inadequacies:

> Etched
> finely, they neither moan nor weep, the
> words, they are neither the experience
>
> nor the telling of it; a barrier of cellophane
> to enmesh you tenderly, or fiercely,
> one is here! one there! one is in two
> or three places at—! or is it
>
> yesterday, what is this, a poem?

In *The Perfect Fiction* (1968), Sorrentino demonstrates an advancement in skill and a continuity of theme. The poems are once again concerned with reality, which is depicted frequently as drab, dark, depressing. "Relief," as Duane B. Schneider writes in his review, "lies only in the futile dreams of something better which never arrives." Evoking the spirit of "the haunt / grim in sunlight: reality," Sorrentino expresses despair in an unusually wide range of voices and tones, touching base with cliche, the vernacular, and the obscene. Occasionally, as in the past, his verse is trite, and there is a tendency toward obscurity.

While the range of poems is broad, they echo previous laments for the "nature of the reality in which we find ourselves." The distressed, afflicted world is briefly jolted with spasms of love, but individuals generally lack the ability to see beneath the surface. Poetry is one way of clearing the reader's vision. In fact, it is the "perfect" way.

Sorrentino worked over a year on *The Perfect Fiction*, writing a unified group of about ninety poems, out of which he took roughly half. The structure of the book, to Donald Phelps, is "a series of contemplations—at best, of the isolate molecular sadness of experience—which are also professions of identity." Phelps explains that these poems, as a commentary on Descartes, are more melancholy than the most rationally pessimistic empiricism because "they deny to the specific any hopeful projected accretion, any logical process." The poet is isolated:

> He walks on the street, in
> his life. The thunder
> gives voice to the heat, a smell
>
> of rain, and trees move.

It is the human condition to face the world alone.

Sorrentino tries to control his content with a form of imposed calm. All fifty-two of the untitled poems have three-line stanzas whose sentences lead

Thomas Victor

from one stanza to the next and, in some cases, into other poems. Sorrentino told Eric Mottram, "When this book was written, I found that my work automatically fell, almost all the time, into three-line stanzas. This was extremely natural to me, but I wanted to be able to use other constructs. In *The Perfect Fiction* I tried to exhaust the three-line stanza, to break, as it were, its hold on my line, by using it in any and every way I could." The predominant mood of this volume is despair:

> It is one man alone, what
> other way
> to say it. I am sick of myself.

5.

XXXXXXXXXXXXXXXXXXXXXXXXXXXXXXXXXXXXXXXXXXXXXXXXXXXXXXXXXXXXXXX

Ultima Despedida del Príncipe Poniatowski de Su Familia

I am he who writes of the Prince of faded colors
Though there are better things to do, like smoke.
I see the subtle patina of despair (sure)
On that face despite his ~~xxxxxxxxxxxxxxx~~ moustache.
Death must be icy blue and Atlantic grey
For those brittle ~~tints~~ have settled in his eyes.
shades

Poniatowski blinks and blinks his frozen eyes
To startle off those wintry frigid colors.
Through his irises his thoughts ~~are seen~~ all grey.
Why doesn't he ~~depart~~ the blood and smoke
And ~~the~~ sobs and corpses and trim his swell moustache?
He has been sent that horrifying ~~gift~~, despair.

The nuns ~~said~~ Judas in ~~dark~~ violet despair
Hanged himself and swayed there with his staring eyes.
The Prince quakes and gags and pulls his royal moustache.
Death is strolling through the fields of autumn colors.
~~He~~ lights a Lucky Strike and in the pearly smoke
Sees that leafless tree ~~and~~ Judas dirty grey.

I'm a Prince, not a ~~draftee in his itchy~~ grey!
He ~~shouts~~, ~~and~~ you know what you can do with your despair!
~~Still~~, Hell keeps manufacturing its smoke.
On his honeymoon the Prince's bride had eyes
That glittered with ~~the decent~~ champagne colors
As he rummaged in her flesh with his moustache.

Now he feels a ~~kindxxf~~ hatred for his trite moustache
And for his hair, less black than sickly grey.
He is but the Prince of wishy-washy colors
Whimpering and crying ~~out~~ a banal despair
And damning God, his wounds, his eyes.
Death slides toward him, a precise and silent smoke.

An interesting fact is that Death doesn't smoke
Nor does he wear a beard or a moustache.
~~Some say~~ that scarlet is the color of his eyes
~~All know~~ his lips and tongue and teeth are grey.
These data may be found under "Death" ~~and~~ "Despair,"
Compiled by the ~~library~~ of Dying Colors.

Suddenly the smoke becomes a man in Oxford grey
He ~~grabs~~ the Prince's moustache~~xxx~~ and exhales despair
~~Xxxxxxxxxxxxxxxxxxxxxxxxxxxxxxxxxxxxxx~~
Deep in his eyes ~~glitter~~ odd barbaric colors.
gleam

"Ultima Despedida del Principe Poniatowski de Su Familia," revised typescript

The world is a bitter place: "Nothing grimmer than dawn at noon. / It is grey and not awake / The people are all dead." The poet is frustrated, but there is the determination to go on: "There is no poetry in me tonight. / Write out of a bitterness: too / many knowing people, wrap / them up: in barbed wire." Yet there remains an inner core of defense:

> Give them a simple
> abstract, say Red.
> Red, Red, Red, Red,
> . . . .
>
> only my friends, standing outside
> this Red I make shall be exempted,
> and my friends are who I name.

The poet is sure of what is important and what can be of lasting sustenance.

While Sorrentino's early books displayed a dry wit and a shrewdly plaintive understatement, in *Corrosive Sublimate* (1971) the wit is often parched and the statement anticlimactic. The spirit of his mentor Robert Creeley broods over many of these poems, which "are replete with short lines, vague abstractions, and deliberately inarticulate statements," as one reviewer observes.

However, although the volume is more uneven than *The Perfect Fiction*, it takes greater chances, using the greater freedom achieved by abandoning the restrictions of the three-line stanza. The book advances thematically, too, as in such poems as "Research, Again" it seeks to come to terms with the poet's memory and past:

> In the center of a peach
> there was a world that he wanted.
> (A poetic fancy fancy. The peach
> was brilliantly real.

Tim Longville points out that the book is about wanting both the "fancy fancy" and the "brilliantly real" simultaneously. It is also about "the indignities and perversions inflicted on both, about what happens in the world to such desires" for "Strange memorable objects: / caught in the most elegant turn of / the mind" ("Rose Room"). Sorrentino unraveled the title for Barry Alpert:

> Corrosive sublimate is a deadly poison, it's also an antiseptic. So that was in my mind. And then simply the idea of sublimation, the chemical process of sublimation which is defined, I believe, as . . . heating a solid material to a gaseous state and returning it to a solid state so that it never passes through a liquid form. In other words, it's purified as a gas and then returns to a solid. And I flattered myself into thinking that somehow the poems worked that way. They were kind of pure, those poems, and yet they had a solidity about them that made them valid for me.

The book's materials are drawn from many sources: New York City, dreams, the imagination, literature, and his own past: "When you leave this town you / Is just campin out (Thus the black porter / to my mother, / on her honeymoon." The poet figure is at the center of this book's focus, as in "The Poet Tires of Those Who Disparage His City":

> I speak now, tell you a bright truth:
> This is a bitter city.
> All the poets in disguise, as if
> They lived here. (You can tell them,
> > They're the ones who
> > have weary smiles
> > and laugh a lot with people
> > who don't know them.

Eric Mottram has pointed out that each poem masters an essential incident from Sorrentino's past and that the structure is in fact "often a rhetoric for recalling an occasion," as in "1947 Blue Buick Convertible":

> The Buick in the driveway
> or parked on the road?
>
> My father in his car, he owned
> a black Fleetwood:
>
> The night was so dark you could not
> see his thin white hair as
> he approached through the sound of crickets.

The best poem in the book, and also one of Sorrentino's longest, is the sixteen-part "Coast of Texas," which describes a love affair in a curious mixture of sentimental and scatological diction. The title translates a phrase from Guillaume Apollinaire ("Sur la côte du Texas"). Sorrentino places the setting in a "blank city" with a "sky / . . . bright blue." The city is hell and the poet is in love. Allusions to Wallace Stevens appear in such phrases as "avenues of green palms." As the poet sits eating chili and drinking rye whiskey, he imagines "A whole novel wrote and discarded in my head." The city is cold and the wind hurts the poet's eyes, and he imagines he can see her face in the palm trees. He wishes to drown in the blue Gulf water. The poem is an attempt to retreat into dream—to avoid the fate of Apollinaire, who "went mad on that hazy coast, dazed / under the blue." But the poet in this poem goes mad, too.

Gilbert Sorrentino

In *White Sail* (1977), Sorrentino takes only those risks he is sure he can meet. For the most part he is not intensely involved, even when writing about emotional subjects (Paul Blackburn's death, for instance). But he is not completely detached from his materials, and there is a fine mixture of lyricism and analysis here.

The poems occasionally seem capricious. He likes to have fun with his titles. For example, there is not a drop of soup in the first poem, "Beautiful Soup," which, as was mentioned earlier, tells the story of a man who took the garbage out and threw himself away. But this deliberate playfulness is once again Sorrentino's way of being absolutely true to his craft and to his developing aesthetic. He continues to maintain the unmitigated integrity of unique experience. It does not matter whether the elements of such experience lend themselves, as one reviewer put it, "to philosophic/intellectual assimilation or not." As Sorrentino writes in "Boilermakers":

> Rich and poor
> of every color and idea
> show themselves
> mannequin and dummy.
>
> Who must apologize
> for tatters
> of integrity?

A typical poem of this volume, "September in Kittery," begins with an allusion to an archetypal poetic comparison of human endeavors with those of a lobster: "Those were the lobsters / many poets write of, compare / to us and our lives: blindly / crawling, dark in the dark," and ends with the unequivocal and undeniable "white sail / on the Sound off Connecticut, breathless!"—an image that serves as the volume's title and is one of the best examples of Sorrentino's figures isolated out of time, pure unto itself.

In *White Sail* appears the first group of Sorrentino's antipodean orange sonnets—14-line poems with variable form and irregular meter that employ in their conceits the unrhymable word *orange*. All of Sorrentino's inherent playfulness emerges in his attempts to undermine conventional frameworks of organization. Some poems are funny; others might cause the reader to pause and think.

All of the orange poems are republished in Sorrentino's recent volume, *The Orangery* (1978). As the dust jacket says, each poem is a variation on *orange*, "which appears and reappears as a color, a fruit, a memory, an intrusion, a word seeking a rhyme, a presence expected and awaited." Such "concept" books are often gross mistakes, but *The Orangery* achieves a notable success. Sorrentino is careful to maintain his usual blend of the serious and the hilarious. Critics were generally laudatory. William Bronk writes, "In *The Orangery* Sorrentino makes things which are hard, gaudy and sometimes scary. They are stark artifacts of our world but not the world. They are made to last." And Carl Rakosi came away from a reading with two impressions: "one of a bright, haunting visual field in which design has primacy; another of a kind of vaudeville in which it is not quite clear what is being mocked." The mockery is inward and literary. The object of the sequence seems to be the "odd things that pop into the mind by chance." Other times Sorrentino's effects are the result of placing real-life objects into otherwise literary scenes. The result often leaves the reader "spellbound."

Sorrentino has always been an angry poet. He has never taken insult to human dignity lightly, and his poems, more often than not, have been fierce reactions against complacent acquiescence before misery. *The Orangery* is not only a clever flight of fancy; it is actually another of his defensive strategies against the foes of happiness. But, as "1939 World's Fair" suggests, these poems leave the reader saddened:

> I still hear those azure carillons
> floating from the Belgium building
> caroming off the Trylon
>
> and the Perisphere.
> . . . .
>> My mother was beautiful
>> in the blue gloom.
>> How she loved me.
>>
>> Sore feet and headaches
>> Depression and loneliness
>> dulled her soft bloom.
>>
>> She died ice-grey in Jersey City
>> with no solitary word.

The poet can retreat into the imagination that provides a momentary respite from responsibility, but just as abruptly the reader is torn from the pretty image—a conscious attempt to harden the sensibilities. For Sorrentino there is ultimately only a single message: "Nothing is the thing that rhymes with orange." —*William Mattathias Robins*

Other:

Sulpicia Elegidia=Elegiacs of Sulpicia, translated by

Sorrentino (Mt. Horeb, Wis.: Perishable Press, 1977).

References:

Barry Alpert, "Gilbert Sorrentino—An Interview," *Vort*, 6 (Fall 1974): 3-30;

Tim Longville, "On Sorrentino's *Corrosive Sublimate*," *Grosseteste Review*, 6 (1973): 91-95;

Eric Mottram, "The Black Polar Night: The Poetry of Gilbert Sorrentino," *Vort*, 6 (Fall 1974): 43-59;

Donald Phelps, "Extra Space," *Vort*, 6 (Fall 1974): 89-96;

Roy Skodnick, "Corrosive Sublimate / Beauty is a Rare Thing," *Vort*, 6 (Fall 1974): 42-43;

Henry Weinfield, "The Image in Time," *Vort*, 6 (Fall 1974): 41-42.

JACK SPICER
(30 January 1925-17 August 1965)

SELECTED BOOKS: *After Lorca* (San Francisco: White Rabbit Press, 1957; London: Aloes, 1957);

Billy the Kid (Stinson Beach, Cal.: Enkidu Surrogate, 1959; Dublin: New Writers' Press, 1969);

The Heads of the Town up to the Aether (San Francisco: Auerhahn Society, 1962);

Dear Ferlinghetti with Dear Jack, by Spicer and Lawrence Ferlinghetti (San Francisco: White Rabbit Press, 1962);

Lament for the Makers (Oakland: White Rabbit Press, 1962; London: Aloes, 1971);

The Holy Grail (San Francisco: White Rabbit Press, 1964);

Language (San Francisco: White Rabbit Press, 1965);

Book of Magazine Verse (San Francisco: White Rabbit Press, 1966);

A Book of Music (San Francisco: White Rabbit Press, 1969);

The Red Wheelbarrow (Berkeley: Arif Press, 1971);

15 False Propositions About God (San Francisco: ManRoot, 1974);

Admonitions (New York: Adventures in Poetry, 1974?);

An Ode and Arcadia, by Spicer and Robert Duncan (Berkeley: Ark Press, 1974);

The Collected Books of Jack Spicer, ed. Robin Blaser (Los Angeles: Black Sparrow Press, 1975);

Troilus, ed. Blaser (Los Angeles: Black Sparrow Press, forthcoming).

Jack Spicer was a San Francisco poet who rejected the traditional centers for poetry—academia and the established publishing houses, using the phrase "English Department" as a derogatory description for analytical approaches to poetry and having his own work published mostly by little magazines and small presses. Because he disliked providing biographical information about himself, little has been written about his life, and his reputation has been limited for the most part to the West Coast. In recent years, however, there has been some critical recognition of his work.

Dissatisfied with traditional poetry, Spicer experimented with language, form, and composition method. The diction in his poetry fluctuates between the commonplace and the sophisticated (the simple diction dominates), while occasionally he strains the limits of language. He was interested in devising new forms for poetry, but he was not averse to using traditional forms, such as the epic, so long as he could experiment within those structures. If his poetry is occasionally unusual or difficult to follow, it is because in 1957 he began to experience dictation by voices other than his own (in the tradition of William Blake, W. B. Yeats, and the French Symbolists). Spicer's poetry is not learned in the fashion of T. S. Eliot's, but his erudition is evident, especially with regard to his knowledge of linguistics and the medieval and renaissance epochs. He has been most popular with readers interested in language theory and in philosophy (despite the seeming simplicity of his verse, his work has attracted the attention of literary critics who discern phenomenological and semiotic philosophical strains), and with persons sympathetic to homosexual love (a topic in Spicer's work). He had a wide following in San Francisco, but the chief figures in his circle were Robert Duncan (who also influenced him), Kenneth Rexroth, and Robin Blaser.

Jack Spicer was born in Los Angeles and spent most of his life in California. He started college at Redlands University in 1943 but transferred to Berkeley in 1944, where he earned two degrees in English (a B.A. in 1947 and an M.A. in 1950). He was a teaching assistant at Berkeley in 1948 while working on his Masters degree and taught there again during the 1952-1953 academic year. During his years in graduate school, he was an announcer and writer for a radio program on KPFA (1948-1950). After completing his graduate studies, he went to the University of Minnesota where he taught linguistics and Old English literature from 1950 to 1952. Following his stay in Minneapolis, he also worked as an instructor at the California School of Fine Arts (1953-1955). In 1955 he went to New York very briefly and then started work as a research assistant in the rare book room of the Boston Public Library (1955-1956). He returned to California permanently in 1956 and found employment as an instructor at San Francisco State (1957) and as a research assistant at Berkeley for David Reed on the Linguistic Geography, a national project to catalogue lexical variations by region (1957-1965). He was the founder of the White Rabbit Press and two magazines, *J* and *Open Space*, in which he published most of his poetry after 1957. After 1957, when he became interested in the spiritual world of "the Other," he sought to collapse the distinction between the inner and outer worlds and described man as a radio set that receives messages. For him, poetry was not something apart from life but of and in man's daily experience. His foremost concern was the struggle with the problem of Being and the poetic form of that Being. The pursuit of this problem, he believed, exacted a personal cost—in his case, alcoholism. Thus, a close friend, Robin Blaser, argues that it was not alcohol but poetry that killed Jack Spicer. Although Spicer taught courses and worked as a research linguist, he devoted his life to poetry, writing by day and holding forth at night in the North Beach bars where he met with the young, contemporary poets.

The dominant themes in his work are love, the dialectic between language (or poetry) and experience, and the relationship between the self and the outside world, which, according to Blaser, he envisioned as a "flowing boundary," leading him to depict the living and the dead as interchangeable and to resort to poetic methods, especially serialization and the revision of myth, that highlight continuity. Thinkers and poets who most influenced him were Ernst Kantorwicz, Robert Duncan, W. B. Yeats, T. S. Eliot, Wallace Stevens, Rainer Maria Rilke, and Garcia Lorca.

The early poetry, written between 1946 and 1956, which Spicer later tried to rewrite and then rejected when rewriting did not accomplish his purpose, concerns poetry and love and makes use of mythic elements, but it is traditional in the occasional inclusion of rhyme and in its use of standard line length, narrative, relatively straightforward language, and imagery. This material appeared in small, obscure magazines, but recently some has been republished in *The Collected Books of Jack Spicer* (1975) and in special issues of the little

magazines *Caterpillar* and *ManRoot*. The early work provides a graphic sense of how far Spicer progressed and is much different from the post-1957 material.

Because of his experiences with dictated poetry, Spicer became dissatisfied with his earlier work. *After Lorca*, written and published in 1957, is the first book that reflects his new approach to verse composition; in it he tried to "empty himself," according to Robin Blaser, "in order to allow his language to receive an other than himself." This is a witty book that includes letters in which Spicer presents his theories on life and poetry, rough translations of Lorca's poetry, and some original poems by Spicer (see Clayton Eshleman in *Boundary 2* for detail on the relation between Spicer's translations and original compositions). Spicer incorporated two Rilkean sets of "correspondences" in *After Lorca*, designed to create links ordinarily considered difficult to accomplish. One is between himself—visible or tangible—and the dead poet Lorca—invisible or intangible—who writes an amusing "introduction" for Spicer's book about him. The second is a link between Lorca's Spanish and Spicer's English when the agent of correspondence—Spicer—knows so little Spanish that he cannot claim to be a competent translator. This link is a symbolic confrontation of the poet's difficulties in communicating his vision of the invisible. Spicer says of the problems with language and communication, for example, that "a really perfect poem (no one has yet written one) could be perfectly translated by a person who did not know one word of the language it was written in.... Words are what sticks to the real. We use them ... to drag the real into the poem. They are what we hold on with, nothing else. They are as valuable in themselves as rope with nothing to be tied to." In this book Spicer introduces, but does not develop, one of his favorite images—ghosts (in this instance, the ghost of Lorca). The translations and poems in *After Lorca*, each dedicated to an acquaintance or friend so as to make them purposeful and alive, are not nearly so provocative as the letters that contain discussions of the poems. The diction and syntax are simple in this varied collection, which consists of an ode and songs but mostly of lyrics and ballads that are somewhat flat in terms of emotion and narrative suspense.

Billy the Kid (1959) is a narrative about how a poet might depict the death of the Western outlaw, Billy the Kid. Brief as this book is, it offers evidence of significant progress in Spicer's creative skill and it constitutes one of his best efforts. The poem reestablishes Spicer's interest in reality, identity, and death, but it also introduces his fascination with myth and the relation among poetry, fictional characters, and real life. It is as much a poem about the creation of poetry and heroes as it is about Billy. As in the past, Spicer's diction and syntax are simple, but the sense of the material here is simultaneously dense, intriguing, and ambiguous. For example, in the prose introduction, he writes: "Let us fake out a frontier—a poem somebody could hide in with a sheriff's posse after him—a thousand miles of it if it is necessary for him to go a thousand miles—a poem with no hard corners, no houses to get lost in, no underwebbing of customary magic, no New York Jew salesmen of amethyst pajamas, only a place where Billy the Kid can hide when he shoots people." Robert Peters appropriately suggests that even though Spicer tries to make his art simple, it is not. In most of Spicer's other poetry, the linguistic simplicity often seems contrived, but in *Billy the Kid* he effectively combines simple and experimental language.

Spicer's choice of Billy the Kid as his subject is important because this figure represents American freedom and resistance to authority. As hero, Billy the Kid is a dubious figure because he is not a good person and seems to have died an ignominious death. He is both mythic hero and fallible human being, as Spicer indicates when he writes:

Nor immortality either (though why immortality should
occur
to me with somebody who was as mortal as Billy the
Kid or
his gun which is now rusted in some rubbish heap or
shined
up properly in some New York museum).

Through this figure, Spicer calls attention to a favorite paradox concerning the relation between reality and poetic creation, between life and death: they are not identical, but despite their distinctive features, they are related and even overlap. Spicer uses Billy to glorify the poet as creator when he notes that God dealt an ace "when he put us alive writing poetry for / unsuspecting people or shooting them with guns." Finally, his rendition of Billy is significant because it indicates Spicer's position vis-a-vis tradition; he draws upon it, yet he persistently experiments with it, making the reader aware that the poem is contemporary and distinct from the tradition upon which it rests.

In *The Heads of the Town up to the Aether* (1962), Spicer accomplished his most successful experimentation with form. The book has three sections that are equally distinctive in structure. Jed Rasula's comment on the purpose of the structural experimentation is illuminating, especially with regard to the shadowy identity of the poetic narrator that Spicer symbolizes by withdrawing the lyrical "I": "Spicer opts for the *insecurity* of an *incredible* fabrication, as will become amazingly clear in *Heads of the Town*. The task of such writing is to avoid submitting to those structural alignments that extend invisibly beyond their active function in the text." Spicer hopes, in other words, to suggest structural possibilities (or ordering principles) to the reader, but he wants to avoid having the structure assume transcendent, commanding influence over the reader's interpretation. This attitude toward structure is a reflection of Spicer's desire to have his poetry actively touch or involve his reader. According to Rasula, Spicer's withdrawal of the authorial pronoun forces the reader to try to create an identity for the poet; in the process, the reader assists in composing the text that he experiences.

On each page of the first section of *The Heads of the Town*—"Homage to Creeley"—Spicer combines a poem with prose commentary. The poems are brief, structurally simple exercises concerning diverse topics—love (with references to Eurydice and Orpheus dispersed throughout), the nature of reality, poetry, and nonsense. This material is witty and mischievous, as the following example from "Hisperica Famina" demonstrates:

Joan of Arc
Built an ark
In which she placed
Three peas
—Can you imagine translating this poem into
New English—

The prose commentary in "Homage to Creeley" offers an occasional incisive revelation, but it consists mostly of obvious statements intended as a satire on academic criticism of poetry (Spicer's despised "English Department of the Spirit"). Given the context in which he makes these statements, the material is amusing. In "Elegy," for example, Spicer opens with the following lines:

Whispers—
Eurydice's head is missing
Whispers
Get out of hell—

Spicer then adds this commentary: "This is definitely a warning to Orpheus which he does not understand—being an asshole. This is too bad because there would have been just as much poetry if he had understood it. The definition of warning has been given constantly. The fact, alone, that Eurydice's head was missing should have warned him."

Spicer contended that he was trying to write without images in "Homage to Creeley" to avoid conscious creation and to allow the voices free rein to dictate to him, but through his repeated references to Eurydice and Orpheus and to ghosts, he initiated a loose symbolic framework for his concern with love and the problem of reality that carries over into the other segments of *The Heads of the Town* and into his later books.

The second segment, "A Fake Novel About the Life of Arthur Rimbaud," is a cryptic, loose, prose rendition of Rimbaud's life as it relates to Spicer's views on love, reality, and the aesthetics of poetry. The titles of several chapters indicate the tone of the work: "The Dead Letter Office," "A Charm Against the Discovery of Oxygen," and "An Ontological Proof of the Existence of Rimbaud." As Jed Rasula indicates, this work is striking because Spicer experiments with the narrative voice, occasionally including autobiographical material, thereby forcing the reader to consider his own identity as it relates to that of Spicer and that of Rimbaud, a poet who fascinated Spicer because of his experiments with conveying a personal, mysterious vision in his poetry. Spicer uses the symbol of the Dead Letter Office to call attention several times to the aesthetic problem of poet-reader communication, suggesting that "inside every Rimbaud was a ready-made dead-letter-officer. Who really mailed the letter? Who stole the signs?" The preceding statement, consisting of allusive hints about Spicer's intention, is as specific or discursive as anything he offers. By employing a symbol such as the Dead Letter Office, he implicitly questions the assumption that literature is an effective means of making the reader aware of the poet's paradoxical dilemma: life and art consist of intriguing mysteries that living beings hope to discuss and resolve with the assistance of other living individuals, the dead (memories of one's own past, other artists, history), and the spiritual realm that Spicer refers to as "the unknown." By leaving the translation of his symbolism and the provision of detail to the reader, Spicer compels the reader to experience the poet's problem concerning communication.

"A Textbook of Poetry," the third segment of *The Heads of the Town*, was written, Spicer says in this section, "to explain. We do not hate the human beings that listen to [poetry]." This statement about the purpose of the work is significant because it presents another aspect of the Spicer paradox. He

was interested in relating life to poetry, and he did not believe in excluding or in deliberately alienating the common reader. At the same time, however, as he strained to invent new perspectives and forms, he wrote verse and theoretical material that was mysterious, sometimes difficult, and often private. "A Textbook of Poetry" is written in an aphoristic style reminiscent of Nietzsche's *Beyond Good and Evil* (1886): it offers incisive, provocative statements in twenty-nine numbered segments, each of which consists of three or four paragraphs, but there is no structural connection among the segments. The link is a loose, thematic concern with poetry, love, and God. In discussing the problem of the metaphor as a means of communicating, Spicer complains, for example, of its inadequacy and notes:

> The ghosts the poems were written for are the ghosts of the poem. We have it second-hand. They cannot hear the noise they have been making.
>
> Yet it is not a simple process like a mirror or a radio. They try to give us circuits to see them, to hear them. Teaching an audience.

The topic here is communication with an audience, but Spicer's comments are not lucid and straightforward. Despite his distrust of metaphors and symbols, he uses three figurative devices within this brief passage to make his point. Two of these figures are important to his symbolic system: the ghost and the radio. The ghost symbolizes the slippery nature of "the text" that each reader discovers in the written words of a book; the book appears to be tangible and fixed, yet each reader transports an individualized emotional reaction to his understanding of the text. This symbol also stands for the poet, the character, or the reader, each of whom is, ironically, tangible and not tangible to the other person. The radio symbolizes communication between the poet and the reader. The poet may transmit a signal that he hopes others will receive, but he may encounter transmission difficulties in his set (the poem), the reader's receiver (his interpretation of the text) may be faulty, or the reader may refuse to turn on his set (to read poetry) or to tune in the specific station (Spicer's poetry).

Two other important issues emerge from Spicer's "A Textbook of Poetry"; Spicer's concern with "astonishment" and with God: "It is up to [poets] to astonish them and Him. To draw forth answers deep from the caverns of objects or from the Word Himself. Whatever that is." Spicer seeks through poetry to awaken a deep sense of wonder that involves God in an inexplicable fashion. He was well read in Calvinist theology and was reluctant to deny the existence of God, but he was also unwilling to commit himself to a system of belief. Consequently, references to God appear frequently but in enigmatic form, as when he makes a pun on God as Logos, the Word, by referring to him as the "Lowghost," a ploy that indicates his equivocation concerning the existence of God: the ghost may or may not exist. Spicer offers provocative, significant theoretical statements on poetry, but he refuses to systematize his thoughts or to present them in a lucid, discursive form. "A Textbook of Poetry" is, then, a valuable yet elusive rendition of his theoretical views.

The Holy Grail (1964) is a narrative poem in which Spicer uses seven medieval characters from Grail epics as a foundation for a discussion of the quest. He had no planned structure for the work when he started, so in some regards the poem seems disjointed. The links that keep the book from losing a center of focus are the Grail motif and the characters whose fictive lives are intertwined. This work offers a particularly good example of Spicer's recourse to and experimentation with myth. The title and the characters' names automatically indicate to the literate reader that Spicer is concerned with man's purpose and how he searches for it. Having alluded to the Grail tradition, however, he begins the poem by indicating that when Gawain simply "followed the markings" he became a symbol of shame, an existential failure who is guilty of bad faith, and that when Percival asked the wrong questions of the wrong individuals and became entangled in his support for war, he was a fool. Each of the other books on a Grail character indicates why that individual failed to discover either the Grail or an appropriate response to man's dilemma about his being. Lancelot failed because he sought love and honor as prizes to be won in battle, refusing to ask "what is the holy grail?" Gwenivere, the skeptic, mocked what she referred to as "spooks and ghosts" and was "sick of the invisible world and all its efforts to be visible." She wished that Lancelot would consume her with passion, but he did not because he was distracted by martial pursuits, honor, and the manners of courtly love. Merlin, whose magic might have conjured the Grail or the spirit world, was imprisoned in a tower that seemed to be political but that was partly his own creation and partly someone else's. He sought to communicate his vision and to create "home without distance," but his self-imposed prison negated his potential. Galahad did not seek the Grail and so found it, but in treating it as

Jack Spicer

a mundane object, he caused it to lose its allure. In "The Book of the Death of Arthur," Spicer indicates that the future king, Arthur, completed the circle of failure because he lost track of why the Grail was significant, thereby making all seem hopeless. Spicer will not, however, succumb to nihilism, despite the grim situation, for he posits the creation of a "monstrous anti-grail none of those knights could have / met or invented." He will not specify how man will rise above the blackness of life, but as the Arthur section ends, he describes a noise in Arthur's head that may provide a reason to hope: "A noise in the head of the prince. Something in God-language / In spite of all this horseshit, this uncomfortable music." Spicer's *Holy Grail* is a contemporary, innovative rendition of mythic material concerning man's universal dilemma about his purpose and about how to live his life in accord with that purpose.

Spicer's last major work, *Language* (1965), is devoted to the same topics as the other books—language, love, and poetry—but here he intensifies his attitudes and the extent of his experimentation. The titles of the segments within the work indicate that there is only a loose thematic coherence: "Thing Language," "Love Poems," "Intermissions," "Transformation," "Morphemics," "Phonemics," and "Graphemics." The loose structure is intentional because in two posthumously published efforts—a Greek play, "Pentheus and the Dancers," and an incomplete detective novel, published in *Caterpillar* (July 1970)—it is clear that, when he wanted to, Spicer was able to create traditional structure and suspense. The random character of the poetry in *Language* results from his attempt to allow the voices to dictate to him and from his dissatisfaction with the present state of poetry and the life that accompanies the pursuit of art. The inadequacy of language becomes symbolic of what is wrong with life and love, as the following passage from "Phonemics" shows:

Tough lips that cannot quite make the sounds of love
The language
Has so misshaped them.
Malicious afterthought. None of you bastards
Knows how Charlie Parker died. And dances now in
                                        some brief
    kingdom (Oz) two phonemes
That were never paired before in the language.

Language has the power to communicate love and to enhance the quality of life, but, for Spicer, it serves instead to exacerbate the existing problems.

The other major issue in this work is Spicer's relation to other people, especially his lovers. He frequently complains about the distance between people and about their failure to bridge gaps, but he makes a telling comment when he writes in "Graphemics" of "being a poet / a disyllable in a world of monosyllables." Spicer wanted to believe that he was an integral part of his society (evident in his love for commonplace pursuits—baseball and the Northshore bars), but he also realized that his knowledge, his sensitivity to life and art, and his life-style set him apart. It is important, then, not to seize upon isolated comments about potential for communication or lack of such potential, because the essence of Spicer and his poetry derives from the tension of the paradox: he perceived himself as both a part of society and apart from society.

The extremity of Spicer's language, which more and more lacks narrative purpose or cognitive sense, seems to reflect a crisis in his mind—that life was not working out as he had hoped. He did not despair, but he seemed increasingly conscious of failure, although it is not clear whether he believed the failure to be his own or that of society.

In the Vancouver lectures, delivered in 1965, Spicer provided a rare discursive outline of his poetic theory. Because these lectures were given in Spicer's last year, they may be taken as the culmination of his views. In his introduction he suggested that poets have three main problems: dictation, the dilemma of the poet as the person in the middle, and the serial poem. Essentially, these problems involve the attempt to clear away obstacles between the poem and the poet and between the poem and the audience. Dictation, he said, involves a sudden "fast take" in which the poet finds himself composing poetry in perhaps one-eighth the time that it used to take him. The poet cannot, however, play tricks with this complicated process; the voices either come or do not. The source of the voices is a mystery to which the poet is most receptive when he practices and becomes adept at ridding the poem of the self. This task, according to Spicer, is quite demanding because it involves the practice of learning to do nothing but wait for the voices, an art that egoistic, Western individuals find trying. The problem for the person in the middle, the poet, is that he must, then, learn to be the agent and not the perpetrator of the poem. He must become like the radio set, said Spicer. Because of his conviction that the self is an obstacle to good poetry, he minimized the significance of individual authorship and refused to permit his work to be copyrighted (hence, problems with piracy were common). When the poet removes the obstacle of the self, he frees the unconscious. Thus, for Spicer, the truly great poem frightens the poet because it transcends the conventional, rising from deep in the unconscious to present the shocking, valuable new insight. When asked about the role of individual ability if poets are merely agents, Spicer hedged and eventually resorted to the argument that the process cannot be intellectualized. On a basic level, the spiritual aspect of dictation defies intellectual exegesis, but Spicer could have argued that there are talented selfless agents and bad selfless agents.

In addition to removing the self, Spicer also sought to divest the poem of artificial, poetic obstacles such as rhyme. In the Vancouver lectures he clarified his reason: "It just seems to me that you swim against all sorts of tides, and everything else, if you exclusively use rhyme." If the poet is worrying with rhyme, in other words, he might miss hearing the voices or he might misconstrue their message. In his drive to minimize obstacles, Spicer even questioned the role of language at its most fundamental level. Early in the Vancouver material, he stated that language is furniture in the poem that the poet must arrange to his advantage. Later he added that language does not have an independent meaning but is merely the structure of the poem. Finally, however, he presented a most unusual theory when he contended that language is "an obstruction to what the poem wants to do, and the more you understand about words and understand about the structure of language, the easier it is for you to see where the obstructions are and prevent them, if possible, from interfering with the message of the poem." The location of the poem, if not in the language, is a mystery that Spicer pursued with dedication. Asked about the role of communication and the purpose of writing poetry, Spicer refused to proffer a solution to the mystery, suggesting "that the answer to the thing of the poem is the same answer that Mallory answered why you climb Everest, not to get to the top or to make an important scientific discovery, but because it's there."

Spicer's devotion to his poetic voices prompted him to "take dictation" on verse that varied significantly in quality, form, and subject matter, but his interest in this spiritual faculty, which he combined with tough intellectual questioning and wit, is the distinguishing feature of his life and art.
—*Richard Ziegfeld*

Periodical Publications:

POETRY:

"To the semanticists," "The chess game," "A new testament," *Occident* (Winter 1946): 39-41;

"Untitled," "4 A.M.," "Chinoiserie," *Contour Quarterly*, 1 (April 1947): 17;

"A night in four parts," "Sonnet," *Berkeley Miscellany*, 1 (1948): 11-12, 14;

"Berkeley in time of plague," "The dancing ape," "Hibernation—after Morris Graves," "Psychoanalysis: An elegy," "The song of the bird in the loins," *Evergreen Review*, 1, no. 2 (1957): 52-58;

"Epithalamium," by Spicer, Ronald Primack, Bruce Boyd, and George Stanley, *Beatitude*, 6 (ca. June 1959): n. pag.;

"Down to new beaches where the sea," "Epilog for Jim," *J*, 2 (Fall 1959): n. pag.;

"The shabby sea where you float in," "Last hokku," *J*, 3 (Fall 1959): n. pag.;

"Jacob," *J*, 4 (Fall 1959): n. pag.;

"Fifth elegy," *J*, 5 (Fall 1959): n. pag.;

"A translation for Jim," "A translation for Jeorge," *J*, 8 (Fall 1959): n. pag.;

"When I hear the word Ferlinghetti / I reach for my g . . n," attributed to Spicer, *Beatitude*, 17 (November-December 1960): n. pag.;

"Three Marxist essays," *San Francisco Capitalist Bloodsucker-N* (Spring 1962): n. pag.;

"This is submitted for your Valentine contest," *Open Space*, 2 (February? 1964): n. pag.;

"Smoke Signals," *Open Space*, 4 (April/May? 1964): n. pag.;

"Pull down the shade of ruin. rain verse," "If your mother's mother had not riven, mother," "What in sight do I have," "It comes May and the summers renew themselves," *Open Space*, 5 (May? 1964): n. pag.;

"Five variations on the earth," *Tish* (Vancouver), issue d (n.d.): n. pag.;

"Lives of the philosophers: Diogenes," *Floating Bear*, 33 (1967): n. pag.;

"A dialogue between intellect and passion," "All hallows eve," "At a party," "Orpheus after Eurydice," "Orpheus in hell," "Orpheus' song to Apollo," "We find the body difficult to speak," "On reading last year's love poems," "Watching a TV boxing match in October," "A heron for Mrs. Altrocchi," "Song for the great mother," "Five words for Joe Dunn on his 22nd birthday," "A prayer for Private Graham Mackintosh on Halloween," *Caterpillar*, 12 (July 1970): 59-82;

"Indian Summer: Minneapolis 1950," "Christmas Eve: 1952," "Lyric for Gary," "Sonnet for Gary," "Portrait of an Artist," "The Inheritance: Palm Sunday," "A Postscript to the Berkeley Renaissance," "The Gardener's Son," "Manhattan," "Untitled," "For Nemmie," "For Ebbe," "For Ed," "For Russ," "For Harvey," "For Dick," "For Billy," "For Mac," "For Joe," *ManRoot*, 10 (Fall 1974-Winter 1975): 99-124.

FICTION:

"The scroll-work on the casket," *Berkeley Miscellany*, 2 (1949): 31-32;

"From a detective novel," *Caterpillar*, 12 (July 1970): 148-161.

DRAMA:

"Pentheus and the dancers," *Caterpillar*, 12 (July 1970): 115-147.

NONFICTION:

"Miller: Remember to Remember," *Occident* (Fall 1947): 44-45;

"The poet and poetry—a symposium," *Occident* (Fall 1949): 43-45;

"Correlation methods of comparing ideolects in a transition area," by Spicer and David W. Reed, *Language Journal of the Linguistic Society of America*, 28 (July-September 1952): part 1, 348-359;

"The Poems of Emily Dickinson," *Boston Public Library Quarterly*, 8 (1956): 135-143;

"Statements . . . ," *Open Space*, 3 (March? 1964): n. pag.;

"Letters to Graham MacKintosh," "Letter to Jim Alexander," "From the Vancouver lectures," *Caterpillar*, 12 (July 1970): 83-114, 162-212;

"An Exercise," "A plan for a Book on Tarot," ed. Robin Blaser and John Granger, *Boundary 2*, 6 (Fall 1977): 3-20.

Interviews:

The Vancouver Lectures—questions following lectures (May 1965), ed. Robin Blaser (Los Angeles: Black Sparrow Press, forthcoming).

Bibliography:

Sanford Dorbin, "A Checklist of the Published Writings of Jack Spicer," *California Librarian*, 31 (October 1970): 251-261.

References:

Robin Blaser, "The Practice of Outside," in *The Collected Books of Jack Spicer*, pp. 271-329;

Michael Davidson, "Incarnations of Jack Spicer: *Heads of the Town up to the Aether*," *Boundary 2*, 6 (Fall 1977): 103-134;

Christopher Dewdney, "Some Statements on Whorf, Spicer, Morphemics, and 'A Palaezoic Geology of London Ontario,' " *Open Letter*, new series, 7 (Spring 1974): 44-47;

Robert Duncan, "Jack Spicer, Poet: 1925-65," *California Librarian*, 31 (October 1970): 250;

Clayton Eshleman, "The Lorca Working," *Boundary 2*, 6 (Fall 1977): 31-49;

Ross Feld, "Lowghost to Lowghost," *Parnassus*, 4, no. 2 (1976): 5-30;

John Granger, "The Loss of the Bride in *Heads of the Town* and the Reclamation of the Text," *Boundary 2*, 6 (Fall 1977): 145-161;

Fran Herndon, "Artwork from *The Heads of the Town up to the Aether*," *Boundary 2*, 6 (Fall 1977): 135-145;

Stephanie Judy, " 'The Grand Concord of What': Preliminary Thoughts on Musical Composition and Poetry," *Boundary 2*, 6 (Fall 1977): 267-285;

James Liddy, "A Problem with Sparrows: Spicer's Last Stance," *Boundary 2*, 6 (Fall 1977): 259-266;

Larry Oakner, "Jack Spicer: The Poet as Radio," *ManRoot*, 10 (Fall 1974-Winter 1975): 3-10;

Stan Persky, "A Note on Robin Blaser and Jack Spicer," *Caterpillar*, 12 (July 1970): 213-216;

Robert Peters, "The House that Jack Built Has an Atwater Kent in the Living Room . . . ," *ManRoot*, 10 (Fall 1974-Winter 1975): 181-191;

Jed Rasula, "Spicer's Orpheus and the Emancipation of Pronouns," *Boundary 2*, 6 (Fall 1977): 51-102;

Peter Riley, "The Narratives of *The Holy Grail*," *Boundary 2*, 6 (Fall 1977): 163-190;

Frank Sadler, "The Frontier in Jack Spicer's 'Billy the Kid,' " *Concerning Poetry*, 9, no. 2 (1976): 15-21;

Gilbert Sorrentino, "Jack Spicer: Language as Image," *For Now*, 5 (n.d.): 28-36;

William V. Spanos, "Jack Spicer's Poetry of Absence: An Introduction," *Boundary 2*, 6 (Fall 1977): 1-2;

George Stanley, "Jack Spicer's *Language*," *Magazine*, 6 (n.d.): n. pag.;

Colin Stuart and John Scoggan, "The Orientation of the Parasols: Saussure, Derrida, and Spicer," *Boundary 2*, 6 (Fall 1977): 191-257.

Papers:

There is a collection of Spicer's papers at the Simon Frasier University Library in Burnaby, British Columbia.

WILLIAM STAFFORD
(17 January 1914-)

BOOKS: *Down in My Heart* (Elgin, Ill.: Brethren Publishing House, 1947);

West of Your City: Poems (Los Gatos, Cal.: Talisman Press, 1960);

Traveling Through the Dark (New York: Harper, 1962);

The Rescued Year (New York: Harper, 1966);

Allegiances (New York: Harper, 1970);

Someday, Maybe (New York: Harper, 1973);

Stories That Could Be True: New and Collected Poems (New York: Harper, 1977);

Writing the Australian Crawl: Views on the Writer's Vocation (Ann Arbor: University of Michigan Press, 1978).

Born in Hutchinson, Kansas, William Stafford was reared in small towns on the Kansas plains. In 1937 he received a B.A. and in 1946 an M.A. from the University of Kansas at Lawrence. He received his Ph.D. from the University of Iowa in 1954. A conscientious objector, Stafford worked in civilian public service camps during World War II. In 1948 he began teaching at Lewis and Clark College in Portland, Oregon, where he still teaches. He has twice taken one-year leaves of absence from Lewis and Clark to teach elsewhere: at Manchester College in 1955, and at San Jose State in 1956. Stafford served as Consultant in Poetry at the Library of Congress in 1970. As a U.S. Information Agency lecturer in 1972, he traveled to Egypt, Iran, Pakistan, India, Nepal, and Bangladesh. Stafford is also the recipient of a number of awards: a Yaddo Foundation Fellowship for 1956; the Oregon Centennial Prize for poetry and short story in 1959; the National Book Award for *Traveling Through the Dark* in 1963; the Shelley Memorial Award in 1964; a National Endowment for the Arts Grant in 1966, and a Guggenheim Fellowship for the same year; and the Melville Cane Award for 1974. He has received two D.Litt. degrees, one in 1965 from Ripon College, the other in 1970 from Linfield College. Stafford married Dorothy Hope Frantz in 1944, and the Staffords have two sons and two daughters.

In addition to six volumes of poetry, Stafford has published many prose articles, and a nonfiction book, *Down in My Heart* (1947), describing his experiences as a conscientious objector in World War II. Many of his articles and three interviews are collected in *Writing the Australian Crawl* (1978). The subject of this book is poetry and how Stafford arrives at it; the volume is the best introduction to his poems. In the essays in *Writing the Australian Crawl*, Stafford meticulously explains both his definition of poetry and his writing routine, tracing the development of a few specific poems. These prose pieces reveal a curious, questing mind resolved to record any impulses that come to it. For Stafford, the poet is a receiver of messages, or at least of impulses hinting at messages. He describes the act of writing as "the successive discovery of cumulative epiphanies in the self's encounter with the world." The poet relies totally on intuition to begin the process of composing; he is willing "to accept the chances the moment brings." While waiting for intuition to lead the way, he clears his mind of any obstructions, aiming for "the exhilaration of discovery, the variety that comes as a result of being yourself." Stafford's typical method of composing is to jot down whatever impulse comes to him (he usually reserves the early morning hours for this) and then follow it. Sometimes it leads to meaningful associations, sometimes not. Such an open-ended thought process entails risks: most of Stafford's "explorations" fail as poems. He publishes only a fraction of what he writes, and some critics, such as Roger Dickinson-Brown, feel even that fraction is too large. Yet Stafford is not discouraged by the failures. He learns from them: "A writer must write bad poems. . . . Finicky ways can dry up sources."

Thus Stafford's poetry is a log of explorations. Just as the journal of a historical voyage of discovery often does not record success in the terms hoped for by those who undertake the trip, so Stafford's poems may disappoint readers who look for orthodox poetic "statements." In other words, as Hazard Adams says, Stafford's readers should not press expectantly for some kernel of truth. The "point" of a poem may be rendered obliquely; Stafford often seems to be marking a trail toward some discovery. To look too hard for the truth of the poem is to miss

it. As he says in *Writing the Australian Crawl*, "Poetry is the kind of thing you have to see from the corner of your eye. You can be too well prepared for poetry. . . . It's like a very faint star. If you look straight at it you can't see it, but if you look a little to one side it is there."

The trails Stafford lays out—he might say, records—in his poems run through space and time. He is vitally concerned with the past, both the remembered, human past and the world's geological past, and how it bears on the present. He feels the slipping away of time as it pulls after him, and he tries to find ways to spend well his brief future. Stafford writes of the American Indian and the lore that kept him in touch with the center of his world. Sometimes in its startling evocation of an animal or event or person, a poem takes on the semblance, and the persuasive power, of myth. Although the reader traces all these elements through a landscape that resembles the American West, Stafford is more than a regionalist. His poetry seeks to take the reader to the frontiers of his own imagination, to the edge of what he knows, and then to induce him to explore farther. The topography of Stafford's country is detailed, concrete, and yet more filled with portent for man than any real terrain. This natural world of the poet is a constantly unfolding process, paralleling the imaginative process of man's mind. The reader confronts this subtly animate land cautiously, aware of its potential, and he abstracts meaning from it much as the pioneers must have done from the American frontier, by touching it, watching it, walking it.

Landmarks and animals from this wilderness, and the phenomena that transpire there, have a curious double nature. They stand immediately as authentically described parts of a world taken to be the West (more often than not the Pacific Northwest). But then each element of this world, at any time, merely by the focus put on it or by the pattern in which it is mentioned, becomes a metaphor, an aid to delineating Stafford's overriding theme: the tension between this natural world, alive with intimations of the spirit that created it, and the artificial, mechanized world man has constructed and now lives in. Stafford builds a poetry that calls forth the intuition, the faculty of mind that can perceive the uniqueness of the natural world. And by doing so, he throws into relief that tension between the two worlds, showing his reader that, consciously or not, he chooses between the two every day of his life.

Stafford convinces the reader of his world's authenticity largely by surprising little turns of

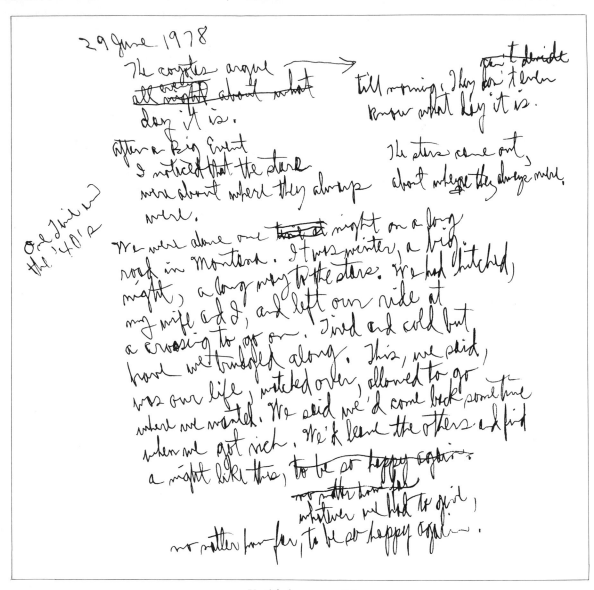

Untitled manuscript

phrases, by word placement. The vocabulary is colloquial and not large; his are homely words, tools the reader knows. But they appear in relationships that are often striking. The syntax is unusual; it is the new ground in which the old tools function. A typical example of Stafford's language technique appears in the poem "Bi-focal" (from *West of Your City*, 1960). Here the words *legend* and *vein* are used initially in the ordinary way, as nouns: "Sometimes up out of this land / a legend begins to move"; "out of the green appears / the vein in the center line...." But then they are twined around each other and used as verbs: "and the legend veins under there," "it legends itself / deep...." First used as nouns, the words have their usual denotations and connotations (although by making *legend* animate Stafford

already begins to enrich the word's meaning). Then, by making the static words active, the poet gives them new life, and imparts in the poem a complex idea that would have required longer, more logical phrases had orthodox grammar been used. Stafford fills his poetry with unusual effects carried off through the couching of ordinary words in extraordinary syntax. This subtle coordination of seeming naivete and artistic contrivance allows rarified intuitions to plane into the reader's mind as effortlessly as the truth of an old saying. As in much good poetry, the reader is often aware that something special has happened, but is at a loss to explain how it was done or what specific elements in the poem did it. He merely knows something else now that *feels* true.

Although Stafford often uses rhymes, even his rhyming poems usually retain an informality (often an irregularity of rhythm) that contrasts attractively with the formality of the rhyme. Several poems have an inherent symmetry hard to describe, yet somehow reflect the keen eyesight and judgment necessary to do justice to a "frontier." This symmetry is not always rigorously maintained. As critics sometimes point out, the meter of Stafford's less formally structured poems sometimes plods; the thought slackens into discursiveness. But in the best poems his wilderness is alive with potential; the pace through it is brisk; and along the way the poet delivers genuine surprises, happy discoveries, with the rectitude of a mapmaker.

Unlike that of many poets, Stafford's work shows little overall development through the years. The voice of his first collection still speaks in his latest. Nor have the themes changed much over the span of his career, although a few reviewers note slight shifts in the proportions of certain ones. In all six book-length collections, the poet favors narrative, tells stories about his world through which the reader glimpses hints of what lies underneath the story, holding up the landscape.

The first of Stafford's book-length collections is entitled *West of Your City*. Fourteen of its poems reappear in *The Rescued Year* (1966). Some critics feel *West of Your City* is Stafford's best book, noting that the language stays sharper more often here, and the thought behind the poems is clearer. This preference may be due, however, to the position of *West of Your City* as the first book-length articulation of Stafford's topics. All of them are here: concern for the past, for the American Indian, for family and home. Many poems are little parables expressing the conflict between man's rationality and his intuition—the one invents cars and rockets and politics, the other can listen to what the world says. Revelation can come at any time. In "Level Light" it comes as evening fades. The dimming light causes an epiphany "that brings to autumn the winter word— / a level shaft that tells the world...." The light's message is one of repudiation and resolution, and it echoes Stafford's descriptions of his own writing process: "*It is now too late for earlier ways; / now there are only some other ways, / and only one way to find them—fail.*"

This poem brings up a point that needs to be stressed. The "message" of many of Stafford's poems is also the "message" of his prose and, one feels, of his life. His is a poetry of commitment; the principles by which he creates it are also those by which he lives. Many of the pronouncements in

Writing the Australian Crawl reveal an intellectual who has the faith to be led by intuition. His poetry is filled with admonitions, usually derived through an almost mystical contact with nature, to live by faith, to use the inner eye all men are born with. Stafford says that "There is something implicit in anything," that life offers man clues to how to live. Man's intuitive abilities give him the responsibility of heeding those clues, of trying to find the pattern behind everyday places and events. That man has done so poorly lately at acknowledging his intuition's purpose accounts for the bleakness of some of Stafford's poems. The instant that the revelation is completed in "Level Light," darkness closes in: "In one stride night then takes the hill." Several poems hint at an apocalypse brought about by man's failure to follow the whispers of intuition. It is no wonder that in "The Well Rising," one of the best poems in *West of Your City*, the poet concludes a thoughtful description of nature with the statement, "I place my feet / with care in such a world."

Stafford makes vivid his world and the lessons it teaches by personifying elements of the landscape and also by describing the actions an explorer might take to try to get along there. The terrain *knows* things. The mountains of "Acquaintance," for example, "hold a grim expression." "Circle of Breath" describes a windmill "giving its little cry." The narrator of "A Survey" recalls tales of a canyon "crammed with hysterical water / hushed by placid sands." The lizard of "At the Bomb Testing Site" "waited for history.... The hands gripped hard on the desert." A sentient world is one worthy of respect; it must be dealt with, questioned. Stafford often describes the questioning process as an action of the hand. In "Ice-fishing" the fisherman waits on the cold ice of a lake, "Not thinking other than how the hand works...." When night comes he checks his line for fish, plunging his hand down "where the tugged river flows over hidden / springs too insidious to be quite forgotten." As the mind searches out beyond what it knows, so the hand searches the hidden places of the wilderness. In "Connections" a raccoon puts his "hand" into the swamp that is its home, "gazing through his mask for tendrils / that will hold it all together." Always the hand is searching for clues to the underlying pattern of existence, the unity beneath all things that, according to intuition, exists.

Stafford looks far and wide for this pattern. In "Walking West" he explores the geological past of the world, searching where "in deep flint another world is / Caught by flint and held forever, / the quiet pace of God stopped still." In "Acquaintance"

William Stafford

the poet acknowledges his search:

> I search in such terrain,
> face flint all the way,
> alert for the unreal
> or the real gone astray.

The poet also explores the human past, in poems tinged with nostalgia. In "The Farm on the Great Plains" the speaker remembers a farm tugging the end of a far telephone line, a farm tenanted by the ghosts of his parents. Once a year he "calls" that line—his heart searches the void that claimed those lives—waiting for the day when a phantom voice will answer and the pattern will become clear:

> Then the line will be gone
> because both ends will be home:
> no space, no birds, no farm.
>
> My self will be the plain,
> wise as winter is gray,
> pure as cold posts go
> pacing toward what I know.

Stafford continues his quest for unity, and for the way of life such understanding would impart, throughout all his volumes. The last line of "Vocation," the concluding poem of *Traveling Through the Dark*, is a sort of commission to poets and to all men: "Your job is to find what the world is trying to be." In "With My Crowbar Key" he reveals how he conducts his search:

> I do tricks in order to know:
> careless I dance,
> then turn to see
> the mark to turn God left for me.

That mark is often hard to find; and most men rarely look for it. Perhaps the anxiety Stafford feels because of the discrepancy between the way men live and the way they ought to live intensifies in *Traveling Through the Dark*. The title poem of the volume deals with the difficulty of finding the right path. The poem's speaker stops his car to push a recently killed doe off the mountain road, where the carcass is a driving hazard, into a canyon. Her belly is still warm: the doe is pregnant, and the fawn inside her is still alive. In this moment, as Dennis Lynch suggests, the poet realizes that everything in the scene—the poet, the deer, the fawn, the car, and the reader—is "traveling through the dark." But although the thoughtless killing seems an ill omen, no despair creeps into the poet's voice, only resolution: "I thought hard for us all—my only swerving—, / then pushed her over the edge into the

river." Even in the dark, the search must continue. In "The Poets' Annual Indigence Report," Stafford asks other poets, and readers, to commit themselves to finding the right road: "Our shadows ride over the grass, your shadow, ours:— / Rich men, wise men, be our contemporaries."

The Rescued Year again includes poems on all Stafford's principal topics, but there may be a few more poems about the human past here than in earlier volumes. Hazard Adams says that the poems of *The Rescued Year* are often "dramas where the point is to recapture something or to face its disappearance, its loss, and yet to gain by having been there." *The Rescued Year* contains many poems in which the speaker confronts memories of relatives, friends, his hometown. In "Some Shadows" he recalls the hard frontier life of his parents. His mother was uncomfortable in the wilderness: she was "foreign—a stranger." His father was "a lean man, a cruel" man. Yet, although his childhood must have been troubled, the speaker cannot let go of

the "shadows" of his past. For better or worse, they are something to hold on to, to gain some sort of resolve from, in a present where "Hawks cling to the barrens wherever I live. / The world says, 'Dog eat dog.' " Just how pervasive these memories are for the speaker is reflected in his choice of images: his father's nickname was Hawk.

One of the finest of these memories is recounted in "Fifteen." The speaker recalls an incident that happened years earlier, when, as a boy, he found an overturned motorcycle and its thrown rider in the grass. The boy righted the motorcycle, which was still running, and "admired all that pulsing gleam, the / shiny flanks, the demure headlights." He led the bike to the road, helped its dazed owner to his feet, and watched as the bike roared out of sight. This experience is savored because, like the tactile image of the exploring hand in other poems, it serves as a metaphor for the questing imagination. Talking of himself and the motorcycle as he stood with it at the roadside, the speaker says, "we indulged / a forward feeling, a tremble. I was fifteen." By reminding the reader of his age here, he makes that *tremble* the important thing in the passage. It was the pulsing of the bike, its urgency to be off down some road, that sent the boy's imagination off beyond what he knew of life at that time—and the memory still spurs the poet's mind to find new roads. These are the memories to cultivate, and *The Rescued Year* imparts several.

Sister Bernetta Quinn interprets the title of *Allegiances* (1970): "To the creatures that compose life's daily procession and the Spirit that sustains it, [Stafford] pledges his allegiances, a term seldom used in the plural." In all his volumes Stafford makes clear his allegiances to all those elements of existence capable of teaching him something about how to live. Often in *Allegiances*, as the transcendent properties of these elements are revealed, the poems take on the proportions of myth. Stafford's approximations of myth have been noticed by George S. Lensing, who attempts to explain the technique by which the poet achieves such effects. According to Lensing, myth seeks to disclose the unity of "the divine, the human, and the sub-human." Stafford works toward such disclosure by "pursuing 'patterns' of allusive but peculiar psychic power." By arranging powerfully evocative images in significant patterns, the poet calls attention to the mythic possibilities of the images. These images are everywhere. In a letter to Lensing, Stafford says, "myth comes at you in the way it did before it was formulated by anyone else. It comes from the influence on us all the time—gravity, wind, time, the

immediacy of near things and the farness of far things—everything that touches you." Stafford constantly tries to jolt his reader into seeing these everyday things in ways that seem fresh, to make each reader apprehend them as if he were the first man to do so, so that their special qualities, forgotten over the long history of civilization, may again be appreciated.

In "Some Autumn Characters" he describes Rain and Cold strikingly, using personification and unusual syntax:

> uninhabited islands hear crisp Rain
> come toward them, their caretaker all winter
> everywhere in the woods trying
> to fasten down the leaves
>
> Cold . . . raps every night
> at doors of lonely farms, moans
> all night around the barn, and cracks
> his knuckles late, late,
> at the bedroom window.

So effective is the poet at realigning his reader's vision of these things, that by the time he gets to the third element described, a special afternoon, the reader is ready to believe the poet's "myth": "And One Afternoon each year / is always yours. . . . where everything counts." Startled a little, the reader, for a moment at least, believes in the import of this afternoon, and of any afternoon.

In "A Sound from the Earth" the famous warrior Crazy Horse's grandfather is turned into a legend, whose voice, "like the thrum of the hills / made winter come as he sang." In his song the old man indicts his audience:

> Boy
> where was your buffalo medicine?
> I say you were not brave enough, Boy.
> I say Crazy Horse was too cautious.

In all his poetry Stafford calls for men to find the spirit once invoked by that buffalo medicine, to recapture a voice "like the thrum of the hills," to reaffirm the allegiances that count.

In *Someday, Maybe* (1973) Stafford investigates, as he does throughout his canon, the steady passing of time. The years figure sometimes as a barrier in the landscape of a poem, sometimes as a disturbance of the weather. In "Friend" the poet muses on the losses coming with years that are described as "a sufficient storm," blowing "over horizons . . . , steady and long." When young, the poet "ran that storm." But he "walks it now," and all but one of his friends are gone, "lost, even on my inner sky." Having learned to treasure whatever time leaves him, the poet keeps this one remaining friend in his thoughts, almost as a talisman, a symbol of the spirit inside any living soul: ". . . that boy: undeterred, / he runs on through the withering world."

Stafford writes well of leave-takings, noting with calm acceptance the death of a beloved pet in "Old Dog": "the far, clear mountains we had walked / surged back into mind." He summarizes what losing someone to time feels like in "A Girl Daddy Used to Know":

> The people we choose are
> the chosen people. But you look back,
> you look back, and the stupid heart,
> too dumb, too honest, never gets lost.

Such loss leaves the poet with two things: a memory of the lost one, to which intuition can bring at least a flicker of life; and a feeling that the dead know what the intuition of the living reaches out to find. In love the poet seeks out these memories as part of his quest. And in some of his finest poems his intuition, guided by that love, leads him unerringly back to his chosen people.

Stafford's latest group of poems is the first section of his volume of collected poems, and the section lends its name to the whole book: *Stories That Could Be True* (1977). The poems have their share of such stories: narratives recounting trips into the poet's terrain; "myths" in which the forces of nature sometimes speak, as in "Heard Under a Sign at the Beach," where the wind says, "When you meet me and bow / I remember our meetings, / the joy." There are poems of moral commitment, and forays into the past. Stafford is still trying to startle the reader, to make him notice the possibilities for revelation around him, trying to mark a true path. The third part of the "Stories That Could Be True" section is entitled "Learning to Live in the World."

In the last fifteen years or so, Stafford's audience has grown, and so has the critical attention paid him. Some critics find fault with him on various accounts: he has published too much; he occasionally lapses into preachiness; the less rigorously structured poems sometimes degenerate into mere discussion; the trail is not always clearly marked (his language is too cryptic to convey meaning). Noting what he considers a growing flaccidity of language in the later collections, William Heyen suggests, "Perhaps the poet is less of an instrument, less of a receiver, and more of a shaper than Stafford believes him to be. Maybe the line between poetry and everyday language is a little thicker than Stafford would concede." Richard Howard says, in *Parnassus*

(Spring/Summer 1974), that the lack of articulation, of development, in his work makes Stafford a minor poet: "the poems accumulate but they do not *grow*; they drift like snowflakes into a great and beautiful body of cancelling work. . . ."

But by far most of the critical response has been favorable. Heyen praises Stafford's best work for its "undefinable sense of myth and prophesy." Linda Wagner concludes that Stafford is "a man ably equipped as a poet, a man who observes his world as naturally as he draws breath." In a brief review in *Harper's* (August 1967) Louis Simpson calls Stafford a true poet. One of the most succinct appraisals of his work comes from the citation of the National Book Award judges who selected *Traveling Through the Dark* for the poetry award in 1963: "William Stafford's poems are clean, direct and whole. They are both tough and gentle; their music knows the value of silence." That Stafford's is an important voice worthy of study, and of respect, cannot be disputed. He offers a unique way into the heart of the world. —*Steve Garrison*

Other:

The Voices of Prose, edited by Stafford and Frederick Candelaria (New York: McGraw-Hill, 1966);

The Achievement of Brother Antoninus: A Comprehensive Selection of His Poems with a Critical Introduction, edited by Stafford (Chicago: Scott, Foresman, 1967);

Poems and Perspectives, edited by Stafford and Robert H. Ross (Chicago: Scott, Foresman, 1971).

Interviews:

Sam Bradley, "Reciprocity vs. Suicide: Interview with William Stafford," *Trace*, no. 46 (1962): 223-226;

"The Third Time the World Happens: A Dialogue between William Stafford and Richard Hugo," *Northwest Review*, 13, no. 3 (1973): 26-47.

References:

Hazard Adams, "Place and Movement," *Poetry*, 110 (April 1967): 42-44;

Roger Dickinson-Brown, "The Wise, the Dull, the Bewildered: What Happens in William Stafford," *Modern Poetry Studies*, 6 (Spring 1975): 30-38;

Charles F. Greiner, "Stafford's 'Traveling Through the Dark': A Discussion of Style," *English*

Journal, 55 (November 1966): 1015-1018, 1048;

William Heyen, "William Stafford's Allegiances," *Modern Poetry Studies*, 1 (1970): 307-318;

Richard Hugo, "Problems with Landscapes in Early Stafford Poems," *Kansas Quarterly*, 2 (Spring 1970): 26-47;

John Lauber, "World's Guest—William Stafford," *Iowa Review*, 5 (Spring 1974): 88-101;

George Lensing and Ronald Moran, *Four Poets and the Emotive Imagination: Robert Bly, James Wright, Louis Simpson, and William Stafford* (Baton Rouge: Louisiana State University Press, 1976), pp. 177-216;

Lensing, "William Stafford, Mythmaker," *Modern Poetry Studies*, 6 (Spring 1975): 1-16;

Dennis D. Lynch, "Journeys in Search of Oneself: The Metaphor of the Road in William Stafford's *Traveling Through the Dark* and *The Rescued Year*," *Modern Poetry Studies*, 7 (Autumn 1976): 122-131;

Tom P. Miller, " 'In Dear Detail, by Ideal Light': The Poetry of William Stafford," *Southwest Review*, 56 (Autumn 1971): 341-345;

Sister Bernetta Quinn, "Symbolic Landscapes," *Poetry*, 118 (August 1971): 288-290;

Alberta T. Turner, "William Stafford and the Surprise Cliche," *South Carolina Review*, 7 (April 1975): 28-33;

Linda W. Wagner, "William Stafford's Plain-Style," *Modern Poetry Studies*, 6 (Spring 1975): 19-30.

ANN STANFORD
(25 November 1916-)

SELECTED BOOKS: *In Narrow Bound* (Gunnison, Colo.: Swallow, 1943);

The White Bird (Denver: Swallow, 1949);

Magellan: A Poem to Be Read by Several Voices (San Jose: Talisman, 1958);

The Weathercock (New York: Viking, 1966);

The Descent: Poems (New York: Viking, 1970);

Climbing Up to Light: Eleven Poems (Los Angeles: Magpie, 1973);

Anne Bradstreet: The Worldly Puritan. An Introduction to Her Poetry (New York: Burt Franklin, 1975);

In Mediterranean Air (New York: Viking, 1977).

Ann Stanford was born in La Habra, California, and has lived most of her life in that state. She was educated at Stanford University (James D. Phelan

Fellowship, 1938), where she received her B.A. in 1938 (Phi Beta Kappa). While still an undergraduate, she made her debut as a writer in Yvor Winters's volume, *Twelve Poets of the Pacific* (1937). She later attended the University of California, Los Angeles, where she received an M.A. in journalism in 1958, an M.A. in English in 1961, and a Ph.D. in English and American literature in 1962. During her student years in Los Angeles she worked as an executive secretary (1957-1958), an instructor in journalism (1958-1959), and a poetry workshop instructor (1960-1961). Since 1962 she has taught English at California State University, Northridge, formerly San Fernando Valley State College. Stanford married Roland Arthur White, an architect, in 1942, and they have three daughters and one son. She currently resides in Beverly Hills, California.

Stanford's poems have appeared in many magazines and have been widely anthologized; she has recorded several for the Library of Congress. Her narrative poem *Magellan* received the Commonwealth Club of California Poetry Silver Medal in 1959. "Pandora" won first prize in the 1960 Borestone Mountain Poetry Awards and appeared in their *Best Poems of 1960* collection; over twenty other poems have appeared in other Borestone Mountain *Best Poems* annual selections. In 1968 she received the Shelley Memorial Award, given each year by the Poetry Society of America to an American poet for distinction in poetry, and in 1976 she won the Alice Fay di Castagnola Award of the Poetry Society of America for *In Mediterranean Air*, then a work-in-progress. In addition to other honors and awards, she has received numerous fellowships and grants, including National Endowment for the Arts Grants (1967, 1974). Stanford has served as critic and juror for various awards, including the James D. Phelan Awards in Literature (1966), the awards to literary magazines of the Kentucky Commission on the Arts (1973), the Avery Hopwood Awards of the University of Michigan (1973), the Bush Foundation Fellowships for Artists (Minnesota) (1977), and the National Poetry Series (1979). She has been cofounder and coeditor of the California State University (Northridge) Renaissance Editions from 1968 to 1970; a member of the editorial board of *Early American Literature* from 1971 to 1973; and a member of the advisory board of the Writing Center at California State University, Los Angeles, in 1977-1978. She is currently a regional vice-president of the Poetry Society of America (since 1970); a member of the advisory board of the Wallace Stevens Society (since 1976); and poetry consultant to the Huntington Library in San Marino, California (since 1976).

Our Town

This is the village where we grew

Our fathers and their sires in line
The trees they planted shade the ~~street~~
And the white houses shine.

We knew the owner of the store.
The preacher was the parson's son
And if one brother went to war
There was another one.

We ~~kept good~~ tended order in the town
Our lawns were trim, the hedges green
And in the country side around
The furrows straight and clean.

We went to church and ~~kept~~ the law
And voted on election day.
~~The soft round hills protected us.~~
The ~~burning towns were~~ far away.
battle always

And when the soldiers came to town
Erect, with our flag overhead
We watched them from the courthouse lawn
Until they shot us dead.

"Our Town," revised typescript

About her poetry Stanford comments: "I try to set down the inner experiences of human beings, especially their relationships to time and the world. The expression is by means of imagery drawn from the visible, especially the natural, scene. The verse forms vary from traditional metrical verse to free verse in long or short cadences." Primarily within the last twenty years Stanford has established her reputation as a significant American poet. In her major volumes *The Weathercock* (1966), *The Descent* (1970), and *In Mediterranean Air* (1977), she is a poet of clarity as well as illusiveness. Her lyricism is always in evidence, especially in the poems of nostalgia and reflection. There is a touch of the metaphysical in her poetry although she is steeped in the classics and obviously enjoys displaying her classical background. Her poems are sometimes intensely personal, often reflecting her California landscape, yet there is a universality to the imagery that more than compensates for any self-indulgency. Her poems are concise and thought-provoking; she employs both rhymed and unrhymed forms, and her originality in the handling of the dramatic monologue is always refreshing and often brilliant.

The Weathercock is divided into two sections: the first contains poems that deal mostly with reminiscences in which the turbulent imagery suggests an underlying disturbance in the poet. Significantly, the first poem in part 2 is entitled "Metamorphosis," and the imagery immediately turns toward a more positive nature: "Toward rivieras turning on the sea, / Designs in apricot on southern walls." As if the title of this transitional poem were not enough, Stanford prepares the reader for the change in tone:

> If we should change
> Is not this the season?
> Rich branches push
> Past frost and night
> And pliant fabrics rush
> Toward the brown shapes of summer.

Part 1 suggests the different directions Stanford takes in her poetry. "The Sailor on Circe's Isle" illustrates her love for the dramatic monologue and anticipates her later use of this form in *In Mediterranean Air*. In this poem she assumes the persona of one who hears "the waves / Crashing like chains to break / The shoreline of a dream." The feeling of futility and loss becomes even more apparent in the final stanza:

> I stay within an isle
> Of acts abruptly ended,
> Of glimpses and detail.
> Offshore the sky
> Echoes the flat sea.
> Sand drifts over the ship.

In the prize-winning poem "Pandora," also in part 1, the narrator again finds unhappiness. Although Pandora's opening the box brings calamity to the world, the poet suggests that she "never suddenly opened the lid." Unfortunately "nothing is changeless," and in the last stanza Pandora's ultimate futility is described: "the silver sifts from the box / On my hair and my tears, and the owner is gone, and I— / I shall never be rid of it." Robin C. Spencer in a review of *The Weathercock* for the *Hartford Courant* (1 May 1966) calls the first eight lines of "Pandora" "brilliantly descriptive and sensuously alive." Indeed, they illustrate well

Amanda Blanco

Stanford's descriptive techniques and confident use of sensuous imagery:

> Never, never again the house new or youth precise
> Or the fresh loaves of hay in the field.
> And the tree bark shimmers black and white
> Only after rain.
>
> The day rose clear-faced and quick
> Breathing lemon and sage, undoubtedly crystal,
> Fog was for coolness, not to get lost in, and the wicked
> Rode to ominous music.

There is a sustained mood of peace and tranquility in "Pastoral on the Back Nine," but there is also a playfulness that may not at first be apparent. By using the back nine of a golf course as a metaphor for the waning years of life, Stanford aptly describes how this area "waits like gentle years for everyman" and how "we come here / Our burdens on our shoulders, and the plan / Defined by hazards." For any golfer who has played a round in the early morning while the dew is still out, these lines are pointedly accurate: "Where in the city is the grass so green / Or made for walking through?" Such lyricism is balanced by her witty description of the air as "a crystal from whose myriad panes / A ball can bounce and veer and ricochet."

The Weathercock has been highly praised by critics. In his review of *The Weathercock* for the *Los Angeles Herald-Examiner* (22 May 1966), Marvin Laser writes: "The sustained lyricism of Ann Stanford's new volume of poems draws its nourishment not only from her acute powers of observation but from her penetration beneath the surface of simple things and common experiences into the paradoxes and mysteries she finds there." Donald B. Johnson, in his review for the *Worcester Sunday Telegram* (1 May 1966), says, "The poetry of Ann Stanford bears the stamp of the classicist. . . . She works easily and well in the traditional poetic discipline—a practice increasingly rare." Stanford describes herself accurately enough in the title poem's last two lines: "In the vast spinning world, I still point true. / I fly here."

The Descent includes translations from Euripides and the *Bhagavad Gita* (her translation of the complete work also appeared in 1970), an elegy to John F. Kennedy, a number of dreamlike allegories, and poems based on well-known paintings. Throughout the volume, there are always the essential Stanford qualities: precise and evocative imagery, classical beauty, and a nostalgic lyricism.

Three poems from *The Descent* serve as excellent examples of her virtuosity. "Night Rain" expresses the love she has for nature: "I am sleepy and warm / I dream of the great horned owl / Snatching birds like plums out of trees," and in "Night of Souls," one of her favorite poems, she suggests a deep understanding of nature's denizens:

> Small beings moving in the midnight grasses,
> Light in the thoroughfares underfoot
> The mole's house hung with the mole's breath
> As with candles, and the busy air
> Clouded with light. . . .

In another of her favorite poems, "The Beating," Stanford displays an awareness of brutality and physical cruelty in lines as memorable for their harshness as the previous poem is for its sensitivity: "The first blow caught me sideways, my jaw / Shifted. The second beat my skull against my / Brain. I raised my arm against the third." May Swenson says of "The Beating," "Psychological blows are told in body-language; through sixteen tight lines the reader feels the knockdowns, is bruised and made sore, but in the two concluding stanzas gathers also the courage to turn from victim to hero."

In *The Descent* Stanford embraces more, experiments more, and accomplishes more than in her earlier work. By choosing to descend "into solidness / . . . where the birds / Alone choose wings for crossing my old sky," she deals more with the actual world and its transience. As May Swenson says, "The rhythms are new in this brave book; in technique, too, Miss Stanford is reborn." Frances Howard in a review for the *Boston Globe* (22 March 1970) calls *The Descent* "a distinguished book. Ann Stanford's voice, in an age of almost hysterical striving for effect, does not shout but speaks eloquently and clearly, with a beautiful economy of phrase, and what she says does not have to be said twice."

Stanford's finest book of poetry is *In Mediterranean Air*. This volume, divided into six parts, begins with the poet's writing of the comfort and security of "the house, the lake, the shore" and of the dangers lurking outside this "ring," where "the enemy waits / Circling and stalking the house in the center." The volume then proceeds through landscape poems, poems of painful and pleasant reminiscences, a classical sequence, and bestiary pieces until the final poem, "The Design," in part 5. Through a careful self-analysis the poet, and reader as well, has learned to accept life outside one's secure circle:

> Happiness itself is a terror.
> I can only conclude with the secret:
> it is the wall of thorns; it is the fruit in the parlor;
> it is the flight and the chase; it is the disillusion;
> it is what we are all afraid of.

Although part 5, the section from which this volume draws its title, is a favorite of Stanford's, her poetic power is never clearer than in the classical poems based on Greek and Roman myth. Part 3, "The Women of Perseus," tells the stories of Perseus and those around him who have suffered. Through a series of dramatic monologues, Stanford includes her interpretation of Medusa. The poet is able to evoke sympathy for Medusa by portraying her rape by a god. Medusa is depicted as a victim of the caprice of "the old man"; she "had never seen a god before." Now she is alone, a prisoner:

> The prisoner of myself, I long to lose
> the serpent hair, the baleful eyes, the face
> twisted by fury that I did not choose.
> I'd like to wake up in another place,
> look for my self again, but there recur
> thoughts of the god and his misdeed always—
> the iron arm, the fall, the marble floor
> the stinking breath, the sweaty weight, the pain,
> the quickening thrust.

Still, part 5 is the highlight of the collection. It is a spy story, and although the reader does not learn all the details of the situation, he nevertheless feels what the pursued and the pursuer feel. It is in this section that the reader becomes completely aware of the confidence Ann Stanford has in her poetic abilities. She moves from the spy to the prey with equal sureness—each is seen through the other's eyes—but sympathy remains with the spy: "I've stayed out here so long my head is ablaze with blossoms." This is the thought of the perennial outsider, and Stanford makes one feel for him, sometimes humorously and sometimes poignantly.

Ann Stanford is a thoroughly modern poet, knowledgeable in the foibles of modern man, yet she is proud of her classical background and enjoys cloaking her poems in mythology. She likes to recall her past; however, she is always reserved in her treatment of personal subjects. Critics generally agree about her place in contemporary poetry. Frederick Shroyer, the *Los Angeles Herald-Examiner* literary editor, calls her "one of the finest poets writing today." Kenneth Rexroth considers her "a very significant poet indeed." James Dickey says, "Her poems are both very quiet and very imaginative—and beautifully written. . . . She's just a pleasure to read." Finally, Carla Hoffman, one of Stanford's former students, in reviewing *In Mediterranean Air*, describes her as "unadorned, unassuming, exquisite. Both the woman and the work."

—*Linwood C. Powers*

Other:

American Literary Scholarship, 1964, includes an essay by Stanford (Durham: Duke University Press, 1966);

American Literary Scholarship, 1965, includes an essay by Stanford (Durham: Duke University Press, 1967);

American Literary Scholarship, 1968, includes an essay by Stanford (Durham: Duke University Press, 1970);

The Bhagavad Gita: A New Verse Translation, translated by Stanford (New York: Herder & Herder, 1970);

"Anne Bradstreet," in *Major Writers of Early American Literature*, ed. Everett Emerson (Madison: University of Wisconsin Press, 1972), pp. 33-58;

Women Poets in English: An Anthology, edited by Stanford (New York: McGraw-Hill, 1973).

Periodical Publications:

FICTION:
"The Burning of Ilium," *Poetry*, 120 (September 1972): 357-359;
"The Old Couple," *Poetry*, 127 (October 1975): 30-32;
'Dreaming the Garden," *New Yorker*, 55 (7 May 1979): 42.
NONFICTION:
"The Experience of the Poem," *Writer*, 80 (December 1967): 20-23;
"May Swenson: The Art of Perceiving," *Southern Review*, 5 (Winter 1969): 58-75;
"Poetry as Work," *Writer*, 85 (October 1972): 18-20;
"The Elegy of Mourning in Modern American and English Poetry," *Southern Review*, 11 (Spring 1975): 357-372.

Reference:

May Swenson, "Cheek by Jowl, Eight Poets," *Southern Review*, 7 (1971): 954-961.

MARK STRAND
(11 April 1934-)

BOOKS: *Sleeping With One Eye Open* (Iowa City: Stone Wall Press, 1964);
Reasons for Moving: Poems (New York: Atheneum, 1968);
Darker: Poems (New York: Atheneum, 1970);
The Story of Our Lives (New York: Atheneum, 1973);
The Sergeantville Notebook (Providence, R.I.: Burning Deck Press, 1973);
Elegy for My Father (Iowa City: Windhover Press, 1973);
The Late Hour (New York: Atheneum, 1978);
The Monument (New York: Ecco, 1978);
Selected Poems (New York: Atheneum, 1980).

Mark Strand was born on Prince Edward Island, Canada, and did his undergraduate work at Antioch College in Ohio, where he completed his B.A. degree in 1957. During the next two years he attended Yale University, receiving the Cook prize and the Bergin prize; his B.F.A. degree was conferred in 1959. The following year he spent at the University of Florence on a Fulbright fellowship. Strand married Antonia Ratensky in 1961; they were divorced in 1972, and in

1976 he married Julia Garretson. Strand received his M.A. degree in 1962 from the University of Iowa, where he worked for three years as an instructor in the department of English. He has lectured and taught at a number of colleges and universities, including the University of Brazil, Mount Holyoke College, the University of Washington, Columbia University, Yale University, Brooklyn College, Princeton University, Brandeis University, the University of Virginia, Wesleyan University, and Harvard University. During this period he was the recipient of a second Fulbright fellowship (1965-1966), the Ingram-Merrill Foundation grant (1966), a National Endowment for the Arts Grant (1967), and a Rockefeller Foundation grant (1968). In addition to these honors, Strand was also the first winner of the Academy of American Poets' Edgar Allan Poe Award for *The Story of Our Lives* in 1974, the same year he received a Guggenheim Fellowship. In 1975 he received an award from the National Institute of Arts and Letters and in 1980 a fellowship from the Academy of American Poets.

Initially, Strand's first volume of poetry, *Sleeping With One Eye Open* (1964), was met with virtually no critical comment, but the questions he raises in the book are provocative foreshadowings of the thematic concerns of all his subsequent verse. The restlessness of his personae—as evidenced by the title poem—and the general sense of apprehension and foreboding form the dark backdrop for all

```
For a moment
in the unpredictable storms that sometimes flame up
things farthest away come back; clouds crack
slipping under their dark hoods, small farms
and houses slide down patched hillsides,
oxen with brown-and-white hides
drift in the immense fields. Trees blaze,
black flies swarm, tiers of screaming gulls
form giant funnels above the slow rolling swells of the bay.
It is a sudden upheaval and a swift return,
and the dead come back, lifted from the dark
of their own dust and clay, sit
in their Sunday best and breathe
the long sea wind looping the hill at dusk.
In this flying arrival of things farthest away,
I see someone enter the shapes of myself, over the years discarded,
and come forth into the parched clearing of the present,
and fall to his knees, and beg me to stay.
```

Revised typescript

Strand's writing. In poems like "The Map," he generates what Richard Howard so perceptively describes as "the tenantless decorum of alienation, of *otherness*":

> For being, the map is as it was:
>   A diagram
> Of how the world might look could we
>   Maintain a lasting
> Perfect distance from what is.

Strand's attempt to maintain a lasting "Perfect distance from what is" contributes to the atmosphere of isolation in poems like "Sleeping With One Eye Open" and "Dreams." In the first, the poet figure is unable to sleep because of the uncanny silence of his house:

>   The shivers
> Wash over
> Me, shaking my bones, my loose ends
> Loosen,
> And I lie sleeping with one eye open,
> Hoping
> That nothing, nothing will happen.

A second kind of isolation occurs in "Dreams," where the speaker observes: "we / Feel dreamed by someone else, / A sleeping counterpart / Who gathers in / The darkness of his person / Shades of the real world." Perhaps an allusion to Descartes's epistemological searching in *The Meditations*, Strand's image sets the stage for what becomes a dominating concern in his later work—the relationship between the objective self of the physical world and the "other" less-definable self that has its being in the subjective consciousness. Likewise, his hope that "nothing, nothing will happen" prefigures his existential wrestling with fundamental ontological issues.

The sense of fear so pivotal in his first book carries over to *Reasons for Moving* (1968), where the settings of many poems are strikingly similar to those in *Sleeping With One Eye Open*. In "Violent Storm," a companion poem to "Sleeping With One Eye Open," the poet figure, who tends "To believe the worst is always waiting," is frightened by the physical storm that makes "an almost human sound." The poet seeks reassurance against the unknown elements of existence, assuming the same wishful posture so characteristic in Strand's first book.

> How we wish we were sunning ourselves
> In a world of familiar views
> And fixed conditions, confined

> By what we know, and able to refuse
> Entry to the unaccounted for.

But the desire for "fixed conditions" does not diminish the violent force of the storm:

> A cold we never knew invades our bones.
> We shake as though the storm were going to hurl us
>   down
> Against the flat stones
> Of our lives. All other nights
> Seem pale compared to this, and the brilliant rise
> Of morning after morning seems unthinkable.
> Already now the lights
> That shared our wakefulness are dimming
> And the dark brushes against our eyes.

The poet's attempts to find relief from the fear occasioned by violence and uncertainty are as futile as his efforts to "hide / Before the duplicating presence / Of . . . mirrors." He realizes the necessity of dealing with himself as he is rather than projecting an image that is fundamentally derivative in nature.

Confrontation with the self is a central motif in Strand's second book, and in "The Man in the Mirror," the poet's persona stands before his own reflection and ponders the mystery of his alter ego: "You seemed to rise and fall / with the wind, the sway / taking you always farther away, farther away."

But the image of the "other" never disappears entirely, and in *Darker* (1970), Strand's third book, the poet continues to dramatize his central theme, man's separation from himself. In "My Life by Somebody Else," the speaker addresses an alien side of his own ego. With mastery of tone and imagery, Strand depicts the split in a typically conversational style, reviewing his own futile attempts to attract and "capture" the alter ego:

> I have done what I could but you avoid me.
> I left a bowl of milk on the desk to tempt you.
> Nothing happened. I left my wallet there, full of
>   money.
> You must have hated me for that. You never came.

> I sat at my typewriter naked, hoping you would wrestle
>   me
> to the floor. I played with myself just to arouse you.
> Boredom drove me to sleep. I offered you my wife.
> I sat her on the desk and spread her legs. I waited.

For Strand, the quest for self-realization is the most formidable obstacle man must overcome if he is to achieve authenticity and wholeness. The speaker in the poem is driven to uncover his "other" self, even though there are inherent dangers in such uncovering. There are clear indications that the poet figure fears the undesirable results of his examination. He leaves a bowl of milk—will the other self be animalistic? He leaves a wallet—will he tempt a thief? He offers his own and his wife's body—will he arouse a homosexual or an adulterer? But for Strand, these considerations are clearly peripheral in light of the overall quest for self-realization. By the final stanza, the poet's declarative style has undergone a complete change; he now questions the possibility of ever achieving union with his other self. In the final lines, even the poet himself has exited, leaving the poem's completion to "Somebody else."

Why do you never come? Must I have you by being
somebody else? Must I write *My Life* by somebody else?
My Death by somebody else? Are you listening?
Somebody else has arrived. Somebody else is writing.

In terms of his philosophical stance in "My Life by Somebody Else," and in other poems like it, Strand exhibits a number of traits characteristic of classic existential thought. In particular, his methodology is reminiscent of Martin Heidegger's, who, in rejecting Platonic interpretations of truth as adherence to Ideal Form, accepts a more primitive notion of truth as *aletheia*, which translates as "to be taken out of hiddenness." "My Life by Somebody Else" might be read as a poetic analogue to this concept of truth when considered in light of Heideggerian standards. As Strand comments in a 1971 interview, "To say that an assertion 'is true' signifies that it uncovers the entity as it is in itself. Such an assertion . . . points out, 'lets' the entity 'be seen' in its uncoveredness. The *Being-true* (truth) of the assertion must be understood as *Being-uncovering*." Instead of attempting to construct an image of himself that will fit into a preconceived pattern, the poet is concerned with uncovering his other self as it is in all its mystery. He does not mold a desired image; rather, he allows it to reveal itself, to demonstrate its own truthfulness. The resemblance of Strand's perspective to Heideggerian existentialism is not limited to the poet's methodology. Like many modern writers, Strand is aware of what it means to confront "Nothing," *das Nicht*. As James Crenner points out in a review of *Darker*, "Strand's nothing" is "similar . . . to that of Heidegger, is the very source of *being*, of whatever there is."

The poet's "black maps" are stark reminders of man's painful and elusive attempts to "rise into being":

The present is always dark,

Its maps are black,
rising from nothing,
describing,
. . . .
its emptiness,
the bleak, temperate
necessity of its completion.
As they rise into being
they are like breath.

In *The Story of Our Lives* (1973), Strand attempts to come to terms with reality through the imagination. Much like the woman in Wallace Stevens's "The Idea of Order at Key West" who must "order words of the sea," Strand's persona in "To Begin" creates a world out of emptiness. It is an effort at imagining a world into existence: "He stared at the ceiling / and imagined his breath shaping itself into words." The poet figure forces himself to say words that, in turn, will prefigure a real world. The process is slow and uncertain. It is ephemeral and unordered, but it is an essential step in the direction of poetic and metaphysical order:

In the dark he would still be uncertain about how to
                                                          begin.
He would mumble to himself; he would follow
his words to learn where he was.
He would begin.
And the room, the house, the field,
the woods beyond the field, would also begin,
and in the sound of his own voice beginning
he would hear them.

But even this successful creation is short-lived because Strand understands that we must create and recreate endlessly if we are to maintain this reality. In "The Story of Our Lives," Strand clearly points to this need for continual creation. In the second part of the poem, he reinforces the notion that we fashion our own existences through our imaginations:

We are reading the story of our lives
as though we were in it,
as though we had written it.

But all must face the pessimistic knowledge that "The book will not survive. / We are the living proof of that. / It is dark outside, / in the room it is darker."

"The Untelling" picks up where "The Story of Our Lives" concludes. The poet figure's attempt to give relatives an account of a day he has recently spent with them illustrates the pain and inherent inaccuracy of any effort to chronicle truth. The more the man tries to describe what he believes has taken place, the more paralyzed he becomes:

Layle Silbert

His pursuit was a form of evasion:
the more he tried to uncover
the more there was to conceal
the less he understood.
If he kept it up,
he would lose everything.

His attempts to "uncover" meet with failure, and the poem concludes with the poet beginning once again to write it. Unlike the situation in "To Begin," where the poet has no objective experience from which to fashion his story, the poet figure in "The Untelling" has all the objective reality he can stand. His problem is that of selectivity, not creation from nothing, and it becomes apparent that the anguish of fashioning truth from reality is as real for Strand as the pain of making a poem out of the raw material of subjective consciousness.

In all of his poetry Strand expresses longing for two things: to understand and come to terms with the self/self split, and to maintain the relationships of love and caring for those close to him. Although five years separate the publication of *The Story of Our*

Lives and the poet's latest major collection, *The Late Hour* (1978), his central concerns are still intact. Likewise, the pivotal imagery of darkness continues to predominate and his introspective demeanor is largely unchanged. In "For Jessica, My Daughter," for instance, he wonders "how it is / such small beings as we / travel in the dark / with no visible way / or end in sight," and he admits to his continuing fear of "the dark and faraway." However, in this poem Strand's fear is at least partially offset by the vague hope that "something" will overcome the darkness, will act as a light "that would not let us stray too far apart!":

Afraid of the dark
in which we drift or vanish altogether,
I imagine a light
that would not let us stray too far apart,
a secret moon or mirror,
a sheet of paper,
something you could carry
in the dark
when I am away.

Although his effort is to pinpoint something that will stay the chaos of separation brought on by "darkness," his imagined hope in *The Late Hour* is clearly overshadowed by the recognition that human relationships cannot be maintained and that the alter ego will always remain an amorphous puzzle as painfully present as it is elusive. In "Poems of Air," perhaps the finest poem in the volume, it is clear that the "sheet of paper" alluded to in "For Jessica, My Daughter" is not the metaphysical "light" that will penetrate the "indelible dark."

The poems of air are slowly dying;
too light for the page, too faint, too faraway,
the one's we've called The Moon, The Stars, The Sun,
sink into the sea or slide behind the cooling trees
at the field's edge. The grave of light is everywhere.

Some summer day or winter night the poems will cease.
No one will weep, no one will look at the sky.
A heavy mist will fill the valleys,
as indelible dark will rain on the hills,
and nothing, not a single bird, will sing.

The skepticism of "Poems of Air" carries over to most of the poems of the book, including "About A Man," where Strand continues to examine the relationship between his authentic self and the "mirror" self. The dramatic situation is identical to that in *Reasons for Moving*, in which his persona confronts his image in the mirror: "Would get up at night, / go to the mirror and ask: / Who's here?" The final two sections of the poem point up Strand's desire for meaning even though he recognizes the "nothing inside":

> Would take off his clothes and say:
> My flesh is a grave with nothing inside.
>
> Would lean to the mirror:
> You there, you, wake me,
> tell me none of what I've said is true.

In the final poem of *The Late Hour*, Strand comes as near as he ever does to explicitly stating the reason for his pessimism.

> down in myself the shouting
> has stopped, has given up.
> I feel we are night,
> that we sink into dark
> and dissolve into night.

Strand's primary poetic quest in all his work is to come to terms with himself through a confrontation with elements of his own psychological makeup that are "unremembered, unorganized, unthought of." His own analysis of this effort in the 1971 interview offers an instructive perspective from which to view his poetry:

> The sense of self I have is coordinated and related in ways that depend on a high degree of selection. It is a chosen self. The way memory is chosen. But the raw self is me, too, just as I am also much more than I choose to remember at any given time. I'm in touch with only a small portion of my experience at any one time and this gives my life as it is verbalized an artificiality that experientially it doesn't have. Also, it could be said, I suppose, that the artificiality is real because it is all we know for sure. The rest is supposition—and maybe metaphorical: that is, the true self may reside in the unremembered, unorganized, un-thought of.

One knows so little about the self that what he does know is reductive and one-sided in favor of "perpetuating a self that will survive because it maintains the illusion of self-control."

Strand's poetry is characterized by a number of basic elements that he shares with many contemporary poets. He emphasizes plainness of diction, relies on occasional surrealistic techniques to provide the imagistic structure of his poems, and makes frequent use of journalistic techniques. Additionally, a strong narrative voice provides the framework for a good number of his finest poems. His striking cadenced voice, first heard in *Reasons for Moving* and developed in *Darker*, sets him apart from his contemporaries. When he achieves this voice and speaks for himself in his poems, he is without rival.

The economy of Strand's verse is a measure of his own ego, his own metaphysical intuitions about the limitations of man's reality. This is not to suggest that because of such limits man is incapable of consequential and meaningful existence, but only that in Strand's work one senses a reduction to the bone of all perception. Strand strips events and situations to their barest essentials, writing like a man who knows only a few words with which he must explain, or at least exhibit, all that one knows of himself. Strand is a sayer, not an explainer. Within the scope of his writing he does not analyze and does not prescribe. He strikes a pose, or many poses, and, quite simply, speaks. In his romantic poems such as "The Man in the Mirror," one finds the shadow of Whitman's persona in "The Looking Glass," although Strand's vision is not of universal harmony but of personal loss. In this respect, his work is both existential and ontological. It is existential because it is dominated by everyday images and rituals of human existence, which are expected to furnish clues for understanding man's philosophical, psychological, and religious make-up. On the other hand, it is ontological because Strand confronts the idea of Being, of what it means to exist, as it were, in the shadow of "Nothing."

At times, Strand is a poet of profound solitude and frightening loneliness. Even the narcissism of poems like "The Man in the Mirror" or "About A Man" is a welcome relief from the stark solipsism so characteristic of much of his poetry. At his best he is a man alone, who, in the solitude of his darkened arena, fights daily battles for sanity and form. But the form he achieves, like that of such disparate precursors as Robert Frost and Wallace Stevens, is temporary.

Strand tells us that we are, like him, fundamentally alone and, by virtue of this loneliness, fundamentally free to determine what sort of existence we want to have. He speaks of sad choices. He is convincing and sure and certainly a deft craftsman. But one senses that Strand is unwilling or unable to liberate his poetry from the restraints of his own artistic control. In the 1971 interview, he speaks of the feelings of liberation he experiences when he reads Kafka, and he defends the "uncontrolled" elements of Henri Michaux's "Prose Poems." But, ironically, Strand's statements reveal his own tendency to back away from things when they begin to get out of control. With all the solipsistic elements of his verse, Strand is perpetually concerned with "keeping things whole," with organizing them and stating them in such a way that they will not fall apart. In a sense this is the effort of all great poetry— to order things that may not really be ordered, to stay confusion if only momentarily, but often Strand steps in too soon to control events that are not yet out of hand. Too often he reacts not to chaos but to the threat of chaos. What the reader is left with after several volumes of significant poetry is a voice crying metaphysical wolf more convincingly than any other poet alive today. If Strand can recognize this tendency and write, as James Dickey puts it, for dear life, he has it in him to become one of the finest American poets of his generation.

—*Thomas McClanahan*

Other:

The Contemporary American Poets: American Poetry Since 1940, edited by Strand (Cleveland: World, 1969);

The Poetry of Mexico, edited by Strand (New York: Dutton, 1970);

18 Poems from the Quechua, edited and translated by Strand (Cambridge, Mass.: Halty Ferguson, 1971);

The Owl's Insomnia: Selected Poems of Rafael Alberti, translated by Strand (New York: Atheneum, 1973);

Carlos Drummond de Andrade, *Souvenir of the Ancient World*, translated by Strand (New York: Antaeus Editions, 1976);

Another Republic: 17 European & South American Writers, edited by Strand and Charles Simic (New York: Ecco, 1976).

References:

Harold Bloom, "Dark and Radiant Peripheries: Mark Strand and A. R. Ammons," *Southern Review*, new series 8 (Winter 1972): 133-141;

"A Conversation with Mark Strand," *Ohio Review*, 13 (Winter 1972): 54-71;

James Crenner, "Mark Strand: Darker," *Seneca Review*, 2 (April 1971): 87-97;

Richard Howard, *Alone With America Essays on the Art of Poetry in the United States Since 1950* (New York: Atheneum, 1969), pp. 507-516.

MAY SWENSON
(28 May 1919-)

BOOKS: *Another Animal* (New York: Scribners, 1954);

A Cage of Spines (New York: Rinehart, 1958);

To Mix with Time: New and Selected Poems (New York: Scribners, 1963);

Poems to Solve (New York: Scribners, 1966);

Half Sun Half Sleep: New Poems (New York: Scribners, 1967);

Iconographs: Poems (New York: Scribners, 1970);

More Poems to Solve (New York: Scribners, 1971);

New and Selected Things Taking Place (Boston: Little, Brown, 1978).

May Swenson was born in Logan, Utah. She earned a B.S. at Utah State University in 1939 and worked as an editor at New Directions Press between 1959 and 1966. She was a poet-in-residence at Purdue University in 1966-1967 and has been instructor in poetry at the University of North Carolina at Greensboro, Lethbridge University in Alberta, Canada, and the University of California at Riverside. In 1976, she was a member of the staff at the Bread Loaf Writers' Conference. She has received numerous awards, fellowships, and grants for her work in poetry, including a Guggenheim Fellowship (1959), National Institute of Arts and Letters Award (1960), a Ford Foundation fellowship for drama (1965), a Rockefeller Foundation grant (1967), two National Endowment for the Arts Grants (1974, 1976), and an Academy of American Poets Fellowship (1979). She has spent most of her life in or near New York City, currently lives at Sea Cliff, New York, and has traveled to the Southwest during recent winters.

What is most immediately impressive about May Swenson's poetry is its visual inventiveness. She is a master sculptor in the medium of language; she is best known for her shape poems, which she prefers to call "iconographs." Her forms, however, are multidimensional, and although their surfaces are finely chiseled and polished, what is even more interesting are the colors and depths of her perception, which are intimately and organically connected to the final form. Her aim, both in visual and verbal image, is to make actual and vivid the natural and mechanical objects of her world. Ann Stanford has called Swenson "the poet of the perceptible. No writer employs with greater care the organs of sense to apprehend and record the surfaces of the world. She is the exemplar of that first canon of the poet—*Behold!*"

Although the technical device of typographical arrangement, as in her shape poems, is the most obvious means Swenson employs to convey her perceptions, she uses almost every available kind of artifice, including elaborate verbal arrangements, metrical variations, rhymes, assonance, alliteration, and onomatopoeia. Her use of capitalization for emphasis and odd marks of punctuation or omission of punctuation are similar to techniques of Emily Dickinson, to whom she is often compared. In her accurate, detailed images, especially of nature, her poems are sometimes like those of Elizabeth Bishop or Marianne Moore. Her shape poems recall the art and craft of George Herbert: both she and Herbert are equally concerned about making the shape more than a mere contrivance, a functional and essential feature of a poem's sense. The shapes Swenson makes on a page are, however, even more daring, real challenges even to the modern printer. Also, like William Blake's deceptively simple poems, Swenson's poems are easy enough for children to read and enjoy but are also often symbolic and visionary. In the simplest of her poems, there are always many things going on, many interconnected levels and poems-within-poems beneath simple surfaces. Her work demands careful reading and rereading.

In her preface to *More Poems to Solve* (1971), a collection of her riddles for children, Swenson comments on the aim and craft of a poet: "The poet works (and plays) with the elements of language, forming and transforming his material to the point where a new perception emerges: something simple or ordinary may be seen as wonderful, something complex or opaque becomes suddenly clear." As a result of her constant search for a unique angle of vision and as a result of novel techniques for recreating familiar images, the most ordinary objects in Swenson's poems—cats, watches, eggs, suns, waves, blankets, lions, kites, DNA molecules, turbojets, birds, trains, fountains—become extraordinary as she forces them into a new light. In a single poem such as "Horse and Swan Feeding," swans, humans, and horses may merge while each retains its own integrity as an object described in intricate detail. In this and other poems, masculine and feminine human images are mixed with animal: "Her kingly neck on her male / imperturbable white steed-like body / rides stately away." This is typical of Swenson's technique, a juxtaposition of simple objects so that they reveal by comparison and contrast elemental features of their natures.

The objects that fill Swenson's poems are not her only subjects, which are often larger and more complex than the surface images. Critics have lamented that Swenson, especially in her early work, rarely attempts to focus on humans and human relationships; but she often approaches the subject of humanity obliquely through poems that, for example, seem on first reading more about animals and other natural objects. As a result, her poems about physical love, described in terms of trees or horses or flowers and bees, are more sensual than most poets generally would dare. Her concern for the art of perception has also led her into questions and problems of epistemology: how do we know what we know?; what perceptions can we trust?; is to-be-bound-by-our-senses a pleasure of life or a curse? Not surprisingly for this "poet of the perceptible," solipsism is the ultimate fear. She is also concerned about metaphysics, especially questions about the nature and state of death and whether or not life outside the physical body is even possible, or preferable. Swenson is wise enough, in most cases, to present the questions and to illuminate the paradoxes of possible answers. Quite naturally, one of her favorite forms is the riddle, again deceptively simple ones. In this form can be seen most clearly her refusal, often noted, to fix objects with names. Richard Howard has said, "The refusal, or the reluctance, to *name* in order that she may the more truly *identify* is what we notice first about May Swenson's poetry." Ironically, a poet who wants her reader to see things most vividly believes sincerely, almost nostalgically, that objects present themselves most directly and powerfully when they are seen simply as themselves, primitively, as in a time before any object was fixed or defined forever, and therefore limited, by a name or a language.

In *Another Animal* (1954), the centaur of the title poem, "straddled between beast and human," is the chief theme and image. In the volume's first poem, "Feel Like a Bird," both Swenson's fine art of accurate detail and her questions about man as an other or as a different animal are evident: "feel like A Bird / understand / he has no hand." The contrasts multiply, all leading to a central question: is a "hand better / than A Wing?" There are advantages to both alternatives, of course, and Swenson does not choose. The theme is reiterated in "Evolution," as natural objects like stones and trees long to assume human characteristics like feeling and speaking; and humans, on the other hand, would like to assume properties of natural objects such as endurance. The contrasts resolve finally in man's favor, for evolution has brought him to the higher pleasure of love and physical relationships with other humans. But more usually Swenson does not resolve the question. She finds instead much pleasure in merging human and animal together in a single image, as in "Beast": "my Brown self / goes on four paws / supple-turning in the lewd Gloom." Double images run throughout the volume, one image a metaphor for the other and neither dominant. A landscape is described in terms of twin jaguars, and both the animals and the features of geography are vivid and exact, as though one is camouflage for the other. A shift in perception, a blink of the eye, transforms one instantly into the other. Swenson's craft in these poems is the art of the magician who, through superimposition, tricks man's perception. Also in these early poems is ample evidence of her keen perception and concern for accuracy of detail; all her images are vivid, especially in their colors and textures: "Colors of horses like leaves or stones / or wealthy textures / liquors of light." Or the eyes of a bird are described: "in neat head like / seeds in A Quartered Apple."

Other subjects in this first volume, subjects to which Swenson returns later, are death, physical love, and poetry. In a short sequence of poems, she alternates contrasting visions of death. In "Why We Die," death is the inevitable wish "because we want to die / and be as dead / as things that / lacking thought beget / no hope and no regret." In the next poem, "I Will Lie Down," the persona becomes one with nature, lying down among grass and leaves, burnt meadows. The calm and beauty of the natural images again make death an attractive state of being. But in "Question," one of Swenson's finest, the poet regrets the loss of the body in death: "Body my house / my horse my hound / what will I do when you are fallen." The physical element is essential, and the persona cannot imagine being separated from it. The fourth poem in the sequence, "The Greater Whiteness," alternates white, gray, and black to indicate that death is a changing and relative state.

The sensuality, even sexuality, of Swenson's poems is oblique but not subtle. The usual method is to employ a single object as a means of describing sexual activity in suggestive terms. The masculinity of the central object in "Sun" is apparent in its "ruthless rip through cumulous" clouds. The sun will "spurn their shy caresses and erect / an immediate stairway to passion's splendid throne." In another poem the accurate and detailed description of an acrobat "astride his swing in space" can be read on a parallel level. And in a poem with the apparently innocent title "Boy in Canoe," the boy "propels his cradle / through uterine blue."

An early argument for organic form and natural images in poetry is in the poem "Satanic Form." Modern, artificial structures, "Things metallic or glass" or "Brick beams receptacles vehicles," are images of "unwilling form," the Satanic form that should be avoided. These are "blasphemies"; what are "blessed" are "Flower and stone not cursed with symmetry / Cloud and shadow not doomed to shape and fixity / The intricate body of man without rivet or nail / or the terrible skirl of the screw." Although Swenson includes many modern images among her poems, images often from life in New York—traffic and subways, office buildings and superhighways— the simple, direct language and natural forms always grow organically out of her subjects.

In *A Cage of Spines* (1958), Swenson includes a number of poems that continue this investigation into the nature of poetry, the form it should take, and the kind of altered perception that makes it possible. In "Her Management" the superiority of Nature's art and her refusal to "place, relate, or name / the objects of her hall" are compared to man's feeble

Thomas Victor

May Swenson [signature]

need to name and define. This is a keynote for this volume, which also introduces Swenson's first series of riddling poems where she, in imitation of nature, refuses also to name. These are simple, fun poems where objects are described so vividly that they finally need no names. Each stanza is a clue: "What's inside? / A sun? / Off with its head / though it hasn't any / or is all head no body / a / One." This is a riddle for an egg. There are others for snow ("Fresh dainty airily arriving"); fire ("a red-haired beast"); butterfly ("little chinks / of mosaic floating"); and hand ("nimble animal or five-legged star").

A witty poem that develops this refusal to name to its logical extreme is "Two-Part Pearable." The problem again is the human practice of naming and defining, and thereby limiting, nature. In the first section of the poem, one pear tree, among many fruit-bearing pear trees, has no fruit: "It is a shock / and a pity to see / a pear tree / that can't be / but is." In the second section, in an imaginary country where the only fruits on pear trees are their leaves, one strange tree bears pears, "not yet named of course." The odd tree in each case violates the code of language, the practice of naming and defining. This is the kind of dogma that Swenson in her use of language persistently negates.

Also about poetry, "The Red Bird Tapestry" and "Fountain Piece" deal with the questions of art and nature and the role of the poet. Like William Butler Yeats's gilded birds, the red bird in the tapestry that the persona is stitching is "more beautiful because he is artificial"—thought instead of actuality. The bird in "A cage of gilded spines" becomes an emblem for the poet who is "the cage that flatters him now." Similarly, in "Fountain Piece," reality and artifice are juxtaposed in the image of a real bird perched upon the stone wing of a fountain shaped like an angel. The actual and the artificial function side by side, but in sensibility they clash. The fountain's "stone cheek smiles / and does not care / that real tears / flow there." Here as in other poems in the volume, Swenson is fascinated with the implications of art and perception and with questions about the ultimate reality of both. In "The Cloud-Mobile," she observes, "Only my watching proves / that island has being, or that bay." Limited by perception, peculiar angles of vision, what is ultimately more real—the city itself or the image of the city upside-down reflected by a pond in the park in "Water Picture"? The images themselves seem constantly to be changing, shifting into each other and yet remaining themselves, as in "To Her Images," where a woman's hands rising and falling on the keys of a piano are also the long necks of

swans dipping to their reflections in water. Or in other poems, the shadow of a poplar tree is also a feather; a forest of pines with "erect tails," "lashes of boughs," "fur needles," and "slits of green light" is also a cat. Swenson's approach to her art is described: "Staring at here, / and superposing then, / I wait for when, / What shapes will appear?"

Other notable poems in this second volume include animal poems, poems about sexuality, about New York, and about death. In "The Centaur," as in Swenson's animal poems of the first volume, animal and human merge, this time in the image of a girl who rides a willow stick for a horse. The girl is both horse and rider in a blend of images that include erotic implications: "I shied and skittered and reared, / stopped and raised my knees, / pawed at the ground and quivered." The first of Swenson's cat poems, "Waiting for *IT*," is also in this volume. Like other poems about cats to follow, her careful observations of cat behavior and her ability to assume thoroughly the angle of vision available to a cat come together in a remarkable poem. Swenson's cats always have something to tell the reader about the nature of reality and the limitations of human perception. In "The School of Desire," another poem about animals and humans and sexuality, the intimate relationship of a horse and horse master are described in detail, straightforwardly on one level and erotically on a parallel level. Also the relationship of two female animals, a tiger and a lion who live companionably together in the Bronx Zoo, is sympathetically described in "Zambesi and Renee." The New York poems contain vivid images of the metropolitan landscape. Swenson's descriptions of trains and train rides are especially good: "Preserved from weather, tidy, on display, / We are chosen fruits in a jar." And Brooklyn is "A shelf of old shoes / needing repair, / but clean knots of smoke / are being tied and untied." Finally, "Death, Great Smoothener" continues her preoccupation with death, this time as a benevolent image.

In *To Mix with Time* (1963), Swenson includes a selection of poems from the two previous volumes and a collection of new poems among which is a group of European poems, images from France, Spain, and Italy. In these poems she strives for something different: a new, more reflective voice, with lines less tightly composed. Her keen observations are still depicted in almost picture-postcard-perfect images, but often this new voice lacks resonance and definition. Occasionally, however, a new dramatic element is redemptive, especially in "Death Invited," where the awful death of the animals in Spanish bullfights is personified in the bull itself. The word *Death* is always substituted for *bull*; after each "Death is dragged from the ring," the cycle begins again: "Here comes trotting, snorting death / let loose again." In a more quietly dramatic poem, "A Boy Looking at Big David," the impact of Michelangelo's statue is conveyed in the boy's lament that he is himself so small that he can touch only David's cold marble toe. The relationship between the small human form, which is sensitive and responsive, to the great art object, which is literally larger-than-life but silent, is the kind of paradoxical juxtaposition that recurs in Swenson's poetry.

Many poems in this volume are again about poetry and perception. In "Let Us Prepare," the persona wants "to get beyond the organic" because the physical body limits perception: "What if it is sight that blinds / hearing that deafens / touch that makes us numb?" This fear that the very nature of humanity forecloses the possibility of ever fully understanding the human dilemma, the nature of the universe, or God is repeatedly stated in this volume. The logical extreme, solipsism, is the fundamental terror of "The Primitive," in which all perceptions are questioned. From the viewpoint of a primitive human, there is no certitude at all that the mountain path he is walking leads anywhere or is in fact anything except a construct of his own eye. Symbolically, his only choice is to continue to walk, "Forward, forward." But he does so without conviction: "am I sure of this? What if, for instance, / I do make the path with my eyes? / And since it is on the mountain, / I am making the mountain?" The series of poems at the beginning of this volume is full of such epistemological and metaphysical questions. These poems are also characterized by unusual patterns of lineation, which are as erratic and unpredictable as the personas' questions are frenetic:

> What
> is it about,
>   the universe
>   the universe
>   about
> us stretching out? We within our brains within it think
>   we must unspin the laws that spin it. We think
>   *why* because
>   we think
>   *because.*

These poems are all trials, lines literally casting out across the page, trying to understand laws of the universe, to "get / out of my / head and / into the / world," to overcome the limitations of flesh, to understand the nature of God, who may Himself

even be a construct of the human mind, a fulfillment of the human search

for what could not be	Found
What can't be	Found
is	Changeless
It is	God
The	Name
is clue The	Thing
is	Lost
	Somewhere

This volume of unusual range, from these unconventional forms and philosophical problems to the softer, longer lines and conventional shapes of the European poems, also demonstrates Swenson's more familiar talent for detail and for inventing novel angles of vision. "Distance / and a certain light," according to one poem, "makes anything artistic." Her subjects are as freshly revealed as ever. The modern art she finds "At the Museum of Modern Art" is not in the galleries but in the lobby, where the forms are more natural and organic: "The shifts and strollings of feet / engender compositions on the shining tiles." In another poem, a cat has difficulty in understanding snowflakes, which seem to him like odd white flies that "have no body and no buzz" and leave his feet mysteriously wet. The most peculiar angle of perception in these poems is the invention of a tourist from another planet who has difficulty in understanding traffic "Southbound on the Freeway": "The creatures of this star / are made of metal and glass. / Through the transparent parts / you can see their guts."

The volume also has Swenson's first poem about man's flight into space, a subject she returns to in subsequent volumes. "Landing on the Moon" expresses the fear that all mystery and imagination will be taken out of the moon when myth becomes reality and is walked upon. She also returns to older subjects, death and sexuality, and there is one riddle poem, but there are not as many poems on these subjects as in the two previous volumes.

Half Sun Half Sleep (1967) is a book primarily of sharp details and wordplay. The first poem, "After the Dentist," is a simple, vivid description of trying to drink coffee, smoke a cigarette, and put on lipstick before the effects of novocaine have worn off. The book has no grand themes or statements but includes simple observations in the company of much fun with language. An intriguing poem is "The Watch," which shows Swenson's power to anatomize an object and all its parts. In this case the watch, personified as a sensitive girl to whom the persona is obviously emotionally attached, is taken to a

MAsterMANANiMAl

	A	M	N
AniMAte MANANiMAl MAttress of Nerves	6	4	4
MANipulAtor Motor ANd Motive MAker	4	4	2
MAMMAliAN MAtrix MAt of rivers red	5	5	1
MortAl MANic Morsel Mover shAker	3	4	1
MateriAl-MAster MAsticAtor oxygeN-eAter	6	3	1
MouNtAiN-MouNter MApper peNetrAtor	3	3	4
iN MoNster MetAl MANtle of the Air	3	3	3
MAssive wAter-surgeoN prestidigitAtor	3	1	1
MAchiNist MAsoN MesoN-Mixer MArble-heAver	4	5	3
coiNer cArver cities-idols-AtoMs-sMAsher	3	2	1
Electric lever Metric AlcheMist	1	2	0
MeNtAl AMAzer igNorANt iNcubAtor	5	2	4
cANNibAl AutoMANANiMAl cAllous cAlculAtor	9	2	4
Milky MAgNetic MAN iNNoceNt iNNovAtor	3	3	7
MAlleAble MAMMAl MercuriAl ANd MAteriAl	8	6	1
MAsterANiMAl ANd ANiMA etheriAl	7	3	3
	73	52	40

M with Title 55

A   77

N   42

52 M = 55
73 A = 74
40 N = 41

40

Correct counts
without title

"MAsterMANANiMAl," annotated typescript

"watchfixer" for an operation: "I / watched him / split her / in three layers and lay her / middle—a quivering viscera—in a circle on a little plinth." Every intricacy is described in human terms. The poem is a curious mixture of sympathy and amusement, for the persona is overanxious about the whole process. Swenson manages these multiple tones with the grace of a master artist. The poem works because it is well tempered and composed, a miniature portrait of the idiosyncrasies of human nature. In another poem in this volume, "The Secret in the Cat," the watch image recurs as the persona takes the cat apart "to see what made him purr." In this volume there is also a response to a letter from Elizabeth Bishop, a poem that echoes and elaborates on Bishop's descriptions of a pair of colorful birds native to Brazil. Colors are in fact a major feature of Swenson's art, and they often assume symbolic importance. In "Colors without Objects," she uses the metaphor of a biological culture under a microscope—all the pure bright colors of moving shapes in miniature—for her own perception of the world, which is likewise full of mostly meaningless but beautiful colors. Only rarely do "a few / iridium specks of idea" float by "in the culture of my eye." Color is so essential, in fact, that in "The Blindman" the different textures of colors, how they taste and feel, are learned as a substitute for vision. In a group of poems, "A City Garden in April," this consuming need to make the natural world vivid in all its shapes and colors is fulfilled in descriptions of objects in a garden.

Swenson takes some risks in her experiments with language in *Half Sun Half Sleep*, the most daring of which is the typographical arrangement of "Of Rounds." The poem is about all the rounds of the sun, its planets and all their moons. The two moons of Mars are repeated "round round," and likewise the twelve moons of Jupiter and nine moons of Saturn are represented visually by repeating the word *round* twelve times and nine times in columns down the page. Finally, words are abandoned altogether, and a cluster of asterisks represents the unknown body around which the whole solar system revolves. The value of this as poetry may be questioned, but the novelty of it, its visual inventiveness, can hardly be doubted. Also depending on typographical arrangement is a riddle, "Out of the Sea, Early," where the words assume the shape of a sun rising above a horizon. But the poem works primarily because its language is exact and vivid, and the typographical form is simply a finishing touch. Another good riddle, "Fable for When There's No Way Out," describes the dilemma of a

chick hatching from his shell. His vision is limited to his embryonic world, but he pecks away at the shell anyway, wondering, "what's the use." And when to his amazement he finds "A way he hadn't known or meant" and the shell begins to crack, he emerges with aphorism: "Rage works if reason won't / When locked up, bear down."

Four poems in the volume deal more directly with metaphysical questions. Both "The Kite" and "The Truth" are on one level vivid descriptions of fascinating objects, a kite and a snake. But the kite is also a face or mask struggling between "The tug of the void" and "the will of the world." The snake is emblematic, even visually in the snakelike arrangement of the poem on the page, of truth that is likewise shifting and unpredictable. Another poem that uses typography symbolically is "The Lightning," which has one continuous slash of space diagonally through the poem. Just in a second's flash there is a glimpse on an "illuminated page" of "Words of destiny." All of nature seems to know the secrets of the universe, cat, kinglet, flower. But the human persona, limited again by his own nature, wonders, "When will I grope my way clear of the entrails of intellect." Similarly, in "Gods / Children," the angle of perception is like the vision of the tourist from another planet in "Southbound on the Freeway," and the final question is the double-meaning one, "Are gods . . . children . . . / *Then are gods children?*" Each of these poems confronts issues about the nature of man, God, and reality.

Half Sun Half Sleep also includes two poems about man's experience in space and three poems describing man's sexuality in terms of natural objects. "After the Flight of Ranger VII" again deals with the impact scientific study has on man's perceptions of the moon, the sad loss of imagination. "August 19, Pad 19" is written from the perspective of an astronaut about to blast off. In "All That Time," two trees embrace and assume masculine and feminine roles; although she seems the passive "upright one" and he the leaner, she also is "the most stubborn" and he the "willing" one. The paradoxes in human sexual relationships are thus made clear. In another poem, "Four-Word Lines," the male and female are identified with a bee and a flower: "I'm a flower breathing / bare, laid open to / your bees' warm stare." And in "Swimmers," the central figures are human but they are not simply swimming, "Tossed / by the muscular sea"; throughout the poem the sealike rhythms of sexual activity are also described.

Swenson's fifth volume, *Iconographs* (1970), is

May Swenson

typographically the boldest and most experimental. The format of the book is larger, to accommodate some of the daring shapes and arrangements of words across the page. Almost every poem is in the shape of its subject: a snake, a flag, a powerhouse, a movie screen, a butterfly, a trellis of roses, a bottle, a turbojet, an island, a rocky crevice. Some of the experiments also include strange nonverbal marks. "Wednesday at the Waldorf" is the oddest, with unusual typographical symbols—plus signs, colons, equal signs, and parentheses typed over each other—placed above selected words. The function of these marks is not clear, but in "Catbird in Redbud," exclamation points placed just above certain words do seem to make visual the nonverbal chatter of the bird in the tree. Two poems that use the shape design most effectively are "How Everything Happens (Based on A Study of The Wave)" and "The Mobile in Back of the Smithsonian." The poems attempt to replicate their subjects. The arrangement for the wave is novel but simple:

```
                                    happen.
                                 to
                              up
                           stacking
                        is
                     something
When nothing is happening

When it happens
              something
                    pulls
                        back
                            not
                               to
                                  happen.
```

The word design for Diego Rivera's mobile at the Smithsonian is more elaborate. On each succeeding page the mobile has assumed a different shape, to indicate the changes in its appearance as it turns; the lines are continuously curving like the shape of the mobile itself. The language of the poem also is a vivid description of the infinite variability of the mobile.

In two of the most daring poems, "The DNA Molecule" and "Science and Religion," Swenson seems to take advantage of outlandish juxtapositions. The DNA molecule is described verbally and visually in terms of Marcel Duchamp's painting *Nude Descending a Staircase*, as though to mock the exclusive worlds of science and art by forcing them together. Whether "Science and Religion" is a poem at all is questionable. It consists in fact of two news

stories taken verbatim from the *New York Times* (30 June 1968), their sentences broken carefully into lines like verse and placed side by side down two columns. One story is about the scientist's dream of placing a telescope in orbit; the other is on the possible discovery of Saint Peter's bones beneath the Basilica. Both end on questions: will America find funds for the telescope; are they really Saint Peter's bones? The gimmick almost works because the language and tone of the two stories, even the pattern of exposition, are so similar that they echo each other and together comment on the nature of the humanity that reveals itself in both stories.

Rarely does Swenson bring in the personal element in her poems. The "I" is conspicuously absent, or when present, it is somehow a remote, impersonal, more generalized first person. But two poems in *Iconographs* benefit from a more personal voice of direct, reflective experience. The persona in "I Look at My Hand" sees in herself the inherited physical marks of both mother and father and struggles with the idea that this inheritance will not be passed on in human form. All energy is going into creations of art rather than nature, and art does not replicate itself. An even better poem, which foreshadows this growing personal voice in *Things Taking Place*, Swenson's next volume, is "Feel Me." The last words of the persona's father were "Feel me to do right," and the ambiguous understandings of possible meanings are the central puzzle of the poem. The lines of this poem are longer and smoother than most of Swenson's best work thus far. This is a new range, and new sensitivities and perceptions emerge. The narrative line also becomes a stronger element: "We cannot feel our father now. His power courses through us, / yes, but *he*—the chest and cheek, the foot and palm, / the mouth of oracle—is calm." In this poem and in "I Look at My Hand," the personal, physical identification with a parent and the need for physical contact—"*Feel* me to do right"—are the full manifestation of an earlier theme in a more personal voice.

New and Selected Things Taking Place (1978) includes a generous selection of poems from five previous volumes as well as sixty-three new poems. Swenson's most characteristic techniques of word-play, riddling, and typographical arrangement are not altogether missing from this new collection, but the power of the poems comes more consistently from the depth and sensitivity of a mature vision than from verbal and visual displays. The surfaces of the poems are less like glittering, expertly cut jewels than like still, deep ponds of reflection. The poems benefit from Swenson's art of accurate detail, but the details now seem to have a larger context, a broader range of vision and perception. The first poem, "A Navajo Blanket," clearly indicates this movement outward from the details of intricate design to the borderless edges where mind is set free. The bright and geometric colors at first "pull you in, and pin you / to the maze," but then, "slipping free of zigzag and / hypnotic diamond," find a way out "by the spirit trail, a faint Green thread that / secretly crosses the border, where your mind / is rinsed and returned to you like a white cup." A strong counterpoint to this theme is evident in the last poem of this collection, "Dream After Nanook," in which more fundamental human needs for food, shelter, and clothing are articulated through the persona's complete identification with the experience of Nanook, who "Lived savage and simple, where teeth were tools." The poems of this volume are similarly more personal and spiritual, and the voice is more direct and hides less behind the masks of verbal play.

Consistent with this new voice and vision, many poems of this volume have as their subjects landscapes and seasons that are often painted as vividly and as delicately as watercolors. The presence of light is a frequent dramatic feature: "A breeze, and the filtered light makes shine / a million bristling quills of spruce and fir." Or dawn is described as "the immense / volcano, sun, about to pour / gold lava over the mountain." The details are there, as they always are in Swenson's poems, but the vistas are wider and more inclusive, and the effect is to improve the eye's farsighted vision as it looks up from separate, exactly observed objects nearer to the eye.

This is the new Swenson, but other poems in the volume are similar to earlier poems in which natural objects are described vividly and from a novel angle of perception. Among these is "The Willets," which is faintly reminiscent of Elizabeth Bishop's "Sandpiper." This talent for detail is lent also to new subjects. In one of the volume's poems about man's ventures in space, "The Solar Corona," the sun "Looks like a large / pizza with too much / tomato sauce." The details of observable human behavior are also new to Swenson in "Dr. Henderson," a warmly humorous portrait of an eighty-year-old man taking his yearly sunbath on the beach, and in "Captain Holm," a thumbnail sketch of another octogenarian who still sails his boat on the bay.

This interest in describing people and relationships to people is also new. Among the best of these personal poems is "That the Soul May Wax Plump," whose subject is the death of the poet's mother. The language is a relaxed, deliberately imperfect blank verse that is graceful and dignified. The personal voice is simple and direct: "My dumpy little mother on the undertaker's slab / had a mannequin's grace. From chin to foot / the sheet outlined her, thin and tall." Similarly composed, "Staying at Ed's Place" succeeds because the tones of the language evoke the atmosphere of personal warmth essential to the poem's meaning: "I like being in your apartment, and not disturbing anything / As in the woods I wouldn't want to move a tree." And again it is this personal voice and these relaxed meters that make the best of Swenson's moon poems, "First Walk on the Moon": "There was no air there, / no motion, no sound outside our heads. / We brought what we breathed / on our backs."

As in her earliest poems, humans and animals are juxtaposed, but here there are fewer point-by-point comparisons. Animals and humans or humans and landscapes do not merge into each other but reveal each other through simple encounters. The occasion for these encounters is less contrived, less artificial, and usually more narrative. The volume's second poem, "Bison Crossing Near Mt. Rushmore," is the best example. A "herd of cars" is stopped to wait for a line of bison crossing the road. At this intersection of humans and animals, the dignity of this "strong and somber remnant of western freedom" is in sharp contrast to the impatient human drivers of "awestruck station-wagons, airstreams and trailers." This theme, the old question of the superiority of beast or human, remains the most persistent in Swenson's work, although the style, tone, metrical arrangement, and manner of presentation have all evolved into a new and more reflective language.

Critical focus has persistently been on Swenson's shape poems, riddle poems, and the verbal and visual gimmicks that immediately capture the reader's attention. Critics, like readers, are fascinated by these experiments with language, which for Swenson more often succeed than fail primarily because her first care has always been to hone the language down to the exact sense. This carefulness and concern for craftsmanship are yielding richer rewards in the best poems of *Things Taking Place*, in which Swenson too seems to have tired of gimmicks and contrivances and to have begun to develop a more directly personal voice for her perceptions. —*Idris McElveen*

Play:

The Floor, New York, 1966; published in *First Stage*, 6, no. 2 (1967).

Other:

Windows & Stones: Selected Poems by Tomas Tranströmer, translated by Swenson and Leif Sjoberg (Pittsburgh: University of Pittsburgh Press, 1972).

Interviews:

"Craft Interview with May Swenson," *New York Quarterly*, no. 19 (Autumn 1977): 14-27;

Karla Hammond, "An Interview With May Swenson, July 14, 1978," *Parnassus*, 7 (Fall/Winter 1978): 60-75.

References:

Daniel Hoffman, ed., *Harvard Guide to Contemporary American Writing* (Cambridge: Harvard University Press, 1979), pp. 601-603;

Richard Howard, "Turned Back to the Wild by Love," *Tri-Quarterly*, 7 (Fall 1966): 119-131;

Dave Smith, "Perpetual Worlds Taking Place," *Poetry*, 135 (February 1980): 291-296;

Ann Stanford, "The Art of Perceiving," *Southern Review*, 5 (Winter 1969): 58-75.

JAMES TATE
(8 December 1943-)

BOOKS: *Cages* (Iowa City: Shepherd's Press, 1966);

The Destination (Cambridge, Mass.: Pym-Randall Press, 1967);

The Lost Pilot (New Haven & London: Yale University Press, 1967);

Notes of Woe (Iowa City: Stone Wall Press, 1968);

Camping in the Valley (Chicago: Madison Park Press, 1968);

The Torches (Santa Barbara: Unicorn Press, 1969; revised and enlarged, 1971);

Row with Your Hair (San Francisco: Kayak Books, 1969);

Is There Anything? (Fremont, Mich.: Sumac Press, 1969);

Shepherds of the Mist (Los Angeles: Black Sparrow Press, 1969);

Amnesia People (Girard, Kans.: Little Balkans Press, 1970);

Are You Ready Mary Baker Eddy, by Tate and Bill Knott (Berkeley: Cloud Marauder Press, 1970);

Deaf Girl Playing (Cambridge, Mass.: Pym-Randall Press, 1970);

The Oblivion Ha-Ha (Boston & Toronto: Little, Brown, 1970);

Wrong Songs (Cambridge, Mass.: Halty Ferguson Press, 1970);

Hints to Pilgrims (Cambridge,Mass.: Halty Ferguson Press, 1971);

Absences (Boston & Toronto: Little, Brown, 1972);

Apology for Eating Geoffrey Movius' Hyacinth (Santa Barbara: Unicorn Press, 1972);

Hottentot Ossuary (Cambridge, Mass.: Temple Bar Bookshop, 1974);

Viper Jazz (Middletown, Conn.: Wesleyan University Press, 1976);

Lucky Darryl: A Novel, by Tate and Bill Knott (Brooklyn: Release Press, 1977);

Riven Doggeries (New York: Ecco Press, 1979).

During the relatively few years of his public poetic career—from the small-press publication of *Cages* in 1966 to the appearance of *Riven Doggeries* (1979) as number eighteen in the prestigious American Poetry Series—James Tate has produced more than thirty books, chapbooks, and broadsides. Such an output is rather remarkable in itself, purely in terms of the volume of poetry and short prose involved. However, when the quality of much of this writing is considered, Tate's importance in contemporary poetry needs no defense. It is true, as his detractors might point out, that many of his volumes are small-press publications and that much of his material is reprinted from one volume to another. Like Robert Kelly, although to a lesser degree, Tate has avoided major publishing houses and national coverage in support of small presses and distribution by bookshops, thereby favoring a more broadly based, grass roots trend in publishing. In the end, however, he has gathered his share of awards and acclaim.

Tate was born in Kansas City, Missouri. He was educated at the University of Missouri from 1963-1964; and he received his B.A. from Kansas State College in Pittsburg, Kansas, which he attended in 1964 and 1965. He studied at the Writers Workshop of the University of Iowa, where he received his M.F.A. in 1967. He has been a visiting lecturer in English, first at the University of Iowa, from 1966 to 1967, and later at the University of California, Berkeley, in 1967-1968. He has been an assistant professor of English at Columbia University from 1969 to 1971; and he has served as poet-in-residence at Emerson College, Boston, in 1970-1971. In 1971 he joined the English faculty at the University of Massachusetts, where he is currently an associate professor. He has also traveled and lived in various places throughout

Europe, including Sweden, Ireland, and England.

Tate is active in other areas of literary endeavor. Since 1967 he has been poetry editor of the *Dickinson Review* (published in North Dakota); and he is currently an associate editor for two presses, the Pym-Randall Press and the Barn Dream Press, both in Cambridge, Massachusetts. From 1971 to 1974 he served as a consultant for the Coordinating Council of Literary Magazines.

In addition to having *The Lost Pilot* (1967) selected to be part of the Yale Series of Younger Poets, Tate has received a number of awards and honors. He has had two grants from the National Endowment for the Arts (1968 and 1969), as well as a National Institute of Arts and Letters Award (1974), and a Guggenheim Fellowship (1976). In 1972 he was chosen to be the Phi Beta Kappa poet at Brown University.

It is difficult, if not impossible, to characterize the poetry of James Tate simply. His style is clearly his own, identifiable; but it is growing and deepening as his themes have grown and deepened. The poems themselves are rooted in landscapes that are often—if not generally—bizarre and surreal. But the worlds he creates are alive. In an essay written for Alberta T. Turner's *Fifty Contemporary Poets* (1977), Tate says, "If I like something it is alive for me. That's not strange: If you can let a plant depress you, why not love a sock?"

"Why not love a sock?" In many ways such a question embodies Tate's approach to poetry, both in theme and in technique. Critic after critic has pointed out the obvious: his imagery is dreamlike, although clear; his stance is often ironical, ranging from involvement to objectivity; his major themes confront (although some would say avoid) the confusion, terror, emptiness, or boredom that define the times. The titles of his volumes indicate his concerns: *The Lost Pilot*, *Notes of Woe* (1968), *Wrong Songs* (1970), *Absences* (1972), and so on. Even one's guardians are *Shepherds of the Mist* (1969). In a chapbook published in 1969 by Sumac Press, Tate poses, in the title, the essential question: *Is There Anything?* One year later, in one of his major volumes, he replies, again in the title, *The Oblivion Ha-Ha* (1970). He recognizes the absences; he faces them as he can; and all he can do is laugh, in the face of the truth, or in spite of it. Thus, his stance is often comic, ironic, clever; his language, his metaphors, are startling. As R. D. Rosen points out, Tate seems to have the "notion that a quality can be transferred from one experience to another, no matter how preposterous the transfer may appear. And, when done well, this is where his surrealism succeeds."

Although a large number of his early poems are narrative in shape, much of his later work has assumed this surreal patterning.

Tate had had two small-press volumes published (*Cages* and *The Destination*, 1967), and some of his poems had appeared in *Heartland: Poets of the Midwest* (1967), prior to the release of *The Lost Pilot* as volume sixty-two in the Yale Series of Younger Poets. The earlier volumes went largely unnoticed by the literary world, but *The Lost Pilot* was received with general enthusiasm and much applause. In his foreword to this volume, editor Dudley Fitts set the tone for the critical reception, calling the poetry "utterly new [and] . . . utterly confident, with an effortless elegance of control, both in diction and in composition, that would be rare in a poet of any age and that is particularly impressive in a first book." Tate was only twenty-three years old. Most reviewers responded to *The Lost Pilot* with simultaneous praise and amazement—praise for the accomplishment and amazement that one so young had done so much so well.

Certainly, not all readers were uniformly impressed. A reviewer for the *Virginia Quarterly Review* found that the poems, in spite of their successes, "lack something vital: a purpose, a sense of direction, a goal." Writing in *Contemporary Poets*, Geof Hewitt states that "in spite of all the fine use of language, only a few of the poems take on enough substance to stick." It is true that the images and juxtapositions in some of the poems, although jolting or comical or stark, often fail to connect clearly with the subject at hand. For example, in "Closing the Chamber Doors" the image of "lagoons / of sawfish coiled in / the clock's alarm" is jolting, yet its thematic function—other than disruption and allusion—is elusive.

Whatever its weaknesses, however, *The Lost Pilot* is quite a significant collection, introducing a new poetic voice, one unique and versatile and imaginative. Perhaps as much as his technique, it is Tate's imagination that elevates the best poems to successes and redeems the weak ones from a comic stance bordering on slapstick. For what he has to say is serious. His themes are, in fact, among those that readers are accustomed to find in poetry. His real people inhabit surreal landscapes; yet their actions and incidents speak of love and anger, life and death, time and loss. In such fine poems as "Coming Down Cleveland Avenue," "Why I Will Not Get Out of Bed," and "The Lost Pilot," Tate moves through various levels of elation, ennui, and sadness. With an uncanny facility he blends childhood memories, personal encounters, and the apparently inexhaustible resources of his unconscious and imagination to create an emotionally successful universe that fronts both comedy and horror. Although his stance is often ironic, he never quails from his subject; instead, he seems to be open to whatever the poems bring, a kind of faith in the creative potential of the unconscious. The end result is a volume that pleases while horrifying. As Donald Justice points out on the dust jacket, "Once despair can be taken for granted, gaiety becomes a possibility, almost a necessity." Although generally *The Lost Pilot* presents poems of loss and chaos, Tate knows how to balance them with wit and humor. He never gives in to the despair that marks much of contemporary literature.

Readers of *The Lost Pilot* saw much promise of things to come in Tate's poetry. He began to fulfill this promise in a rapidly produced string of seven small-press volumes, beginning with *The Torches* (1969). In this volume (which was enlarged and reprinted with six additional poems in 1971), he continues the themes he considered in his earlier works. The opening poem, "The Initiation," is a poem of death and darkness; and from there the poems move through a world of loneliness and despair. The landscape is frozen, as in "Vengeance" and "The Children's Indictment"; and the people are predominantly victims of violence, witnesses, or outsiders in unusual places. Yet, as in *The Lost Pilot*, the poems here do not capitulate to despair. On one level, they are elevated by Tate's wit and comic instincts; on another, there are notes of joy, as in "Little Misery Island": "I do not remember the last spoken word / only the wet joy / of your emerald body."

As if to underline a belief that joy only serves as a counterbalance, Tate entitled his next volume *Notes of Woe*. The territory is familiar: detached characters, surreal imagery, comic and ironic stance, sudden turns at the ends of the poems, and tones of loss and despair. The language is essentially the same, too, except that Tate allows his lines to run longer than the predominantly three-beat lines that characterize the preceding collections. All in all, *Notes of Woe* does not fare too well when compared to *The Lost Pilot*, and critics such as Ronald Moran were quick to say so. Writing in the *Southern Review*, he suggests that "Tate is apparently determined to be *new*, at whatever cost"; and he feels that the poems fail in not "coming to terms with subject matter."

Row With Your Hair (1969) continues Tate's thematic concerns, especially moods and ideas relating to love and death. The technique varies from

a successful use of surrealism to language that seems little more than clever. As R. D. Rosen has pointed out, in reference to Tate's poetry in general, "Tate has a weakness for the dream-image which is not convincing, but 'sounds right.' " In other words, when Tate's "faith in the unconscious" is not justified, his poems do not seem quite so successful. Nevertheless, this volume does succeed in its presentation of a coherent pattern of despair, from "Up Here" ("I would like to help, / believe me, but up here nothing / is possible, nothing is clear") to "Consumed" ("You are the stranger / who gets stranger by the hour").

Tate does not seem to have the need to settle matters clearly, either for himself or for the reader. He appears to be content with a balance. The opening poem of *Shepherds of the Mist*, for example, is "The Artificial Forest." And the elves of this forest walk this balance: "None knows happiness or woes." In this volume the imagery is again surreal; Tate seems most comfortable when his poems walk the line between sleep and consciousness. The comic tone likewise remains. However, the "darkness" of the earlier poems has intensified in this volume. For example, in "Mercy" "The people are killing the people / for the people." Also, in "Shepherds of the Mist," the poet says, "Piercing the silence / I yell, I'll tell you the truth / if you'll tell me! / How to suffer." Yet the balance between extremes and opposites continues even in despair, and the poem ends with a sigh of resignation: "Life is such a disappointment. / I can't go on, I'll go on." In some slight way, there seems to be an uneasy acceptance here of the realization found in "Coda" (in *Notes of Woe*): "I regret everything." But it is an acceptance with balance.

Tate's second major volume, *The Oblivion Ha-Ha*, is in some ways a collection of selected poems, for many of its sixty poems are from the volumes published after *The Lost Pilot*, including twenty-three poems from *Row With Your Hair*. As in his other books, the title is an indication of the contents: laughter in the face of—and perhaps because of — despair, a kind of laughing to keep from crying. Indeed, at least since Albert Camus, this theme has become so common that the entire thematic thread of these poems risks cliche.

In spite of its risks and repetitions, however, *The Oblivion Ha-Ha* is an important and impressive collection. The poems represent the best of James Tate to date, exclusive of the poems in *The Lost Pilot*. In this later volume the strengths and weaknesses of his style become evident. For Tate is a skilled poet, a turner of metaphors and a shaper of images. When he is terrifying, the fear is universal, as it is in "The Salute," where he "dreamed a black widow dream all night" and says "I salute / this lady with obedient white fingers / for she is a widow by choice, / and I her mate." And when his stories are captivating, there are few poets who can be more successful, as illustrated in "The Day Lost."

Tate's best poems are those that are lyrical, generally personal, surreal, and witty. Yet there is a danger in too much facility with a single style and focus, as many critics have stressed. The concensus is that Tate occasionally falls victim to such a curse. Writing in *Poetry* magazine, James Atlas says that sometimes in Tate's poetry, "The metaphor becomes a clever joke, where things appear as other things; what I find unnerving about all this is that the precision of symbolism has broken down, the clarity that graced its usage tempered by ennui." In other words, when Tate's poems fail, they fall short because the devices themselves are not sufficient to sustain the poems, because wit and jarring imagistic leaps do not fulfill the poems' promises. Or else they fail because the glibness and wit are all there is, as in "Diane Linkletter Haikus" (in *Are You Ready Mary Baker Eddy*, the 1970 volume Tate coauthored with Bill Knott): "Do not go gentle into / that ha-ha."

As Tate's career has progressed, so has his poetry. In *Absences* his development is seen clearly. The first section of the volume is comprised of sixteen poems that provide a cross section of his past performance, and it includes the difficult "The Distant Orgasm," reprinted from *Wrong Songs.* Here the themes are echoes of earlier ones; the style is identifiable; the persona is personal, highly subjective; lyricism and wit dominate. In the second section, however, Tate gives the reader something different. Entitled "Absences," this section has an epigraph from Guillaume IX of Aquitaine, part of which says: "I'll write a song about nothing at all, / Not about myself, nor about anything else." The setting is the world of sleep, and the persona is "put under a spell one night / On a high hill." The epigraph takes the reader to the heart of *Absences*, where he finds a searching through the processes and recesses of sleep and dream. The landscape is uncertain, and in the end Tate can say, "Toto, I don't think we're in Kansas." Where they are is, in fact, unknown; very little is known. It is a state of "absences," a place where "nothing comes," not even sleep ("The eye wants to sleep / but the head is no mattress"); even "His age is not known." It is a negative, if not negated, universe; and it is all created from the internal universe, where fear and confusion are bred out of the absences.

The remainder of *Absences* shows Tate lengthening his lines until the poems approach prose—in "Deaf Girl Playing" published in a separate volume in 1970), in "Two-Hundred-and-One" (first included in *Wrong Songs*)—and returning to his accustomed style. But the whole of the volume is quite successful in spite of the mixed (or cautious) reviews. Tate creates memorable lines ("Mother sings as she bundles me up so tight" in "As a Child"), startling images ("A dirty comb in the house / of the recently deceased" in "Absences"), and clever and interesting anecdotes (like the one titled "Man with Wooden Leg Escapes Prison"). Although it may be true, as some critics suggest, that the volume suffers under the burden of scholarly allusions, the burden is a light one, a weight that grows negligible quickly. These poems are grounded in realities, internal and external; and they clearly demonstrate the moral and emotional emptiness that has become associated with the twentieth-century consciousness.

In a poet who takes such joy in playing with words and language, it is difficult to tell when he is serious, when he has blundered, and when he is toying with the craft. The poems in *Viper Jazz* (1976) present such a problem. As with *Absences*, the critical responses to this volume were mixed, ranging from clear praise to lament. The word *jazz* in the title suggests that Tate has allowed himself more freedom from precision, from the denotative meanings of the words, than in earlier poems; for he takes liberties, knowing that his meaning can evolve from the jazzlike accumulation of image and impression. As usual, the imagery is surreal, and here perhaps it is even more startling than in previous volumes ("She has a nipple on her eyeball"). The humor and irony also remain; his experimentation with prose poems and longer lines continues and grows. The narrative persona has become more central; and, as William Logan points out in *Poetry*, "The world has shrunk to that central 'I,' and each of those sentences, those sad, short bits of prose, admits either an irrecoverable loss or a failure of knowledge. The presence with which these poems are most comfortable is nothing. . . ." Thematically, *Viper Jazz* continues Tate's exploration of the gaiety in the midst of the absences, the laughter in the face of death and oblivion. Above the games ("Who Gets the Bitterroot?"), beyond the use of words simply for their sounds or for humor ("Once I Was Young in the Land of Baloney"), *Viper Jazz* reaches farther and farther beyond conventional narrative. Tate is stretching more deeply into the unconscious, the illogical, the surreal, to show anew the world he sees.

The progress of Tate's career indicates an increasing concern with the manipulation of form while focusing on the same essential subjects. The critical response to his work is mixed, but the sum is nevertheless positive. Tate's poetry provides a lively and jolting characterization of the universe. His language is fresh and highly suggestive. And unlike many surrealists—including those who are his followers—he is clearly able to control the situations he creates. —*Stephen Gardner*

Other:

Lucien Stryk, ed., *Heartland: Poets of the Midwest*, includes poems by Tate (Dekalb: Northern Illinois University Press, 1967);

"A Box for Tom," in *Fifty Contemporary Poets: The Creative Process*, ed. Alberta T. Turner (New York: David McKay, 1977), pp. 315-321.

Interview:

The Making of Poetry (New Haven: Yale University Press, 1967).

Reference:

R. D. Rosen, "James Tate and Sidney Goldfarb and the Inexhaustible Nature of the Murmur," in *American Poetry Since 1960: Some Critical Perspectives*, ed. Robert B. Shaw (Chester Springs, Pa.: Dufour Editions, 1974), pp. 181-191.

HENRY TAYLOR
(21 June 1942-)

SELECTED BOOKS:*The Horse Show at Midnight: Poems* (Baton Rouge: Louisiana State University Press, 1966);
Breakings (San Luis Obispo, Cal.: Solo Press, 1971);
An Afternoon of Pocket Billiards: Poems (Salt Lake City: University of Utah Press, 1975).

Henry Splawn Taylor was born in Loudoun County, Virginia, to Thomas Edward and Mary Splawn Taylor. His father owned and operated a large family farm and was an educator, a high school principal, as well. Taylor attended the Loudoun County public schools until 1958 when he entered George School. In 1960 he entered the University of

Virginia from which he graduated with a B.A. in English in 1965. He spent 1965-1966 at Hollins College where he took an M.A. in creative writing. In June of 1965 he married Sarah Bean of Charlottesville, Virginia. The marriage was ended by divorce in 1967. In 1968 he married Frances Ferguson Carney of Norfolk, and from that union he is the father of two sons—Thomas and Richard. Since 1966 Taylor has held a number of teaching positions. Until 1968 he was an instructor of English at Roanoke College in Salem, Virginia. From 1968 to 1971 he served as an assistant professor at the University of Utah, and he was director of the University of Utah Writers' Conference from 1970 through 1972. In 1971 he became an associate professor of literature at the American University in Washington, D. C., and he was promoted to professor in 1976. From 1972 to 1975 he was the associate editor of *Magill's Literary Annual*, and he was a contributing editor for the *Hollins Critic* from 1970 to 1978.

Perhaps most significantly, Taylor's background is not only southern and rural but also Quaker. He was born into a Quaker family, within the context of a largely Quaker community, that has been located in the same place since the late eighteenth century. A deeply assumed sense of place, a constant awareness of tradition and continuity, and the serious and profoundly charitable faith of the Quakers are essential in his art. So also is his experience as a horseman. About this experience he has written: "I grew up with horses, and in fact thought my vocation would be tied up with them—thought that until I was maybe 21 or 22. In 1961 I tried out, not successfully, but not disgracefully either, for the U.S. Equestrian Team. . . . I still do enough riding to preserve my nerve and touch, and I think in terms of analogies to equitation when I'm writing. Nerve and touch, and timing."

Academically, Taylor has earned an enviable reputation as a teacher of writing, not only in college but also in the Poetry in the Schools program. His combination of anthology and textbook, *Poetry: Points of Departure* (1974), is highly regarded as a handbook of contemporary poetry. He has written significant critical studies of a number of poets, including Richard Wilbur, John Hall Wheelock, May Sarton, and William Meredith. Taylor has published translations from French and Italian poetry, and his verse translation of Euripides' *Children of Herakles*, done in association with the late Robert A. Brooks, is scheduled for publication by Oxford University Press. Finally, one should mention Taylor as performer, as a public reader of poetry, both his own and the work of others. A gifted

Recueillement   Charles Baudelaire

Sois sage, ô ma Douleur, et tiens-toi plus tranquille.
Tu réclamais le Soir; il descend; le voici:
Une atmosphère obscure enveloppe la ville,
Aux uns portant la paix, aux autres le souci.

Pendant que des mortels la multitude vile,
Sous le fouet du Plaisir, ce bourreau sans merci,
Va cueillir des remords dans la fête servile,
Ma Douleur, donne-moi la main; viens par ici,

Loin d'eux. Vois se pencher les défuntes Années,
Sur les balcons du ciel, en robes surannées;
Surgir du fond des eaux le Regret souriant;

Le Soleil moribond s'endormir sous une arche,
Et, comme un long linceul traînant a l'Orient,
Entends, ma chère, entends la douce Nuit qui marche.

GETTING HIMSELF TOGETHER   from _Desperado_

                takes
He ~~brings~~ his pain to the woods, to settle down.

Wanting the dark, he shuts the cabin door

while the town he left lies buried in thick air

he once breathed freely, watching others drown.

Back there, they run like cattle down a chute

to moo at horny theater marquees
          slobber over rubber
or ~~gag on rubber adult~~ novelties;

so he carries his pain here to shake it out

away from them. On the gray planks upstairs

old calendars are curling up like scrolls
              he can see
until all ~~that remains~~ is the painted scene

of a mermaid combing starfish from her hair
       flyspecked   Toward midnight
or a ~~faded~~ sunset. ~~At last~~ he unrolls

his sleeping bag and beds down with his pain.

                (After Baudelaire)

"Getting Himself Together," revised typescript

323

Henry Taylor

reader, he has given a great many highly successful readings all over the United States. An added, if necessarily somewhat limited, attraction to these performances is Taylor's almost uncanny ability to *impersonate*, by voice, gesture, facial expression, and often with appropriate parodic verses, any number of prominent poets of our time. Surely there is nobody else who can do a brief skit offering swift impersonations of, for example, Howard Nemerov, John Frederick Nims, James Dickey, Robert Bly, and J. V. Cunningham.

Taylor was only twenty-four when his first book, *The Horse Show at Midnight* (1966), appeared. It is, as might be expected, a brilliant and mixed performance. Not mixed in its bright virtuosity, for Taylor was from the first a skilled and demanding craftsman. Rather, the book seems widely various in its interests and potential. There are lyrics and short, amusing anecdotal vignettes he names "Snapshots." There is a whole section of parodies, sparkling parodies of the poetry of Dickey, Cunningham, Nemerov, Robert Creeley, Denise Levertov, James Wright, and Bly, most of these done on assignment for Bly's magazine, the *Sixties*, until Taylor volunteered one on Bly himself, thus ending that amiable relationship. And there are a number of longer narrative poems of remarkable accomplishment, including the title poem, and "A Blind Man Locking His House," as well as the longest, 250 lines, "Things Not Solved Though Tomorrow Came." The title poem, "The Horse Show at Midnight," shows, in essence, the sort of dramatic tension and poetic narrative structure Taylor was seeking to develop and exploit. Its flaw, if any, is that at least rhythmically it is under the spell and influence of the work (up to that point) of James Dickey. But, in an interview in *The Writer's Voice*, (1973), Taylor cheerfully announces this influence and allows that he chose to leave the title poem intact and in place for an amusing reason: "I wrote a number of poems that are very much influenced by James Dickey," he says, "the title poem, for example. I let it stand because I know that James Dickey is afraid of horses and couldn't have written it." In the same interview Taylor explains the narrative outline of the poem as simply as possible but nonetheless suggests the complex resonances of it and the mystery:

> It's in two sections. The rider speaks in the first section, and he says he has a dream vision in which everything goes absolutely right for him until the very end when he feels a distance between himself and the horse. And the horse goes out of the ring, back into his stable in a kind of dreamlike way. Then the story is retold from the point of view of the horse. . . . As he's lying in the stable, he hears the rider's call, and the heart, and the heartbeat, you know, the two heartbeats, the rider's and the horse's join together. He goes to the ring, he goes through these motions, and what happens is that we see somehow that the rider's vision carries over

From such a long, tight-knit poem it is hard to excerpt any parts without some distortion and minor damage; but perhaps these few lines at the beginning of the second section, "The Horse," can convey something of the lyrical flavor of the whole:

> In the darkened stable I move in my sleep
> And my hoof stirs the straw and wakes me.
> I rise, breathing softly, inhaling
> The moonlight outside like perfume,
> Straining to hear the command
> That moved my hoof in the straw.
> In my huge, shining shape I stand
> Listening, and I hear the calling again.
> Through the locked door of my stall.

Henry Taylor

Obeying, I march to the show ring,
Beside horses I cannot see, but feel
As their hoofs shake the air around me.

The language is simple and easy to follow by ear. But the action and the images are complex, appropriately hallucinatory. Rhythmically the poem appears to be at once formal and fairly simple, using as its ground base the kind of anapestic line that, for that time, was indeed James Dickey's trademark (a line form that poet David Slavitt, also in *The Writer's Voice*, described as being about as musical as banging a spoon on a plate a couple of times). In Taylor's hands, however, the line becomes supple and subtle, richly various with a mixture of end-stopped and run-on lines, with delicately, constantly shifting caesuras, with graceful assumptions of iambic and trochaic lines without loss of the shadowing primary rhythm. Technically it is a superbly realized poem and demonstrates much of what Taylor could do and has subsequently done. Many of these characteristics—strong narrative line and structure, the poem as contained story; simple, straightforward, auditory language wrapped in a syntax that is intended to be appropriate to the action and thus may be extremely complex; an emphasis on form, which may manifest itself in a structure of rhymed stanzas or may, also, be shown in and through the subtle use of a clearly defined rhythmic base; a subject matter of country life and matters, often including horses and riders—continue to be strongly evident in Taylor's later work even as his skills increase and are increasingly refined and as his interests and concerns shift slightly with his own growing maturity.

Breakings (1971) showed further development of several of the stances taken in *The Horse Show at Midnight*. There are no parodies this time, but there are satires of several kinds. There is an unmerciful attack on Nixon's Vietnam actions and policy in "Speech." The words of the president become molasses that pours from the poet's radio and "flows to the rug, spreads / into a black, shining puddle / slowly expands, covers / the rug with dark sweetness." This, of course attracts flies—"I can barely hear the speech / above the buzzing of their wings." After the speech is over, the flies remain.

At night, sometimes,
I can hear them
making soft liquid sounds
of contentment.

"Buildings And Grounds," on the other hand, is at once gentler and funnier, an easygoing picture of

manicured and well-tended Salt Lake City as seen by a southern boy, a country boy a long way from home, living among strangers:

I will set up on cinderblocks in the front yard
a '38 Ford with no tires or headlights,
to shelter the hound and the chickens,

I will sit in the gutted driver's seat
with a bottle of Old Mr. Mac, glaring at my
neighbors, reading aloud from *God's Little Acre,*
I will be a prophet of wildness and sloth!

But the Puritan gaze of my neighbors cuts through
my desperate vision of home—my dream house
will not flourish here.

There is one sixty-line narrative poem of considerable distinction (and horror)—"Burning a Horse"—and there are some "Snapshots." But the title poem, "Breakings," is a personal lyric, its pain and sorrow at once contained and distanced, turned to music by a deft rhyming stanza. Here is the last stanza of that poem, which, by its honesty and specificity, has earned the right to consider general implications:

So nothing changes, nothing stays the same,
and I have returned from a broken home
alone, to ask for a job breaking horses.
I watch a colt on a long line making
tracks in dust, and think of the kinds of breakings
there are, and the kinds of restraining forces.

An Afternoon of Pocket Billiards (1975) includes the seven poems that made up *Breakings* and adds to them thirty-eight new poems, making it Taylor's largest and most inclusive gathering to date. It is also, unquestionably, his best work so far, clearly marking growth and progress to match his own changes in the years since *The Horse Show at Midnight*. *An Afternoon of Pocket Billiards* is carefully structured. It is put together in four separate parts—"Breakings," "Learning To Face Extinction," "From Porlock," and "Harvest." "Breakings" and "Harvest" deal, seriously and freshly, with his favorite subjects, taken out of country life and his own and family history, as well as including a translation or two. "Learning to Face Extinction" offers some "Snapshots" and a number of witty vernacular and occasional poems. "From Porlock" is concerned, as this subtitle suggests, with aspects (chiefly satirical) of the literary life and scene. It includes the wonderfully brutal and matter-of-fact epigram "To An Older Poet":

Young for my years, impertinent, perhaps
a poet and perhaps not—so you said.

I remind you, in a momentary lapse
of taste, that when I'm your age you'll be dead.

In both the beginning and ending sections and the middle two, which serve in part as scherzo to the whole, there is a wide range of verse forms, traditional and redesigned, including two full-fledged working sestinas. There are several extensive narrative poems—"Smoking in Bed in the Fire Chief's House," "Harvest," "My Grandfather Works in His Garden," "Miss Creighton," "An Old Rhodes Scholar"—each in a different verse and stanzaic form, and, most important, the elaborate and extensive title poem of the collection, put together out of eleven ten-line, rhymed stanzas, a complex, closely observed account of the inner and outer drama of a long afternoon of billiards. (Taylor wields a pretty fair cue stick in "real life.") Chance and skill, the desire for order "beyond love's sudden vagaries," the choice to cultivate "cold skill and a force like love" in the place—"a green field of order"—"where there is neither hope nor haste," become the elements of an encompassing metaphor for the poet's personal life, half-hidden, half-confessed; for his art and craft, thus all of ours, all arts and crafts; and, in the largest sense, for all our efforts to act freely in the face of a programmed and often wholly predictable fate. It is his biggest and most ambitious poem, around which the others cluster, giving and taking warmth and meaning.

Not surprisingly, perhaps, *An Afternoon of Pocket Billiards* gained a good deal of favorable attention. May Sarton, never lavish or careless with critical praise, was unequivocal in her judgment, offered on the book jacket— "I regard Henry Taylor as the best poet of his generation." Howard Nemerov praised Taylor's "steady and grave truthfulness to the experience," adding that he "is not a fancy poet full of poetical diction, but a poet who has the art to conceal art, not to let the language get in the way." Malcolm Cowley expressed delight in the poet's voice, a voice he could describe as "unmistakably his own." In a chronicle review, in the *Sewanee Review*, Paul Ramsey celebrated the poet's "magnificent lyricism" and his "high power of generalization, gravely, passionately won." The *Virginia Quarterly Review* called the book "an exceptionally fine collection of poems" and named Taylor, without qualification, as "a major talent." Most recently, reviewing Taylor's career up to this point and treating *An Afternoon of Pocket Billiards* in some depth in *Book Forum*, poet and novelist Kelly Cherry calls the second book the expression of Taylor's "deeper, sweeter, and truer talent, the

ability to penetrate and render the characteristic rhythms of other *lives*." She continues, pointing out that "Taylor gives us more than poems; he gives us people, a series of portraits that are, above all, lifelike, as realistic as Roman sculpture, so that the old Rhodes scholar, the father and the grandfather, that fat man, the president—each is unmistakably himself, the poet respecting his material at the most profound level, on the purely ontological plane." But if Taylor's work has received some recognition from poets of an older generation and some serious and favorable attention from some of the poets of his own age, his work is not nearly so well known, yet, as it might be. In forms and content, style and substance, he is not so much out of fashion as deliberately, determinedly unfashionable. His love of forms is (for the present) unfashionable. His sense of humor, which does not spare himself, is unfashionable. His preference for country life, in the face of the fact that the best known of his contemporaries are bunched up in several urban areas, cannot have made them, the others, feel easy about him, or themselves for that matter. They have every good reason to try to ignore him.

His feeling of contempt (expressed during an interview published in 1976) for "the New York literary scene, where everybody's expending so much valuable energy stabbing other people in the back," cannot have warmed the cockles of the hearts of any number of temporary movers and shakers in the New York poetry world.

Never mind, his reputation grows as his work builds up, as he continues to write his poems. The poems keep appearing in places like the *Virginia Quarterly Review*, the *Southern Poetry Review*, the *Washingtonian*, and the *Hollins Critic*, and he reports that he is working on two separate books— "The Flying Change," whose title poem has already appeared in *New Southern Poets* (1975), and "Desperado," a fairly wild and woolly sonnet sequence of, so far, undetermined length. Some of these sonnets were published by Unicorn Press in 1979 and give a sense of what the shape and direction may be. Desperado, as *character*, shares experiences with the poet, but describes them and reacts to them in a much more rowdy, rough and ready way, albeit always within the fourteen lines of the sonnet form. When Taylor left McLean, Virginia, not long ago to build a house and a road and to live on Ferris Hill, part of the Taylor family's farm, Desperado departed from the District and its suburbs also. Leaving this insulting message behind:

POTOMAC FEVER AS LOW-GRADE INFECTION
Desperado left the suburbs of D.C.

where he had lived among politicos
and Big Names always seemed to stand too close.
On Sundays in the Drug Fair line he'd see
buying his *New York Times*, Mr. Richardson,
say, or Colson, who bought the *Star*. Now those
are days he rarely mourns in his repose
far out from town, but he had ignorant fun

strung out in downtown lobbies, where he could shout
Italian at the backside of Earl Butz
or fashion limericks on the interim
'twixt jail and Jesus, or contrive ersatz
occasions to say "Say what you like about
Mao Tse-Tung, but that old slope could swim."

It seems likely that Desperado will have more ignorant fun and will make more mischief before he's done. It seems possible that readers who care about the state of contemporary poetry will have some fun, too, discovering Desperado and through him the whole impressive body of Henry Taylor's work. —*George Garrett*

Other:

Poetry: Points of Departure, edited by Taylor (Berkeley: Winthrop, 1974);
The Water of Light: A Miscellany in Honor of Brewster Ghiselin, edited by Taylor (Salt Lake City: University of Utah Press, 1976).

Periodical Publications:

"The Halt Shall be Gathered Together: Physical Deformity in the Fiction of Flannery O'Connor," *Western Humanities Review*, 22 (Autumn 1968): 325-338;
"Two Worlds Taken as They Come: Richard Wilbur's *Walking to Sleep*," *Hollins Critic*, 6 (July 1969): 1-12;
"Letting the Darkness In: The Poetic Achievement of John Hall Wheelock," *Hollins Critic*, 7 (December 1970): 1-15;
"Vantage and Vexation of Spirit," *Georgia Review*, 25 (Spring 1971): 17-26;
"Poetry of the Movies: A Panel of Experts on *Blind Alley* Discuss the Influence of Cinema on Modern Poets," *Film Journal*, 1 (Fall/Winter 1971-1972): 36-49;
"A Road Sufficient for the Purpose," *Washingtonian*, 14 (December 1978): 81-88;
"In Charge of Morale in a Morbid Time: The Poetry of William Meredith," *Hollins Critic*, 16 (February 1979): 1-15.

Interviews:

George Garrett and John Graham, "Henry Taylor," in *The Writer's Voice: Conversations with Contemporary Writers*, ed. George Garrett (New York: Morrow, 1973), pp. 120-140;
Dan Johnson, "An Interview With Henry Taylor," *Window*, 1 (Spring 1976): 1-21.

Reference:

Kelly Cherry, "Watersmeet: Thinking About Southern Poets," *Book Forum*, 3 (1977): 264-274.

JOHN UPDIKE
(18 March 1932-)

BOOKS: *The Carpentered Hen and Other Tame Creatures* (New York: Harper, 1958); republished as *Hoping for a Hoopoe* (London: Gollancz, 1959);
The Poorhouse Fair (New York: Knopf, 1959; London: Gollancz, 1964);
The Same Door (New York: Knopf, 1959; London: Deutsch, 1962);
Rabbit, Run (New York: Knopf, 1960; London: Deutsch, 1961);
The Magic Flute (New York: Knopf, 1962; London: Deutsch & Ward, 1964);
Pigeon Feathers and Other Stories (New York: Knopf, 1962; London: Deutsch, 1963);
The Centaur (New York: Knopf, 1963; London: Deutsch, 1963);
Telephone Poles and Other Poems (New York: Knopf, 1963; London: Deutsch, 1964);
Olinger Stories (New York: Vintage, 1964);
The Ring (New York: Knopf, 1964);
Assorted Prose (New York: Knopf, 1965; London: Deutsch, 1965);
A Child's Calendar (New York: Knopf, 1965);
Of the Farm (New York: Knopf, 1965; London: Deutsch, 1966);
Verse (Greenwich, Conn.: Fawcett, 1965);
The Music School (New York: Knopf, 1966; London: Deutsch, 1967);
Couples (New York: Knopf, 1968; London: Deutsch, 1968);
Bath After Sailing (Stevenson, Conn.: Country Squires, 1968);
The Angels (Pensacola, Fla.: King & Queen Press, 1968);
On Meeting Authors (Newburyport, Mass.: Wickford Press, 1968);

John Updike

Three Texts from Early Ipswich (Ipswich, Mass.: 17th Century Day Committee, 1968);

Midpoint and Other Poems (New York: Knopf, 1969; London: Deutsch, 1969);

Bottom's Dream (New York: Knopf, 1969);

Bech: A Book (New York: Knopf, 1970; London: Deutsch, 1970);

Rabbit Redux (New York: Knopf, 1971; London: Deutsch, 1972);

The Indian (Marvin, S. D.: Blue Cloud Abbey, 1971);

Seventy Poems (London: Penguin, 1972);

Museums and Women (New York: Knopf, 1972; London: Deutsch, 1973);

Warm Wine (New York: Albondocani Press, 1973);

A Good Place (New York: Aloe Editions, 1973);

Six Poems (New York: Aloe Editions, 1973);

Buchanan Dying (New York: Knopf, 1974; London: Deutsch, 1974);

Cunts (New York: Hallman, 1974);

Query (New York: Albondocani Press, 1974);

A Month of Sundays (New York: Knopf, 1975; London: Deutsch, 1975);

Picked-Up Pieces (New York: Knopf, 1975; London: Deutsch, 1976);

Couples: A Short Story (Cambridge, Mass.: Halty Ferguson, 1976);

Marry Me (New York: Knopf, 1976);

Hub Fans Bid Kid Adieu (Northridge, Cal.: Lord John Press, 1977);

Tossing and Turning (New York: Knopf, 1977; London: Deutsch, 1977);

The Coup (New York: Knopf, 1978; London: Deutsch, 1979);

From the Journal of a Leper (Northridge, Cal.: Lord John Press, 1978);

Sixteen Sonnets (Cambridge, Mass.: Halty Ferguson, 1979);

Too Far to Go (New York: Fawcett Crest, 1979);

Problems (New York: Knopf, 1979);

Talk from the Fifties (Northridge, Cal.: Lord John Press, 1979).

John Updike was born in Shillington, Pennsylvania. Following graduation (*summa cum laude*) in 1954 from Harvard University, where he was an English major and editor of the *Harvard Lampoon*, he studied for one year on a Knox fellowship at the Ruskin School of Drawing and Fine Art in Oxford, England. On 26 June 1953 he married Mary Entwistle Pennington with whom he had four children: Elizabeth, David, Michael, and Miranda. His first marriage ended with divorce, and on 30 September 1977 he married Martha Ruggles Bernhard.

Updike has long revealed that his true ambition was to be a cartoonist, if not for Walt Disney then at least for the *New Yorker*: "What I have become is a sorry shadow of those high hopes." Still, the beginnings of his career as a writer are associated with the *New Yorker*, for that magazine published his first professional story, "Friends from Philadelphia," on 30 October 1954. Following his return from Oxford in 1955, he joined the staff of the *New Yorker*, and for the next two years he contributed to the "Talk of the Town" column. Although he ended his formal ties with the magazine's editorial staff in 1957 and moved to Ipswich, Massachusetts, to concentrate on writing, he continued his relationship with the periodical, which has been publishing his poems, stories, essays, and reviews regularly for more than twenty-five years. The move from New York to Ipswich brought the anticipated results, for by 1959 Updike had had three books published: *The Carpentered Hen and Other Tame Creatures* (poems, 1958), *The Poorhouse Fair* (novel, 1959), and *The Same Door* (short stories, 1959). His career, which would eventually earn him the reputation as a major American author, was well launched.

Critical recognition soon followed. In 1959, he was awarded a Guggenheim Fellowship and the Rosenthal Foundation Award of the National Institute of Arts and Letters for *The Poorhouse Fair* in 1960; his novel *The Centaur* (1963) won the National Book Award for fiction in 1964; his short stories have been honored with O. Henry Awards and he was elected to the National Institute of Arts and Letters in 1964, and to the American Academy of Arts and Letters in 1977.

Although his popular reputation rests primarily on his novels, Updike has proved himself a master of the various genres. Those who mistakenly think of Updike as only a novelist should examine his nonfiction prose pieces, most of which were written for the *New Yorker* and are numerous enough to fill the major portions of two books, *Assorted Prose* (1965) and *Picked-Up Pieces* (1975). In addition to the novels, volumes of short stories, and collections of essays, he has also published a play, *Buchanan Dying* (1974), and four books of poetry: *The Carpentered Hen, Telephone Poles* (1963), *Midpoint* (1969), and *Tossing and Turning* (1977). Updike takes his poems seriously, as much more than diversions between completing one novel and planning the next, but the public wrongly defines his poetry as merely light verse in the spirit of Ogden Nash. This misconception is unfortunate, for his collections of poems show a change of tone and mood from the humor of *The Carpentered Hen*, through the lyrics of *Telephone Poles* and the autobiographical poems of *Midpoint*, to the meditations on death in *Tossing and Turning*. This is not to say that he abandons humor after *The Carpentered Hen* but only to suggest that the poems of comic rhyme and verbal pyrotechnics are but one side of Updike the poet. The place to begin a reading of his verse is not with *The Carpentered Hen* but with his essay "Rhyming Max," a review of Max Beerbohm's parodies first published in the *New Yorker* (7 March 1964) before being collected in *Assorted Prose.*

Updike's appreciation of authors like Beerbohm and James Thurber and of parody in general is an outgrowth of his early desire to be a cartoonist. Understanding Beerbohm's verse parodies to be a kind of verbal cartooning, he points to the art of rhyme as an agency of comedy. Replete with regularity and rigidity, rhyme reflects the mechanical action that Henri Bergson termed a primary cause of laughter. Updike writes, "By rhyming, language calls attention to its own mechnical nature and relieves the represented reality of seriousness." Assonance and alliteration perform a similar function and join rhyme as means by which man asserts control over things. Light verse for Updike "tends the thin flame of formal magic and tempers the inhuman darkness of reality with the comedy of human artifice. . . . it lessens the gravity of its subject." Admitting in the foreword to *Assorted Prose* that his theory of rhyme as set forth in "Rhyming Max" may be wrong, he nevertheless reiterates his belief that rigidity, rhyme, and comedy go together. *The Carpentered Hen* illustrates his argument.

Steering a course between what the dust jacket calls "playfulness and sobriety," the volume begins with a quotation from Boethius's *The Consolation of Philosophy*, which associates the muses of poetry with "poison sweets" and philosophy with "healing remedies." Updike, of course, ignores this dismissal of the muse, but the epigraph indirectly warns the reader that more is going on in *The Carpentered Hen* than the surface comedy of puns and play. Beneath his celebration of the delightful artificiality of words is a respect for language itself.

Many of these early poems take to task the inane writing of journalists, advertisers, and editors. Combining verbal acrobatics such as puns and traditional stanza forms organized with amusing twists, he often parodies the venerable art of the occasional poem when he appends to many of the verses prose statements usually lifted verbatim from an ad or editorial. Thus "Duet, with Muffled Brake

Thomas Victor

Jan V pdike [signature]

Drums" pokes fun at an advertisement in the *New Yorker* that claims that the meeting of Rolls and Royce made engineering history, while "An Ode: Fired into Being by Life's 48-Star Editorial, 'Wanted: An American Novel' " comically exposes the muddled thinking of those who argue that the Great American Novel may be written to order to reflect the surface prosperity of the 1950s. Quoting parts of the editorial, and designating sections of his poem as strophe, antistrophe, and epode (parts of the Pindaric ode), he writes a parody of inspiration.

Not all of the poems are this amusing. As if foreshadowing the more somber poetry of his later collections, Updike also includes serious pieces of social observation like "Ex-Basketball Player" and "Tao in the Yankee Stadium Bleachers." These poems illustrate his lifelong interest in sports, but more important, they comment upon the ephemeral nature of physical prowess, reputation, and life itself. Readers of the story "Ace in the Hole" (*The Same Door*) and the novel *Rabbit, Run* will recognize the situation in "Ex-Basketball Player" as

John Updike

Updike describes the plight of the aging athlete whose current circumstances no longer equal the glory of past headlines. "Tao in the Yankee Stadium Bleachers" is a better poem, which muses on the proposition that "Distance brings proportion." Referring to passages of Eastern philosophy such as the dead rule longer than any king, Updike couches his thoughts on mutability in a metaphor of athletics. The inner journey is "unjudgeably long," and every man eventually files out while small boys in the grandstands wait to take their places.

These two poems do not rely upon comic rhyme and verbal play. They look forward to the short stories in which Updike effectively comments upon the sense of diminishment and loss that age inexorably brings. Yet the dominant tone of *The Carpentered Hen* is not melancholy but joy. Celebrating the vitality of language, Updike offers rhymes like *eschewed / egritude* ("Even Egrets Err"), exposes cliches ("Poetess"), and takes pleasure in the vocabulary of *iginous, xanthic,* and *zebuesque* ("Capacity"). The book appropriately ends with the twelve-page poem "A Cheerful Alphabet," which is an updated *McGuffey's Reader* designed to teach his son the wonders of a versatile vocabulary. *A* stands no longer for the apple of sin and Eden but for the still lifes of Paul Cézanne. Designating *T* for trivet, for example, and *X* for xyster, Updike shows that alphabets are cheerful and that language is alive.

His witty efforts to guard language from the stultifying effects of jargon and cliche, a primary feature of *The Carpentered Hen*, are continued in the first half of *Telephone Poles*. The occasional poem is again parodied, as in "Recital," which quotes a headline in the *New York Times*, "Roger Bobo Gives Recital on Tuba," and which goes on to play with the outrageous rhymes associated with light verse. Other poems in this section celebrate authors like Agatha Christie and Beatrice Potter for their "perfect craft," and in "The Menagerie at Versailles in 1775," Updike bows to Dr. Samuel Johnson, one of the great post-Renaissance preservers of a lively vocabulary. As a gesture of homage, Updike arranges words taken verbatim from Johnson's notebook. The point of the poem is not what it means but how it illustrates the vivacity of language used by those who care.

For all of the pleasures of the light verse, however, *Telephone Poles* is a significant collection primarily because of the serious lyrics in the second half. These poems treat many of the themes that readers of Updike's fiction have come to expect: the attractions of memory, the threat of mutability, and the pleasure of the mundane. As Updike writes in the foreword to *Olinger Stories* (1964), he needs the "quiet but tireless goodness that things at rest, like a brick wall or a small stone, seem to affirm." These poems look more to Shillington than to Ipswich as if he were trying to secure a still point before facing the changes of middle age. A testimony to his close observation of common things, the volume illustrates his statement that "a trolley car has as much right to be there, in terms of aesthetics, as a tree."

The title poem is the center of the collection. Praising the relative permanence of manmade objects and their place in the modern imagination, Updike writes, "The Nature of our construction is in every way / A better fit than the Nature it displaces." He does not mean that trees, for example, are less valuable than telephone poles but that poles testify to man's ingenuity in meeting his needs in the natural world, which must endure the yearly cycle of death and rebirth. Telephone poles may not offer much shade, but unlike elms they are both stable and utilitarian. Since their "fearsome crowns" at the top may literally "stun us to stone," the poles also serve as updated versions of ancient myths, in this case the myth of the Gorgons' heads.

Other fine poems, such as "Shillington" and "Suburban Madrigal," show Updike finding significance in the unglamorous items of the quotidian. His need to reaffirm the permanence of the past is poignantly expressed in the former when he insists upon the necessity for memory to counter the erosion by time. Sidewalk cracks are mended and vacant lots give way to buildings, but one may visit the constantly diminishing past through memory and art. The town's children who today reenact the actions of his own youth will soon face the same predicament because change is a condition "of being alive."

Perhaps the best poem in *Telephone Poles* is "Seven Stanzas at Easter." Noting how contemporary man is caught between the demands of reason and faith, Updike insists that the miracle of Resurrection must withstand the challenge by the mind if the Church is to survive: "Make no mistake: if He rose at all / it was as His body." The dilemma is nicely suggested in the key word *if* and in the speaker's description of the miracle in the rational discourse of scientific language. *If* Christ rose, He did so not metaphorically but literally. Symbols may not replace fact as the cornerstone of faith. The poet's uncertain tone reflects the predicament of intelligent modern man who would believe even while he doubts.

Updike's most ambitious collection of poems is *Midpoint.* Published when the poet was thirty-seven

330

TASTE

I have, alas, no taste (talleyrand; that
taste, that instructor of
between the draped and the
that

that advocate of the right as is reckless

My first wife had taste

I know a man with taste

"Taste," manuscript

years old, the title poem is a forty-one-page analysis of his life to age thirty-five, midpoint in the biblical span of three score and ten years. "Midpoint" is an impressive combination of autobiography, homage to past poets (Dante, Spenser, Pope, Whitman, and Pound), scientific knowledge, experimental typography, and comic tone. Defining the intellectual bearings of his first thirty-five years in order to prepare for the second half of his life, Updike explains that the poem is both "a joke on the antique genre of the long poem" and "an earnest meditation on the mysteries of the ego." "Midpoint" is not entirely successful because the parts are more impressive than the whole, but it must be read carefully by those interested in Updike's career.

The poem is too long and complex for a thorough analysis here, but some observations may be made. The general movement illustrates the poet's growth from youthful solipsism to an acceptance of his connection with all of humanity. *Point* is the key word both thematically and in terms of the poem's arrangement, for Updike not only shows that he needs an acceptable point of view to understand his relationship with the highpoints of man's history, but he also fills the second canto with a maze of black and white dots that take shape as photographs from his family album when held at arm's length.

From his current perspective, he understands that as a child he saw himself as the most prominent point in a radius of dots all secondary to him. Each person may view his experience from a single point of view at a given moment in his life, but the solipsism of the child must be toned down if he is to accept his place in the world. The pointillistic photographs illustrate his most immediate connection—the family, and the opening line parodies Whitman's celebration of self: "Of nothing but me, me / —all wrong, all wrong—." Whitman may be a significant dot in the myriad points of Updike's past, but nineteenth-century beliefs are not necessarily reliable for a twentieth-century man. The importance of appropriate points is again established in the third canto about the composition of solids, which Updike now understands to be made up of compressed particles and dots. Finally, he accepts the truth that identity depends upon love and the willingness to see life as a progression toward a metaphorical point that clears the vision of the eye / I.

Three other sections join the title poem to make up *Midpoint*: "Poems," "Love Poems," and "Light Verse." Of the three, "Love Poems" is the most impressive because the mixed emotions of desire and

guilt that are a hallmark of Updike's best short stories are poignantly expressed. These poems reflect what the shift from remembering his past to concentrating on his present has meant to his imagination. Especially good is "My Children at the Dump." Taking his children on an outing, the poet understands the parallel between the shattered dolls and toys thrown away on the dump and the children who will soon be discarded in divorce. Happy and unaware, the children feel the lure of the junk pile, but the poet knows that his need to preserve is negated by the sheer size of this hill of loss. He may love and even clutch, but his own end is clearly foretold.

Updike's recognition in *Midpoint* that he is on the down side of what he calls the "Hill of Life" forms the emotional center of *Tossing and Turning*, his best volume of poetry. He does not abandon the subject of his past, as the fine "Leaving Church Early" shows, but he focuses more than ever upon the challenges of success and suburbia. The persistence of memory, a primary factor in his earlier poems and tales, gives way to the encroachment of age. The title of the collection suggests his restlessness, and a line from "Sleepless in Scarsdale" describes his dilemma: "Prosperity has stolen stupor from me."

Two of the three long poems in *Tossing and Turning* recall boyhood in Shillington and youth at Harvard: "Leaving Church Early" and "Apologies to Harvard," the Harvard Phi Beta Kappa Poem for 1973. The aloneness that later becomes insomnia is detailed in the former as Updike describes the absence of communication in his family "kept home by poverty, / with nowhere else to go." The need to forgive is a condition of their misery. The latter poem may be read along with "The Christian Roommates," a story from *The Music School* (1966), as one of Updike's few accounts of university days. The third long poem, "Cunts," celebrates the beauties of female sexuality in explicit terms even while it criticizes the exploitation of the new sexual freedom by those who see themselves as "swingers" at "groovy" parties. The poem is comic and to the point as Updike urges an exchange of the demure Venus de Milo for the sensual Botticelli Venus.

Yet the best poems in *Tossing and Turning* are the shorter lyrics in which Updike acknowledges his step across midpoint in the direction of what he metaphorically calls *Nandi*. Surrounded in suburbia by the trappings of material success and a happy family, he nevertheless finds himself restless and afraid. The stupor that prosperity steals has a double meaning. He cannot find the stupor he needs to sleep because his life is now "too clean," and his success has lulled him into a stupor that clouds his artistic vision, his spiritual sustenance. Too much success "pollutes the tunnel of silence."

It also makes him afraid. More than any of the other collections, *Tossing and Turning* shows the poet's uncertainty about death and annihilation. In "You Who Swim" and "Bath After Sailing," two of his finest poems, Updike uses water to illustrate the unbeatable immensity of nonhuman otherness. The former is a sixteen-line description of his lover, who is such an expert at the dead man's float that she seems at home on both land and water. She splashes and plays and excels at love, but death lurks just out of sight. The final line—"We swim our dead men's lives"—suggests that all men return to the water that made them. The fear is just as great in "Bath After Sailing." Safely back from another confrontation with the deep, the poet is aware of the ironic change from overwhelming ocean to soothing tub. The "timeless weight" of the sea may threaten, and the gentle swell of the bath may cleanse, but the tub so resembles a coffin that his fingertips shriveled by the water remind him of death. The last trip to the final destination is described in "Heading for Nandi" as the lonely poet takes a night flight across the endless ocean.

Not all of the poems in *Tossing and Turning* are as bleak, for Updike also includes a section of light verse that recalls the verbal antics and dedication to a lively language that characterize *The Carpentered Hen*. Burlesques like "The Cars of Caracas" and "Insomnia the Gem of the Ocean" are fun to read. But the public's misconception of Updike the poet as a mere versifier of witty rhymes and sparkling puns could be corrected by close reading of his best poems, especially the second half of *Telephone Poles* and most of *Tossing and Turning*. Updike will continue to write both light and serious poetry, as the recent publication of the limited edition *Sixteen Sonnets* (1979, 250 copies numbered and signed) shows. His poetry may never replace his fiction in importance and execution, but it is a significant part of his considerable achievement. —*Donald J. Greiner*

Bibliographies:

C. Clarke Taylor, *John Updike: A Bibliography* (Kent, Ohio: Kent State University Press, 1968);

B. A. Sokoloff and David E. Arnason, *John Updike: A Comprehensive Bibliography* (Norwood, Pa.: Norwood Editions, 1973);

Michael Olivas, *An Annotated Bibliography of John Updike Criticism 1967-1973, and a Checklist of His Works* (New York: Garland, 1975).

References:

Rachael C. Burchard, *John Updike: Yea Sayings* (Carbondale: Southern Illinois University Press, 1971);

Robert Detweiler, *John Updike* (New York: Twayne, 1972);

Edward R. Ducharme, "Close Reading and Teaching," *English Journal*, 59 (October 1970): 938-942;

David D. Galloway, *The Absurd Hero in American Fiction*, revised edition (Austin: University of Texas Press, 1970), pp. 21-50;

Alice and Kenneth Hamilton, *The Elements of John Updike* (Grand Rapids, Mich.: Eerdmans, 1970);

Hamilton and Hamilton, *John Updike* (Grand Rapids, Mich.: Eerdmans, 1967);

Hamilton and Hamilton, "Theme and Technique in John Updike's *Midpoint*," *Mosaic*, 4 (Fall 1970): 79-106;

Howard M. Harper, Jr., *Desperate Faith* (Chapel Hill: University of North Carolina Press, 1967), pp. 162-190;

Granville Hicks, *Literary Horizons* (New York: New York University Press, 1970), pp. 107-133;

John S. Hill, "Quest for Belief: Theme in the Novels of John Updike," *Southern Humanities Review*, 3 (September 1969): 166-178;

Jane Howard, "Can a Nice Novelist Finish First?," *Life*, 61 (4 November 1966): 74-82;

Joyce B. Markle, *Fighters and Lovers: Theme in the Novels of John Updike* (New York: New York University Press, 1973);

Elizabeth Matson, "A Chinese Paradox, but Not Much of One: John Updike in his Poetry," *Minnesota Review*, 7 (1967): 157-167;

Arlin G. Meyer with Michael Olivas, "Criticism of John Updike: a Selected Checklist," *Modern Fiction Studies*, 20 (Spring 1974): 121-133;

Modern Fiction Studies, special Updike issue, 20 (Spring 1974);

Michael Novak, "Updike's Quest for Liturgy," *Commonweal*, 78 (10 May 1963): 192-195;

Joyce Carol Oates, "Updike's American Comedies," *Modern Fiction Studies*, 21 (Autumn 1975): 459-472;

Charles Thomas Samuels, *John Updike* (Minneapolis: University of Minnesota Press, 1969);

Samuels, "John Updike: The Art of Fiction XLIII," *Paris Review*, 12 (Winter 1968): 85-117;

Arthur Schlesinger, Jr., "The Historical Mind and

the Literary Imagination," *Atlantic Monthly*, 233 (June 1974): 54-59;

William T. Stafford, "The 'Curious Greased Grace' of John Updike: Some of His Critics and the American Tradition," *Journal of Modern Literature*, 2 (November 1972): 569-575;

Tony Tanner, *City of Words: American Fiction 1950-1970* (New York: Harper & Row, 1971), pp. 141-152;

Larry E. Taylor, *Pastoral and Anti-Pastoral Patterns in John Updike's Fiction* (Carbondale: Southern Illinois University Press, 1971).

MONA VAN DUYN
(9 May 1921-)

BOOKS: *Valentines to the Wide World: Poems* (Cummington, Mass.: Cummington Press, 1958);

A Time of Bees (Chapel Hill: University of North Carolina Press, 1964);

To See, To Take: Poems (New York: Atheneum, 1970);

Bedtime Stories (Champaign, Ill.: Ceres Press, 1972);

Merciful Disguises: Published and Unpublished Poems (New York: Atheneum, 1973).

Mona Van Duyn was born in Waterloo, Iowa. She was educated at the University of Northern Iowa, where she received a B.A. in 1942, and at the University of Iowa, where she obtained her M.A. in 1943. She married Jarvis A. Thurston in 1943. She was an instructor in English at the University of Iowa (1943-1946) and at the University of Louisville (1946-1950); lecturer in English at Washington University, St. Louis (1950-1967); and lecturer for the Salzburg (Austria) Seminar in American Studies in 1973. She has served as a poetry consultant for the Olin Library Modern Literature Collection at Washington University. From 1947 to 1967 she edited, with Jarvis Thurston, *Perspective: A Quarterly of Literature*. Her awards include *Poetry* magazine's Eunice Tietjens Memorial Prize, 1956; two Helen Bullis Prizes from *Poetry Northwest*, 1964 and 1976; a National Endowment for the Arts Grant, 1966; the Hart Crane Memorial Award from American Weave Press, 1968; the Harriet Monroe Memorial Prize from *Poetry* magazine, 1968; first prize in the Borestone Mountain Poetry Awards, 1968; the Bollingen Prize, 1970; the National Book Award for *To See, To Take*, 1971; a Guggenheim Fellowship, 1972; and D.Lett.

degrees from Washington University in 1971 and from Cornell University in 1972.

In Mona Van Duyn's world, love and its possibilities are intimately related to the transforming qualities of art. In poetry, as in love, nothing is easy, and perfection is not a realizable goal. Yet, according to Van Duyn, these are the best and finally the most satisfying aims we can have: to love life and each other with commitment; to create art that is rooted in that love.

However serious these concerns, Van Duyn's poems are filled with wit and wry humor, most of it cased in relatively formal verse. Rhyme and slant rhyme, the frequent use of couplets, and strong but irregular rhythms are characteristic of her work. She says in her 1971 National Book Award acceptance speech, "Poetry honors the formed use of language particularly, being concerned with both its sound and its meaning, and a poet spends his life's best effort in shaping these into a patterned experience which will combine an awareness of earlier patternings with the unique resonance of his own voice. He tries to do so in such a way that the experience may be shared with other people. This effort assumes a caring about other human beings, a caring which is a form of love."

Mona Van Duyn's poems are about people—people whose ordinary lives include sickness and death, disappointment and despair, as well as faith and humor and love. The particulars of these poems often center on domestic activities: birthdays, christenings, gardening, cocktail parties, and dealings with relatives. Yet the commonness of her subjects is misleading, for the poetry encompasses far more than such a catalogue suggests. Van Duyn's acquaintance with philosophy, psychology, and the arts is clearly evident. Santayana, Plato, Schrödinger, Henry James, Freud, Christopher Smart, Camus, and other writers, painters, composers, and scientists appear in titles, epigraphs, and the poems themselves, side by side with characters from nursery rhymes, the Bible, and Greek mythology. Hers is a generous mixture of the ordinary and the unusual, the natural and the sophisticated.

The basis of many poems is a complex metaphor extended into all its imaginative possibilities. Indeed it is her language, especially, that is admired by most reviewers. Marjorie Perloff takes a minority view, however. Complaining of "delicate little insights" and narrow thematic range, Perloff dislikes the very aspect of Van Duyn's writing that earns high praise from other critics. According to Perloff, "If poetry is, as Pound put it, 'language charged with meaning to the utmost possible

Herb Weitman

degree,' hers has a fairly low voltage. Too often, poems that begin with dazzling metaphors peter out because they go on too long." A more representative statement comes from the *Virginia Quarterly Review*: "She is a poet of great wisdom, skill, and versatility; she is able to sustain locally intense language over long narrative and meditative poems in a variety of modes and voices. . . . she has been here for more than twenty years, writing some of the finest poetry we have."

In Mona Van Duyn's first collection of poems, *Valentines To the Wide World* (1958), her voice is already assured, her manner confident. In the title poem she explores the nature of innocence and the continuing but impossible desire to maintain it. Part 1 of this three-part poem deals with a gangly eight-year-old girl who, despite some limited experience with evil ("Her friend has a mean Dad, a milkman always kicks the dog"), is able to dismiss the darker side of life in favor of a simple confidence in God and man:

> Mother, is love God's hobby? At eight you don't
> even look up from your scab when you ask it. A
> kid's squeak, is that a fit instrument for such a

question? Eight times the seasons turned and cold snow tricked the earth to death, and still she hasn't noticed.

Despite the tone of mock annoyance with the child, the poem ends with the speaker's memory of her own youthful awkwardness and easy belief and her wish that the child might retain naturalness and a sense of hope in a world "where anything is still possible—or almost anything."

Part 2 continues an examination of what that possibility consists of. To Van Duyn, the most "useful" way to make sense of the world, and the one offering the greatest likelihood of understanding, is through art—through the poem, which contains "simultaneous / recovery and reminiscence." For Van Duyn, as for other poets, art itself is a mode of reality, and the act of poetic creation is literally a way of remaking the universe, of harmonizing what seems most inharmonious. Needing to create order out of the confusion of people and activities the earth contains, she finds the poem the only vehicle that "starts with the creature / and stays there, assuming creation is worth the time it takes, / from the first day down to the last line on the last page. / And I've never seen anything like it for making you think / that to spend your life on such old premises is a privilege."

The theme of art and love justifying life is a recurrent one in Van Duyn's work. In part 3 of "Valentines to the Wide World," she explores the effects of time on one's perceptions of the possible and the important. The poem concludes with a couplet indicating that maturity and the certain knowledge of death help one understand the two things that make life worth living: "but against that rage slowly may learn to pit / love and art, which are compassionate."

The final poem in the volume is equally significant as a statement of Van Duyn's belief in the importance of love and is perhaps the finest piece in the collection. "Toward a Definition of Marriage" questions and affirms married love, with all its turbulence and variation. The love she celebrates is frequently violent, sometimes destructive: "Think of it as a duel of amateurs /.... Now, too close together for the length of the foils, / wet with fear, they dodge, stumble, strike, / and if either finally thinks he would rather be touched than touch, / he still must listen to the clang and tick of his own compulsive parrying." In five sections comparing married love to building a world's fair island, a picaresque novel, an unpublished poem, a circus of acrobats and animals, and last to the shuffling of historical documents, she always keeps its ideal in mind:

> Say for once that the start is a pure vision
> like the blind man's (though he couldn't keep it.
> Trees soon bleached to familiar) when the bandage
> came off and what a world could be first fell on
> his eyes.

When the poem ends, the conclusion of the poet is that despite everything, love remains the foundation of the marriage, although that foundation may crack or need repair and often groans under the pressure of a shifting and unstable world. Whatever strains are put on it, however, Van Duyn concludes that married love must be preserved and restored, for she believes it is crucial to civilized human survival.

The poems in *A Time of Bees* (1964), Van Duyn's second collection, range from an exploration of the self in relation to the four primary elements: air, earth, water, and fire; to a stay in a mental institution and subsequent recovery; to gardens and suburbia; to the nature of friendship; to the meaning of civilization itself. Using her characteristic half-rhymes, sometimes in quatrains, sometimes in couplets, Van Duyn creates poems impressive for their intelligence and their determined attempts to find reason in an unreasonable world.

"A Serious Case," for example, is about what often happens to the artist, or to any misfit in the society—a society that values conformity and adjustment far above art and individualism. The poem begins with an epigraph from Plato's *Republic*. The most significant portion of the quotation is: "The Artist knows nothing of true existence.... Let this be our defence for sending him away ... for the safety of the City." Plato was right, of course, in identifying artists as enemies of the status quo, as rebels who might upset an often precarious balance in a society. But the price the maladjusted have to pay for the society's stability, Van Duyn reminds us, is exceedingly high.

Identifying inmates in the hospital according to letters in the alphabet (roughly analogous to the institutional substitution of impersonal numbers for people's names), she presents their individual torments in detail, letting the reader know that whatever the real causes, the patients consistently and unfairly blame themselves for their ills: "Held together, all agree that delay is despair / although nothing has ever defined the foe but the mirror." The poet speaks with irony and bitterness about the cost of such incarceration and treatment as the persona and others have experienced at the hands of those who support the Ideal: "We'll pay, of course, for the privilege of saying goodbye / to past ideas. Electricity, chemistry, industry, understanding, love and time all took us away / from the classic statesman. A hard democracy / reinstates us." Finally, she describes the former patient as one who "becomes, in fact, a survivor / of the kind Plato banished, knowing he would scramble all over / and scuttle the Ark." Angry at the necessity to conform to a world that fears her, the speaker nevertheless knows what must be done to live. She is not sure how successful she can be, but at the end of the poem she seems to have her own values in balance.

In "Recovery," a second poem on the same subject, Van Duyn uses chilling metaphors to dramatize the terrors of both treatment and recovery: "Come Prince of Pills, / electric kiss, undo us, and we will appear / wearing each other's pain like silk, the awful / richness of feeling we blame, but barely remember." And "To trust perception again is like learning to lean / on water. The water, moving over minnows, is haunted." In this poem, the anger is less apparent; fear and bewilderment dominate. The poem ends with a poignant simile revealing the speaker's uncertainty, now, about her future. After the electroshock and the pain, "Memory will come, like some quiet girl, / slow-spoken and friendly, to tell me whatever it was / I knew I wanted in this grassy world." The loose form—a stanza length that is fixed in each section but varies from section to section, with a heavy reliance on assonance while avoiding any consistent rhyme scheme—suggests both the need for an informing order to help make sense of things and at the same time an understandable hesitation about coming to any firm conclusion or resolution. In this poem the power of exceptional imagination is shown to be the clear enemy of sanity, and the wish to be healthy often wars with the need to be individual and creative. The theme is certainly not new, but Van Duyn's treatment of the conflict is especially sensitive and convincing.

The excellent title poem of this volume, "A Time of Bees," is a narrative describing a married couple's determined efforts to get rid of a hive of bees that infests their porch. After the successful rooting out of the pests, the speaker and her husband go to a party, where they tell their bee story and discover that a scientist-friend needs an enzyme from bees' wings. Going through the garbage after the party, the three people discover some of the bees still alive, some actually in the process of being born. Van Duyn draws an analogy between this miracle and human love, which also "makes a claim on the future, grasping." Identifying with the bees, perhaps with all vulnerable creatures, the speaker says, "And / I feel it start, a terrible lifelong heave / taking direction. Unpleading, the men prod / till all that grubby softness wants to give, *to give*." Always it is the man who "takes hold," who makes "fierce sallies." Near the end of the poem is the line "The men do it." The speaker recognizes the justification for what they are doing, but says, "I can't touch it." She regrets the necessity of these deaths, which the men can deal with matter-of-factly, as she cannot. She finds in this episode a parallel with the mystery of love and with the differences between men and women.

To See, To Take (1970) received the National Book Award in 1971. Her strongest collection, it contains the poems for which Van Duyn is likely to be best remembered. Among the finest of these are "Leda," "Leda Reconsidered," "The Voyeur," and "The Creation."

Using a quotation from William Butler Yeats's famous sonnet "Leda and the Swan" as an epigraph, Van Duyn's "Leda" answers Yeats's question: "Did she put on his knowledge with his power / Before the indifferent beak could let her drop?" The answer is a firm No. Van Duyn's skill in extrapolating from the Yeats poem is admirable, for her wit and tone give a surprising twist to the old story. Making both figures

dully ordinary, Van Duyn characterizes Zeus as the kind of man who always seeks his own reflection in the eyes of women: "collecting these rare pictures of himself was his life." Finally, after the drama (which turns out not to be so dramatic or traumatic after all), she says of Leda:

> She tried for awhile to understand what it was that had happened, and then decided to let it drop. She married a smaller man with a beaky nose, and melted away in the storm of everyday life.

The poet's unromantic view of Leda's life is humorous, partly by contrast with the elevation in Yeats's poem. But the much longer "Leda Reconsidered," although it also relies heavily on wit, is a far more serious and sympathetic treatment, especially of the male figure. Here the poet speaks of likenesses between women and gods and between men and gods, and in both cases she finds more similarities than between women and men. The complexity of sexual love is again at the heart of the poem. Van Duyn gives Leda sympathy for the swan: "She saw what he had to work through / as he took, over and over / the risk of love, / the risk of being held," but she suggests that Leda lacks the god-male capacity for transformation: "To love with the whole imagination— / she had never tried. / Was there a form for that? / Deep, in her inmost, grubby female center. . . ." Van Duyn views women as generally less imaginative but wiser and more practical than men; and she portrays women as always willing to submit: "To give: women and gods / are alike in enjoying that ceremony, / find its smoke filling and sweet." The poem concludes with Leda's abandonment to love, which gives her pleasure, even as she recognizes the male as "the utter stranger." Again, as in "A Time of Bees," there is the emphasis on the weaker creature's *giving*.

A related theme is treated in "The Voyeur." A reviewer in *Antioch Review* says, "No one, perhaps, has made a poem of feminine sexuality as fine as 'The Voyeur.' " Here passion is anonymous and in some ways purer than the married love in many of Van Duyn's other poems: "She has shed belief / that the strongest love is habitual." The woman in the poem is alone in a cabin deep in the woods. She spots someone or something on the path outside her window. Man or beast, he arouses her, and she slips from nakedness into a sleek new dress, feeling his eyes every moment upon her. She so much gives herself over to the experience of being watched, of displaying herself to the male, that "she believes if he winked / out there in the moonlight / one side of her

After the supper dishes
three & four couples will walk down the road
to the neighbors, and will sit
around the heating stove,
and talk about Emma Harles,
who is finally giving away cuttings
of her famous orange-blooming Kalanchoe,
and about Ed Lelands,
on food stamps all year,
out with a brand new pickup
in their yard, and about
Old Lady Kerner, who was seen
in the drugstore buying Oil of Olay
to smooth out the wrinkles
eighty-five years have hammered
into her face

who is finally giving away cuttings
of her famous orange-blooming
Kalanchoe, and about the Ed Lelands,
On food stamps all year,
but with a brand new pickup
... cold or harsh
in their front yard, and about
Old Lady Kerner, who was seen
in the drugstore buying Oil of Olay
to smooth out the wrinkles
eighty-five hard years have hammered
into her indomitable face.

Untitled manuscript

338

would go numb." As in the Leda poems, the male figure seems potentially threatening, but the woman is excited by the prospect of what he may do: "She wants his eyes to find the / pure recipience she has turned to / and bring it . . . What? Anything, / sweet, sacred, or evil, / in his attention." The idea of woman as willing victim is reinforced; sex has an aspect of desirable violence.

In "The Creation," Van Duyn again links the process of making art with that of loving another person. Creating a portrait of a woman who is now dead, she compares her poetic method to Rauschenberg's erasing parts of a de Kooning drawing to make a "new" work. The metaphor of erasing is used throughout the poem, as the speaker delineates her friend's outstanding qualities and then claims to blot out difficult memories with a few strokes of rubber. The poet admits the urge to turn everything—even the most important intimacies— to her own use, and to transform life into art—not entirely to make painful experience more manageable, but also for the pleasure of creation itself. Regretting, finally, her own selfish motives, the poet says:

> Swept empty by a cyclone
> inside, I lift the paper.
> But before I blow it clean,
> sketched now in rubber crumbs,
> another face is on it—mine,
> Sneak, Poet, Mon-
> ster, trying to rob you with words.
>
> Your death was your own.

Bedtime Stories (1972) is a departure for Van Duyn. These are narrative poems told in a German-American dialect from the point of view of the poet's grandmother. The poems are versions of the old woman's stories as remembered by the poet, who grew up with them. The cumulative effect is powerful and convincing. In them, the reader meets people whose lives have been filled with the hardships typical of immigrants and first-generation Americans, whose appraisal of their own lot is remarkably good-natured and accepting. Van Duyn's ear for this dialect is acute:

> You know Gust, he alwus said there
> was no Easter Rabbit, that's what he said.
> He alwus said it was us that did it, colored
> them eggs. Well so then one day it was the day
> before Easter, they hadda plant tatoes so Mother
> took the two kids along in the fields, she helped
> plant tatoes that day. I didn't have to.

There is a patient matter-of-factness about poverty, especially, that rings true: "To school, when we was at school, we had white lard / and a little salt sprinkled over on our bread, / and that was what we eat at school."

These poems are intended as a tribute to the poet's grandmother. Van Duyn says in the last line of the final poem of the collection, "If artless love makes you live again, you live." The poems accomplish the purpose. The grandmother is the kind of woman Americans traditionally admire: full of pioneer virtues, she is tough, courageous, loving, and imbued with quiet folk wisdom.

Merciful Disguises (1973) is a collection of published and unpublished poems. It includes generous selections from Van Duyn's four previous volumes as well as a section titled "Unpublished Poems 1965-1973." The first poem in that section, "The Fear of Flying," is yet another exploration of married love. Here Van Duyn seems at first more cynical than in earlier work, but at the poem's end she reinforces what she has always said about the necessity for marriage and married love. In puzzling out the source of her panic at the airport just before a trip, the speaker suggests the possible reasons why she might dread leaving her husband behind, rejecting each obvious explanation:

> It's not as if we were young
> and couldn't bear to part—
> far from it. We've been yoked together so long
> it doesn't even hurt
>
> that we both forget every anniversary.
> There were good years together,
> one has to remember that toward the end, surely—

She records her husband's various ploys with other women, "each clever image" he seduces them with, and recalls earlier years when she could play the role of sensualist with him. Regretting age and the inevitable loss of passion, she concludes finally, although she calls him her "familiar monster," that "it would seem that I still love you, / and, like a schoolgirl deep in her first despair, / I hate to go above you." While this comment does not really explain her hysteria at the airport, it is clear that marriage continues to be a mixed blessing in Van Duyn's view—one she values despite its failings.

Another of the newest poems, "Midas and Wife," presents the figure of King Midas, who finally succumbs to his wife's desire to be transformed to gold. The wife, like the poet, believes art is more enduring than love, although the relationship between the two remains critical: "Changing under your touch, I'll prove / whatever holds perfectly is stronger than love, / but subject still to love's artless imperative." The irony is that the husband's love dies while his wife's lives, since they cannot touch; but as in ordinary human relationships, the fixed image is easier to revere than the real person and, paradoxically, "touching" always involves the risk of loss.

From the beginning, Van Duyn's poems have dealt with life's "motley and manifold." Her vision is clear, her philosophy pragmatic. Although she writes of a fallen world, it is also a world full of human potential. And although despair emerges from time to time, the poet knows how to combat it with love and poems. In a poem titled "The Challenger," she says of the darkest enemy, Death: "I will fight you with nuance and with clearness, / with the making and breaking of form and measure. / with a greedy face and with an immaculate." The words *love, possibility, art,* and *poetry* appear with significant frequency in Van Duyn's poems. They are the passwords to her world. —*Susan Ludvigson*

References:

Richard Howard, Review of *Merciful Disguises, American Poetry Review*, 2 (November-December 1973): 9;

Howard, Review of *To See, To Take, Nation*, 210 (4 May 1970): 536;

Thomas H. Landess, Review of *To See, To Take, Sewanee Review*, 81 (Winter 1973): 150-151;

Herbert Leibowitz, Review of *Merciful Disguises, New York Times Book Review*, 9 December 1973, p. 4;

Marjorie Perloff, "Sometimes a Great Notion," review of *Merciful Disguises, Washington Post Book World*, 6 January 1974, p. 3;

Review of *Merciful Disguises, Virginia Quarterly Review*, 50 (Winter 1974): xi;

Review of *To See, To Take, Antioch Review*, 30 (Spring 1970): 134.

PETER VIERECK
(5 August 1916-)

BOOKS: *Metapolitics: From the Romantics to Hitler* (New York: Knopf, 1941);

Terror and Decorum: Poems 1940-1948 (New York: Scribners, 1948);

Conservatism Revisited: The Revolt Against Revolt, 1815-1949 (New York: Scribners, 1949; London: Lehmann, 1950); revised and enlarged as *Conservatism Revisited, and The New Conservatism: What Went Wrong?* (New York: Collier, 1962);

Strike Through the Mask! New Lyrical Poems (New York: Scribners, 1950);

The First Morning: New Poems (New York: Scribners, 1952);

Shame and Glory of the Intellectuals: Babbitt Jr. vs. the Rediscovery of Values (Boston: Beacon Press, 1953);

Dream and Responsibility. Four Test Cases of the Tension Between Poetry and Society (Washington, D.C.: University Press of Washington, 1953);

The Persimmon Tree: New Pastoral and Lyrical Poems (New York: Scribners, 1956);

The Unadjusted Man: A New Hero for Americans: Reflections on the Distinction Between Con- *forming and Conserving* (Boston: Beacon Press, 1956);

Conservatism: From John Adams to Churchill (Princeton: D. Van Nostrand, 1956);

The Tree Witch: A Poem and Play (First of All a Poem) (New York: Scribners, 1961);

New and Selected Poems: 1932-1967 (Indianapolis: Bobbs-Merrill, 1967).

Peter Robert Edwin Viereck was born in New York City. He graduated *summa cum laude* from Harvard College in 1937 with a B.S. in history and literature. He did graduate work on a Henry fellowship at Christ Church, Oxford University, and returned to Harvard to earn an M.A. in 1939 and a Ph.D. in 1942, both in history. During World War II, he served with the U.S. Army Psychological Warfare Branch in Africa and Italy, where he analyzed radio propaganda, including Ezra Pound's anti-American broadcasts. In Rome in 1945, he met and married Anya de Markov, the daughter of Russian immigrants. They had two children and were divorced in 1970. In 1972, Viereck married Betty Martin Falkenberg.

In 1946, Viereck began a teaching career in history, first at Harvard, then at Smith College, and since 1948 at Mount Holyoke College, where he currently holds the William R. Kenan chair as professor of European and Russian history. He has traveled widely in Europe, lecturing on poetry at universities or working on research projects in history. He has served as visiting lecturer at numerous universities including Oxford in 1953 and the University of Florence on a Fulbright fellowship in 1955. In 1954 and again in 1963, he was Library of Congress Whittall lecturer in poetry.

Since his Harvard days, when he won both the Garrison prize medal for the best undergraduate verse and the Bowdoin prize medal for the best philosophical prose, Viereck has continued to devote his attention equally to history and poetry. He is the only American scholar who has received separate Guggenheim Fellowships in the two fields. His first volume of poetry, *Terror and Decorum* (1948), won the 1949 Pulitzer Prize.

Viereck's poetry and poetic theories are rooted in the social and political philosophy he has worked out and articulated repeatedly in the prose works he has continued to produce since his doctoral dissertation, *Metapolitics: From the Romantics to Hitler*, was published in 1941. His early passion for his own brand of conservatism stems at least in part from his reaction against his father's public support of Nazism during both world wars.

In poetry and politics, Viereck identifies himself as a "value-conserving classical humanist," always searching for a middle way, a synthesis of extremes that emerges in political theory as "the revolt against revolt" and in poetry as "twentieth-century baroque" or "Manhattan classicism." Because he wants extremes resolved, Viereck walks a fine line. Among other conservative political theorists and practitioners, such as Frank Meyers (writing for the *National Review*, 11 August 1956), he has been labeled a "counterfeit," accused of "passing off his unexceptionably Liberal sentiments as conservatism." Viereck justifies his own position not by the current practices of those who call themselves conservatives but by tracing the origins of conservatism to the English philosopher Edmund Burke, who was staunchly opposed to the Romantic radicalism and revolution that characterized nineteenth-century France. Viereck, like Burke, argues for the importance of traditions and values that have functioned positively to protect man against his own irrational appetites and ego. But Viereck is cautious of the opposite extreme, and he opposes conformity and the submergence of the self in a mechanized and dehumanized society. His hero is not the "Adjusted Man," who buys wholesale the current ideology, who keeps up with the Joneses or acquiesces under the pressures of authority. Viereck's hero is the soul-searching "Unadjusted Man," who is constantly seeking his own way: "The meaningful moral choice is not between conforming and nonconforming but between conforming to the ephemeral, stereotyped values of the moment and conforming to the ancient, lasting archetypal values shared by all creative cultures."

At precisely this point, Viereck's political and poetic theories intersect and support one another, for he believes that man's salvation is through his cultural heritage, especially his literature and his imagination, which have the continuing potential to unite the individual with his universe. Throughout his poetry, he attempts to adjust the inner life to the outer life through the sheer power of language and imagination. His poetry is at once a poetry of ideas and lyricism. In thought and craftsmanship, his language is articulate and tough, and his conceits are often metaphysical, intelligent, and shocking. The lyrical element is present in finely crafted lines of sounds and rhythms. When Viereck is at his best, he can have both intelligence and lyricism in the same poem. In his poetry as in his political theory, he insists on synthesis, on yoking extreme opposites however he can, with high seriousness or low buffoonery. As a result of this risk-taking, his range in tone and in subject matter is exceptional. Also as a result, he often fails disastrously and conspicuously.

Viereck has repeatedly articulated a literary credo that focuses on three major elements: the necessity for morality, form, and clarity. His insistence on the presence of these three in good poetry has led him frequently into controversy. He objected to the selection of Ezra Pound as recipient of the Bollingen Prize in 1949 because he could not accept the judges' argument that "artistic form can be considered apart from its content." He has continued to be adamant in his belief that "moral implications must be present in great art but not as the explicit blueprint mechanically imposed; rather the morality is often the by-product of a responsible use of words for their own sake." As a result of this insistence on morality, Viereck's poetry is frequently characterized by a strong sense of its own ideological importance. He has on one hand been praised by Josephine Jacobsen in *Massachusetts Review* (Summer 1968) for his "cosmic sense," and on the other hand, he has been criticized for overloading his poems with ideas, for overexplaining in prefatory notes, footnotes, and poem titles. For example, a good poem that otherwise illustrates well Viereck's art of orchestrating lyricism and philosophy suffers from the much too explicit title "Crass Times Redeemed by Dignity of Souls." He tells too much;

Peter Viereck

his aim is to make his moral stance clear, but in the process he detracts from the poem's chief purpose and merit, the sense of joy and humanity that comes through primarily in the finely wrought rhymes and meters. To balance moral ideas with lyricism is not easy, but Viereck will persistently risk trying and he often succeeds.

Viereck has similarly been outspoken in his arguments in favor of form in poetry: "Just as political liberty is not based on a radical smashing of traffic lights but on law and traditional established institutions, so poetry must be subjected to the challenge of form, the more rigorous and traditional and conservative the better, to bring out the response of beauty." More recently, he has sparked controversy in his statement that there is a biological basis for meter and rhyme. But in practice as well as in theory, Viereck follows his own dicta. He never writes in free verse, which he deplores "on principle," and his typical poem almost always includes rhyme as well as meter. No poet in the twentieth century is a more inventive rhymer, although the fact that he is so good at it sometimes leads him away from the poem into rhyming for the sheer fun of it. For Viereck, rhyme is equally effective as the principal stylistic feature in his philosophical poems as well as in his lyrical, satiric, and comic poems. What he strives for is "spontaneity," which emerges most effectively from the order of conventional forms, just as in political theory he wants the passion of the free individual to be tempered by traditional values and cultural practices. His aim is for a "strict wildness," which he defines as "spontaneous absent-mindedness accompanied by the strictest, most conscious discipline of craftsmanship."

Viereck's third insistence is on clarity, on poetry that communicates fully with the greatest possible simplicity. He justifies this aim in terms of social utility: "Today, when reality is itself an obscure nightmare-poem of uncontrolled association, then a poetry which is lucid and lofty and calm and ennobling—a clear-water communicative poetry—is more creative and a truer criticism of its age." But again, he synthesizes and does not want to sacrifice "legitimate difficulty," which is sometimes necessary for the sake of profundity or originality. What he wants is a "difficult simplicity" that is the "tragic affirmation that follows the dark night of the soul." Although Viereck's poetry is occasionally difficult and demands second and third readings, as all good poetry should, it is seldom difficult for the sake of impressing the reader with its own intelligence, a practice among his contemporaries that Viereck

deplores. On the contrary, his insistence that his point of view be intelligible leads him to repeat, to return again and again to the same themes, and to invent as many ways as possible to gain his reader's attention and state his ideas in yet another novel way.

Viereck's first volume of poetry, *Terror and Decorum*, was favorably received by reviewers, many of whom recognized his energetic control of language for purposes of wit and variety in tone and subject matter. The volume presents a full view of his art at its best and worst, and it includes samples of all the major themes and stylistic features. "Poet," the first poem in the book, states clearly in rhymed iambic pentameter (Viereck's favorite form) his view of the poet's role as benevolent monarch whose responsibility is to maintain a tight rein upon the excesses of language and whose power is absolute: "all things are because he willed them so." The design of the poem is daring. Under the reign of the monarch-poet, certain parts of speech have been silenced or exiled. But on news of the monarch's death, "Lush adverbs, senile rhymes in tattered gowns" begin to express themselves in "notes to exiled nouns / And mutter openly against his reign." In spite of all the chaos, there is comfort in the knowledge that the dead poet lives "on in form" and in his grave "Not worms, not worms in such a skull / But rhythms, rhythms writhe and sting and crawl." In the hands of a less skillful poet, the personifications would easily lapse into absurdity, and the poem would fail. Viereck accomplishes what in theory would seem impossible; he not only risks the elaborate metaphor, but he also maintains a serious tone with a serious subject, his first articulation of his poetic credo, which has remained essentially unchanged.

In "Dolce Ossessione," another poem about poetry, Viereck declares openly that he will assume any shape, perform any trick, to gain attention, and in other poems in the volume he does just that. In "To a Sinister Potato," one of his best-known poems, the potato is personified as one who is "Puffed up with secret paranoias" because he is merely functional: "In each Kiwanis Club on every plate / So bland and health-exuding do we wait / That Indiana never, never knows / How much we envy stars and hate the rose." A potato talking in rhyme could easily disintegrate into doggerel, but the poem works and not simply as a comic poem but also as a satiric commentary on man's own "secret paranoias" about the roles he is doomed to play.

In this volume also is Viereck's first tree poem. "You All Are Static; I Alone Am Moving" relies on personification and paradox. The talking tree pities

342

mankind, who is static and perhaps by comparison not alive at all. The voice asks, "Can non-trees feel?," and it wishes it could "reel / You through my thousand outstretched ways of loving." Other modern poets have compared and contrasted the roles of man and tree, but usually the human voice controls the poem. Viereck turns this around: his trees do the talking, and whether sympathetic or perturbed, they are always perceptive and articulate.

"Kilroy," one of Viereck's most daring poems, also appears in this first volume. It is perhaps the best example among all his poems of the kind of circus act that he alone would risk. He manages the subject, the mock-epic war hero who scrawled "Kilroy was here" everywhere he went, with a curious combination of wit and sensitivity to the sad comedy of the anonymous soldier's role in time of war. In his poem, Kilroy is every soldier who ever went to war for whatever reason but whose primary gain was a liberating sense of adventure and foolhardiness. He is the perfect personification of Viereck's "free individualism," the human spirit set loose to find his own way in a meaningless, chaotic time. Kilroy is principally the American soldier of World War II, but he is also Orestes, who was chased by Furies; Ulysses, who was unrecognized and misunderstood when he returned from Troy; and Icarus, who took the ultimate risk on "hopeless wings" and left his "Exultant Kilroy-signature / Upon sheer sky." Kilroy is sign and symbol of the adventuresome spirit, whether Chaucer's mild pilgrims telling tales on the way to Canterbury, or G.I. Faustus, or God. This is the final verbal feat: in Viereck's poem, Kilroy is not like God; "God is like Kilroy; He, too, sees it all; / That's how He knows of every sparrow's fall." Kilroy, not God, is the standard to emulate. According to the poem, the word, in fact, means, "the world is very wide. / He was there, he was there, he was there!" And all the boys who could not or would not go to war weep that they have not had Kilroy's adventure and wide-ranging experience.

The most important poems of *Terror and Decorum* deal, not surprisingly, with antitheses and the resolution of antitheses. The theme and all its philosophical implications are fully worked out in "Two Girls Setting Out in Life," where the choices made by Marquis de Sade's character Justine are contrasted to those made by her friend Juliette: one revels in the grand life of fun and lust; the other's chief aim is to remain virtuous. Viereck's resolution is that elements of both life-styles are necessary; the characters are in fact counterparts of one shared humanity.

This vision of the nature of man as a curious combination of good and evil recurs in the major poems of this volume. In "For An Assyrian Frieze," the powerful, conquering King of Assyria boasts that in one town he "freed nine pearl-caged nightingales, and built / A pillar of skulls so high it stabbed the sun." This is the evil voice that seems to come from the lion's face on the frieze. Down through the ages, the poem suggests, the evil has spread: "Earth spawns no gangrene half so luminous / As the contagion of those molten eyes." Viereck fully accepts the idea of inherited sin, but the other half of his theme is that God, or whatever ultimate reality there is, is not always so benevolent either. The nature of God, in fact, is not at all certain. In "From Ancient Fangs," Viereck, as he frequently does, identifies ultimate reality with *sky*, the final, natural fact, always beyond man's ability to know. When everything else is falling (poison from ancient fangs, bombs, tennis balls), the pitiful human voice in the poem implores "good old sky" not to fall. Sky answers remotely and viciously, "When worlds grow honest, noble, clean, or clever, / I fall and smother them forever." And sky advises: "All sights bore Me now but blood. / The main thing is to kill. And kill. And kill."

The ultimate perplexity that Viereck presents and attempts to resolve is these two visions of man and ultimate reality. If both are at best unreliable, forever marked by original sin or unknowable and apparently indifferent, what can man depend on? Viereck's answer is humanistic, whether expressed as "dignity of souls" or simple human love. In "Crass Times Redeemed by Dignity of Souls," the speaker, who is "Torn out of blackness, soon to choke on black, / Leaning on nothingness before and back," finally turns to human love that "Heals and / shreds and / liberates the night." Similarly, in one of Viereck's strongest short poems, "Well Said Old Mole," the speaker bemoans, "How frail our fists are when they bash or bless / the deadpan idiot emptiness of sky." His conclusion, not unlike the final lines of Matthew Arnold's "Dover Beach," is a clear vision of his doom: "We are alone and small, and heaven is high; / Quintillion worlds have burst and left no trace; / A murderous star aims straight at where we lie." And his final suggestion is: "Quick—let me touch your body as we die."

The problem of not being able to understand the human dilemma, not being able to hear any sure voice to explain or make sense out of meaningless events, is the subject of three major poems in *Terror and Decorum*: "A Walk on Snow," "*Vale* from Carthage," and "Six Theological Cradle Songs." "A

343

Walk on Snow" is written in blank verse, a rare form for Viereck. Walking out on a pine trail to an odd clearing, a circle of snow, the persona begins with a series of questions that probe inscrutable mysteries: "are stars cold for all their brightness, / Deaf to our urgencies as snowflakes are?" At first the answers that seem to present themselves are encouraging; the "reachable star" is warm and sympathetic. But the persona knows this answer is a hoax of his own imagination; the star is a "rocket of my unbelief." The poem concludes: "Shivering I stood there, straining for some frail / Or thunderous message that the heights glow down. / I waited long; the answer was / The only one earth ever got from sky." The answer is no answer, and Viereck, whose weakness in many other poems is that he says and explains too much, has no other commentary.

"*Vale* from Carthage," also a strong poem, concludes similarly. The poem is an elegy in memory of Viereck's younger brother, whose "humanistic ideas" Viereck greatly admired and who was killed in action in 1944. In the opening lines, Viereck recalls their last encounter when they both in semi-jest wondered if one or the other "Wears doom, like dungarees, and doesn't know." Now in Carthage, having word that his brother is "shot dead at Rome," he reads the inscription on an ancient Roman soldier's tomb, contemplates the injustices of war, and compares the fate of the two soldiers, one who will never again see Times Square, the other never to see Rome. The final line is plain: "What's left but this to say of any war?" Like "A Walk in Snow," the poem is classical in restraint. Viereck may elsewhere write more explicitly of "dignity of souls," but in these poems dignity is inherent in the simplicity of style and in the deliberate choice not to say too much.

Viereck's theological vision in these poems is perhaps even more profound than his political ideology. The vision is clearest in "Six Theological Cradle Songs," although it is not stated with as much dignity as in "A Walk in Snow," "*Vale* from Carthage," or "Well Said, Old Mole." He has suggested that these "cradle songs" should be read on two levels: as "humorous nursery rhymes for children" and as "sinister allegories for adults." But there is, in fact, little about them that is humorous or for children, although their subject is a naive, innocent child who does not yet know the sinister realities of the world and whose assumptions about life and death and God are gradually undercut. "IF there's no God" (a big *if* that he reluctantly grants), "then at least there's no devil." The chorus of

grownups responds, "If only you KNEW." The child also naively imagines Death as a pitiful "Blind flamingo, hunting fishes," who "does not mean to gobble you or me." And God is a friend, who "watched me from the sky. / Maybe he never lived at all. / Maybe too much friendship made him die." The child rationalizes and apologizes, even for God. In the last of the six songs, "Hide and Seek," the children, playing near a dark forest at dusk, are shouting, "Come OUT, come OUT, wherEVer you are." They grow "puzzled," then "lonely," and finally are "shivering" with fear as one boy fails to respond to their repeated calls. Unknown to them, the boy has gone through the forest and come out on the "farther side." The simple allegory, told in terms of a child's game and from a child's perspective, repeats Viereck's persistent preoccupation with death and with the inscrutable nature of ultimate reality.

While *Terror and Decorum* does include these and other successful poems, there are many others that do not work for the majority of readers, that fail conspicuously when all Viereck's risk-taking techniques disintegrate into contrivances and verbal clowning. In a poem about the tragic career of Hart Crane, "Look, Hart, That Horse You Ride Is Wood," the mixture of tones is not satisfying. The seriocomic tones of "Kilroy" work to underscore each other, but how is a reader to respond to such comments about Crane as "the clerks his daddy hired / Plus gin plus sea; then Hart felt tired, / Drank both and drowned"? Other failures often noted by critics and reviewers are the result of problems in diction that often occur in poems otherwise carefully crafted. In "Dolce Ossessione," the poet, who is transforming himself into any shape to get the reader's attention, finally settles on becoming, in lovely, lyrical lines, "A flame-scaled trout" who will "shimmer through your nets— / Like lies? like truth?" In the last line of the poem, the poet-trout asks, "What child will scoop me up, what pudgy hands?" The choice of "pudgy" is regrettable, as is the image, in "From Ancient Fangs" when sky is being implored not to fall, "Hold tighter, sky. Be roof to us, not rug." Or there is some question about the effectiveness of one of Viereck's most important lines in "*Vale* from Carthage": "And what if one of us," asks one brother of the other as they separate in war, "Wears doom, like dungarees, and doesn't know?" The choice of the word "dungarees" is a risk that can be justified in terms of its connotations. Doom and death are as casual and common to man as are the dungarees he wears. But in a poem that is otherwise elegiac in tone, this line glares. These are typical of the kinds of faults Viereck's poems occasionally have.

In 1950, Viereck's second volume of poetry, *Strike Through the Mask*, was published a little more than a year after his first book. It was a disappointment to many critics and reviewers who had seen in *Terror and Decorum*, which won the Pulitzer Prize in 1949, a more than usually promising young poet. *Strike Through the Mask*, a slim volume of twenty-four poems, has proportionately fewer good poems. As a result, Viereck's occasional and characteristic lapses are more obvious. More important, the book lacks the kinds of poems that make the first volume successful, poems of genuine wit and poems that synthesize lyricism with a philosophical and theological vision. Most notable in the volume are the four new tree poems, which continue Viereck's fascination with trees who think themselves superior to humans. There is a running debate between the values of lyricism, identified with the "willow lyre," and "true tree-reality," identified with the oak. The most interesting tree poem, "To My Playmate, with Thanks for Carefree Days Together," does show again Viereck's unconventional wit. In this macabre poem, the tree's playmate is a hanged man whose corrupt human flesh has rotted down to "the perfect bone within." A "sacrament of rope" has "married blood and wood," and the tree and corpse make a mutually supportive pair. Whenever the tree is in despair, he need only "twitch my branch and you'll dispel / All spells by rattling me some joyous jig." And for the corpse, the tree has provided the ultimate service of ridding him of his corrupt human flesh, rotted by weather or cleaned out by birds and worms until all ego is out and the skull is a hive for honeybees. This curious synthesis of death and joy, reminiscent of themes from William Butler Yeats, whom Viereck claims is a major influence on his verse, is also found in another poem, "Ennui." The speaker is the body of a man who died trapped in ice. The corpse, envious of its "bodiless sisters" who escaped in "twirling ghost-swarms," is the "only ghost on earth who isn't gay." Only the boredom of being trapped in ice with nothing to do makes him "almost wish" sometimes that he were alive. One other poem about death, which is also perhaps Viereck's strongest love poem, is the first one in the volume, "Which of Us Two." The speaker who has been physically severed from a loved one by death is so overwhelmed by loneliness and despair, "such black as stuffs a tomb, / Or merely midnight in an unshared room," that he is led to wonder "which of us has died." The vivid description of the loss, especially of physical closeness, elevates the poem's final question above the level of mere sentiment.

Also in *Strike through the Mask*, two poems about poetry should be noted. "Small Perfect Manhattan" is an oblique statement, which Viereck has clarified elsewhere, about "Manhattan classicism," his term for his own modern, synthetic style. The poetic creed that the poem articulates is that it is better for classicism "to build its small, quiet perfection right inside the largest, noisiest . . . industrial center of the world" than to flee "into an ancient lifeless Hellas, whose artificial revival leads not to the classicism of Athens but to the dead sterility of the Sahara." In the other poem about poetry, "Some Lines in Three Parts," his subject is "the birth of song," which is the slow, agonizing, even ugly transformation of the owl (wisdom and reality) into the nightingale (lyricism). Both of these poems are important statements in verse of Viereck's beliefs about the form and function of his poetry.

The First Morning (1952) shows most clearly that Viereck was turning in the direction of lyricism. The better poems in the volume are more deliberately lyrical, like "Stanzas in Love with Life and August" and "Arethusa, The First Morning," the first two poems, both written in longer, looser lines characterized by fluidity and motion. Both poems celebrate natural phenomena that have metaphorical implications for humanity. Arethusa was a sea nymph changed by Artemis into a spring that feeds a stream in Sicily. Arethusa herself is the speaker, commenting on her feelings, perplexed by her dim memory on the first morning after the transformation. Viereck takes full advantage of this myth to suggest indirectly the stages of awareness and of movement through life toward death. Influences along the way include obstacles in the stream, animals who live in it or drink from it or step through it. The most dramatic event in the course of Arethusa's life is the sense of "hoofprints on my mirror," a harmless, trembling doe who pauses in the stream: "I splashed those moss-mild willowy shanks and knew her; / Softer than snails and all my little stones; / Warmer than fish or lilies; good to know." Each wants to pause longer where their paths have crossed or at least "go a while together," but "soilward, seaward, each gropes graveward separately." When Arethusa reaches her final waterfall and takes "one last jump," she expresses Viereck's own vision of the emptiness and indifference of ultimate reality or *sky*. Her last thought, and fear, is that she will "find no hoofprints on the sky."

"To Be Sung," perhaps Viereck's most lyrical poem, also appears in this volume. The lines here are shorter, in dimeter, unusual for Viereck, and with unaccented syllables at the ends of each line to replace rhyme, also unusual for Viereck. The poem is for a daughter, and for the most part it is light and loving: "For what is a song for / If not to smooth ringlets / Of daughters too hurt by / the prose of the world?" But the poem ends in its last section with an abrupt shift to the image of a death camp and of the father digging graves for both of them before they are shot: "For what is love here for / If not to smooth ditches / For all the world's daughters / Whose dying we share?"

One section in *The First Morning*, "Irreverances," includes a cycle of short rhyming verses that mock the aims of the New Critics, with whose major tenets Viereck has frequently disagreed: "discarding the *relevant* historical, psychological, and ethical aspects, they are often misreading the text itself. What do they know of poetry who only poetry know?" Viereck's prose attacks are much more effective than the mocking tones of the poem, "1912-1952, Full Cycle." This poem and others in this section, including a poem of self-mockery, tend to trivialize issues that seriously concern him. Fortunately there are better examples of his rhyming wit put to good use.

Louise Bogan, in reviewing *The First Morning* for the *New Yorker* (31 January 1953), complained that Viereck "now appears to be a writer of verse that is fundamentally not serious." What is missing from this volume, as well as from *Strike through the Mask*, which came before, and from *The Persimmon Tree*, which followed in 1956, is the "tragic sense" that seemed to be emerging in his philosophical and theological poems in his first book, *Terror and Decorum*. This is not to say that *The Persimmon Tree* does not contain some fine poems, but again the merits are chiefly lyrical. "To My Isis," the first in the volume, is a remarkable poem, combining Viereck's powers for lyricism and wit. The speaker is a modern Osiris, who, like Viereck's personae, has assumed the shape of any and everything, "fanning forth from man / To worm and back," to defy death and celebrate life. Sometimes he is as trivial as dust or dandelion fluff, as beautiful as birch or trout, or more fundamental like mud: "All gross masks I'll try / But hairy spiders. These I still can't stomach." Even in death, he is lively and "just as real as you are . . . merely scattered." Whereas this poem is about the role of the poet, two other important poems in

this volume are about the nature of poetry. In a 1966 article for the *Christian Science Monitor*, Viereck used "At the River Charles" and "Etruria" to illustrate his poetic credo. The "sunstruck spray" of the River Charles is for him the perfect symbol of the kind of synthesis he wishes to make of contraries that continually fascinate him, earth and sky, the outer and inner life, what is constant and what is changing. In "Etruria," the companion poem, he asserts finally his belief that ideas and ideals cannot survive apart from reality, which is specific and physical: "My vines are vines . . . no symbol and no dream. / That dust is three-dimensional. The olives / Are really there. I am the land I seem." In these poems, in the title poem "The Persimmon Tree," and in others in this volume, Viereck seems more than usually concerned with the role of imagination, which, to be effective, must constantly recognize and adjust itself (like Viereck's "Unadjusted Man") to realities that are often painful or ugly. In "Decorum and Terror: Homage to Goethe and Hart Crane," he brings together the conflicting voices of two poets who argue wittily and satirically about their separate visions of reality and poetry, their classic and romantic polarities. Viereck pays homage to them both.

Two poems in *The Persimmon Tree* return briefly to Viereck's concern for the metaphysical. In "Looking Up Again and Again While Walking," the image of the poet's sister is "translated into sky," the antithesis of Viereck: "I used to try to sing her to my clay; / She used to try to pray me to her sky." In spite of the conflict between them, which is never resolved, there is much praise and envy of the kind of vision the sister had, where the blue of sky is "undespairing blue" and where "will lets go." From another more negative perspective, the voice in "Nostalgia" is the voice of a deity who has abandoned earth "eight thousand years" and returns now because of guilt perhaps or a sudden nostalgia for the physical beauty of earth and its seasons. Nothing has changed about the natural beauty of earth; but humanity itself has changed. The people he created no longer worship him with harp and goatskin. Criticism of such a deity is by implication rather than by explicit statement, but again the vision is of a deity who is remote, vindictive, and capricious.

The Tree Witch: A Poem and Play (First of All a Poem), published in 1961, is a verse play, which, according to Viereck, has been performed several times, including at Harvard's Loeb Theater. Although the play contains some of his loveliest lyrics and develops fully the idea of the tree in all its naturalness as superior to humans who are corrupted by flesh and the modern pressures of a technological society, it is hard to imagine all of Viereck's social and political ideas dramatized in this manner. The conflict is clear enough: a dryad (SHE—the personification of all that is natural and lovely) and a chorus of "hygiene-spraying and jargon-spraying aunts" (THEY—the personification of a decadent conformity) compete for the attention and soul of WE, "the enlightened and emancipated technologizing moderns." The poem is full of talk and argument and draws on every conceivable kind of modern opinion, theory, and dogma. It is Viereck's philosophy and circus act carried to their logical extremes. The combat between his antitheses takes place in a garage, where the dryad is captured after being separated from her tree, which was cut down to make way for an eight-lane highway. The outrageous risk Viereck takes in attempting to dramatize his ideas in this unorthodox manner is alone fascinating and indicative of the personality behind it all.

The chief merit of Viereck's best book of poetry, *New and Selected Poems: 1932-1967* (1967), is the arrangement of the poems so that they comment on one another. Most of the poems are from the four earlier volumes of verse, the majority from *Terror and Decorum*, and there are selections also from *The Tree Witch*. The ten sections bring together his major themes and subjects. They include his tree poems in "The Tree Menagerie"; his antitheses in "Earth" and "Sky"; his poems about poetry in "Persimmons"; his theological poems in "Cradle Songs and Elegies"; and his "grotesques," like his "sinister potato," in another section. This arrangement will forever plague editors and critics, but much is gained by avoiding the simplicity of a chronological arrangement. The best of the new poems is "Five Walks on the Edge," which appears in a section called "Walks," where earlier poems on this subject are also collected. The poem uses features of the New England coast, rocks and waves, water and sun, gulls and leaves, to make symbolic and philosophical statements. Again, Viereck's antitheses are present; in "Coming to terms with rock," one must choose between sense and will, between the passive and active stance. What humankind longs for, he suggests, is just a little responsiveness, "just a little / Resonance in so much waste." And his advice is to "Wade without foresight or don't wade at all. / Plunge without seeing or you'll never find. / There's only insight." The final line is a halfhearted acknowledgment: "Well, we have got this far." The poem is typical of Viereck's struggle to reconcile romanticism with reality, a high, unreachable aim that he at last dismisses reluctantly with a shrug.

Forthcoming is a new volume of poetry, "Applewood: A Conflict in Three Voices," which after over a decade without the publication of a collection of poems promises to be important for the direction of Viereck's verse and reputation. Poems to appear in "Applewood" already published in journals indicate that he has continued to be concerned with articulating his social and political visions and with developing his lyrical talents. The title poem is concerned again with Viereck's antitheses, and one of his loveliest lyrics, published first in *Terror and Decorum*, "Gladness Ode," is greatly expanded and revised. Although to date he has published five major volumes of verse, Viereck has been ill-served by readers and critics who have responded negatively to his boldness, his unorthodox subjects, and his daring linguistic feats, the very features that make him an exciting and important poet. He is in many respects his own worst enemy, having acknowledged long ago his "inability to discriminate between my worse and better poems." This inability to select and edit his own poems is especially apparent in his revisions from one volume to the next. But in spite of these lapses in language and in spite of his persistent desire to make his ideas about morality and society clear and persuasive, Viereck has already established himself as a poet with a unique talent for merging the separate disciplines of poetry and social philosophy in a language that is at once lyrical and humane, witty and risk-taking. —*Idris McElveen*

Other:

"Beyond Revolt: The Education of a Poet," in *The Arts in Renewal*, ed. Scully Bradley (Philadelphia: University of Pennsylvania Press, 1950), pp. 35-66;

"My Kind of Poetry," in *Mid-Century American Poets*, ed. John Ciardi (New York: Twayne, 1950), pp. 16-49;

"Conflict and Resolution," *Christian Science Monitor*, 29 December 1966, p. 8;

"Conservatism," *Encyclopaedia Britannica*, 15th edition (1974), pp. 62-69;

"Strict Form in Poetry: Would Jacob Wrestle with a Flabby Angel?," *Critical Inquiry*, 5 (Winter 1978): 203-222.

References:

John Ciardi, "Peter Viereck—The Poet and the

Form," *University of Kansas City Review*, 15 (Summer 1949): 297-302;

Marie Henault, *Peter Viereck* (New York: Twayne, 1969);

John Lawlor, "Peter Viereck, Poet and Critic of Values," *Etudes Anglaises*, 7 (July 1954): 280-293;

Claes G. Ryan, "Peter Viereck: Unadjusted Man of Ideas," *Political Science Review*, 7 (Fall 1977): 325-366.

DAVID WAGONER
(5 June 1926-)

SELECTED BOOKS: *Dry Sun, Dry Wind* (Bloomington: Indiana University Press, 1953);

The Man in the Middle (New York: Harcourt Brace, 1954; London: Gollancz, 1955);

Money Money Money (New York: Harcourt Brace, 1955);

A Place to Stand (Bloomington: Indiana University Press, 1958);

Rock (New York: Viking, 1958);

The Nesting Ground (Bloomington: Indiana University Press, 1963);

The Escape Artist (New York: Farrar, Straus & Giroux, 1965; London: Gollancz, 1965);

Staying Alive (Bloomington: Indiana University Press, 1966);

Baby, Come On Inside (New York: Farrar, Straus & Giroux, 1968);

New and Selected Poems (Bloomington: Indiana University Press, 1969);

Where Is My Wandering Boy Tonight (New York: Farrar, Straus & Giroux, 1970);

Riverbed (Bloomington: Indiana University Press, 1972);

Sleeping in the Woods (Bloomington: Indiana University Press, 1974);

The Road to Many a Wonder (New York: Farrar, Straus & Giroux, 1974);

Tracker (Boston: Atlantic/Little, Brown, 1975);

Whole Hog (Boston: Atlantic/Little, Brown, 1976);

Travelling Light (Port Townsend: Graywolf Press, 1976);

Collected Poems 1956-1976 (Bloomington: Indiana University Press, 1976);

Who Shall Be the Sun? (Bloomington: Indiana University Press, 1978);

In Broken Country (Boston: Atlantic/Little, Brown, 1979);

The Hanging Garden (Boston: Atlantic/Little, Brown, 1980).

David Wagoner was born in Massillon, Ohio. He was educated at Pennsylvania State University, where he received a B.A. in 1947. In 1949, he earned an M.A. in creative writing from Indiana University. Formerly an instructor at DePauw University (1949-1950) and Pennsylvania State University (1950-1954), Wagoner has taught at the University of Washington since 1954, and since 1966 he has been a professor of English. He has also served as the editor of *Poetry Northwest* since 1966 and as editor for the Princeton Poetry Series since 1978. In 1978, he was elected to succeed Robert Lowell as a chancellor of the Academy of American Poets. His work has been recognized with a Guggenheim Fellowship (1956), a Ford fellowship (1964), a National Institute of Arts and Letters grant (1967), *Poetry* magazine's Morton Dauwen Zabel Prize (1967), a National Endowment for the Arts Grant (1969), *Poetry's* Oscar Blumenthal Prize (1974) and Eunice Tietjens Memorial Prize (1977). *Sleeping in the Woods* (1974) and *Collected Poems 1956-1976* (1976) were nominated for National Book Awards. *In Broken Country* (1979) was nominated for a 1980 American Book Award.

Writing now for more than twenty years, author of nine novels and eleven volumes of poetry, the recipient of numerous awards and honors, Wagoner has remained, nevertheless, relatively unnoticed over the years, and his work has been conspicuously omitted from the major anthologies of contemporary verse. A number of reasons for these oversights might be advanced—Wagoner's reputation as a poet suffered from constant comparisons with his friend and teacher, Theodore Roethke; Wagoner's subject matter, consisting chiefly of the American Northwest, frequently leads reviewers to bypass his work with only an acknowledgment of his obvious lyric gift for writing about the natural world; and finally, Wagoner's poems suffer ironically from being too "readable." As X. J. Kennedy admitted, "Wagoner is so readable a poet, that coming to him after, say an evening with Pound's later *Cantos*, one practically has a twinge of Puritan guilt, and feels shamelessly entertained—refreshed instead of exhausted." But while Wagoner's poems are indeed entertaining, his best work is no less complex than Robert Frost's; and the natural world in Wagoner's poems, as in Frost's, is Wagoner's means of speaking about our largest concerns—how we are to go about "finding the right direction" in "broken country" so that we may, in time, with luck, arrive with a full and earned understanding of this "worn-down, hard, incredible sight / Called Here and Now," an understanding that involves the acceptance that our lives are what we make of them, a continued "journey without regret." And while Wagoner's poetic journey is not unlike Roethke's—to "become one with the world by empathy" (as John Gardner rightly noted in his review of the *Collected Poems*)—his means of travel is completely his own. Wagoner is more of a "thinking" poet than Roethke, and his characteristic voice is a curious and inimitable mixture of the matter-of-fact "Here and Now" and the calm astonishment over the way in which the "Here and Now" is, nevertheless, an "incredible sight."

After growing up in Whiting, Indiana, Wagoner attended Pennsylvania State University where Roethke was his teacher. (Roethke was later instrumental in Wagoner's move to the University of Washington in 1959.) Wagoner's tribute and debt to Roethke are worked out in the early volumes of poetry, most notably in *Dry Sun, Dry Wind* (1953), a first volume that Wagoner completely omits from his *Collected Poems*. *Dry Sun, Dry Wind* consists of two parts: twenty-two short lyrics and eight longer quasi-dramatic monologues. In the first part, the book broods over and mourns the loss of the ordinarily fertile and life-giving aspects of the world; the wind that once set the strings of the aeolian harp in motion is, for Wagoner, "drier than left husks" and the sun "carries death to leaves" ("Sun, Wind"). As Richard Howard has commented, these twenty-two lyrics "operate by an alienation effect"—the world around the speaker is continually seen as hostile and estranged. Without a "holding place," in a world that continuously shifts, we are finally lost, the way sandbars are buried by the constant alterations of sand dunes:

> Like retarded water
> Sweeping to a shore of houses,
> The dunes alter.
> Last year, this rippling hill,
> Slanted and sheer against the windfence,
> Was a gulley, and the larch sapling
> Stood on toes of root above the furze.
> . . . .
> Wind looks like this:
> Curving through shallows of land
> Lifting and letting fall,
> Taking cover around and from the stone,
> Caressing all.
> But the eye turns feebler, year by year:
> Mound and hollow do not lodge in the mind.
> Eyes are tossed like sandbars

> Along whatever crossway the wind takes,
> Buried at random with the tree, with love,
> With last year's certain light.

This poem—"Afternoon of Sand"—also illustrates the basic structure of these early lyrics: a series of natural observations that suggest the imperfection of the world in which we live followed by a more direct linking to the speaker's predicament and estrangement. The poem also illustrates the basic flaws of these early poems: they too neatly explain themselves—here is a landscape and this is what it means (Wagoner's later poems will implicitly trust the landscape to carry the meaning of the poem); and they are marked by a somewhat mawkish tone of lamentation ("O drier than time / they know no counterparts but love and rhyme"; "O all distance turning cold / with age, stilling the white lake"; "I look for a mooring place, / But leaves are light").

A number of Wagoner's most distinctive and prevalent traits are already apparent: the clarity of descriptive detail (although the concreteness of the detail in these poems is often lost in the vagaries of place)—"Moss points all one way on the stone"; "like water / In a pose, the thatch of knuckle-grass has frozen"; a wonderful feel for the metaphorical implications of ordinary situations—"The walls are broken: / Like curious hanging gardens, / The lathwork and wire / Sway in the circling air"; and a blank-verse line that becomes less regular in the later poems, frequently building in a kind of low-keyed but steady way toward emotional intensity—"and above, the leaves of the hemlock whisk / Like the sounds of wasps, as, maundering and uncertain, / In an air already greyed to the thinnest light, / The thinnest noise, the first snow too late." Besides these technical aspects of Wagoner's verse, *Dry Sun, Dry Wind* introduces the almost "religious" yearning for fullness and communion between the self and the world that runs throughout the Wagoner canon. (Sam, the aerialist, longs for flight, for the knowledge that the birds will not give up; Silas, the tree surgeon, for the health of earlier times when "apples once, / after blossoms, hung there and fell / Into my baskets"; and Luke of Sippo Heights for the "bedlam of things.") Although Wagoner's formal Christianity waned early, his writing has, from beginning to end, sought to discover what in nature is common with himself. For Wagoner, the imaginative act is a means of communion (he calls himself a "lost preacher," "doing time in the hard woods"). He sees poem-making as a constant attempt to break through the barriers between interior and exterior so that whatever lies behind "the dark window" might be revealed, as in "Note from Body to Soul":

> Each word a rock
> The size of a fist—
> I throw them one by one
> At the dark window.

Two novels (*The Man in the Middle*, 1954; *Money Money Money*, 1955) and five years later (Wagoner was at the time teaching with Roethke at the University of Washington), Wagoner published his second volume of poems, *A Place to Stand* (1958). Like the earlier *Dry Sun, Dry Wind*, this volume is concerned with identity and ultimate questions: "What called me? Why? When will the flame and foam make sense? / How shall I quicken? Who are these animals? Where *am* I?" ("Admonition"). The journey to answer these questions leads the speaker backward to his beginnings, "follow[ing] water down" ("The Migration"), toward the "crippled underhalf of the mind" ("Lullaby through the Side of the Mouth"). Unfortunately, and Wagoner's self-editing for the *Collected Poems* (only ten poems from his second volume are included) suggests his awareness of this problem, the journey echoes Roethke too obviously, both in the song-poems with Roethkean rhythms and in lines like "(Why shall I curl? How may I touch? / Who echoes me to death?)." But Wagoner's best work to date is included here as well. In what may be his first poem in his own voice, "To My Friend Whose Parachute Did Not Open," Wagoner brings together one of his most persistent concerns—that words are not enough, that only a song that transcends words, coming "miraculously" from somewhere outside the self can sustain—with the lyrical and technical resourcefulness one associates with his more mature poems. Perhaps most important is the possibility of hope (although limited) both in this poem and in *A Place to Stand*. Wagoner's journeyer (in "The Hero with One Face," for example) seems ready now to learn:

> Now, like Ulysses, master of
> The world under, world above,
> The world between—and one beyond
> Which was not near enough to find—
> I wait, and wonder what to learn:
> O here, twice blind at being born.

Wagoner's search for "a place to stand" finally is successful in *The Nesting Ground* published in 1963, five years after *A Place to Stand* and his third novel, *The Rock*. In a publisher's note to the volume, Wagoner remarks: "Many of the poems use the objects and creatures of the natural world, in action, to recreate dramatically the emotional and spiritual trials of man." Indeed, for there is a wholly new trust in the landscape to be its own source of meaning. Perhaps this trust in the natural world is related to Wagoner's new "home"; his poems have abandoned the arid landscapes of the Midwest for the teeming life of the Pacific Northwest; and he has moved from lamentation and complaint to his more typical stance of cataloguing the world around him, as in "Guide to Dungeness Spit":

> Those whistling overhead are Canada geese;
> Some on the waves are loons,
> And more on the sand are pipers. There, Bonaparte's
>   gulls
> Settle a single perch.

X. J. Kennedy, in discussing Roethke's "influence," has commented wisely on Wagoner's relation to the Pacific Northwest: "I suspect that the most valuable service Roethke ever performed for Wagoner was to bring him to the Pacific Northwest and expose him to rain forests. As in Roethke's late masterwork 'Meditations at Oyster River,' the landscape provided Wagoner with better objective correlatives than the smokestacks of Chicago-side Indiana." Wagoner himself has acknowledged the necessity of leaving the Midwest. In "A Valedictory to Standard Oil of Indiana" (from *Staying Alive*, 1966), Wagoner first asks the question, "What should his high school classmates do, now that 'Standard Oil' has automated," and then answers by instructing them to "Get out of town."

The Nesting Ground contains a number of fine poems that are "essential" Wagoner. Besides "Guide to Dungeness Spit," a kind of prototype for Wagoner's best poems, which are written as a series of instructions for survival in life, there are "Homage," where the poet is "bent down" by the protective attacks of a male hummingbird only to notice what has been clear all along—"its mate . . . perched silent at my elbow"—and "Standing Halfway Home," where the poet "suddenly stand[s] still" so long that he becomes enough a part of the natural world for a "seedy, burr-sized wren" to "burst into song" an "arm's length" away as if the poet "were a stalk." Similarly, poems like "The Nesting Ground" and "Plumage" suggest that by patience and by sinking into the natural world, one will learn to decipher the "source" from the semblance, the way one can "see" a hiding pheasant perfectly matched to its environs "at the end of sight." And finally, there are poems like "Advice to the Orchestra" that once again implore us to give ourselves over to song:

Offer yourselves through the mold on brass, through
  skins and bones.
Your music must consume its instruments
Or die lost in the elbow-joints and valves, in snaggle
  and crook, ratchet and pinchbeck, in the folded winds.

After publication of his fourth novel, *The Escape Artist* (1965), considered by many critics as his best, Wagoner produced his fourth book of verse. The new direction of his poetry begun in *The Nesting Ground* is continued in *Staying Alive*. "The Words" from that volume expresses Wagoner's changing perspective:

> Wind, bird, and tree,
> Water, grass, and light:
> In half of what I write
> Roughly or smoothly
> Year by impatient year,
> The same six words recur.
>
> . . . .
>
> I take what is:
> The light beats on the stones,
> And wind over water shines
> Like long grass through the trees,
> As I set loose, like birds
> In a landscape, the old words.

"I take what is" becomes, in many respects, Wagoner's motto. For Wagoner, taking what is involves: an acceptance of our fragmented selves, which through love we are always trying to patch together; an acceptance of our own darkness; and an acceptance of the world around us with which we must reacquaint ourselves. All of these ideas are at work in the title poem, "Staying Alive," which is in the characteristic guide-to-survival mode for which he has been deservedly praised. Laurence Leiberman suggests that Wagoner's "instructional" poems ("Staying Alive," "Crossing Half a River," "The Middle of Nowhere," "The Other Side of the Mountain," "Slow Country," "Sleeping in the Woods," the nine "New Poems" section of the *Collected Poems*, and twelve new poems that conclude *In Broken Country*) are "his own unique stakeout in contemporary writing." *Staying Alive* is frequently said to be the volume where Wagoner comes into his own as a poet. Perhaps it is more than simply a coincidence that the title poem is Wagoner's first, and in some respects most enduring, mastery of a style that, as Sanford Pinsker has noted, "links ostensibly scattered strands of the Wagoner canon into something like a cohesive vision."

"Staying Alive," along with "Sleeping in the Woods," prefigures Wagoner's most recent instructional poems, establishing a groundwork of concerns that Wagoner returns to again and again. For this reason, they can serve as a focus for a discussion both of Wagoner's favorite themes and his thematic development from *Staying Alive* to *Sleeping in the Woods* (1974). "Staying Alive" (and the others) is a series of directives. (Wagoner's use of this form is closer to Henry Reed's "Lessons of War" than Frost's "Directive.") Wagoner's instructions, like Reed's, operate within a framework that is quite literal—for Wagoner, the practical advice of a manual, given by a woodsy guide.

The plot of "Staying Alive" is quite simple: should the neophyte "you," lost in the wilderness, stay put, "Trusting to others" for rescue or "start walking and walking in one direction." Both choices are considered, although the neophyte begins with the "safer choice"—to stay put. This part of the poem serves as a kind of initiatory stage in preparation for the time when "you" may "decide at last" to "break through / In spite of all danger." Thus the "you" learns to "watch," to build a lean-to, to make a fire, and most important to "stand still." "Waiting" for Wagoner plays an essential role in other poems as well: all demonstrate how the alien world of nature opens to us when we "wait." The "you" in "Staying Alive" must become more open to the world around him; before "finding himself" he must begin by letting the woods "find him." And it is "openness" that lies beneath the progress of Wagoner's "you" from "Staying Alive" to "Sleeping in The Woods." The "you" in "Staying Alive" "must learn" how to change from someone who is "uprooted," "pruned," and "transplanted" into someone who "follows" the "columbine and bleeding hearts" ("Moving Into The Garden"). Only when we are "comfortable" in the alien woods will we be "at last" ready to "break through / In spite of all danger."

When Wagoner's "you" does decide to "start walking," another continuing "lesson" in Wagoner's verse is suggested—when finding one's way in the wilderness in life one must let the woods, rather than the mind which may perceive wrongly, be the guide. Only sense perception and the objective world will bring the "you" "safe to nightfall".

Remember the stars
And moss when your mind runs into circles. If it
                                      should rain
Or fog should roll the horizon in around you,
Hold still for hours

David Wagoner

Or days if you must, or weeks, for seeing is believing
In the wilderness.

Wagoner repeats these instructions (in different guises) in the more recent series. In "Tracking" from "New Poems" in *Collected Poems*, the guide instructs:

    in this empty country
    You must learn to read
    What you've never read before: the minute language
    Of moss and lichen,
    The signals of bent grass, the speech of sand
    The gestures of dust

And in "Finding the Right Direction" from *In Broken Country*:

Those times when too much stands between you and
                                    the sky—
Tree crowns and clouds of mist—when the hidden sun
Makes nothing of your shadow
To guide you south, you turn to stones, to slopes and
                                    trees,
To flowers, even to birds for your directions.

If we "learn" our lore correctly—to naturalize ourselves to the world's ways, to follow the pathway of the world as it is, rather than our minds—then

There may even come, on some uncanny evening,
A time when you're warm and dry, well fed, not thirsty,
Uninjured, without fear,
When nothing, either good or bad, is happening.
This is called staying alive.

"Staying Alive" concludes with the "you" finally left alone in the woods with only his preparation, his knowledge of how to "stay alive." There is only his "self" into which he must "burrow / Deep for a deep winter"; for it is the self's "deep," not some higher assistance, that must finally counter the imminent death suggested in "deep winter." "Staying Alive" begins Wagoner's search for the "pathway" that leads out of the "wilderness," a search that continues in his most recent work. It presents us with Wagoner's most characteristic stance and voice: "we" are instructed in a voice that is, at once, matter-of-fact, self-mockingly witty, and quietly reverential to accommodate the most negative and disintegrative aspects of life, balancing the good against the bad.

"Sleeping in the Woods," published eight years later, forms a kind of companion piece. Written in the same instructional manner, it seems to begin where the earlier poem ends. In "Sleeping in the Woods," Wagoner's "you," still "Not having found

[his] way out of the woods," learns to sleep in peace come nightfall. The process of learning is similar in both poems: the "you" is instructed once more to naturalize himself with the surrounding world. Only after the "you" has familiarized his body with the ground, only after he is "lying still / At last" may he:

    watch the shadows seeking their own level,
    The ground beneath you neither rising nor falling,
    Neither giving nor taking
    From the dissolving cadence of your heart, identical
                                    darkness
    Behind and before your eyes. . . .

In language reminiscent of the definition of "staying alive," Wagoner reminds us that the moment of sleep is a moment of equilibrium, of balance between the internal and external worlds of the self. Finally beyond the fearful world of "Staying Alive," the "you" goes to sleep "without a ceiling, / For the first time without walls."

Unlike the failure of communication in "Staying Alive" (the "you" is not rescued), "Sleeping in the Woods" suggests that once we "rely on" (Wagoner's pun on "lie on") the self, we may reach a compromise with the world we live in. That is, although the imagination may have "its snout half sunk in blood / And the mind's tooth gnaw all night at bone and tendon," it also has the capability to create light, to transform the familiar universe so that "stars, shut out / By leaves and branches in another forest" may "burn / At the mattering source / Forever." Put another way, the imagination in Wagoner's poem makes matter (the stuff of the world) matter (give importance to) by establishing a compromise, a balance between the "imponderable / Dead and living / Earth." Besides simply "staying alive" in the world, the "you" has learned to see the familiar world as mysterious and significant.

In "Sleeping in the Woods," release from the woods comes by "making light of it." To "make light" means to concede and accept our limitations, the "darkness" in which we are lost. The "problem of recognition" ("Staying Alive") is solved, then, by realizing that "identical darkness" is "behind and before your eyes." If we recognize ourselves for what we are, by "simply being here" we will find the "right way out."

Between *Staying Alive* and *Sleeping in the Woods*, Wagoner produced two volumes of poetry, *New and Selected Poems* (1969) and *Riverbed* (1972), two novels, *Baby, Come On Inside* (1968) and *Where is My Wandering Boy Tonight?* (1970), and edited *Straw for the Fire: From the Notebooks of Theodore*

Roethke, 1943-1963 (1972). *New and Selected Poems* begins (as does the later *Collected Poems*) with ten poems from *A Place to Stand* and ends with thirty-five new poems, eight of which Wagoner pared for *Collected Poems*. It seems that Wagoner's acceptance of both himself and the world opened a much wider range of subject matter for his poems. The poems are peopled with bums, convicts, burglars, shoplifters, garbagemen, and an escape artist (the jacket note to *A Place to Stand* mentions that Wagoner "has worked at times as a railroad section-hand, a concentrated soup-scooper in a steel mill, a park policeman, and a restaurant grillman"). Wagoner always seems to have "one ear to the ground," able to find poems in even the most offhand comments; often his poems are responses to newspaper clippings, comments on the news, casual advice from strangers. No wonder, then, that he has been so prolific over the years—he has an uncanny ability of turning any subject into poetry, an ability that might be related to the "magical" role that he sees for poets.

Since Wagoner is a member of The Society of American Magicians, it is not surprising that a number of his poems take magic as their motif (between "New Poems" and "Sleeping in the Woods," there are "Magic Night at the Reformatory," "The Escape Artist," "The Inexhaustible Hut," "The Extraordinary Production of Eggs from the Mouth," "Last Words of the Human Fly," "The Floating Lady," "The First Trick," and "The Uncanny Illusion of the Headless Lady"). Writing about Wagoner's novel *The Escape Artist*, Richard Howard provides a rationale: "the poet can be not only the 'emergency maker' but the magical entertainer who by delighting us all saves his own neck and ours as well." Over the years magic, like love, and like poetry, has been a life-sustaining force that counters the disintegrative aspects of life. In fact, magic, love, and the imagination are all interconnected in Wagoner's work since as lovers "we believe in magic," and as magician-lovers we "believe" that magic "can break suddenly out of stone or out of dry air" like words suddenly become song. As in Wagoner's wilderness-guide poems, the focus of his "magic" poems is the way in which illusion, like the imagination, can "produce something from nothing," and more importantly, how the poet's and the magician's sleight-of-hand are essential to staying alive"; in the words of a very recent poem ("Getting There"): "what you make of it / the Here and Now / means everything."

Although in *Riverbed* and *Sleeping in the Woods* there are an extraordinary number of unsentimental, but reverential poems concerning man's relationship with the natural world like "Riverbed," "The Death and Resurrection of Birds," "Waiting with the Snowy Owls," "The Gathering of the Loons," "Talking to Barr Creek," "The First Place," "An Offering for Dungeness Bay" (to name just a few)—one should consider another type of poem that Wagoner has turned to again and again. *Riverbed* ends with three poems ("Old Man, Old Man," "Lost," and "Fog") in Wagoner's voice, but using a kind of Indian cosmology to express his ideas, as in "Lost":

> Stand still. The trees ahead and bushes behind you
> Are not lost. Wherever you are is called Here,
> And you must treat it as a powerful stranger,
> Must ask permission to know it and be known.
> . . . .
> If what a tree or bush does is lost on you,
> You are surely lost. Stand still. The forest knows
> Where you are. You must let it find you.

Similarly, *Sleeping in the Woods* concludes with seven more poems of this nature, "Seven Songs for an Old Voice." The poems chart the progress of the "old voice," as he learns to accept even death as natural, an acceptance that hinges upon full recognition of the cyclic polarities of nature:

> I have praised the rising and the dying wind,
> Water falling or vanishing, even the end of grass.
> I have welcomed the seasons equally
> And been one with all weather from the wild to the
> silent.

In Wagoner's more recent work, he returns to plumb this vein more fully. In *Collected Poems*, the poems in sections 3 and 4 of "New Poems" are loosely based on Indian legends, and in *Who Shall Be the Sun?* (1978), Wagoner has collected all of these previous poems and added fifty-one new poems based on the "Lore, Legends, and Myths of Northwest Coast and Plateau Indians." The use of these Indian legends gives Wagoner's narrative and lyrical gifts free rein. Or put another way, Wagoner finds in these legends a way to combine the concerns of his magic and wilderness poems—as he writes in the author's note to *Who Shall Be the Sun?*, the "spiritual trait" of the American Indians that he admires most is their lack of ego and awe. "they did not place themselves above their organic and inorganic companions on earth but recognized with awe that they shared the planet as equals with animals, fish, birds, trees, rivers, bushes, stones and such phenomena as weather and natural disasters." If comparisons are drawn between Wagoner's group

David Wagoner

of nine backpacking poems in the "New Poems" (a group of which, Vernon Young has said, "In all of American literature there is not, I think, a sequence of poetry more remarkable") and these recast, embellished Indian legends, the unity and achievement of Wagoner's work makes itself felt. For just as the Indian legends are concerned with humility, with connections to the landscape, with the transforming possibilities of dream, and with coming to terms with one's own death, Wagoner's nine-poem sequence maps the recontinued journey of Wagoner's "you," a journey that involves: "Breaking Camp" after "having spent a hard-earned sleep"; losing one's ego ("Meeting A Bear," "Walking in a Swamp"); finding oneself by losing oneself to the landscape, which is never "lost" ("Tracking," "Missing the Trail," "From Here to There"); knowing one's self ("Being Shot"); experiencing the kinship between one's body and the natural world ("Waiting in the Rain Forest"); and finally, "travelling" to the "world of our first selves" where the dictum of "Staying Alive"—"seeing is believing" —becomes at last the more complete "believing is once more seeing."

In Broken Country, Wagoner's most recent volume of poetry, carries on many of these same concerns, and relies more than ever on the instructional mode of his backpacking poems. Besides another twelve-poem sequence that continues the search in the wilderness, there are a number of other poems employing the same approach— "Stunts" (a poem in five parts that finds its metaphors in a handbook of magic stunts), "Cutting Down a Tree," "Judging Logs," "Buck Fever," "Duck-Blind," "Setting a Snare," "Trapline," and "Posing with a Trophy." All of these poems do not work; sometimes they are too preachy. This type of poem seems to work best when the instructions are given more in the form of a handbook than as the disguised social commentary of such poems as "Cutting Down a Tree":

Having picked your tree and cleared its base of suckers,
You size it up roughly, looking as toplofty
As it, deciding now which way it should topple
By the lay of the land or its own inclination,
Even walking off the bed-ground, where you will put it
In its place for bucking and scaling, to make certain
No hidden stumps or cross-fallen logs
Will shelter it and cost you half your profit.

But the sequence of twelve poems that concludes *In Broken Country* can stand with Wagoner's finest poems, and Wagoner's best poems are, as John Gardner has said, "among the best anyone has

written". In this new sequence of backpacking poems, Wagoner's landscape is the desert rather than the rain forest. The change is related to the kind of journey Wagoner's "you" must now make; that is, how does one find himself in "broken country" where everything "seems in favor of dying." "Finding the Right Direction" in this "graveyard" involves constant "guesswork," and as "In Broken Country" suggests, the best Wagoner's walker (and poetry?) can do is:

put two and two
Together, take them apart,
And put them together again and again in baffling
pieces,
Seeing the matter of all your sensible facts
Jumbled to the horizon.

Despite the obvious difficulty of making headway in a world without "footholds and handholds," and despite the fact that this journey has "nothing at the end of it / But the end of it" ("Climbing Alone"), the "you" pushes on, "Crossing A River" by following alongside it until the river "goes underground" (all is temporary in this desert landscape), leaving him halfway, "Standing in the Middle of a Desert." At this point, Wagoner's walker "reconsiders," but learns that in a world of death, only one thing matters—life. And living means moving on, "marking your time in this intractable sand." Past the "point of no return" (the sixth poem appropriately), all directions the same in the desert, the journey continues in the "blowing sand" where the only hope is the "rooting place" a boot mark makes for "an hour," a place where seeds may strain to rise "root and branch," to "postpone their burial."

The next three poems in this sequence— "Living Off the Land," "Reading the Landscape," "Seeing Things"—concern the necessary adjustments to this landscape. Survival means facing oneself, living face to face with death, a death which reminds "you" that

Your mind's voice and mind's eye
Are equally vulnerable in their pastimes
and desolations,
Their taste for all the flavors of light
and shade
And the sweet nothings
Of casual, elaborate, or desperate speech.

And survival means "go[ing] along" with a world of "disguises," choosing a direction in a directionless, "speechless" world.

Finally, after a "night of reckoning," Wagoner's

"you," having learned how to live "by the sweat of [his] brow," is rewarded with life-giving water. As in Wagoner's other wilderness poems, the way to this water lies in both listening "hard," "Not to the ragged pulse in your mind's ear / (That deserted music)," but "For the actual droning of bees, for actual birdsong," and in following these bees and birds "To the place where they've made their lives over and over." For making our lives over and over is all we can ever do. The only "lasting impression" of our lives, as the last poem of the sequence, "Getting There," instructs, is the imprint of our erratic, slipshod, and "meandering" attempts. What has been implicit all along is now accepted: "in broken country," our lives are a continual beginning, and what we make of them is the "end of endings."

It remains to be said that many of these poems— from *Collected Poems* to *In Broken Country*—are major achievements. At their best, they balance a remarkable range of emotions and tone, bringing together Wagoner's wit and lyrical pacing in a new, quieter, more personal, and more powerful way than ever before. Although he continues to write novels (*The Road to Many a Wonder*, 1974; *Tracker*, 1975; and *Whole Hog*, 1976) it is Wagoner's poetry on which his reputation will rest. For Wagoner has evolved over the years a kind of poem and voice that is all his own, and that, more importantly, can speak about large questions, while remaining honest to his own and his audience's distrust of easy answers. As Laurence Leiberman has written, "the resultant effect, unlike anything I have encountered in American poetry, is that of an apparently low-keyed, spare lyricism, of moderate emotional intensity which gathers force and verve from a steady build-up of pitch accruing from the perfect control of nuances and overtones over a wide stretch of purely hypnotic, clean writing." In short, Wagoner's poetry demands reading and justifies the high praise that Robert Boyers gave to him early on: "David Wagoner seems to me one of our best poets, perhaps one of the best we have had in this country." —*Robert K. Cording*

Play:

An Eye for an Eye for an Eye, Seattle, 1973.

Other:

Robin Skelton, ed., *Five Poets of the Pacific Northwest,* includes poems by Wagoner (Seattle: University of Washington Press, 1964);
Straw for the Fire: From the Notebooks of Theodore Roethke, 1943-1963, edited by Wagoner (Garden City: Doubleday, 1972).

Interview:

"An Interview with David Wagoner," *Crazy Horse,* no. 12 (1972).

References:

Robert Boyers, "The Poetry of David Wagoner," *Kenyon Review,* 32 (Spring 1970): 176-181;
John Gardner, Review of *Whole Hog* and *Collected Poems, New York Times Book Review,* 2 January 1977, pp. 7, 10;
Richard Howard, *Alone With America Essays on the Art of Poetry in the United States Since 1950* (New York: Atheneum, 1969): pp. 533-551;
X. J. Kennedy, "Pelting Dark Windows," *Parnassus,* 5 (Spring/Summer 1977): 133-140;
Laurence Leiberman, "David Wagoner: The Cold Speech of the Earth," in his *Unassigned Frequencies: American Poetry in Review 1964-1977* (Urbana: University of Illinois Press, 1977), pp. 152-181;
Sanford Pinsker, "On David Wagoner," in *Contemporary Poetry in America,* ed. Robert Boyers (New York: Schocken Books, 1974), pp. 360-368;
Vernon Young, "Poetry Chronicle," *Hudson Review,* 29 (Winter 1976-1977): 629-632.

DIANE WAKOSKI
(3 August 1937-)

BOOKS: *Coins and Coffins* (New York: Hawk's Well Press, 1962);
Discrepancies and Apparitions (Garden City: Doubleday, 1966);
George Washington Poems (New York: Riverrun Press, 1967);
Greed, Parts one and two (Los Angeles: Black Sparrow Press, 1968);
Inside the Blood Factory (Garden City: Doubleday, 1968);
The Diamond Merchant (Cambridge, Mass.: Sans Souci Press, 1968);
A Play and Two Poems, by Wakoski, Robert Kelly, and Ron Loewinsohn (Los Angeles: Black Sparrow Press, 1968);
Thanking My Mother for Piano Lessons (Mount Horeb, Wis.: Perishable Press, 1969);

Greed, Parts 3 and 4 (Los Angeles: Black Sparrow Press, 1969);

The Lament of the Lady Bank Dick (Cambridge, Mass.: Sans Souci Press, 1969);

The Moon Has a Complicated Geography (Palo Alto: D. Alexander / Odda Tala, 1969);

The Magellanic Clouds (Los Angeles: Black Sparrow Press, 1970);

Black Dream Ditty for Billy "the Kid" M seen in Dr. Generosity's Bar Recruiting for Hell's Angels and Black Mafia (Los Angeles: Black Sparrow Press, 1970);

On Barbara's Shore (Los Angeles: Black Sparrow Press, 1971);

Greed, Parts 5-7 (Los Angeles: Black Sparrow Press, 1971);

The Motorcycle Betrayal Poems (New York: Simon & Schuster, 1971);

The Wise Men Drawn to Kneel in Wonder at the Fact so of Itself, by Wakoski, David Bromige, and Robert Kelly (Los Angeles: Black Sparrow Press, 1971);

Smudging (Los Angeles: Black Sparrow Press, 1972);

Form is an Extension of Content (Los Angeles: Black Sparrow Press, 1972);

The Pumpkin Pie (Los Angeles: Black Sparrow Press, 1972);

Greed Parts 8, 9, 11 (Los Angeles: Black Sparrow Press, 1973);

Dancing on the Grave of a Son of a Bitch (Los Angeles: Black Sparrow Press, 1973);

Stillife: Michael, Silver Flute and Violets (Storrs: University of Connecticut Press, 1973);

Winter Sequences (Los Angeles: Black Sparrow Press, 1973);

Trilogy: Coins and Coffins, Discrepancies and Apparitions, The George Washington Poems (Garden City: Doubleday, 1974);

Looking for the King of Spain (Los Angeles: Black Sparrow Press, 1974);

Abalone (Los Angeles: Black Sparrow Press, 1974);

The Wandering Tattler (Driftless, Wis.: Perishable Press, 1974);

Virtuoso Literature for Two and Four Hands (Garden City: Doubleday, 1974);

The Fable of the Lion and the Scorpion (Milwaukee: Pentagram, 1975);

Creating a Personal Mythology (Los Angeles: Black Sparrow Press, 1975);

G. Washington's Camp Cups (Madison, Wis.: Red Ozier Press, 1976);

The Last Poem, with *Tough Company* by Charles Bukowski (Santa Barbara: Black Sparrow Press, 1976);

Waiting for the King of Spain (Santa Barbara: Black Sparrow Press, 1976);

The Ring (Santa Barbara: Black Sparrow Press, 1977);

The Man Who Shook Hands (Garden City: Doubleday, 1978);

Pachelbel's Canon (Santa Barbara: Black Sparrow Press, 1978);

Trophies (Santa Barbara: Black Sparrow Press, 1979);

Cap of Darkness (Santa Barbara: Black Sparrow Press, 1980);

Toward A New Poetry (Ann Arbor: University of Michigan Press, 1980).

Diane Wakoski was born in Whittier, California, and, according to her own account, began writing poems when she was seven years old. She received her B.A. from the University of California at Berkeley in 1960. In 1965 she married S. Shepard Sherbell and, after divorcing Sherbell, married Michael Watterland in 1973. Wakoski has been awarded the Bread Loaf Writers' Conference Robert Frost fellowship (1966), the Cassandra Foundation Award (1970), a grant from the New York State Council on the Arts (1971), a Guggenheim Fellowship (1972), and a National Endowment for the Arts Grant (1973). She has held poet-in-residence positions at the California Institute of Technology, the University of Virginia, Colorado College, Willamette University, Hollins College, the University of California at Irvine, Macalester College, Lake Forest College, Michigan State University, the University of Hawaii, Whitman College in Walla Walla, Washington, the University of Wisconsin, and Emory University. Wakoski is currently a professor of English at Michigan State University.

Wakoski considers herself primarily a narrative rather than lyric poet, and she suggests further that her work is better called "personal," rather than "autobiographical" or "confessional." "When people call me confessional," she says in a 1979 interview, "what they usually mean is that I write autobiographical poetry and I often talk about pain and loss and the general problems that middle class Americans associate with neurosis and mental disorders which I think are great human problems." Her "personal narrative," on the other hand, "implies that there is no way that a poem could ever, ever, ever have any kind of meaningful existence unless you felt there was a person behind it," while at the same time reminding the reader that the "I" of the poem is not necessarily Wakoski herself. Poets invent personae, masks, various voices, says

Wakoski, to liberate themselves from the "obsessive muse," to distance themselves from the terror and eventual boredom in the relentless mental repetition of an image, word, or phrase that leads to the writing of a poem.

In many of Wakoski's poems the obsessive muse focuses on the idea of beauty. Taken as a whole, her work may be regarded as a linguistic/poetic quest for beauty. Believing that the role of the artist is "to focus on the conflict between the desire for beauty and the natural ugliness the world imposes on us, to create beautiful artifacts that in some way give other people a sense of beauty . . . ," she writes poems that affirm the world's beauty while lamenting human blindness to it. Her early poems manifest this affirmation of beauty in two main ways: in the attempt to resolve difficult or unpleasant situations and events and find beauty in them, and in the use of a narrative line composed of stark, intense, but finally beautiful, images. The events or dramatic situations in these early poems are often fantastic, or at least improbable; the second phase in her development may be noted in her gradual preference for more everyday events, which begins to be apparent about the time of *Inside the Blood Factory* (1968).

The Wakoski canon may be divided into three phases. The first, which one may call her imagistic phase, begins with *Coins and Coffins* (1962), her first published book, and continues roughly until *Inside the Blood Factory*. The second phase, characterized by a movement away from the extraordinary and toward a search for beauty in the everyday, begins approximately with *Thanking My Mother For Piano Lessons* (1969) and ends at about the time of *Virtuoso Literature for Two and Four Hands* (1974). A third phase, illustrated by an increasingly self-conscious use of musical forms and rhythms, begins about this time and continues to the present, reaching a high level of clarity in *The Man Who Shook Hands* (1978), a book whose best poems wed Wakoski's primary themes—beauty and music—with a digressive structure.

In her early poems Wakoski remembers being influenced by T. S. Eliot, Robinson Jeffers, Allen Ginsberg, and Robert Lowell. Later, as her style matured, William Carlos Williams, Charles Olson, and especially Wallace Stevens and Robert Creeley became poets of importance to her, as did Robert Duncan and Jerome Rothenberg. Her fascination with what she calls Creeley's contemplation of "the possibility of using the principle of digression as a structure" begins early in her career, and comes into conscious focus in the opening essay of *The Man*

Who Shook Hands—"The blue swan, an essay on music in poetry"—where admiration for Stevens is also clearly shown by her use of "Peter Quince at the Clavier" as one of the bases for her essay.

"Justice is Reason Enough," a poem in *Coins and Coffins*, exemplifies Wakoski's first-phase poetry. In it, a young woman relates the story of her brother David. The poem begins with a description of David's body lying on the sand at the base of a cliff bordering the sea and tells of the narrator's irritation with her mother, who constantly asks "why?" The narrator then describes a dream David had had about a gull "beating its wings / effortlessly together until they drew blood" and explains that this dream led her brother to her room to seduce her. The poem ends with the narrator posing this answer to her mother's question: "justice. Justice is / reason enough for anything ugly. It balances the beauty in the / world." At one point, the narrator responds to her mother's constantly asking why by saying that she "wanted / never to hear of David any more." At the poem's end, however, the narrator affirms, "I will never forget / him, who was my brother, who is dead."

Three characteristics make this poem a good example of Wakoski's early work. The first is the use of a series of images in an associative process. The second is the use of an unforgettably dramatic situation narrated in the first person, and the third is the narrator's attempt to resolve or be at peace with the situation. The poem also illustrates the importance of Wakoski's distinction between the personal narrative and a confessional poem, for the failure on the part of some readers to distinguish a narrator separate from the poet led them to believe that the poem describes a piece of Wakoski's biography: "For years, people thought this was a true story," she says in *Creating a Personal Mythology* (1975), and she explains that although the event is imaginary it is as psychologically true as any other part of her biography: "It is, I think, as much a part of my history now as whatever is real about my history." The poem derives a peculiar power from the narrator's stance, which is very near the events of the poem but still matter-of-fact about them, embodying Wakoski's maxim, "if you want to write personal poetry (that great luxury) you have to be absolutely impersonal about yr experiences and life."

"Apparitions Are Not Singular Occurrences," from *Discrepancies and Apparitions* (1966), is a first-phase poem built almost solely on the associative process and imagistic technique. The poem opens with the startling images of an unnamed "I," wearing only strings of diamonds, riding on a zebra past the door of an unidentified "you." The person inside, "a bird wearing the mask of a bird," is having drinks with Death. Wakoski suggests in the introduction to *Trilogy* (1974) that the use of such bizarre images is "a way of making the reader accept the specialness of the feelings of speaker in the

Layle Silbert

poem." The effect of this series of images is certainly unique. In a fundamental way, however, the three extraordinary images—a naked woman riding a zebra, a masked bird, Death drinking a cocktail—and the process of their making are the true subjects of the poem. The narrator's sharp focus on the image of a trapeze artist swinging up on the bar to escape death brings the other images into clear resolution: the person in the house has rejected life for death. The narrator's final accusation that treating Death like an honored guest is "sharing something you had no right to share" makes the images represent both a human betrayal and the final, great betrayal symbolized by death.

Inside the Blood Factory marks a breakthrough for Wakoski, for she says, "At the point in my life

when I wrote *Inside the Blood Factory*, I was beginning to perceive beauty through myself." Thus, in the poems of this volume, the narrator, as persona for the poet, becomes the single most important structuring element in the poem. For example, "Ringless," a poem of approximately eighty lines, may be divided into three sections, all dealing with the narrator's response to her own ringless fingers. The first section begins with a simple statement, "I cannot stand the man who wears / a ring / on his little finger," then progresses through a series of embellishments and elaborations on this statement. She compares the man with the ringed little finger to a white peacock who walks the moon and contrasts the peacock with "the great man, George," who breaks in two in the narrator's living room one day and proves to be made of marble. The section then presents, almost dialectically, an argument as to whether the man's wearing the ring on his little finger is justified by Jean Cocteau's having worn one or by the precious and semiprecious stones associated with Gustave Flaubert, Garcia Lorca, Dante, Robert Browning, and George Washington. The narrator maintains that these examples from the past do nothing to justify the man's ringed little finger, and she concludes the section by asserting that this man "may indeed / run the world; / that does not make him any better in my needlepoint eyes," adding suspense in the final lines: "Why / is a story."

The second section of "Ringless," the longest, presents a series of "hot" images—red and black and gold—and a vision of a life more primitive than any American has known. This series closes with a simple statement: "There was hot sun and there was no talk." The narrator returns to the image of George Washington from the first section of the poem and asks, "How do I reconcile these images with our cool president, / George Washington, walking the streets?" Her answer to this question implies that such a reconciliation is impossible, for despite the fact that her bones all are engraved "America," her head draws her "away from furniture and pewter / to the sun tugging at my nipples and trying to squeeze under my toes." This contrast between the hot and the cool, between the sun and pewter, continues with a vision of the sun and moon, both appearing as men with rings on their little fingers. Alexander Hamilton, whom the narrator loves, appears, and he too has a ring on his little finger. Lorca is once more invoked, with rings on both little fingers, and the narrator comments: "and suddenly everyone I knew appeared, / and they all had rings on their little fingers, / and I was the only one in the world left without any / rings." With an almost dreamlike logic, the second section concludes with George Washington walking the aisles of the Senate with a ring on his finger, "managing *my* world."

The third and concluding section of "Ringless" is also the shortest. It begins with a statement, "This is what I mean," and relates, in the juxtaposed images of a nameless, ringed "you" and the "ringless ringless" narrator, the source of the narrator's dislike of the man with the ring on his little finger. The poem ends with a repetition of the opening lines ("I cannot stand the man who wears / a ring / on his little finger"), followed by a semicolon, a space, and the final line, "not even you." The reader retains a residue of descriptions that are both the process and substance of the poem: the man with the ring on his little finger, the narrator with no ring, the contrasting visions of people working in the sun in a society where rings are unimportant and George Washington walking the aisles of government with a ring, a symbol of power, on his little finger. In America, rings represent power, the ability to act and to control. The narrator has no ring and can stand no man who flaunts his power by wearing a ring on his little finger.

"Slicing Oranges for Jeremiah," also in *Inside the Blood Factory*, makes an interesting comparison to the far more imagistic "Ringless." The poem relates a simple event: a woman slices oranges for her son, Jeremiah, who was born without a thyroid and craves some nutrient the fruit provides. The first section of the poem sets the scene: "rosy Jeremiah, with long eyelashes," grabbing the orange slices from the wooden cutting board "like a little raccoon running to prepare them." The second section presents a contemplation of the significance of the opening scene in more abstract terms: "What does it mean / if a child cannot talk when he is six, / if he shits in the toilet one day; in his pants the next?" These questions are followed by other questions about meaning: about a man who drinks and fails to earn enough money, contemplates adultery but will not commit it, and about his wife, who may take sleeping pills or walk in front of a car. This section closes with a description of Jeremiah, who "takes the sun / and slices it up / like the oranges and eats a little fire / thirsty for the juice," providing a transition back to the opening scene, and the third section muses once more on the significance of a mother slicing oranges for her son.

The fourth section begins with the narrator watching Jeremiah eat the oranges his mother has sliced for him, "orange after orange, / until I felt the juice in my own mouth, / just watching." The narrator considers Jeremiah's lost thyroid, speculates that "even this baby animal, / your son, / must know that it was you who kept him alive," and "how his father knew too / it was you who kept him, your husband, alive," and concludes that "they both resented it, / depending on you as they did, / men needing the woman more than any man could admit."

The fifth section is a contemplation on the strength of women, this strength that men depend on and resent. The images are more precise evocations of the wife in the second section of the poem, images that assert that not weakness but strength leads women toward death: "It isn't weakness that points us towards death, / but strength, men dying earlier than women, / trying to show their strength, / women taking their own lives with gas, in ovens with their gold-clock babies under their aprons, / with sleeping pills glistening like amber necklaces poured into / the stomach's cave, / stepping quietly under car wheels." The melodic precision of the second section gives way here to full harmonic richness; the chains of images digress from the main narrative, but add resonance and depth.

The final section of "Slicing Oranges for Jeremiah" contains twenty-six lines. The narrator reminisces about her childhood, beginning with an image of an orange tree, whose "dusty dark citrus leaves" make "black smudges" on her sweater. She then speaks of a gypsy within her "who wants to run / with all those oranges in a bag / and trade them for the sun," or to "find someone who will cut them for me / the way you slice them for Jeremiah." The poem ends with the narrator's wish that "I might have / an orange tree / growing just behind my throat / straining to stay alive, to endure."

"Slicing Oranges for Jeremiah" is a tribute to the masterful use of the mundane. An action of everyday ordinariness, a mother slicing fruit for her son, becomes the emblem and medium by which the poem explores notions about the strength of women, self-sufficiency, and relationships within families. The language of the poem is casual, conversational; it masks the intensity and importance of the poem's themes so successfully that the careless reader is likely to take the quiet narrative at its surface value, missing what lies beneath.

Wakoski's preference for simple words and rhythms that mirror the patterns of speech can mislead the reader into reading her poems too literally. This mistake in turn leads the reader to consider her themes trivial, for by reading on only the literal level, one misses the substance and

Diane Wakoski

complexity provided by the emblematic level, and the poem may appear flat, two-dimensional. The strength of poetry, in Wakoski's estimation, is that both sides of a paradox can be presented together, equally and simultaneously, a situation that life cannot duplicate. At its best, Wakoski believes, poetry employs the objects, events, and experiences of life in a way that allows the reader to experience their emotional substance. Her emblematic use of language is one of her methods for obtaining this result.

The Motorcycle Betrayal Poems (1971) revolves around a central theme of the failure of love. The dedication reads: "This book is dedicated to all those men who betrayed me at one time or another, in hopes they will fall off their motorcycles and break their necks." The quiet malice of these words informs many of the poems in the volume, and as one betrayal follows another, the incautious reader is tempted to toss the book aside, weary and depressed at the pain and anger that never quite mount to rage. But it is a mistake to assume that the betrayals so pointedly portrayed are merely literal betrayals, and the best poems in the volume, including the first, "I Have Had To Learn To Live With My Face," make clear the difference.

The poem opens with a short section of four lines, which contains a statement by the narrator, or controlling consciousness: "You see me alone tonight. / My face has betrayed me again, / the garage mechanic who promises to fix my car / and never does." In the second section the narrator expresses contempt for her face and ends by wishing that "you would bruise and batter / and destroy, napalm it, throw acid in it, / so that I might have another / or be rid of it at last." Later, in the fifth section, however, the narrator asserts that "Learning to live with what you're born with / is the process / the involvement, / the making of a life."

This statement signals an epiphany on the part of the narrator, who then traces the steps in the process of her acceptance of her face. She is stern at first, although hating the sternness; she laughs at "this ridiculous face / of lemon rinds / and vinegar cruets / of unpaved roads / and dusty file cabinets," but she finds the anger returning. Passing through envy of others, pain of isolation, and self-pity, the narrator returns once more to anger: "and it is anger I want now, fury, / to direct at my face and its author, / to tell it how I hate what it's done to me." Wishing to make her face "look at itself every day, / and remind itself / that reality is learning to live with what you're born with," she recalls also "that pride and anger and silence will hold us above beauty."

The poem becomes a reverie about beautiful things—"etched tile faces, old gnarled / tree trunks, anything with the beauty of wood, teak, lemon, cherry"—but returns with a jolt to the narrator's lament that she lost her children, husband, "everything a woman needs, wants," because of her face, "shimmering and flat as the moon / with no features."

In the next two sections the narrator recounts her efforts to sculpt her face, to mold it into something "articulate" and thereby "almost beautiful," and the last sections suggest a softening, an acceptance of her birthright. The eleventh section presents two questions—"Am I wrong I constantly ask myself / to value the struggle more than the results? / Or only to accept a beautiful face / if it has been toiled for?"—and the final section implies that the narrator has answered these questions: "Tonight I move alone in my face; / want to forgive all the men whom I've loved / who've betrayed me." The narrator intimates that "the great betrayer is that one I carry around each day, / which I sleep with at night."

The poem ends with a comparison of the narrator's face and an arid mountain, "a killer, rocky, water hard to find, no trees anywhere." The substance of the poem lies in the conflict between "natural" and "artificial" beauty. Beauty in nature exists alongside ugliness, and to appreciate that beauty one must accept a certain amount of ugliness. People do love desert mountains and the moon, although its cold light is merely a reflection. The great betrayer in "I Have Had To Learn To Live With My Face" is not the narrator's face but her mind, her set of expectations about herself, people, and the world. Learning to live with one's face is a metaphor for accepting the fact that the world does not often meet one's expectations of it; the poem itself is both metaphor and example: metaphor for the process of learning to accept the ambiguous beauty in the world, and example of the process by which human beings may create beauty. This process of creating beauty is simultaneously a way of perceiving it. Thus at the end of the poem, the narrator is able to forgive the men who have betrayed her, realizing that the "great betrayer" is the one she sleeps with each night—her dream of the way the world should be.

"Thanking My Mother For Piano Lessons," also in *The Motorcycle Betrayal Poems*, continues to explore the themes presented in "I Have Had To Learn To Live With My Face." It opens with three sections that compare sitting down to play the piano to "walking on the beach" and finding "a diamond

Diane Wakoski

Red runner
she comes cast me in red tights
showing satin skin underneath,
and red shorts,
a red runner's jacket
like a bird I don't expect to see
in the rain

Thinking of fires I have built
and how ~~that~~ flames are not
gratuitous
how hard it is to get even
combustible material / to burn
I wonder how she
burns through the continuous
                          rain

of Juneau
this runner, young woman

"Red runner," manuscript

as big as a shoe," or finishing a piece of furniture, or escaping a pursuer. The fourth section discusses more specifically the narrator's "relief / of putting your fingers on the keyboard" when the "bare floors and a few books" of her home depressed her. Sections five and six thank the narrator's mother and examine the mother's dedication to her child's piano lessons that led her to neglect herself and the household debts to pay for the lessons. The seventh section presents a striking portrait of the narrator as a child, "a quiet child, / afraid of walking into a store alone, / . . . afraid of not having any money." The reader sees the narrator seated at the piano, playing her way through fear, through grimness and poverty, through lonely days "empty as a rusty coffee can," through the loss of her father, and through all the ugly little indignities visited upon the child by a world that seems too spiteful to ignore, too terrible to resist.

The tenth section reveals the fantasy life of the quiet child at the piano, "wanting only to be touched by a man who loved me, / who would be there every

361

night" and "dreaming of pianos that made the sound of Mozart / and Schubert without demanding that life suck everything / out of you each day, / without demanding the emptiness of a timid little life." The eleventh section is once more a song of thanks from the narrator to her mother: she is grateful for the piano she laid her books on each afternoon after school. The narrator has not played the piano in ten years, "perhaps in fear that what little love I've been able to / pick, like lint, out of the corners of pockets, / will get lost." She then describes love as "a man / with a mustache / gently holding me every night," and she explains that the touch of this man halts the "pounding, banging / battering" in her brain of the music from her past.

The twelfth section of "Thanking My Mother For Piano Lessons" draws the poem together in a way typical of Wakoski's work. Here again the emblematic use of image and event gives a sharp intensity to the not unfamiliar story of a timid child who excels at music. The child, now grown up, realizes that her youthful piano playing brought beauty into her otherwise bleak life, and that, by extension, her poetry making—the creation of "the man / with a mustache / gently holding me every night"—brings beauty to her adult world. In the final lines of the poem, the narrator invokes the image of Beethoven, the tormented artist, suggesting the theme of the poem: "When I touch the man / I love, / I want to thank my mother for giving me / piano lessons / all those years, / keeping the memory of Beethoven, / a deaf tortured man, / in mind; / of the beauty that can come / from even an ugly / past."

In the preface to *Virtuoso Literature for Two and Four Hands*, perhaps the last book in her second phase, Wakoski states her intent: "In this book of poems, I am trying to explore the images of fantasy and my past. My keyboard now is the typewriter." This volume continues the themes discovered and refined in the previous volumes, and further explores the emblematic and metaphoric use of language in search of beauty. One poem, "Driving Gloves," illustrates this process through the question of the impact of the past on the present. The first three sections present the controlling consciousness's attitude about her past and about the respective influences of heredity and environment on the shape of her life. She capsulizes her position with a statement, "A bud is not a summary. / But it is the total / in a reduced form," and with a vision of heredity as "The perverse mimic / the desire to repeat / whatever's heard / or seen." The poem then jumps to the narrator's account of her learning to drive, how "From the / beginning, I insisted on what my friends considered an affectation. / I wore gloves for driving." She lists her reasons: "I said the / wheel got too hot or cold, that my / hands got sweaty or stiff from rheuma- / tism, that I did not feel in control without gloves."

The fifth section explains that Californians never wear gloves or hats because they consider them affectations, particularly when worn by members of the social class the narrator was born into. She relates her surprise at remembering, while on an automobile trip between the East Coast and California, that her mother, "improbable as it seems," wore driving gloves, and she then clarifies her surprise: "My mother . . . who never wore gloves on / any occasion I can remember, . . . who never even had a job she had to dress up for, she, / she wore gloves when she drove a car."

The narrator returns to the idea of heredity, elaborating on her description of it: "It is the perverse voice that speaks in us, / going back to old inflections, / old fictional language of other characters. . . ." She shifts suddenly to a conversation she has had with a woman named Anne, whom she is teaching to drive. Anne's father has written ten novels no one would publish, and he is a terrible driver. Anne believes herself to be like him, explaining "how we're all like some parent or ancestor," and how she has waited many years before seeking a driver's license. The narrator argues that Anne is hardly like her father, recounting that he had four or perhaps five wives and taught basic English all his life, whereas Anne has one husband, "a faithful one you would never leave," and is a Greek scholar, "a 'bluestocking' / if we use that term anymore." Still, Anne fears she is like her father, and the narrator queries, "what are these mimicries that we all look for, / that we fear?"

The seventeenth section gives the narrator's answer to her own question: always she has been terrified of being like her mother. She describes her mother, "heavy and unfashionable," "a high polite voice," and "a sad life, / discreet of imagination," giving her fear substance and human texture, and she ends by comparing her own use of driving gloves to a mole on her left shoulder, "which has its mysterious twin somewhere." The next two sections juxtapose the narrator's fear of being like her mother with Anne's fear of being like her father, and the twentieth section asks the question that is the first step toward facing those fears: "Do we have no courage to live our own lives? / Do we hope the past will live them for us?"

"No," the narrator answers as she explains that Anne learned to drive precisely because she is not her father, and that she herself wears driving gloves not for any reason she gives when pressed and not because her mother did, but simply because she likes to. The final section asserts that "Our lives *are* our own," and insists that "We must ask grace from ourselves. / Our memories. / Let them / release us from the past." The poem concludes with this definition of the past: "Only something / we have all lived / through."

The process described in "Driving Gloves," where the individual breaks from the past, away from both heredity and early environment, apparently was very much in the mind of the poet at this time, for the poems that follow those in *Virtuoso Literature for Two and Four Hands* express a fundamentally different attitude toward the past. Elements of the narrators' pasts still appear in the poems, but in each case the speaker, in becoming aware of the past, is liberated from it. Wakoski's concern with "personal mythology" moves to the fore here, and her continued preoccupation with George Washington is joined by a similar interest in another mythic character, the King of Spain, who is the embodiment of the world as one wishes it would be.

Waiting For The King Of Spain (1976) may be a high point of her third phase as well as Wakoski's finest book of poems. Her style here is polished and capable of expressing subtle variations of irony and feeling, and the sonatalike structure, where a theme or image is introduced, varied, counterpointed, and harmonized (as in "Ringless"), is fully developed. The strength of Wakoski's sense of beauty lends the poems in this volume an element of affirmation, an uplifting spirit that is sometimes wanting in her earlier poems. She seems sure of herself in these poems, and this surety passes to the reader as a confidence in her vision and a belief in the truth of it.

"To the Thin and Elegant Woman Who Resides Inside of Alix Nelson" is an especially fine poem. The first section begins with an image of a child, "Curly-head / plump little mother's girl, / like a delicious peach in August," who is growing up "into a Vogue model with peacock eyes and slinky hips that / are like swan-necks, even in the bulky clothes from Autumn Saks." Asserting that "this is an invocation to dump / fashion," the narrator invites the young woman "to love your own soft peachy cheeks," "and to let men be lovers, / not faggots." The section ends with an invitation to "proclaim / men AND / women / as lovers; and proclaim / our own Rich / American bodies."

The second section suggests that "once a country has produced flesh that it does not deny or

destroy, / civilization has come a long way, baby." Ironically extolling the virtues of American civilization, the narrator turns suddenly solemn: "So / how / can we live with these punishing ideas, / that a woman with a boy's body is beautiful, till she has to starve / herself on rye-thins and non-fat cottage cheese." Wakoski's exploration of the relationship between natural and artificial beauty reappears here, and the narrative favors nature's side.

The third section presents a letter, sent by "a critic of life" to the narrator, criticizing her "thin lips, / and the life of constant movement." "But," the narrator argues, "I am like water / or fire, / never still." Despite her "sturdy Polish, German, American body," it is the narrator's nature to be ever in motion. When the "critic of life" complains of the narrator's "thin veneer," she rejoins "but I am a new painting, / not an old one." She demands her "American prerogatives": "Forget faggots and their thin bodies. / The confusion of Pentimento. / Clarity: like Goethe, / I want more light, more clarity, more vision." Essentially, the narrator evokes America as the new Eden. Thin "faggots," the "unnatural" inhabitants of the old world, give way to the "natural" pioneers; "the confusion of Pentimento," where the original lines the artist paints appear through the ones painted over them as the painting ages, obscuring both pictures, gives way to the simple clarity of a line drawing. The reference to Goethe concerns both his theory of optics (which, contrary to Newton, held that the phenomenon of sight resulted from particles emitted from the eyes) and his powerful and omnivorous mind, which devoured sciences as diverse as masonry and botany. The fourth section concludes with a picture of the California landscape: "the thin palm trees on their pencil-like stalks, which are imports. / The fat stubby palms, which are native to the landscape."

In the fifth section, the narrator begins by asserting that she "will not diet on toast and lettuce," but feast on a multitude of lettuces, "with crumbled roquefort, thick fresh olive oil from / the Mediterranean and vinegar aromatic with tarragon." Her body, she attests, "is full of the juice of poetry," and despite a lack of love, she is not thin, having learned "that Americans, / we, have so much, we all love too much, / or, perhaps, better stated, not 'too much' but more than anyone / can ever receive."

The sixth section opens with the germ of the poem, the poet's "obsession": "Alix, inside your body of pears and peaches, and mine of thick / leafy salad, is delicacy, yes. But never thinness." She then moves to a celebration of American art forms: "Give us the rich chorus / of American drama. The substantial narrative, the loud Country- / Western singer, not the thin lyrics of an English past." After praising American food, the narrator asseverates, "I will not starve myself / in order to dance on European yachts, for we have our / square dances here. And hoe downs. And most of all, / the dance of our daily bread."

The final section is a variation on the Lord's Prayer, inspired perhaps by the last line of the preceding section. Wakoski's wit appears here at its finest, in the ironic malice that, although gentle, cuts in many directions at once: "Give us this day . . . / yes, and forgive us, / as we forgive those who want us to be thin. For this is the / kingdom. / Yes, and the power and glory / forever. / Ah, men. / (The sigh of a well-fed woman)."

"To the Thin and Elegant Woman Who Resides Inside of Alix Nelson" represents the work of a mature artist; it contains examples of many of Wakoski's major themes and techniques. Her concern with aesthetics is plainly evident in the subject matter of this poem, as the narrator seeks to convince someone other than herself to accept a new standard for beauty. The use of "associative process," where one image suggests and implies another although one may not follow the other logically, demonstrates accomplished talent, for the images harmonize and cohere, leaving few rough edges. The narrative itself manages to balance the hostile and the sentimental, suggesting both without a plethora of either.

Wakoski's most recent volume of poetry, *The Man Who Shook Hands*, shows a sharp awareness of her past course and presents, after a fashion, a credo for her poetry. It begins with "The blue swan, an essay on music in poetry," an essay that Wakoski calls "a key to the book," a key, "However, not to the poems but only to where my philosophies and meditations are leading me." It is built around three things: the Wallace Stevens poem "Peter Quince at the Clavier"; Robert Creeley's idea of digression as a means of structure; and the story of the man who shook hands, who has, in Wakoski's words, "become a totemic figure, an obsession of mine, someone constantly present in my attempt to understand the world."

The essay itself "is an attempt to show you the process of making an idea into music," and it encapsulates Wakoski's growth as an artist and person. Couched in the form of a letter to friends, the essay begins with eight lines from "Peter Quince at the Clavier": "Music is feeling, then, not sound; / And thus it is that what I feel, / Here in this room, desiring you, / Thinking of your blue-shadowed

silk, / Is music. / . . . . / Beauty is momentary in the mind— / The fitful tracing of a portal; / But in the flesh it is immortal." Wakoski has long acknowledged her affinity for Stevens, but in this essay the relationship between Stevens and such poems as "Thanking My Mother For Piano Lessons" is quite apparent. The concern with beauty, the metaphoric invocation of music, the notion that an idea not clothed in flesh is not lasting suggest that Wakoski and Stevens share a similar, anti-Platonic concept of metaphor.

Wakoski begins by saying that she considers herself a pragmatist rather than a realist, and her poetry, the creation of her personal mythology, stems from her pragmatism. "When you are denied the life you want, you invent one for yourself. . . . I am not a realist. . . . I am a pragmatist. I have learned to live with both my dreams and my reality. My dreams are the mythic me." She relates also that her idea of finding the perfect man—her King of Spain— and her idea of poetry are the same, "the same concept, the same spirit, the same holy quest, for beauty, embodied in the flesh, not denying, but attesting to the spiritual life."

She then proposes that digression is a form of music, "for music is that movement which we follow, that sound which we recognize not because it says anything but because it is motion, which does not ask for dialogue or response," and she asks whether "to speak seriously is not the most serious form of making love." Classical forms of rhetoric invoke the courtly age when "to make love" was to woo, to win the physical affection by word and stylized gesture. Wakoski then suggests that she will explore digression as a form of music through the story of the man who shook hands.

After a false start in which digression interferes and stalls the story, Wakoski introduces a definition of music: "The nature of music is that you must hear all the digressions," what composers call rhapsodies, reveries, or overtures. A "Second attempt at the story of the man who shook hands" leads, once again, far away from the story, this time into "Peter Quince at the Clavier." When this attempt stalls, a third attempt is begun, opening with a statement that addresses a concern central to much of Wakoski's poetry: "Digression has led me to the bourgeois dilemma of art: how to speak of the deep things which concern, when you know, either, that they are not cosmic concerns or when you are not willing to attest to all of the facts because they concern your feelings or responses to people who do not feel or respond the same way you do." This statement illuminates and clarifies Wakoski's contention that her use of startling or bizarre images is designed to induce the reader to "accept the specialness of the feelings of the speaker," and it aids in interpreting her assertion that "poetry is the art of saying what you mean but disguising it."

Three further attempts to tell the story of the man who shook hands all fall victim to digression. After admitting that the story is actually about the lack of reciprocity described in the third attempt at the story ("people who do not feel or respond the same way you do"), the story begins in earnest. It is a simple story; the lonely protagonist, who "could have been at the ends of the earth," meets a man. The man is similarly isolated, and although he thinks himself "brilliant, radical, unusual, and unique," she finds him "ordinary, foolish, doctrinaire, and just another young man of fashion." Their lives entangle nonetheless, and she reports: "I felt old and wise enough to carry on a relationship without burdening it with a future or with fairy-tale endings." The protagonist's original dislike of the man alters, however: "maybe this impossible man would become the perfect man." She also reports being "excited by many impossibilities." At their parting, instead of embracing, the man shakes her hand.

This is a logical enough ending to a story with the title "The Man Who Shook Hands," but the protagonist's response to the man's action—sheer unreasoning terror—adds a twist to the plain event. As always in Wakoski's mythopoeic worlds, it is not the event itself that is significant, but the responses of the people who participate, and most important, *why*: why did the event happen, why did the speaker respond so intensely? These remain pertinent questions in treating any of Wakoski's poems, for the answers to these questions lie near the heart of obsession-inspired poetry. What is it about the images, phrases, or words of the poem that stung the poet long or hard enough to lead her to make the poem?

The rest of the story of the man who shook hands concerns the protagonist's attempts to understand her response to the event. The protagonist compares the rejection by this man to the form letters sent by magazines to aspiring authors—formal, politic, impersonal—and she finds her response surprising because of her dislike of the man. She is obsessed with the man who shook hands, and she thinks it is "because, I did, for the first time, encounter someone who wished to try formally to explain that terrible subject—lack of reciprocity—to me." Her response to the event is emblematic, representative of a more intense emotional and

Diane Wakoski

Robert Turney

intellectual response to a concept. "So now we do not have a man rejecting a woman. You are all right. How common. But we have a poet perceiving reality and within twelve hours being told her perceptions are completely wrong."

"The blue swan, an essay on music in poetry" is a fascinating study, for it presents in compact form a treatise on Wakoski's poetry. The structure of the essay is a prototype of her poems. An event is presented, usually in the form of a striking image: David's body on the beach in "Justice is Reason Enough," the girl on the zebra in "Apparitions are not Singular Occurrences," the man who shook hands in the essay. The first third of the piece then presents a series of embellishments and elaborations, usually in the form of digressions, that make the original image three-dimensional and give it substance and texture. The middle third of the piece puts forth, in the manner of a sonata, a second image or series of images that may complement, conflict, or even contradict the original image; and the final third, to continue the musical metaphor, presents the coda, the resolution of images and the attempt to explain them. Sometimes, as in "Ringless," the coda is plainly announced: "This is what I mean." Other times it is more obliquely heralded, as in "Justice is

Reason Enough": "Mother asked me why / every day for a year; and I told her justice." At still other times it is not announced at all, but simply presented in an image that combines the images that precede it. The narrator's wish for "an orange tree / growing just behind my throat" typifies this third manner of coda.

"The blue swan, an essay on music in poetry" closes with an invitation for the reader to recite "*Blue Monday* or *The Pink Dress* or a poem such as *The Magellanic Clouds* in my voice or his own." Wakoski herself wishes to "render the whole of Wallace Stevens' wonderful *Peter Quince at the Clavier*." Before doing so, however, she gives one further comment on her poetry, a comment that summarizes her work to date and suggests her future direction, for it is certain that the process she describes will continue: "first comes the story. Then comes the reaction to the story. Then comes the telling and retelling of the story. And finally . . . comes boredom with the story, so that finally we invent music, and the nature of music is that you must hear all the digressions." —*Mark Harris*

Other:

Four Young Lady Poets, includes poems by Wakoski (New York: Totem Press / Corinth Books, 1962);

The Magi, includes poems by Wakoski (Los Angeles: Black Sparrow Press, 1971).

Interviews:

A Terrible War: A Conversation With Diane Wakoski, ed. Philip L. Gerber and Robert J. Gemmett (Winnipeg: University of Manitoba Press, 1970);

"An Interview With Diane Wakoski," *Contemporary Literature*, 18 (Winter 1976): 1-19;

"A Colloquy With Diane Wakoski," *Gypsy Scholar*, 6 (Summer 1979): 61-73.

THEODORE WEISS
(16 December 1916-)

BOOKS: *The Catch* (New York: Twayne, 1951);

Outlanders (New York: Macmillan, 1960);

Gunsight (New York: New York University Press, 1962);

The Medium (New York: Macmillan, 1965);

The Last Day and the First (New York: Macmillan, 1968);

The World Before Us: Poems 1950-1970 (New York: Macmillan, 1970);

The Breath of Clowns and Kings (London: Chatto & Windus, 1971; New York: Atheneum, 1971);

Fireweeds (New York: Macmillan, 1976);

Views and Spectacles (London: Chatto & Windus, 1978; enlarged edition, New York: Macmillan, 1979).

Theodore Weiss was born in Reading, Pennsylvania. His childhood was spent in various small Pennsylvania towns, and he was educated at Muhlenberg College in Allentown. Weiss received his B.A. from Muhlenberg in 1938 and his M.A. from Columbia in 1940. In 1941, he married Renee Karol, a violinist and author of children's books, and began a teaching career. He has served on the faculties of the University of Maryland (Summer 1941), the University of North Carolina at Chapel Hill (1942-1944), Yale University (1944-1946), and Bard College in Annandale-on-Hudson, New York (1947-1966). Most recently, he has been associated with Princeton University, first as poet-in-residence (1966-1967) and, since 1968, as a professor of English and creative writing. Weiss has also been a lecturer at the New School for Social Research in New York (1955-1956), a visiting professor of poetry at the Massachusetts Institute of Technology (1961-1962), and a lecturer at the New York City Young Men's Hebrew Association (1965-1967). He has contributed poetry and criticism to numerous magazines. Since 1943, the Weisses have edited and published the *Quarterly Review of Literature*.

Despite his important contributions as teacher, critic, and editor, Weiss's reputation rests primarily on his poetry. His achievements have been recognized by numerous honors and awards. Weiss has received a Ford Foundation fellowship (1953), the Wallace Stevens Award (1956), a grant from the National Endowment for the Arts (1967), and an Ingram-Merrill Foundation grant (1974). He was a member of the Wesleyan University Press Poetry Board (1963-1968) and has acted as poetry editor for

Princeton University Press's Series of Contemporary Poets (1974-1977). He has been an honorary fellow of Ezra Stiles College at Yale since 1964, and has received honorary degrees from both Muhlenberg College (1968) and Bard College (1973), as well as a Brandeis University Poetry Citation (1977). Made the W. and A. S. Paton Foundation Professor for Ancient and Modern Literature at Princeton University in 1977, Weiss was the Visiting Hurst Professor of Creative Literature at Washington University in 1978 and read and lectured for the United States Information Agency in South Korea, Thailand, Taiwan, the Philippines, and Japan in 1979.

Weiss's poetry is characterized by rich language, dense syntax, complex structure, and an elitist flavor. He is interested in tradition, in making poetry's past relevant to its present, in narrative and dramatic verse as well as lyric, and in the challenges and opportunities presented by the long poem. Weiss is a vigorous independent. Although he joyfully acknowledges his debt to poets from Homer to Shakespeare, Browning, Wordsworth, and moderns such as Ezra Pound, T. S. Eliot, Robert Frost, Wallace Stevens, and William Carlos Williams, Weiss meticulously avoids alliance with any school or movement. "I'm not a joiner, and that also makes me a modern man."

Weiss has openly discussed his individualistic views. He is an outspoken critic of many modern poets: "They are gradually giving up altogether; they've given up rhyming—okay; they've given up metre—okay; there are those who are giving up metaphor—okay. Now it's the verse line. They're writing lots of things which are often neither fish nor fowl, neither prose nor poetry, and offering them—a sort of final collapse into what they can do. I have no great sympathy for such writing. . . . I love the idea of defying easy poetizing. I want the hard things in life that will challenge us and say, 'ah-hah! Can you make a poem of this?'. . . I don't like modern poetry's crazy notion that a poet must find his voice and be stuck with it. I want many voices, not just one lumpy little dull voice!" He sees "the deliberate, passionate pursuit of mindlessness" as the most dangerous trend in contemporary poetry. "Most of us need, not mind-blowings, but what little mind we have and can cultivate."

In his own work, Weiss wants "as mixed and abundant a mash as I can find." This means "releasing, as much as I can, the whole life of words." His work also combines the immediacy of the present with the richness of the past. "Oppressive as the past can be, especially in its evils and mistakes,

Layle Silbert

one can well understand revulsion from it. Yet to throw it all away, to pretend to be Adam all over again, is to be fatuously prodigal." Weiss is especially reluctant to deny his literary heritage. Like many modern artists, he feels a sense of homelessness. Nevertheless, he asserts that he lives "in all kinds of literature: English, French, Russian, Greek; they're homes, too. I don't know why modern man, particularly in the arts, is so frightened of admitting that the mind is a place he lives in and that works are also places he lodges in."

Weiss attempts to reconcile the virtues of freedom on the one hand and technique on the other. "If you give up metric, at least conventional metric, and to a large degree I have, syntax then becomes especially crucial. . . . For me syntax is the lifeline of a sentence or a poem. Syntax and its play of syllables—the skimming skein of sounds, rippled at times to the surface, at others caught deep down in the undertow, yet swaying insinuatingly as in a dance—helps to insure the shape and unity of a poem. Syntax satisfies both sides of me, the voluptuary and the puritan."

Theodore Weiss

Although he is aware that many believe this to be "the age of the short poem," Weiss's longing for comprehensiveness has led him to the long one. "I've always been impatient with the single, simple lyric, despite its purity of voice, because it's a little too one-dimensional." He dislikes poetry's relinquishing its traditional narrative and dramatic roles to other genres, particularly the novel.

Much of what Weiss says seems to imply that he is a literary reactionary, but his work is revolutionary as well. In some ways, he is beyond the avant-garde. Weiss himself has described his poetry as "a moving toward conventional form and then a sidestepping. Building up expectations only to shake them with something else."

The Catch (1951), like most of his work, received good critical reviews. Weiss notes that the title "was supposed to suggest the haul as of fish that the poems comprised and the round or a song to be repeated—that is, the poems in their echoing of each other thematically and otherwise." He goes on to comment about the book's theme: "In general the book meant to explore the diverse ways we are caught: in *this* time, *this* place, *this* occasion, in war as in the warrings of peace, in nature as in our natures, and in the designs the past set going." Although most of the verses in this first volume are relatively short, *The Catch* does include "Shades of Caesar," a poem in which he combines some of the modern techniques he admires with elements of the narrative he fears have been surrendered to the novel. Weiss calls it "the first long poem I felt realized enough to venture into print."

Almost ten years separate *The Catch* from the appearance of *Outlanders* in 1960. "My second book," Weiss states, "in contradistinction to *The Catch*, emphasizes the basic American sense of going out, the various ways of meeting the dilemmas of our day. This pioneering spirit, however, has brought in its train a feeling of uprootedness, of being lost in the boundless desert of time and space. Gradually the book organized itself around the theme of the homelessness of our time. . . . Against the desperate modern struggle to subdue nature through technology I posed a number of worthies, outlanders like Thoreau and the nineteenth-century painter Albert Ryder, who were, in their personal stands, heroic replies to, if not solutions of, the outrages unleashed."

"Barracks Apt. 14," one of the poems in *Outlanders*, contains a concise statement of Weiss's poetic theory. His attempt to reconcile all sources is explicit in the first line: "All must be used." Everything is there: references to the classics, nature, and the contemporary world of a makeshift apart-ment, its occupants and contents. Furthermore, the effort to bring the diverse elements together is successful. This poem, like many of his others, ends affirmatively. Harmony does come: "the music will confound you."

Outlanders also contains one long monologue, "The Generations," which "presents an old woman, resolute in her Christian fundamentalism as ever, working over her garden and thoughts of her sons." The poem grew out of Weiss's interest in Browning and his conviction that "poetry can and must renew its older, larger interests in people and a world past the poet's self-preoccupation."

Weiss's next book, *Gunsight*, builds on these ideas. Although *Gunsight* was published in 1962, just two years after *Outlanders*, Weiss actually "worked intermittently on it for almost twenty years." Originally only twenty lines long, the finished poem is book length. As he explains, *Gunsight* "seeks to extend the dramatic monologue, to enrich it with modern poetry's accomplishments, tries to put those accomplishments to more ambitious uses." The central figure is a young American soldier who undergoes surgery after being wounded in World War II. "As the anesthesia takes effect, he descends into his own hell; he becomes the theater to a flock of memories, each clamoring for his attention which has till now been denied." Voices from the past, differentiated by various type styles, drift in and out, summoning him to relive, from childhood on, his painful past. The soldier suffers, but he endures. Indeed, the poem contains one of the finest examples of Weiss's humanism:

> Some things—the crag, the granite sea, the slug,
> this mouth that grinds incessantly in you—
> cannot be turned into the human. All
> that we can do is try, while we are men,
> to meet them humanly.

During the years spent on *Gunsight*, Weiss also collected a backlog of both "other shorter poems" and "a group of monologues beyond them." The shorter poems make up the bulk of his fourth book, *The Medium* (1965). Weiss comments that "The title and the poems have to do with language—whatever its distortions and seductions and whether it be words, paint, or notes—as it makes our lives possible, ordering them and enabling us to live with each other and with the objects, known and unknown, of the world. At the same time some of the poems concentrate on the resources—the secret, vibrant life, of language itself, as on the endless transactions between it and the world and ourselves. Beyond that I find myself frequently turning to the

AUTOBIOGRAPHIA ILLITERARIA

It's the lost, the hidden,
sections of my life, those pages
not yet come to, I keep
looking for.
                So I continue
sniffing and probing, like Hoppy
whirled round and round
on the mat
                he's sat on countless
times. And missing it in this
spot and that, a long trail
scored with ruts,
                        I think
my missing means it's somewhere
there. Like the woman who
collects dolls still.
                        "Sometimes
I look at them, bangles, satin
sashes, mousy little shoes,
cluttering up the house.
                                What
do I do? Rush out and buy some
new ones. O a few do work:
this Japanese,
                        its swivel-neck;
the Hopi too--that Mud-Head Clown
akimbo--images the children
can grow used to
                        of divinities
who sadly down from the hills
to live with them a certain
portion of the year."
                        Still
there is a side to the ubiquitous
familiars I've little inkling
of; still,
                beyond the smell
of myself, the strangeness that
goes out from me far as the world,
far at least as time.

"Autobiographia Illiteraria," revised typescript

Theodore Weiss

notion of ourselves as a medium, though for who knows what purpose and used by who knows whom."

Both the interest in language and the title of the last section of *The Medium*, "Airs for Caliban," point to the triumphs of *The Last Day and the First* (1968). Although it also includes a group of shorter poems and a section of adaptations from Boris Pasternak, the volume's showpieces are three long poems: "Caliban Remembers," "Mount Washington," and "Wunsch-zettel." All three are excellent, but the Caliban monologue is a masterpiece. One critic places it "among the finest poems of the decade." Praise for the poem has centered on its gorgeous language and the rich resonance that comes from allusions to Shakespeare and Browning. However, Weiss himself stresses the poem's contemporary relevance. "My poems . . . are of no consequence if all they do is remember abjectly and studiously the originals. . . . The Caliban poem, for example, is really under it all a comment on the excess of power that Prospero exercised. . . . I was thinking of nuclear energies."

The World Before Us: Poems 1950-1970 (1970) contains well-chosen selections from all of the earlier books except *Gunsight* plus a section of new shorter poems. Although Weiss published a critical study of Shakespeare's early work, *The Breath of Clowns and Kings*, in 1971, no books of poetry appeared between *The World Before Us* and the publication of *Fireweeds* in 1976.

Fireweeds are hardy plants that grow easily on land that has been cleared or burned over; they symbolize both destruction and renewal. The dual theme is not new to Weiss. *The Last Day and the First*, pointing as it does to both apocalypse and creation, sounds much the same note. In *Fireweeds*, however, Weiss applies the theme to art:

> Well, is it not the virtue of art
> that it, somehow surviving, happens again
> and again?

The theme of depleted soil producing new growth is specifically relevant to Weiss's work. Many of the poems in *Fireweeds* are reconsiderations of subjects treated earlier. However, the new verses are anything but repetitious. *Fireweeds* proves that Weiss can use his old concerns not only to make art again but also to make it fresh and strong.

One good example is his long poem, "The Storeroom." Possibly the best selection in *Fireweeds*, the piece is, nevertheless, only the latest of his many treatments of Homer's Odysseus and Penelope. The difference here comes from Weiss's focusing not on the wanderer but on the wife and her storeroom of memories and memorabilia. Important to both "The Storeroom" and Weiss's latest works are the twin themes of acceptance and endurance. Although much admired, he is too demanding to be a popular poet. Far from regretting his status, Weiss glories in it:

> You know now that you will not sit
> in that one's fat and glamorous pants
> and never will be fit for that one's
> antic shoes.
> > And still you choose
> to feel superior.

This mood continues into *Views and Spectacles*, Weiss's most recent volume. The book takes its title from a poem in *Fireweeds*, and other entries from as far back as *Outlanders* are included. Although the 1978 British edition is made up entirely of poems from earlier books, the 1979 American edition has a section of new poems. One of them, "Autobiographia Illiteraria," illustrated here, shows Weiss still "sniffing and probing," still persisting in multiplicity of vision. He explains in "Views and Spectacles":

> But most of all I want
> glasses that, quicker than knives,
> eliminate glasses.
> > I don't want
> my nose everlastingly squashed
> up against the candy windows
> of the world
> > but rather both sides
> of Olympus or simply something
> godly: to wit, at once to see
> and, seeing, be.

—*Katherine Knight*

Other:

Selections from the Notebooks of Gerard Manley Hopkins, edited by Weiss (New York: New Directions, 1945);

"Gerard Manley Hopkins: A Realist on Parnassus," in *Accent Anthology*, ed. Kerker Quinn and Charles Shattuck (New York: Harcourt, Brace, 1946);

"Franz Kafka and the Economy of Chaos," in *The Kafka Problem*, ed. Angel Flores (New York: New Directions, 1946);

"Towards a Classical Modernity and a Modern Classicism," in *Poets on Poetry*, ed. Howard Nemerov (New York & London: Basic Books, 1966).

Periodical Publications:

"T. S. Eliot and the Courtyard Revolution," *Sewanee Review*, 54 (Spring 1946): 289-307;

"Science and Poetry A Symposium," *Review of Metaphysics*, 15 (December 1961): 248-255;

"How To End The Renaissance," *Sewanee Review*, 73 (Autumn 1965): 636-658;

"A Suite for Boris Pasternak," *Delos*, 1 (1968): 49-61;

"Old, New, and Newest Criticism," *Encounter*, 37 (December 1971): 67-74;

"Joining *The Donner Party*," *Parnassus*, 1 (Fall / Winter 1972) : 36-46;

"Between Two Worlds or on the Move (Donald Davie)," *Parnassus*, 3 (Fall / Winter 1974): 113-140;

"The Writer's Sense of Place," *South Dakota Review*, 13 (Autumn 1975): 88;

"Lucretius: The Imagination of the Literal," *Salmagundi*, 35 (Fall 1976): 80-98;

"E. P.: The Man Who Cared Too Much (Ezra Pound)," *Parnassus*, 5 (Fall / Winter 1976): 79-119;

"Springs of Imagination," *Times Literary Supplement*, 22 April 1977, p. 482;

"The Blight of Modernism and Philip Larkin's Antidote," *American Poetry Review*, 6 (1977): 39-41;

"Friends of Promise: Four Editors Look Back at Outstanding Periodicals of Their Youth," *Times Literary Supplement*, 16 June 1978, p. 667;

"QRL: Hallelujah on a Straw," *Tri-Quarterly*, 43 (Fall 1978): 164-183;

"Lunching with Hoon: Wallace Stevens," *American Poetry Review*, 7 (September / October 1978): 36-45;

"The Many-Sidedness of Modernism," *Times Literary Supplement*, 1 February 1980, p. 24.

Interviews:

"An Interview with Theodore Weiss," *Crazy Horse*, 10 (March 1972): 25-34;

Colette Inez, "An Interview with Theodore Weiss," *Parnassus*, 5 (Spring / Summer 1977): 161-174.

References:

Harry Berger, "A Local Enclave: The Poetry of Theodore Weiss," *Fat Abbot*, 3 (Summer/Fall 1961): 39-79;

Warren Carrier, A Facade of Modernity, and a Personal Poet," review of *The Catch, Western Review*, 16 (Spring 1952): 251-255;

Bruce Cutler, Review of *The Medium, Poetry*, 108 (July 1966): 269-272;

Philip Dacey, Review of *The World Before Us, Crazy Horse*, 10 (March 1972): 35;

James Dickey, "The Death and Keys of the Censor," review of *Outlanders, Sewanee Review*, 69 (Spring 1961): 329-330;

Reginald Gibbons, "Cure: Theodore Weiss's Poetry," *Modern Poetry Studies*, 9 (Spring 1978): 18-33;

Edward Hirsch, "To Hell with Holy Relics: on Theodore Weiss," *American Poetry Review*, 5 (1976): 35-36;

Daniel Hoffman, Review of *The Last Day And The First, Poetry*, 114 (August 1969): 335-344;

John Holmes, "A Feeling For Life," review of *The Catch, New York Times*, 28 October 1951, p. 22;

Richard Howard, *Alone With America Essays on the Art of Poetry in the United States Since 1950* (New York: Atheneum, 1969), pp. 552-574;

Howard, "Poetry Chronicle," review of *Gunsight, Poetry*, 102 (July 1963): 250-259;

Howard, *Preferences* (New York: Viking, 1974), pp. 299-303;

John T. Irwin, "The Crisis of Regular Forms," review of *The World Before Us, Sewanee Review*, 81 (Winter 1973): 158-171;

John Koethe, "The Poetry Room," review of *The World Before Us, Poetry*, 120 (Spring 1972): 49-51;

P. Leary and R. A. Kelly, eds., *Controversy of Poets* (Garden City: Doubleday, 1965), pp. 553-554;

Laurence Lieberman, "Recent Poetry: Exiles and Disinterments," *Yale Review*, 61 (October 1971): 82-100;

Edward L. Mayo, "Two Twayne Poets," review of *The Catch, Poetry*, 81 (February 1953): 324-327;

J. D. McClatchy, review of *Fireweeds, Poetry*, 130 (April 1977): 45-47;

John Mole, "Celebrating the Crumbs," review of *Views and Spectacles: Selected Poems, Times Literary Supplement*, 20 October 1978, p. 1215;

M. L. Rosenthal, *The New Poets: American and British Poets since World War II* (New York & London: Oxford University Press, 1967);

William Stafford, Review of *Fireweeds, New York Times Book Review*, 2 January 1977, p. 8.

Anne Stevenson, "Choosing To Feel Superior," review of *Fireweeds, Times Literary Supplement*, 27 May 1977, p. 656;

Robert Stock, "The Hazards Of Art," review of *The Last Day And The First, Nation*, 208 (24 March 1969): 370-379.

Theodore Weiss

Papers:

There is a collection of Weiss's manuscripts in the Firestone Library, Princeton, New Jersey.

REED WHITTEMORE
(11 September 1919-)

BOOKS: *Heroes and Heroines* (New York: Reynal & Hitchcock, 1946);

An American Takes a Walk (Minneapolis: University of Minnesota Press, 1956; London: Oxford University Press, 1956);

The Self-Made Man (New York: Macmillan, 1959);

The Boy from Iowa (New York: Macmillan, 1962);

The Fascination of the Abomination: Poems, Stories, and Essays (New York: Macmillan; London: Collier-Macmillan, 1963);

Little Magazines (Minneapolis: University of Minnesota Press, 1963; London: Oxford University Press, 1964);

Return, Alpheus: A Poem for the Literary Elders of Phi Beta Kappa (Williamsburg, Va.: King & Queen Press, 1965);

Ways of Misunderstanding Poetry (Washington, D.C.: Library of Congress, 1965);

From Zero to Absolute (New York: Crown, 1967);

Poems, New and Selected (Minneapolis: University of Minnesota Press, 1967);

Fifty Poems Fifty (Minneapolis: University of Minnesota Press, 1970; London: Oxford University Press, 1970);

The Mother's Breast and the Father's House (Boston: Houghton Mifflin, 1974);

William Carlos Williams: Poet from Jersey (Boston: Houghton Mifflin, 1975);

The Poet As Journalist (Washington, D.C.: New Republic Books, 1975).

Reed Whittemore's eight collections of poems deploy elements of astringent wit and metrical grace along a broad front of wry social commentary ("Americanized Auden" is James Dickey's phrase for the tone of much of Whittemore's verse). Whittemore is often compared with Ogden Nash in a context of usually dismissive references to light verse, and many critics feel that his poetry lacks the high seriousness needed to complement his infallible ear for verse rhythms. Admirers like Howard Nemerov, however, laud Whittemore's civility and wit, lamenting that the humor and accessibility of his poems have hurt him unfairly among the New Critics. All observers nevertheless praise the agility with which his syllables sort themselves out and his sharp eye for vanities both personal and social. Furthermore, his own criticism has a sparkling surface attributable to an urbane mind familiar with much of the best that has been thought and said in the world.

Edward Reed Whittemore was born in New Haven, Connecticut. His father was a physician, and Whittemore reports that the family was "fairly rich until the Crash." He was educated at Phillips Academy, Andover, and at Yale, where he says he "immediately became a literary entrepreneur." He was drafted into the army after graduating from Yale in 1941 and spent three years in the Mediterranean area as an officer in the Twelfth Air Force—in his own words, "a non-flying, headquarters officer who earned a Bronze Star for writing fine memoranda and keeping records of one-hundred octane gas consumption."

Following a brief postwar term as a graduate student in history at Princeton, Whittemore took a teaching post at Carleton College in Northfield, Minnesota, where he revived *Furioso*, a literary magazine that he had helped originate while a sophomore at Yale and that was ultimately revived a second time in 1960 as the *Carleton Miscellany*. During two decades at Carleton, Whittemore abandoned attempts at fiction writing and found that his "real interest was in extended discursive statements in prose and verse."

Whittemore's involvement in the literary establishment has been extensive. He served in 1964-1965 as Consultant in Poetry to the Library of Congress; he has been a director of the Association of Literary Magazines of America; and he was literary editor of the *New Republic* from 1969 through 1973. He has received numerous honors and awards: the Harriet Monroe Memorial Prize from *Poetry* magazine in 1954, the Emily Clark Balch Prize (*Virginia Quarterly Review*) in 1962 for "The Music of Driftwood," the Award of Merit Medal of the American Academy of Arts and Letters in 1970, a grant from the National Institute of the Arts, and a Guggenheim Fellowship. He has been since 1968 a professor of English at the University of Maryland.

Whittemore's first volume of poetry, *Heroes and Heroines* (1946), comprises forty-three rather slight works, fifteen of them sonnets, most of the others under thirty lines, and a high percentage written in rhyme. More than half have as subject either a character from literature or a quotation that inspired the poem as a gloss, and the remainder take up the traditional topics of war, death, and nature. *Heroes and Heroines* is self-consciously literary and not especially robust, pleasant enough in its verbal skills but seldom arresting in conception.

"The Heart of Darkness," for instance, is a sketchy drama, based on Joseph Conrad's *Heart of Darkness* (1902), with Marlow, Kurtz (condemned to speak in sonnets), and a chorus of two drunken sailors. The poem is burdened by improbabilities, but Marlow's summation stands out as one of the better moments in the volume:

You see, the glamour's off.
The secrets of jungles, fabulous gardens off, out, and
                                        beyond,
Better were dark than blazing, hidden than—this.

Where there were spheres of wonder and hush, and
                        where there was darkness,
Idiots play in the sun.

Two other poems—"Jim" and "Patusan"—also derive from Conrad, and the other heroes and heroines include such fictive folk as Moll Flanders, Gulliver, Guinevere, Hester Prynne, Lady Brett Ashley, and Sherlock Holmes. Among the other poems, the fine meditation "A Winter Shore" remains one of Whittemore's best statements of his personal vision, although not all of its stanzas have the rightness of this one:

Caught in an offshore breeze
A butterfly will turn
Too late to fight the air,
Will turn, then, to another shore
Flapping off despair.

The image here snaps sharply into focus, but *Heroes and Heroines* seldom surprises elsewhere with such happy inventions.

An American Takes a Walk (1956) collects forty-three new poems and fifteen from *Heroes and Heroines*. Although the new poems are abundantly allusive, they no longer depend on other works of literature for their subjects. (One exception is "Abbreviated Interviews with a Few Disgruntled Literary Celebrities," which quotes Miss Ulalume's account of how "Edgar cut in at the dance down at Yaanek's, and Lethe / Got terribly angry.") Nature and the seasons continue to be fruitful topics. "Moving among the Seasons" glances at man's transience on earth, "the flaw in creation we daily confront," and mocks the "illiterate" self that "takes offense" at the weather, "lifts its chin up and huffs stiffly off / To bolt the doors double, and draw up the covers, and frown." "Thoughts of the California

Desert" develops a witty image of an "indolent desert" that "slouches, half an eye closed / And half an eye out for men of affairs whose cares / Keep them from keeping their gaudy gardens hosed." "Spring Again" celebrates that durable subject, opening with somber images of death ("The refuse of a dead season—leaves and stalks / And all possible forms of pastness, withered and brown—") and closing "as shoots of green began groping / Their way in the dark to the surface of things, / And robins appeared on schedule, and buds swelled."

An American Takes a Walk includes several sprightly treatments of themes from contemporary culture. "Ladders" is sly and mocking:

I am frightened by ladders, Freud, by ladders,
Ladders that rock and shudder and sink in the ground.
As I rise to dangerous roofs and windows and branches,
My soul, Freud, my soul sinks in the ground.

"An Address to the Holder of Some High Government Office" asks for relief "Of worry of what lies in store for us from your store, / Of ray guns and nuclear speedboats." "The Summer People" neatly catches its gin-drinking bridge and tennis players:

Makeshift though our mansions are,
And seedy though our courts,
Our lives are rich and full at the shore
Because our kind are sports.

"God's Acres" is a funny rejection of the delight in nature taken by those, for instance, "who can tell a grosbeak from a grackle," and its tone is far from that of "On a Summer Sunday," with its pleasant, soothing close:

And that day
That somnolent summer Sunday day,
Crept away, crept away
To deep but delicate distances, as the den
And the wood and the wind unobtrusively darkened,
And the birds and the children slept, and the doors
                                        were still.

But the best—at least, most hilarious—poem in the volume is probably "A Day with the Foreign Legion." Its opening lines are exceptionally surprising and pleasing as they tear a set of cliches to shreds, and it is unlikely that light verse can do much better than the following comic vignette:

And as they sat at the iron tables cursing the country,
Cursing the food and the bugs, cursing the Legion,
Some sergeant or other rushed in from The Fort
Gallantly bearing the news

From which all those the remorseless desert serves
Take their cues:
"Sir!"
    "What is it, Sergeant?"
        "Sir, the hordes
March e'en now across the desert swards."

In *The Self-Made Man* (1959) Whittemore's poetic identity takes on firm outline: a mild curmudgeon in a sweater, devoted to pipes, martinis, seed catalogues, and musings on the weather, the seasons, and the commonplaces of everyday life. A few sonnets are tucked away among the forty-five poems collected here, but free verse with longish lines predominates.

No other poet has observed himself at work with so much wit, making poems out of the writing business itself. A sample of quotations should bear out this claim. "Notes on a Certain Terribly Critical Piece" concludes with self-deprecation:

Here is a beautiful world full of beautiful, beautiful
Unwritten poems (in every ephemeral flower),
Which, as I understand it, are mine to transcribe
Into beautiful written poems for all time to admire.
And what am I doing, what in the world am I doing?
I?

I am busy writing a critical piece.

In "Lines on Being Refused a Guggenheim Fellowship," the frustrated poet asks,

What curses should I choose?
What curses would a muse choose
If she had been, as I have been, refused,
Muse?

One more example in this vein will suffice. It comes from "Waves in Peoria," which describes the insistence with which a "rhythmic rumble" builds up in the poet's head:

It is like an unwritten poem pounding and pounding
A vast cranial shore until nothing else
Can be heard and the poet grows nervous,
Loses his appetite, and starts to conduct
Himself like a frustrated Renaissance lover.
The remedy
Is to get the thing down on paper and stuff the paper
In a drawer, a postbox or even a small magazine,
Thus escaping it
By the process which is most frequently called creation
Except by psychiatrists,
Who think of it, rather, as cure for psychic distress.

The slightness of such subjects is evident, but so are the beguiling whimsies in which they are dressed.

Whittemore finds topics lying around everywhere to suit his many fancies. In "Purity" a pedantic physicist reminds that all falling bodies would fall equally fast "if you took / All the air away." The poet is enraged by this supposition:

All the air away?
Who would take all the air away? Is there anyone,
Anyone present, anyone living,
Who would make such an issue of purity that he'd take
All the air away?

In *Framley Parsonage* (1861) Anthony Trollope innocently has Dr. Thorne sit down to enjoy a mutton chop. Alas, "A Finnish critic in London" came upon this passage "as he lay / Moodily on his pallet / Late on a critical day." The result for the Finnish critic is a trilogy, *Chops, the English Heritage*; for Whittemore, a poem, "The Mutton Chop." "The Tarantula" allows that unloved creature to tell of his hurt at reading what "One Alexander Petrunkevitch, of Yale, now retired, " has said of the tarantula's lonely fate:

When I am born
I dig a burrow for me, and me alone,
And live in it all my life except when I come
Up for food and love (in my case the latter
Is not really satisfactory: I
"Wander about after dark in search of females,
And occasionally stray into houses," After which I
Die). How does that sound?

Other riches of expression abound. "The Farmhouse" speaks "Of all that wood and busheldom and breeze / It once served." Not too many poets would have plucked that perfect "busheldom" from their word-hoard. In "A Storm from the East" the speaker is weary of freezing gales and, with his housebound family in mind, sings this lovely question: "Oh, when will the wind die down, weatherman, and let / What is so be so, what prevails prevail?"

The Boy from Iowa (1962) and *The Fascination of the Abomination* (1963) are both miscellaneous collections of poetry and prose. No surprises occur, but a pang for the passing of time is sensed more frequently. Whittemore's wit is nowhere sharper, nor his rhythms defter, than in the best poems in these two books. In "The Renaissance Man" the middle-class writer in middle age is caught perfectly in all the facticity of that condition, the "noises, distractions, bills, visitors / Thrusting themselves upon him." The writer as "cultural messenger" is sketched wryly in "The Cultural Conference," while

Maxwell Mackenzie

Reed Whittemore

"No Retreat," "More Heroics," "Cover," and "The Dawn Walker" scrutinize with despair and tenderness the ambiguous place of the individual in an unnamed world.

The graces of Whittemore's light verse—a term not used pejoratively here—should not obscure the genuine plaintive strain he masters in lyrics like "The Music of Driftwood" and "Our Ruins." The music of driftwood "comes from deep water" and is

> true to the temper and pulse
> Of each flutelike, bassoonlike image that pads or
> flutters
> Within the midnight recesses, yet true too
>
> To its own poor selfless self, bare, bearing
> From way, way over yonder its theme of old
> blossomings.
> Temples in orchards, rites, supplications,
> art.

"Our Ruins" considers America's short past and concludes:

> Antiquity doesn't matter. In but a decade

> An empty house can gain centuries, and old mills
> Can lure the bright trout and slim pike for miles and
> miles
> To swim in the depths by their old wall by falls
> Or lurk in their rotten wheelways, savoring the shade.

The new works in *Poems, New and Selected* (1967) constitute the best collection among Whittemore's eight volumes. At least one of these poems—"Clamming"—belongs in every anthology of American verse. Its subject is "The self, what a brute it is," and its germ of incident is "how, at the age of four, I was trapped by the tide / As I clammed a sandbar." The poet loves to tell the story, explaining:

> It serves my small lust
> To be thought of as someone who's lived.
> I've a war too to fall back on, and some years of flying,
> As well as a high quota of drunken parties,
> A wife and children; but somehow the clamming thing
> Gives me an image of me that soothes my psyche
> Like none of the louder events. . . .

The tone in these lines is perfect, the gaze in squeaky-bright focus. The self and its tantrums provoke "The Bad Daddy," the story of a grousy father "who has been angry with the whole family, one by one," and "retires to his study to be sullen and think of death." In this sour funk he writes splenetic memos to his family, leaving him at peace:

So now the bad daddy feels much much more like
                            himself.
His typewriter pants pleasantly in its shed; the beast is
                            fed.
Down the long waste of his years he sees, suddenly,
                            violets.
He picks them and crushes them gently, and is at
                            peace.
Gettem all, bad daddy, and sleep now.

Not since Emily Dickinson's locomotive stopped at its own stable door has a machine been so animated as bad Daddy's typewriter.

Several of these new poems ponder deep themes, and one merits special attention for its religious statement. "Wordsworth and the Woman" is an irritable reaction to a passage in book 7 of *The Prelude* where Wordsworth reports how for the first time in his life he heard "The voice of woman utter blasphemy" and prissily confides, "I shuddered." The poet's retort to "Old shuddering Wordsworth" is "You make me angry." Whittemore's directness in the final stanza reveals much:

An honest woman or man has a moral duty,
Man, to use god's name in vain when the
                            establishments
Which put his name on their doors are vain,
Including that temple of rocks and fastidious naturals
Of yours, man.
So, from the other ranks,
I send to the girl who defiled that temple: thanks.

"Dear God" muses at length on existential freedom and slavery, war and peace, and what these tensions and antinomies signify for the artist. It concludes with the poet's admission of shame for "the spectacle of the self, the pompous self, / The miniscule godlet strutting behind the wall."

"The Seven Days" is one of Whittemore's longest poems, a moving humanistic affirmation of man. It is a narrative of a week of lonely confrontation with the self at Crotched Mountain in New Hampshire. The fifth day constitutes a crisis:

On the fifth day the first god made great whales
And creeping things.
I got up late with a head, and barely made breakfast

And sat in my cabin still fuzzy from too much beer,
Wondering what I was doing there.
The mountains were clear, the air had a rinsed look,
But the land was dry, unchanged. I was still in the
                            museum.
My wife and children were half a country away.
The sun kept tearing around in the empty sky.
I was forty-five. I was old. I wanted to cry.

After this confrontation with his Furies, the hero rises on the sixth day to survey the man (himself) he has created ("hairy, tan, middle-aged, arrogant"). The seventh day offers whatever affirmation is possible:

There, then, was the world. The man surveyed it.
He doubted it was his duty to call it good.
He knew it to be but a world like any other.
He knew that his god, now resting, had made what he
                            could.

Lisel Mueller called "The Seven Days" "a beautiful and highly inventive combination of tongue-in-cheek brightness and the sadness that comes with understanding." It is a superb poem in Whittemore's finest collection.

Fifty Poems Fifty (1970) is a disappointment. It has all the expected subjects—much scrutiny of the "pompous self" ("A Fascinating Poet's Diary"), literature feeding on literature ("The Fall of the House of Usher" is about "a big boxy wreck of a house / Owned by a classmate of mine named Rod Usher"), and the manipulation of nature into stances useful to the poet ("Mountains"), but it carps and carps. The frowsy curmudgeon reveals too much bile in these poems.

For example, "The Sad Committee Shaggy" bemoans the loss of "paradize" when the king is replaced by a chairman. "The Silent Teacher in the Disappearing Classroom Shaggy, Wiz No Book" takes a swipe, all too easy, at progressive education, making a villain of "zat nice old guy, Rousseau." Modern art displeases in "The Quest" because "the best pizzas in town have been framed for the art gallery." These examples, of course, are a small part of the whole, but they exemplify a kind of endemic querulousness that sullies *Fifty Poems Fifty*.

The two longer pieces—"The Sick One" and "The Parable of the Past"—are just dull after the sparkling ingeniousness of such a long work as "Return, Alpheus: A Poem for the Literary Elders of Phi Beta Kappa" in *Poems, New and Selected*. Exceptions such as "Death" and "The Mind" can be pointed to, but *Fifty Poems Fifty* is a weak collection.

The Mother's Breast and the Father's House

(1974; the title is from an essay by Ralph Waldo Emerson) collects twenty-seven new poems from the period 1970-1974, along with twenty-seven from previous volumes. The new poems are generally satisfying, displaying the customary range in tone. The usual disgruntlement with institutions seems even stronger in *The Mother's Breast and the Father's House*, but the tone is clearer and without whine and sneer. "Money" gets in a lot of licks:

The IRS crooks are stealing from the installment-plan
                                                    crooks
And the banker crooks
And the conglomerate crooks.

The angry poet wants to know "Where are the new radicals?" His answer is,

—they are writing books about woodsy communes
Picketing for women's lib
Telling us not to eat meat smoke obey teacher.

A lot of the grumbling of this sort in *The Mother's Breast and the Father's House* may be pretty old stuff and the curmudgeon may be betraying his age, but the style still works.

Many of the same complaints are heard in an ambivalent "Ode to New York," in which the real villain is unmasked when the poet admits "I know that when I speak of you I speak of me." "The Wolf" and "Oh There You Are!" make good, clean, cynical fun of political alliances, the former concluding with a big bad wolf who is really a "misunderstood" wolf and an industrious third pig who is simply "an anal and driven pig." Since "both need therapy," "they shake hands. / And apply for a joint grant." Again, there is a feeling that perhaps this lode has been mined out, the poet poking around in slag and scoria.

No reservations apply to the best of the traditional light-verse pieces. "The Abominable Snowman," for instance, catches that creature, with his "abominable green eyes," "abominable paws," "abominable fur," and "abominable teeth," as he stands "abominably on a lawn pushing snow down a chimney." "Frankie and Johnnie Revisited" tells how those lovers "certainly had a nice hook-up / (Frankie was a girl)" and how "theirs was a glorious interpersonal relationship for many and many a year."

Whittemore has another voice that speaks on a deeper level with much feeling, and it is nowhere heard more affectingly than in "On Looking Through a Photo Album (Of Viet Cong Prisoners)." The album is studied closely, with its "pictures of blindfolded females, / And slim males with their

heads in sandbags." The conclusion reveals the generosity of the poem:

Yet I am sold out to this enemy; I like his small ears.
I am struck by his wide forehead, his high cheekbones.
His suppleness pleases me, and his spirit.
When I look at the gun at his chest, the knife at his
                                                    bowels,
I fear for him.
When I see him hung by the heels I am sick.
The griefs that I find in his wrinkles, his patience in
                                                crossed legs,
The sullen undauntedness issuing from him
Swamp me with traitorous feeling.
Don't I know that this is a war? that this is the enemy?

The same reflective tone suffuses "Where the Path Ends," which ends with this speculation:

Many of the two-legged ones do indeed imagine that
                            they see out from those depths.
They are severe at parties.
They stand talking with drink in hand of the id and
                                                the afterlife,
Of bottomless canyons of soul.
They have not been out past the path's end either.
They know no more of the dark than any child.
They project their own melodramatic notions out
                                        past the path's end,
A common fallacy.
Could it be that behind the demons of tree trunks,
And the glacial stonery,
Could it be that the soul of the wild chews placidly like
                                                    a cow?

I project the image.
I fear death,
But once when it was close to me it was cowlike,
It went moo.
The cabin may be the darker place.

Whittemore will probably be best remembered as a writer of light verse. Although many of his inventions fail, a few such as "A Day with the Foreign Legion" have enough exuberance polished by wit to endure. In *The New Book of English Light Verse* (1978) Kingsley Amis has an observation useful to Whittemore's readers: "We are told that all poetry refers to all the other poetry extant at the time of composition. With high verse this reference will usually be distant, often imperceptibly tenuous; with light verse it is intimate and essential. To this degree it is altogether literary, artificial and impure." Precisely so with Whittemore's light verse. Amis further observes that "Light verse makes more stringent demands on the writer's technique," and

Whittemore has always met the most stringent tests of technique. He is a craftsman whose work offers great finish, the whole projected from a literary and worldly sensibility.

Whittemore's other voice deserves its due. It too is immensely civilized and is what James Dickey had in mind when he remarked, "Of the two (or more) poets in Whittemore, I should like most to see the one who wrote ["A Winter Shore"] emerge." This poet does emerge, but he is cautious, guarded, often undercutting himself when he finds himself approaching large sentiments and themes. When he speaks straight, as in meditations such as "Still Life," "Death," "The Mind," and "Lines," this poet is totally sober, and one hears briefly the voice Dickey responded to, the voice that Dickey said hints of "all the latent terror of the natural world." Modern American poetry has been enriched by the notes of both voices. —*Frank Day*

References:

James Dickey, *Babel to Byzantium: Poets and Poetry Now* (New York: Farrar, Straus & Giroux, 1968), pp. 49-52;

Laurence Lieberman, Review of *Poems, New and Selected, Yale Review*, 57 (Winter 1968): 267-268;

Lisel Mueller, Review of *Poems, New and Selected, Shenandoah*, 19 (Spring 1968): 67-68;

Howard Nemerov, "The Poetry of Reed Whittemore," in his *Poetry and Fiction: Essays* (New Brunswick, N.J.: Rutgers University Press, 1963), pp. 167-182.

Richard Wilbur

Richard J. Calhoun
Clemson University

BIRTH: New York, New York, 1 March 1921, to Lawrence L. and Helen Purdy Wilbur.

EDUCATION: A.B., Amherst College, 1942; A.M., Harvard University, 1947.

MARRIAGE: 20 June 1942 to Charlotte Hayes Ward; children: Ellen Dickinson, Christopher Hayes, Nathan Lord, Aaron Hammond.

AWARDS: Harriet Monroe Memorial Prize (*Poetry* magazine), 1948; Oscar Blumenthal Prize (*Poetry* magazine), 1950; Guggenheim Fellowships, 1952-1953, 1963; American Academy of Arts and Letters Rome Fellowship (Prix de Rome), 1954; Edna St. Vincent Millay Memorial Award, 1957; National Book Award for *Things of This World*, 1957; Pulitzer Prize for *Things of This World*, 1957; L.H.D., Lawrence College, 1960; L.H.D., Washington University, 1964; Sarah Josepha Hale Award, 1968; Bollingen Prize, 1971; Shelley Memorial Award (Poetry Society of America), 1973; L.H.D., Williams College, 1975; L.H.D., University of Rochester, 1976; D.Litt., Amherst College, 1967; D.Litt., Clark University, 1970; D.Litt, American International College, 1977; D.Litt., Marquette University, 1977; D.Litt., Wesleyan University, 1977.

SELECTED BOOKS: *The Beautiful Changes and Other Poems* (New York: Reynal & Hitchcock, 1947);

Ceremony and Other Poems (New York: Harcourt, Brace, 1950);

Things of This World (New York: Harcourt, Brace, 1956);

Poems 1943-1956 (London: Faber & Faber, 1957);

Candide: A Comic Operetta Based on Voltaire's Satire, lyrics by Wilbur, book by Lillian Hellman, and score by Leonard Bernstein (New York: Random House, 1957);

Advice to a Prophet and Other Poems (New York: Harcourt, Brace & World, 1961; London: Faber & Faber, 1962);

Loudmouse (New York: Crowell-Collier; London: Collier-Macmillan, 1963);

The Poems of Richard Wilbur (New York: Harcourt, Brace & World, 1963);

Walking to Sleep, New Poems and Translations (New York: Harcourt, Brace & World, 1969);

Opposites (New York: Harcourt Brace Jovanovich, 1973);

The Mind-Reader (New York & London: Harcourt Brace Jovanovich, 1976);

Responses, Prose Pieces: 1953-1976 (New York: Harcourt Brace Jovanovich, 1976).

Richard Wilbur was born in New York City, one of two children of Lawrence L. and Helen Purdy Wilbur. His father was an artist, a portrait painter. When Wilbur was two years old, the family moved to a pre-Revolutionary stone house in North Caldwell, New Jersey. Although he did not live far from New York City, he and his brother Lawrence grew up in rural surroundings, which, he later speculated, led to his love of nature.

Wilbur showed an early interest in writing, which he has attributed to his mother's family because her father was an editor of the *Baltimore Sun* and her grandfather was an editor and a publisher of small papers aligned with the Democratic party. At Montclair High School, from which he graduated in 1938, Wilbur wrote editorials for the school newspaper. At Amherst College he was editor of the campus newspaper, the *Amherst Student*. He also contributed stories and poems to the Amherst student magazine, the *Touchstone*, and considered a career in journalism.

Immediately after his graduation in June 1942, Wilbur married Charlotte Hayes Ward of Boston, an alumna of Smith College. Having joined the Enlisted Reserve Corps in 1942, he went on active duty in the army in 1943 in the midst of World War II and served overseas with the 36th (Texas) Division, first in Italy at Monte Cassino, later at Anzio, then along the Siegfried Line in Germany. It was during the war that he began writing poems, as he later said, borrowing Robert Frost's phrase, as "a momentary stay against confusion" in a time of disorder. When the war ended, he found himself with a drawer full of poems, only one of which had been published.

Wilbur went to Harvard University for graduate work in English to become a college teacher, and he decided to submit additional poems for publication only after a French friend read his manuscripts, "kissed me on both cheeks and said, 'You're a poet!'" (as Wilbur said in a 1970 interview). In 1947, the year he received his A.M. from Harvard, his first volume of poems, *The Beautiful Changes and Other Poems*, appeared. He spent the next three years as a member of the Society of Fellows at Harvard, first projecting a scholarly book on the concept of the dandy and then working on a book about Poe, neither of which he ever completed.

With the appearance of his second book of poems, *Ceremony and Other Changes*, in 1950, Wilbur was appointed an assistant professor of English at Harvard, where he remained till 1954, living in Lincoln, Massachusetts, with his wife and three (later four) children. He spent the academic year 1952-1953 in New Mexico on a Guggenheim

Fellowship to write a poetic drama. When his attempts at a play did not work out to his satisfaction, he turned to translating Molière's *Le Misanthrope* instead, beginning his distinguished career as a translator. A grant of $3000, the Prix de Rome, permitted Wilbur to live at the American Academy in Rome for a year. On his return to America his translation of *The Misanthrope* was published and performed at the Poets' Theatre in Cambridge, Massachusetts.

In 1954 Wilbur was appointed an associate professor of English at Wellesley College, where he taught till 1957. His third volume of poetry, *Things of This World*, was published in 1956 and was his most honored book: he received the Edna St. Vincent Millay Memorial Award, the National Book Award, and the Pulitzer Prize. The same year the musical version of Voltaire's *Candide*, with lyrics by Wilbur, the book by Lillian Hellman, and a score by Leonard Bernstein, was produced at the Martin Beck Theatre in New York City.

In 1957 Wilbur began a long tenure as professor of English at Wesleyan University and as advisor for the Wesleyan Poetry Series. He received a Ford Foundation grant in drama and worked with the Alley Theater in Houston. *Advice to a Prophet and Other Poems*, his fourth book of poetry, appeared in 1961, and his translation of Molière's *Tartuffe* (1963) earned him an award as corecipient of the Bollingen Poetry Translation Prize. The Lincoln Center Repertory Theatre brought his translation of *Tartuffe* to the stage in New York City in 1964. His collected poems, *The Poems of Richard Wilbur*, had appeared in 1963, and his fifth book of poetry, *Walking to Sleep, New Poems and Translations*, followed in 1969. In 1976 his sixth volume of poems, *The Mind-Reader*, was published, and in 1977 he moved to Smith College as writer-in-residence. He now lives in Cummington, Massachusetts.

Richard Wilbur has always been recognized as a major literary talent and as an important man of letters—poet, critic, translator, editor—but he has never quite been ranked as one of the two or three best contemporary American poets. Early in his career he was overshadowed as a poet by Robert Lowell, who won the Pulitzer Prize for *Lord Weary's Castle* in 1947, the year Wilbur's first book of poems, *The Beautiful Changes*, was published, and whose *Life Studies* (1959) was given principal credit for important new directions in poetry that Wilbur chose not to take. In the 1960s comparisons between Lowell and Wilbur as important new poets became comparisons between Lowell and James Dickey as quite possibly the country's two most important poets. Presently, in the 1970s, more critical attention has been given to such poets as John Ashbery, A. R. Ammons, James Wright, W. S. Merwin, and James Merrill than to Wilbur.

Wilbur's status as an important poet may have changed, but for more than thirty years his poetry has remained pretty much as it has always been—skilled, sophisticated, witty, impersonal. In 1949 when Philip Rahv in *Image and Idea* divided American writers into two camps—"Palefaces," elegant and controlled, and "Redskins," intense and spontaneous—Richard Wilbur was clearly a "Paleface." After Robert Lowell made his break in 1959 with modernist impersonality in poetry, he gave Rahv's distinction new currency by describing American poets as either "cooked" or "raw." Wilbur's "marvelously expert" poetry was undeniably one of the choice examples of "cooked" poetry. Then in 1964, at a time when poetic styles were moving away from impersonality, Leslie Fiedler, one of the advocates of the reemergence of the "I" at the center of the poem and of a neo-Whitmanesque rejection of objectivity and the entire metaphysical-symbolist tradition, found the influence of T. S. Eliot's formalistic theories especially strong on Richard Wilbur: "there is no personal source anywhere, as there is no passion and no insanity; the insistent 'I,' the asserting of sex, and the flaunting of madness considered apparently in equally bad taste." Wilbur's poetry seemed resistant to change. His poetry was judged too impersonal for the early 1960s; it was not politically involved enough during the literary protests against the war in Vietnam in the later 1960s, and, in the 1970s, not sufficiently postmodernist. Yet during each decade many readers conceded that he was one of the most skillful poetic craftsmen, to be compared more accurately, not with Robert Lowell, but with Marianne Moore, Elizabeth Bishop, and Howard Nemerov.

Wilbur has seldom compared his poetry with that of his contemporaries. Instead he has described his art as "a public quarrel with the aesthetics of E. A. Poe," a writer on whom he has written some significant literary criticism. In Wilbur's view, Poe believed that the imagination must utterly repudiate the things of "this diseased earth." In contrast, Wilbur believes, "It is the province of poems to make some order in the world but poets can't afford to forget that there is a reality of things which survives all orders great and small." Poets are not philosophers: "What poetry does with ideas is to redeem them from abstraction and submerge them in sensibility. . . ." Consequently, Wilbur's main concern is to maintain a difficult balance between the intellectual and the emotive, between an appreciation of the particulars of the world and their spiritual essence. If he is explicit in his prose about his quarrel with Poe, it might also be said that he has had an implicit quarrel with the "raw" poetry in Donald Allen's *New American Poetry 1945-60*, (recognized in the 1960s as a manifesto against the "academy"), and also with the extremely personal, seemingly confessional poetry of Robert Lowell, W. D. Snodgrass, and Anne Sexton, for Richard Wilbur as critic and as poet clearly accepts a doctrine of impersonality and does not advertise his personal life in his poetry. "I vote for obliquity and distancing in the use of one's own life, because I am a bit reserved and because I think these produce a more honest and usable poetry," he says in a 1962 interview. A description of his six books of poetry published from 1947 to 1976 sustains this view.

Wilbur's first volume of poetry, *The Beautiful Changes*, contains the largest number of poems (forty-two) and the fewest number of translations (three) of any volume so far. Although he began writing his poetry to relieve boredom while he was in the army in 1943, there are only seven war poems, and they are more poetic exercises on how to face the problems of disorder and destruction than laments over the losses occasioned by war in the traditions of the World War I British poet Wilfred Owen and the best American war poet, Randall Jarrell.

The first of Wilbur's war poems, "Tywater," presents the paradox of the violence illustrated in a Texas corporal's skill in killing—"The violent, neat and practiced skill / Was all he loved and all he learned"—contrasted with the quietness of his death—"When he was hit, his body turned / To clumsy dirt before it fell." The compassion of Jarrell's war poetry is clearly missing. Instead, there is an ironic detachment more like John Crowe Ransom's but without the precise characterization that distinguishes Ransom's best poems:

> And what to say of him, God knows.
> Such violence. And such repose.

Another war poem, "First Snow in Alsace," suggests the theme implied by the title of the volume, *The Beautiful Changes*. The beautiful can change man even in war. War is horrible because man permits it in spite of such perennial desires as the simple childlike pleasure of a soldier at war on being "the first to see the snow," as the night guard repeats the pattern of his childish delight. In another poem, "On the Eyes of an SS Officer," Wilbur uses one of the villains of the Holocaust for a poetic exercise on the extremes of fanaticism: first, that of the explorer

Roald Amundsen, a victim of the northern ice that he desired to conquer; then that of a "Bombay saint," blinded by staring at the southern sun; and, finally, the fanaticism of the SS officers. The implication is that the SS officer in his fanaticism may combine what is symbolized in the eyes of the first two fanatics, ice and fire, for his eyes are "iced or ashen." The persona stays detached, not explicitly condemning this terrible kind of fanaticism. The poem ends a bit tamely with his request to "my makeshift God of this / My opulent bric-a-brac earth to damn his eyes."

If there is a predominant theme in Wilbur's first volume, it is how the power of the beautiful to change can be used as a buttress against disorder. The initial poem, "Cigales," suggests the necessity and the beauty of mystery in nature. The song of the cigales (better known as the cicada) can change those who hear it, but the reason for the song is beyond even the scientist's ability to explain it. It is spontaneous, gratuitous, and consequently, a mystery to be appreciated as an aesthetic experience and described by a poet in a spirit of celebration.

"Water Walker" postulates an analogy between man and the caddis flies or "water walkers," which can live successfully in two elements, air and water.

Layle Silbert

A human equivalent would be the two lives of Saint Paul, described as "Paulsaul." He serves as an example of a "water walker," a man who was converted from service in the material world to service in the spiritual but who remained capable of living in both. The speaker in this poem desires a similar balance between two worlds, material and spiritual; but he is kept from transcendence, like the larva of the caddis held in the cocoon, by the fear that he might be unable to return to the material world.

In his first book, imagination is a creative force necessary to the poet, but Wilbur touches on an important theme developed more thoroughly in his later poetry, the danger that the imagination may lead to actions based entirely on illusions. His interpretation of Delacroix's painting, the subject of the poem "The Giaour and the Pacha," seems to be that in his moment of victory the Giaour realizes that by killing his enemy, at his mercy in the painting, he will lose his main purpose in life, which has been based on a single desire that proves valueless, illusory.

Another poem, "Objects," stresses what is to become a dominant theme in Wilbur, the need for contact with the physical world. Unlike the gulls in the poem, the poet cannot be guided by instincts or imagination alone. His imagination requires something more tangible, physical objects from the real world. He must be like the Dutch realist painter Pieter de Hooch, who needed real objects for his "devout intransitive eye" to imagine the unreal. It is only through being involved in the real world that the "Cheshire smile" of his imagination sets him "fearfully free." The poet, like the painter, must appreciate the "true textures" of his world before he can imagine their fading away.

One of the best lyrics in the collection is "My Father Paints the Summer." It has an autobiographical basis because Wilbur's father was a painter, but it is not a personal poem. The lyric develops the second meaning implied by the title *The Beautiful Changes*—the existence of change, mutability. It praises the power of the artist to retain a heightened vision in a world of mutability. The last stanza begins with the kind of simple graceful line that is to become characteristic of Wilbur at his best: "Caught Summer is always an imagined time." Again the concern is balance in the relationship of the imagination and the particulars, the physical things of this world. The imagination needs the particulars of a summer season, but the artist needs his imagination for transcendence of time, "to reach past rain and find / Riding the palest days / Its perfect blaze."

The title poem of the volume is the concluding poem and serves at this stage of Wilbur's poetic career as an example of his growing distrust of Poe-like romantic escapes into illusion and of his preference for a firm grasp of reality enhanced by the imagination. In "The Beautiful Changes" Wilbur gives four examples of how the beautiful can change: the effect of Queen Anne's lace on a fall meadow, the change brought about by the poet's love, a chameleon's change in order to blend in with the green of the forest, and the special beauty that a mantis, resting on a green leaf, has for him. The beautiful changes itself to harmonize with its environment, but it also alters the objects that surround it. The ultimate change described is the total effect of the changes of nature on the beholder, written in Wilbur's most polished lyric manner:

> it turns
> Dry grass to a lake, as the slightest shade of you
> Valleys my mind in fabulous blue Lucernes.

Wilbur's first volume was generally well received by the reviewers, and it was evident that a new poet of considerable talent had appeared on the postwar scene. Many of his first poems had a common motive, the desire to stress the importance of finding order in a world where war had served as a reminder of disorder and destruction. There were also the first versions of what was to become a recurring theme: the importance of a balance between reality and dream, of things of this world enhanced by imagination.

Wilbur spent three years between the publication of his first volume of poetry in 1947 and the appearance of his second book of poetry in 1950 as a member of the Society of Fellows at Harvard, working on his uncompleted studies of the dandy and Poe. What he did complete, though, was *Ceremony and Other Poems*, continuing his concern with the need for a delicate balance between the material and the spiritual, the real and the ideal. In finding order in a world of disorder, poetry as celebration of nature is a "Ceremony," something aesthetically and humanly necessary. The concept of mutability, secondary in his first volume, is now primary, leading to a consideration of death, both as the ultimate threat of disorder and chaos and as motivation for creating order in the human realm. One of the poems concerned with facing death has come to be among Wilbur's most frequently anthologized poems, "The Death of a Toad." Wilbur finds in the toad a symbol for primal life energies accidentally and absurdly castrated by a tool of modern man, a power mower. The toad patiently and silently awaits his death with his "wide and antique eyes" observing this world that has cost him his heart's blood. His antiquity mocks a modern world that is already in decline.

"Year's-End," another poem on the threat of death, even more clearly contrasts the death of natural things, in their readiness to accept it, and the incompleteness and discord that death brings in the human realm. A dog that "slept the deeper as the ashes rose" is contrasted with "the loose unready eyes / of men expecting yet another sun / To do the shapely thing they had not done." This poem demonstrates Wilbur's skill in describing objects but also his sometimes functional, sometimes not, desire to pun. Some reviewers found the first line of the poem to be Wilbur close to his worst: "Now winter downs the dying of the year." In contrast, his description of winter is Wilbur near his best:

> I've known the wind by water banks to shake
> The late leaves down, which frozen where they fell
> And held in ice as dancers in a spell
> Fluttered all winter long into a lake.

"Lament" is a poem about death, about expressing regret that the particulars of the world, what is "visible and firm," must vanish. This time a pun is functional: "It is, I say, a most material loss." "Still, Citizen Sparrow" is one of Wilbur's best-known poems and, along with "Beowulf," introduces a new and important theme: whether heroism is possible in a world of disorder. In "Beowulf" the stress is on the loneliness and isolation of the hero. In "Still, Citizen Sparrow," in contrast to the common citizens (the sparrows), the hero appears as "vulture," a creature the sparrows must learn to appreciate. The poem is tonally complex, beginning as an argument between Citizen Sparrow and the poet over a political leader as a vulture and ending with an argument for seeing the faults of leaders in a broader perspective because they perform essential services, accept the risks of action, and are capable of dominating existence. The "vulture" is regarded as heroic because he is capable of heroic action: he feeds on death, "mocks mutability," and "keeps nature new." Wilbur concludes: "all men are Noah's sons" in that they potentially have the abilities of the hero if they will take the risks.

Another poem, "Driftwood," illustrates what some of Wilbur's early reviewers saw as the possible influence of Marianne Moore: finding a symbol or emblem in something so unexpected that the choice seems whimsical. In this poem the driftwood becomes an emblem for survival with an identity. It has "long revolved / In the lathe of all the seas." It is isolated but has retained its "ingenerate grain."

In Wilbur's second volume, as in his first, the need for a balance between the real and the ideal that avoids illusions and escapism is a significant theme. In "Grasse: The Olive Trees" the town in its abundance exceeds the normal and symbolizes reaching beyond the usual limits of reality, the overabundance of the South, that can become enervating and illusionary:

> and all is full
> Of heat and juice and a heavy jammed excess.
>
> Whatever moves moves with the slow complete
> Gestures of statuary. . . .

Only the "unearthly pale" of the olive represents the other pole of the reality principle and "Teaches the South it is not paradise."

"La Rose des Vents" is the first dialogue poem for Wilbur, a dialogue between a lady and the poet, a format reminiscent of Wallace Stevens's "Sunday Morning." The lady argues for the sufficiency of accepting the reality of objects, while the poet desires symbols at a remove from reality. In Wilbur's version the lady has the last word:

> Forsake those roses
> Of the mind
> And tend the true,
> The mortal flower.

"A World Without Objects is a Sensible Emptiness" is a poem with perhaps the quintessential Wilbur title. Visions, illusions, oases are the objects of quests for people in a wasteland world, but the questing spirit, "The tall camels of the spirit," must also have the necessary endurance to turn back to the things of this world as a resource:

> Turn, O turn
> From the fine sleights of the sand, from the long empty
> oven
> Where flames in flamings burn
>
> Back to the trees arrayed
> In bursts of glare, to the halo-dialing run
> Of the country creeks, and the hills bracken tiaras made
> Gold in the sunken sun.

Extravagant claims are made for visions that are firmly based on life. A supernova can be seen "burgeoning over the barn," and "Lampshine blurred in the steam of beasts" can be "light incarnate."

In *Ceremony* Wilbur shows greater variety than in his first book. He can express his major themes in lighter poems, even in epigrams. The importance of

a delicate balance between idealism and empiricism, speculation and skepticism, is concisely and wittily expressed in his two couplets "Epistemology." Samuel Johnson is told to "Kick at the rock" in his rejection of Berkeleyan idealism, but the rock is also a reminder of the molecular mysteries within the rock: "But cloudy, cloudy is the stuff of stones." Man's occasional denials of the physical world he so desperately needs are wittily mocked in the second couplet:

> We milk the cow of the world, and as we do
> We whisper in his ear, "You are not true."

In his review of Wilbur's third volume of poetry, *Things of This World* for *Poetry* magazine (September 1956), Donald Hall concluded: "The best poems Wilbur has yet written are in this volume." His judgment was confirmed: Wilbur received both the National Book Award and the Pulitzer Prize for *Things of This World*. Three poems should certainly be ranked among his very best: "A Baroque Wall-Fountain in the Villa Sciarra," "Love Calls Us to the Things of This World," and "For the New Railway Station in Rome." The last two show the influence of his year spent in Rome on a Prix de Rome fellowship. As the title would suggest, there is even a greater stress on the importance of the use of the real in the poems in this volume. If the imagination does create a world independent of objects, it is made clear in "Love Calls Us to the Things of This World" that love always brings one back to the world of objects. Even nuns move away from pure vision back to the impure, "keeping their difficult balance."

It is not always the simpler forms that are the most inspiring. "A Baroque Wall-Fountain in the Villa Sciarra" is based on Wilbur's daily observation of a "charming sixteenth- or seventeenth-century fountain . . . that appeared to me the very symbol or concretion of Pleasure" (*Poet's Choice*, ed. Paul Engle and Joseph Langland). The elaborate baroque fountain is described as an artistic embodiment of the pleasure principle. Human aspiration may be more clearly seen in the simpler Maderna fountains, but the elaborate forms on the baroque fountain:

> are at rest in fulness of desire
> For what is given, they do not tire
> Of the smart of the sun, the pleasant water-douse
>
> And riddled pool below,
> Reproving our disgust and our ennui
> With humble insatiety.

It is indicative of Wilbur's penchant for impersonal-

Richard Wilbur

?

What is a question-mark?
A flowering stone
It is, and is its own
Answer. Dark
And hard is a stone, its skin
Is manifold,
And rolled tight to hold
What within?
A stone has no insides
And its perfection
Is to be sheer protection.
What it hides
Is what it is. We,
Saying it back
Brazen in daylight, ask
What can it be?
Then does the graceful flower
By wonder grown
Over the world-shaped stone
Bend for an hour.

"?," manuscript

ity that he ends the poem not by indicating the personal delight he feels in the fountain but by imagining what Saint Francis of Assisi might have seen in the fountain: "No trifle, but a shade of bliss."

The final poem in the volume is one of the best, "For the New Railway Station in Rome." The impressive new station becomes a symbol of how man's mind must continually work on things of this world for the imagination to have the power to recreate and to cope with disorder:

What is our praise or pride
But to imagine excellence, and try to make it?
What does it say over the door of Heaven
But *homo fecit?*

Donald Hill has said of Wilbur's early poetry that Wilbur has seemingly taken William Carlos Williams's slogan "No ideas but in things" and altered it to "No things but in ideas." Beginning with his third volume, *Things of This World*, Wilbur still recognizes the importance of the imagination, but his emphasis has clearly shifted toward Williams's concept "No ideas but in things" in his stress on the need for things of this world, both for effective endurance in a world of death and disorder and for creativity.

Wilbur's fourth volume of poetry, *Advice to a Prophet*, was not published till 1961, after he had moved in 1959 from Wellesley College to begin a long tenure as a professor of English at Wesleyan University. *Advice to a Prophet* is a larger volume of poetry than *Things of This World*, with thirty-two poems, including four translations and a passage translated from Molière's *Tartuffe*, as well as "Pangloss's Song" from the comic-opera version of *Candide*, and the collection received favorable comments from such critics as Babette Deutsch, Dudley Fitts, M. L. Rosenthal, William Meredith, and Reed Whittemore. But the praise for *Advice to a Prophet* was tempered by criticisms that it had an academic, privileged, even ivory-tower perspective. The title poem is vaguely topical, suggesting the threat of the ultimate atomic holocaust that became a near reality in October 1962 with the Cuban Missile Crisis. Even here Wilbur might be accused of aesthetic detachment: his poem is not humanistic in its concerns but aesthetic and phenomenological, envisioning a world without its familiar objects, without things rather than without people:

Nor shall you scare us with talk of the death of the
race.
. . . .
Ask us, ask us whether with the worldless rose
Our hearts shall fail us. . . .

Perhaps still showing the influence of Marianne Moore's passion for oddities, Wilbur stresses in this volume what the imagination can do with apparently mundane things. In "Junk" he suggests that intimations of the ideal can be found in the rubbish, the junk of the world, and in "Stop," in the grim everyday objects at a train stop. In "A Hole in the Floor" Wilbur even compares the potentials of his discoveries in the floor with those of a great archeologist: "As Schliemann stood when his shovel / Knocked on the crowns of Troy."

In "Grasshopper," he adds to the poetic bestiary that he had collected in his volume *A Bestiary* (1955). He admires the grasshopper for having achieved a delicate balance between stasis in its pause on a chicory leaf and action in its springs from the leaf. Donald Hill calls the poem "a minor masterpiece," but some reviewers believed that Wilbur seemed too content with "minor masterpieces," both in form and in subject matter. He showed an unwillingness to undertake major experiments in form or to introduce new and possibly socially relevant subject matter at a time when that was becoming expected. To some reviewers and critics, he seemed a poet reluctant to take risks of any sort. In fairness, one must say that he does experiment with "new" lines in his poetry, such as his use of the Anglo-Saxon alliterative line in "Junk." But in comparison with what other poets, Robert Lowell and John Berryman for example, were doing by 1961, the experimentation is comparatively minor. Wilbur seemed almost to be writing his poems in a cultural and political vacuum. By 1961 the tremendous impact that Lowell had made in *Life Studies*, by apparently confessing disorder in his own family, had been felt. Two years after *Life Studies* Wilbur opened his volume with what he thought to be a more dramatic poem, "Two Voices in a Meadow," a dialogue between two objects from the world of the mundane, a milkweed and a stone. The drama in this poem and in the title poem, "Advice to a Prophet," seemed humanly insignificant compared to Lowell's more personal approach. Wilbur fails in his attempts to indicate more dramatically and more positively how order might be restored, what his personal "stays against confusion" are, much as Robinson Jeffers's attempt at a tragic poetry had failed before, because he seems too exclusively concerned with objects, with symbolic things, rather than people. Wilbur's message appears to be that when man becomes familiar with the world's own change, he can deal with his own problems as something related to the reality of things. Wilbur calls those who do not respond to the things of this world, those who prefer their dreams and who move to illusions, "the Undead," vampires.

In "Shame" Wilbur attempts to define the kind of human behavior that disturbs him—irresoluteness, a failure to deal with reality. He attempts to provide positive examples of heroic behavior, but he fails to create convincing examples as Robert Lowell does even with the symbol of the mother skunk, "refusing to scare" in "Skunk Hour." In the dialogue poem "The Aspen and the Stream," the Aspen is the positive heroic example because it seems to escape its existence by delving into flux, experience—symbolized by the stream—even if the result is only "a few more aspen-leaves."

It was eight years before Wilbur's next volume

of poetry, *Walking to Sleep*, appeared in 1969. (His collected poems, *The Poems of Richard Wilbur*, and his translation of Molière's *Tartuffe* were published in 1963.) The volume is rather slim, with fewer original poems (only twenty-two) and more translations (eleven) than in previous volumes. What overall unity there is in the four sections of the volume is suggested by the title: these are poems on the subject of how to "walk"—symbolically, how to live before sleep and death. There is once again, as in "Junk," experimentation with the Anglo-Saxon alliterative line divided by a caesura. In "The Lilacs" these flowers are used as a symbol of the cycle of death and rebirth in nature, with the "pure power" of nature that may compensate for the "depth" of death. The poem concludes:

These lacquered leaves
    where the light paddles
And the big blooms
    buzzing among them
Have kept their counsel,
    conveying nothing
Of their mortal message,
    unless one should measure
The depth and dumbness
    of death's kingdom
By the pure power
    of this perfume.

A kind of balance between life and death may be seen if one can appreciate "the pure power" of life. "In the Field," the title poem of the first section, also suggests that the power in life may be sufficient to compensate for the ultimate disorder, death. Wilbur finds in the field "the heart's wish for life, . . . staking here / In the least field an endless claim." And he believes that the same principle is in man. It "is ourselves, and is the one / Unbounded thing we know."

Wilbur also believes that in man's desires lies the answer to his questions. "Running" is, like "In the Field," a longer poem than Wilbur usually writes. It is divided into three parts and describes the act of running at three different times in the poet's life. The poem is intended as not only an affirmative statement about human aspiration but also one about the ultimate meaning of human activities. Wilbur's running becomes a symbol of aspiration at different stages in life. What keeps man running? It *is* human aspiration:

What is the thing which men will not surrender?
It is what they have never had, I think,
Or missed in its true season.

The poem is by Wilbur's own admission one of his most personal poems. It also implies the middle-aged poet's belief that his own life is satisfying and worthwhile.

The title poem, "Walking to Sleep," begins with a discussion of going to sleep that soon becomes a meditation on how to live and a warning against a life of illusion. It is also an argument for accepting death without illusions by literally staring it down. This might be regarded as a climactic poem on a major thematic concern. What is recommended is once again a balance, a life in which reality and "strong dream" work together.

One of the few poems in the volume to be almost immediately anthologized, "Playboy," describes the imaginative response of an adolescent stockboy to the impact of a centerfold in *Playboy* showing a beautiful naked girl. "High on his stockroom ladder like a dunce," he examines "her body's grace," engrossed in "how the cunning picture holds her still / At just that smiling instant when her soul, / Grown sweetly faint, and swept beyond control, / Consents to his inexorable will."

Other poems are also atypical of Wilbur's usual themes. He even includes a protest poem addressed to President Lyndon Johnson; the occasion is not the Vietnam War but Johnson's refusing the official portrait painted by the artist Peter Hurd. The protest is more artistic than political. The poem makes a contrast between Johnson and the culture of Thomas Jefferson with his Rotunda and "Palestrina in his head." Although the poems were published in the midst of the Vietnam vortex, Wilbur is once again primarily concerned with advocating the life of "a difficult balance" between reality and the ideal as the way to personal fulfillment.

Wilbur's sixth volume of poetry, *The Mind-Reader*, appeared in 1976, with twenty-seven new poems (nine previously published in the *New Yorker*) and nine translations. The reviews were again mixed, with some reviewers praising his craftsmanship and defending him from what they regarded as unfair attacks on his conservatism as a poet; others found his new volume simply more of the same and lamented his not taking risks by seeking new directions. The translations provide new examples of Wilbur's superb ability to translate from the French, and he also included translations from the Russian, poems by Andrei Voznesensky.

There are new things in the volume, especially in Wilbur's clearly discernible movement toward simpler diction and more direct poems. Except for the title poem there are no long poems in the book. Wilbur seems to enjoy working with shorter poems

as in the six-line, three-couplet "To the Etruscan Poets," on the theme of mutability exemplified by the Etruscan poets, who "strove to leave some line of verse behind / . . . Not reckoning that all could melt and go."

Some reviewers found "Cottage Street, 1953" to be provocative. It is an account of Wilbur's meeting a young Sylvia Plath and her mother at the home of his mother-in-law, Edna Ward. A contrast is made between Sylvia Plath's destructive tendencies and Edna Ward's power of endurance. A few reviewers treated the poem as if it were a personal attack on Plath by a poet hostile to confessional poetry. The poem is undoubtedly intended as a variation on Wilbur's theme of a need for balance, which he later came to realize Sylvia Plath had always lacked. He opposes love as a principle of order to the "brilliant negative" of Sylvia Plath in her life. What makes the poem exceptional is that Wilbur is dealing with real people characterized rather brilliantly:

> And Edna Ward shall die in fifteen years,
> After her eight-and eighty summers of
> Such grace and courage as permit me no tears,
> The thin hand reaching out, the last word *love*.
>
> Outliving Sylvia, who, condemned to live,
> Shall study for a decade, as she must
> To state at last her brilliant negative
> In poems free and helpless and unjust.

In this poem Wilbur deals with the human problem of survival and death without his usual detachment and with a directness his poems usually lack.

More representative of his usual type of poem is "A Black Birch in Winter." It could have appeared in any of Wilbur's first five volumes. A symbol (the black birch) is found for nature's ability to survive and grow to greater wisdom each year. Except for slightly simpler diction, the poem is a variation on a usual theme, and the conclusion seems a parody of the conclusion of Tennyson's "Ulysses":

> Old trees are doomed to annual rebirth,
> New wood, new life, new compass, greater girth
> And this is all their wisdom and their art—
> To grow, stretch, crack, and not yet come apart.

One poem would seem on the surface to be atypical, Wilbur taking the unusual risk of involving his poetry in the political protest against the war in Vietnam. "For the Student Strikers" was written at the time of Kent State for the Wesleyan *Strike News*. Wilbur's support is not, however, for student protests but for their canvassing programs, house-to-house visits to discuss the student point of

Charles Morales

Richard Wilbur

view about the war. Typically, he urges dialogue—order—instead of protests—disorder:

It is not yet time for the rock, the bullet, the blunt
Slogan that fuddles the mind toward force.
Let the new sound in our streets be the patient
                                                            sound
Of your discourse.

Not much good protest poetry was written about the 1960s, but there is a difference in perspective, in dramatic intensity, and in contemporary relevance between Wilbur in this poem and Robert Lowell in *Notebook 1967-68.*

What is encouraging for those who want more variety in Wilbur's themes or a less impersonal Richard Wilbur is a new emotional directness in the poems about his daughter. Whereas Lowell, Anne Sexton, W. D. Snodgrass, and even James Dickey have told much about their families, until *The Mind-Reader* a reader might not know that Wilbur had a family. Two poems about his children mark a change. His son Christopher's wedding is described traditionally and indirectly in "A Wedding Toast." But "The Writer" is one of Wilbur's most personal poems and, even more important, perhaps one of his best. As a father and as a writer he empathizes with

his daughter's attempts to write a story. He describes her creative struggles "In her room at the prow of the house," and he is reminded of another struggle that he saw before at the same window:

I remember the dazed starling
Which was trapped in that very room, two years ago;
How we stole in, lifted a sash

And retreated, not to affright it,
And how for a helpless hour, through the crack of the
                                                            door,
We watched the sleek, wild dark

And iridescent creature
Batter against the brilliance, drop like a glove
To the hard floor, or the desk-top.

Wilbur is slightly more personal in a few poems; the persona in the title poem, "The Mind-Reader," helps that poem achieve more of the dramatic intensity he has been trying to get into his recent work. He seems to be seeking even firmer and more affirmative statements of the need for order and responsibility; and his tone in the later poems is more confident, more self-assured, as if he is assured that his own artistic life has been worthwhile, that he has himself maintained a balance between reality—

the things of this world—and imagination—things enhanced. Wilbur's perspective is concisely stated in "C-Minor," a poem about switching off "Beethoven at breakfast" to turn back to the reality of the day:

There is nothing to do with a day except to live it.
Let us have music again when the light dies
(Sullenly, or in glory) and we can give it
Something to organize.

To some critics Richard Wilbur may not now be legitimately the major poet anticipated in 1947 and seemingly arrived in 1956. An approach to his poetry alone cannot, however, evaluate properly his importance as a man of letters. For a balanced view of his literary importance, it should be stressed, first of all, that among all his literary contemporaries he is undoubtedly the most sensitive and accurate translator of poetry and of drama in verse. His ability to translate from the French has been rivaled among postwar poets only by Randall Jarrell's skill in translating from German. Unlike Robert Lowell, Wilbur has been a *translator*, not, as Lowell called himself, a writer of "imitations," a poet who uses a poem in another language as a medium for expressing his own poetic sensibility. Wilbur's view of translating is an extension of his view of writing poetry. He has consistently set for himself the goal of accurate verse, of translating not just language but also verse forms. The importance of stressing Wilbur's translations in an evaluation of his poetry is neatly summed up by Raymond Oliver: Wilbur's "degree of accuracy is almost always very high and his technical skill as a poet is just about equal to that of the people he translates." The degree of praise is realized when one considers the writers that Wilbur has translated. If the quality of his translations is high, the quantity is equally impressive. His work with Molière, especially his translations of *Le Misanthrope* and *Tartuffe*, not only read well as verse but have been performed with success. Most celebrated of all was his collaboration with Leonard Bernstein in producing *Candide*.

Wilbur's intentions as a translator have been clearly stated in his introduction to *The Misanthrope* and provide faithful testimony to his technical interests in the craft of verse making. He has a craftsman's interest in a wide variety of poetry: dramatic, lyric, even light verse. His "wit" in his use of rhyme and in his tendency toward puns in his more serious poetry has not always been treated kindly by critics. He has, however, written an amusing volume of light verse for children, *Opposites* (1973), with considerable grace, wit, and humor.

Wilbur also has considerable importance as a literary critic. One could contend that he has surpassed, with the possible exception of Randall Jarrell and Karl Shapiro, his contemporaries and near contemporaries as a poet-critic. He has written perceptively on his poetic opposite, Edgar Allan Poe, and he has contributed a major essay on Emily Dickinson. In 1976 his reviews and critical essays were collected in a volume titled *Responses, Prose Pieces: 1953-1976*. Several of the essays are on his own work. His insight into his own creative powers compares in quality, if not quite in quantity, with James Dickey's attempts in *Self-Interviews* (1970) and *Sorties* (1971) to describe his own creativity.

The question remains about the future of Wilbur's reputation as a preeminent poet. Has Richard Wilbur really changed much or developed far enough in more than thirty-five years of writing poetry? In 1950, for John Ciardi's *Mid-Century Poets*, he not only declared his unvarying motivation for writing but identified what has always been the major theme in his writing: "The poem is an effort to articulate relationships not quite seen, to make or discover some pattern in the world. It is conflict with disorder. . . . "

Wilbur's conflict with disorder has perhaps led him to be satisfied with traditional patterns and traditional themes and old ways to solve old problems. He is consistently a poet of order, of affirmation. His job as a poet, as he sees it, has always been to order his experience, to give his responses to two extremes of disorder: chaos and destruction on the one, and illusions and escapism on the other. His response as a humanist and as a poet is to keep a firm focus on reality as represented by objects, by the things of this world. As a poet he must be modestly heroic, see more, range further than the ordinary citizen. He writes in an early poem, "Objects":

I see afloat among the leaves, all calm and curled,
The Cheshire smile which sets me fearfully free.

If one is content to judge Richard Wilbur in terms of his intentions, he has achieved them well. But, to make the kind of pun Wilbur is capable of himself, he has not invariably been a poet for all decades. In 1950 his view of poetic creation was compatible with that of the dominant critical view of his generation of emerging poets, the "rage for order view" of creativity promulgated by the formalistic New Criticism. Times and critical tastes have changed. Formalism is no longer the dominant critical approach. Modernism has been replaced by a neo-Romantic postmodernism, and man's rage for order has now been balanced by a view of man's rage for chaos. Recent literature can disturb, and poetic forms can be "open" as well as "closed."

What has not changed sufficiently in thirty-five years to satisfy his detractors is Wilbur's poetic style or themes. His concern with a poetry of ideas and his passion for order have resulted in near distaste for dealing with raw experience. His critical reputation today must, of course, bear the consequences. What his critics and his readers must not miss, however, in their concern for the lack of current relevance of his ideas and poetic forms are his mild irony, his sophisticated wit, his humor. Then, finally, there is his craftsmanship, his skill with words and traditional poetic forms. For many readers, his sheer talent, his poetic art, is enough.

Other:

A Bestiary, compiled by Wilbur (New York: Spiral Press for Pantheon Books, 1955);

Molière, *The Misanthrope*, translated with an introduction by Wilbur (New York: Harcourt, Brace, 1955; London: Faber & Faber, 1958);

Poe: Complete Poems, edited with an introduction by Wilbur (New York: Dell, 1959);

Emily Dickinson: Three Views, includes an essay by Wilbur (Amherst: Amherst College Press, 1960);

Molière, *Tartuffe*, translated with an introduction by Wilbur (New York: Harcourt, Brace & World, 1963; London: Faber & Faber, 1964);

Molière, *The Misanthrope and Tartuffe*, translated with a note by Wilbur (New York: Harcourt, Brace & World, 1965);

William Shakespeare, *Poems*, edited by Wilbur and Alfred Harbage (Baltimore: Penguin, 1966); revised and republished as *The Narrative Poems and Poems of Doubtful Authenticity* (Baltimore: Penguin, 1974);

Molière, *The School for Wives*, translated with an introduction by Wilbur (New York: Harcourt Brace Jovanovich, 1972);

Molière, *The Learned Ladies*, translated by Wilbur (New York: Harcourt Brace Jovanovich, 1978).

Interviews:

David Curry, "An Interview with Richard Wilbur," *Trinity Review*, 17 (December 1962): 21-32;

Robert Frank and Stephen Mitchell, "Richard Wilbur: An Interview," *Amherst Literary Magazine*, 10 (Summer 1964): 54-72;

Willard Pate, "Interview with Richard Wilbur," *South Carolina Review*, 3 (April 1970): 15-23;

Edward Honig, "A Conversation with Richard Wilbur," *Modern Language Notes*, 91 (October 1976): 1984-1998;

Peter Stitt, Ellesa Clay High, and Helen McCoy Ellison, "The Art of Poetry," *Paris Review*, 19 (Winter 1977): 69-105.

References:

Louise Bogan, *Achievement in American Poetry* (Chicago: Regnery, 1951), pp. 133-134;

Robert Boyers, "On Richard Wilbur," *Salmagundi*, 12 (1970): 76-82;

Paul F. Cummings, *Richard Wilbur: A Critical Essay* (Grand Rapids, Mich.: Eerdmans, 1971);

James Dickey, *Babel to Byzantium: Poets and Poetry Now* (New York: Farrar, Straus & Giroux, 1968), pp. 170-172;

Frederic E. Faverty, "Well-Open Eyes; or, the Poetry of Richard Wilbur," in *Poets in Progress*, ed. Edward Hungerford (Evanston, Ill.: Northwestern University Press, 1962), pp. 59-72;

Leslie A. Fiedler, *Waiting for the End* (New York: Dell, 1964), pp. 218-221;

Donald Hall, Introduction to his *Contemporary American Poetry* (Baltimore: Penguin, 1962), pp.17-26;

Hall, "The New Poetry: Notes on the Past Fifteen Years in America," in *New World Writing* (New York: New American Library, 1955), pp. 231-247;

William Heyen, "On Richard Wilbur," *Southern Review*, 9 (July 1973): 617-634;

Donald L. Hill, *Richard Wilbur* (New Haven, Conn.: College & University Press, 1967);

Randall Jarrrell, *Poetry and the Age* (New York: Vintage, 1953), pp. 227-240;

Kenneth Johnson, "Virtues in Style, Defect in Content: The Poetry of Richard Wilbur," in *The Fifties: Fiction, Poetry, and Drama*, ed. Warren G. French (Deland, Fla.: Everett / Edwards, 1970), pp. 209-216;

Ralph J. Mills, Jr., *Contemporary American Poetry* (New York: Random House, 1965), pp. 160-175;

Raymond Oliver, "Verse Translation and Richard Wilbur," *Southern Review*, 11 (April 1975): 318-330;

Anthony Ostroff, ed., *The Contemporary Poet as Artist and Critic: Eight Symposia* (Boston: Little, Brown, 1964), pp. 1-21;

M. L. Rosenthal, *The Modern Poets: A Critical Introduction* (New York: Oxford University Press, 1960), pp. 253-255;

Rosenthal, *The New Poets: American and British Poetry Since World War II* (New York: Oxford

University Press, 1967), pp. 328-330;

Donald Barlow Stauffer, *A Short History of American Poetry* (New York: E. P. Dutton, 1974), pp. 385-387;

Hyatt H. Waggoner, *American Poets: From the Puritans to the Present* (Boston: Houghton Mifflin, 1968), pp. 596-604;

A. K. Weatherhead, "Richard Wilbur: Poetry of Things," *ELH*, 35 (December 1968): 606-617.

Papers:

Most of Richard Wilbur's papers are in the Robert Frost Library, Amherst College. Additional manuscripts, mostly early works, are in the Poetry Collection, Lockwood Memorial Library, State University of New York at Buffalo.

PETER WILD
(25 April 1940-)

BOOKS: *The Good Fox* (Kalamazoo, Mich.: Goodly Company, 1967);

Sonnets (San Francisco: Cranium Press, 1967);

The Afternoon in Dismay (Cincinnati: Art Association of Cincinnati, 1968);

Joining Up and Other Poems (Sacramento: Runcible Spoon, 1968);

Mad Night with Sunflowers (Sacramento: Runcible Spoon, 1968);

Mica Mountain Poems (Chapel Hill: Lillabulero Press, 1968);

Love Poems (Northwood Narrows, N.H.: Lillabulero Press, 1969);

Poems (Portland: Prensa de Lagar, 1969);

Three Nights in the Chiricahuas (Madison, Wis.: Abraxas, 1969);

Fat Man Poems (Belmont, Mass.: Hellric, 1970);

Terms & Renewals (San Francisco: Twowindows, 1970);

Dilemma: Being An Account of the Wind That Blows the Ship of the Tongue (Poquoson, Va.: Back Door, 1971);

Grace (Pennington, N.J.: Stone, 1971);

Peligros (Ithaca: Ithaca House, 1971);

Wild's Magical Book of Cranial Effusions (New York: New Rivers, 1971);

Cochise (Garden City: Doubleday, 1973);

New and Selected Poems (New York: New Rivers, 1973);

The Cloning (Garden City: Doubleday, 1974);

Tumacacori (Berkeley: Twowindows, 1974);

Cavalryman (Tannersville, N.Y.: Tideline, 1976);

Chihuahua (Garden City: Doubleday, 1976);

Health (Berkeley: Twowindows, 1976);

Island Hunter (Tannersville, N.Y.: Tideline, 1976);

Pioneers (Tannersville, N.Y.: Tideline, 1976);

House Fires (Santa Cruz: Greenhouse Review, 1977);

Barn Fires (Point Reyes Station, Cal.: Floating Island, 1978);

Gold Mines (Iola, Wis.: Wolfsong, 1978);

Zuni Butte (Bisbee, Ariz.: San Pedro, 1978);

Pioneer Conservationists of Western America (Missoula, Mont.: Mountain Press, 1979);

The Lost Tribe (Iola, Wis.: Wolfsong, 1979);

Enos Mills (Boise, Idaho: Boise State University Press, 1979);

Jeanne d'Arc: A Collection of New Poems (Memphis: St. Luke's, 1980);

Wilderness (St. Paul, Minn.: New Rivers, 1980);

Pioneer Conservationists of Eastern America (Missoula, Mont.: Mountain Press, forthcoming 1980).

Although central to his poems is the landscape of America's Southwest, Peter Wild's poetry sweeps across the continent of human experience and fantasy. Born in Northampton, Massachusetts, Wild's fascination with the West began in his youth, and after graduation from high school he went west to work on a ranch. By the end of the summer, his enthusiasm for ranch work had declined, and he entered the University of Arizona, Tucson. During his summer vacations Wild remained in the West doing ranch work and fighting fires for the U.S. Forestry Service. After receiving a B.A. (1962) and an M.A. (1967) from the University of Arizona, he went on to the University of California, Irvine, which awarded him an M.F.A. in 1969. In 1971 he returned to the University of Arizona to teach in the English department, where he is now a full professor. Wild's love for the western landscape is reflected not only in his poetry but in his prose books about conservation and his service as contributing editor for *High Country News*, a newspaper reporting on environmental affairs in the Rocky Mountain area.

Wild often uses the myths and legends of the Indian West to suggest a disturbing and visionary perception of man living in the midst of enormities. The cosmic world is exemplified by far horizons, towering mountains, and landscapes whose receding distances trouble the mind and excite the senses. He writes of the most essential and basic human conditions by using language alert to particularization and vivid in its dreamlike quality. Nearly always his poems probe into the fragility that human beings share and the patience with which they confront their transitory lives. This exploration usually takes place in the heart of a landscape that reinforces man's own smallness. Merciless storms, far-reaching vistas, and violent threats reappear in Wild's work. Man to some extent controls and dominates what he finds with language and rhythm. At the same time he is able to revel in love and glorify his ability to survive those threats brought about either by nature or by his own emotions.

Whatever the case, Wild's poetry frequently suggests that there exists something beyond the cognitive world. Like a man who quietly folds back a cardboard facade or parts gradually a heavy curtain on which is painted an idealized landscape, Wild infuses his poems with convoluted and unexpected images that run rampant. Wild leads the reader into a land beyond a land, a region where, following the poet, he can track his own fears, doubts, and joys in Natty Bumppo fashion. Piling image upon image, Wild acts as a guide into a visually exciting realm the reader knew existed but seldom thought to enter. Although Wild scouts the territory, he usually avoids teaching or conducting lessons in the meaning of experience.

Like all worthwhile poetry, his batters the sense of the ordinary and rewards with a seriously considered perception of the art of living. Using a persona, Wild seems as awestruck and as enthralled with these beautiful and terrible landscapes as readers are. But this poeticized world is not unpeopled. The reader meets characters loving, hoping, killing, and dreaming. Compared often with surrealists, Wild is not solely interested in phantasmagoria or distorted vision. He is equally concerned with the people who have taken up fictive residences in mythic lands where the topography brings about, nevertheless, feelings of deja vu. Yet one could not appreciate this illusory world had he not the ability to return to the world ordered by the mundane and grounded in reality. Readers come away from Wild's work and turn to their own concerns, glad for the excursion he has provided but happy to be home again in more familiar surroundings.

The Afternoon in Dismay (1968) is Wild's first major collection of poems. (His *Sonnets* and *The Good Fox*, both appearing in 1967, preceed it and are incorporated in this 1968 publication.) The volume is generally a sustained presentation of imagery and a delving into the fantastic world Wild creates brilliantly. Two of his best sonnets are included here; "Ram" and "Watchman" repay a reader's attention.

Written in the classic Italian pattern, they follow a basic iambic pentameter line. The Ram, the symbol for Aries, which begins spring on the zodiac table, also seems to announce the passing of the years, the passing particularly of youth. The times are both good and bad. Caught in the flow of the seasons and anticipating advancing middle age, the persona bemoans his conditions: "I straddle the fence, see dying moths in an old man's eyes, squirming / hooks of sperm in the genitals of a sleeping youth." The watchman, patient and on guard, exemplifies Wild's use of people carefully at sentinel, facing terror, real or imagined. In characteristic fashion, Wild ends the poem with an image of nature not ordinarily perceived by man: "Dogs nibble on slices of the moon." The title poem of the collection, "Afternoon," tells of a man who, "lacking in talent / but not wisdom," goes off to a beach by himself and builds a house "on a pile of rocks." He learns how "to sleep passive" and "how to sit patient." He may be Wild or at least the artist figure who catches "himself playing / imaginary games / with the pelicans."

Mica Mountain Poems (1968) establishes Wild's credentials as a poet whose talent at creating visually disturbing poetry is undeniable. Although their language is more conventional than that of his later books, the poems in this collection anticipate the full range of Wild's verbal prowess as it appears in subsequent volumes. "Flight (I)" certainly is a poem whose imagery is both startling and unified:

> Learning how fragile life is
>   easily crushed
> or punctured
>   letting the life-air out;
> the bones not really living bone
>   but more like plaster structure
> the skin a thin cover
>   stretched over cavities
>   and juices,
> . . . .
> sometimes lying in the darkness
>   I feel the birds
>   about to rush up my throat.

Other phrases from other poems illustrate just as well Wild's inventive and laudable ability to make language do more than readers expect it can. In "Aeon," for instance, "Our desert grumbles"; in "Midnight" "a chain of camels / appears stiff against the stone horizon."

Wild is a prolific writer. Whether the publications are chapbooks or collections, he has

Peter Wild

Everett Peirce

[signature: Peter Wild]

come out with something impressive nearly every year since 1967. In 1969, for example, three books, *Love Poems, Three Nights in the Chiricahuas,* and *Poems* were published. In *Love Poems* Wild's skill at producing lyrical, sensuous images comes to the foreground. These conceits cascade across the pages, and all but one of them, "Ventana," are brief. The love expressed in the poems takes two forms: the love of women and the love of nature. Wild seems equally eager to embrace both. "Cielo" depicts a young girl in whose "mouth / are storms / of brown lilies." In "Silencio," "the shattered desert tilts into sunlight, / and the brown hills / and your brown arms / move / into day." The mental anguish, the sorrow, of the person described in "Dolor" is made vivid by Wild's having the person denounce natural things. It is a wonderful poem characterizing the outsider who cannot love:

> you understood
>   only as rocks became fire,
> water turned to steam—
> the earth pained
>   the soles of your feet;

> you denounced the sun
>   for not sinking
>   to your darkness.

> you hefted your life
>   like a broken arm.

Like the far mountain ranges, the person stands solitary and barren. The description is frightening and masterfully wrought. The word *heft,* for instance, conveys all the pain and suppression Wild wants it to carry. The entire book is an admirable achievement.

Poems explores a variety of subjects, but the overriding topic is the idea of displacement and an attempt by people to order the world immediately surrounding them. The displacement can be caused by sleep, by travel, or by fear. In "Waking" Wild describes the return of consciousness:

> When I wake
> those rivers I've been crossing all night,
>   freezing my waist,
>   sink into the ground
> and the horizon stands out fringed
> with puppets and bone saints clapping
>   soft hands

The dream state is carried into the day, and the images that appear at poem's end are as nightmarish as any deep sleep could inflict.

Fat Man Poems (1970) is a series of sketches, some humorous, which is by and large free of the Southwestern locale. Most are concerned with capturing scattered bits of imagery. "God is A Helicopter With A Big Searchlight" shows Wild poking the reader gently in the side with his comic, fictive elbow. Wild continues to startle readers with the boldness and aptness of his perceptions. For instance in part 2 of "Resolution," he writes that "a shadow walked along the wall / like a bruise, / like the reflection of a putrid cloud." The title poem, "Fat Man," may explain some of Wild's intentions: "He walks through seas of himself, / always deeper; horizons fade."

Terms & Renewals (1970) is set in a Mexican landscape and is another of Wild's surrealistic settings in which the characters attempt to survive the rigors of the country. "Snakes" is an interesting poem, but it relies too heavily on Wild's continued concern with fear and the natural order of things. "Last Night Emily Dickinson" seems out of place in the collection; however, the last lines are memorable: "In the imminent darkness / like a butterfly / my heart tore / in two."

Grace and *Wild's Magical Book of Cranial*

Effusions were published in 1971. "A Traveller Sitting Beneath a Mimosa Tree Looking Out At An Ancient Landscape," a poem included in *Grace*, asserts Wild's interest in exploring distances, both physical and spiritual: "He's a long way / from where he's come, / a land where they speak no language." *Wild's Magical Book of Cranial Effusions* is a tour into the meaning of lunacy and sanity, marked once again by his ability to blend images and distortions with whimsy and horror. Both of these collections reinforce the complexity of Wild's verbal authority. His poetry is not obscure, but it can be cryptic. Undoubtedly his poems have a muscular brashness about them.

Peligros (1971), a title that means *hazard* or *jeopardy*, concentrates on depletion, risk-taking, and violence. Several of the poems are distinguished. Among them are "Curses" and "Thinking on the Plains," which ends: "People who love me / don't seem to understand / what parts I leave and what I take, / what muscle they strip / from my bones." A bit self-absorbed, the persona presents a thought hardly new but whose poignancy remains effective.

New and Selected Poems (1973) takes poems from *The Afternoon in Dismay, Sonnets, Mica Mountain Poems, Love Poems, Terms & Renewals, Dilemma: Being An Account of the Wind That Blows the Ship of the Tongue*, as well as *Wild's Magical Book of Cranial Effusions, Grace,* and *Peligros*. Included also are new and previously uncollected poems. The edition is further enhanced by the brief introduction written by William Matthews. Besides the book's giving a reader an overview of Wild's poetry to 1973, the preface provides some indication of what the reader may expect. Matthews believes that the poems collected here "are obviously the work of a man who wants above any other literary ambition to write good poems, and who can." One always hopes for good poetry; what one longs for, of course, is great poetry. Matthews has also said that "every time I see a new poem of his I read it with great anticipation." His choice, then, of the word *good* seems somewhat of an equivocation; however, his liking Wild's work cannot be disputed. Wild has received more favorable reviews than he has unfavorable. Nearly all the critics agree that there is in his work something compelling.

Wild's use of landscape takes a maturer or perhaps a more significant turn in *Cochise* (1973). It may be that the countryside, whose splendid trappings he so meticulously details, is the self, depicted according to the symbolist technique of creating interior landscape, the place where inner and outer environments either collide or coalesce. Cochise is literally both place and person. A county in Arizona, Cochise also refers to a man who is living out his days in a culture depleted and enervated. The title poem is replete with the fantasy world of dreams and expectations that Wild charges with vigorous surrealism. Like many of his poems, this one begins simply and in a straightforward manner; it grows increasingly more complicated, as if readers were facing a revolving mirror whose one side is concave, the other convex. Cochise is a great warrior, and the speaker of the poem tracks him because he is "our stronghold." A woman with the speaker, perhaps herself an Indian, is an unwanted visitor; the persona drifts into his fantasy because of her boring talk. Lost in a myth of glory and innocence, the speaker swears "never to go back," never to leave the illusion. The idea of attaining spiritual heights informs the collection with the notion that there is indeed a life behind or beyond the life we recognize. For example, in "The Climbers" this metaphysical adventure is grounded in breath-demanding labor:

> The further they go
> the less they leave behind.
> though they start out snorting,
> stamping their feet, the wind
> like teeth in their ears. spreading out
> the meadows burn white, the cows
> loom in the trail. . . .

The distances charted in the landscape are the distances found between man and his spirit, man and his sense of place, man and his aspirations. The Indian culture, now "one-eyed," is a fearful remembrance of past civilizations whose cultures have been destroyed by wars, greed, and people overly zealous to champion practicality.

To contrast the spirit and place of Cochise are poems like "The Candidate," whose biting contempt may be derivative, but whose imagery is totally Wild's own concoction:

> Mornings he spits out a few
>   rotten teeth with the toothpaste
>   and a little green blood.
>   gold doubloons roll from his belly.
>   and with a crust of toast
>   still wedged in his mouth
>
> he begins running through the day
>   in his rubber suit . . .

Threatened by his lack of confidence and security, modern man is the Babbitt figure gone finally and perversely berserk. *Cochise* relies heavily on

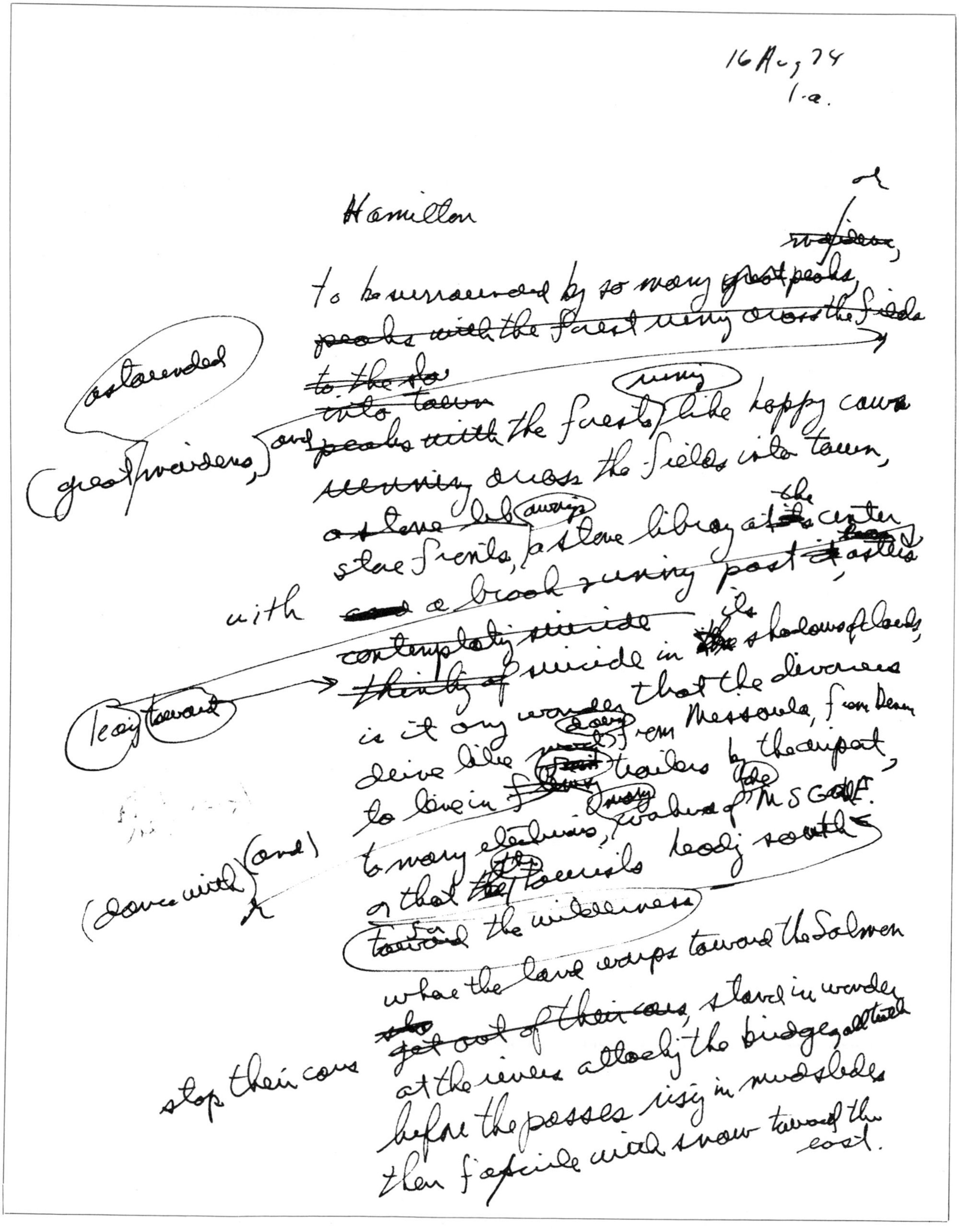

"Hamilton," manuscript

unexpected twists and turns in thought, and at times the images come close to being used for their own sakes. Like the speaker in "The Night-Blooming Cereus," Wild seems to be a poet whose "whole life is a trance / I hope to break from / once or twice a year."

Published in 1974, *The Cloning* reestablishes Wild's ability to focus on characterization as well as setting. Surrealism remains a powerful ally, but its use here is more constrained and more selective. His interest also returns to nightmare and waking, the difference between what is factual and what is fictitious. Readers are also exposed to the intruder threat, whether it be nature or man, tourist or native. Several noteworthy poems help keep Wild's reputation elevated. Among them are "Dreams," "Bamboo," "Termites," "The Wilderness," and "After Rain." Wild continues to be a master of verbal surprise. Consequently the reader finds himself in a land where "flaming words begin to fall," where the "sun has his children," where a warrior can look "down the hole of his throat." Perception and vantage points are jangled and seem double-jointed. *The Cloning* perhaps best proves that Wild's poems retain their individual lusters if they are read separately rather than in tandem or at one sitting. His techniques are exciting, but they can also wear thin and be distracting. His poetry often reads so well that it hurts. Other times his imagery is disarming simply for the sake of being disarming. Readers attuned to contemporary literature want contemporary, innovative techniques, not a clever use of imagery that clones itself into stagnation. There is, without doubt, a delicate line between nonsensical whimsy and the revitalization of the English language.

Three chapbooks published in 1978, *Gold Mines*, *Barn Fires*, and *Zuni Butte* suggest what future direction Wild will choose. *Gold Mines* begins with a quote from Edward Abbey: "Is not all gold fool's gold?" The reader is not certain if this quotation is a warning about what is to come or a comment followed by a question mark. The booklet is made up of seventeen nuggets, some of which maintain in high fashion Wild's visual language. "The Shy Person" has beguiling imagery, but it is more like an out-of-focus snapshot than it is a deliberate attempt at portraiture. Of course, Wild may have been after neither:

Disrobing, she threw her skin toward the fire,
                    and being shy
missed.

All we find is a raincoat
on a bench by the furnace
            of the daffodils.

If readers enjoy poetry whose meaning seems hidden by the very language that tries to convey that meaning, then Wild has achieved something special in *Gold Mines*.

Barn Fires and *Zuni Butte* are reminiscent of *Cochise* and *The Cloning*. Containing longer poems than *Gold Mines*, the pamphlets underscore the almost frenetic pace at which Wild produces poetry. Returning to familiar topics and landscapes, the poems mirror his previous subjects, including that of human beings living in a realm—both mental and physical—that is beautifully distorted.

Wild's latest collection of poems, *Wilderness* (1980) reaffirms some of Wild's basic interests, but his concerns are shaped with a growing sophistication of presentation. In most of his poetry published before that in *Wilderness*, Wild has seen man as living in a natural world represented by vast, remote areas of land. Wild first investigates seriously a soul's being mirrored by the surrounding landscape in *Cochise*. *Wilderness* takes this approach a step further. The characters who populate the poems are modern men, and they run the gamut from a prospector in "Midas" to a middle-aged jogger in "German Shepherd." Nevertheless, the book explores the notion that human beings carry a wilderness within themselves and that their visions of nature shape the worlds they call their lives. Man may accept the stultifying routine of modern man's day-to-day existence; he may be caught up in the rampant growth of materialism, attended by a rapid decline in hope; or he may see the harmony of natural cycles. The third possibility, of course, is the ideal choice. As Wild implies, the other two perceptions seem to be the "criminals" people "harbor" within themselves. Some of the characters in *Wilderness* continue to aspire nobly to mine the gold, and they run "after a fat, kicking heart" in hopes of rejuvenating their waning idealism. A growing number, however, forego climbing the mountain or mining the ore, and they are content to sit "on the edge of the bed . . . like an emphysemiac." Clearly, Wild has set up the contraries deliberately, and his poems continue to be both athletic and sensitive. They are themselves statements glorifying that side of man's nature which is spiritual. Ideas and thoughts may appear to creep into the poems surreptitiously, but Wild continues to be a master of word choices that at their best remain both clever and haunting.

                                        —*Walter Freed*

Other:

Brown Miller, ed., *Lung Socket*, includes poems by Wild (San Francisco: Open Skull, 1968);

Phil Perry, ed., *Mad Windows*, includes poems by Wild (Notre Dame: Lit, 1969).

Periodical Publications:

"Wild's Magical Book of Cranial Effusions," *Little Magazine*, 5 (Spring 1971): supplement, 9-46;

"Eighteen Poems," *Little Magazine*, 9 (Spring 1975): 11-30.

References:

William Matthews, Introduction to *New and Selected Poems*, pp. 11-13;

Robert Peters, "Mud Men Mud Women," *Margins*, 14 (October-November 1974): 57ff; republished in his *The Great American Poetry Bake-Off* (Metuchen, N.J.: Scarecrow Press, 1979);

Ormond Seavey, "Peter Wild: An Introduction," *Little Magazine*, 9 (Spring 1975): 4-10.

NANCY WILLARD
(26 June 1936-)

SELECTED BOOKS: *In His Country* (Ann Arbor, Mich.: Generation, 1966);

Skin of Grace (Columbia: University of Missouri Press, 1967);

The Lively Anatomy of God (New York: Eakins Press, 1968);

A New Herball (Baltimore: Ferdinand-Roten Galleries, 1968);

Testimony of the Invisible Man: William Carlos Williams, Francis Ponge, Rainer Maria Rilke, Pablo Neruda (Columbia: University of Missouri Press, 1970);

19 Masks for the Naked Poet (Santa Cruz: Kayak Books, 1971);

Childhood of the Magician (New York: Liveright, 1973);

Carpenter of the Sun (New York: Liveright, 1974);

Sailing to Cythera and Other Anatole Stories (New York: Harcourt Brace Jovanovich, 1974);

The Island of the Grass King: the Further Adventures of Anatole (New York: Harcourt Brace Jovanovich, 1979);

William Blake's House: Poems for Innocent and Experienced Travelers (New York: Harcourt Brace Jovanovich, forthcoming 1980).

The poetry of Nancy Willard seems quite different in theme and tone from much of the literature written by women during the 1960s and 1970s. The major social and personal issues of the feminist movement are not centrally addressed in her five volumes. Instead, as Stanley Poss declares in his review of *Carpenter of the Sun* (1974), Willard "seems very much at home with herself and her world which, in comparison to [Adrienne] Rich's, is viable rather than not," and as Francine Danis writes in her essay "Nancy Willard's Domestic Psalms," "Willard's poetry, bright, graceful, and often playful, radiates womanly fullness, contentment, and reverence." Yet if the writer's voice is not angry nor desperately troubled, neither is it complacent nor trite. At the heart of Willard's poetry lies a commitment to order, unity, and permanence, but this commitment grows out of her clear perception of contrary, potentially disruptive forces that she must, as woman and artist, both encompass and counter.

Central to her first two volumes, *In His Country* (1966) and *Skin of Grace* (1967), is the motif of healing; for Willard, healing is achieved through perceiving, recording, and reconciling the divergent elements of human experience as constructs for her life and art. Thus, as "The Tapestry Makers" (*In His Country*) reveals, "making" is equated with "healing," but "healing" is envisioned as an "agony / of lights," and as "In the Hospital of the Holy Physician" (*Skin of Grace*) asserts, the "cure" is made "In the pulse of my ruin." The conception that order can be achieved only through the recognition of potentially disordering forces is again suggested by the third volume of poetry, *A New Herball* (1968). Here the perfections of the woodland flora are both threatened and enhanced by the dragon that lies waiting on the forest's floor and by the soldier who brings his grenades to the scene. *19 Masks for the Naked Poet* (1971), though quite different in tone and technique from the first three volumes, reiterates their concerns. By assuming numerous masks, the poet encounters, becomes, and ultimately transforms all things into a larger, more comprehensive whole. Willard's last volume of poetry to date, *Carpenter of the Sun*, focuses upon the author's roles as wife, mother, and writer, roles that she integrates with clear contentment and grace. Yet, once again, the unity forged between herself and her universe encompasses, not ignores or dismisses, the complexities built into the human experience. Throughout her poetry, Willard emphasizes the necessity for exactness of perception and expression; it is this ability to perceive, express, and fuse possibly discordant elements of her world that gives her work its excellence.

Born in Ann Arbor, Michigan, Nancy Willard earned her B.A. (1958) and Ph.D. (1963) degrees from the University of Michigan and her M.A. degree (1960) from Stanford University; at Michigan she won the Avery Hopwood Award in poetry, and at Stanford she was a Woodrow Wilson Fellow. Among her other honors are the Devins Memorial Award for *Skin of Grace* (1967), an O'Henry Short Story Award for "Theo's Girl" (1970), and Lewis Carroll Shelf Awards for two children's books, *Sailing to Cythera and Other Anatole Stories* (1974) and *Island of the Grass King: the Further Adventures of Anatole* (1979). In addition to her five books of poetry, Willard has published two collections of short stories—*The Lively Anatomy of God* (1968) and *Childhood of the Magician* (1973), one critical book, and twelve volumes for children, with another forthcoming in 1980. She teaches in the English department at Vassar College and has also taught since 1975 at the Bread Loaf Writers' Conference. She is married to Eric Lindbloom and has one son, James.

Aesthetic principles central to Willard's own poetry are defined in her critical book, *Testimony of the Invisible Man: William Carlos Williams, Francis Ponge, Rainer Maria Rilke, Pablo Neruda* (1970). These four writers, whom Willard labels the *Ding*-poets, are united, she says, by their scrupulous examinations of concrete things. For these poets, Willard contends, the truth of the world resides in particular objects themselves, not in the conventional ideas that men impose upon these things. Thus, all "stereotyped modes of thinking or seeing," whether the result of the writer's personality or of his cultural-intellectual heritage, must be destroyed so that he can, as "invisible man," truly perceive objects in their "inexhaustible variety." New ideas, new unities arise from the *Ding*-poets' fresh mode of seeing; for, as Willard states, "Art is not a [mere] selection from the world but a transformation of it into something that praises existence."

Moreover, to achieve his goals, the *Ding*-poet must not only clearly see but also accurately express his world: he must create a "rhetoric of things" that, Willard believes, operates in two different ways for the writers she examines. The Americans, Williams and Neruda, demand a freshness of language associated with a freshness in sense perceptions, and through this new language they hope "to renew man's vision of things . . . [and] to break down his

isolation by renewing his vision of himself"; the Europeans, Ponge and Rilke, employ the "rhetoric of things" as the "rhetoric of revelation" transmitted from the outsider-poet, who is in contact with the "silent world," to other men, who are bound by their less important human involvements: "The word becomes the Word and the poet the god who utters it." Willard, in her own work, clearly shares the *Ding*-poets' concern for accuracy of perception through the examination of concrete things. In addition, she embraces the exactness and freshness of language that she praises in Williams and Neruda. If she does not finally agree with the Europeans that the poet is a god separate from other human beings, she does adopt much of the language of revelation in her work. Willard's *Testimony of the Invisible Man* clearly helps define aesthetic principles underlying her own poetry.

Themes and techniques particularly characteristic of Willard's first three volumes are illustrated by two works from her initial book, *In His Country*. "Picture Puzzles" portrays a family effort to assemble a jigsaw puzzle of Fra Angelico's *Nativity*, yet behind this apparently serene and trivial activity lies a darker motivation: "It's because we're broken / that we love / puzzles; pictures / cut all askew, / fifteen hundred / pieces, salvage / of divine catastrophe." In the jumble of pieces, the speaker finds an image of the broken human psyche whose repair, like that of the puzzle, seems an "impossible assemblage":

> Peacocks, kings, horses
> sleep in the rubble, peasants,
> angels, and gillyflowers
> cocked for resurrection.
> Pieces like grey stones,
> piece like a bloody star,
> pieces like bones.

The extraordinary beauty of the figures portrayed suggests their potential for resurrection, but the shapes and colors of the individual pieces imply disordering counterforces, unyielding, bloody, and stark. Still the speaker persists in her efforts to bring unity to the "senseless floes": "Excavating / a lost language, / we dredge / for the verb that binds / image to image in one word, / clear / sheaf in the makers' minds." And the repairing verb, exactly perceived and exactly expressed, ultimately comes in the word *flowers*:

> The saint, the king flowers
> not from our knowing but our being born
> in every leaf and wing

397

prophesied by men
  who arrived before.
We know
  we make the picture to find again
the simple paradise
  of Fra Angelico,
hymning in broken chords
  how without this bloody star
the angel could not stand,
  how the shapes of our healing lie
  dumb in our hand.

In *Testimony of the Invisible Man*, Willard uses the image of flowering to suggest that moment when a thing reveals its essence to its viewer. Rejecting stereotyped and therefore false perceptions ("our knowing") while surrendering to the puzzle-piece things themselves (the "shapes" of "leaf and wing"), the speaker is able to achieve her flowering, her healing. Yet the order thus created is not the "simple paradise" of Fra Angelico but instead a construct unifying the angel and the bloody star. Without one, the other cannot stand.

The principle that order can be achieved only through the true perception of objects in all their forms is reiterated and further clarified in "Saint Nicholas is the Patron Saint of." Here Willard declares that scholars and children are similar because they are capable of loving things for themselves, not for their uses; scholars will "fall / in love with the print / and forget the poem," and children will prefer "the small tag" on a costly doll's gown to the doll itself. Yet each group, in focusing upon the small, particular thing, is perceiving its true value:

The worth of a guinea springs
from no solvent powers.
Its cameo world rejoices,
is therefore saved,
ranking with shells and with pressed flowers,
amphoras, apes'
skulls, words, and wings
not to fly with but to delight
the eye as things,
caps and categories loved
for their smooth shapes
and voices
calling nouns home for the night.

The precisely expressed catalogue of objects in this stanza fuses the apparently grotesque with the obviously beautiful, the abstract with the concrete, much as "Picture Puzzles" unites the angel with the bloody star. And, again, as in the preceding poem, the principle for the objects' union can be perceived only through true, unstereotyped modes of thinking and seeing:

Their order belongs to eyes
that the earth chooses
to edit a work much vexed:
    de verietate rerum,
an occult, particular text.

The "work," composed of all the ambiguities of man and his world, *is* "much vexed," but through scrupulous examination of concrete things, the observer can understand the difficult "text," which is, at once, both "particular" and "occult."

Willard's second volume, *Skin of Grace*, again focuses upon the role of perception in achieving healing unities. The poem "String Games," like "Saint Nicholas is the Patron Saint of," considers an object not in terms of its function but in terms of its inherent qualities discerned by the true observer. The cat's cradle fashioned by a child is, of course, useless: " 'It wouldn't warm a mouse,' / says the old woman, her needles / chattering over the slow growth / of sweaters and socks, necessary / as lexicons and oatmeal." Yet, in the object and in the act of its creation, Willard suggests, lies an image fusing order and disorder. The cat's cradle is constructed "to hold the Protean act / together, shaking it / inside out"; the figure thus both connects and disarranges its elements, reflecting in the process the Protean fluidity of all systems of order. "Rapid as argument, / acrobatic as a conversation / of mutes," the string figure "leaves nothing behind, / arrives with nothing, stands / nowhere but ravels its simple cradles / and familiar space like proverbs / stuck on your hands." The unity created, then, is one that encompasses nothing and everything, a paradox clear and acceptable only to the careful observer of the thing itself.

Three other poems from *Skin of Grace*—"The Church," "The Insects," and "Crewel"—variously illustrate unities achieved through the fusion of apparently contradictory elements. And, again, in these works, principles of order are discovered only through true perception of the objects themselves. Among the icons and whitewashed purity of "The Church," the poet envisions "a mural of monkeys pressing wine," "a cock," "a dancing bear or a boy / riding on a wild boar," "a dragon," and "a griffin"—for these profane, exotic beings are part, too, of the greater union, "the communion / of saints and men." In the creatures closely observed under the microscope in "The Insects," Willard finds images of beauty, power, and permanence that contradict

Carpenter of the Sun

My child goes forth to fix the sun,
a hammer in his hand and a pocketful of
nails.
Nobody else has noticed the crack.

Twilight breaks on the kitchen floor.
His hands clip and hammer the air.
He pulls something out,

something small, like a bad tooth,
and he puts something back,
and the kitchen is full of peace.

All this is done very quietly,
without payment or promises.

Nancy Willard

"Carpenter of the Sun," manuscript

man's conventional, inaccurate conceptions of the tiny beings: "Our boundaries break / on their jeweled eyes, / . . . the creature / we understood disappears. / . . . the roach / cocks his enormous legs at your acre, / eyes like turrets piercing / eons of chitin and shale." Transformed into the "shape of your oldest fear / of a first world / of monsters," the insects, in their finally acknowledged power, give man a clear view of his relationship with his world; he is simply part, not master, of the greater unity of things. And in "Crewel," Willard observes an old woman's quilt-making, which fuses fine materials, lovingly worked stitches, exotic creatures, and a magical vision of the world:

> In the crewel world of my grandmother
>   a leopard bares satin teeth,
> its jaws open loop for hunting
>   than singing. Trees round as puddings

fan into fruit where a monster
    parrot hangs like an earring in starstitch

and whipped spider's web.
. . . .
herringbone for a hummingbird
wing, filoselle and crow's-foot
    for the flounched hills, knotted
cross furring the red deer that floats
    to a blue pagoda sunk in strawberries
where the tree of life hardly feels
    the fernstitch bobbinay twice its size.

In conceiving and creating her quilt, the old woman forges unity from incredible variety; and as she works, she achieves the ultimate fusion of the artist with her art, "a promise / of lion and lamb and herself wed." Here, as in much of Willard's best poetry, order and unity result only when an object reveals, to the eyes of a true observer, the principle reconciling apparently contradictory elements.

Exactness in perception and expression becomes absolutely central to Willard's third volume of poetry, *A New Herball*, a collection of twelve poems celebrating garden and woodland flora. In these works, each natural object is portrayed in its concrete particularity, and this penetration of the thing itself often yields secrets important to the observer's conception of unities between man and nature. "Hyacinth" illustrates Willard's dual purpose in these poems:

> Hyacinth: ceremonial
> plumes in a
> tournament of riders
> charging under the
> turf. Dense
> as a sponge
> to the touch, yet
> splayed, starred
> like cloves; someone
> has sunk a
> chandelier in the
> garden.
>
> When I used to cut
> spinneys and scepters
> of white paper, it was
> your substance I
> dreamed of.

The visual and tactile imagery in the poem exactly conveys the concrete reality of the flower; moreover, the "substance" of this reality is said to provide the impulse for the observer's art as she tries to capture and reproduce, in ornate paper cutting and in the poem itself, the hyacinth's totality. Again, in "Iris," the flower's precise portrait and the object's implications for its perceiver exist side by side:

> The iris shoot unsheathes
> itself crumpled and wet
> as the folds of a stomach,
>
> then straightens, summoned
> into the elegant blades,
> sealed, calked, one on
>
> the other, a print of
> leaves, brushed on the
> air. This is the tongue
>
> of marriage: we grow,
> we cleave without asking.
> With our skin
>
> we know.

Here, the iris—"crumpled" and "elegant," "sealed" and "calked," inevitably and intuitively cleaving and growing—becomes an emblem for marriage, for the union of man and woman with one another and with the natural object itself.

The small verse portraits of *A New Herball* fuse each flower's diverse elements into a comprehensive whole; yet a unification process of a different sort is defined in two of the volume's poems. "Out of War" and "News from the Interior" describe predators upon the woodland scene—a man who would kill what he can no longer understand, "the weather / of inward mornings, of play / between fox and man's child"; and a dragon who moves the air, "grieves the saints and / the young men in the / fields," "shakes the cold stream," and tears bees "from huge oaks snapping / under his harsh boots." Yet both of these figures, the human interloper and the dragon sleeping on the forest's floor, become part of the unified processes of the natural scene; in response to their guileless brutality, the woodland produces its exotic growth—"Mandrake unfolds" in the dragon's footprints—and the fox and the child continue to "lie down together." The unity of nature thus encompasses both the beautiful and the terrible.

19 Masks for the Naked Poet, though more surrealistic in subject matter and technique than the three earlier volumes, shares their concern with the forging of unities from diverse elements. In these quite whimsical works, the poet becomes, through the many masks he adopts, a Proteus: he is, as "The Poet Folds to his Heart a Thousand Women" declares, "the hunter and the whipper-in, / yes, and the dogs, the fiddler and fiddle, / the ape and garden, / their snow and water; / the man and woman, / with heavy hair and a soft chest." He knows, becomes, and ultimately transforms all things. In "The Poet's Wife Watches Him Enter the Eye of the Snow," for example, the protagonist, as he "gather[s] the dark strands / of the poem like a tide," appropriates his wife's familiar household objects—her sink, her dustpan, her eyeglasses, and her "five masks praising the sun." Through them he ascends into the heaven of creation, and when the objects are returned, the poet's wife senses their transformation;

> In the morning she calls to the newsboy:
> "How can I, wife of the poet,
> know what he saw and did there?
> It is enough that I open my eyes
>
> and my glasses perch on my nose
> and show me the brittle dreams of parrots.
> Enough that my dustpan believes it shoulders
> the broken bones of those warriors the stars,

that my sink gurgles for joy,
and my five masks tell me more
than I knew when I made them."

The household objects, then, become both the vehicles for and the recipients of the poet's magic, and their transformation unites them, the poet, and the poet's wife in a special knowledge and communion.

Again, in "The Poet Turns His Enemy into a Pair of Wings," the artist encounters, assumes, and ultimately reconciles all experience. His enemy, a dragon who "picked his pockets, hid his poems, / beat its tail on his head at night, / blew the nose off his wife's face," leaps onto the poet's back, and the man carries the creature through the streets ignoring his every command and his every transformation. Finally, when the dragon identifies himself as Salamander, fireman of the stars, and directs his bearer to "Go up," the poet attends:

How shall I go? asked the poet.
Just as you are, said the dragon,
day in night, night in hand,
hand in pocket, pocket in poem,
poem in bone, bone in flesh!
flesh in flight.

The catalogue brings together all of the diverse elements—concrete and abstract, ridiculous and sublime, contradictory and complementary—of the poet's life and art. By subduing his supernatural enemy and thereby receiving his blessing, the protagonist is able to achieve "flesh in flight," a true union of man and god, of the earth and the skies, of physical reality and artistic imagination. The poet, thus, encompasses and reconciles all elements of the natural and supernatural worlds.

The previously uncollected poems that compose just over two-thirds of Willard's last volume of poetry to date, *Carpenter of the Sun*, seem increasingly personal, increasingly domestic in subject matter and tone. The best of these works focus upon the author's roles as wife, mother, and poet, roles that she, unlike many women writers of her generation, finds quite reconcilable. Yet her contentment, her sense of unity among her many selves and the other people or elements in her world, results from her confronting and embracing, not simply ignoring, disparate currents in her life. The pattern in these domestic poems is, in short, identical to that in the earlier works, as "Marriage Amulet" reveals:

You are polishing me like old wood.
At night we curl together like two rings

on a dark hand. After many nights,
the rough edges wear down.

If this is aging, it is warm as fleece.
I will gleam like ancient wood.
I will wax smooth, my crags and cowlicks
well-rubbed to show my grain.

Some sage will keep us in his hand for peace.

The poem beautifully celebrates the union of two people in marriage; "the rough edges wear down," and the amulet-couple becomes the emblem of "peace." Yet the work also suggests the importance of retaining individuality within the marital union; the speaker's unique "crags and cowlicks" are polished to "show," not to obscure, her "grain." Thus, marriage is union, but it is union that recognizes and encompasses the individual qualities of the people involved.

"Why I Never Answered Your Letter" more directly reveals the careful probing of disparate elements so necessary to the creation of a sense of unity:

It's true I make books, but not often.
Mostly I am always feeding someone,
nine cats whose tails flag me down each morning
. . . .
My man comes home, dreaming of sirloin.
I ravage the house: three eggs and half a potato.
I embalm them in amorous spices with beautiful
names.
It's true I make books, but mostly I make do.
The chapters of hunger are filled but nothing is
finished.

At night a baby calls me for comfort and milk.
Someday I'll teach him to sing, to dance, and to
draw,
to learn his letters, to speak like an honest man.
Right now I teach him to eat, and I tell him a story,
how an angel came to Saint John with a book in its
hands,
saying, *Take and eat. It shall make thy belly bitter,*
but thou shalt know all people, all prophets, and all
lands.

The speaker envisions herself in her several domestic roles as a "feeder" of others—cats, husband, and child. Yet she also describes her writing activities in terms of "feeding" herself; she makes books as she might make dinner, and "the chapters of hunger are filled but nothing is finished." As the poem concludes, the two apparently different types of feeding are merged. The protagonist literally teaches her child to eat while she imaginatively tells him a

Nancy Willard

story of a book that is to be eaten. Through the merging of the physical act and the intellectual one, of the rather mundane domestic lesson and the highly important creative one, the child and his mother-poet are prepared to comprehend everything, sweet and bitter, "all people, all prophets, all lands." Again, a sense of unity and contentment is achieved, but at its foundation lies a clear recognition and appreciation of the disparate, potentially discordant elements in human experience.

At first glance Willard's characteristic subjects—jigsaw puzzles, crewel embroidery, cat's cradles, flowers, the activities of the domestic life—seem unpromising as substance for poetry. Yet, through her acute powers of perception and her unfailingly deft and evocative language, she manages to invest these small objects, these quietly familiar situations, with enormous significance. In them she finds diverse, potentially discordant elements; but in them, too, she discovers patterns for order, permanence, and unity. Combining a remarkable vision with polished craftsmanship, Nancy Willard proves herself a superbly gifted and accomplished poet. —*Judith S. Baughman*

References:

Francine Danis, "Nancy Willard's Domestic Psalms," *Modern Poetry Studies*, 9 (Spring 1978): 126-134;
Stanley Poss, "I Never Go Anywhere Without my Raccoon," *Western Humanities Review*, 29 (Autumn 1975): 391-393.

C. K. WILLIAMS
(4 November 1936-)

BOOKS: *A Day for Anne Frank* (Philadelphia: Falcon Press, 1968);
Lies (Boston: Houghton Mifflin, 1969);
I Am the Bitter Name (Boston: Houghton Mifflin, 1972);
With Ignorance (Boston: Houghton Mifflin, 1977).

Charles Kenneth Williams was born in Newark, New Jersey. He was educated at Bucknell University and at the University of Pennsylvania, where he took the B.A. in 1959. Since 1972 he has been a contributing editor for *American Poetry Review*. In 1974 he was awarded a Guggenheim Fellowship, which resulted in the publication of his latest book, *With Ignorance* (1977).

Williams's long poem, *A Day for Anne Frank*,

was first published in a limited edition in 1968 before it was included in *Lies* (1969), a collection of lyrical invectives against the bitterness and lying that, in the poet's view, are at the root of much of the world's daily activity. The world is not a place for sensitive and articulate beings; Anne Frank, for instance, is "a clot/ in the snow, / blackened, a chunk of phlegm / or puke." The epigram from *A Day for Anne Frank* reads: "God Hates You!" and, indeed, the world of Williams's poetry is one of futility and despair arising from a hostile universe. God himself is the author of much destruction, and in "Loss" the poet experiences an apotheosis, becoming an accomplice of God as each witnesses the "tall weeds come up dead / and the house dogs, snapping / their chains like moths, howl / and point towards the withering / meadows at nothing."

Williams's achievement lies in his depiction of the power of terror. He is at his best when he creates a scene that becomes the image for a besieged world. For example, in "Ten Below" he describes "an old cart-horse covered with foam" that stands as the symbol for an uncommunicable array of miseries. On the other hand, Williams is at his worst trying to create the same effect with allegory and sermonizing. In "It Is this Way with Men" the poet tells the reader that men are driven down in a hostile universe, but he does not say who drives them and for what purpose. Williams is susceptible, at times, to the dilemma illustrated so well by the correspondent's attitude in Stephen Crane's short story, "The Open Boat" (1898). He sometimes fails to distinguish between a hostile universe and an indifferent one. As Crane suggests, in an indifferent universe there are no temples and no bricks to throw at them. Likewise, in Williams's early poetry, there is often a lack of clearly defined target and ammunition. As he concludes in "Ten Below": "You can't cut your heart out. / Sometimes, just what is, is enough."

Williams's least successful images are those that are most unnatural and nightmarish—images that seem to have been created rather than experienced. This kind of macabre mawkishness is easy to spot in *Lies*: it has a specialized vocabulary of its own, abounding in such words as *scum*, *scab*, *testicles*, *genitals*, *vagina*, *womb*, and *urine*. This semi-scatological language goes hand in hand with the poet's attempt to shock the reader into some kind of eschatological revelation, but it does not always work.

Yet Williams's rage against the world and against the lying platitudes that somehow keep the world in motion is often poignant and powerful. His vocabulary is usually simple, direct, and often forceful; the lines of his poems are arranged to ensure the impact of the horror he depicts. Nevertheless, *Lies* rarely offers a glimmer of hope, and paradoxically, this omission lessens the impact of the terror. Bludgeoned by the repetition of impending doom, the reader becomes less sensitive and strangely acclimatized to the aura of suffering and injustice. The poet's exhaustive catalogue on a single theme has a deadening effect. Tentative notes of hope are only irregularly sounded. In "To Market" a kind of compromised but viable love exists. The reader may also discover a momentary glimmer of hope in "What Is and What Is Not," in which the poet admits that innocence flourishes in children even though it and they eventually will be "consumed."

In 1972, three years after *Lies*, Williams's third book, *I Am the Bitter Name*, was published. The Bitter Name is the main character who appears in a variety of guises. This volume of poetry is appropriately titled, for it is Death with whom the entire generation of the 1960s, like Abraham, felt all too well acquainted, and much of Williams's poetry shows the influence of the times. *I Am the Bitter Name* is characterized by the fear and hatred nurtured by America's involvement in Southeast Asia. The first poem of the collection, "A Poem for the Governments," is an invective against "you mr old men" [sic], criticizing political and bureaucratic complacency that condones the horror of the twentieth century. (Five of the most political poems in the volume, "A Poem for Governments," "Keep It," "The Spirit The Triumph," "Madder," and "The Nickname of Hell," were reprinted in an anti-Nixon anthology of drawings and poems called *The Sensuous President*, 1972, edited by "K," a pseudonym for Williams.) In *I Am the Bitter Name*, Williams's rage, previously undirected, finds a target, although one cannot say that his poetry necessarily benefits as a result. The effect of terror on the human consciousness is sometimes more profound and debilitating when it is ill defined, and thus the vaguely malign universe of *Lies* is potentially more terrifying than the corrupt world of *I Am the Bitter Name*.

Much of Williams's anger is expressed in the formlessness of the contemporary poetic. Rarely do the lines sing and never do they make an attempt to create a sense of order. Images are often chosen for their ability to shock rather than their ability to convey meaning. For example, lines like "the baby was easy / the baby went up in the thin air / I remembered in dostoevsky where they talked . . . ," from "The Rabbit Fights for His Life The Leopard Eats Lunch," are characterized by the abrupt transition and juxtaposition of incongruous images that are the hallmark of the unmediated feeling from groups such as the Beats and the hip poets of the 1960s. These farfetched images, shocking diction, and disregard for poetic form drive many readers away and create a void between the poet's attempt to communicate and the reader's willingness to listen. Thus in a poem like "The Nickname of Hell," the first two lines, "the president of my country his face flushed / horribly like a penis is walking . . . ," divert the reader's attention from a consideration of the metaphor's meaning.

In *I Am the Bitter Name* there is one poem of undeniable power, a poem that conveys an entire generation's apprehension at world events out of control. The last poem in the book, "In the Heart of the Beast," is the longest poem in the book and is devoted to one subject—the dissolution of faith in a

Layle Silbert

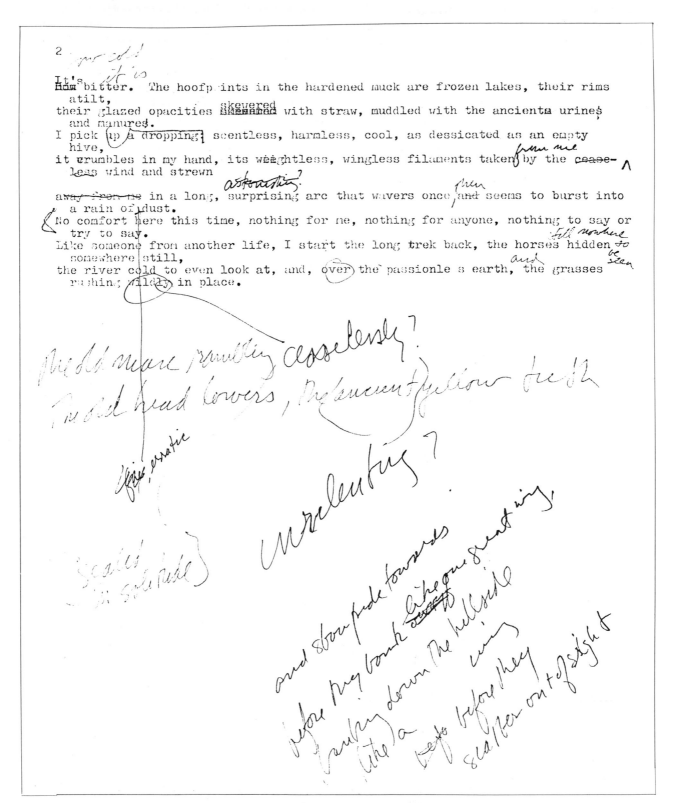

2

It's
How bitter. The hoofprints in the hardened muck are frozen lakes, their rims atilt,
their glazed opacities skimmed with straw, muddled with the ancients urines and manures.
I pick up a dropping, scentless, harmless, cool, as dessicated as an empty hive,
it crumbles in my hand, its weightless, wingless filaments taken by the cease- less wind and strewn
away from me in a long, surprising arc that wavers once and seems to burst into a rain of dust.
No comfort here this time, nothing for me, nothing for anyone, nothing to say or try to say.
Like someone from another life, I start the long trek back, the horses hidden somewhere still,
the river cold to even look at, and, over the passionless earth, the grasses rushing wildly in place.

Work-in-progress, revised typescript

404

rational world. The epigram sets the scene: "May 1970: Cambodia, Kent State, Jackson State," mentioning names that were symbols to a generation rebelling against the violence it perceived, and Williams is at his very best choosing the images that emerge from those tragic places. The poem complements its subject by rejecting all traditional forms and cadences. Indeed, it is a collection of images and questions arranged in as haphazard a fashion as the time they describe. Recalling the famous photograph of one of the students killed by the National Guard at Kent State, Williams says:

On the front page of the times a girl is screaming
she will be screaming forever
and her friend will lie there forever you wouldn't know
she
wasn't sleeping in the sun except for the other
screaming.

Williams also uses a portion of the *New York Times* editorial exonerating the National Guard for their actions and responds with a single cry: "o my god / my god," the cry of helpless resignation that not even poetry can overcome.

Williams's most recent book, *With Ignorance* (1977), is a departure in style and subject from earlier work. Once again the verse is unstructured, but now the lines are longer, recalling the exuberant effusiveness of Walt Whitman. Moreover, many of these poems deal with the same subject that fascinated Whitman—the investigation of the complex American sensibility. Some of Williams's best work is here, perhaps because the poet has now achieved more distance from his subjects. Two superior elements in the poetry of *With Ignorance* reveal themselves immediately: the first is a dramatic quality—these poems are stories; secondly, there is a probing quality—the poet now wants to explore, not excoriate. Here Williams has a series of phenomena in view, mysterious and inscrutable, and he turns to his poetry as a method of savoring the events and discovering answers.

The first poem, "The Sanctity," is a remarkable vignette, a successful dramatic rendering of a ubiquitous mystery. The poet recollects his life at a time when he worked as a construction worker, recounting an experience he had at the home of an older worker, a carpenter who served as his protector and teacher. When he visits the older man's house for dinner, the carpenter has an argument with his wife that ends in an explosion. The man goes berserk, smashes furniture, and terrifies the children, his mother, and his wife; but he shows up at work the next day as if nothing happened. How are we to account for the dual nature of this carpenter, who, like all the men on the job, vacillates between good nature during the day and potential murderousness after hours? What unhappiness or suffering drives these men to violent acts, and what is it about work that soothes their turmoil? Williams does not feel the need to answer that question for us. Instead, he recounts the experience with a dramatic vividness, recalling that "I think I've never had as much contentment as I did then, before work, the light just up, / everyone sipping their coffee out of the heavy white cups and teasing the middle-aged waitresses." Williams has hit on a mystery too profound, too common, too inscrutable to draw easy conclusions. What makes these men this way? What makes the simple assume religious overtones, become sanctified? Merely the thing itself; and Williams celebrates the thing itself with perhaps the best poem he has written yet. The last two lines have all the answer that can be given:

Listen to the back-hoes gearing up and the shouts and
somebody cracking his sledge into the mortar pan.
Listen again. He'll do it all day if you want him to.
Listen again.

In his most recent book of poetry, Williams has come closest to his own definition of what he would like to do in poetry. He is quoted in *Contemporary Poets* as saying: "What I would really like would be to sing without meaning anything. There's a song: a man making a canoe, he's singing

I am making a canoe
I am making a canoe

. . . yes, like that."

Williams comes as close as he can to his ideal in *With Ignorance*. Like "The Sanctity," most of the poems here are stories with embedded meanings. They encourage the reader to explore the action of the poem and derive what he may. They are moments frozen in time, instances of the real preserved. They are generally very good. Only the last, the title poem, "With Ignorance," is a return to the abstract meditation without the drama.

Williams is becoming less bitter, less strident, less insistent, and his poetry improves as a result. He has realized the importance of little things as well as gigantic things, and the balance makes for promising expectations. —*Thomas Goldstein*

Other:

The Sensuous President, edited with contributions

by Williams as "K" (New York: New Rivers Press, 1972).

References:

Stephen Berg, "Paragraphs on the Poetry of C. K. Williams' Book, *Lies*," *December*, 9 (1967): 201-202;

Morris Dickstein, "Politics and the Human Standard," *Parnassus*, 1 (Fall 1972): 125-129;

Richard Howard, Review of *Lies*, *American Poetry Review* (November-December 1972): 45.

JONATHAN WILLIAMS
(8 March 1929-)

SELECTED BOOKS: *Red/Gray* (Black Mountain, N.C.: Jargon, 1952);

Four Stoppages (Stuttgart: Jargon, 1953);

The Empire Finals at Verona (Highlands, N.C.: Jargon, 1959);

Amen / Huzza / Selah (Highlands, N.C.: Jargon, 1960);

Elegies and Celebrations (Highlands, N.C.: Jargon, 1962);

In England's Green & (San Francisco: Auerhahn Press, 1962);

Emblems for the Little Dells, and Nooks, and Corners of Paradise (Highlands, N.C.: Jargon, 1962);

Lullabies Twisters Gibbers Drags (Highlands, N.C.: Jargon, 1963);

Lines About Hills Above Lakes (Fort Lauderdale, Fla.: Roman Books, 1964);

Affilati Attrezze Per I Giardini De Catullo (Milan: Perici Editore, 1966);

The Lucidities (London: Turret Books, 1967);

Polycotyledonous Poems (Stuttgart: Edition Hansjorg Mayer, 1967);

Descant on Rawthey's Madrigal: Conversations with Basil Bunting (Lexington, Ky.: Gnomon Press, 1968);

Sharp Tools for Catullan Gardens (Bloomington: Indiana University, Fine Arts Department, 1968);

An Ear in Bartram's Tree (Chapel Hill: University of North Carolina Press, 1969);

Mahler (New York: Grossman, 1969; London: Cape Goliard, 1969);

Strung out with Elgar on a Hill (Urbana, Ill.: Finial Press, 1970);

Blues & Roots / Rue & Bluets (New York: Grossman, 1971);

The Loco Logodaedalist in Situ (London: Cape Goliard, 1972);

The Personal Eye, text by Williams and photographs by Clarence John Laughlin (New York: Aperture Monograph, 1974);

The Family Album of Lucybelle Crater, text by Williams and photographs by Ralph Eugene Meatyard (Highlands, N.C.: Jargon, 1974);

Hot What? (Dublin, Ga.: JW. Mole Press, 1975);

Elite / Elate Poems (Highlands, N.C.: Jargon, 1979);

Portrait Photographs (Frankfort, Ky.: Gnomon Press; London: Coracle Press, 1979).

Jonathan Williams was born in Asheville, North Carolina, to Thomas Benjamin and Georgette Williams, a lively couple who soon moved the family to Washington, D.C. They were straight from the gracious strictures of Southern semiaristocracy (yet stubborn mountain folk to the bone). Williams's father was a multigifted self-made man, and his mother a talented decorator. In Washington, Williams attended that most British and Episcopalian of schools, St. Albans, attached to Washington Cathedral, and left with acute anglophilia and a lifelong taste for cathedrals.

Consecutively, without taking a degree, he studied art history at Princeton, painting with Karl Knaths at the Phillips Memorial Gallery in Washington, etching and engraving with Stanley William Hayter at Atelier 17 in New York, and the whole range of arts at Chicago's Institute of Design. Then, in 1951, he returned to his native North Carolina mountains where the Bauhaus-influenced school, Black Mountain College, was in force with poet Charles Olson as rector. There, he distinguished himself on the softball team, hosted rambles through Southern drawing and dining rooms as well as drive-in cinemas, once dropped a pot of asphalt on a raw canvas from his room window, became friends with what were to become some of the best-known painters, poets, composers, and dancers of today, wrote his first signal poems, and began to produce a series of the finest examples of the bookmaker's art since William Morris. To publish poetry alongside the work of contemporary painters, photographers, and typographers, he founded The Jargon Society in 1951, and he has remained its editor, publisher, and designer up to the present—with some ninety titles to his credit. He has taught at the Aspen Institute for Humanistic Studies, Maryland Institute College of Art, the University of Kansas, Wake Forest University North Carolina School of the Arts, Salem College,

Winston-Salem State University, and the University of Delaware. He has held fellowships and grants from the Guggenheim Foundation (1957-1958), the Longview Foundation (1960), the National Endowment for the Arts (1968, 1969, 1970, 1973), and has received an honorary degree from Maryland Institute College of Art (1969).

One of the happiest legacies of Ezra Pound is the idea that any healthy society is in debt to its imaginative gadflies. Jonathan Williams is one of the wittiest and most daring. Precocious, with early influences ranging from Edith Sitwell, Kenneth Patchen, Robinson Jeffers, Kenneth Rexroth, and William Carlos Williams to Charles Olson, Robert Duncan, and Robert Creeley, Williams has created a distinctive line, sure of foot in a stream of syllables, clearly witty in the splash of its consonants—a line well informed by ear and eye, though innocent of metrics.

He has been deemed "democratic" by William Carlos Williams, "our best greek poet" by Guy Davenport, "salty" by James Laughlin, "unequalled" by A. R. Ammons, "Indispensable!" by Buckminster Fuller, a "joyous laborer" by James Dickey. Robert Duncan calls him a "veritable male Marianne Moore"—and Thomas Lask says, "of all the Black Mountain poets (teachers and disciples alike), Jonathan Williams is the wittiest, the least constrained, the most joyous." And also a satirist. The typical attender of Williams's heretofore unexpected undercurrents, founts, and sidelights of art would find all of the above to be true. The person behind all this hoopla is the crafter of an athletic style, each phrase to be read as if it were a basketball swishing through a net, each dribbled syllable contributing to a never-before-seen game of words. It is true that his more curious stretches of restless imagination may depend for their resultant point on humor dropped in the totally unsuspecting lap, but as poems they are always easy on the tongue and sharp as chitchat in a barber's shop. All get up and go, he sets us straighter. He has learned, the listener leans back to hear, from both socked flyballs and Charles Olson's "And the mind go forth to the end of the world." He knows that each one makes an arc.

Alert for eccentrics, roadside cafes with the accent over the *f*, stray-cat-scratched wisdoms of the urinal, foibles and follies, slips of the tongue, seers and doers, masters of schtick and spiel from sidewalk to bedroom and back, he seldom errs with eye or ear. This kind of Catullan spunk may be side by side with deep, moving, bucolic lyrics, one after another extolling the cow bells and cuckoos in Mahler, or Thoreau coming on a muskrat. Here, puns are a kind

of *gloire*; musics of the spheres may be traced through the relation of *o*'s and *a*'s both stressed and muted throughout what seems but brusque statement and rude sentiment.

Amongst this ruckus, Jonathan Williams's strength as a poet lies in a nearly tireless questioning of the extratraditional lyric, in a time that believes with him that "form is only an extension of content" (Robert Creeley's words). If we take lyric in its first sense as song from a lyre, then we understand that in Williams's poetry, from the early book "Jammin' The Greek Scene" (only published in scraps and pieces), in which he turns up rather like Edith Sitwell playing Ovid on the saxophone in a New Orleans dive, to the masterly later poems written one each to movements of Mahler symphonies, his words present themselves, one after the other, as equivalents of notes of music plucked still ringing from the air. He stands as one always in dialogue with Orpheus himself.

In the splendid books clustered around "Jammin' The Greek Scene," *Amen / Huzza / Selah* (1960) and *Elegies and Celebrations* (1962), the reader's ideas of music are stretched to include the lilts of energetic local speech, speech furthermore in terms vastly unconscious, yet honed to his most polished, terse wit. The intensity of psychic thrust in these poems is undiminished after two decades. "Enthusiast" and "The Distances to the Friend" (both elegies to older writer figures) are poems in which "song sweats through the pores" and the depths of one man swim before us "stifling all repulsion" "into the sounding keyboard."

Although published in 1959, his first widely remarked book, *The Empire Finals at Verona*, was written largely after the three books noted above. It includes the poems Williams wrote in correspondence with Louis Zukofsky at the time they both decided to translate Catullus—Williams in the argot of American jazz and Zukofsky after the sound of Latin. The volume also contains some of the best sports poems ever written, and surely some of his most democratic, witty, and lovely work:

> mute, flat on the planet,
> eyeing a jet-stream eight miles out,
> full of fall-out, waste and fragrance
> from Nevada
>
> going out to seed the plankton,
> sink atolls
>   and burst the livers of great whales.

This book contains three especially fine short lyrics: "Autopsy," "A Vulnerary," and "The Grounds."

The first is Walt Whitman's autopsy report and contemporary newspaper obituaries. The second is Williams at his most sparely beautiful, in a poem dedicated to Robert Duncan; while the third, under a feisty epigraph culled from an Edward Dahlberg letter, stakes itself out squarely on the boundaries of Eden—a place he is to return to often in later work.

With *In England's Green &* (1962), he continues to walk this new imagined realm, propelled by Blake although arm in arm with Emerson and Thoreau:

> in the monocular sunlight
>
> three miles wide
> lid to lid.

Note also, in this book, the end lines of a Southern poem titled "Cobwebbery," which is among the best of Williams's recreations of common talk:

> Maw, rip them boards off
> the side the house
>
> and put the soup pot on
>
> and plant us some petunias
> in the carcass of the Chevrolet
>
> and let's stay here
> and rot in the fields
>
> and sit still.

In that soup pot seems to stew the nurture of the whole blasted South, to Williams's mind, a pap of spiders. "Cobwebbery" indeed. The concluding poem of this volume is called "The Familiars," which relates a strange myth of a poet-planted "Rattlesnake Master" who takes "masses of rattlers large as washtubs" "into the crevice into / the central den." From this inner center, perhaps Jonathan Williams's Eden, words shed their skin to hear in a world where *paine* is become *paean*, and where common experience is scripture plain as birds singing in a tree. He finds a spot where each bud or bulb or den is literally a "crawl" of exits. It is a wonderful tale.

Since these books of the early 1960s, Jonathan Williams's productions have multiplied, sometimes to the point of ephemerality. Among this work, his *Mahler* (published first in 1967, then further expanded in 1969) stands paramount in its sustained maturity and lyric zest. These splendid poems were written both out of a long early listening to the music of Gustave Mahler during a time when Jean Sibelius was the darling of the concert hall, then a further compressed listening during the months of May and June of 1964 at his mountain home in Highlands,

North Carolina. In a complex series of intro-, retro-, and circumspections, the images appear in interlacing circles like the first drops of rain on a reflecting pond, deceptive as to depth. Certain of these images appear to float through whole gilt clouds of unknowing that some black (or even ever bluer) empyrean might support. Witness from two movements of "Symphony 5":

> II. *Stormily agitated*
>
> to be a block of flowers
> in a wood
>
> to be mindlessly in flower
> past understanding
>
> to be shone on
> endlessly
>
> to be *there*, there
> and blessed
>
> III. *Scherzo*
>
> one two three
> one two three
>
> little birds waltz to and fro
> in the piano
>
> at Maiernigg on the
> Wörthersee
>
> and up the tree:
> cacophony
>
> one two three.

Every page bears the stamp of Williams's rangy intelligence, from local reference, to Eros Creatrix, and back to the heart. This collection has justly remained Williams's most popular book with critics, fellow poets, and readers alike. Yet one might equally praise *Blues & Roots / Rue & Bluets* (1971), which the author called a "Garland for the Appalachians" of "common words in uncommon orders—conversations quoted exactly but cast into line to reveal their native invention." Along the way there are also road signs, more snakes off the road, and a lot of whittling on porches. Take "The Hermit Cackleberry Brown, On Human Vanity":

> caint call your name
> but your face is easy
>
> come sit
>
> now some folks figure theyre
> bettern
> cowflop they
> aint

not a bit

just good to hold the world together
like hooved up ground

thats what.

These poems should sit on our shelves alongside *Uncle Remus* (1880), a book Jonathan Williams's father used to read to company. Alone, they would make another poet's reputation.

No one should miss, either, "Excavations from the Case-Histories of Havelock Ellis" (published in the 1972 selected poems *The Loco Logodaedalist in Situ*). The title is unusually direct for Williams, and what he unearthed in these texts is by and large his most direct work to date—if also his most dark. Stark history after stark history is revealed, each in a kind of Piranesi of closets. Their only kin are such as Henry James's "The Jolly Corner" (1908), long snatches of Proust, and Poe at his best. One "History" reads baldly: "it is a dark crimson / it affords me relief." It could be the burnt scraps of Count Dracula's memoir. Another affords this little vision of hell:

the sight of the naked
river,

increased by
a young Turk smoking
below the waist.

We have no other poems as naked (and smoking) as these.

At the height of his career, what later explorations might we expect? Not since James, certainly, has there been an artist so in touch with everyone, so aware (a lesson he learned, as did Olson, from Edward Dahlberg) that style could be built soundly. Grit and vision seem to sum up the career of this strange man. His support of other artists is unparalleled in our time. Because of this younger man, some now undenied elder masters have been published again, among them, Kenneth Patchen, Louis Zukofsky, Basil Bunting, Stevie Smith, Mina Loy, and Lorine Niedeker. He has also republished early editions of Olson, Creeley, Duncan, Levertov, and many others. At his table one can meet anyone from Buckminster Fuller to William Burroughs, and often at the same time.

The fate of multitalented men, from Leonardo da Vinci to the composer Lord Berners who dyed tumbler pigeons shades of mauve, cerise, and chartreuse, all for delight of a guest, is often that their art is not comprehended by more direct minds. It may be, though, peeping through exactly these so

often cranky, cross-grained, quirky minds, that one focuses best on a complex time. It is easy to imagine a future critic's zeroing in on Jonathan Williams as a window to what could comfortably be called a "period." Jonathan Williams is like Ezra Pound and Ruskin before him, that rare breed of proselytizing exemplar to whom each act of art constitutes an impetus for freedom. —*Ronald Johnson*

Other:

Edward Dahlberg: A Tribute, edited with notes on contributors by Williams (New York: Tri-Quarterly, 1970);

The Appalachian Photographs of Doris Ullman, preface by Williams (Penland, N.C.: Jargon, 1971);

Epitaphs for Lorine, edited with an introduction by Williams (Penland, N.C.: Jargon, 1973);

Lyle Bonge, *The Sleep of Reason*, edited with a preface by Williams (Highlands, N.C.: Jargon, 1974);

The Land: Twentieth Century Landscape Photographs, text by Williams and others (London: Gordon Fraser, 1975);

I Shall Save One Land Unvisited, Eleven Southern Photographers, edited with an introduction by Williams (Frankfort, Ky.: Gnomon Press, 1978).

Periodical Publication:

"The Southern Appalachians," *Craft Horizons*, 26 (1966): 46-67.

JAMES WRIGHT
(13 December 1927-25 March 1980)

BOOKS: *The Green Wall* (New Haven: Yale University Press, 1957; London: Oxford University Press, 1957);

Saint Judas (Middletown, Conn.: Wesleyan University Press, 1959);

The Lion's Tail and Eyes: Poems Written Out of Laziness and Silence, by Wright, Robert Bly, and William Duffy (Madison, Minn.: Sixties Press, 1962);

The Branch Will Not Break (Middletown, Conn.: Wesleyan University Press, 1963; London: Longmans, 1963);

Shall We Gather at the River (Middletown, Conn.: Wesleyan University Press, 1968; London: Rapp & Whiting, 1969);

Collected Poems (Middletown, Conn.: Wesleyan University Press, 1971);

Two Citizens (New York: Farrar, Straus & Giroux, 1973);

Moments of the Italian Summer (Takoma Park, Md.: Dryad Press, 1976);

To a Blossoming Pear Tree (New York: Farrar, Straus & Giroux, 1977).

James Arlington Wright was born in Martins Ferry, Ohio. He grew up in this steel-mill town, living for a while on a small farm nearby; both places appear in his poetry. He served with the army in Japan in World War II and later went to Kenyon College from which he graduated in 1952, receiving the Robert Frost Poetry Prize. Wright spent 1953 at the University of Vienna on a Fulbright scholarship to study the work of Theodor Storm. Returning to the United States, he entered the University of Washington at Seattle, where he studied with Theodore Roethke, and received his M.A. in 1954 and his Ph.D. in 1959. During this period, he received Borestone Mountain Poetry Awards in 1954 and 1955, the Eunice Tietjens Memorial Award from Poetry magazine in 1955, and in 1957 his first volume of poetry, The Green Wall, was selected for publication in the Yale Series of Younger Poets.

He taught at the University of Minnesota (1957-1964), Macalester College in St. Paul, Minnesota (1963-1965), and from 1966 until his death in 1980 he taught at Hunter College in New York City. He spent 1965-1966 studying on a Guggenheim Fellowship. In addition to this fellowship, Wright also received the Kenyon Review poetry fellowship (1958-1959); a Longview Foundation award (1959), a prize from Chelsea magazine (1960), the Ohioana Book Award in poetry for Saint Judas (1960), the Oscar Blumenthal Prize from Poetry magazine (1968), the Brandeis University Creative Arts Award (1970), the Academy of American Poets Fellowship (1971), the Melville Cane Award from the Poetry Society of America (1972), and the Pulitzer Prize for Collected Poems (1972). His second wife was the former Anne Runk. He had two sons from a previous marriage.

Wright was always haunted by human suffering, not only his own, but also the suffering of the social outcast—the murderer, the rapist, the untrue lover, the Judas. He was also amazed by the inexplicable beauty of nature, not in the sweeping Romantic sense, but in its particular manifestations: a bronze butterfly, a blue jay on a branch, two Indian ponies, the body of a fish. His poetry documents his attempt to understand suffering and beauty and to express them.

Wright, along with Robert Bly, Louis Simpson, and William Stafford, is one of a group that has been variously called poets of "emotive imagination," or the "deep image"—surrealistic and subjective. He was a willing experimenter. As he commented in Contemporary Poets, "I have changed the way I've written, when it seemed appropriate, and continue to do so." The primary change that marks his career is a move from a preference for rhyme and traditional poetic meter and syntax to the use of a series of images and the rhythms of the spoken language. Reasons for these changes may be found both in Wright's work as a translator of George Trakl, Hermann Hesse, and Pablo Neruda, as well as other Latin American poets, and in his association with Bly and the Sixties (now Seventies) Press.

The Green Wall (1957), volume fifty-three of the Yale Series of Younger Poets, is a collection of forty poems, arranged in five sections: "Scenes and Laments," "To Troubled Friends," "Loves," "Stories and Voices," and a final untitled section of three poems. The names of these divisions reveal Wright's concerns. Descriptions of people with serious problems, of places that cause violent reactions in the poet, and of people he loves fill the book.

"A Poem about George Doty in the Death House" is characteristic of this collection and of Wright's early poetry in general. The poem describes a speaker's meditation on a murderer. The speaker (the poet in this case and in most of Wright's poetry) is concerned not with the soul of the innocent girl who was murdered, nor with the souls of the other prisoners, but with that of George Doty, the guilty one. Wright is fascinated by guilt; at times, he is obsessed with it. He wants to experience the collective guilt of humanity, which he personifies in the characters of his poems: a troubled friend, a defeated savior, a fugitive, a whore, a parent of a deaf child, and a murderer. A second characteristic of this volume is the formal diction associated with traditional poetry. For example, Wright describes a criminal in lines that could never be mistaken for prose: "He is the one for wonder, / Who sways his fingers under / The cleanly shaven chin." Such lines stand in stark contrast to his subject matter.

When discussing the poetry of this collection, Wright always acknowledged his debt to both Edwin Arlington Robinson and Robert Frost. Part of this debt manifests itself in the technical brilliance of Wright's early poetry. The poems of A Green Wall consist of well-developed, logically arranged images, rhyme, and, frequently, iambic meter. His ability to employ these conventions influenced the critical reception that this book received. Reviewers who preferred the traditions of Robinson, Frost, Wallace Stevens, and the Fugitives praised Wright's technical achievement. In contrast to these critics, another group believed that his true talents were being masked by his insistence on using traditional form and focused on his attitude toward his subject matter, his desire "to make the poems say something humanly important instead of just showing off with language." This disagreement between those who praise the virtue of technique and those who desire significant comment on the human condition recurs with each of Wright's books.

Wright's second collection, *Saint Judas*, appeared two years later in 1959. In contrast to *The Green Wall*, the poetry of his second volume is generally much less formally structured and much more pessimistic. In the thirty-one poems of this collection, Wright continues to write about particular places and about people who have been rejected by society.

In "Offering for Mr. Bluehart," Wright uses one of his typical patterns of development: description followed by a comment that expresses his personal reactions to the situation. The first stanza describes a field from which the poet and some of his friends once stole apples. The second stanza describes the "lean satanic owner" who "fired his gun across the gray / Autumn where now his life is done." The final stanza is an apology; Wright mourns Bluehart by not taking any more of his apples. Confessing that with maturity has come a respect for the property of others, the poet continues, "now may my abstinence restore / Peace to the orchard and the dead." The last line, "We shall not nag them anymore," illustrates his awareness of colloquial language and his increasing willingness to use it. This poem, like most in the volume, mixes poetic diction and less affected language, and the juxtaposition often bothered both readers who preferred traditional conventions and those who preferred more open poetry.

The last poem of the collection, "Saint Judas," illustrates Wright's increasing identification with society's misfits. This sonnet tells of Judas, the betrayer of Christ, who, on his way to commit suicide, becomes a Good Samaritan. The poem begins with Judas's recounting how he had forgotten his own intention at the moment when he "caught / A pack of hoodlums beating up a man." His first reaction was to help "this victim beaten, / Stripped, kneed, and left to cry." Only then does he remember the "bread my flesh had eaten, / The kiss

that ate my flesh." The poem closes with the enigmatic lines, "Flayed without hope, I held the man for nothing in my arms." The ambiguity of the phrase "for nothing" mirrors Wright's problem in facing human suffering; does the phrase mean "without hope of payment, monetary or otherwise," or does it mean "for no good reason, without any benefit for either him or me"? The biblical imagery in this poem completes the book's epigraph:

> They answered
> and said unto him,
> Thou wast altogether born in sin,
> and dost thou teach us?
> And they
> cast him out

Wright takes his responsibility to humanity seriously.

Although "Saint Judas" paints the poet as rejected prophet, ineffective savior, and useless martyr, another poem in the collection, "The

Layle Silbert

James Wright

411

James Wright

Morality of Poetry," comments on the poetic craft with less discouraging words. Wright wishes to offer another writer the "careful rules of song." The poet thinks he has found them in the flight of a single gull above the rest:

> It thrives on hunger, and it rises strong
> To live above the blindness and the noise
> Only as long as bones are clean and spare,
> The spine exactly set, the muscles lean.
> Before you let a single word escape,
> Starve it in darkness; lash it to the shape
> Of tense wings skimming on the sea alone . . . .

He finds, however, that he is mistaken. He decides that the moon, its light, and its power over the earth's tides are more significant than the gull's flight. Instead of recording rules to send his friend, he offers

> shoreward echoes of my voice:
> The dithyrambic gestures of the moon,
> Sun-lost, the mind plumed, Dionysian,
> A blue sea-poem, joy, moon-ripple on wave.

The poet's trying to capture the "moon-ripple," like Saint Judas's willingness to take the victim in his arms, constitutes whatever morality poetry or life may offer.

Wright's poetry changed drastically between *Saint Judas* (1959) and *The Branch Will Not Break* (1963). As early as the publication of his second volume of poetry, Wright had announced that his future verse would be different. He first published this new poetry in *The Lion's Tail and Eyes*, a collection of poems by Wright, Bly, and William Duffy, in 1962. The poems that Wright included in this volume are reprinted along with other new poems in *The Branch Will Not Break*.

Generally avoiding traditional meter, rhyme, and discursive reasoning, Wright focuses on human emotion, which has its own intuitive logic. One of the most representative and controversial poems of this third volume is "Lying in a Hammock at William Duffy's Farm in Pine Island, Minnesota," which ends:

> Over my head, I see the bronze butterfly,
> Asleep on the black trunk,
> Blowing like a leaf in green shadow.
> Down the ravine between the empty house,
> The cowbells follow one another
> Into the distances of the afternoon.
> To my right,
> In a field of sunlight between two pines,
> The droppings of last year's horses
> Blaze up into golden stones.

> I lean back, as the evening darkens and comes on.
> A chicken hawk floats over, looking for home.
> I have wasted my life.

Academic critics find the last line totally unjustified and, therefore, unacceptable, but those critics such as Crunk (Robert Bly) and others who favor a move away from what they call formulaic, intellectual poetry praise it because it does not mouth "any recognizable moral and philosophical platitudes." The admirers point to the beauty of the images and their appropriateness to the theme of searching for a home. The butterfly is at rest in its natural habitat and the cows are going home for the day. The hawk is headed for a place of rest. Only the poet, lying in someone else's hammock, is the last to discover his failure to have found a home. The final line does not, however, preclude hope. On the contrary, it implies that because the speaker has realized his predicament, he can and will set about restructuring his life.

A recurring theme in this volume is darkness, the darkness of evening and night, of violence and death, and of fear, yet all of these are examined and explained in the brightest of lights. Wright mediates contrasting images of darkness and light throughout the collection. In "Eisenhower's Visit to Franco, 1959" the poet uses imagery of light and dark to criticize American foreign policy in the 1950s. The poem begins, "The American hero must triumph over / The forces of darkness" and ends with the image of "clean new bombers from America," which glide down to Madrid to assist Franco in fulfilling his promise that "all dark things / Will be hunted down." The "shining circle of police," glittering smiles, and "glare of photographers" contrast sharply with the descriptions of "the slow dusk / Of Spain."

Two characteristics of the poetry in this collection are the easing of Wright's guilt about society's outcasts and his heightened sense of beauty. His descriptions of people are as compassionate as his earlier ones, but these poems do not exhibit preoccupation and identification with murderers, prostitutes, and others who have offended society. More evident, however, is his emerging willingness to describe and celebrate the beauty of nature. In addition to poems such as "Lying in a Hammock at William Duffy's Farm," in which Wright is somehow separated from nature, are poems such as "A Blessing," which illustrate a different attitude about his relationship with nonhuman otherness. Perhaps Wright's most frequently anthologized poem, "A Blessing," describes his experience as he and a friend momentarily startle two Indian ponies in a field. Like the two humans, the two animals "love each other. / There is no loneliness like theirs." He continues his description of the horses and the twilight: "Suddenly I realize / That if I stepped out of my body I would break / Into blossom." This three-line conclusion is the kind of non sequitur Wright's critics dislike, even though it clearly transmits the emotions that resulted from this experience. Furthermore, these lines capture both the surprise and the suddenness of the feelings. The best of Wright's new poetry succeeds in describing, without trying to explain, personal realizations. Not all of his poems work as well as this one; even Crunk, one of Wright's supporters, admits that some of the poetry in this third volume does not reach its goal because it fails to re-create the experience for the reader or because it fails to convince him of the significance of the experience for the poet.

The title *The Branch Will Not Break* is appropriate for several reasons. The line itself is the last line of "Number Two: I Try to Waken and Greet the World Once Again," the second of a pair of poems entitled "Two Hangovers." Wright laughs as he watches a "brilliant blue jay . . . springing up and down, up and down / On a branch." The jay abandons "himself / To entire delight" because both the jay and the poet know "the branch will not break." As an ending to the poem, the line illustrates Wright's playfulness and his faith in nature, both of which appear repeatedly throughout the collection. As the title of the book, the line summarizes some of what the poet has learned about his craft. It is flexible enough to withstand great varieties of experimentation and change, even those as extreme as his own. Finally, the line represents what Wright has learned about himself, that he, too, can endure and change as he needs to in order to face his own private struggles.

Shall We Gather at the River appeared five years later in 1968. The title, an allusion to the old Protestant hymn, promises renewal, faith, and hope; the poetry in this volume, however, offers only the opposite. The rivers mentioned in the book, and there are many, are all associated with death or some other great loss. Wright returns to his earlier fascination with the miserable and the pitiable. The book is dedicated to Jenny, a lost love who had "broken her spare beauty / In a whorehouse old." References to Jenny, other prostitutes, and whorehouses occur throughout as do references to the dead and dying who are bereft of hope for this life or any other. The first poem, "A Christmas Greeting," is typical of the poetry of despair that permeates this volume. A monologue written, with the exception of the last line, in couplets, the poem tells of Charlie, an old drunk who committed suicide by jumping off a bridge and who has returned to haunt Wright at the Christmas season. The poet can only recollect Charlie's miserable life and complain about his own problems: "I'm afraid to die, / It hurts to die, although the lucky do." He has little to say to Charlie, except for the usual social amenities, "Good Evening, Greetings, and Good Night, / God Bless Us Every One," the last of which ironically mocks the meaning of the holiday by alluding to Dickens's *A Christmas Carol*. In desperation, the poet ends, "What are you doing here?," but he receives no answer.

The unanswered questions continue throughout the volume, all variations of a query Wright poses in "Lifting Illegal Nets by Flashlight": "What does my anguish / Matter?" Instead of answers, he finds and offers only descriptions of human suffering, his own as well as that of others. He devotes three poems, "Inscription for the Tank," "In Terror of Hospital Bills," and "I am a Sioux Brave, He Said in Minneapolis," to the destitution and sorrow of an American Indian. The last of these poems is composed of two parts, the second of which is characteristic of the "deep image" poetry with which Wright's poetry is often associated:

> The black caterpillar
> Crawls out, what with one thing
> And another, across
> The wet road.
> How lonely the dead must be.

The resolution of the poem's last line and the image it follows are the result of an affective or intuitive logic, not a deductive one. The poet avoids an explanation; he merely offers his response to a situation, hoping that his readers can share or at least understand his reaction.

Wright's *Collected Poems* appeared in 1971 and won the Pulitzer Prize in 1972. It contains thirty-five of the forty poems in *The Green Wall*, all of the poems in the three succeeding volumes, twenty-nine translations, and thirty-three new poems. The translations separate the more traditional poetry of the first two volumes from the more innovative poetry of the third and fourth volumes.

The new poems illustrate the contrast between tradition and innovation that has always been evident in Wright's work. Several of the poems employ various kinds of end rhyme and poetic meter while others illustrate a bolder use of informality and looseness of style and structure. This increasing looseness parallels his attempt to capture and express his excitement and anxiety about living. The book's epigraph, a line from Jorge Guillén, "The flowers on the wallpaper spring alive," characterizes Wright's emotions. Two of the new poems, "The Quest" and "Sitting in a Small Screenhouse On a Summer Morning," begin the volume and set the mood for the collection. "The Quest" is a love poem celebrating the poet's search and success:

> So, as you sleep, I seek your bed
> And lay my careful, quiet ear
> Among the nestings of your hair
> Against your tenuous, fragile head
> And hear the birds beneath your eyes
> Stirring for birth, and know the world
> Immeasurably alive and good,
> Though bare as rifted paradise.

Wright's celebration of human love and the beauty of the natural world dominates the new poems of this collection although the despair of earlier poems is noticeably present.

Brooding introspection permeates "Many of Our Waters: Variations on a Poem by a Black Child," the Phi Beta Kappa poem delivered at the College of William and Mary on 5 December 1969. The poem begins with a journal entry recounting an experience with Garnie, a black boy, and recording a lengthy comment made by the child. The second section of the poem is a diatribe against the Ohio River and the land in which Wright grew up; the section ends with his begging for help in his loneliness and failure. Section 3 deals explicitly with Wright's own poetry and his desire to write poetry. It begins, "The kind of poetry I want to write is / The poetry of a grown man." The poets of New York, he continues, "have little pity / For the clear pure word." The last few lines of the section contrast the attitude of the New York poets with the image of a grown man who is doomed to suffer, to remain silent, to die, but to grow. Section 4 continues with commentary on poetry; "the kind / of poetry I want / Is to lie down with my love," he states as he curses the drudgery of having to go to work each day. The poet, as all grown men, is predestined to hurt, to work, and to fail to fulfill his desires. The next two sections return to Garnie and another black, a beautiful baby, Gemela. The poem's final section, "A Message from the Mountain Pool Where the Deer Come Down," addresses Jack Wright, the poet's brother to whom the poem is dedicated, and attempts a reconciliation with his brother or at least an understanding previously unknown between the two men. Wright again speaks openly of his own poetry:

All this time I've been slicking into my own words

The beautiful language of my friends.
I have to use my own, now.
That's why this scattering poem sounds the way it does.

Although he apologizes for the "scattering" poems that do not please him, he, by virtue of continuing to write, struggles to create "the poetry of a grown man." He concludes the poem with a mixed tone: "Pity so old and alone, it is not alone, yours, or mine, / The pity of rivers and children, the pity of brothers, the pity / Of our country, which is our lives." Life is neither positive nor encouraging, but humans have the slight consolation that they all suffer together and can perhaps comfort one another.

Two other poems that illustrate similar concerns but with more affirmative resolutions are "Small Frogs Killed on the Highway" and "Northern Pike." The former contrasts tadpoles "dancing / On the quarter thumbnail / Of the moon" with those frogs that "crouch there, too, faltering in terror / And take strange wing" when they cross the road. Wright shows that he would like to take the risk of leaving the pool, like those dead frogs that "are alive forever in the split second / Auto headlights more sudden / Than their drivers know." The poet identifies himself not with the tadpoles, nor with those that never tried to escape the oncoming cars, but with those that leapt into the light. As a writer, he searches constantly for those significant experiences that epitomize life as a series of intense, short-lived events and then describes them. "Northern Pike," the last of the new poems, captures such an event. In technique much like "A Blessing," the poem begins by describing a situation in Wright's past, in this case, catching and cleaning a fish; then follows a catalogue of the prayers of fishermen, including a prayer for "the gamewarden's blindness." The men eat their catch, and the poem closes, "There must be something very beautiful in my body, / I am so happy." Critics argue about whether or not the last lines are justified, given the lines that precede them, but the lines do illustrate one of Wright's convictions, that the world is "immeasurably alive and good." The poetry of this volume suggests an assurance of the goodness of life that is stronger than that in any of Wright's earlier works. He does not hold such an attitude naively, but only after great struggle and only with great reservation.

Two Citizens appeared in 1973. Many of the thirty-one poems in this volume were written, or at least begun, while Wright and his wife, Annie—the two citizens—were traveling in Europe. For the most part, the poems of this collection may be divided into

Oct. 11, 1977:

AT PEACE WITH THE OCEAN OFF MISQUAMICUT

*sent to
D. of portland 1/23/78
[accepted]
for broadside*

A million rootlets,
Shifting ~~and curling~~ *their dunes*
Quiver a little on the deep
Clavicles of some body,
Down there, a while.
It is still asleep, it is the Atlantic,
A sting-ray drowsing his fill of sunlight, a moulting angel
Breathing the grateful water,
Praying face downward to a god I am afraid
To imagine.
What will I do when the sting-ray
And the angel
Wake?
Whose mercy am I going to throw
Myself upon?
When even the Atlantic Ocean
Is nothing more than
My brother the sting-ray, ~~my sister the grateful wanderer~~   *delete*
~~The poet, and my child the wind?~~

~~That is awake.~~

think?

The mercy of the wind

"At Peace with the Ocean off Misquamicut," revised typescript

two groups, those in which Wright reflects on his American background and upbringing and those in which he celebrates Europe and the love of his wife. The difference between settings or subjects is, however, not the only distinguishing characteristic of the two categories. Those poems that treat American subjects tend toward a bitterness reminiscent of Wright's earlier poetry of despair; those which concern Europe and more precisely, his love of Annie Wright, tend to be light and even effusive. Perhaps Wright, having spent a great deal of his career studying, analyzing, and giving words to human suffering, writes more easily about pain than about joy. Critics either praise the poetry of this volume as another step toward skillful, perceptive analysis of human emotion or rebuke it as a further move toward boring, self-indulgent confessionalism.

Two Citizens opens with "Ars Poetica: Some Recent Criticism," a poem that treats everyday life as poetry. The poem begins with an idea that appears throughout the collection: "I loved my country / When I was a little boy," implying that his feelings have changed. Wright rails against the United States, even entitling one poem, "I Wish I May Never Hear of the United States Again." Although that poem is not devoted to criticism of the United States, others, including "Ars Poetica," are. In it, Wright tells of a crazy aunt, Agnes, now dying in "the nuthouse in Cambridge," who had tried to rescue an escaped goat from neighborhood boys who were stoning it. "Aunt Agnes, / Who stank and lied, / Threw stones back at the boys / And gathered the goat, / Nuts as she was, / Into her sloppy arms." Wright then comments on America and its faults:

> Reader
> We had a lovely language,
> We would not listen.
>
> I don't believe in your God.
> I don't believe my Aunt Agnes is a saint.
> I don't believe the little boys
> Who stoned the poor
> Son of a bitch goat
> Are charming Tom Sawyers.
>
> I don't believe in the goat either.

He then complains of his former love for his country, concluding "Hell, I ain't got nothing. / Ah, you bastards. / How I hate you." Wright's scathing damnation of his country prevails in other poems such as "Son of Judas," "The Young Good Man," and "Ohio Valley Swains." On occasion, he directly criticizes the country and its values by name; other times, he presents a specific situation from his past that criticizes by implication. In "Ohio Valley Swains," Wright describes his anger after the rape of a girl by Johnny Gunball and his gang. He confesses that he "loved her only in my dreams, / But my dreams meant something," indeed not only imagined images of mining-town girls, but also of his own country.

In evident contrast to the somber poems about America are the poems set in Europe. Being in another culture, imprisoned and at the same time liberated by not speaking the language, frees the poet and allows him to celebrate joys that others might pass over as insignificant, particularly day-to-day experiences shared with his wife as they travel. Poems such as "Bologna: A Poem about Gold" and "Hotel Lenox" are in praise of love. The last few poems of the collection combine Wright's despairing side with his warmer, more optimistic one. "Well, What are You Going to Do?" describes the experience of watching a calf being born. "October Ghosts" recalls Jenny and the unrealized past. The final poem, "To the Creature of the Creation," concerns the writing of poetry: "No, I ain't much. / The one tongue I can write in / Is my Ohioan." Several critics have taken issue with this statement, claiming that much of Wright's work sounds not conversational and "Ohioan" but artificially poetic. These readers fail to realize that the "Ohioan tongue" is not a single way of speaking but a variety of moods and emotions, even contradictory ones simultaneously.

Moments of the Italian Summer, published in a limited edition in 1976, is a series of fourteen prose poems introduced by a poem written by his wife. These poems are based on journal entries and, as such, are discursive but incompletely developed. The pieces represent one further step in the development of Wright as a poet, one in which he has moved from the traditionally structured verse in his first volumes to poetic prose. He creates, often photographically, a scene and then expresses his reaction to it.

Seven of these prose poems, some of which had undergone considerable revision, prose pieces, and nearly two dozen other poems constitute *To A Blossoming Pear Tree* (1977). Many of the pieces describe scenes in Europe while others document life in America. Wright matches form with function to produce some of his finest poetry in spite of occasional images that are too personal or too cryptic to be deciphered. The contents of this volume demonstrate his increasing ability to manipulate the language beautifully and skillfully and provide a break from his earlier bitterness and despair.

The three final poems of the collection express Wright's philosophy well. "Hook" recalls an encounter years earlier with an Indian on a cold street corner in Minneapolis: "the young Sioux / Loomed beside me, his scars / Were just my age." The speaker asks the Indian about the scars, only to have him raise "his hook into the terrible starlight" and slash it about. The poem ends with these lines:

> Did you ever feel a man hold
> Sixty-five cents
> In a hook
> And place it
> Gently
> In your freezing hand?
>
> I took it.
> It wasn't the money I needed.
> But I took it.

The two, momentarily united, are forever separate, yet there is none of the despair of the earlier poetry here, only description and brief comment.

A similar but contrasting experience occurs in the title poem. After beginning with a beautiful description of the pear tree in blossom, Wright begins to tell "something human," a story about an old man in the "unendurable snow" in Minnesota who, desperate for love, has unsuccessfully propositioned the poet. "Give it to me, he begged. / I'll pay you anything." Both "slunk away / Each in his own way dodging / The cruel darts of the cold." Addressing the beautiful tree, Wright shares his amazement at and pity for the old man:

> Young tree, unburdened
> By anything but your beautiful natural blossoms
> And dew, the dark
> Blood in my body drags me
> Down with my brother.

This conclusion, more desperate and poignant than many of those of earlier poems, is also more effective in its juxtaposition of the momentary beauty of nature with the enduring darker sides of human life.

The final poem, "Beautiful Ohio," is Wright's peacemaking with the river that in a sense spawned him. Many earlier poems have criticized the river, its ugliness, its pollution, and its sorrow. This poem does not pretend that the situation has changed; on the contrary, the poet sits "on a railroad tie / Above the sewer main," watching the Ohio send "a shining waterfall out of a pipe." In spite of the river's unappealing characteristics, Wright concludes, "I have my own song for it, / And sometimes, even today, / I call it beauty." He has resolved a conflict of many years; he no longer needs constantly to curse the river. He can see that, even if only occasionally and not for long, the river deserves its name of Ohio, "beautiful river." Wright can accept nature as it is, seeing past the detrimental changes man has brought about. He seems to have reached some sort of equilibrium in his attitude toward nature and man.

Wright spent a large part of 1979 in Europe, "keeping a notebook and writing some new pieces." He died in New York City on 25 March 1980. In a 1975 *Paris Review* interview, Wright had commented, "I do not have a talent for happiness. Some people do. . . . I tried to come to terms with that in the clearest and most ferociously perfect form that I could find and in all the traditional ways." Many readers may question Wright's technique or his achievement, but they must respect his dedication, perseverance, and vision. —*Keith Walters*

Other:

George Trakl, *Twenty Poems*, translated by Wright, John Knoepfle, and Robert Bly (Madison, Minn.: Sixties Press, 1961);

César Vallejo, *Twenty Poems*, translated by Wright, Bly, and Knoepfle (Madison, Minn.: Sixties Press, 1962);

Theodor Storm, *The Rider on the White Horse*, translated by Wright (New York: Signet, 1964);

Pablo Neruda, *Twenty Poems*, translated by Wright and Bly (Madison, Minn.: Sixties Press, 1968; London: Rapp & Whiting, 1968);

Hermann Hesse, *Poems*, translated by Wright (New York: Farrar, Straus & Giroux, 1970);

Neruda and Vallejo, *Selected Poems*, translated by Wright, Bly, and Knoepfle (Boston: Beacon Press, 1971);

Hermann Hesse, *Wandering: Notes and Sketches*, translated by Wright (New York: Farrar, Straus & Giroux, 1972; London: Cape, 1972);

"Letters from Europe, Two Notes from Venice, Remarks on Two Poems, and Other Occasional Prose," in *American Poets in 1976*, ed. William Heyen (Indianapolis: Bobbs-Merrill, 1976), pp. 424-457.

Interviews:

William Heyen and Jerome Mazzaro, "Something to be said for the light: A Conversation with James Wright," ed. Joseph R. McElrath, Jr., *Southern Humanities Review*, 6 (1972): 134-153;

Peter Stitt, "The Art of Poetry XIX," *Paris Review*, 16 (Summer 1975): 34-61.

Bibliography:

Belle M. McMaster, James Arlington Wright: A Checklist," *Bulletin of Bibliography*, 31 (1974): 71-82, 88.

References:

Edward Butscher, "The Rise and Fall of James Wright," *Georgia Review*, 28 (Spring 1974): 257-268;

Crunk [Robert Bly], "The Work of James Wright," *Sixties*, 8 (Spring 1966): 57-78;

Madeline De Frees, "James Wright's Early Poems: A Study in 'Convulsive' Form," *Modern Poetry Studies*, 2 (1972): 241-251;

John Ditsky, "James Wright Collected: Alterations on the Monument," *Modern Poetry Studies*, 2 (1979): 252-259;

Bruce Hendriksen, "Poetry Must Think," *New Orleans Review*, 6, no. 3 (1979): 201-207;

Richard Howard, *Alone With America Essays on the Art of Poetry in the United States Since 1950* (New York: Atheneum, 1969), pp. 575-586;

G. A. M. Janssens, "The Present State of American Poetry: Robert Bly and James Wright," *English Studies*, 51 (April 1970): 112-137;

Paul A. Lacey, *The Inner War: Forms and Themes in Recent American Poetry* (Philadelphia: Fortress Press, 1972), pp. 57-81;

George S. Lensing and Ronald Moran, *Four Poets and the Emotive Imagination: Robert Bly, James Wright, Louis Simpson, and William Stafford* (Baton Rouge: Louisiana State University Press, 1976), pp. 87-132;

Laurence Liebermann, *Unassigned Frequencies: American Poetry in Review, 1964-77* (Urbana: University of Illinois Press, 1977), pp. 182-189;

William Matthews, "Entering the World," *Shenandoah*, 20 (1969): 80-93;

Ralph Mills, Jr., "James Wright's Poetry: Introductory Notes," *Chicago Review*, 17 (1964): 128-143;

Charles Molesworth, "James Wright and the Dissolving Self," in *Contemporary Poetry in America: Essays and Interviews*, ed. Robert Boyers (New York: Schocken Books, 1974), pp. 267-268;

James Seay, "A World Immeasurably Alive and Good: A Look at James Wright's *Collected Poems*," *Georgia Review*, 27 (Spring 1973): 71-81;

Stephen Stepanchev, *American Poetry Since 1945: A Critical Survey* (New York: Harper & Row, 1965), pp. 180-184;

Peter A. Stitt, "The Poetry of James Wright," *Minnesota Review*, 2 (1972): 13-32;

Cor van den Heuvel, "The Poetry of James Wright," *Mosaic*, 7 (Spring 1974): 163-170;

Stephen Yenser, "Open Secret," *Parnassus*, 6 (1978): 125-142;

Paul Zweig, "Making and Unmaking," *Partisan Review*, 40 (1973): 269-273.

PAUL ZIMMER
(18 September 1934-)

BOOKS: *A Seed on the Wind* (San Francisco: Privately printed, 1960);
The Ribs of Death (New York: October House, 1967);
The Republic of Many Voices (New York: October House, 1969);
The Zimmer Poems (Washington, D.C. & San Francisco: Dryad Press, 1976).

Paul Zimmer was born in Canton, Ohio. He attended Kent State University beginning in 1952, but his education was interrupted from 1954 to 1955 by service in the army. He was back at Kent State from 1956 until 1959, but he did not receive his B.A. until 1968. After college he held a variety of jobs—all of them related to books. He managed book departments in California for such stores as the San Francisco News Company (1963-1964) and the University of California at Los Angeles bookstore (1964-1966). From 1967 to 1979 Zimmer has served as the assistant director of the University of Pittsburgh Press and editor of the Pitt Poetry Series. In 1970 he served as the poet-in-residence at Chico State College (now California State University, Chico). He received a Borestone Mountain Award in 1971 and three years later he was given a grant from the National Endowment for the Arts. He is now the director of the University of Georgia Press.

Zimmer's first book of poetry, *A Seed on the Wind* (1960), privately printed in a limited edition of 200 copies, is a slight volume, containing nineteen lyrics on a variety of topics. The poetry is spare and not "academic," but intellectual in that it often is a

A Seed on the Wind is the appropriate title for this first collection: each poem is a seed for the complex configuration that occurs in the engaged imagination. Zimmer strives to simplify, and he succeeds if one grants that a successful poem may have a limited scope. The last poem in the collection, "Seed on the Wind," culminates the poet's desire to arrive at the foundation of poetry; this poem is literally a celebration of sound and a metaphor for the action of reading the poem:

> Whisked to wet things, a
> Cracking rudiment will
> Bud a worm from
> Husks, and nose a hill
>
> Of sad aside to shine
> Its teeming genesis.
> In rain it rots
> And cannot kiss.

Zimmer's second book, *The Ribs of Death* (1967), not only represents a more dramatic achievement than *A Seed on the Wind*, but also marks a move toward the kind of poetry that Zimmer now likes to write. In *Contemporary Poets* (1975), Zimmer says, "When I began writing poetry . . . I began casting my voice into characters I had made up: Peregrine, Mordecai, Phineas, Alphonse, Wanda, Imbellis, Cecil, Willis, etc. . . . I look upon this period of my work as an apprenticeship for making the autobiographical-type poems I have been working on in recent years—the Zimmer poems." *The Ribs of Death* exemplifies his early concentration on persona poems. The book is divided into five sections: the first is devoted to his various characters, the fourth explores the established personae of great poets and inventors in specific situations, such as "Keats in Rome," "Wordsworth in Summer," and "First Mate Joseph Conrad." Sections 2, 3, and 5 are devoted to lyrics and contemplative poems in the style of those in *A Seed on the Wind*.

The characters the poet creates have certain enduring and identifiable characteristics that give them continuity from poem to poem. The reader knows how they will act, and each character is the center of what Zimmer calls a "cluster" of poems devoted to one persona. Phineas is the least clearly drawn of the group, for he serves occasionally as nothing more than a cardboard figure on which the poet can heap his irritations. In "The Poet Bequeaths his Frustrations to Phineas," for example, poor Phineas becomes a private scapegoat and takes on all the poet's worst woes—storms, mud, wind, bird droppings. Zimmer's primary goal in

determinedly self-conscious celebration of the imagination. Its sparseness stems from its simple subjects; for example, there are poems about birds, flowers, spiders, meadows, and seeds. The illustrations by Jerome Jensik complement the poems' simplicity by using the fewest lines possible to convey the subjects and indicate the poetry's mood, small celebrations of words and images. In "A Hunting Song," three five-line stanzas of unrhymed, unmetrical lines set up the contrast between a flower, the foxglove, and an unseen fox. A hunting club pursues the fox somewhere in the unseen distance, and the dogs' barking penetrates the silence, marking the doom of the cornered fox. All this must be imagined; Zimmer gives but the barest suggestion. Yet he salutes the survival of the most frail of the foxes:

> Bruised by insect wings and
> Crushed perfumeless by
> Stumbling feet, they will
> Yet survive alone, defying
> The probings of our greenest thumbs.

Paul Zimmer

these persona poems is, of course, humor, and none of his characters is funnier than Lord Fluting, who is ripped apart by the intrusion of reality on his imaginary world. In "Lord Fluting Dreams of America on the Eve of his Departure from Liverpool," the good peer defines his particular version of the American dream: "Purple Indians pas de bourree / Around a Chippendale totem pole. / The Ute dips to the Crow, / And curtsies to the Navajo, / While the forest in its wig and stole / Claps its leaves politely." Two more stanzas of idyllic reverie follow, but in "Lord Fluting in America" reality has already made its unceremonious entry. The poem begins: "Some ass has slapped mud / In the chinks of my house, / But the wind grinds through / To fray my ripening nostrils." The humor works. One can easily imagine the staid, fussy gentleman making his way west amidst the barbarity of pioneer America. Zimmer's other characters, Wanda and Alphonse, are not always innocently funny. "Alphonse Imagines What the People's Thoughts Will Be When He Is Gone" is an example of the sardonic quality that occasionally infests the laughter. The reader watches Zimmer's characters struggle with their personal problems and dilemmas real or imagined, and experiences a certain affection for them whether he laughs or cries.

The fourth section of *The Ribs of Death* is entitled "The Poet Projected into Shapes," and here, rather than create characters, Zimmer takes established personalities or memories of them and projects them into novel situations so that the reader may share their dubious wisdom. Of course, this method is nothing new in poetry; from Dante to T. S. Eliot poets have felt they could benefit by resurrecting other sensibilities in order to have the advantage of another pair of eyes. Zimmer, characteristically, is not above a little fiendish humor at this tradition's expense. In "Wordsworth in Summer," for example, the epigraph is taken from *The Journal of Dorothy Wordsworth*, the entry dated 28 July 1800: "Intensely hot. I made pies in the morning. William went into the wood, and altered his poems." These six lines follow:

William's lines were simmered like blueberries
That July. Beneath the trees
He smelled the lacquer of their juice,
And heard their seeds fall loose
To crackle like old meters in the heat;
And later on he ate them with his tea.

In contrast to the tone of irreverence in "Wordsworth in Summer," other poems reveal the poignant, quiet suffering of the individual, unsure

```
A FINAL AFFECTION

I love the accomplishments of trees,
How they try to restrain great storms
And pacify the very worms that eat them,
Even their deaths seem to be considered.

I fear for trees, loving them so much.
I am nervous about each scar on bark,
Each leaf that browns.   I want to
Lie in their crotches and sigh,
Whisper of sun and rains to come.

Sometimes on summer evenings I step
Out of my house to look at the trees
Propping darkness up to the silence.

When I die I want to slant up
Through those trunks so slowly
I will see each rib of bark, each whorl;
Up through the canopy, the subtle veins
And lobes touching me with final affection;
Then to hover above and look down
One last time on the rich upliftings,
The circle that loves the sun and moon,
To see at last what held the darkness up.
```

"A Final Affection," typescript

of his position in the world. In "Reverend Animus Closes the First Church of Christ and His Saints," the good Reverend wonders if he does the right thing, unable to detect, as the reader does, that his own silent arrogance causes his anguish: "Years ago, in deep theology, / I laid the pious plans which somehow failed. / I would have had them love God with their fear. / I would have had God look like me to them." The rest of the poems in *The Ribs of Death* recall the earlier book, and one poem, "The Witch of Benjamin County," is reprinted with only minor changes.

Zimmer's next book, *The Republic of Many Voices* (1969), is similar to *The Ribs of Death* except that this time there is a startling new character— Zimmer himself. Recalling Zimmer's statement about his move from casting his voice into personae to speaking in his own voice, one realizes that the autobiographical poems represent a definite achievement for him, even though readers may have suspected that his fictitious characters were variations on Zimmer's own personality. The results are mixed. He employs the same humorous, anecdotal style, but he remains as distant to the reader as the caricature, Lord Fluting, and never approaches the solidity of some of his other "real" characters, for example, "First Mate Joseph Conrad," or even a fully imaginary character such as Reverend Animus. The Zimmer in the poetry emerges as a confused, uncoordinated misser-of-trains, a dangerous hunter, an incompetent mechanic, and an indefatigable schlemeil. In "Zimmer and his Turtle Sink the House," one can at least forgive his bungling on account of his youth. Here he recounts the experience of filling the sink for his pet turtle. Unfortunately, for both him and the turtle, he never turned off the faucet and "All the towels, old underwear and mops / That I could muster never dried / The house up, never turned / The meter back from what it told."

The Zimmer Poems (1976) continues in the vein of the autobiographical poems in *The Republic of Many Voices* and includes three poems from this earlier volume. Of the forty-four poems in *The Zimmer Poems*, only one does not have Zimmer's name in the title. While one may question the seriousness of such a narrow focus, the character Zimmer serves a useful purpose for Zimmer the poet, who has created this version of himself as a scapegoat on which to heap his frustrations with the world. Just as no real person's life can be as glorious as the lives of heroes in fiction, the fictional characters in these poems loom large over the poet's own persona. Even Lord Fluting seems big to the character Zimmer. Throughout the collection, Zimmer's inadequacies are treated with humor and sometimes parody, as in the warning contained in this parody of A. E. Housman's "The Shropshire Lad," "A Zimmershire Lad":

> Oh lads, ere your flesh decay.
> And your sigh grows dimmer,
> Beware the ale foam in your way

Or you will end like Zimmer.

Zimmer is forever creating characters to inhabit the home of his poetry, and one gets the impression that the poems are often secondary to the creation of personalities. His characters all have heavy doses of self-consciousness; rarely can they forget their roles. This use of characterization may cause his verse to be labeled "light." Nonetheless these poems are enjoyable, in the same way that puzzles and musicals are fun and occasionally profound. As Zimmer says in the last poem of *The Republic of Many Voices*, "Zimmer Bids Farewell and Greeting to the Republic of Many Voices":

> Built by Peregrine, defended by Imbellis,
> Shamed by Mordecai, and peopled by
> All of them and me, this Republic,
> By God, will stand because of
> And despite me.

—*Thomas Goldstein*

Other:

"The Importance of Being Zimmer," *American Poets in 1976*, ed. William Heyen (Indianapolis: Bobbs-Merrill, 1976): 460-466.

References:

Robert Boyers, "Mixed Bag," *Partisan Review*, 36 (1969): 306-315;
Hayden Carruth, "Making It New," *Hudson Review*, 21 (Summer 1968): 399-412.

Louis Zukofsky

Steven Helmling
Rutgers University

BIRTH: New York, New York, 23 January 1904, to Pinchos and Chana Pruss Zukofsky.

EDUCATION: M.A., Columbia University, 1924.

MARRIAGE: 20 August 1939 to Celia Thaew; children: Paul.

AWARDS: Longview Foundation award, 1961; Union League Civic and Arts Foundation Prize (*Poetry* magazine), 1964; Oscar Blumenthal Prize (*Poetry* magazine), 1966; National Endowment for the Arts Grants, 1967, 1968; National Institute of Arts and Letters grant, 1976; Honorary Doctorate, Bard College, 1977.

DEATH: Port Jefferson, New York, 12 May 1978.

BOOKS: *Le Style Apollinaire*, by Zukofsky and René Taupin (Paris: Les Presses Modernes, 1934);
First Half of "A" 9 (New York: Privately printed, 1940);
55 Poems (Prairie City, Ill.: Decker, 1941);
Anew: Poems (Prairie City, Ill.: Decker, 1946);
A Test of Poetry (New York: Objectivist Press, 1948; London: Routledge, 1952);
Some Time / Short Poems (Highlands, N.C.: Jargon, 1956);
5 Statements for Poetry (San Francisco: San Francisco State College, 1958);
Barely and Widely (New York: Celia Zukofsky, 1958);
"A" 1-12 (Kyoto, Japan: Origin Press, 1959; London: Cape, 1966; Garden City: Doubleday, 1967);
It Was (Kyoto, Japan: Origin Press, 1961);
16 Once Published (Edinburgh: Wild Hawthorn Press, 1962);
I's Pronounced "Eyes" (New York: Trobar Press, 1963);
Bottom: On Shakespeare (Austin, Tex.: Ark Press / University of Texas Press, 1963);
Found Objects 1962-1926 (Georgetown, Ky.: H. B. Chapin, 1964);
After I's (Pittsburgh: Boxwood Press / Mother Press, 1964);
An Unearthing: A Poem (Cambridge, Mass.: Privately printed, 1965);
Iyyob (London: Turret, 1965);
I Sent Thee Late (Cambridge, Mass.: Privately printed, 1965);

Finally A Valentine (Stroud, Gloucestershire, U.K.: Piccolo Press, 1965);
"A" Libretto (New York: Privately printed, 1965);
All: The Collected Short Poems, 1923-1958 (New York: Norton, 1965; London: Cape, 1966);
All: The Collected Short Poems, 1956-1964 (New York: Norton, 1966; London: Cape, 1967);
"A" 9 (Cologne: Hansjörg Mayer, 1966);
"A" 14 (London: Turret, 1967);
Prepositions: Collected Critical Essays of Louis Zukofsky (London: Rapp & Carroll, 1967; New York: Horizon Press, 1968);
Little, a fragment (San Francisco: Black Sparrow Press, 1967);
From Thanks to the Dictionary (Buffalo, N.Y.: Gallery Upstairs, 1968);
Ferdinand, Including It Was (New York: Grossman, 1968; London: Cape, 1968);
"A" 13-21 (Garden City: Doubleday, 1969; London: Cape, 1969);
Catullus Fragmenta (London: Turret, 1969);
Catullus (New York: Grossman, 1969; London: Cape Goliard, 1969);
Autobiography (New York: Grossman, 1970);
Little (New York: Grossman, 1970);
All: The Collected Shorter Poems, 1923-1964 (New York: Norton, 1971);
"A" 24 (New York: Grossman, 1972);
Arise, Arise (New York: Grossman, 1973);
"A" 22 & 23 (New York: Grossman, 1975);
"A" (Berkeley: University of California Press, 1978);
80 Flowers (Lunenburg, Vt.: Stinehour Press, 1978).

If the twentieth century still harbors a major but undiscovered poet, that poet is surely Louis Zukofsky. Not that he has been entirely unrecognized; indeed, early he earned the praise of an older generation of Titans, of Ezra Pound, T. S. Eliot, Marianne Moore, William Carlos Williams. Among figures nearer his own age, E. E. Cummings, Sir Herbert Read, and Kenneth Rexroth long and consistently expressed their admiration for his work; and among a generation of younger poets, talents as diverse as Robert Creeley, Robert Duncan, Hayden Carruth, and Charles Tomlinson have all acknowledged the deepest sorts of indebtedness to Zukofsky and his poetry. Kenneth Cox has said flatly that

Zukofsky is the most important poet born since 1900, and similar judgments have been implied by such forceful critics as Hugh Kenner and Guy Davenport. Yet despite the extravagant praises of so many talented poets and critics, Zukofsky's work remains all but unknown to most readers of poetry. His work is rarely (and poorly) represented in college anthologies, and his books, when they do manage to find their way into print, are generally unreviewed, undiscussed, and unread. Among the unimpressed, some complain that his poetry is trivial or overly simple, while others find it too ambitious, too difficult, and obscure. To be sure, there are reaches of Zukofsky's work that might invite either judgment. Zukofsky glosses the matter whimsically in *"A"* section 12:

> Everything should be as simple as it can be,
> Says Einstein,
> Not simpler.

Those who dismiss his work as "minimalist," precious, and narrow have obviously not looked at *"A"*, surely the most inclusive poem ever written, which finds occasions to treat Castro and Catullus, Eisenhower, Eskimos, Ghengis Khan, Geiger counters, Spinoza, sputnik, Vivaldi, and much more. (Next to *"A"*, Pound's *Cantos* seem restricted and exclusive in their subject matter.) No poet is in touch at so many points with so much of the world around him; no poet has written so comprehensively of domestic life; and no poet has undertaken so sustained and original an effort to make political poetry possible in this century of poetic and political extremes. Something of the complexity of his achievement might be suggested by the observation that he chose a recondite troubadour verse form, the sestina, for his "Mantis," a poem about the Depression poor set in a New York subway. The result, passionate but unsentimental, urgent but deliberate, is certainly one of the greatest and most moving political poems of the century.

A slender, fastidious, unathletic man, described by one observer as "a virtuoso of hypochondria," Zukofsky's emblem would seem to be the imperious, slow-moving creature whose pace ("eyes, pins, bright, black and poor") he captured so masterfully in "Mantis." Yet his own deepest psychic affinities were for galloping horses: "your horse complex," exclaims the poet's wife in *"A"* 14, "what a preoccupation." (The index Zukofsky supplied to the 1978 one-volume University of California edition of *"A"* lists 106 page references to "horses.") His life was a quiet one of steady and concentrated work; it was not a career rich in outward events,

punctuated every few years by the publication of another book. His books were mostly published long after they were written, and he habitually worked on several projects at once, so that a single book, even a slight one, might be the work of a decade or more. And a major work, like *"A"*, might be rearranged as its composition proceeded: the twenty-four serially numbered sections of the poem are not in chronological order. He preferred his writing desk to almost any other recreation; he read widely in philosophy, politics, economics, and history; he passionately loved classical music (his wife Celia Thaew is a composer, and their son, Paul, is a well-known concert violinist and conductor). All of his interests were deep and longstanding, and all found their way into his poetry. An oeuvre composed with such devotion exacts a like care from its readers.

Louis Zukofsky was born 23 January 1904 in a tenement in New York City's Jewish ghetto on the Lower East Side. Zukofsky's first language was Yiddish. His parents were recent emigrants from Russia; neither spoke English. A precocious child, Zukofsky learned English on his own and distinguished himself in school. His record entitled him to free enrollment at New York's City College, but his parents sacrificed to send him to Columbia, where, at the age of 20, he was awarded the M.A. degree. He had the usual interest of intellectuals in that time and place in politics; history—how to make sense and meaning of it—was a theme he would never forsake. He was interested in Marx, but tempered Marx's reading of history with the very different one of Henry Adams, whose book *The Education of Henry Adams* (not commercially published until 1918) was still a new book. One of Zukofsky's earliest and most ambitious projects was a long essay, "Henry Adams: A Criticism in Autobiography," often revised, but which originated in this period. He had begun writing poetry in his late teens. Imagist in feeling and technique, these early poems exhibit great craft often in the service of slight perceptions; but there are also magnificent lyrics, like "Tall and singularly dark you pass among the breakers." Political themes are treated sometimes obliquely, as in the 1925 tribute to Lenin, "Memory of V. I. Ulianov," sometimes more directly, as in "During the Passaic Strike of 1926." Studious, quiet, and intensely intellectual, Zukofsky was not a dominating figure, but the writers and artists (among them Tibor Serly, Charles Reznikoff, and George and Mary Oppen) he met in New York in the 1920s seemed tacitly to acknowledge that Zukofsky was the most prodigious talent, the true genius, of their circle.

Louis Zukofsky

Zukofsky's first ambitious project in verse was "Poem Beginning 'The,'" written in 1926. It has six "movements" and 330 numbered lines; its cultural despair, probing psychologistic themes, and its freight of literary allusions (all scrupulously annotated by the author himself) make it seem very much a post-*Waste Land* performance. Its youthful fervor and arch, over-erudite self-consciousness communicate, as does Samuel Beckett's *Whoroscope* (1930), the excitement young and ambitious writers felt in that period, when all things seemed possible. "Poem Beginning 'The'" utterly eschews the explanatory or obvious; progress from line to line is elliptical; sudden changes of mood and direction, without transitional cues, are the rule; and everywhere the surface bristles with signs of the author's learning and avant-garde sophistication. In the first twenty-five lines alone, the tone shifts from satiric to something like mantic, while allusions to the Oedipus complex, D. H. Lawrence, Norman Douglas, Pound, Eliot, Joyce, François Villon, and Marianne Moore flash by.

The poem asks, as so many young men's poems do, how to write poetry given the miseries of the historical and political situation. The miseries in question are partly continuous (as are the dense allusiveness and the free-verse technique) with those that concerned Pound and Eliot in that period—the exhaustion of culture following the Great War, the ominous political chaos of Europe. But there is much that is specifically Zukofsky's own, in particular the problem of reconciling a provincial Jewish folk heritage with ambitions in the direction of an international high literary modernism. The poet pictures himself as an impoverished outsider, hungrily looking through restaurant windows, in a bravura passage that parodies Edgar Allan Poe's "To Helen":

> Engprof, thy lectures were to me
> Like those roast flitches of red boar
> That, smelling, one is like to see
> Through windows where the steam's galore
> Like our own "Cellar Door."

Of course this satirizes not the poet's longing but the fatuous self-assurance of the Engprof, who ends by dismissing even Poe: "Poe / Gentlemen, don't chewknow, / But never wrote an epic." (Zukofsky was already nursing epic ambitions of his own; he was to commence writing "*A*" a year later.)

For all its modernist trappings, "Poem Beginning 'The'" addresses itself to the folk culture from which the poet springs. The poem repeatedly apostrophizes the speaker's mother, while a note directs the reader to associate "the word Mother" with the Bible, ur-text and ultimate genetrix of all Jewish culture. The maternal theme is treated seriocomically: in one moving passage Zukofsky has adapted a traditional Jewish folk song, a lullaby a mother croons to her infant son, while elsewhere there is ironic acknowledgement that Freud's preoccupations with the mother-son relationship ("Oedipus-faced wrecks," and "Tear the Codpiece Off, A Musical Comedy") seem to have something specifically Jewish about them. Elsewhere we hear of a "Helen Gentile" and are assured that "Assimilation is not hard, / And once the Faith's askew / I might as well look Shagetz just as much as Jew." But the poem ends, "I have not forgotten you, mother." The assurance lies not in the poet's readiness to renounce the alien culture but in his recognition that origins are never abandoned; even assimilated, one's nature cannot really change.

Large in scope, passionate, even declamatory, and intensely personal, "Poem Beginning 'The'" is unique among the reticent, severe, and slighter poems of Zukofsky's early canon. If the latter call to mind Pound's imagism, the larger ambitions of "Poem Beginning 'The'" answer to the *maius opus movebo* announced in such poems of Pound's as *Hugh Selwyn Mauberley* (quoted in Zukofsky's poem) and the *Cantos*. "Poem Beginning 'The'" most resembles the so-called "ur-*Cantos*" that Pound published in *Poetry* magazine in 1917 and had reprinted often (twice in book form) before scrapping them. It seems likely that Zukofsky knew these early versions of *Cantos* I-III well; the present versions were not in print until 1925. By 1927 Zukofsky was exchanging letters with Pound, and "Poem Beginning 'The'" appeared in the *Exile*, Pound's little magazine, in spring 1928. The older poet's encouragement was characteristically brisk and extravagant, Pound recommending Zukofsky to friends as "the only intelligent man in America." Among those who thus heard of Zukofsky was William Carlos Williams. Williams was impressed with the work Zukofsky showed him, and before long Zukofsky was helping Williams edit the revived version of his little magazine, *Contact*. It lasted for three issues in 1932, but Williams and Zukofsky had launched a friendship that only grew warmer as time went on.

For some time Zukofsky had been meditating a long poem, and in 1928 he began writing. He had already decided that it was to be called "*A*"; it was to have twenty-four sections or "movements," and it was to be a life's work, accommodating whatever the fortunes of a lifetime might provide for subject matter. The random deliverances of "fortune" were to be ordered throughout the poem by a concern with music: the local lyricism of verbal music, the formal structuring of themes and variations, developments and resolutions, and an intellectual ordering of ideational play that aimed at a "music of thought." The spirit and example of Bach were to preside over the whole, and the poem's first line is:

> A
> Round of fiddles playing Bach.

The single letter *A*, the poem's title, functions here as the indefinite article for the opening sentence, and the title *"A"* is perhaps as appropriate to an open-ended project as the definite article is to the shorter, thematically more pointed "Poem Beginning 'The,'" whose theme is the intractability and ineradicability of identity, of heritage and aspiration and their conflict. Even the indefinite article, of course, specifies something: that the noun that follows must begin with a consonant. As if to evade that specification, *"A"* 14, headed "beginning *An*," announces that it and subsequent sections of the poem, eleven in all, will begin with *an*, although not always, it turns out, in the guise of the indefinite article: *"A"* 17 begins with the word *anemones*; *"A"* 21 with *an* in the Elizabethan sense of "if"; *"A"* 24 with *and*. The index to *"A"* lists dozens of references to both *a* and *an*, and more to *the* than to both *a* and *an* combined. In 1946, in "Poetry: For My Son When He Can Read," Zukofsky wrote that "a case can be made for the poet giving some of his life to the use of the words *the* and *a*: both of which are weighted with as much epos and historical destiny as one man can perhaps resolve."

If, on a large scale, the poem was to entertain by enacting them, the metaphysical imponderables of such linguistic gestures as assigning articles to nouns, it was also to agitate *ad lib* whatever other associations the letter *A* might arouse: with "concert A," for example, the musical note to which "fiddles" (like those in the poem's first line) tune themselves, or with the legs (A-shaped) of police sawhorses, or with vitamin A, or the A-bomb.

When Zukofsky began *"A"*, in the late 1920s, the A-bomb had not been foreseen, and it may be that some of these themes had not been foreseen either; they seem to characterize later phases of the poem's composition. The earliest sections of *"A"* are far more concerned with politics and economics and their relation to art. The poem opens with the poet leaving a concert performance of Bach's *St. Matthew Passion* in New York. It is Easter (and Passover) 1928; the music, composed in 1729, seems more vivid

Louis Zukofsky

to the poet than do the crowds—small-talking art consumers—with whom he now steps out into a street where beggars panhandle and headlines report strikes and lockouts. Art's "Desire longing for perfection" seems compromised by a social milieu that reduces art to a mere distraction, an occasion for gossip and amusement for an elite leisure class.

> The next day the reverses
> As if the music were only a taunt:
> As if it had not kept, flower-cell, liveforever,
> before the eyes, perfecting.

But the poet recognizes that he cannot smugly rebuke others, in Art's name, for their failure rightly to value Art; he, too, must answer to the perfection Art posits and celebrates, "Everything which / We are and never quite live."

These themes are sustained through *"A"* 6, and interwoven with others: an elegy for a dead friend and, again, the theme of "Poem Beginning 'The,'" assimilation. The contrast of Art's perfection and history's chaos is enforced again and again; as in the passage just cited, Art ("flower-cell, liveforever") is linked with Nature:

> Natura naturans—
> Nature as creator,
>
> Natura naturata—
> Nature as created.
>
> He who creates
> Is a mode of these inertial systems—

The flower—leaf around leaf wrapped
around the center leaf

Nature in its formal perfection and slow patient processes, in turn, is linked with music, and by implication Bach is linked with Spinoza. In *"A"* 6, a lengthy passage speaks about the poem's own music and offers a distinction between the poem's "voices" whose importance to the rest of the poem will grow. Music, the text says, is

My one voice. My other: is
An objective—rays of the object brought to a focus,
An objective—nature as creator—desire
for what is objectively perfect
Inextricably the direction of historic and
contemporary particulars.

The distinction between the musical voice and the "objective" one agitates succeeding sections of the poem, but how to reconcile "historic" matter with the claims of a "desire for what is objectively perfect" is a problem *"A"* 6 confronts immediately. Bach's music is a "particular," the reader is told, but so is an incident from the Napoleonic Wars, when a barrel containing the severed phalluses of hundreds of massacred soldiers was sent to their commander as a gesture of defiance. How to make Art, something "objectively perfect," from such horror?

This question concerns *"A"* 6, written in 1930 with the Depression looming large; *"A"* 7, composed from 1928 to 1930, offers a kind of answer to it. *"A"* 7 consists of seven sonnets, in consonance with the movement's number. The poem makes elaborate play with the conceit of police sawhorses, closing off a New York street, metamorphosed by the power of words into real horses. The poem begins by declaring the helplessness of the imagination before sheer fact, then affirms the contrary: that words have the power to transform the prosaic donnees of circumstance into poetic perception. Sawhorses become horses of flesh and blood; a Chinese laundry becomes an emblem of the cleansing and making new of the world; words quoted from the text of Bach's *St. Matthew Passion* direct the reader to see the poem's activity as redemptive, a kind of resurrection, raising the universe of death to life. Verbal motifs from preceding movements of the poem recur, but the effect of *"A"* 7 is to present itself as distinct from all that precedes it. Despite ellipses and sudden transitions, the first six sections of *"A"* are fluent and forward moving, their free verse proceeding, in Pound's words, "in sequence of the musical phrase," and making audible a distinct and recognizable voice and sensibility. In *"A"* 7, though, easy forward movement and access to an authorial presence are severely restricted: the diction is dense and artificial, the syntax distorted, and the reader must divine and assemble meanings that the extreme formal elaborateness of the whole seems at first more to bury than express.

"A" 7 exhibits what Joseph Frank has called "spatial form," and presents itself as an autonomous art object. *"A"* 6 offers a distinction (quoted above) between the poem's "musical" and "objective" voices; taking these as poles of Zukofsky's poetic range at this period, one may say that *"A"* 1 through 6 exemplifies the "musical" voice, *"A"* 7 the "objective." Indeed, *"A"* 7 stands out as the most comprehensive example in Zukofsky's early canon of everything he meant to imply by the word *objectification* in an essay that dates from 1930 (the same year that *"A"* 7 was completed) and was published together with *"A"* 7 in Harriet Monroe's *Poetry* magazine. The essay was called "Sincerity and Objectification." By the first of these terms, Zukofsky meant devotion to technique, and his thinking obviously follows Pound's 1913 dictum that technique is the only test of an artist's sincerity. The other term, *objectification*, is more ambiguous, and implies values that Zukofsky was forever adjusting. At various places in the essay Zukofsky speaks of lenses focusing on an object, as if to imply a quasi-scientific objectivity (this was doubtless meant to irk those who regard science and poetry as inimical, and who prize the latter for being subjective); he also used the word *objective* in the military sense. But the essential suggestion of "objectification" was that the finished poem should be an autonomous object, self-sufficient, resolved, exhibiting a "totality of perfect rest."

This suggestion has a New Critical sound to it, implying as it does a severance of the poem from its author, but the objectivist "impersonality" (Zukofsky never uses that word) is not, like Eliot's, a strategy for keeping the author and his personae distinct. Indeed, the whole effect of the bizarre syntax and impacted diction of *"A"* 7 is to frustrate any sense of encountering a voice or a sensibility or a personality. Recognizing that technical "sincerity" easily becomes "style," and hence self-regarding, Zukofsky wants to insist that the poem should in no way interpose the author between the reader and the object the poem presents. The poet's power of imagination is not entirely effaced—consider, after all, the extravagant wit of *"A"* 7—rather it becomes merely another among the objects of the poem's attention. In contrast to imagism's tendency toward mere visual impressions, in the objectivist effort (writes William

Carlos Williams), "The mind rather than the unsupported eye entered the picture." But—and this is crucial—Zukofsky refuses to celebrate the "mind" that thus enters his poems as his own: mind is immanent in the surrounding world just as, he insists, flesh-and-blood horses are immanent in police sawhorses. The desire for redemption that "A" 7 "objectifies" depends on this insistence; the desire cannot be redemptive unless it is, or can be imagined to be, not personal to the poet but universal.

The "Sincerity and Objectification" essay had been written for an occasion. Ezra Pound had long been urging Harriet Monroe to install Zukofsky as guest editor for one number of *Poetry* magazine. Monroe at last consented, but she wished the issue to represent a nameable movement, and to contain some sort of manifesto to be supplied by Zukofsky. Accordingly, when the Objectivist number appeared in February 1931, it contained "Sincerity and Objectification," "A" 7, and poems by William Carlos Williams, Carl Rakosi, Robert McAlmon, Charles Reznikoff, Basil Bunting, Kenneth Rexroth, and George Oppen. Zukofsky's essay maddened many readers; it appeared needlessly obscure, and arrogantly dismissive of all poets not "objectivist." Response from subscribers was so negative that in the subsequent number Monroe denounced the essay and, in turn, each of the poets Zukofsky had presented. Letters to the editor complained of a tendency among the objectivists to advance "Jewish nationalism disguised as a Greek chorus"; Zukofsky in particular was chided for his supposed lack of political commitment in such parlous times, and his poetry was pronounced "introverted and minor." In the debate that ensued, Zukofsky's attempts to explain his explanation were unavailing—the impression remained of a cliquish and self-important coterie—and, no polemicist, he soon ceased to concern himself with the matter. One who followed the objectivist controversy with keen interest was William Carlos Williams; always fascinated by the problems of formulating issues of poetic value, Williams remained interested in the questions "objectification" had opened long after Zukofsky had put the matter behind him. In the early 1050c, Williams asked Zukofsky again what he had meant by the word, and Zukofsky replied that "Objectivist poetry equals poetry, and that's that.... A poem has an expressed shape, form, love, music (or what other word have you?), and that goes for a poem in anytime, for any time." A decade later, it was Williams who contributed the entry on "Objectivism" to *The Princeton Encyclopedia of Poetry and Poetics*.

During this time, Zukofsky's relations with Pound were deepening. By 1930, Zukofsky was at work on a long essay about the *Cantos*; in 1931, Pound, with Eliot and Marianne Moore, sponsored (unsuccessfully) Zukofsky's application for a Guggenheim Fellowship; also in 1931, Pound, who had been urging Zukofsky to come abroad, sent the younger poet a check for $112 to cover the cost of a steamer ticket. Zukofsky was moved, but felt he could not accept; he kept the check as a memento of Pound's kindness. But the following year he accepted money that had been gathered by his friends in New York for the same purpose, and in June 1933 he was greeted in Cherbourg by René Taupin. Armed with introductions from Pound, he visited Fernand Leger, Constantin Brancusi, and Andre Masson in Paris, met Tibor Serly in Budapest, then journeyed to Rapallo to meet Pound himself.

Pound was cordial and even "fatherly," but he had already become preoccupied with politics and economics, and disliked the quiet skepticism with which Zukofsky met his vehemences. Zukofsky's left-leaning views, of course, squared badly with Pound's enthusiasm for Mussolini, and politics were to divide the two men in coming years. When Zukofsky edited An "Objectivists" Anthology (1932), Pound and Eliot contributed, lending the "movement" a prestige it had not garnered from the scandal in *Poetry*; and when Pound's *Active Anthology* appeared in late 1933, it featured poetry and a note on the *Cantos* by Zukofsky, along with new work by Eliot, Williams, Hemingway, Marianne Moore, E. E. Cummings, Louis Aragon, and others. But by 1935 Pound had lost patience with Zukofsky's politics, rejecting new work of Zukofsky's with the comment that "the next anthology will be econ / conscious and L / Z wont be in it."

But if politics were driving Zukofsky and Pound apart, they were bringing Williams and Zukofsky closer together. Both men abhorred the direction of Pound's politics, but both shared a more fundamental distrust of the effect political fervor—whatever the politics—could have on a literary imagination. At a time when many voices were urging Williams to serve various good causes, Zukofsky encouraged him in his natural bent, to put his art first. As time went on, and Zukofsky's pursuit of "art" led to more obscure and more private poetry, Williams, always the populist, objected. But his reservations about the poetry did not extend to his estimate of Zukofsky's critical acumen; Williams continued to offer his manuscripts to Zukofsky for criticism and comment, and the two remained warm friends. When Williams died in 1963, Zukofsky responded with "A Coronal, for Floss," addressed to the poet's widow; it consists of passages of Zukofsky's and Williams's writings intertwined, poetry, prose, and correspondence between the two men. It later assumed a place in Zukofsky's magnum opus, becoming "*A*" 17. A more elaborate elegy is "*A*" 15, which links Williams's death, on 4 March 1963, with two others that occurred the same year, Robert Frost's (29 January) and John F. Kennedy's (22 November).

Under Pound's sponsorship, Zukofsky's work had been fairly well circulated; indeed in a hostile review of *An "Objectivists" Anthology*, Yvor Winters complained about seeing so much of Zukofsky's work in poetry magazines, but he confidently (and happily) predicted that it would soon sink from view. It began to: Pound's enthusiasm had cooled, and in any case, Pound's authority as a literary impresario was eroding because of his isolation in Rapallo and his increasingly virulent fascism and anti-semitism. In 1938, Pound dedicated *Guide to Kulchur* to Zukofsky and Basil Bunting, and when Pound visited the United States in 1939, the two poets met and amicably aired their differences. In a famous exchange, Zukofsky rebuked Pound for his susceptibility to fascist rhetoric, saying, "Whatever you don't know, Ezra, you ought to know *voices*." Zukofsky later reported, "I told him that I did not doubt his integrity had decided his political action, but I pointed to his head, indicating something had gone wrong." About Pound's bigotry, Zukofsky insisted that "I never felt the least trace of anti-Semitism in his presence. Nothing he ever said to me made me feel the embarrassment I always have for the 'Goy' in whom a residue of antagonism to 'Jew' remains." Years later, when Pound was in custody at St. Elizabeths Hospital near Washington, D.C., Zukofsky and his family stopped there for a visit; they were on their way to North Carolina, where Paul, ten years old but already a formidable violinist, was to give a concert. The youngster brought his instrument to the hospital, and there, outdoors under the trees, played Mozart, Bach, and Corelli, and, to Pound's intense delight, the Janequin "bird music" that Pound had transcribed for his Canto LXXV. Zukofsky's subsequent relations with Pound were warm, if circumscribed: Pound took a great interest in Paul Zukofsky's career, but poetry and politics were subjects the two poets avoided thenceforward.

During the Depression poets were being urged to serve the revolution, and some of them, like Zukofsky's friend and fellow poet George Oppen, were forsaking poetry altogether in favor of complete political commitment. But the technical and formal ambitions of "objectification" were urging Zukofsky toward greater "estheticism" at just the time that the surrounding social situation was turning desperate. Whether it was that irony that inhibited him, or simply that he was short of time—he was no longer teaching, but putting in long hours on government projects sponsored by the New Deal—Zukofsky wrote little during those years. During 1933 and 1934, only ten poems were written, all of them short; there was no criticism, no fiction, no work on "*A*". But among the output of this period was the important poem "Mantis." A praying mantis inexplicably stranded in a New York subway seems doomed to certain extinction in that infernal place of machines and noise, where throngs of the city's poor hurry about their business. Everyone is too rushed, too hardened, to rescue the creature, to "save it!" Besides, being city people, they are frightened of insects anyway. As the poem proceeds, this hardheartedness and unwillingness to help the helpless but majestic insect are implicated in the larger structures of indifference and acquiescence, the dehumanizing, self-interested "tunnel vision," literalized by the poem's subway setting, in which the human poor are themselves trapped. In a breathtaking reversal (all the more breathtaking for the poem's formal intricacy and halting, deliberate, mantislike movement), the mantis becomes an emblem of that larger nature that encloses human history, and might (the poem urges) "save it." "Mantis" is a sestina, but the poem has a free-verse coda, " 'Mantis,' An Interpretation," which is less an "interpretation" of the poem than an account of its writing from original perception to finished poem. Poem and "interpretation" both are key texts for the student of Zukofsky.

From 1935 to 1940, after a hiatus of five years, Zukofsky resumed work on "*A*", and "*A*" 8, 9, and 10 surely belong with the best of the poetry of the 1930s. The conflict, if there was one, between objectification's artier ambitions and political urgency resolved itself firmly in favor of politics as the Spanish Civil War, the Munich Crisis, and at last the outbreak of war and the fall of France took place. "*A*" 8 (1937) draws heavily on the techniques for presenting historical material then being pioneered by Pound in his *Cantos*, although Zukofsky's materials, to a much greater extent than Pound's, are contemporary. "*A*" 10 (1940) laments the fall of France: its plangency and intensity recall Picasso's *Guernica*, and its almost operatic tone succeeds, even after forty years, in conveying a sense of the horror of those events far more vivid than the restrained and ironic "affirming flames" more characteristic of the verse that moment inspired. *"A"* 8 and *"A"* 10 are in the "musical" free verse of the earlier sections of *"A"*; *"A"* 9 presents the elaborate formalism and density that signals Zukofsky's "objective" manner. Only the first half of the present *"A"* 9 was written during this period; it is an interrogation of the theme of value in terms suggested by Zukofsky's reading of Marx and of books on atomic physics; carrying impersonality and objectification to an extreme, the poem is actually spoken by objects, mass-produced manufactured goods. This strange amalgam of thought and speech is tortuously wrought into the rigid and complex rhyming and syllabic schemes of the canzone form of Guido Cavalcanti's *Donna Me Prega*, in which, Pound explained, "Each strophe is articulated by 14 terminal and 12 inner rhyme sounds, which means that 52 out of every 154 syllables are bound into pattern."

The passion with which *"A"* 10 laments the fall of France in 1940 is climactic: the war, of course, was only just beginning. Following *"A"* 10, Zukofsky's poem again went into suspended animation. During the war years he wrote short poems and prose pieces such as "Ferdinand"; he also completed *A Test of Poetry* (1948), "a comparative study, in English, of poetry from Homer to the present time." The book juxtaposes, with little or no comment, passages of poetry from various times, so that "a means for judging the values of poetic writing is established." The book's didactic aims owe much to Pound's *ABC Of Reading* (1934), although its scheme, unlike Pound's, is ahistorical, implying that some poetic values are universal and perhaps even absolute. Such suggestions animate another prose text written in the 1940s. "Poetry: For My Son When He Can Read" (1946) argues that poetry can transcend history by reason of its music, which appeals to physiology, and by reason of its exactitude and precision, comparable to science's: "In poems, as in works of science, the involved susceptibilities always function with respect to some concept of exactness of utterance." During the war Zukofsky had worked for an electronics firm, "writing," Peter Quartermain reports, "instruction manuals for radios, bombsights, and such like." An interest in science is evident in several of the poems published in *Anew* (1946), especially #12 ("It's hard to see"); *A Test of Poetry* for that matter has as epigraph a quotation from Michael Faraday. In 1947 Zukofsky took a teaching post at Polytechnic Institute of New York in Brooklyn, teaching technical writing and occasional literature and creative-writing courses to engineering students. The poet Hugh Seidman, a student of Zukofsky's there, remembers asking

Zukofsky if he would have been happier at a liberal arts college; Zukofsky replied that "the engineer or scientist was closer to his concept of poetry than was the liberal arts student who has less contact with and respect for design, form, and invention and who would perhaps tend to imitate other poets and conventions." In 1950, in *"A"* 12, Zukofsky enunciated a poetic calculus:

About my *poetics*—

An integral
Lower limit speech
Upper limit music

Starting in 1948 when Zukofsky again resumed work on *"A"*, history and politics remained as themes in the poem, but their treatment was very different than it had been. Increasingly, history's events are merely cited, as if from a great distance, as if from a transhistorical vantage point. This change may be attributed partly to the intractable horror of World War II, but it probably reflects a more fundamental change in orientation in Zukofsky's life as well as his art. In 1933 he had met Celia Thaew, a composer; in 1939 they married; in 1943 their son Paul was born. Henceforth Zukofsky's poetry was to view experience from the vantage point of domestic values. In 1948, he again took up *"A"* 9, which had elaborated Marxian themes of value through Cavalcanti's most elaborate canzone form. In returning to it, Zukofsky doubled its length, making it a double canzone. Incredibly, the new strophes employ all the same rhyming words as the old ones, but now the theme is love, pursued in the language of Spinoza. Impersonality reigns still: in the first half of the poem, "things" had spoken; in the second half, love speaks.

"A" 9 was completed in 1950, and in that year the poet also wrote *"A"* 11, a song to comfort his wife and son after his death, and began *"A"* 12, a long autobiographical movement that solemnizes the poem's shift from political to domestic themes. The spirit of Bach presides again and is joined by Spinoza and Aristotle; Celia and Paul are celebrated; Zukofsky mourns the death of his father; and the theme of "love and eyes" from *A Midsummer-Night's Dream*, later to be the basis for the enormous *Bottom: On Shakespeare* (1963), appears in the poem for the first time. "History" is registered in the experience of people Zukofsky knows, particularly a

half-literate draftee, Jackie, killed in the Korean War, whose letters from boot camp, Japan, and at last Korea are quoted. The poem offers meditations on hate and love and thought, many of which are delivered in the form of aphorism. There is an inventory of the poet's unpublished or unfinished projects, and the movement ends with Zukofsky's translation of the opening of the *Odyssey*, a gesture as complex as Pound's opening the *Cantos* with a translation of the Homeric *nekyia* (or descent into hell). Coming as it does at the end of the poem's first half, it affirms that the second half of the poem will assay a new beginning and pursue domestic themes (as *"A"* 12 ends, Telemachos is rising from sleep); this consonance of beginnings and endings also has a musical effect suggestive of the art of fugue, and so climaxes one movement of the poem's elaborate homage to Bach. *"A"* 12 quotes Bach's treatise, *The Art of the Fugue*, and plays elaborately with the formula "Blest Ardent Celia Happy," much as one of Bach's own themes consists of the four notes B flat, A, C, and for H, B natural.

"A" 12 alone is as long as the preceding eleven sections of the poem. It was written in 1950 and 1951, and then, for another decade, *"A"* was set aside while Zukofsky worked on other projects. Preeminent among these was *Bottom: On Shakespeare*, which Zukofsky had begun writing in 1947. This long, dense, and demanding work ("the most original meditation on Shakespeare since Coleridge," Guy Davenport calls it) is a sort of commonplace book in which Zukofsky has collected and commented upon heteroclite texts bearing on love, considered as an epistemological problem. The difficulty of knowing, much less saying, what love is is acknowledged from the beginning by a speech of Bottom's from *A Midsummer-Night's Dream* ("I have had a dream, past the wit of man to say what dream it was. Man is but an ass, if he go about to expound this dream . . ."); and the central problem Zukofsky is addressing is stated by Helena in a passage from the first scene of the play:

> Things base and vile, holding no quantity,
> Love can transpose to form and dignity.
> Love looks not with the eyes but with the mind,
> And therefore is wing'd Cupid painted blind.
> Nor hath Love's mind of any judgment taste;
> Wings and no eyes figure unheedy haste;
> And therefore is Love said to be a child,
> Because in choice he is so oft beguil'd.

How love can "transpose" vileness "to form and dignity," even though it is "so oft beguil'd," is the question the whole book agitates: Zukofsky's presentation of the issue is related to the modernist poetic of particularity and concreteness rather than abstraction and generalization. Love, like poetry, goes astray when it "looks not with the eyes but with the mind." Love, says Zukofsky, is a "desire to project the mind's peace," and that formulation will do also to describe Zukofsky's conception of the "totality of perfect rest" achieved by poetry. The theme of Bottom "is simply that Shakespeare's text throughout favors the clear physical eye against the erring brain. . . . " Bottom orchestrates many and lengthy quotations—chiefly from Aristotle, Plato, Spinoza, Wittgenstein, but also from Freud, William James, Cardinal Newman, William Blake, Francis Bacon and many others—that discuss the relation of the senses to intellection; and these quotations are interwoven with passages from Shakespeare and other poets. All of this elaborates an epistemology in which love emerges as the force that, if fed by accurate sensuous perception, can redeem the relation of humankind to nature. As the poet of "blind love," Shakespeare presents "love as the tragic hero. He is Amor, identified with the passion of the lover falling short of perfection—discernment, fitness, proportion—at those times when his imagination insufficient to itself is an aberration of the eyes." There is also, of course, the corresponding comic possibility: "when reason and love are an identity of sight its clear and distinct knowledge can approach the sufficient realizations of the intellect." This formulation has little to do, of course, with Shakespeare's comic vision, but it does define Zukofsky's own claim to be a comic poet.

Zukofsky's objectivist poetic grew in part from a conviction that the poet's "major aim" (as he wrote in the 1946 essay, "Poetry: For My Son When He Can Read") "is not to show himself but that order that of itself can speak to all men." Such a formulation is open to question in an age that assumes, as ours does, that all perception and expression are inescapably subjective. In *Bottom* Zukofsky quotes Wittgenstein's remarks on the subject, especially the dictum (*Tractatus Logico-Philosophicus*, 1922) that "The subject does not belong to the world but it is a limit of the world," and that "solipsism strictly carried out coincides with pure realism. The I in solipsism shrinks to an extensionless point and there remains the reality coordinated with it." Wittgenstein goes on to affirm what is, in effect, the basis of Zukofsky's stance as a poet: "There is therefore really a sense in which in philosophy [and, Zukofsky would add, in poetry] we can talk of a non-psychological I. The I occurs in philosophy through the fact that the 'world is my world.' The philosophical I is not the man, not the human body or the human soul which psychology treats, but the metaphysical subject, the limit—not a part of the world."

Zukofsky probably resisted the afterthought here, that the "philosophical I" is "not a part of the world." The immanentism he shared with Spinoza implies rather a conviction that the philosophical or poetic "I" is so deeply implicated in the world that deviation from the world's exactions is not really possible. Thus (and this signals his distance from Wittgenstein), the poet need not worry about either solipsism or obscurity. The argument that "solipsism strictly carried out coincides with pure realism" substantiates Zukofsky's conviction that the poet can be most objective when exploring at the very "limit of the world" that his philosophical and poetic "I" imposes. It does not concern him that the poetry resulting from such effort may look more subjective than objective, more solipsistic than realistic, or that it may be personal and obscure to a degree that affords most readers little access. In the Wittgenstein quotation about solipsism and realism, there is no third party, no reader interposed between the "extensionless point" and the "reality coordinated with it."

These remarks bear on the extreme difficulty and obscurity of the second half of "A". Zukofsky's apparent unconcern with his audience can be attributed to his objectivist poetic and to his immanentist, Spinozistic sense of the self in the world, but it has its springs also in his alienation from the literary scene and his bitterness at the indifference and worse that had greeted his work. Once in the late 1950s, George Oppen asked Zukofsky about the obscurity of his work, and received an exasperated reply: "It doesn't matter, they don't care if they understand you or not." The same impatience is audible in an interview conducted a decade later. Zukofsky had been speaking of "having done away with epistemology" in *Bottom*, to which the interviewer responded with the observation that *Bottom* seemed, to him, all epistemology. "The questions are their own answers," said Zukofsky; "You want to say 'yes,' say 'yes'; you want to say 'no,' say 'no.' " As to what *Bottom* was about, then, if not epistemology, Zukofsky answered, "If you want to live, you love; if you don't want to live, you hate—that's all. . . . It's as simple as that."

By the time Zukofsky resumed work on "A" in 1960, Pound was back in Italy; Zukofsky's friendship with Oppen had cooled; and it had been years since Zukofsky had been much published or read. Across the Atlantic, younger British poets, especially Charles Tomlinson, associated with the little magazine *Agenda*, were paying homage to Zukofsky, but contacts with them were few, and their approaches tended to be reverential and honorific rather than critical and challenging. Williams was still a warm friend, but he had long been complaining that Zukofsky's poetry was too obscure, and the friendship seems to have sustained itself more on mutual affection than intellectual and imaginative exchange.

Zukofsky's late work evinces a disregard for its audience, in short, because Zukofsky considered— and he was nearly right—that he had no real audience. His world consisted of his family and his work, and in his poem he felt free to consult only his own pleasure, with the consequence that much of "A" 13-24 is forbiddingly difficult. The poetry of "A" 1-12 is self-consciously "modernist," elliptical and allusive, but it presents no difficulty to anyone who has learned to read the *Cantos*, or Williams's *Paterson*, or Charles Olson's *Maximus*. If its viewpoint is special, still its materials are largely public, or if private, universal: marriage, fatherhood, death. But in "A" 13-24 the difficulty of the poem becomes extreme. The poem's most accessible materials—the incidents of domestic life, the emergence of Paul as a violin prodigy, the public events of the Kennedy-Johnson years—lie on the surface, along with others more arcane: philosophical speculation, alchemical lore, recondite vocabulary drawn from the natural sciences, especially geology, botany, and ornithology. But even the most public of the poem's "objects" are incorporated into an imaginative organization whose principles lie hidden. The two voices, the "musical" and the "objective," that alternate in the first half of "A" are fused in the second half; the formal games are simple and easily discerned, usually involving small stanzas based on the novel (but in Zukofsky's hands, impressively effective), principle of word count rather than syllable or stress count. But the language, the diction and syntax, are skewed decisively from the norms of grammar and common usage, especially in the late sections, "A" 22 and 23, where Zukofsky seems to be continuing in verse the Joyce- and Stein-flavored experiments he had earlier undertaken in prose pieces like "Thanks to the Dictionary." Eliot's remark concerning Joyce and Milton, that each wrote in a language of his own based on English, is applicable to the later sections of "A".

"A" 13 and 14 develop to a gnomic impenetrability Zukofsky's penchant, first explored in "A" 12, for aphorism. Aside from "A" 16, which is only four words long, and *"A"* 17, the "Coronal" for William Carlos Williams's widow, perhaps the most accessible of the late sections of the poem is *"A"* 15. It opens with a rendering of part of the book of Job, in which Zukofsky "translates" the Hebrew into a tortured English whose syllables duplicate so far as possible the actual sounds of the original. The body of the poem laments the deaths of Robert Frost, William Carlos Williams, and John F. Kennedy, and lengthy passages from Edward Gibbon concerning barbarism and civilization follow. At the close allusions to the scene in the *Iliad* in which the Nereids mourn because Achilles must soon die bind the movement into an emotional whole. *"A"* 18 begins with a love poem to Celia but quickly shifts to coarse humor and a satirical narration of certain events in Vietnam, closing with references to Jonathan Swift and his Scriblerian friends. *"A"* 19 narrates the adventure of Zukofsky's son Paul entering a violin competition in Europe. Next comes a short movement, only two pages long, written for Paul's twentieth birthday (this is *"A"* 20), a "respond" for a tone row Paul had composed. *"A"* 21 is an idiosyncratic translation of Plautus's *Rudens*, which evidently attracted Zukofsky because of its resemblances to Shakespeare's *Pericles*. *"A"* 22 and 23 are the most obscure (and last written) sections of the poem, reverting (as in the first half of *"A"* 9) to a manner in which "things" speak, announcing geological and anthropological themes. *"A"* 24 is titled "L. Z. Masque," and a prefatory note explains that it is a "five part score—music, thought, drama, story, poem. Handel's 'Harpsichord Pieces' are one voice. The other four voices are arrangements of Louis Zukofsky's writings. . . . " The "Thought" voice speaks excerpts from the prose criticism; the "Drama" voice recites lines from Zukofsky's play, *Arise, Arise*; the "Story" voice presents excerpts from "It Was"; and the "Poem" voice quotes earlier sections of *"A"*. The music and the four voices are heard simultaneously; "Dynamics are indicated by type point size." Guy Davenport compares *"A"* 24's "polyphonic voices" to the music of Charles Ives, and suggests that *"A"* 24 enacts a "family reunion" of Zukofsky's works, "a grand Jewish family affair, with everybody cheerfully talking at once." *"A"* 24 was performed in New York City in June 1973. The juxtapositions of texts it orchestrates are, of course, more easily assayed on the printed page; approached that way, *"A"* 24 provides, for all its chaotic appearance, a lucid and even analytic retrospective view not only of *"A"*, but of Zukofsky's whole career.

There is one more "movement" to be mentioned in *"A"*: the index Zukofsky prepared for the poem's first corrected, complete, one-volume printing, published by the University of California Press in 1978. Its inclusions (*a, an, the*) are as telling as its omissions (Stalin, Robert Frost, Vietnam). As idiosyncratic as anything in the poem itself, the 1978 index bristles with fascinating hints at the poet's mature sense of what his poem was about; it is more a concordance to the poem's themes than a mere index.

Throughout the 1960s, as the last half of *"A"* was being composed and Zukofsky's writing was becoming more obscure, the poet and his work were at last gaining some of the recognition that had been withheld for so long. The surest sign was that mainstream publishers were bringing out Zukofsky's long-neglected work. The short poems were first collected in 1965; in 1967 *Prepositions: Collected Critical Essays* appeared; "Ferdinand" and "It Was" were reprinted together in 1968; *Little*, a whimsical mini-fantasia about a violin prodigy named Little Baron Snorck von Chulnt, appeared in 1970. But the most remarkable new work to appear during these years (new movements of *"A"* aside) was *Catullus*, which came out in 1969. Zukofsky had begun translating Catullus in 1958, working through the canon in order. Initially he was translating in the accepted sense of the word, so that, for example, *Cui dono lepidum novum libellum / arido modo pumice expolitum* is rendered "Whom do I give my neat little volume / Slicked dry and made fashionable with pumice?" But as he proceeded, Zukofsky decided to try to retain so far as possible the sounds of the Latin. (Another manifestation of this aim is the "translation" from the Hebrew Job that opens *"A"* 15.) As a consequence, in the later poems a very strange English results. Carmen 92's *Lesbia mi dicit semper male nec tacet umquam / de me: Lesbia me dispeream nisi amat* becomes "Lesbia may dicker simper maul or nag talk at whom, come / dear me: Lesbia my despair ay my uneasy mate." At worst Zukofsky's *Catullus* is unreadable; at best it is likeliest to disclose its wit to the reader whose knowledge of Latin enables the original text (on the facing page) to serve as a trot. But the whole effort testifies to Zukofsky's belief in the primacy of sound in poetry, of sound as one of the absolutes of the art (because it is physiological). The relevant gloss is to be found in Zukofsky's 1950 essay, "A Statement for Poetry," quoted in *"A"* 24: poetry's music "permits anybody who does not know Greek to listen and get something out of the poetry of Homer: to 'tune in' to the human tradition, to its voice which has developed among the sounds of natural things, and thus escape the confines of a time and place, as one hardly ever escapes them in studying Homer's grammar."

At the time of his death in 1978, Zukofsky was seeing into print *80 Flowers*, a small book of short poems full of flower lore. He meant the poems to gesture toward his eightieth birthday (which would have been in 1984); as Hugh Kenner notes, the word *flowers* (in the book's title) can be a verb.

In 1978 Zukofsky was also correcting the text of *"A"* and preparing the index for the poem's first complete printing in one volume. Throughout his life, *"A"* had appeared only in small excerpts, printed on small presses in limited numbers. Not until 1959 was a substantial portion of the poem printed in hardcover, and that was not in America, but Kyoto, Japan. An American edition, photo-offset from the Kyoto printing, appeared eight years later, but quickly went out of print. *"A" 13-21* appeared in England and America in 1969; *"A" 24* was published in 1972; and *"A" 22 & 23* followed in 1975. The reader who wanted all of *"A"* would be put to some pains to assemble four volumes, all very different in size, typeface, paper, and format. In the mid-1970s the University of California Press undertook to publish *"A"*, and the prospect of a corrected, uniform, one-volume edition issuing from a well-respected university press can only have been the more gratifying for having been deferred so long. Unhappily, Zukofsky died in May 1978 with *"A"* still in press.

Hugh Kenner has called *"A"* "the most hermetic poem in the language, which they will still be elucidating in the 22nd century." Perhaps one must wait till then to assess with any assurance Zukofsky's place in the poetry of this century. At present, though, there can be no question that he is vastly more important a poet than is generally recognized. He is the most formidable inheritor in English or American poetry of the modernist legacy not only of Pound but also of Joyce and Stein. For all their difficulty, *"A"* 7, 9, 11, and 12 are masterpieces of twentieth-century poetry; so are dozens of passages from elsewhere in *"A"*, and so are many of Zukofsky's shorter poems, especially "Poem Beginning 'The,'" "Mantis," and (William Carlos Williams's favorite of all Zukofsky's works) #43 of *Anew*, "You three." His long career of patient and adventurous work, undertaken with the minimum of public recognition, has much to tell about the fate of an ambitious and original imagination when it must make its way in the world unattended by the personal flamboyance of a Pound, the appealing folksiness of

a Williams, the charisma and egotism of an Olson. His work illustrates both the perils and the possibilities of working out of the public eye, for if obscurity is his work's besetting vice, his willingness to risk obscurity is also the condition of his greatest achievement. His reputation can only grow as his work becomes better known. His discovery by the next generation promises to be one of the signal events of the literary history of the coming years.

Other:

An "Objectivists" Anthology, edited by Zukofsky (Le Beausset, Var, France & New York: To Publishers, 1932);

Ezra Pound, ed., *Active Anthology*, includes poems and a note by Zukofsky (London: Faber & Faber, 1933);

"Addenda to *Prepositions*," *Journal of Modern Literature*, 4 (September 1974): 91-108.

Bibliographies:

Celia Zukofsky, *A Bibliography of Louis Zukofsky* (Los Angeles: Black Sparrow Press, 1969);

Zukofsky, "Year by Year Bibliography of Louis Zukofsky," *Paideuma*, 7 (Winter 1978): 603-610.

References:

Barry Ahearn, "The Adams Connection," *Paideuma*, 7 (Winter 1978): 479-493;

Ahearn, "The Aesthetics of '*A*'," Ph.D. dissertation, Johns Hopkins University, 1978;

Ahearn, "Notes On A Convocation of Disciplines," *Montemora*, 4 (1978): 251-259;

Ahearn, "Origins of '*A*': Zukofsky's Materials For Collage," *ELH*, 45 (Spring 1978): 152-176;

Marcella Booth, *A Catalogue of the Louis Zukofsky Manuscript Collection* (Austin: University of Texas Press, 1975);

Don Byrd, "The Shape of Zukofsky's Canon," *Paideuma*, 7 (Winter 1978): 455-477;

Hayden Carruth, "The Only Way To Get There From Here," *Journal of Modern Literature*, 4 (September 1974): 88-90;

Samuel Charters, "Essay Beginning 'All,'" *Modern Poetry Studies*, 3 (1973): 241-250;

"Conversations with Celia Zukofsky," *Paideuma*, 7 (Winter 1978): 585-600;

Cid Corman, "The Transfigured Prose," *Paideuma*, 7 (Winter 1978): 447-453;

Kenneth Cox, " 'A'-24," *Agenda*, 11 (Spring-Summer 1973): 89-91;

Cox, "Louis Zukofsky," *Agenda*, 13/14 (Winter-Spring 1976): 127-130;

Cox, "Louis Zukofsky," *Agenda*, 16 (Spring 1978): 11-13;

Cox, "The Poetry of Louis Zukofsky: 'A'," *Agenda*, 9/10 (Autumn-Winter 1971): 80-89;

Robert Creeley, "For L. Z.," *Paideuma*, 7 (Winter 1978): 383-385;

Creeley, "Louis Zukofsky's *All*," *Agenda*, 4 (Summer 1966): 45-48;

Guy Davenport, "Scripta Zukofskii Elogia," *Paideuma*, 7 (Winter 1978): 394-399;

Davenport, "Zukofsky's 'A' 23-21 and *Catullus*," *Agenda*, 8 (Autumn-Winter 1970): 130-137;

Davenport, "Zukofsky's 'A'-24," *Parnassus*, 2 (Spring-Summer 1974): 15-24;

Fielding Dawson, "A Memoir of Louis Zukofsky," *Paideuma*, 7 (Winter 1978): 571-579;

L. S. Dembo, "Louis Zukofsky: Objectivist Poetics and the Quest for Form," *American Literature*, 44 (March 1972): 74-96;

Thomas A. Duddy, "The Measure of Louis Zukofsky," *Modern Poetry Studies*, 3 (1973): 250-256;

Robert Duncan, "As Testimony: Reading Zukofsky These Forty Years," *Paideuma*, 7 (Winter 1978): 421-427;

Allen Ginsberg, Robert Creeley, Hugh Seidman, Celia Zukofsky, "Memorial Celebration For Louis Zukofsky," *American Poetry Review*, 9 (January-February 1980): 22-27;

David Gordon, "Zuk and Ez at St. Liz," *Paideuma*, 7 (Winter 1978): 581-584;

William Harmon, "*Eiron* Eyes," *Parnassus*, 8 (Spring-Summer 1979): 5-23;

Burton Hatlen, "Catullus Metamorphosed," *Paideuma*, 7 (Winter 1978): 539-545;

David Ignatow, "Louis Zukofsky: Two Views," *Paideuma*, 7 (Winter 1978): 549-551;

"Interview with Louis Zukofsky," *Contemporary Literature*, 10 (Spring 1969): 155-219;

Hugh Kenner, "Bottom on Zukofsky," *Modern Language Notes*, 90 (December 1975): 921-922;

Kenner, *A Homemade World: The American Modernist Writers* (New York: Knopf, 1975), pp. 162-193;

Kenner, "Loove in Brooklyn," *Paideuma*, 7 (Winter 1978): 413-420;

Kenner, "Louis Zukofsky: All the Words," *Paid-euma*, 7 (Winter 1978): 386-389;

Warren P. Lang, "Zukofsky's Conception of Poetry and a Reading of his Poem of a Life 'A'," Ph.D. dissertation, Indiana University, 1974;

Stephen Roy Mandell, "The Finer Mathematician: An Introduction To The Work of Louis Zukofsky," Ph.D. dissertation, Temple University, 1976;

Mary Oppen, *Meaning A Life: An Autobiography* (Santa Barbara: Black Sparrow Press, 1978);

Peter Quartermain, "I Am Different, Let Not A Gloss Embroil You," *Paideuma*, 9 (Spring 1980): 203-210;

Quartermain, "Recurrencies: No. 12 of Louis Zukofsky's *Anew*," *Paideuma*, 7 (Winter 1978): 523-538;

Burton Raffel, "No Tidbit Love You Outdoors Far As A Bier: Zukofsky's *Catullus*," *Arion*, 8 (Autumn 1969): 435-445;

Harold Schimmel, "Zuk. Yehoash David Rex," *Paideuma*, 7 (Winter 1978): 559-569;

Hugh Seidman, "Louis Zukofsky at the Polytechnic Institute of Brooklyn (1958-61)," *Paideuma*, 7 (Winter 1978): 553-558;

John Taggart, "Intending a Solid Object: A Study of Objectivist Poetics," Ph.D. dissertation, Syracuse University, 1975;

Taggart, "Zukofsky's 'Mantis,' " *Paideuma*, 7 (Winter 1978): 507-522;

C. F. Terrell, ed., *Louis Zukofsky: Man and Poet* (Orono: University of Maine Press, 1979);

Charles Tomlinson, "Objectivists: Zukofsky and Oppen, A Memoir," *Paideuma*, 7 (Winter 1978): 429-445;

William Carlos Williams, "An Extraordinary Sensitivity," *Poetry*, 60 (September 1942): 338-340;

Williams, "Louis Zukofsky," *Agenda*, 2 (December 1964): 1-4;

Williams, "A New Line Is A New Measure," *New Quarterly of Poetry*, 2 (Winter 1947-1948): 8-16;

Williams, Review of *An "Objectivists" Anthology*, *Symposium*, 4 (January 1933): 114-116;

Phillip R. Yanella, "On Louis Zukofsky," *Journal of Modern Literature*, 4 (September 1974): 74-87.

Papers:

Zukofsky's manuscripts and correspondence are held by the Humanities Research Center, University of Texas, Austin, Texas.

Books for Further Reading

This is a selective list of general studies relating to contemporary American poetry. Fuller bibliographies may be found in Lewis Leary, *Articles on American Literature, 1950-1967* (Durham: Duke University Press, 1970), Leary with John Auchard, *Articles on American Literature, 1968-1975* (Durham: Duke University Press, 1979), the annual MLA International Bibliographies, the annual bibliography of *Journal of Modern Literature*, and *American Literary Scholarship: An Annual Survey* (Durham: Duke University Press, 1965-).

Allen, Donald M., ed. *The New American Poetry: 1945-1960*. New York: Grove, 1960.

Allen and Warren Tallman, eds. *Poetics of the New American Poetry*. New York: Grove, 1974.

Berg, Stephen and Robert Mezey, eds. *Naked Poetry: Recent American Poetry in Open Forms*. Indianapolis: Bobbs-Merrill, 1969.

Berg and Mezey, eds. *The New Naked Poetry: Recent American Poetry in Open Forms*. Indianapolis: Bobbs-Merrill, 1976.

Bigsby, C. W. E., ed. *The Black American Writer*. Deland, Fla.: Everett / Edwards, 1969.

Boyars, Robert, ed. *Contemporary Poetry in America*. New York: Schocken Books, 1974.

Cambon, Glauco. *Recent American Poetry*. Minneapolis: University of Minnesota Press, 1962.

Cargas, Harry J. *Daniel Berrigan and Contemporary Protest Poetry*. New Haven, Conn.: College & University Press, 1972.

Carr, John, ed. *Kite-Flying and Other Irrational Acts: Conversations with Twelve Southern Writers*. Baton Rouge: Louisiana State University Press, 1972.

Charters, Samuel. *Some Poems/Poets: Studies in American Underground Poetry Since 1945*. Berkeley: Oyez, 1971.

Conversations with Writers, 2 vols. Detroit: Bruccoli Clark / Gale Research, 1977, 1978.

Cook, Bruce. *The Beat Generation*. New York: Scribners, 1971.

David, Lloyd and Robert Irwin, eds. *Contemporary American Poetry: A Checklist*. Metuchen, N. J.: Scarecrow, 1975.

Deodene, Frank and William P. French, eds. *Black American Poetry Since 1944: A Preliminary Checklist*. Chatham, N. J.: Chatham Bookseller, 1971.

Dickey, James. *Babel to Byzantium: Poets & Poetry Now*. New York: Farrar, Straus & Giroux, 1968.

Dickey. *Spinning the Crystal Ball: Some Guesses at the Future of American Poetry*. Washington, D. C.: Library of Congress, 1967.

Dickey. *The Suspect in Poetry*. Madison, Minn.: Sixties Press, 1964.

Dodsworth, Martin, ed. *The Survival of Poetry: A Contemporary Survey*. London: Faber & Faber, 1970.

Duberman, Martin. *Black Mountain: An Exploration in Community*. New York: Dutton, 1972.

Feldman, Gene and Max Gartenberg, eds. *The Beat Generation and the Angry Young Men*. New York: Citadel, 1958.

First Printings of American Authors, 4 vols. Detroit: Bruccoli Clark / Gale Research, 1977-1979.

Fox, Hugh, ed. *The Living Underground: An Anthology of Contemporary American Poets*. New York: Whitsun, 1973.

French, Warren, ed. *The Fifties: Fiction, Poetry, Drama.* Deland, Fla.: Everett / Edwards, 1970.

Gayle, Addison, Jr., ed. *Black Expression: Essays by and about Black Americans in the Creative Arts.* New York: Weybright & Talley, 1969.

Gershator, Phillis, ed. *A Bibliographic Guide to the Literature of Contemporary American Poetry, 1970-1975.* Metuchen, N. J.: Scarecrow, 1976.

Glicksberg, Charles I. *The Sexual Revolution in Modern American Literature.* New York: Humanities Press, 1972.

Guttman, Allen. *The Jewish Writer in America: Assimilation and the Crisis of Identity.* New York: Oxford University Press, 1971.

Hamilton, Ian. *A Poetry Chronicle.* New York: Barnes & Noble, 1973.

Hassan, Ihab. *Contemporary American Literature, 1945-1972: An Introduction.* New York: Ungar, 1973.

Henderson, Stephen, ed. *Understanding the New Black Poetry.* New York: William Morrow, 1973.

Heyen, William, ed. *American Poets in 1976.* Indianapolis: Bobbs-Merrill, 1976.

Hill, Herbert, ed. *Anger and Beyond: The Negro Writer in the United States.* New York: Harper & Row, 1966.

Hoffman, Daniel, ed. *American Poetry and Poetics.* Garden City: Doubleday, 1962.

Hoffman, ed. *Harvard Guide to Contemporary Writing.* Cambridge: Harvard University Press, 1979.

Hoffman, ed. *New Poets 1970.* Philadelphia: Department of English, University of Pennsylvania, 1970.

Hollander, John, ed. *Modern Poetry: Essays in Criticism.* London, Oxford & New York: Oxford University Press, 1968.

Howard, Richard. *Alone With America: Essays on the Art of Poetry in the United States Since 1950.* New York: Atheneum, 1969.

Howard, ed. *Preferences: 51 American Poets Choose Poems From Their Own Work and From the Past.* New York: Viking, 1974.

Ignatow, David, ed. *Political Poetry.* New York: Chelsea, 1960.

Juhasz, Suzanne. *Naked and Fiery Forms: Modern American Poetry by Women, A New Tradition.* New York: Harper & Row, 1976.

Kalstone, David. *Five Temperaments.* New York: Oxford University Press, 1977.

Kazin, Alfred. *Contemporaries.* Boston: Little, Brown, 1962.

Kostelanetz, Richard, ed. *The Young American Writers: Fiction, Poetry, Drama, and Criticism.* New York: Funk & Wagnalls, 1967.

Lacey, Paul A. *The Inner War: Forms and Themes in Recent American Poetry.* Philadelphia: Fortress Press, 1972.

Leary, Paris and Robert Kelly, eds. *A Controversy of Poets.* Garden City: Anchor, 1965.

Lensing, George S. and Ronald Moran. *Four Poets and the Emotive Imagination: Robert Bly, James Wright, Louis Simpson, and William Stafford.* Baton Rouge: Louisiana State University Press, 1976.

Lepper, Gary M. *A Bibliographical Introduction to Seventy-Five Modern American Authors.* Berkeley: Serendipity Books, 1976.

Levertov, Denise. *The Poet in the World.* New York: New Directions, 1973.

Lieberman, Laurence. *Unassigned Frequencies.* Urbana: University of Illinois Press, 1977.

Malkoff, Karl. *Crowell's Handbook of Contemporary American Poetry.* New York: Crowell, 1973.

Malkoff. *Escape from the Self.* New York: Columbia University Press, 1977.

Margolies, Edward. *Native Sons: A Critical Study of Twentieth-Century Negro American Authors.* Philadelphia & New York: Lippincott, 1968.

Mazzaro, J., ed. *Modern American Poets.* New York: McKay, 1970.

Mersmann, James F. *Out of the Vietnam Vortex: A Study of Poets and Poetry against the War.* Lawrence: University Press of Kansas, 1974.

Mills, Ralph. *Cry of the Human: Essays on Contemporary American Poetry.* Urbana: University of Illinois Press, 1975.

Moss, Howard, ed. *The Poet's Story.* New York: Macmillan, 1973.

Myers, Carol Fairbanks. *Women in Literature: Criticism of the Seventies.* Metuchen, N. J.: Scarecrow, 1976.

Oberg, Arthur. *Modern American Lyric.* New Brunswick: Rutgers University Press, 1977.

O'Brien, John, ed. *Interviews with Black Writers.* New York: Liveright, 1973.

Packard, William, ed. *The Craft of Poetry: Interviews from the New York Quarterly.* Garden City: Doubleday, 1974.

Paolucci, Anne, ed. *Dante's Influence on American Writers, 1776-1976.* New York: Griffon House for the Dante Society of America, 1977.

Parkinson, Thomas, ed. *A Casebook on The Beat.* New York: Crowell, 1961.

Pinsky, Robert. *The Situation in Poetry: Contemporary Poetry and Its Tradition.* Princeton: Princeton University Press, 1976.

Poulin, A., Jr., ed. *Contemporary American Poetry.* Boston: Houghton Mifflin, 1971.

Ransom, John Crowe, Delmore Schwartz, and John Hall Wheelock. *American Poetry at Mid-Century.* Washington, D. C.: Library of Congress, 1958.

Rexroth, Kenneth. *American Poetry in the Twentieth Century.* New York: Herder & Herder, 1971.

Robson, Jeremy, ed. *Corgi Modern Poets in Focus 4.* London: Corgi, 1971.

Shaw, Robert B., ed. *American Poets Since 1960: Some Critical Perspectives.* Cheadle, England: Carcanet Press, 1973.

Spears, Monroe K. *Dionysus and the City: Modernism in Twentieth Century Poetry.* New York: Oxford University Press, 1970.

Stepanchev, Stephen. *American Poetry Since 1945: A Critical Survey.* New York: Harper & Row, 1965.

Turner, Alberta T., ed. *50 Contemporary Poets: The Creative Process.* New York: McKay, 1977.

Turner, Darwin T. *Afro-American Writers.* New York: Appleton-Century-Crofts, 1970.

Tytell, John. *Naked Angels: The Lives and Literature of the Beat Generation.* New York: McGraw-Hill, 1976.

Vendler, Helen. *Part of Nature, Part of Us: Modern American Poets.* Cambridge: Harvard University Press, 1980.

Vinson, James, ed. *Contemporary Poets.* New York: St. Martin's, 1975.

Wakoski, Diane. *Creating a Personal Mythology.* Los Angeles: Black Sparrow Press, 1975.

Writers at Work: The "Paris Review" Interviews. 4 vols. New York: Viking, 1958, 1963, 1967, 1976.

Contributors

Michael Adams	*Louisiana State University*
Alex Batman	*University of South Carolina*
Ronald Baughman	*University of South Carolina*
Judith S. Baughman	*University of South Carolina*
Caroline G. Bokinsky	*University of South Carolina*
Ashley Brown	*University of South Carolina*
George F. Butterick	*University of Connecticut*
Keen Butterworth	*University of South Carolina*
Richard J. Calhoun	*Clemson University*
Robert K. Cording	*Holy Cross College*
David Cowart	*University of South Carolina*
Frank Day	*Clemson University*
Robert DeMott	*Ohio University*
Beth Fleischman	*University of South Carolina*
Benjamin Franklin V	*University of South Carolina*
Charles Frazier	*University of South Carolina*
Walter Freed	*Winthrop College*
Stephen Gardner	*University of South Carolina at Aiken*
George Garrett	*York Harbor, Maine*
Steve Garrison	*University of South Carolina*
Thomas Goldstein	*University of South Carolina*
Donald J. Greiner	*University of South Carolina*
Bob Group	*University of South Carolina at Salkahatchie, Allendale*
Mark Harris	*University of South Carolina*
Eric Hartley	*Columbia, South Carolina*
Steven Helmling	*Rutgers University*
Jeffrey Helterman	*University of South Carolina*
Robert W. Hill	*Clemson University*
Charles Israel	*South Carolina State College*
Ronald Johnson	*San Francisco, California*
Katherine Knight	*University of South Carolina*
Susan Ludvigson	*Winthrop College*
Jerry B. McAninch	*Midlands Technical College*
Thomas McClanahan	*South Carolina Arts Commission*
Kenneth McCullough	*Columbia, South Carolina*
Idris McElveen	*Spring Valley High School*
James Mann	*University of South Carolina*
Anthony Manousos	*Cook College, Rutgers University*
Carolyn Matalene	*University of South Carolina*
Keith Moul	*Seattle, Washington*
Dan Murray	*Suffolk County Community College*
Anne Newman	*University of North Carolina at Charlotte*
Stephen A. Parris	*University of South Carolina*
Linwood C. Powers	*Richmond, Virginia*
William Mattathias Robins	*University of South Carolina*
H. Meili Steele	*University of South Carolina*
Willard Spiegelman	*Southern Methodist University*
Joan Taylor	*University of South Carolina at Beaufort*

Contributors

William B. Thesing	*University of South Carolina*
Deno Trakas	*University of South Carolina*
Keith Walters	*University of South Carolina*
Holly Mims Westcott	*University of South Carolina*
Richard Ziegfeld	*University of South Carolina*

Cumulative Index Volumes 1-5

Cumulative Index to Volumes 1-5

*Indicates master entries

Cumulative Index

A CHRISTMAS STORM

~~All Sunday & Sunday night,~~
~~All day, all night,~~ the cold water ~~comes~~ down
at the will of heaven, freezing where it hits
glazing the windshields and the ~~roads and walks~~
~~if you wanted a world without friction,~~ here,
sheathing ~~the lines,~~ the branches ~~and till up~~
in leaden insulations uniform
across the counties and the towns, until
connections ~~give~~ and ~~power~~ lines come down
~~and limbs~~ that had sustained the horizontal
a hundred years unstrained crack ~~with~~ the weight
of stiffened wet and short transformers out
~~until~~ ten thousand homes ~~out~~ suddenly off
go ~~dark~~ and silent, and the cold comes in
slowly at first, then faster, drifting through
the window frames ghostly, and under doors,
while night comes on and provident families
remember where the candles and ~~lanterns~~ were
from last year, and other families don't;
while lucky families light fires, and others
but bundle up in blankets or skid downstreet
to the ~~mercy~~ of the neighbors or their kin,
and cars caught out are paralyzed at hills,
and it is clear ~~from portable radios~~
~~as from a look outdoors~~ that the relentless rain
will go unrelentingly on till it relents.

Which it does do ~~at last~~ next day at dawn,
when sunrise ~~lights the splendor of the~~ world
in radiant brocades and fevere'd
drainpipes and eaves and ~~till the~~ brilliant far
of bush and tree and ~~start~~ the region 'round;
~~where every twig is bright, being itself,~~
its ~~outline~~ in transparent ice, and ~~then~~ less
the halo of that in light, as in the great
museum of mind the million ~~crystal~~ trees
~~light up at once~~ their diamonded display,
~~their crystal magnificence, their~~ candelabra
of silver ~~winking~~ ruby and emerald and gold
~~according to~~ the sun and ~~falling~~ wind,
~~giving away~~ the treasures of ~~the~~ world
before the powerful ~~and the poor alike.~~

8 i 79